Praise for *The Pentago[n]*

"This concrete behemoth—the largest office buil[ding]
the product of considerable human ingenuity [and]
Steve Vogel amply demonstrates in his interesting account. . . . This is
not, of course, the first account of the [9/11] attack, but with its Clan-
cyesque action and firsthand detail . . . it is surely the most vivid."
    —*The New York Times Book Review*

"The saga of the construction of the Pentagon, skillfully recounted by
Steve Vogel . . . is as enthralling as it is improbable. . . . It was one of the
greatest engineering feats of the twentieth century—driven by the intelligence and willpower of larger-than-life figures prepared to cut corners
and demand the impossible. Mr. Vogel has brought to our notice a thrilling achievement."
    —*The Economist*

"Engrossing and revealing   Vogel's account shines   [He] provides a
first-rate account of the transformation of a dilapidated Arlington neighborhood into what Norman Mailer called 'the true and high church of the
military industrial complex.' "
    —*San Francisco Chronicle*

"[Vogel] puts on display his superlative skills as a journalist with capturing
human detail. Above all, he reminds us that history is made by living people, and he has a biographer's fascination with the details of dozens of
personalities who made the Pentagon what it is today."
    —*The New York Sun*

"Vogel vividly depicts the horror of those inside the Pentagon on September 11, 2001 and then skillfully describes the rebirth of the Pentagon
through the Phoenix Project. His intimate knowledge of the construction
process and his years of research energize these pages. . . . There is simply no better book on the massive construction—and then restoration—
of the building itself."
    —*The Christian Science Monitor*

"Steve Vogel's marvelous work recounts the construction of one of the world's most iconic buildings—the Pentagon. But more compelling by far, he relates the human stories underlying this huge construction effort. . . . All this would of itself be enough to warrant a book but Vogel plunges on to an appropriate second story: the terrorist assault of 9/11 and the Pentagon's subsequent resurrection. This section of the book, due perhaps to the proximity of the event, is all the more compelling."
—*New York Post*

"Every building of any size and complexity has a story; few of them are this compelling."
—*The Hartford Courant*

"A thrilling biography of a building."
—*GQ* (essential reading selection)

"Among books dealing with seemingly impossible engineering feats, this easily ranks with David McCullough's *The Great Bridge* and *The Path Between the Seas*, as well as Ross King's *Brunelleschi's Dome*."
—*Kirkus Reviews* (starred review)

"A brilliant and illuminating study of this singular (and, in many ways, sacred) American space."
—*Publishers Weekly* (starred review)

"Steve Vogel has provided two excellent books in one: an interesting account of the frenetic effort to build the world's largest office building in order to support the U.S. entry into World War II, and an equally fascinating study of how the building survived and was reborn in the renovation effort so rudely interrupted on Sept. 11, 2001. . . . Vogel has done a great service to a historic structure and its people."
—*The Virginian-Pilot*

"A fascinating story, told in lively style."
—*St. Louis Post-Dispatch*

"Vogel's writing coupled with the dynamic, conflict-strewn history of the Pentagon provides for a fascinating and comfortable read while giving new insight into an old Washington landmark."
  —*Roll Call*

"Vogel's book starts off like a runaway freight train, with the rush to construct the Pentagon amid the turmoil of World War II. . . . *The Pentagon* can easily be recommended to anyone—the history buff, the political layman or anyone with an ear for an interesting account."
  —*Winston-Salem Journal*

"An amazing story, expertly researched and beautifully told. Part history, part adventure yarn, *The Pentagon* is above all else the biography of an American icon."
  —RICK ATKINSON, author of the Pulitzer Prize–winning *An Army at Dawn*

"Superb! Not only the best biography of a building ever written, but a fascinating look at the human architecture behind the Pentagon—the saints and scoundrels of our national defense. With his decades of experience covering the military and a web of insider connections, Steve Vogel has produced a book that's not only timely and a treat to read, but a stellar example of how to write history in the twenty-first century."
  —RALPH PETERS, author of *Never Quit The Fight*

"This book, like the Pentagon itself, is a stunning and monumental achievement."
  —ANDREW CARROLL, editor of *The New York Times* bestsellers *War Letters* and *Behind the Lines*

"Students, writers and historians will use *The Pentagon* as a reference book for years to come. Vogel has created an admirable, timely and immensely readable book. It is a must read for anyone who has ever worked in the building."
  —*Pentagram*

THE

PENTAGON

Random House Trade Paperbacks New York

THE
PENTAGON

A HISTORY

The Untold Story of the Wartime
Race to Build the Pentagon—and
to Restore It Sixty Years Later

STEVE VOGEL

To my parents,

Donald and Joan Vogel

2008 Random House Trade Paperback Edition

Copyright © 2007 by Steve Vogel

Credits for photos and illustrations are located beginning on page xv.

Library of Congress Cataloging-in-Publication Data

Vogel, Steve.
Pentagon : the untold story behind the creation of the symbol
of American might / Steve Vogel.
p. cm.
Includes bibliographical references and index.
ISBN 978-0-8129-7325-9
1. Pentagon (Va.)—History. 2. Public buildings—United States—Design and
construction—History—20th century. 3. Buildings—Repair and reconstruction—History.
4. United States—Dept. of Defense—Procurement—History. I. Title.

UA26.A745V64 2007
355.60973—dc22   2006050873

Printed in the United States of America

www.atrandom.com

2 4 6 8 9 7 5 3 1

Book design by Carol Malcolm Russo

GO SIR, GALLOP, AND DON'T FORGET THAT THE WORLD WAS MADE IN SIX DAYS. YOU CAN ASK ME FOR ANYTHING YOU LIKE, EXCEPT TIME.

—NAPOLEON BONAPARTE

CONTENTS

PART I
THE MAKING OF THE PENTAGON

PART II
THE REMAKING OF THE PENTAGON

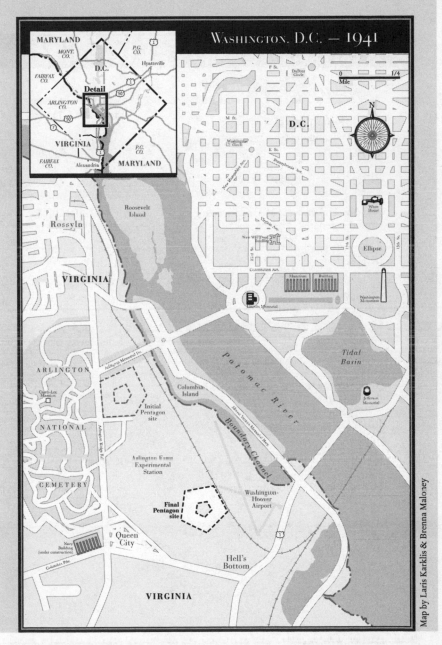

Map showing Washington, D.C., Arlington County, Virginia, and environs in the summer of 1941.

1941

July 17: Brig. Gen. Brehon Burke Somervell launches the Pentagon project

July 24: President Roosevelt approves the project

Aug 14: The project receives approval from the Senate

Aug. 29: FDR orders the site moved to its present location

Sept. 11: Ground is broken at the new site

Dec. 7: The Japanese attack Pearl Harbor

1942

April 30: First employees move into the Pentagon

July 21: Decision is made to add a full fifth floor

Nov. 14–15: War Department high command—George C. Marshall and Henry Stimson—move in

1943

Mid February: Building completed

Architectural style: **Stripped Classical**

Materials: Reinforced concrete made from **680,000 tons of sand** and gravel dredged from the Potomac River and supported by **41,492 concrete piles**; the design saved enough steel to build one battleship during wartime.

Height of building: **71' 3.5"**

Number of floors, plus mezzanine and basement: **5**

Total length of corridors: **17.5 miles**

Area covered by building: **29 acres**, large enough to accommodate five U.S. Capitol buildings

Access highways built: **30 miles**

Overpasses and bridges built: **21**

Parking space: **67 acres**

THE PENTAGON

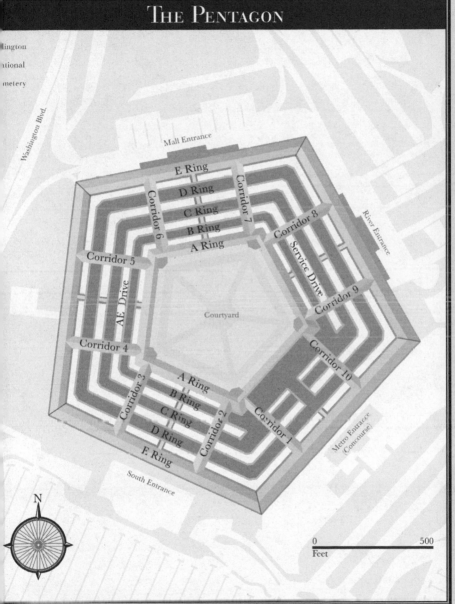

Arlington
National
Cemetery

Washington Blvd.

Mall Entrance

E Ring
D Ring
C Ring
B Ring
A Ring

Corridor 7

Corridor 6

Corridor 8

River Entrance

Corridor 5

Service Drive

AE Drive

Corridor 9

Courtyard

Corridor 4

Corridor 10

Corridor 3

A Ring
B Ring
C Ring
D Ring
E Ring

Corridor 2

Corridor 1

Metro Entrance
(Concourse)

South Entrance

N

0   500
Feet

Map by Laris Karklis & Brenna Maloney

ILLUSTRATIONS

CAST OF CHARACTERS

PART I

(Ranks and titles are primarily as of 1941)

The Builders—Army

Brigadier General Brehon B. Somervell, chief of the Army's Construction Division, later commander of Army Services of Supply

Colonel Leslie R. Groves, chief of operations and later deputy chief of Construction Division, later head of the Manhattan Project

Lieutenant Colonel Hugh "Pat" Casey, chief of design for Construction Division

Captain Clarence Renshaw, constructing quartermaster/engineer for the Pentagon project

Lieutenant Robert Furman, executive officer for the Pentagon project

The Builders—Contractors and Architects

John McShain, chief contractor for the Pentagon project

J. Paul Hauck, job superintendent for the Pentagon project

G. Edwin Bergstrom, chief architect for the War Department

David Witmer, chief assistant to Bergstrom, later his replacement

Luther Leisenring, chief of the architects' specifications section

Ides van der Gracht, chief of production for the Pentagon design team

Socrates Thomas "Red" Stathes, a draftsman

Larry Lemmon, a draftsman

The White House
President Franklin D. Roosevelt

Harry Hopkins, special adviser to FDR and former head of the Works Projects
Administration

Major General Edwin "Pa" Watson, the president's military aide

Harold Smith, director of the White House budget office

Harold Ickes, secretary of the interior

The War Department
Henry L. Stimson, secretary of war

General George C. Marshall, Army chief of staff

Robert Patterson, under secretary of war

John J. McCloy, assistant secretary of war

Robert Lovett, assistant secretary of war for air

William Hastie, civilian aide to Stimson

Members of Congress
Senator Harry S. Truman, Democrat of Missouri, chairman of Senate special committee investigating national defense; in April 1945 succeeded FDR as president

Representative Clifton Woodrum, Democrat of Virginia, member of House Appropriations Committee

Representative Merlin Hull, Progressive of Wisconsin

Senator Carter Glass, Democrat of Virginia, chairman of Senate Appropriations Committee

Representative Albert Engel, Republican of Michigan, member of House Military Appropriations subcommittee

Civilian Commissioners and Staff
Gilmore Clarke, chairman of the Commission of Fine Arts

Frederic Delano, chairman of the National Capital Park and Planning Commission and
uncle to the president

William Delano, member of planning commission; friend of Somervell's and distant
cousin to Frederic Delano

Hans Paul Caemmerer, secretary of the fine arts commission

Jay Downer, highway consultant, associate of Clarke and Delano

Paul Phillipe Cret, architect and member of fine arts commission

Army Officers and Staff
Colonel Ernest Graves, Corps of Engineers officer, mentor to Somervell and Groves

Brigadier General Charles "Baldy" Hartman, Somervell's predecessor as chief of construction

Brigadier General Eugene Reybold, chief of supply, later chief engineer

Major General Edmund Gregory, quartermaster general

Major Garrison "Gar" Davidson, an aide to Groves and the former West Point football coach

George Holmes, Somervell's public relations man

Captain Donald Antes, an aide to Groves

Brigadier General Wilhelm B. "Fat" Styer, deputy to Somervell

Brigadier General Alexander D. Surles, chief of the Bureau of Public Relations

Colonel Thomas F. Farrell, executive officer to Groves

Brigadier General Thomas M. Robins, Somervell's replacement as chief of construction

Brigadier General Dwight D. Eisenhower, chief of war plans; later Allied commander for landings in North Africa and Europe; Marshall's successor as Army chief of staff

Lieutenant General Henry H. (Hap) Arnold, commander of Army Air Forces

Major Franklin Matthias, an aide to Groves

Navy Department

Henry Knox, secretary of the Navy

Admiral Ernest King, commander in chief of the United States Fleet

Workers

Stanley "Joe" Nance Allan, a carpenter

Donald Walker, a steelworker

Hank Neighbors, a payroll witness

The First Pentagon Employees ("The Plank Walkers")

Helen McShane Bailey, administrative assistant, Office of the Chief of Staff

Marjorie Hanshaw, secretary, Ordnance Department supply section

Opal Sheets, "Miss 10,000," administrative assistant, Services of Supply

Marian Bailey, a telephone operator and later supervisor

Lucille Ramale, file clerk, Transportation Corps

Henry Bennett, clerk, Ordnance Department

Jimmy Harold, assistant engineer, Ordnance Department field service

PART II

The Early Cold War Years

James Forrestal, secretary of defense, 1947–49

Louis Johnson, secretary of defense, 1949–50

George C. Marshall, secretary of defense, 1950–51

Clark Clifford, aide and later special counsel to President Harry Truman 1946–50; secretary of defense, 1968–1969

Marx Leva, aide to Forrestal, Johnson and Marshall, 1947–51

The Vietnam Years

Robert McNamara, secretary of defense, 1961–1968

General Harold K. Johnson, Army chief of staff, 1964–1968

David McGiffert, under secretary of the Army, 1966–69

Lieutenant Colonel Ernest Graves Jr., son of Ernest Graves and aide to the secretary of the Army, 1967–68

Captain Phil Entrekin, commander of C Troop, 1st Squadron, 6th Cavalry Regiment at the Pentagon, 1967

Abbie Hoffman, marcher at the Pentagon, cofounder of Youth International Party (Yippies)

Norman Mailer, marcher at the Pentagon, author of *The Armies of the Night*

Bill Ayers, marcher at the Pentagon, later member of Weather Underground

Rita Campbell, custodial foreman for Pentagon's fourth floor cleaning crew

The Post-Vietnam Years

Donald Rumsfeld, secretary of defense, 1975–77, 2001–2006

Colin Powell, military assistant to secretary of defense Caspar Weinberger, 1983–86; chairman of the Joint Chiefs, 1989–93; secretary of state, 2001–05

John Hamre, Department of Defense comptroller, 1993–97; deputy secretary of defense, 1997–99

Paul Wolfowitz, deputy secretary of defense, 2001–2005

Pentagon Management

David O. "Doc" Cooke, the "Mayor of the Pentagon"

Steve Carter, building engineer; assistant building manager on 9/11

John Jester, chief of Pentagon police force

The Pentagon Renovation and Phoenix Project

Lee Evey, chief of the Pentagon Renovation Program, 1997–2002

Frank Probst, a communications contractor

Les Hunkele, a renovation project manager

Allyn Kilsheimer, structural engineer in charge of demolition and redesign for the Phoenix Project

Stephen Ludden, a Phoenix Project construction foreman

Inside the Pentagon on 9/11

Lieutenant Kevin Shaeffer, action officer in the Navy Command Center

Colonel Phil McNair, executive officer to the Army Deputy Chief of Staff for Personnel

Paul Gonzales, office supervisor, Defense Intelligence Agency comptroller's office
Peter Murphy, counsel for the commandant of the Marine Corps

Rescuers
Alan Wallace, Pentagon heliport firefighter
Lieutenant Colonel Paul "Ted" Anderson, Army congressional liaison office
Captain Mike Smith, Arlington County Fire Department
Assistant Chief Jim Schwartz, Arlington County Fire Department incident commander

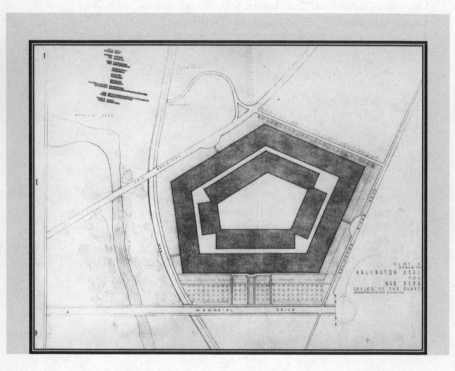

*Early plot plan for a new War Department headquarters
at Arlington Farm.*

PRELUDE

A pentagon

On a warm and rainy Thursday evening in July 1941, inside a War Department office in Washington, a small group of Army officers hastily assembled for a meeting and listened in disbelief to the secret plan outlined by their commander.

The general spoke in the velvety southern accent of his native Arkansas, but at a cadence far too rapid to be called a drawl. He was not in uniform—Army policy kept officers in civilian clothes so as to disguise from Congress the burgeoning military population in Washington—but he cut an immaculate figure, with his trim build, combed-back graying hair, and neatly groomed mustache. Over the past eight months, the officers of the Army's Construction Division had grown accustomed to bold and quick action from their chief. At age forty-nine, Brigadier General Brehon Burke Somervell had earned a reputation as a tough and "ruthless expediter." Somervell, it was said, could spot red tape before it even turned pink. Now he turned his eyes—"the keenest, shrewdest, most piercing eyes one is likely to meet," in the words of one observer—toward his chief of design, Lieutenant Colonel Hugh "Pat" Casey.

"Pat, we're going to build a new War Department Building, and we're not going to build it in Washington," Somervell said. "It's going to be built over in Virginia."

The building Somervell wanted to create was too big to fit in Washington and would have to go across the Potomac River in Arlington. It would be far larger than all the great structures of the city, including the U.S. Capitol. It would surpass any office building in the world. Somervell wanted a headquarters big enough to hold forty thousand people, with parking for ten thousand cars. It would contain four million square feet of office space—twice as much as the Empire State Building. Yet it must be no more than four stories high—a tall building would obstruct views of Washington and require too much steel, which was urgently needed for battleships and weapons.

The War Department would occupy the new headquarters within half a year, Somervell instructed. "We want 500,000 square feet ready in six months, and the whole thing ready in a year," the general said.

The War Department's chief architect would immediately assemble the people and equipment needed for the job, Somervell said. "Now, don't question his requirements," the general told his staff. "That isn't your job." Somervell gave no written instructions. The project was moving too fast, and its details were too sensitive. He ended the meeting with orders to have the general layout, basic design plans, and architectural perspectives for the building on his desk by 9 A.M. Monday.

"That," Casey later said, "was a big order." Somervell's engineers and architects were in for a long weekend.

Washington was consumed by war anxiety. Three weeks earlier, Adolf Hitler, already in control of much of Europe, had launched a surprise attack on the Soviet Union. The German army was already halfway to Moscow and had 300,000 Russian soldiers encircled around Smolensk. President Franklin D. Roosevelt, alarmed by Nazi gains, had declared a national emergency on May 27, triggering furious military preparations. The War Department in Washington was growing at an explosive rate, its 24,000 workers scattered in seventeen buildings around the area, including apartment buildings, warehouses, private homes, and several rented garages. Somervell's own headquarters was nestled in a new five-story federal office building on Capitol Hill known as the Railroad Retirement Building; he and other Army commanders spent hours every day traveling from office to office.

The dispersion of the War Department, inconvenient during peace-time, was unacceptable in a national emergency. General George C. Marshall, the Army chief of staff, racing to prepare the military for a conflict he believed the country could not avoid, needed a quick solution, and turned to Somervell, the Army's chief of construction. Marshall pictured a complex of temporary buildings on one site. Somervell took the concept further, envisioning a single, huge headquarters to house the entire War Department. A powerful Virginia congressman signaled interest on July 17 in finding a solution to the War Department's problem. Somervell launched the project that evening.

Working around the clock over the weekend, Somervell's staff brainstormed on a design. The restrictions were confounding, given the space they needed. The easiest solution, constructing a tall building, was out. They would have to spread out horizontally. But how? Pat Casey visualized a city of 40,000 people, not traveling by car, but instead moving by foot through one vast building. Casey and chief architect Edwin Bergstrom, working with harried assistants, toyed with different layouts. A square building that size—with the enormous interior distances to be covered—was too unwieldy, as was a rectangle. An octagon seemed too awkward. Finally, guided by the odd shape of the plot of land on which they hoped to build, they sketched a five-sided ring, curiously reminiscent of an old fortress: a pentagon.

PART I

THE MAKING
OF THE PENTAGON

Lieutenant Colonel Brehon B. Somervell
in November 1940, upon taking command
of the Construction Division.

CHAPTER 1

DYNAMITE IN
A TIFFANY BOX

Stimson looks for the right man

Henry Stimson was agitated. At age seventy-three, the secretary of war was the elder statesman of President Franklin D. Roosevelt's cabinet in both age and demeanor, known for his dignity, wisdom, and Yankee reserve. To his staff at the War Department, Stimson seemed "like the Rock of Ages." But he also was imbued with a deep streak of Old Testament temper, and an agitated Stimson was a fearsome thing. "Everybody always seemed to think of Stimson as a wonderful old gentleman," one officer later said. "He was old all right, but he was a tough guy. If he had to, he knew how and when to use profanity."

Stimson was swearing regularly in the fall of 1940. The largest peacetime military mobilization in American history had begun that spring, and it was bogged down. France had fallen in May, the Low Countries were overrun, and Britain was in grave danger. Roosevelt responded with a call to dramatically build the armed forces, and Congress answered with legislation raising the authorized strength of the Army eightfold, from 174,000 to 1.4 million. But before this great Army could be raised, it needed a roof.

Dozens of military camps had to be built immediately around the country to house and train hundreds of thousands of draftees. Work was flowing into the Army Quartermaster Corps's once-sleepy Construction Division at unprecedented levels; the division's monthly budget of less than $10 million soared to a figure eventually seventy times that amount. Orders to construct camps, munitions plants, housing projects, airfields, and ports were piling up. Construction headquarters took on the air of a Middle East bazaar, with some offices so crowded that workers had to hop over desks to move around. "The halls teemed with visitors, as contractors, materialmen, equipment dealers and a good many others beat a path to the men with a billion dollars to spend," the Army's official account of World War II construction in the United States notes.

The men with a billion dollars struggled and spent mightily, but soon fell on their faces. "They had gotten into desperate confusion," in Stimson's view. The mobilization of the entire Army was dangerously delayed by the construction mess. Almost nothing could be done until the facilities were built. General George C. Marshall, the Army chief of staff, had set ninety-day deadlines to build the camps, an order that proved hopelessly unrealistic. By November 1940, good weather for construction was vanishing, and the pressure was increasing. With few camps finished, Marshall's ambitious schedule had to be drastically revised, and only token numbers of draftees called up. Guardsmen had quit jobs, vacated apartments, and left families to find they had no place to report. The Army was being portrayed by the press as an organization of dunces. "Even sadder than the delays were some of Mr. Stimson's excuses," scolded *Time* magazine, which laid the blame on "the bumbling quartermasters."

Stimson was on his second stint as secretary of war, having served in the same job almost three decades earlier for President William Taft during the years leading up to World War I. Back then, he had seemingly endless time to get the Army ready for war, but no money. Now, Congress had appropriated fantastic streams of money, but there was no time.

"I am not satisfied [the Construction Division] is doing as rapid work as I think should be done," Stimson noted in his diary. As the delays stretched on, the secretary grew "more and more agitated," observed John J. McCloy, the "gnomelike" assistant secretary of war often at the old man's side. McCloy, an astute Wall Street lawyer, had been recruited by Stimson earlier that year and quickly earned a reputation as the secretary's top troubleshooter.

Stimson told McCloy they needed someone with the "necessary drive" to speed up the construction program. "If only a good man could be found the problem would be solved," Stimson said. But who? The secretary's attention was directed to a dynamic Army Corps of Engineers lieutenant colonel, Brehon Somervell, who had turned around the Works Progress Administration program in New York City in four years as administrator. Stimson instructed McCloy to check with his New York connections about Somervell's temperament and ability. McCloy found Somervell had a "reputation as a driver and almost fearless energetic builder. . . . They all added up to the conviction that whatever the form of the organization, he was the man to head it."

Somervell was already slotted for a humdrum assignment with a training command in the Midwest, but Marshall intervened. "Have him assigned for temporary duty here in the office of the Chief of Staff," Marshall instructed his chief of personnel on November 8, 1940. ". . . Confidentially, the Secretary of War wants to get a look at him without Somervell being aware of this."

Stimson wanted to see this man for himself.

I suppose the fellow who built the Pyramids was efficient, too

None of Brehon Somervell's seven predecessors had fared well trying to tame New York City's work-relief system. "Several had resigned in despair or disgust, one had died, probably of overwork, and none had lasted a year," the *New Yorker* noted. There was no doubt that the New York office of the Works Progress Administration—the New Deal agency providing emergency public employment for the nation's jobless—was in dire need of assistance. The New York WPA was one of the largest employers in the nation, providing jobs for 200,000 workers, and it spent one out of every seven WPA dollars in the nation. The program was grossly inefficient, in part because of its immensity but also because the city was home to powerful unions and left-wing parties that drew their support from the huge ranks of unemployed. WPA head Harry Hopkins had turned to the Army Corps of Engineers to bring some military discipline and engineering expertise to the agency.

Hopkins appointed Somervell Works Projects Administrator for New

York City in the summer of 1936. "I consider it to be the most difficult WPA job in the nation," he said. Funding cuts that spring forced thousands off the WPA payrolls in New York, sparking almost daily picketing and sit-in strikes. Somervell's immediate predecessor, Victor Ridder, a philanthropist and liberal, had ended up foaming at the mouth about "Communist rats and vermin." He suffered a nervous breakdown and resigned. The communist newspaper *Daily Worker*, which had campaigned against him under the slogan "Get Rid of Ridder," crowed in victory. A similar fate was widely predicted for Somervell.

The only one not worried was Somervell. His first public comment on the fate of his predecessors was to cheekily suggest a new slogan for the *Daily Worker*: "Sink Somervell." Somervell found the idea of workers on relief going out on strike "just fantastic" and tried a different tack from his predecessors. Instead of sending police to forcibly eject the protesters—a step that guaranteed screaming headlines—Somervell simply locked the bathrooms. Strikers held out as long as their bladders did, then filtered off one by one.

Somervell imposed Army discipline on the WPA, threatening to fire any workers who interfered with the program. Leaving his office one day to find protesters had laid down in the pavement directly in front of his car, the colonel did not hesitate. He ordered his driver to start the car, hopped in, and slammed the door. When they realized Somervell was not stopping, the protesters leapt to their feet and fled. His war against shovel-leaners so aggrieved the Workers Alliance—the major WPA union—that it distributed cartoons depicting Somervell as Simon Legree, whirling a huge blacksnake whip above a terrified WPA worker. But Somervell soon made peace with labor; picket lines grew infrequent, and strikes a thing of the past. He cut administrative costs by two-thirds, bringing the WPA in line with private construction. Somervell transformed the sprawling, dysfunctional office into a quietly efficient billion-dollar business enterprise that laid sewers, built parks and playgrounds, battled child malnutrition, and constructed enough roads to reach Denver, by one estimate. "Charges of boondoggling, once the order of the day, have been rare during the Somervell administration," the *New York Times* reported. The local union head was obliged to admit Somervell had done an able job getting the WPA's management in hand, adding bitterly, "I suppose the fellow that built the Pyramids was efficient, too."

Somervell cut a dapper figure in his mufti and trademark bow tie, and his dry and carefree sense of humor won over the New York press. "Well, girls, what's wrong today?" he'd ask reporters, generally all men. He even chatted amiably with the *Daily Worker* reporter. "His manner is pleasant and shrewd, and there is a touch of Will Rogers in his public personality," the *New Yorker* said.

His amiability could not always mask his ferocious temper, made all the more striking by his otherwise elegant ways. "Dynamite in a Tiffany box," was how one industrialist would later describe Somervell. "He is out of the tradition of the Elizabethan Englishman, all lace and velvet and courtliness outside, fury and purposefulness within," a journalist wrote.

Somervell was one of only two men who could hold his own with New York City Mayor Fiorello H. La Guardia using the "Little Flower's" weapon of choice—a pair of lungs. The other, Robert Moses, the city's powerful redevelopment czar, would actually outyell La Guardia, while Somervell's technique was to beat the mayor to the first shout. "Either way," said an admiring witness, "it was no mean feat."

Somervell, hardly a New Deal liberal, had little sympathy for the more humanistic aspects of the WPA program. He paid an unannounced visit to Bellevue Hospital, where the WPA was assisting with a therapeutic finger-painting class for mentally disturbed patients. One of the patients had just disrobed, and the colonel walked into the classroom to find a naked man with paint all over his hands. Somervell "went up like a torch," a witness said, and the program was stopped. A furor arose when Somervell accepted a complaint that airport murals painted by August Henkel included a likeness of Joseph Stalin and depicted the Wright Brothers in Russian-style uniforms. Somervell had the murals burned in a pot-bellied stove.

Yet it was hard to argue with his results. Somervell's tenure culminated in the biggest WPA project ever undertaken. Ground was broken for a new airport at North Beach in Queens in September 1937. The airport was La Guardia's vision, but it was built with Somervell's whip. "The day before yesterday" was Somervell's invariable reply every time the architect asked when drawings were needed. It was the sort of project Somervell loved. Much of the $45 million, 558-acre airport was built on land reclaimed from the East River. Somervell built a steel trestle over Bowery Bay to reach a trash dump on Rikers Island, allowing trucks to transport a great mound of cinders, and rubbish to be used as fill at the airport site. Overseeing a workforce that reached 23,000, Somervell relentlessly rushed the project to completion in little over two years. An excited crowd of 325,000 people attended the airport's dedication on a cloudless day in October 1939. Many public officials took bows, but La Guardia—for whom the airport would soon be named—later said the real credit lay with Somervell.

Among those who toured the new airport that month was George C. Marshall. "I was much impressed," the Army chief of staff wrote in a note to the colonel. War had come to Europe in September, and Marshall added Somervell's name to his list of officers whose services he might depend upon in the near future.

Just a country boy from Arkansas

"I'm just a country boy from Arkansas trying to get along in the big town," Somervell would invariably say. The claim was preposterous. There was nothing of the bumpkin about Brehon Burke Somervell. He had been born in Little Rock, and his parents, hardly country farmers, came from prominent, well-established families. In the 1740s, James Somervell, of Kennox, Scotland, had immigrated to St. Mary's County in southern Maryland and built a great plantation, Mulberry Fields, on the banks of the Potomac. His grandson, Richard Bullock Somervell, was a prestigious planter in west Tennessee who helped lead the state into secession during the Civil War.

Richard Somervell's son, William, raised amid wealth and sent to fine schools, was practicing medicine in Little Rock when his wife gave birth to a son, Brehon, on May 9, 1892. The boy's mother, Mary Burke Somervell, an elegant, sophisticated schoolteacher, was the dominant force in her son's life. She raised her only child to believe his upbringing and ancestry made him special; it was a lesson he took to heart.

After William Somervell lost much of his hearing and gave up his medical practice, the family moved in 1906 to Washington, where Mary Somervell established a girls' finishing school. Belcourt Seminary was soon one of the most fashionable in the city. There Brehon was raised "in an atmosphere of tittering young girls, classical literature, and relentless application of the principles of good breeding." The boy was so handsome his mother made him sit with his back to the girls at dinner.

Brehon had a wild streak, and, irked by Belcourt's genteel atmosphere, he frequently escaped to play sandlot baseball. He was known as "the irrepressible one" at Washington's Central High School. "Brehon is about the liveliest one we have come across lately and no one knows what he is going to do next," the class yearbook, *The Brecky,* noted upon his graduation in 1909. But Brehon knew. Army officers were a common sight in the capital, and the boy was mesmerized by them. "One day in Washington I saw a couple of West Point cadets. They looked perfect to me," he later said.

Somervell won an appointment from an Arkansas congressman to enter the U.S. Military Academy in 1910. There, he shone in all he did. He was a superb marksman and rider, and a star fencer; he was a natural in a sport demanding quick rapier thrusts. With his elegance and fine looks, Bill—as most friends called him—earned a reputation as a dandy, but he was also near the top of his class in all major areas of study. Fellow cadets marveled at his powers of organization. "If you could take Bill's mind out and examine it you would find it pigeonholed and arranged like a card index," the class yearbook, *The Howitzer,* reported. His major deficiency was one that would plague him throughout his life: his volcanic temper. Somervell forfeited his chance at the cadet captaincy by throwing china at mess. He graduated sixth in the Class of 1914, a ranking that easily won him assignment to the Corps of Engineers, the branch that traditionally drew the brightest from West Point. Small and elite, with only 190 officers when Somervell was commissioned as a second lieutenant, the corps saw itself as separate from and better than the rest of the Army. It was an elitism for which Somervell was perfectly suited. Besides, with projects such as building dams and canals, the engineers offered the most hope for an interesting career during the peaceful times most of the world enjoyed in the spring of 1914.

Touring Europe on two months' graduation leave, Somervell wasted no time thrusting himself into great events. In August 1914, the German army crashed across the Belgian frontier near Liège, the beginning of a great, wheeling offensive into France. Somervell immediately reported to the U.S. Embassy in Paris, where he was named assistant military attaché and put to work aiding Americans trying to escape ahead of the advancing Germans. To speed the exodus, the battleship USS *Tennessee* was dispatched to France carrying a million dollars in gold stuffed into ten kegs.

Young Somervell hired special trains and ships to rescue stranded Americans and distributed money to panicked tourists clamoring to get home. His handling of the crisis quickly earned him a reputation as a man who could size up a problem, find a solution, and drive it through to completion.

Reporting for duty in the United States, which was still years from entering the war, Somervell was sent to Texas to map the country along the Mexican frontier. It was a somnolent assignment at first, but adventure found him again. "I was hard at work when (Pancho) Villa raided the border and made it unnecessary to finish the maps," Somervell later said. The Mexican bandit attacked Columbus, New Mexico, in March 1916, killing eighteen Americans and leaving the small border town a smoking ruin. A punitive expedition was launched by President Woodrow Wilson under the command of General John "Black Jack" Pershing, and Somervell, to his joy, found a new opportunity.

He wasted no time making a name for himself, displaying what became a lifelong knack for impressing his superiors while infuriating his peers. Reporting to duty at expeditionary headquarters two hundred miles into Mexico, he came bearing a large box of Havana cigars preferred by his commanding officer, Captain Ernest "Pot" Graves. Somervell was placed in charge of building and operating a section of highway for the truck convoys supplying Pershing's cavalry with rations, grain, and water.

The Pershing expedition marked the first time the Army had used motor transportation of any significant amount in a military operation, and it showed. The Army old guard insisted mule trains were more reliable, and at times it seemed they indeed were. The motorized expedition was hampered by breakdowns in the supply chain. Somervell, assigned to a new job as regimental supply officer, struggled to get the tremendous amounts of gasoline and oil required to keep the trucks running.

Motoring down a rough trail one hot afternoon, Pershing came across one of his trucks stalled by the road. "Black Jack" was outraged to see the crew idling in the shade with no officer in view, and he sprung from his car. "Where is the officer in charge?" Pershing demanded.

"Here, sir," a voice underneath the truck answered. It was Somervell. Covered with grease from head to foot, he crawled out from under the truck, stood, and saluted. Half-scowling and half-smiling, Pershing silently returned the salute and drove on.

Somervell's performance in Mexico won him a spot in the first Army engineering detachment sent to France after America entered the Great War in 1917. Assigned to the 15th Engineer Regiment—with Pot Graves again his immediate superior—Somervell landed in France with the unit on July 25. Now a captain and soon to be a major, Somervell constructed a great munitions dump at Mehun-sur-Yèvre, a hundred miles south of Paris, and then was sent to straighten out a mess near Dijon at Is-sur-Tille, where poorly trained engineer troops building an advance depot were floundering. Somervell shook the troops from their lethargy with reveille at dawn and worked them from first light until dark, with barely a break for meals. Somervell's hurry-up style was evident in all he did. Finding no proper sleeping quarters for the regiment, he bought new tents without waiting for a purchase order. The Army billed him for $17,755 and threatened to deduct the cost from his pay, but Somervell argued his way out.

For over a year Somervell toiled, building dumps, barracks, and a poison-gas depot, and he was awarded with a temporary promotion to lieutenant colonel and the Distinguished Service Medal for his record of "unusual vision [and] initiative." Somervell was far from satisfied. He begged for transfer to combat duty, but he had made himself too useful to supply commanders, and they refused to spare him. Given leave in the fall of 1918, Somervell spurned the chance to relax in Paris, instead pleading with Pot Graves to lend him his Army sedan, a big Cadillac, so he could make "just a little visit" to the front. It was not merely adventure he was seeking; calculating as always, Somervell was also thinking of his career. "I have yet to hear a hostile shot and I'm not going home with that on my record," Somervell insistently told Graves.

The gruff but good-natured Graves finally capitulated and did not see his Cadillac again until after the armistice. Somervell's timing, as usual, was prescient. He arrived at the front October 31, the day before the final phase of the Meuse-Argonne offensive that would break the German army. Somervell worked his way to the headquarters of the 89th Division, which was taking part in the push to the Meuse River. The division's operations officer had just been captured by the Germans while on reconnaissance, and a replacement was needed.

"What do you know about military tactics?" Somervell was asked.

"Practically nothing," he admitted.

"An ideal man for the job," replied a sardonic officer. But the 89th was in a fix, and Somervell got the post.

The division chief of staff, Colonel John C. H. Lee, found his new operations officer to be "truly an answer to prayer. He learned with lightning-like rapidity, was fearless and brilliant." By November 5, the 89th had reached the Meuse opposite Pouilly in northeast France, where the retreating Germans were thought to have destroyed all bridges in the area. Late in the day, the division learned that the Germans had failed to blow a bridge leading to town. Somervell accompanied Lee on a reconnaissance to the frontline, along a canal that paralleled the river. Reaching the approach to the bridge, they found it had been damaged, but in the darkness could not tell how badly. Shortly before midnight, Somervell went forward with two scouts, moving more than five hundred yards beyond the last American outposts and fording three branches of the Meuse. Across the river, they encountered a German detachment and drove it off with a brief exchange of fire. Somervell considered chasing them but wisely turned back. The bridge was passable, Somervell reported to his superiors. The division crossed the river several days later and was advancing when word came after sun-up on the morning of November 11 that an armistice was to go into effect at 11 A.M. that day.

For his exploits at Pouilly, Somervell was awarded the Distinguished Service Cross, the nation's second-highest decoration for bravery. Now a certified war hero—one of only nine officers to win both the Distinguished Service Cross and the Distinguished Service Medal during the conflict—Somervell's reputation was made. Pot Graves's evaluation of the subordinate who absconded with his car was succinct: "This is the best officer I ever saw, or hope to see." It was high praise, but Graves's words hinted at the ambivalence some officers felt about Somervell. His brilliance was darkened—and in part fueled—by an aggressive and opportunistic nature so powerful that his peers, many of them quite aggressive themselves, were taken aback. "He called himself a mean son-of-a-bitch, and he was," said William Hoge, an engineer officer who would cross swords with him. "Watch Somervell," it was said around the Army, and not always meant favorably.

Assigned to the Army of Occupation in the Rhineland, Somervell enjoyed life stationed in the ancient city of Koblenz, founded by the Romans at the strategic confluence of the Rhine and Mosel rivers. His reputation among friends as "a gay blade" suffered after he met Anna Purnell, a young YMCA volunteer from a privileged Chicago background who helped entertain the 89th Division troops. She was lovely, with wavy, Titian hair, a woman of "rare personal charm," in the judgment of Colonel Lee. Somervell married her on August 28, 1919, in the Kaiser's private chapel in Koblenz. A year later, Somervell returned to the United States with his wife and the first of three daughters.

Magnitude never seemed to bother him

More than one major controversy in Somervell's career presaged the splash he would make with the Pentagon, including the tempest that arose while he served as District Engineer for Washington, D.C. In 1929, Somervell pondered a grandiose scheme to make the Potomac River the national waterway by connecting it with the Ohio River. It was a dream first pursued 135 years earlier by George Washington, who began building a canal that would have tied the fledgling country to the lands west of the Allegheny Mountains. The modern project would construct twenty-seven dams to turn 185 miles of the Potomac's upper reaches between Washington and Cumberland, Maryland, into navigable water; it was an enormous undertaking that Somervell reluctantly concluded would be prohibitively expensive. Instead—perhaps as a consolation—he advocated tackling a portion of the project. Somervell wanted to dam the Potomac at two points upriver from Washington, including at Great Falls, a scene of primeval beauty where the powerful river cascades over a series of jagged boulders, falling seventy-six feet in less than a mile.

Somervell was pitted against a formidable foe: Lieutenant Colonel Ulysses S. Grant III, grandson of the Union general, who was executive officer of the National Capital Park and Planning Commission. He was well-known in Washington, having led what the newspapers dubbed the "war on neckers" during the summer of 1928. Grant demanded that visitors to Washington parks sign a pledge promising to "refrain from any action, posture or public display of amorousness that might be offensive to

others or could set a bad example to the children." Despite his disapproval
of park romances, Grant was a lover of nature, and he was appalled by
Somervell's proposal to flood majestic Great Falls. His planning commission came down squarely against the plan.

Somervell was not the least intimidated about taking on a brother officer of the Corps of Engineers, even one who outranked him and bore such
a famous name. To the contrary, Somervell publicly ridiculed Grant, issuing a statement to the press calling Grant's criticism "too far-fetched to
claim the attention of any thinking person, much less an engineer who is
supposed to know about such matters." Congress, however, sided with
Grant and soon passed a bill that established an extensive park system
along the Potomac, including at Great Falls.

The whole affair was vintage Somervell, from the supremely confident
case he made for building the dams to his fury at anyone—Grant, in this
case—who tried to stop him. Most notably, it laid bare Somervell's deep, almost megalomaniacal passion for operating on a grand scale. Building
huge ammunition depots during the Great War had merely whetted his appetite. He saw himself as a builder, and the bigger the project, the better.
"Magnitude never seemed to bother him," said General John Hardin, a fellow Army engineer. "I think he loved the bigness of things."

Somervell was bitterly disappointed by the outcome of the Great Falls
debate, but before long he had another canal to build, this one even
grander. In 1934, President Roosevelt appointed Somervell to a board
studying the feasibility of building a canal across northern Florida, connecting the Gulf of Mexico to the Atlantic Ocean, an idea that, like Washington's Potomac canal, had been contemplated for centuries. The board
recommended the project, and, a year later, Roosevelt allocated $5 million
in relief money as a means of putting men to work. To no one's surprise,
Somervell—now a lieutenant colonel—was placed in charge.

Congress was decidedly dubious about the project because of its high
cost and environmental problems. Where the estimated $120 million needed
would come from, nobody knew. But Somervell was not to be dissuaded and
tried to force congressional approval with a *fait accompli*. In the town of
Ocala, Florida, just five days after Roosevelt's announcement, Somervell
presided as a thundering blast sent a geyser of dirt into the air, tearing out

the first hole for the canal. Within three weeks, Somervell had three thousand men on the job and was pressing Washington for another $20 million. "He got his orders one morning and before Congress could get around to stopping the project he had that great ditch well along in construction in a matter of a few weeks," an Army engineer later wrote. "I doubt if there are many equals to that performance."

Somervell was completely in his element. The canal, running 195 miles across Florida, would be of a suitably Somervellian scale, twice as long as the Suez Canal and four times the length of Panama's. There was no other job in the world he would rather have, he said.

Attracted by the grand scope of the canal, a roving newspaper columnist for the Scripps-Howard chain visited the project headquarters in Ocala in the spring of 1936 to interview Somervell. Arriving at Camp Roosevelt at 5 P.M. on a Sunday, Ernie Pyle walked into the administration building and found one person at work. It was Somervell—at forty-four, his hair turning silver—wearing blue trousers with a light-gray pullover. He wasted no time in charming the columnist. "I'm glad you came. I wanted to quit work anyhow," said Somervell, rising to greet Pyle from behind a desk covered with foot-high piles of charts and reports.

"Somervell surprised me," Pyle—who became the greatest American reporter of World War II—told his readers. "I had expected to see an old, hard-bitten engineer veteran, tough as a horse-hair lariat and meaner than Pilate. Somervell is tough all right, I guess, but he doesn't look it. . . . It would make him sore to say so, but he is a handsome man."

In full, folksy Will Rogers mode, Somervell regaled Pyle with tales of Arkansas, Pancho Villa, and the copperhead snake one of his daughters had killed, skinned, and made into a bandeau the previous summer. "He's a fellow you can sit down and talk with," Pyle wrote. "He's a tremendous reader, and seems to know something about everything." Somervell, the columnist predicted, might well take his place among the storied engineers of past great projects. "Panama had its Goethals, the Brooklyn Bridge its Roebling, and the Florida Canal will have, I suppose, its Somervell," Pyle wrote.

It was not to be. Several months after Pyle's visit, Congress cut off all further funding for the canal, and the project was shut down. Somervell would have to make his mark elsewhere.

A gleam of light on the horizon

Somervell's time in Florida was not entirely wasted. Among those he met in Ocala was a slim, somewhat wan former social worker from Iowa whose mild-mannered appearance completely belied the power he bore as confidante and alter ego of the president. Harry Lloyd Hopkins, the impassioned and resilient New Deal high priest leading the largest work-relief effort in the nation's history, was impressed with Somervell's performance putting thousands of men to work on the canal. When that enterprise collapsed, Hopkins saw Somervell as the ideal man to straighten the embarrassing New York WPA mess. Somervell cultivated his relationship with Hopkins, recognizing the aide's tremendous influence with Roosevelt. Somervell's accomplishments in New York over the next four years solidified a deep bond between the soldier and the social worker. More importantly, Hopkins appreciated what Somervell might still accomplish. Though by then terribly frail from a cancer operation that removed three-fourths of his stomach, Hopkins became Somervell's great champion.

Somervell needed one. By the summer of 1940, he was agitating to get out of New York, worried he would miss the boat if war came and he was stuck at the WPA. For years, Somervell had believed another war with Germany was inevitable. ("If I hadn't," he said, "I would have got out of the Army long before.") The stunning evacuation of British troops from Dunkirk in late May 1940 convinced him the time was near. Somervell began "frantically pulling wires" to get back on active service, pressing his case with a senior officer on Marshall's staff.

La Guardia, by now a fervent believer in Somervell's abilities, twice blocked his efforts to leave the city with appeals to the White House. Somervell used his own White House entrée to appeal directly to Roosevelt in October, arguing that the WPA was running smoothly and that he could better serve the country if he were back on military duty. After FDR promised La Guardia he would appoint a worthy successor, the mayor reluctantly agreed to Somervell's departure. "It hurts," a disappointed La Guardia told reporters when the news was announced November 7. Somervell, the mayor said, "leaves here permanent and impressive monuments to his executive skill."

Leaving New York was only half the battle. Somervell's performance did not earn him much credit among his peers in the Army, who held a low regard for the WPA and its decidedly unmilitary projects. Somervell spoke briefly with Marshall, asking to be considered for a field command and reminding the general of his highly decorated combat service in World War I. Marshall, though impressed with Somervell's work building the airport in New York, was noncommittal. To his dismay, Somervell subsequently learned that the chief of engineers, Major General Julian Schley, who viewed Somervell as a bit too ambitious and a bit too shrewd, was assigning him to a respectable but lackluster position as executive officer for a new engineer training center to be established in the Midwest. No location had been selected yet, giving Somervell a reprieve.

Arriving in Washington in November 1940, Somervell began desperately fishing about for a better assignment. He need not have worried. Unknown to Somervell, Stimson and Marshall were watching him with another job in mind. The secretary of war, fretting over the Army's camp-construction debacle, was impressed with what he saw. After meeting Somervell, Stimson wrote in his diary, "A gleam of light . . . came into my horizon."

Waiting in the wings

Brigadier General Charles "Baldy" Hartman, chief of the Army's Construction Division, had heard the rumors for a week that his head was on the block; stubborn, proud, and a bit nervous, he ignored them and went about his work. He was not surprised when his superior, Major General Edmund Gregory, showed up unannounced at the division headquarters in the Railroad Retirement Building on Capitol Hill early in the afternoon of December 11, 1940. "I knew by the scared look on his face he had bad news for me," Hartman later said. He was right.

Being chief of construction was the culmination of a quarter-century of dedicated service for Hartman. He was a West Point graduate who had been one of the Army's youngest colonels in World War I, and he was beloved by his staff for his honesty and modesty. But his timing was bad. He was appointed to the job in March 1940, just weeks before the national emergency prompted by the fall of France overwhelmed the Construction Division. "The Lord Himself could not meet the construction timetables and cost estimates," reported a construction expert sent to assess the situation for the government. But that did not matter. Angered by the delay in the Army's mobilization, Marshall's staff complained that Hartman was "making a complete mess of the construction program." Baldy, one critic said cuttingly, was a "nice old gentleman who was used to being bawled out by colonels' wives over furnaces." It was a cruel judgment, unfairly smearing an officer who in ordinary times would have been a fine construction chief. But Hartman's best was not good enough, not now.

Marshall had come to Stimson's office the morning of December 11 to tell the secretary he intended to replace Hartman with Somervell. Stimson felt a bit queasy about axing Hartman, despite his deep dissatisfaction with construction progress. "It is a pathetic situation because Hartman has been a loyal and devoted man," he wrote in his diary that day. ". . . But he apparently lacks the gift of organization and he has been running behind in the work." Stimson approved the change.

The pressure had been building for weeks. The White House had threatened to take the construction program away from the Army and put it under civilian control. Momentum for the move waned as soon as Army officials let the White House know that Somervell would be put in charge. That satisfied the critics. Harry Hopkins, in particular, gave Somervell an "enthusiastic" endorsement.

Gregory, who was the Army's quartermaster general and who in theory should decide who would head the Construction Division, still balked at the switch, not out of loyalty to Hartman, but because he did not in the least trust Somervell, whom he considered "brilliant, but slick." Marshall's deputy chief of staff, Major General Richard C. Moore, warned Gregory that unless he accepted Somervell, the entire construction program would be stripped from the Quartermaster Corps.

Gregory finally saw the light. Arriving in Hartman's office, he wasted no time with pleasantries and informed Baldy that he was relieved at once from the Construction Division. "I did not give him the courtesy of a reply," Hartman later said. He closed his desk and left his office.

Somervell was waiting in the wings. "Somervell walked in one door, and Hartman walked out the other," Hartman's secretary later recalled. Somervell had been eagerly preparing since November, when a Stimson adviser had asked if he would be interested in the position; before the job was even his, Somervell had launched a "whirlwind" four-state inspection tour and produced a fourteen-page report criticizing the construction program.

Somervell's appointment was announced to the press December 13; reporters were told the construction delays "had no bearing" on the change of command. Hartman checked himself into Walter Reed Army Hospital, on the verge of a nervous breakdown. It was curiously reminiscent of the fate that had befallen Somervell's predecessor at the WPA. The War Department announced he had entered the hospital "for observation and treatment following a long period of overwork." In part, it was a convenient fiction, Stimson noted in his diary, "designed to protect poor old Hartman, who has been as faithful as could be and has broken down under the task, from being unjustly criticized." Hartman was indeed broken, as was his heart. He soon suffered coronary problems, retired, and cut off contact with old friends.

The deed done, it was soon forgotten, as Stimson was much enamored of his new construction chief. "Somervell was like a breath of fresh air," the secretary recorded after the two talked the job over. Stimson proudly showed off his new construction chief at a press conference December 19, an appearance that had the desired effect: "I think the sight of Somervell was enough to show the point to the Press that progress was being made."

Clifford Berryman cartoon in the Washington Evening Star,
August 29, 1941.

CHAPTER
2

THE SOMERVELL BLITZ

I will just move

The officers of the Army's Construction Division filled a government auditorium near the division's Capitol Hill headquarters on the morning of February 22, 1941. Though 120 had been invited and 150 chairs set out, the officers spilled over into the aisles. No one, it seemed, dared miss hearing the new chief speak about his principles of organization.

Brigadier General Brehon Somervell commanded the floor. "Napoleon used to say—I'm very glad he said it because I have repeated it two or three hundred times—'There aren't any poor regiments; there are only poor colonels.'" Somervell then drove home the point, in case anyone had missed it: "Everybody here is a colonel, in a sense."

Doubtlessly, many officers shifted uncomfortably in their seats. After waiting a decade and a half during the slow interwar years to make lieutenant colonel in 1935, Somervell had jumped two ranks to brigadier general in January 1941, and he was not the least bit shy about using his new power. Since taking command of the Construction Division a little over two months earlier, Somervell had purged the organization, sweeping out Hartman loyalists, older officers who had lost their steam, incompetents, fools, or anyone else he concluded was not up to the job. It had become known as the Somervell Blitz.

"I will not talk . . . ," Somervell told Brigadier General Eugene Reybold, the Army's chief of supply, a week after taking command. "I will just move."

That he had done. The new construction chief filled key positions with his own men, bringing in engineers from his days at the New York WPA and the Florida Canal. With Marshall's blessing, he raided other War Department staffs, trolling for the most aggressive officers and the smartest operators. Somervell streamlined the division, reducing it from eleven branches to five. "If he continued any of Hartman's policies, it was purely coincidental," a division officer later said.

The Somervell Blitz was more than a bloodletting. It was accompanied by record-breaking construction. Somervell pressed forward as if the nation were already at war, calling the Construction Division "the shock troops of preparedness." He drove his staff relentlessly, seven days a week, leaving officers exhausted. "We members of the Construction Division in Washington had a major campaign under our belts before the shooting war for Americans got underway," said Major Gar Davidson.

The first battle was to get the Army's stalled mobilization moving. Dozens of camps were needed to house troops across the county by the spring. Workers fought bad weather and material shortages but quickly finished fifty major camps and twenty-eight troop reception centers. By spring 1941, they had finished enough facilities to accommodate the entire Army, now one million strong.

"The new Army is housed," Somervell boasted in a press release. The tally under construction by the summer also included nine hospitals, forty-five munitions plants, fifty-two harbor facilities, ten chemical-warfare plants, and twenty-one storage depots. "In terms of speed it represents the most remarkable achievement in rapid large scale construction in the annals of this or any other army," the War Department claimed.

A new story emerged, replacing the image of bumbling quartermasters from the previous fall. In this, Somervell took his cue from one of his heroes, Theodore Roosevelt. The Rough Rider had known the value of publicity, and so did Somervell. In his first week on the job, he created a new section in the Construction Division—public relations—and immediately hired a veteran newspaperman, George S. Holmes, a former Washington correspondent for the Scripps-Howard chain, to run it. Somervell ordered every construction office in the country to put public relations men on their staffs and supply the local press with regular stories about construction projects. They were instructed to send Holmes progress reports and photographs every Friday via airmail.

Holmes and his staff were soon putting out an "exuberant" flood of press releases extolling the accomplishments of the Construction Division and, by extension, Somervell. The effort paid off with national publicity, including a seventeen-page layout in *Fortune* magazine that told how "half horse, half alligator" quartermasters had "conjured forty-six cantonments and tent camps out of prairie mud or pine barrens or rocky defiles." Somervell distributed thousands of copies of a forty-four-page booklet saluting "the greatest Army building program of all time." He appeared at groundbreakings and construction-industry conventions around the country and wrote articles for industry publications saluting "this unparalleled achievement."

Somervell handled congressional relations with equal aplomb. Hartman, his predecessor, had let congressmen cool their heels in the hallway when they came visiting. But anytime congressmen came calling, Somervell would sweep out anyone who happened to be in his office and usher in the legislators.

The support Somervell had from the top was more than Hartman could have imagined. Somervell, according to Quartermaster General Gregory, had a "pipeline to General Marshall," and thus did not pay any attention to his nominal chain of command—including Gregory. The quartermaster general watched sullenly as his subordinate was granted his every wish.

Somervell had another trump card, one that intimidated his rivals even more than the unstinting backing he received from Marshall: Harry Hopkins. Every senior officer in the department knew the president's closest aide was Somervell's protector. If they didn't, Somervell let them know. Gregory believed Hopkins "was always moving around back of the curtain." How true this was did not matter. The perception was daunting enough.

For Somervell, it was a perfect situation: an unlimited mandate to build, coupled with unlimited power and an unlimited budget. "You can't do anything without money," he told the Construction Division officers gathered in the auditorium on that February morning. "It may be the curse of humanity but we all like to be cursed every once in a while."

Somervell was amply cursed. The Army's earlier cost estimates for the construction program had been woefully inadequate, and Somervell had been given another $338 million.

"Congress has given us practically a blank check on this construction," he told the officers, adding as an afterthought, "that makes it all the more incumbent upon all of us to pay close attention to our financial transactions." In truth, Somervell was little concerned with cost overruns. "We're buying time, and time is the most expensive commodity in the world," he told a newspaper columnist. "Time and economy don't mix."

That attitude alarmed the junior senator from Missouri, who was beginning to poke into the nation's enormous defense spending. Somervell was exactly the sort of regular Army officer that Harry S. Truman had resented as a Missouri National Guard captain commanding an artillery battery in France during World War I. Truman considered Somervell a martinet who "cared absolutely nothing about money." Somervell, Truman once noted with a touch of pride, did not like him "because I stuck pins in him."

Somervell did despise Truman, considering him a headline-hunting hypocrite. The story Somervell told close associates over the years was that Truman's enmity toward him, as well as the special Senate committee Truman created to investigate defense spending, resulted from Somervell's refusal to select a contractor favored by the senator. "They threatened to form the committee to make our lives miserable if we did not give the contract for the St. Louis Small Arms Plant" to Truman's choice, Somervell later wrote in a letter, and he claimed to have proof of the threat in a safe-deposit box.

The skill Somervell normally used to assuage members of Congress quickly deserted him in his dealings with Truman. Major Gar Davidson, summoned to Somervell's office one day in early 1941, listened in alarm as the general and the senator went at it over the telephone. "Mr. Senator," Somervell concluded the conversation, "as far as I'm concerned you can go piss up a rope." That remark, Davidson believed, "was the straw of insolent independence that broke the camel's back and precipitated the Truman Committee."

The committee was established in March 1941, and its first target was

Somervell's construction program. Whether instigated by Somervell's invective, Truman's spite, or simply the senator's dismay at wasteful spending, the committee quickly became a thorn in the general's side. The committee's report that summer charged that the Army camp construction program had wasted "several hundred million dollars," and Truman told the Senate he was "utterly astounded" at evidence of negligence and inefficiency on the part of the War Department.

Truman's slings and arrows dented Somervell's armor, but he was hardly vanquished. At the White House and at the top of the War Department, Somervell was seen as a miracle man. Stimson called him a man "who could throw away the book and get results in the face of unexpected handicaps and obstacles." Truman was correct that there had been terrible budget overruns: The cost of 229 troop facilities, originally estimated at $515 million, came to $828 million. But much of the added cost was due to early, ridiculously low War Department estimates that predated Somervell's tenure. Under Secretary of War Robert Patterson stoutly defended Somervell against Truman's attacks, denouncing "the namby-pamby attitude now assumed toward the men who were called for the purpose of creating an army."

The new Army was housed. Somervell's next task would be to create a home for the War Department itself.

Who is this stinker?

One man in particular deserved credit for the remarkable turnaround in the Construction Division, in the opinion of Colonel Leslie R. Groves, the paunchy Corps of Engineers officer who served as Somervell's chief of operations. That would be Groves himself. And it was Groves whom Somervell would rely upon most to build the new War Department headquarters.

Groves was bemused by Somervell's mania for publicity, calling it a "disease." Somervell had "tremendous ability, more than anybody I have ever seen in some respects," Groves later said. But Somervell overlooked one thing in modeling himself after Teddy Roosevelt, in the view of Groves, who keenly studied his superior's methods. Somervell forgot that Teddy just didn't build up Teddy; he built up the Rough Riders too.

Leslie Groves was, if anything, even more supremely confident than Somervell. Beneath his thick and graying dark hair—iron gray, he called it—were fine facial features, including a trim mustache and penetrating, unblinking blue eyes that moderated his jowls.

"Ruthless" was the word used to describe Groves almost as often as it was Somervell. The difference, in the view of an officer who knew them both, was that Somervell "was a gentleman as well as a driver." While Somervell could be quite charming and urbane, Groves biographer Robert S. Norris noted, this was "something rarely said about Groves." Blunt and brusque, with the grace of a bulldozer, Groves had consistently won high marks from superiors for his engineering and administrative skills, and consistently lower marks for his tact and military bearing.

"When you looked at . . . Groves," a fellow engineer officer remembered, "a little alarm bell rang 'Caution' in your brain."

Groves, sent to help the struggling Construction Division months before Somervell's arrival, had issued a series of stinging critiques. Captain Donald Antes, a normally good-natured construction officer, was so outraged he wanted "to get a shotgun and go looking for someone" after reading one Groves report. "Who is this stinker?" Antes asked.

Hartman had been forced in November 1940 to accept Groves, then a major, as his deputy. The Quartermaster Corps viewed him as a spy for the Corps of Engineers, their historical rival, which they correctly suspected was trying to wrest control of construction. Groves—who adroitly parlayed the new job into a promotion two ranks to colonel—was soon issuing orders to older, more experienced quartermaster officers who seethed at the interloper's impertinence. But Groves's competence and coolness were beyond question.

Groves could not walk out of his office without being accosted by frantic construction officers needing immediate decisions on projects around the country. "Usually 4 or 5 other men would keep trailing me to take the place of the man who had first gotten hold of me," he later said. Groves figured he was making one multimillion-dollar decision for every hundred feet of corridor walked. It was no sweat for Groves. "Once you have made decisions like that you are not scared when you get to the bigger ones," he said.

Groves, known as Dick to his family, was the son of an Army chaplain who served in posts around the world, from the Philippines to China during the Boxer Rebellion to Fort Apache in Arizona. The boy's imagination was stirred by the tales he heard from old Indian fighters at the western posts where his father was stationed. His mother's death when he was sixteen—possibly from ptomaine poisoning—marked the end of a carefree childhood. Fired by a competitive spirit, Dick excelled in school and earned admission to West Point in 1916. At the academy he kept largely to himself, devoting endless hours to study; he earned a reputation as a scold for lecturing other cadets against squandering opportunities. Classmates called him "Greasy" in honor of his thick, oily hair.

Groves's class graduated from West Point in November 1918, nearly two years early because of the American entry into World War I, but too late to see any action. Ranking fourth in his class, Groves was commissioned a second lieutenant in the Corps of Engineers. Over the next two decades in various assignments, Groves built a solid record of accomplishment and a reputation as an officer who completed projects ahead of schedule.

The Corps of Engineers was a small world, and Groves eventually encountered Somervell, four years his senior. They shared a mentor. Colonel Ernest "Pot" Graves, Somervell's old commander in Mexico and France and by then a minor deity in the corps, had taken Groves under his wing when the latter was assigned in July 1931 to the Office of the Chief of Engineers in Washington. The gruff and husky Graves, who had been a star lineman and coach for West Point, imparted his football-as-life philosophy during the long walks the two took most mornings from their homes off Connecticut Avenue to their office in the Munitions Building on the Mall. Graves was deaf and Groves had to raise his deep voice to a shout to be heard. No master of the King's English, Graves would respond in the blunt and taciturn language he had employed as a coach. "It must have been a sight to behold," Groves's son recalled many years later. But Groves absorbed Pot's message: Brains, willpower, and integrity were the core standards by which men were measured.

Graves's protégés ran in the same circles, and Pot would sometimes have the younger engineers over to his house to drink some of his homemade wine, described by one partaker as "potent, though not a vintage variety." Even Groves, not easily impressed, found himself drawn to Somervell when they first met in 1932. He quickly sized up Somervell as someone on his way to the top. Somervell also thought well of Groves and asked the younger officer in 1935 to join him in Ocala to help build the Florida ship canal. Groves declined, as he had been selected to attend the Command and Staff School at Fort Leavenworth—an important career stepping-stone. Somervell was nonetheless shocked and upset. "It was quite apparent to me that he felt that anyone who was offered the opportunity to be one of his assistants should jump at it no matter what other prospects he might have," Groves later said.

The incident dampened relations between the two. The next time Groves had more than a casual meeting with Somervell was in late 1940 when Somervell took over the Construction Division, inheriting Groves as his deputy. The two officers, alike in so many fundamental ways and so different in others, formed an uneasy relationship, not hostile but not warm. Neither was under any illusions about the other, both respecting but not fully trusting the other. Both were elemental forces, and it was not surprising that the two would sometimes clash, given their outsize ambitions, intellects, and egos.

"Somervell was a man of great capabilities, extremely intelligent and had every attribute of an outstanding leader, with a few exceptions," Groves later said. He had no complaints about the bloodletting that accompanied the Somervell Blitz. In most respects, Groves believed Somervell wielded his ax fairly. To his amusement, Groves was often left to do the actual axing for Somervell. "It distressed Somervell when he had to personally handle matters of this kind, although he always heartily approved of such action," said Groves.

Somervell, for his part, valued Groves's ability to drive projects forward, unmatched by anyone except Somervell himself. Groves always suspected Somervell did not like him because of his intelligence; Somervell did not want to be too close to anyone so smart, Groves once said, a comment that revealed more about Groves than it did Somervell. "I doubt if he ever had any personal affection for me but he did have respect for what I could do towards making his organization a better one," Groves wrote on another occasion. Without question, this was true. The next test would be building a new headquarters for the War Department.

A new headquarters

The War Department already had a spanking-new headquarters building, a big, neoclassical structure at 21st Street and Virginia Avenue in the Foggy Bottom neighborhood of Northwest Washington. The New War Department Building, as it was officially known, had been planned for years, built for $18 million, and was set to open in June 1941. Henry Stimson was not particularly impressed, complaining the façade looked like the entrance to a provincial opera house. Looks were the least of its problems. The new building, meant to replace the temporary headquarters in the Munitions Building on the Mall, was far too small.

Through much of the 1930s, the Army had been clamoring for a new home and more space. General Malin Craig, Marshall's predecessor as chief of staff, found it not only humiliating but potentially dangerous to have the department dispersed in so many locations, which included offices in Washington, Virginia, and Maryland, various shacks, apartment buildings, and Leary's Garage at 24th and M streets. The problem "results in unavoidable delays and difficulties that could not be expected to have other than the most serious consequence in the event of an emergency," Craig warned in February 1938.

Congress finally approved funding that year for a new War Department headquarters in Foggy Bottom, on a rectangle of land along Constitution Avenue that federal planners had marked earlier in the decade as the future home for the War and Navy departments. Roosevelt personally approved the site and in 1939 sketched out an idea for a colonnade connecting the two proposed buildings to a neutral meeting area. "That is a small office where the Secretary of War will meet the Secretary of the Navy," Roosevelt explained. "You know, neither one will go to see the other."

Construction of the New War Department Building had proceeded apace. But when Stimson inspected it on the morning of April 25, 1941, the secretary was dismayed. Though the building had 500,000 square feet, only 270,000 square feet were available for office space. "It is a most wasteful building . . . ," Stimson noted that day in his diary. "There was great difficulty in fitting in what we want. . . . So at present we are considering my staying in the old building, but I confess I don't like that very much."

A month later, Stimson told Roosevelt that the War Department needed more space. The world picture was darkening. The London Blitz reached new heights, and German bombers had badly damaged the House of Commons and Westminster Abbey. In the Pacific, U.S. fears of Japanese aggression were growing. The 24,000 War Department workers were now spread out in twenty-three buildings. The New War Department Building could accommodate perhaps four thousand workers and reduce the scattering to seventeen buildings, but it would be a temporary reprieve: New employees were arriving in Washington at the rate of a thousand a month. By the end of the year, the number of workers was expected to reach thirty thousand.

It was a far cry from the year 1800, when the War Department moved from Philadelphia to the new capital with a total of eighteen employees, or nineteen including the secretary of war. Its first home in Washington, a rented three-story brick private home on Pennsylvania Avenue, was soon destroyed by fire. A subsequent headquarters nearby fared no better; it went up in flames when the British burned Washington in 1814. A permanent home was then built for the War Department near the White House on the southeast corner of Pennsylvania Avenue and 17th Street. The War Department building, with drab-painted brick and a Corinthian colonnade across its façade, was completed in 1820 and housed the department for nearly six decades, including momentous days during the Civil War when Abraham Lincoln would walk over from the White House to the War Department telegraph office and read the latest dispatches from the field. The building was razed in 1879 to make way for the enormous and ornate State, War and Navy Building, whose construction curiously presaged that of the Pentagon in some respects. With its thick granite walls, sixteen-foot ceilings, and almost two miles of black-and-white marble tile corridors, the 662,000-square-foot building was reputed to be the largest office building in the world; many said it was also the most unsightly. The flamboyant French Second Empire architecture stood in startling contrast to the sober classical revival buildings common in Washington. Mark Twain called it "the ugliest building in America," while Henry Adams labeled it an "architectural infant asylum."

Ugly or not, the building provided a good home to the War Department for another sixty years. But its prime location was coveted by the White House, which also needed more space, and during the 1930s many

War Department offices were forced out. In late August 1939—as German troops massed along the Polish border—Marshall and then Secretary of War Harry H. Woodring were moving out of the department's longtime headquarters.

When World War II erupted in Europe September 1, the War Department found itself newly headquartered in a factory-like temporary building on the Washington Mall. The Munitions Building—located between Constitution Avenue and the Reflecting Pool, roughly equidistant from the Lincoln and Washington memorials—was one of many temporary buildings constructed on the Mall during World War I. The curse of the Munitions Building, utterly without ornamentation, was that it was built too well to fall down on its own. Marshall actually preferred the Munitions Building to his old office, finding it more efficient to be reunited with War Department offices previously evicted from the State, War and Navy Building.

Yet it was no solution. With the eruption of war, the issue became not one of convenience, but one on which lives might depend. To those trying to coordinate the Army's mobilization—what Marshall called "a great Army in the making"—the inefficiencies of a scattered War Department were endangering American readiness. The lost time, wasted motion, lack of supervision, and absence of personal contact were causing problems.

"The matter of office space for the War Department has become one of greatest urgency," Under Secretary of War Patterson, who was overseeing the mobilization, warned Stimson in a confidential memo on November 29, 1940. ". . . There is no question but that the congestion is materially retarding the National Defense program." Marshall insisted he needed his key commanders close at hand for "almost hourly conferences these days when the military establishment is being tremendously enlarged." That fall, the chief of staff reversed a plan to turn some of the Army's space in the Munitions Building over to the Navy. The War Department was "already suffering seriously from an unfortunate dispersion," Marshall told the chief of naval operations, Admiral Harold Stark.

Even with the New War Department Building in Foggy Bottom nearing completion, the War Department was short a million square feet of office space in Washington. Stimson was so disgusted that he declared he would rather stay in the Munitions Building than move as planned into "so inadequate" a building—or as he called it, "this abortion that has just come into use." In May 1941, Stimson directed that only Patterson's office and the headquarters for the Corps of Engineers move into the New War Department Building.

To help house the War Department, Congress approved funding to construct temporary buildings in Washington. But the War Department, concerned about heavy traffic and parking problems in downtown Washington, was scouting locations in Virginia. The Army had recently acquired a large tract of land in Arlington, just across the Memorial Bridge from Washington. Directly east of Arlington National Cemetery, the land had been used for decades by the Department of Agriculture as a farm for experimental crops. The Army wanted to build seven two-story frame temporary buildings on the site, which was only a four-minute drive from the Munitions Building, "with no stop light at all" to slow traffic, as Marshall enthusiastically told a congressional committee. Roosevelt sent a letter to House Speaker Sam Rayburn on June 4 asking for legislative authority to build federal structures in Arlington, complaining that lack of space in Washington had "seriously retarded" defense activities. A week later, Marshall appeared before a subcommittee of the House Appropriations Committee and asked that the department be allowed to build in Virginia. "To be able to build our temporary office buildings on the Arlington Farm site means everything to us," Marshall testified. "We can do business if our buildings are placed there."

But Somervell would have a bolder idea. It was obvious to him that something much bigger and more permanent was needed, and fast.

The overall solution

The real business at Representative Clifton Woodrum's congressional hearing on July 17, 1941, came after the meeting ended.

Woodrum, a powerful Democrat from Roanoke in southwest Virginia and acting chairman of a House Committee on Appropriations subcommittee, had called the hearing to gather testimony about the proposal to build temporary office buildings for the War Department and other overcrowded federal agencies. Portly, with white hair and ruddy cheeks, Woodrum had the shrewd face of the pharmacist he had once been. The southern progressive had risen to power on the Appropriations Committee and regularly floor-managed important spending bills through the House. Though he often voiced support for fiscal conservatism, Woodrum had no problem supporting projects that brought home the bacon for the Commonwealth.

The proposal before the Subcommittee on Deficiencies was to spend $6.5 million to build temporary structures, including three for the War Department on the Arlington Farm site. Woodrum was dissatisfied with this proposal, the latest of several of what he considered "piecemeal" approaches to solving the War Department's problem. After the testimony ended, he approached Brigadier General Eugene Reybold, the War Department's representative at the hearing. In his deep baritone—Woodrum had a fine voice and was known as "the singing congressman"—he challenged the general. Why doesn't the War Department work out an "overall solution" to its space problem, he asked Reybold.

Reybold promised Woodrum the War Department would report back to the subcommittee with a plan by the following Tuesday, five days hence. The bespectacled Reybold, a sturdy and low-key engineer who in manner and looks was more like a country doctor than an Army officer, quickly turned the matter over to Somervell.

With typical brio, the construction chief immediately took Woodrum's words as an invitation for something much grander than a few temporary buildings. If it was an overall solution that was desired, then Somervell would construct a building big enough to house the entire War Department—a nerve center for the enormous military force gathering to fight a global war. Exactly when Somervell conceived this idea is not known; likely it had been percolating in his head for at least several weeks. In any event, on the evening of July 17, 1941, Somervell seized the opportunity presented by Woodrum's question. The project that would become known as the Pentagon was launched that evening.

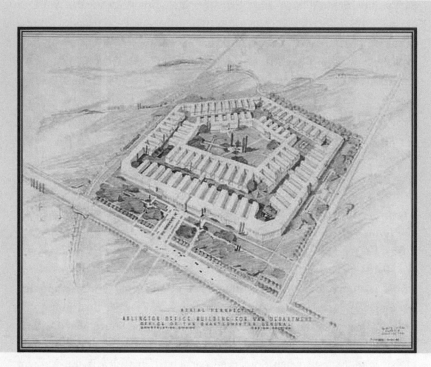

Aerial perspective of proposed War Department building by Socrates Thomas Stathes, July 1941.

CHAPTER
3

DREAM BUILDING

Incidentally, the largest office building in the world

The first problem was where to put it. Major Pat Casey's mind was still reeling from the secret instructions Somervell had given him the previous night, July 17, for constructing a massive new War Department headquarters—"incidentally, the largest office building in the world," Casey later noted dryly. Energetic and experienced, Casey was one of the Army's most brilliant engineers, an up-and-coming officer Somervell had quickly snagged upon taking control of the Construction Division.

Somervell wanted the plans on his desk Monday morning, July 21, and it was already Friday. Casey quickly saw big problems with the location Somervell had designated for constructing the building, the Washington-Hoover Airport along the Potomac River in Arlington. A week earlier, the Army had taken an option on the 147-acre airport, a hopelessly inadequate airfield at the foot of the 14th Street Bridge. Washington-Hoover had been the principal airport for Washington for fifteen years, but a modern airfield, National Airport, had opened in June about a mile downriver. After the congressional hearing July 17, Woodrum had suggested to Brigadier General Reybold, the supply chief, that the Army use the old airport in his home state for office buildings. Somervell—eager to win the Virginian's blessing for the project—had seized upon the airport as the right site for his enormous new headquarters building.

But the foundation conditions at the airport worried Casey. The low-lying riverbed land was barely better than a swamp and subject to flooding. Reybold, who had similar concerns, went out to look at the site and con-cluded that the problem was even worse than realized. "It would be haz-ardous for us to build a building of a permanent nature there," Reybold warned.

When Casey asked Somervell whether other sites near the airport might be used, the general did not rule it out. "So we looked over the map of Washington, and I tried to figure out other suitable areas," Casey later said.

Obviously, it would have to be a big site. Somervell had ordered the building to be no higher than four stories, so as to not spark protests against a tall building along the river, as well as to avoid using the amount of steel a high-rise would need. "And not going vertically and requiring that amount of office space meant getting a vastly spread out area," Casey said.

Casey's practiced eye quickly zeroed in on a sixty-seven-acre tract about a half-mile upriver from Washington-Hoover, on a plateau sixty feet above the Potomac, just east of Arlington National Cemetery. It was Ar-lington Farm, the spot Marshall had endorsed a month earlier for temporary buildings. The site seemed ideal from the standpoint of foundation, utili-ties, water supply, elevation, and existing roads. A small party—operating discreetly to avoid any word leaking out—surveyed the terrain and reported back favorably. Reybold also recommended the site, and Somer-vell quickly approved the switch.

Like the adjacent cemetery, Arlington Farm had once been part of the grand estate of Robert E. Lee that had been confiscated by Union troops in the spring of 1861 for the defense of Washington. In 1900, Congress trans-ferred four hundred acres of the Arlington estate to the Department of Agriculture to use as an experimental farm to improve agriculture. Arling-ton Farm served as an Ellis Island for plants sent to the United States by Americans traveling on government or private missions abroad. Scientists studied everything from new methods of breeding corn to ways of com-bating tomato wilt to new uses for hemp, and over the years thousands of foreign plants were naturalized there for domestic use.

The threat of war brought an end to this agricultural idyll. Marshall wanted to use the land for the garrison of infantry and cavalry troops at neighboring Fort Myer, which was responsible for the defense of Washington. In September 1940, Roosevelt personally approved the return of Arlington Farm to the War Department.

Perched on a hill above the Potomac, just below the Lee mansion and overlooking Memorial Bridge, Arlington Farm was one of the most prominent sites in the Washington area. In approving the site, Somervell and his planners agreed that the height of the proposed building should be reduced from four stories to three to keep it in harmony with the surroundings. The lower height, Somervell figured, would take care of any aesthetic concerns that might be raised.

Bergstrom gets to work

Late on Friday afternoon, July 18, Somervell directed George Edwin Bergstrom to get to work. A formal man with a brusque manner, his dark hair whitening at the temples, the War Department's chief architect was an intimidating figure to the young officers assigned to work with him. He looked "the way architects should appear, like a Frank Lloyd Wright," according to one. Bergstrom's influence on the project would be profound, but his involvement would end in disgrace and personal tragedy.

Bergstrom—known by his middle name all his life—was born and raised in Neenah, Wisconsin, the son of a Norwegian blacksmith who had immigrated to America and built a successful foundry manufacturing plows and stoves. Edwin was sent to Phillips Academy in Andover, Massachusetts, and then earned a degree in architecture from Yale University in 1897, with further study at the Massachusetts Institute of Technology. Young Bergstrom headed west and founded an architectural firm that soon became a leading force in the building explosion around Los Angeles in the early years of the twentieth century. The firm, Parkinson and Bergstrom, specialized in "Class A" commercial buildings—structures built with steel frames and reinforced concrete—and designed more of them than any architectural firm in the West. In 1921, Bergstrom helped found the Allied Architects Association of Los Angeles, a cooperative society of thirty-three architects who collaborated on public works projects; the society designed the Pasadena Civic Auditorium and the curved wooden frame that served as the first shell sheltering musicians at the famed Hollywood Bowl.

By 1941, Bergstrom was sixty-five years old, an accomplished and experienced architect, but that was not the real reason Somervell had hired him in February to be chief of the Construction Division's architectural unit. Bergstrom was president of the American Institute of Architects, the country's preeminent professional organization of architecture; as such, he carried a cachet that Somervell coveted. In the same vein, Somervell hired the presidents or past presidents of the American Society of Civil Engineers, the American Society of Mechanical Engineers, and the American Society of Landscape Architects. Two dozen prominent engineers, architects, professors, and attorneys—a veritable who's who in their fields— were brought in as consultants. They represented "the best in the country," Somervell boasted.

It was essentially a public relations ploy, and an expensive one at that. Somervell's hires were not the dollar-a-year men of lore; the consultants were drawing as much as $100 a day plus expenses. Luther Leisenring, a longtime civilian employee with the Construction Division who had served as supervising architect since 1930 until Somervell demoted him and put Bergstrom in his place, groused that the various society heads "just sat around in fancy offices and signed a few papers" and did no appreciable work.

Bergstrom, at least, was no figurehead. His patriotism fired by Nazi atrocities, including in his father's native Norway, Bergstrom took his assignment seriously and became Somervell's key adviser on architectural matters. He worked "every day and long into the nights," assisting in the design of the camps, munitions plants, and buildings the Construction Division was putting up around the country, and bringing in private architects to help.

Now Bergstrom was in charge of the biggest project of his long career. Captain Robert W. Colglazier, a Construction Division officer, was under orders from Somervell to get everything Bergstrom needed—people, equipment, office space—and to get it without question. Bergstrom wanted a lot. "He literally, and I mean literally, wanted hundreds of people," Colglazier recalled. He scrambled to meet the chief architect's demands.

Meanwhile, Bergstrom and his assistants gathered with Casey's team

Friday night at the division headquarters in the Railroad Retirement Building in Washington to plan the new project.

It fit

The Arlington Farm tract had a peculiar shape, bound on five sides by roads or other divisions. It was roughly a square, with a triangle sliced off one corner, leaving an asymmetrical pentagon. The site was bound on the north for 1,360 feet by Arlington Memorial Drive, the stately road that connected Memorial Bridge to Arlington National Cemetery. On the west the border ran for 1,340 feet along Arlington Ridge Road, an old and important thoroughfare connecting Georgetown to Alexandria. To the south, a double row of oak trees bounded the site, dividing it from a field used for training troops at Fort Myer. Another planned highway would run on a north-south route, forming the southeast border of the site. On the east-northeast side, the borderline followed a branch of the Pennsylvania Railroad and a proposed truck highway for 1,150 feet.

Though he had reduced the number of floors from four to three, Somervell still wanted four million square feet of office space. The design team gazed at maps, trying to figure out how to fit such a large building in.

Bergstrom led the deliberations, working closely with Casey and Frederick H. Fowler, president of the American Society of Civil Engineers, another Somervell hire. Roy C. Mitchell, Bergstrom's longtime chief engineer in Los Angeles who had followed his boss to Washington, brought expertise in structural design and mechanical work. Also detailed to the team was Socrates Thomas Stathes, a young War Department draftsman who had studied architecture at Washington's Catholic University.

Stathes was known to friends as Red, in honor of his auburn hair and freckled face. His father and mother had emigrated in 1900 from the Greek village of Isari and settled in Washington, where they opened a restaurant. Red, the second oldest of their five children, was the pride of the Stathes family. He earned an architecture degree at Catholic University and after winning the Paris Prize in 1938 went to study at the Ecole des Beaux Arts. Caught in France with no good way home when the war broke out the following year, Stathes used the Greek he had spoken since childhood to befriend several Greek crewmembers aboard a freighter. They let him stow away back to America. Stathes went straight to work for the War Department, and the gifted draftsman now found himself assigned to sketch the first drawings of the new building.

Despite the layout of the tract, a pentagonal shape was not immediately obvious to the designers; rather, it gradually dawned on them that it might make sense. The team tried "different setups and layouts, such as square, octagonal and rectangular and so on," Casey later said, "and finally we came up with sort of a joint expression of views and thoughts and ideas and ended up with this five-sided pentagon structure." Stathes's sketch showed an irregular pentagon, like a square with a corner cut off, more or less matching the shape of the tract. It was really two buildings, a five-sided ring surrounding a smaller one of the same shape.

All through the weekend they refined the design. The interior of the outer ring was lined with forty-nine barracks-like wings, sticking in like the teeth of a comb. The smaller ring had thirty-four exterior wings, all pointing toward the outer ring. The wings were 50 feet wide and 160 feet long, separated from each other by thirty-foot-wide open-air "light courts." Corridors connected the two rings on the ground and third floors. The whole structure had a gross area of 5.1 million square feet, including 4 million square feet of office space and the remainder for services facilities. Only the most senior officials would have private offices; everyone else would work in enormous open areas. Allowing a hundred square feet per worker, the building could hold forty thousand employees.

By Sunday night, the plans were completed. Bergstrom had come up with an estimate of $17.5 million for the project; to be on the safe side, Somervell would double that to $35 million. The figure was startlingly high for a single building, yet would prove woefully inadequate. Stathes's drawings were prepared for presentation to Representative Woodrum's House subcommittee on Tuesday.

Two years before his death in 1981, Casey could not conceal his pride over meeting Somervell's challenge: "I might say that on Monday morning he did have our layout plans, the architectural perspectives, and the general description of this structure conforming generally to his instructions. As I say it was a busy weekend."

While all the designers contributed, it was Bergstrom, more than anyone else, who conceived the pentagonal shape. "I would say Bergstrom probably has the greatest credit for it," Casey said in 1979. Contemporary records reach the same conclusion. "The original conception, the general layout and the overall direction of the design . . . were the responsibility and the contribution of Mr. Bergstrom," according to a 1943 Corps of Engineers memorandum.

There were many problems with the irregular design. The pattern was awkward and the routes between wings of the two buildings were circuitous. Lacking symmetry, with rows of wings sticking out, the building was frankly quite ugly.

Yet given the five-sided site, the pentagonal design had one virtue that overrode all other considerations, Red Stathes remembered more than sixty years later: "It fit."

It should not ever come to pieces

The whole idea seemed nonsensical to Henry Stimson, still disgusted with the debacle over the last New War Department Building. How could the War Department propose to build a new headquarters when it had just opened one last month?

Under Secretary of War Robert Patterson had telephoned Stimson early the morning of Tuesday, July 22, to inform him about the building Somervell had dreamed up—big enough "to hold the entire War Department and take the place of the present new building and the old building and the seventeen other buildings that we are scattered in all over the city," Stimson related to his diary. "[Patterson] said that plans had been drawn on the chance to see whether such a building could be done and he asked me if I would see the architect and the various other people. . . . So I said, 'All right.' "

Somervell had leapt into action upon getting the plans and elevations Monday morning, immediately taking them up the chain of command. He presented the proposal to General Moore, the Army deputy chief of staff, who thought it "very logical." He won quick approval the same day from Marshall and then Patterson. Now he had to convince Stimson.

Soon after the telephone conversation with Stimson, Patterson arrived at the secretary's headquarters in the Munitions Building, accompanied by Somervell, Reybold, and Bergstrom. As they presented their case, the dubious Stimson found himself slowly drawn to the logic. The secretary examined the plans for the building, which struck him as being "on practical and simple lines." How long would it take to finish, Stimson asked. One year, Somervell promised. It would be built on War Department land, allowing the Army to control the construction rather than depending on the vagaries of the Public Buildings Administration. The efficiency of the War Department would improve 25 to 40 percent by having everyone under one roof, Stimson was told.

Finally, the secretary conferred his blessing on the endeavor. "I had at first been very skeptical of it, because the whole thing seemed to be silly to start now just when we have gotten one new building, but that has been such a failure that gradually I got interested and finally I came to the conclusion that it would probably be a good thing," Stimson recorded in his diary. Stimson noted that the new building would free space for the Navy, also bursting at the seams, to move into the Munitions Building. "Of course it will cost a lot of money but it will solve not only our problem . . . it will solve a lot of other problems," he wrote.

Sound it out with the Appropriations Committee and see what they think, Stimson told his visitors. A hearing was already set for that afternoon before Woodrum's subcommittee; Reybold was supposed to report back with the War Department's solution for the space crisis. At the suggestion of Moore, Somervell first went to Woodrum's office to show the proposal privately to the congressman. The Virginian's support for such a grandiose project would be critical, they knew. Woodrum was impressed, particularly by Somervell's claim that the building would free 2.1 million square feet now occupied by the War Department in offices around Washington, easing the government's space problem.

At the hearing, Woodrum invited Somervell to speak. "Suppose you tell us where the building is to be, and what kind of building it is proposed to construct," the congressman said.

Exuding confidence, Somervell presented his plan. The building would be three stories high, a height conforming to its prominent setting by the Memorial Bridge. The first employees would move in within six months. The building would be completed in twelve months. He blithely reported that construction and planning would take place simultaneously.

"We will have to develop the plans contemporaneously with the building, or we cannot do the job," Somervell said. Though there would be room for forty thousand people, the War Department expected it would hold thirty thousand for the time being and that the remaining space would be used for storage. The efficiency of the War Department would be increased by one quarter. The building would be of reinforced concrete with a brick exterior, he said. There would be no marble or other fancy materials. The cost would be $35 million, and that covered everything except parking lots for ten thousand cars.

"How long do you think your estimate will stand without an increase?" Representative Louis Ludlow, an Indiana Democrat, asked suspiciously.

"We do not want it to stand for more than a year," Somervell parried. "We will have it finished within a year."

"This thing would not come to pieces very easily, would it?" asked Representative John Taber, a New York Republican.

"It certainly should not," Somervell assured him. "It should not ever come to pieces."

"What would you say would be the life of the building?" Ludlow asked.

"The life of the building would be a hundred years unless it became obsolescent," the general replied.

"If you had the money, how soon could you get under way on it?" Woodrum asked.

"We could get under way on it in two weeks," Somervell replied.

No one questioned Somervell's stunning promise. As for the huge size, it was no time for restraint, the general told the congressmen. "Every time we have asked for what we thought was just what we needed, by the time the building was finished it was not enough, and I think it would be the height of folly to cut this thing right to the edge and not have any leeway," he said.

"Would this probably be the largest single government building constructed, if undertaken?" Ludlow asked.

"Oh, I do not think so," Somervell replied dismissively. "Of course we always have to build the biggest."

Conceivably, Somervell did not know the full scope of what he was proposing; more likely, he was merely being coy. The Chicago Post Office, then the biggest government building in the country, covered six acres, reached fourteen stories in its northern corners, and contained 1.7 million square feet of space. The Empire State Building, the tallest building in the world at 102 floors, had 2.25 million square feet of office space. The War Department building as proposed by Somervell was far larger; it would contain 4 million square feet of office space and have total space of 5.1 million square feet.

Somervell had sold them; the subcommittee unanimously approved funding for the new building, sending the recommendation to the full committee.

Stimson decided it was time to tell the president what was afoot, although he was still embarrassed about asking for another War Department building on the heels of the last one. On Thursday, July 24, he told the president's military aide, Major General Edwin "Pa" Watson, that he wanted to speak with Roosevelt after that afternoon's cabinet meeting about a new War Department headquarters in Arlington. "It has now reached the stage where the Appropriations Committee has heard of it, and Stimson wants you to know that he is not [the] author, but that the plan has a lot of merit," Watson reported to the president.

Shortly before the cabinet meeting, an objection to Somervell's plan was finally raised. Harold D. Smith, Roosevelt's budget director, a former Kansas farm boy known as "a beagle for bargains," had got wind of the project. He smelled trouble. Smith too sought the president's ear. Watson reported to Roosevelt that Smith "is very anxious that the President does not commit himself on the proposition" until the planned building's impact on traffic, water supply, sewers, and the like was studied.

Smith's request went unheeded. Somervell's proposal was reaching the president at an opportune time, as Roosevelt had concluded that America likely could not avoid war with Nazi Germany. Earlier that month the president had agreed to take over the defense of Iceland from Britain, a decision of "first-rate political and strategic importance," in the estimation of Winston Churchill, the British prime minister. Roosevelt biographer James MacGregor Burns later wrote that "If ever there was a point when Roosevelt knowingly crossed some threshold between aiding Britain in order to stay out of war and aiding Britain by joining in the war, July 1941 was probably the time."

When the proposal was raised during the cabinet meeting July 24, Roosevelt breezily approved the building, to the secretary's relief. Later that afternoon, Stimson sent a letter to Woodrum, who was awaiting word: "In response to your inquiry I am authorized by the President to advise you that he has approved the construction of the proposed War Department building at Arlington Farms. I may say that an urgent need exists for this building, and I hope that we may have the approval of the Congress for it at an early date."

In exactly one week, Somervell had proposed constructing a building of unprecedented size and scale, produced preliminary plans out of thin air, won the strong support of the War Department leadership including a skeptical secretary of war, sold it to key Congressional leaders, and received a green light from the president of the United States. Nothing, it seemed, could stop him.

Lebensraum

On July 24, 1941, the same day that Roosevelt approved the new building, Representative Merlin Hull, the seventy-year-old Progressive Party member and dean of the Wisconsin delegation to the House, sat at his desk on the floor, looking over House Resolution 5412, a bill just reported by the Appropriations Committee. The House of Representatives had convened at noon that day to consider the $8 billion supplemental spending request for national defense, including money to boost the Army's size by 300,000 to 1.7 million soldiers. Routine passage was expected.

Hull's eye stopped at the last item listed in HR 5412. On page 34, under the heading "War Department, civil functions, Quartermaster Corps," there was an authorization for the construction of a new War Department building across the Potomac River, to cost $35 million. Hull was astonished. It was an enormous amount of money for a single building. It was also against congressional rules. Woodrum had added the $35 million to the appropriation bill as a rider, but the legislation should have originated with the Committee of Public Buildings and Grounds. To get around this inconvenience, Woodrum had enlisted the aid of Representative Fritz Lanham, the Texas Democrat who chaired the buildings committee. Lanham's committee had met the day before and unanimously agreed to support the measure and ignore the fact that there was no authorization act.

Now Lanham took the House floor to sing the building's praises and to urge Congress to lay aside the rules. "I doubt if, during the many years I have served on the Committee on Public Buildings and Grounds, a more practical, feasible and sensible building project has been presented to us than this particular one," he said. "It is not to be a monumental building, ornate in its details, but a permanent workshop on Government-owned land."

Hull, for one, was not going to stand for it. He was known as a stickler for rules and for his diligence, never missing a committee meeting and almost always on the House floor for roll calls. When the House clerk read the last paragraph of the bill—the one for the building's construction—Hull raised a point of order: The paragraph was unauthorized legislation.

Woodrum was in a bind. Hull was correct, he responded, but the matter was too important to be stopped by a technicality. "Nothing that we could do in this bill or anywhere else would give such an impetus to the efficiency of our defense program as to be able to get the War Department under one roof in order that they may attend to the business for which we are appropriating these large sums," Woodrum said.

Hull would not budge. This building was too big. "It is sufficient to build four capitol buildings the size of the one we are now working in, so I am going to insist on my point of order," he said. Woodrum had no choice but to postpone the bill until the Rules Committee could consider the matter. The entire $8 billion defense supplemental bill was on hold.

The cat was now out of the bag. For the press and for Washington, the contretemps was the first word of what was being planned. Even within the War Department, few knew about it; high officials approached by reporters that day said they had never heard of the project. The War Department hurriedly put out a press release late in the day announcing that the president and secretary of war had approved construction of a new building to house the entire department. "It is believed that it will constitute the largest office building in the world," the release said, taking pains to emphasize the spartan nature of the project: "The building will be strictly utilitarian in character and will be devoid of facilities except those relating directly to the business functions of the War Department."

The *Evening Star* hit the streets with the news that night, and all the papers ran big stories the following morning. The *Washington Post* called it "a 35 million dollar 'dream' building" and ran a big illustration showing Red Stathes's rendition of the odd-shaped structure. The *Washington Daily News* described it as a "proposal to carpet 67 acres of Virginia farmland with brick and concrete" and sardonically referred to the War Department's need for *Lebensraum*. The Arlington County manager confessed to being "dizzy" at the prospect of a single building housing almost as many people as the rest of the county.

None of the planning agencies that had say over such projects had been consulted. Nor had anyone with the Arlington County government been notified. The *Star* was shocked. "The $35,000,000 War Department building project planned for Arlington County, Va., is so staggering in its proportions as to be difficult to grasp on short notice," the paper editorialized, adding that "surely Congress will not adopt so far-reaching and revolutionary a project" without review by the proper agencies.

But that was precisely the intention. On Friday morning, Woodrum appeared before the House Rules Committee to report that Roosevelt and Stimson were urging quick congressional approval. The committee voted to recommend that the rules be waived and the $35 million appropriation be attached to the bill.

When the House reconsidered the matter on Monday, Hull was not ready to concede. "This proposition is so staggering, so astounding, that if my point of order did nothing more, it served to give the Congress and at least some of the press an opportunity to consider what was being brought in here under the guise of national defense," he told the House. It seemed to him that before approving a building comparable in cost to and greater in size than "the great Empire State Building . . . the House at least ought to have the opportunity to learn more about what the proposition really means." The cost, Hull warned, might be twice the $35 million estimated by the War Department.

Others took up the cry, incredulous that the War Department was again seeking a new building. "Think of it—after two months of occupancy of the present building they find that it is too small and they want to go somewhere else," said Representative Robert Rich, a Pennsylvania Republican.

Representative Everett Dirksen, the flowery-speaking Republican from Illinois, broached the question that many would soon be asking: What possible use would this huge building have after the war? "Every Christian man or woman in the world hopes that somehow this great conflagration will come to an end speedily, and when it does, will we need a $35,000,000 monument on the other side of the Potomac?" he asked. August Andresen, a Minnesota Republican and part-time farmer, voiced suspicion of Roosevelt's true intentions. "I understand that the report is quite current around here that they want these big buildings and large facilities so we can police the world after the war is over."

Woodrum was ready to allay such concerns. War Department officials, he said, had assured him they could use the building after the war to store their increasingly voluminous records. (General Marshall, ever the soldier, had another suggestion, telling Somervell he wanted to move in an infantry regiment after the war and use the building as a barracks.)

Ominous global events loomed over the debate. Hitler was advancing steadily into the Soviet Union. A week earlier, Nazi aircraft had started bombing Moscow, and a spearhead of the German army was nearing Leningrad. Why was the War Department spending money on a new headquarters when money was desperately needed for American bombers, some congressmen wanted to know. "We cannot win wars with buildings," Andresen declared. Woodrum countered by painting a dire picture of a "handicapped" American army preparing for war in badly overcrowded buildings. As for accusations that the building was a "palatial" waste, Woodrum insisted, "There are no frills or ruffles. There are no elevators, no trimmings, no gymnasiums or the like. It is to be a building designed for maximum service."

Hull and his supporters tried three times to kill the proposal; each time they were beaten back without recorded votes. In the end, the House sent the $8 billion defense bill to the Senate with only eleven dissenting votes and the $35 million for the building intact. Woodrum had carried the day, and in the view of many, won a grand prize for his state. "We are giving Virginia a great deal," said Representative Adolph Sabath, Democrat of Illinois. "When this structure is built we shall have given them the greatest building ever constructed anywhere by any nation."

Sensitive to appearances, Woodrum put out a press release disavowing his role in launching the project: "I would like to point out . . . the project was wholly and entirely the idea of the War Department, of their own initiative, without any suggestions whatsoever, so far as I know, from anyone in Congress." Technically, this was true. But it was Woodrum who had inserted the project into the appropriations bill and put his considerable clout behind building it in Virginia. Somervell and Woodrum in partnership were driving the project forward.

Harold Ickes, Roosevelt's curmudgeonly secretary of the interior, had no illusions. "It was easy to see how this greased pig went through the hands of Congress," Ickes recorded in his diary. "Of course, it had the support of Congressman Woodrum in the House. Woodrum is all for economy except when the State of Virginia is concerned."

Ickes was alarmed at the prospect of this enormous edifice along the Potomac. "Here was another example of acting before thinking," he fumed in his diary, annoyed that Roosevelt had so blithely agreed to the project. "As is so often the case . . . instead of seeing how vicious the plan was and what it would do in the way of dislocating the carefully considered plan for . . . the protection of Washington, [the President] gave a nod of approval," he wrote. But Ickes was encouraged by a rising tide of opposition from Roosevelt's advisers, federal agencies and boards, the press, and the public. As opponents recovered from Somervell's surprise, the battle over the building was only beginning. The immediate focus was turning to the Senate, which would consider the matter later in the week.

Monitoring the progress of the opposition, Somervell was not daunted in the least; he barreled ahead, convinced that there was no time to waste. "There is an emergency, and we want to get to work . . . in the next few days so we can get a large part of this done before the bad weather in January," Somervell said the day after the House vote. He had already lined up a builder.

A grand fellow

Across the Potomac, a little less than a mile downriver from where Somervell wanted to build his new War Department headquarters, another edifice was rising on the south side of the Tidal Basin. It looked like a Roman temple under construction, its neoclassical dome and white marble columns surrounded by cranes and hoists. A sign in front of the site read "John McShain, Inc.—Builder."

Viewing the progress of the Jefferson Memorial with particular interest was the occupant at 1600 Pennsylvania Avenue. Franklin D. Roosevelt often would watch the construction work while breakfasting at the White House and had even ordered some trees trimmed so that he might have an unobstructed view across the Ellipse to the rising memorial.

Roosevelt was a great admirer of Jefferson, feeling himself closer in spirit and style to the Renaissance man who wrote the Declaration of Independence than to any other Founding Father, and he had been deeply involved in the memorial's creation. He had approved the memorial's Pantheon design despite furious attacks from critics who considered the conservative Roman style to be hackneyed and pedantic. (Frank Lloyd Wright called it an "arrogant insult to the memory of Thomas Jefferson," while the *Washington Times-Herald* compared it to "an old-fashioned, overturned crockery thing of the sort you never see in anybody's bedroom any more.") There had been further controversy over the need to cut down or transplant some of the lovely Japanese cherry trees that ringed the Tidal Basin in order to make room for the memorial. A group of Washington society ladies chained themselves to the trees and threatened to disrupt Roosevelt's groundbreaking ceremony on December 15, 1938. ("Dowager Row May Peril Rite at Memorial," a *Washington Post* headline warned.) Roosevelt was undaunted. "If . . . the tree is in the way, we will move the tree and the lady and the chains, and transplant them to some other space," he said. The dowagers eventually retreated. At the request of McShain, the contractor, Roosevelt returned to lay the cornerstone at the memorial in November 1939—with the condition "that there be some guarantee that we would bar the cherry tree ladies from the site," McShain later wrote.

Roosevelt by then had become quite taken with the charming little Irishman building the memorial. At age forty-two, handsome with auburn hair and sharp blue eyes, McShain still looked young despite the neat mustache he had grown years earlier to make people think he was older. McShain stood only five feet seven inches but was a dynamo of nervous energy. He was a perpetual presence at his jobs, "trotting like a coon dog," as described by one of his workmen. A natty dresser even at construction sites, he would briskly ask questions and issue orders in a voice a listener once described as sounding like a "Mummer's parade." McShain was a rarity among builders in that he never used profanity; a Catholic who attended Mass daily, he summarily ripped down any nude pinups he found in construction shacks.

McShain's parents had emigrated from County Derry in Ireland in the early 1880s and settled in Philadelphia, where his father struggled but eventually established himself as a builder, constructing churches, rectories, and schools for the city's Catholic archdiocese. John was born in 1898, the youngest of four children. He was four when his mother died in premature labor, possibly caused by her exertions when she rushed young John to a doctor after he cut himself falling from a rocking chair. Her death left a hole in his life, a loss that he still felt as an old man. "He was a deprived youngster, deprived emotionally because of his mother's death," McShain's daughter, Sister Pauline McShain, said many years later. "His father didn't give him a lot of affirmation." The boy struggled at school.

In the summers he worked construction jobs for his father, who paid him a pittance. When the boy asked for a raise, his father told him he was not worth a raise. Young John quit to work in a shipyard. On his deathbed in 1919, John McShain, Sr., asked his eldest son, Jim, to take over the business. When Jim declined, the father asked his only other son, John, then twenty, who quietly said, "I'll try."

With a modest inheritance, McShain oversaw the firm from a one-room office over a garage at 1610 North Street in Philadelphia, surviving some lean years and slowly building up business. He was a familiar sight in his raccoon coat and derby hat, dashing around the countryside in his Ford Model T roadster to check on the progress of his jobs. He earned a reputation as a highly competitive builder who delivered projects on schedule and on budget. By the time he won his first federal contact in 1932 to build the twelve-story Philadelphia Naval Hospital, McShain had become a force in the city's building industry.

What set McShain apart was his genius for pricing jobs. He would pore over estimate sheets and, with a sharp pencil, scribble in savings and shortcuts to underbid his competitors but still make a profit. Arriving at a construction site, McShain would ask a superintendent what he was paying for concrete or for moving dirt and instantly know whether he was making money. "John McShain can figure a job tighter than most men alive," Matthew McCloskey, McShain's friend and great rival for the title of king of Philadelphia contractors, once said. In 1936, McCloskey beat McShain by $1,600 on a $6 million job at Pennsylvania State College. A few minutes after the award was announced, McShain encountered McCloskey in the elevator. McShain was "fighting, snarling mad" and told McCloskey that "friendship was one thing, but it was him or me" from there on.

"I'll beat you, McCloskey," McShain spat, "if it's only by the price of a nail. And I'll beat you every chance I get." That McShain did, "too often and by more nails than I want to remember now," recalled McCloskey, who would become John F. Kennedy's ambassador to Ireland.

The building business in Depression-era Philadelphia was not big enough for McShain, and he soon set his sights on Washington, where New Deal dollars were flowing. His first jobs in the capital came in 1934, when he built foundations for the Internal Revenue Building and a Library of Congress annex, and more soon followed. "We were on our way," McShain later wrote. "Each month we continued to win larger contracts."

It was glory, and not cash, that most motivated McShain. "I'd rather break even on a monumental building than make a million on an uninspired warehouse," he would say, and his construction of the Jefferson Memorial proved him true to his word. McShain's impetus for building the memorial came soon after he started in Washington, when he brought his family down to see the sights. They rode around town in a limousine, with his young daughter Polly in the jump seat. Walking up the steps to the Lincoln Memorial, his daughter asked, "Daddy, did you build this?" The proud father somewhat abashedly admitted he had not. "Right away I got a great inspiration," McShain said years later. In 1939, when the Thomas Jefferson Memorial Commission put out a request for bids, he got his chance. "I sent word to all my competitors: 'Don't waste your time bidding; it's going to be our structure,' " he said. "When they submitted the bids, I reduced the price to a point where I barely could see the possibility of coming out even." McShain's bid of $2.157 million was low enough to win the contract though not enough to break even; he ended up losing $43,000. The prestige of building the memorial might have been reward enough for McShain, but

it was good for business too. The job had an incalculably valuable side benefit: It made him Franklin Roosevelt's personal builder.

McShain was just a few months into the construction of the Jefferson
Memorial when he bid on another project even dearer to the president's
heart. In the latter half of his second term, at a time when he was contem-
plating retiring to Hyde Park and writing his memoirs, Roosevelt had become consumed with the idea of creating the nation's first presidential
library. With one eye on his historical legacy, Roosevelt wanted a reposi-
tory for his vast collection of papers, books, and memorabilia that would
be turned over to the government and open to the public, yet that he could
use as a private office. He carved a sixteen-acre lot from his Hyde Park estate for the library, raised private funds for the project, and in July 1939
signed legislation passed by Congress authorizing the whole deal. Now he
had to select a builder. Roosevelt, who had not yet met McShain, did some
checking on the man building the Jefferson Memorial. He asked the Democratic senator from Pennsylvania, Joseph F. Guffey, about McShain's ability. "He is the best builder in the country," replied Guffey, who added a
caveat: McShain was an ardent Republican.

On September 5, 1939, McShain learned that he had been awarded the
contract to build the Roosevelt Library with his bid of $291,400. Three
days later, McShain received word that the president wanted to see him the
following morning in Hyde Park. After McShain arrived on the grounds of
the estate, Roosevelt drove up in his dark metallic blue 1936 Ford Phaeton,
specially equipped with hand levers that allowed the president to control
the brakes and throttle despite the polio that left his legs partially paralyzed.
The top was down, and Roosevelt invited McShain to take a seat in the
front. McShain was coming to him "with a splendid reputation," Roosevelt
said. "I've checked on you," the president added. "I find you're a Republican." But Roosevelt "hastened to assure me that such a situation would in
no way interfere with our plans," a relieved McShain wrote in a diary he
kept of his encounters with the president.

The two men hit it off. Though in the midst of a great international
crisis, Roosevelt was unable to resist taking time out for the library. Hitler
had invaded Poland a week earlier, and England and France had declared
war on Germany. German troops had reached Warsaw and the battle for

the city was under way. Roosevelt told McShain he had just been on the telephone with Ambassadors Joseph Kennedy in London and William C. Bullitt in Paris, and the president appeared "nervous and alarmed" by the news; FDR said he would be unable to stay long from the house. But looking over the library site, Roosevelt soon forgot his cares and expounded on his vision for the building. They drove around surrounding Dutchess County looking at examples of the Dutch colonial architecture and stonework that the president wanted McShain to emulate. After touring for two hours, Roosevelt dropped McShain off with a hearty farewell and an invitation to return with his family in two weeks, when news crews would be on hand to film the start of work. McShain was soon a regular at Hyde Park, visiting generally once a month in the ensuing year to supervise construction with the president.

McShain's Republican leanings were strongly held—inherited from his father and reinforced by his wife's family—and he never wavered from them in his entire life. (McShain would later refuse to apologize about all the work he received during the Roosevelt and Truman administrations, replying with irritation when a newspaper columnist asserted he was the darling of Democrats: "Great guns, is it my fault that they've been the only ones around for the past 20 years to sign the contracts?") Yet McShain genuinely liked Roosevelt, finding him "a high-class gentleman" and relishing the president's joviality. "He was like a young boy, joking and he told wonderful stories," McShain later wrote. The two shared a vitality, a love of life, and supreme self-confidence.

Roosevelt treated McShain warmly, the president lighting cigarette after cigarette as he gossiped about presidential politics and fretted over developments in Europe, speaking as if the builder were a trusted confidant rather than a hired contractor. Roosevelt quickly gleaned that the way to McShain's heart was through a promise of glory. When McShain approached him with a plan for presenting him with an engraved silver trowel to lay the cornerstone at the library, Roosevelt was enthusiastic and assured McShain that for "the next two centuries, people would view this trowel with great interest and that everyone that did so, would see my name inscribed thereon," a pleased McShain wrote afterward.

Accordingly, Roosevelt invited McShain to speak at the handover of the Roosevelt Library to the federal government on July 4, 1940. The proud builder sailed with his family up the Hudson River from New York City aboard his power boat, *Poll-O-Mine,* named after his daughter. With the handsome stonework of the library as a backdrop for the ceremony, McShain assured the president the building would last for many centuries and then turned over the keys. Roosevelt pronounced himself delighted with the final product.

McShain sealed Roosevelt's affection with a final gesture a year later, at the building's formal dedication on June 30, 1941. "After viewing the Library I was convinced that there was still something lacking in order to make a perfect layout," McShain wrote to Roosevelt on July 8, 1941. The builder enclosed several sketches showing a little stone guardhouse, to be constructed at the gate leading to the library, "which I would like the privilege of building for you at this time.

"Of course, I am aware that you have already given the new Library to the Government and in view of this action I would be delighted to erect this new structure for the large sum of One ($1.00) Dollar," McShain continued.

Roosevelt—who had previously bemoaned the lack of funds to build a guardhouse—immediately accepted. "You are not only a grand fellow but you are a real friend in time of need!" the president wrote back July 12. "I am thrilled by your splendid offer to build us a Guard House . . ." There was nothing surreptitious about the matter—Roosevelt publicly acknowledged McShain's gift in remarks to a Hyde Park audience—but it all served to deepen the ties between the builder and the president.

As work commenced on the $18,000 guardhouse, Roosevelt boarded his special presidential train on the night of July 24 and retired to his comfortable sleeping compartment for the overnight trip to Hyde Park, where he planned to spend a long weekend. Earlier that day, at the cabinet meeting, the president had given his approval for the new War Department building in Arlington. Arriving in Hyde Park the following morning, Roosevelt at some point spoke to McShain and confided that a big project was brewing back in the capital. "During our conversation he told me that they were planning to build the largest building in the world in Washington and it was a great secret," McShain later wrote. "He also told me that he would have no influence in making the selection of the contractor but he was hopeful our firm would be given every consideration."

Roosevelt, apparently unaware that Washingtonians were waking up the morning of July 25 to word of the building in their newspapers, was wrong about the matter still being secret. In any event, though he said nothing about it to the president, McShain already knew all about the new building. He had already been tapped by Somervell to build it.

No greater worlds to conquer

Somervell had started selecting a contractor on July 22, the same day that Stimson approved the new War Department building. The size, complexity, and financing demands of such a huge project meant that more than one contractor would be needed. That day, Brigadier General Wilhelm "Fat" Styer, Somervell's deputy, instructed the department's Construction Advisory Committee to recommend contractors who could build a new headquarters at "the utmost speed."

McShain, well plugged in to Washington, had been tipped by a friend in the government that "the largest building in the world" was in the works even before Somervell or Roosevelt said anything to him. "Naturally I was quite interested," he wrote. McShain made inquiries around town, filed all the necessary papers with the War Department, and learned that his firm was one of twenty being considered for the job. "The rumors circulated that the building would cost approximately forty million dollars and would be required to be completed within a year," McShain wrote. His appetite was further whetted by word that the job would be awarded on a cost-plus basis, meaning that the contractor would get a set fee over and above the final construction cost and thus be guaranteed a profit—making "the proposition much more attractive," McShain wrote.

The Construction Advisory Committee, made up of civilians prominent in the industry, had the task of selecting builders for cost-plus contracts, which could not be put out to the low bidder because the fees were fixed. The committee had been established by Hartman, Somervell's predecessor, as a way of making sure contractors were chosen by merit and not by influence-peddling. Somervell found this annoying. "The board was in

Somervell's way," committee member Ferdinand J. C. Dresser, director of the American Construction Council, later told Army historians. Hartman had resolutely guarded against allowing politics to interfere with the process, but Somervell believed he had a God-given right to keep the politicians happy. "It didn't take the boys on the Hill long to catch on that Somervell was more easy to get to than Hartman," Dresser said. The huge amount of building contracts being signed by the War Department "was too big a thing for the politicians not to get mixed up in it," Dresser added. "They were on our necks. Believe me, the heat was terrific."

On July 24, the committee recommended to Somervell that the new headquarters be built by three firms: John McShain, Inc., of Philadelphia, Turner Construction Co. of New York, and the George A. Fuller Co., also of New York. McShain's credentials for the job were unquestionable. So were those of Turner and Fuller, both titans of the construction industry. Turner had a strong presence in Washington and was considered a pioneer in building concrete structures. Fuller was in the midst of compiling a construction record in Washington that rivaled McShain's, building the Lincoln Memorial, the Department of Justice, the National Archives, the Supreme Court, and Washington National Cathedral. When McShain's firm was at the height of its success, the only larger contractors in the country were Fuller and Turner.

Somervell heartily endorsed the recommendation for McShain, noting his record of completing War Department projects "in a highly satisfactory manner and well within the time allowed for construction." But Somervell immediately telephoned Under Secretary of War Patterson and pressed him to substitute Turner and Fuller with two far smaller firms. "As was explained to you in our phone conversation of July 24, it is my opinion that the following combination of firms is best qualified to handle construction of this important project," Somervell wrote to Patterson the following day. The general listed three contractors: John McShain, Inc., of Philadelphia, Doyle & Russell of Richmond, Virginia, and Wise Contracting Company, Inc., also of Richmond.

War Department policy was that, all other criteria being equal, a contractor from the region where a project was being built would receive preference. However, Doyle & Russell and Wise were not remotely in the same league as the big New York firms. The two Virginia firms had recently built Camp Lee, a quartermaster training center near Petersburg, Virginia, but the project was nothing close to what was envisioned in Arlington. However, they offered something that Fuller and Turner could not: Both were based in Virginia, Clifton Woodrum's home state. By happy coincidence, Virginia was also the home of Senator Carter Glass, the powerful chairman of the Senate Appropriations Committee, which would soon be considering the proposed building in Arlington.

Patterson was usually reluctant to deviate from the recommendations of the Construction Advisory Committee, but this time he approved Somervell's request. Committee member Dresser, for one, was under no illusions as to why the general insisted on the switch. It was done at the behest of Woodrum, who "put together" the Virginia firms, Dresser said.

As to why Somervell chose to keep McShain over Fuller or Turner among the recommended out-of-state firms, the general, beyond his respect for McShain's capabilities, was doubtless aware of Roosevelt's affinity for the builder and may well have seen it as a way to keep the president happy. Indeed, Roosevelt's reaction when Somervell informed him of McShain's selection "was very favourable," the general told McShain. The president "assured them he was delighted we did receive the contract and authorised them to make the award immediately," McShain wrote.

Dick Groves saw "political reasons" behind the selection of the Virginia companies, but he approved of the choice of McShain, whom he admired as "a tough little Irishman who would do a good job."

Whatever the reasons, the selection of McShain would prove inspired. In McShain, Somervell and Groves had a contractor who could rise to meet their quite unreasonable demands for speed and scale. The Virginia firms, in contrast, would lend little more than their names and financial support to the construction, while reaping easy profits.

Principals of the three companies unanimously agreed to name McShain general contractor. Given charge of constructing the largest office building on earth, McShain believed he had reached "the pinnacle" of his life. "I felt, at that stage, there were no greater worlds to conquer," McShain later wrote.

Just as losing money on the Jefferson Memorial had proven a good investment for McShain, taking a bath on the Roosevelt Library paid off. Mc-

Shain certainly saw it that way, according to his friend and business associate, Atlantic City attorney Thomas Munyan. "He was a smart fellow," Munyan recalled more than sixty years later. He may have lost more than $100,000 building the library, McShain once told Munyan, but he got the Pentagon.

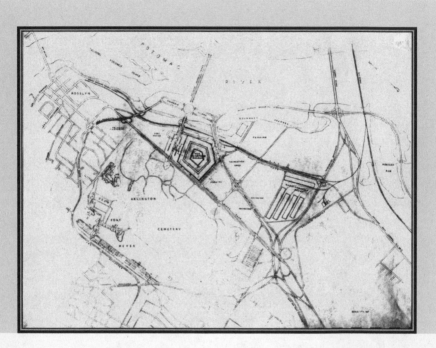

Map depicting the original site proposed for the War Department building near the foot of Memorial Bridge.

CHAPTER 4

CARRYING L'ENFANT'S
BANNER

The resurrection of Pierre L'Enfant

The men digging up the grave at the old Digges farm in Maryland worked in silence, stopping only for a short time when a thunderstorm passed through on that April day in 1909. The grave was unmarked, except by a tall, slender red cedar tree planted eighty-four years earlier, at the same time as the body for which they searched. The men dug down about four feet before their spades reached any trace of the remains, a layer of discolored mold about three inches thick. That soil, along with two bones and a tooth, were all that remained of Pierre Charles L'Enfant, the designer of Washington.

The Paris-born architect and engineer had served as a major in the Continental Army under George Washington during the Revolutionary War. At Washington's request, L'Enfant rode to the port of Georgetown on the Potomac River in March 1791, arriving alone on horseback on a rainy evening. Washington wanted him to survey the surrounding untamed countryside, where Congress had agreed to establish a new capital for the United States. But in typical grand fashion the Frenchman opted to do much more than a topographical survey. "Through days of almost incessant rain he crisscrossed the woods and fields between the Eastern

Branch and the Potomac, glimpsing through fog and mist, pleasant land-scapes, splendid views, bubbling springs and splashing creeks, and visualizing a stately city in that setting," according to one account. The city L'Enfant laid out in the following months was magnificent, one of grand avenues, beautiful open expanses, and stirring views. The plan received a positive, though subdued, reception.

L'Enfant, however, managed to alienate all sides with his capricious ways and refusal to observe deadlines. Washington dismissed the Frenchman in February 1792. Among many other insults, L'Enfant was never paid for his services designing the capital. He lived out his last years at the farm of his friend, Thomas Digges, in Prince George's County a few miles south of the new capital, and died a pauper in 1825, unnoticed and forgotten.

But no more. After being pulled from the grave on April 22, 1909, L'Enfant's scant remains were placed in a casket and wrapped in an American flag. Escorted by a military honor guard, the casket was taken five days later to the Capitol Rotunda to lie in state. There, as throngs of citizens paid their respects, President William Howard Taft presided over a memorial ceremony attended by senators, diplomats, and Supreme Court justices. "He whose mortal remains—a few scattered bones—we today transfer from the obscure resting place of nearly a century to live with the nation's great, served us in arms and civil life with rare and masterful genius," declared Vice President James "Sunny Jim" Sherman.

It was not just L'Enfant's body that had been resurrected. L'Enfant's plan for Washington had been rehabilitated. The builders of the federal city had followed the general layout drawn by the French engineer, but over the course of the nineteenth century much of the grandeur envisioned in the plan was marred by a hodgepodge of buildings, depots, carriageways, and clusters of trees that filled in open spaces and destroyed vistas. Celebrations of Washington's centennial in 1900 triggered a rediscovery of L'Enfant and his vision for a monumental city. L'Enfant's champions were inspired by the burgeoning "City Beautiful" movement then coming into fashion in architectural and civic circles around the country, the notion that the beautification of a city could boost personal morals, cultural values, and economic growth. In this vein, the Senate created the McMillan Commission, an illustrious committee including architectural luminaries such as Daniel Burnham and Frederick Law Olmsted, Jr. The commission issued a momentous report in 1902 that recommended Washington be restored in accordance with L'Enfant's vision. The commission recorded many triumphs, none bigger than persuading the Pennsylvania Railroad to move its train depot off the great National Mall, freeing it of unsightly train tracks, sheds, and smoke that had long spoiled the view. Commissioners even extended the grand sweep of the L'Enfant plan, proposing to push the monumental core farther west and south by filling in swampland, building a memorial to Abraham Lincoln along the Potomac, and connecting it with a bridge across the river to Arlington National Cemetery.

It was to Arlington that L'Enfant was taken at the conclusion of the April 28, 1909, ceremony in his honor at the Capitol Rotunda. L'Enfant's casket was placed on a caisson and drawn by six bay horses down Pennsylvania Avenue, across the Potomac to the cemetery, and then carried to his new burial place, high on a hill looking back to Washington. "His last resting place . . . is a tribute to the memory of the man who above all others President Washington selected to plan the site of the Capital," *The Washington Post* noted. "It is directly in front of the historic old Lee mansion and in full view of the fruits of his labors."

Arlington Cemetery by then was the most hallowed burial ground in all the land, with a noble history that added to its mystique. The Greek Revival hillside mansion that capped the grounds had been built beginning in 1802 by George Washington Parke Custis, the first president's adopted grandson. Custis wanted to build a great stone home on the wooded 1,100-acre estate as a memorial to Washington, but, short on cash, he settled for a brick-and-wood structure with a faux marble and sandstone finish. It looked grand, at least from a distance, and from the portico visitors gazing back toward Washington enjoyed what the Marquis de Lafayette proclaimed in 1824 to be "the finest view in the world."

Custis's daughter, Mary Anna Randolph Custis, was married under the arches of the drawing room in 1831 to a dashing young Army lieutenant named Robert E. Lee. There the couple lived for a happy thirty years and raised seven children, though Lee was absent for extended periods with Army duty. The Lees left Arlington forever in the spring of 1861, when Colonel Lee, after a long night of pacing on squeaking floorboards in his upstairs bedroom, declined command of the Federal Army and instead accepted that of the seceding state of Virginia's forces. Union troops soon crossed the river to occupy Arlington's high ground, creating a vast military encampment on the land and using the house as headquarters for the Army of the Potomac. In the beginning, the home was treated respectfully, but as hopes for a quick victory faded after the First Battle of Manassas and the war turned into an awful and bloody ordeal, bitter feelings arose. The house was looted and great stands of virgin oak that covered the grounds were cut for timber and firewood. In 1864, with the Union Army in need of a new location to bury its ever-increasing numbers of dead, the federal government designated the Arlington grounds as a cemetery. At the order of Brigadier General Montgomery Meigs, commander of the Union garrison at Arlington, some of the first bodies were planted next to the mansion in a semicircle around Mary Lee's beloved flower garden, a message of cold reproach to the Lee family. General Lee had long since accepted that Arlington was lost. "They cannot take away the remembrances of the spot, & the memories of those that to us render it sacred," he wrote his wife on Christmas Day 1861. "That will remain to us as long as life will last, & that we can preserve."

At first the cemetery was little more than a potter's field, a place to bury Union soldiers whose families could not afford to ship their bodies home; their sad number reached sixteen thousand by war's end. But the burial in subsequent years of some of the giants of the Civil War—particularly General Philip Sheridan in 1888—greatly increased Arlington's national stature. A crowd of 25,000 attended the burial of 163 crew members killed when the USS *Maine* blew up in Havana harbor in 1898. But nothing could compare to Armistice Day in 1921, when the burial of an unknown soldier felled in the Great War sparked the greatest traffic jam Washington had ever known.

So many thousands of cars followed the caisson procession from the Capitol to Arlington that traffic on the bridges leading to Virginia came to a complete standstill. Many abandoned their automobiles to walk across the bridges, and others took canoes. President Warren G. Harding arrived at Arlington only minutes before he was supposed to open the noon ceremony, and his mood was grim. "It is understood that the President more than once during the journey expressed himself very forcibly regarding the confusion," the Washington *Star* reported.

The capital was so traumatized by the monumental jam that Congress was finally persuaded to approve funding for a new Potomac crossing, the Memorial Bridge, fulfilling the McMillan Commission's recommendation two decades earlier, and by extension L'Enfant's plan. As the commission had suggested, the bridge was sited on a perfect line between the Lee Mansion and the recently completed Lincoln Memorial across the Potomac, thus extending monumental Washington to the Arlington Heights. When it was completed in 1932, the Memorial Bridge, with its covering of North Carolina granite and its sculpted eagles from Italy, was instantly celebrated as one of the treasures of the capital. Most breathtaking of all was the graceful linear vista created: The river separating Lincoln and Lee, twin pillars of North and South, had been bridged. From his perch of restored glory in front of the Lee mansion, L'Enfant was presumably well satisfied with the view.

L'Enfant rolls in his grave

In July 1941, L'Enfant, or what was left of him, was surely rolling over in his second grave. Gilmore D. Clarke, chairman of the Commission of Fine Arts, was certain of that. It suddenly seemed L'Enfant's view would be destroyed by the enormous new War Department headquarters Somervell was planning for just a few hundred yards below the major's tomb. Clarke was dumbfounded by the proposal for a building large enough to hold forty thousand people—"a population as large as Poughkeepsie, New York, or Shreveport, Louisiana," Clarke wrote soon after learning of the plan. "It is proposed to place this 'city' at the very portals of the Arlington National Cemetery, thus resulting in the introduction of 35 acres of ugly, flat roofs into the very foreground of the most majestic view of the National Capital that obtains . . . from a point near the Tomb of Major L'Enfant, the architect of Washington."

The Commission of Fine Arts was the keeper of L'Enfant's flame. Created by Congress in 1910 to permanently carry on the work of the McMillan Commission, the Commission of Fine Arts had established itself as the "arbiter of public taste in the capital," guiding the architectural development of the city and passing judgment on the location, arrangement, and treatment of buildings, monuments, and sculptures. It carried no legal authority to block projects, but Congress generally followed the judgments passed down by the distinguished architects, sculptors, and landscape architects who made up the commission.

Clarke, a New York City native, had a reputation as one of the nation's finest landscape architects and had helped design some of the country's first parkways. He was not a building architect, but that did not stop him from passing judgment on those who were. "I've been around architecture so long that I'm arrogant enough to think that I know something about it," he once said. Clarke had a "gift for forceful expression," in the view of the *Star*. He employed it vigorously during the fierce debate over the design of the Jefferson Memorial. Clarke derided architect John Russell Pope's pantheon dome as "indefensibly pedantic" and "slavishly classical," and he led the commission's unsuccessful campaign to persuade Congress and Roosevelt to change the design. Clarke would never guard his opinions for political expediency, no matter the political clout of the applicant.

Clarke was accustomed to getting respect. But Somervell had not bothered to notify the commission about the massive new War Department building, much less consult with it. When Clarke, working from his office in New York City, finally got word of what was afoot, the project had already been approved by the House of Representatives.

Clarke declared war. "It is inconceivable that this outrage could be perpetrated in this period of the history of the development of this City, a city held in the highest esteem by every citizen who visits it," he wrote in a letter to the Senate.

Clarke saw himself as the guardian of good taste in the nation's capital, and that meant he had to stop Somervell.

If Hitler would postpone his war

Somervell had also ignored the National Capital Park and Planning Commission, charged with preparing and maintaining "a comprehensive, consistent and coordinated plan for the National Capital and its environs." Somervell had assured Congress that there was no need to consult the commission about constructing the world's largest office building inside those environs.

Not everyone agreed, including the planning commission chairman.

His name was Frederic A. Delano, or, as President Roosevelt called him, "Uncle Fred."

Delano, younger brother of Roosevelt's mother, Sara, was a pioneer in the field of city planning, for which he had no professional training but endless passion. City planning had been rare in America until after the turn of the century, when it was spurred on by civic activists like Delano; he was a leading force in resurrecting L'Enfant's plan and clearing out the Mall. Delano pushed Congress to bring order to the capital's development by creating the National Capital Park and Planning Commission; he had served without pay as chairman since its inception in 1924.

Somervell's assurances aside, the law creating the commission clearly gave it oversight over the proposed building in Arlington. On short notice, Delano called a special meeting of the planning commission with Somervell for July 29, the day after the House approved funding for the building.

Uncle Fred had the sardonic wit and boundless energy of his nephew, though at age seventy-seven he was slowing down a tad. Delano had many concerns about the building, particularly potential transportation problems for a site across the river in Virginia. But he appeared to be in no mood for a fight against a project already endorsed by his nephew, nor was he inclined to challenge the War Department on an issue painted as being of the utmost importance for national defense. When the meeting began at 2 P.M. in Room 7118 of the Department of Interior Building in Washington, the chairman threw in the towel during his opening statement. "General Somervell, I want it made clear that I do not want to be made a party to any obstructions to a project that is very much needed at this time," Delano said. That set the tone for the whole hearing.

Commissioners raised a few questions about the size of the building and the lack of roads, but Somervell brushed them aside with the simple message that the building was an urgent necessity and that there was no time to waste on nitpicking questions. "I ask that nothing be done to kill this," the general told the commissioners. "This seems to be an opportunity to get it when we need it most."

No one challenged Somervell. Delano absolved Somervell of his plan's imperfections. "I don't want to play the role of a troublemaker when it looks as though it is pretty evident that the arguments for this are so strong that you won't be listened to," Delano said after Somervell departed. "You will only give them the satisfaction of saying I told you so."

Commissioner Charles W. Kutz made a wistful suggestion: "If Hitler would postpone his war a year or two . . ."

My God, what will that boy do next?

Yet Delano had not been one in the past to shy away from arguments about architecture, planning, and buildings, even with his nephew.

In 1938, the Navy pushed plans to replace its hospital in downtown Washington with a new one in nearby Bethesda, Maryland, featuring a sixteen-story, 215-foot high tower. Delano was appalled—the tower far exceeded the 130-foot limit established by law in the District, and even if it was in Maryland, it was a bad precedent. At a joint hearing before the planning and fine arts commissions, Delano and Gilmore Clarke resolved to oppose the tower, which stuck up "like a sore thumb," in Clarke's words. There was one problem. Rear Admiral Ben Moreell, who presented the plans for the hospital to the commissions, pulled out a crude sketch showing the tower flanked by two-story wings. The sketch was drawn on White House stationery and bore the initials "FDR."

Delano turned to Clarke. "My God," Delano whispered, "what will that boy do next?"

"That boy," Franklin Roosevelt, had long fancied himself a respectable amateur architect, drawing on a childhood interest that continued through his schooling, into his early public life as assistant secretary of the Navy, and on through his presidency. He was particularly active in and around Hyde Park, poking his nose into the design of several local post offices and collaborating with architect Henry Toombs on a Dutch colonial cottage on his estate in 1938. *Life* magazine published the plans for the cottage with the legend "Franklin D. Roosevelt, Architect." Professional architects were aghast. "After seeing the title Architect after F.D. Roosevelt in your magazine, I give up," John Lloyd Wright, son of Frank Lloyd Wright, wrote to *Life*. "Put me in a concentration camp."

Roosevelt was not apologetic, suggesting to his private secretary, Missy LeHand, that the following response be given to critics: "By the way, did Thomas Jefferson have a license when he drew the sketches for Monti-cello, the University of Virginia and a number of other rather satisfactory architectural productions?"

In architecture, as in other pursuits, Jefferson was Roosevelt's role model. Next to the Virginian, Roosevelt was the American president most engaged with architecture, though, as art historian William B. Rhoads has written, "his taste was Jeffersonian without Jefferson's inventiveness." For federal buildings in Washington, Roosevelt favored a conservative and conventional look and was especially fond of neoclassicism, an affinity he shared with the leader of Germany, Adolf Hitler, himself an amateur ar-chitect.

Whatever his talent and taste, Roosevelt had an aesthetic sensibility and understood the power of architecture to convey meaning. He believed the buildings his administration left behind would outlive his policies and that "the ongoing presence of buildings could serve as a bond between gen-erations and even centuries," Rhoads wrote. Roosevelt thus had a deep in-terest in the look and placement of buildings in Washington, leaving his stamp on the Jefferson Memorial, National Airport, and the Pentagon. However, no federal building was more purely a Roosevelt production than the Naval Hospital in Bethesda.

Roosevelt had been itching to build a government tower ever since a 1936 campaign stop in Lincoln, Nebraska, where he had been deeply im-pressed by the new twenty-two-story art deco state capitol, the first in the country to feature a tower. Roosevelt decided the new Navy hospital would be the perfect opportunity to build his own tower. He drew his sketch in December 1937, basing it on the Nebraska capitol, and turned it over to the Navy's Bureau of Yards and Docks, which prepared drawings for the sixteen-story tower under the direction of architect Paul Cret. The follow-ing summer, Roosevelt inspected several sites before settling on a farm along Rockville Pike in Bethesda, about three miles from the District bor-der. To passersby it appeared to be a rundown cabbage patch, but the pres-ident, spotting a spring-fed pond on the grounds, was reminded of the Pool of Bethesda, the Biblical place of healing and renewal. He decided it would be the perfect spot for a towering hospital.

After Delano's planning commission and Clarke's fine arts commission raised objections, the Navy came back with new plans in the fall, this time for a twenty-three-story tower rising 250 feet. "They exceed in monstrosity the original plans," an exasperated Delano wrote the president.

"Dear Uncle Fred," Roosevelt wrote on December 1, 1938, from Warm Springs, Georgia, where he would often visit to bathe his crippled legs in the healing waters.

> I have very carefully studied hospital design and, frankly, I am fed up with the type the Government has been building during these past twenty years. Therefore, I personally designed a new Naval Hospital with a large central tower of sufficient square footage and height to make it an integral and interesting part of the hospital itself, and at the same time present something new— getting away from colonial brick or ultramodernistic limestone. All of the doctors who have seen the design are tremendously keen about it as a practical and useful building for the needs it will serve.

The president went on to paint a pastoral image of the hospital he envisioned, likening the effect of his Navy tower to church spires in "the English countryside."

That reference was too much for Delano. "Oh Sire!" he wrote his nephew on December 14. ". . . Since the beginning of time the formula has been that 'the King can do no wrong.' However, from the time of Solomon and even further back, the King found it necessary to surround himself with soothsayers, astrologers, and other wise men to warn him of the pitfalls and dangers lying ahead of him."

It was no use. Roosevelt braved a driving rainstorm on Armistice Day, 1940, to lay the tower's cornerstone. The president stood beside the contractor—John McShain, of course. Grasping a silver trowel, Roosevelt dabbed at the wet cement. "I've done it before and I can do it better than John McShain," he assured his audience. To complete the English countryside effect, Roosevelt ordered the grounds of the tower enclosed by a sheep fence.

Despite his failure to stop the tower, Delano had occasionally managed to rein in his nephew's grander architectural impulses. Delano had objected, for example, to the size of the Jefferson Memorial—"an effort to outdo the Lincoln Memorial," he called it—and Roosevelt had agreed to scale it back.

Delano decided it was time to rein in his nephew again. Sometime between the end of the planning commission meeting at 5 P.M. July 29 and the following afternoon, Uncle Fred changed his mind about the new War Department building in Arlington. He would be a troublemaker after all.

Uncle Fred goes to bat

At 3 P.M. on Wednesday, July 30, Frederic Delano walked into the Oval Office for a meeting with his nephew about the proposed War Department building. Accompanying Delano was Harold Smith, director of the president's budget office. Smith had the look and sensibilities of a Midwestern justice of the peace. In his off-the-rack suit and department-store shoes, with calm gray eyes behind his rimless spectacles, he presented the very image of frugality. His opinions, delivered in slow, judicial tones, were held in high regard by Roosevelt.

The visitors had a very direct message: "It was a great pity to construct this building," the president was told.

Roosevelt had returned the previous day from a five-day visit to Hyde Park, where he had decamped after approving the new building at the Cabinet meeting July 24. Now, faced with his uncle's protests, the president admitted that perhaps he had been a bit hasty. "After he got to thinking it over he was a good deal disturbed," Delano related two days later. "Of course I asked how a matter of such tremendous import as that could be passed through without giving it any real consideration." Roosevelt noted in his defense that most of the Cabinet had raised no objection to the building.

Smith's concerns about the building were not aesthetic. He just did not think it made any sense. The proposal had been hurriedly and incompletely considered. He could not understand why a huge, permanent building was needed when the growth of the War Department was supposed to be a temporary response to the emergency.

Delano and Smith told the president that moving forty thousand people back and forth across the Potomac River between Washington and Virginia every day would create "terrific" traffic problems and overwhelm the capacity of the bridges and scant road network in Arlington. By the end of the meeting, the president had come to an agreement with his visitors. Somervell's building would be cut back considerably in size.

Reporters were waiting outside the White House after the meeting, and an unnamed federal official—more than likely Smith—said that the president had agreed to pare down the building. "The problem of getting 40,000 persons to and from the proposed 35 million dollar War Department Building in Arlington County, Va., has so concerned President Roosevelt that, with his blessing, Federal officials have taken steps to modify drastically original plans for the structure," *The Washington Post* reported on the front page the following morning.

Delano was fortified by Smith's support. "I am glad to know that the Director of the Budget is fighting as hard as he can on it," Delano told his commission colleagues.

Delano sent the Senate Appropriations Committee a letter on July 31 outlining the commission's view on the project. Gone was the bonhomie of the planning commission meeting two days earlier at which Delano had vowed not to interfere with the building. The project "will have a very serious retarding effect on the National Capital," Delano warned the senators. It would cause traffic chaos, disrupt Washington's rental-office market, upend long-considered plans for the federal city, and place financial burdens on Arlington County. He questioned the entire rationale for the building: "Is it wise to put the entire general and official staff of the Army in one place where many of them might be subject to being put out of action?"

Delano urged the size of the building be halved, at least temporarily. "We are strongly of the opinion that while the War Department is justified in planning an office building for a maximum of 40,000 employees, it would be unwise to build more than for say 20,000 employees, until some experience shall have been acquired in concentrating this number in an outlying suburban location," his letter concluded.

No one was more delighted with the turn of events than Gilmore Clarke, chairman of the Commission of Fine Arts. At the Interior building later that morning, Clarke's commission held a joint session with Delano's National Capital Park and Planning Commission to coordinate the assault. Clarke played the role of firebrand, passionately urging that the two commissions marshal public opinion and form a united front to defeat the proposal, appealing to the commissioners' sense of duty to posterity.

"We wouldn't want to take this thing on alone," Clarke said. "We wanted some support. It would seem to me the public is rather stirred up about this and now is the time to make a constructive suggestion which might fire the imagination of some of the gentlemen on the Hill."

Delano glumly warned that there probably was not time to change the site. "One trouble we are up against is that time is pretty nearly the essence of this whole thing," he said.

The building's five-sided design with a big courtyard in the middle was atrocious, Clarke said. "The building is designed with a bull's eye. It is about as bad a plan as could be designed," he said. "We just wouldn't have the answer ten years from now for the reason we put that thing there." He mocked Somervell's contention that putting the entire War Department staff in one building was necessary for efficiency. "He won't walk half a mile around that building. He will pick up a telephone. Unless I am greatly mistaken these people do not move around very much—they are glued to their chairs. They get in a car and go someplace."

Clarke conceded that the War Department needed some solution to cope with the emergency. "What is the answer?" he mused. "It is sort of bad business to condemn things and not have an answer up your sleeve."

Nobody had an answer up his sleeve. Delano resigned himself to waging further battle. "All right," he said, addressing the planning commissioners before they left. "We may have to go to bat on this thing."

Roosevelt's fishing expedition

Two days later on August 3, at 10:40 on a hot and humid Sunday morning, the American flag flying over the White House came down from its staff, signaling the president's departure. Roosevelt was escaping a Washington August so hot that "the heat was melting the tar on Massachusetts Avenue," according to one press account. The presidential limousine carried Roosevelt and several top aides across town to Union Station, where a special train waited to take the president to New England for what press spokesman Stephen Early told reporters would be a relaxing ten-day fishing cruise.

Before leaving town, Roosevelt had taken care of a pressing matter. After huddling with Harold Smith at noon on Friday, Roosevelt signed a letter to Senator Alva Adams, chairman of the Senate Appropriations subcommittee that was to consider the new War Department building. The letter offered a revisionist account of the green light the president had given Stimson at the cabinet meeting a week earlier. "When this project was first brought to my attention, I agreed that it should be explored," Roosevelt's letter read. "Since then I have had an opportunity to look into the matter personally and have some reservations which I would like to impart to your committee."

Those reservations were directed solely at the building's size and not its location, Roosevelt added. "While I am in full accord with this general objective of providing additional permanent space and have no objection to the use of the Arlington Farm site for an office building for the War Department, I do question the advisability of constructing the entire 4,000,000 sq. ft. on the proposed site without first being reasonably sure that the present and proposed traffic and transportation facilities can accommodate" all the expected workers, he said.

The letter, drafted by Smith and using language very similar to that sent by Delano to the Senate the day before, urged the Senate to approve "a smaller building" limited to twenty thousand employees. More space could be added later if needed, Roosevelt said.

With all final business attended to, Roosevelt appeared not to have a care in the world as he headed out of town. The presidential train pulled out of Union Station at 11 A.M. on August 3, headed for New London, Connecticut, where Roosevelt's yacht, the USS *Potomac,* was waiting. The president looked relaxed and cheerful, boasting of the number of fish he expected to catch. "It was no more than the start of a vacation for a man who has . . . longed for some sea air," *The New York Times* reported.

It was a good deal more than that. *Potomac* was scheduled for a surreptitious night rendezvous off Martha's Vineyard with the heavy cruiser USS *Augusta,* flagship of the U.S. Atlantic Fleet. *Augusta,* in turn, escorted by another heavy cruiser and five destroyers, would carry Roosevelt to waters off Newfoundland for a secret meeting—his first as president—with Winston Churchill, prime minister of Great Britain.

Almost everyone back in Washington, even senior government officials, was in the dark about the president's mission. Congress remained in session, and in the president's absence the debate over the new War Department building erupted into a full-fledged controversy.

Somervell confidently moved forward to construct the building on his own terms, making no adjustments to shrink it. The Office of Production Management, the government agency overseeing war-mobilization efforts, approved his contract with McShain on August 4. The following day Somervell ordered test borings of the Arlington site.

Yet there was no denying Somervell had suffered quite a reversal. In the first two weeks since launching the project July 17, he had rolled to one victory after another. But as July turned to August, the stiffening resistance from the fine arts and planning commissions had begun to turn the tide. Harold Smith—whom Henry Stimson considered to be "the most dangerous opponent" of the building—was fighting an effective battle behind the scenes at the White House. Skepticism was growing in Congress. Now, worst of all, Roosevelt wanted the building's size cut in half.

A hearing was set before Senator Adams's appropriations subcommittee on August 8. Somervell's burgeoning league of opponents was taking aim not only at the building's size, but also its location. Harold Ickes, Roosevelt's own interior secretary, complained the president's proposal to halve the size of the building was no solution. "In other words, Lee House and the Washington Monument would look down upon only 17½ acres of roofs instead of about 35 acres," the interior secretary noted sardonically in his diary. Contradicting the absent president's views, Ickes telephoned Adams and strenuously objected to the building's location.

Clarke, the fine arts commissioner, also lobbied senators, sending an impassioned letter August 2 to the Appropriations Committee and distributing copies to reporters. "Are we going to create a blot upon the landscape which can never be erased and which will be regretted for decades after this emergency is past history in the minds of future Americans?" Clarke asked.

As an afterthought, Clarke sent a copy to Somervell. The general's one-sentence reply to Clarke on August 5 was curt, but it spoke volumes of disdain: "I acknowledge receipt of your letter of August 2 to the Committee on Appropriations of the United States Senate, previously published in the newspapers."

The newspapers had indeed picked up the cry. The *Star* photographed the proposed site from the Goodyear blimp, floating high above the Lee mansion. The picture was run across five columns with an accompanying declaration by the paper that "the unparalleled view of Washington from the heights of Arlington Cemetery would be distorted by acres upon acres of ugly flat roofs." A *Star* editorial declared such a building "certainly would be an act of vandalism," and the newspaper blamed Somervell. "In the course of a few hours, an Army officer with no experience in city planning and without consulting any planning agency, 'sold' a House Appropriations Committee on a new scheme—to . . . build a stupendous War Department Building." Out-of-town papers weighed in with their own criticism. "Defense is a necessity, but it is not necessary that structures erected for any of its purposes should be an offense against esthetics," *The New York Times* lectured.

The National Association of Building Owners and Managers contended such an enormous building would hurt the rental market and be an "economic liability" after the war. Prominent senators criticized the notion of the War Department abandoning Washington. "Once you do this, we may have all our federal departments scattered all over the United States," warned Henry Cabot Lodge, Jr., of Massachusetts. "This city may be a ghost town after the emergency," echoed Robert R. Reynolds, chairman of the powerful Military Affairs Committee.

Reynolds, with support from other senators, proposed that the building instead be constructed on the grounds of the Soldiers' Home, a venerable retirement facility for veterans established in 1851 with booty brought home from the Mexican War on a large, leafy oasis in the northern reaches of the city. Rolling fields around the home held what a newspaper described as "one of the world's finest herds of Holstein Friesian cows; plus an equally distinguished flock of White Leghorn chickens" that helped provide food and sustenance to the veterans. All of them—old soldiers, chickens, and cows—should be evicted, lock, stock, and barrel, in the view of the *Star*, which heartily endorsed Reynolds's proposal.

Lodge, on the other hand, favored razing poor, primarily black neighborhoods in Washington to keep the War Department in the city, thus killing two birds with one stone, in his opinion. Citizens came forward with their own suggested locations, among them amid the trees of the National Arboretum in Northeast Washington or surrounded by juvenile delinquents on the nearby 350-acre grounds of the National Training School for Boys, a reform school.

Barely noticed in all the uproar was an informal suggestion from Jay Downer, a consultant for the Public Roads Administration, who had often worked with Gilmore Clarke on parkway projects in New York. He was now planning roads to tie northern Virginia together with the District of Columbia, and was intimately familiar with the land in the area.

On the morning of August 6, Downer telephoned Hans Paul Caemmerer, the longtime secretary of the Commission of Fine Arts and a passionate L'Enfant disciple who served as Clarke's eyes and ears in Washington. The War Department owned another vacant plot of land in Arlington, Downer told him, this one immediately south of the Arlington experimental farm and adjacent to Washington-Hoover Airport. The War Department had just broken ground for a quartermaster depot on the site. Why not use this land for a temporary headquarters, Downer suggested.

Caemmerer quickly contacted Clarke in New York. The chairman liked the idea. There would be no aesthetic concerns about building on this low-lying, ignoble tract of land. A telegram was sent the same day to Delano, in Salt Lake City on business, asking his reaction. Delano telegrammed back his approval the next day, calling it "much more agreeable" than Somervell's proposal.

A consensus was settling in many quarters around town that the new War Department simply could not be built at the foot of Arlington Cemetery, a location where it would desecrate the view from the tomb of Pierre L'Enfant. Surely these were plans that the War Department "will gladly give up in the light of fuller information," *The New York Times* told its readers. In this the *Times* was quite mistaken; like many others, it had failed to reckon with General Somervell.

Clifford Berryman cartoon from the Washington Evening Star,
Aug 20, 1941.

CHAPTER 5

A FIRST-CLASS BATTLE

A hell of a mess with Congress

Brigadier General Brehon Somervell, brimming with righteous purpose and armed with maps and figures, strode into the Senate Appropriation Committee's meeting room on the first floor of the Capitol on the morning of August 8, 1941, ready for the showdown over the War Department building in Arlington. Newspaper reporters lurked in the hallway outside as senators and witnesses arrived. The hearing was closed to the public, and frustrated reporters tried to get a fix on the fate of Somervell's building.

"What do you think of this proposal?" a reporter called to Senator Carter Glass of Virginia, the imperious, white-haired chairman of the Senate Appropriations Committee, who everyone in the Capitol knew would have enormous influence determining the outcome. "I'm going to tell the committee how I feel, not the newspapers," Glass snapped.

Inside the committee room, Gilmore Clarke, chairman of the Fine Arts Commission, wasted no time denouncing Somervell's proposed building. "We think it would be one of the most serious and worst attacks on the plan of Washington that has ever been made," he testified.

Senator Alva Adams, the subcommittee chairman, tried to broker a compromise, asking about Roosevelt's declaration that the building's size should be cut in half. "That reduction in capacity doesn't meet your criticism at all?" the senator asked.

"No, sir; that wouldn't meet our sanction at all," Clarke replied. "We are opposed to any building whatever on that Arlington site."

The strident opposition rubbed senators the wrong way. Clarke "was too sarcastic and unbending," Harold Ickes noted in his diary. "Then General Somervell, whose pet this scheme seemed to be, had his turn and he swept all before him."

Somervell summarily rejected the sites proposed by his opponents. No other site but Arlington Farm would do for the War Department, the general insisted. Foggy Bottom, the Washington neighborhood where the New War Department Building was located, could not possibly accommodate a building of this scale; the area was congested and parking nonexistent.

Somervell reserved his greatest scorn for the quartermaster depot site, set in a picaresque neighborhood known as Hell's Bottom. "The Chairman of the Fine Arts Commission thinks it is all right to put the War Department down among a lot of shanties, brickyards, dumps, factories and things of that kind, but I think the War Department is worthy of a little better place," he said.

Arlington Farm should be put to a more important use than expanding a cemetery, Somervell said, launching into a deadpan comic tangent. "My hope is that we can make this a city for the living and not for the dead," he said. ". . . If it is important to get dead ones in that area, I can guarantee you as many per acre in the building . . . as there would be otherwise."

The general was likewise ready when asked about spoiling the view from the Lee mansion. "If there is anything inappropriate in standing on the steps of the home of the greatest soldier we ever produced in this country and looking at the War Department, I do not know what it is," he said

It was a tour de force presentation, and Clarke knew it. The fine arts chairman asked to speak again and did his best to belittle the general. "The Commission of Fine Arts has been thinking about the problem of the development of Washington for 30 years. General Somervell has been thinking about it for, maybe, 6 months. It seems inconceivable to me . . ."

Somervell angrily interposed. "Do you not think you had better stick to what you have been doing yourself?" he snapped at Clarke.

Clarke ignored the interruption and again pushed for the quartermaster depot site. "The general passed that off to say that he does not want to place the War Department around some Negro shacks," he said. "Well, it is not going to be very long before the improvement of the War Department building will eradicate any of the objectionable buildings that are in the vicinity of the site."

Somervell was incensed by Clarke's comments. In the hallway afterward, Clarke saw Somervell. He walked over to the general, greeting him with his hand extended. Somervell refused to shake it and walked away.

Clarke gloomily filled in waiting reporters on what had transpired. "It looks like the War Department is going to win," Clarke said. "The only question remaining is esthetic, and the War Department can't understand that." As Clarke predicted, the subcommittee unanimously approved money for the building at Arlington Farm on August 11.

When the full Appropriations Committee considered the measure the next day, four dissenters spoke against the building, including Senator Theodore Green of Rhode Island, who considered the building "a monstrosity."

But the only opinion that really mattered was that of Glass. At eighty-three, the committee chairman was a living link to antebellum Virginia, born in Lynchburg three years before the Civil War. Except for a stint as secretary of the treasury under Woodrow Wilson, Glass had represented Virginia in Congress since 1902, first in the House and since 1920 in the Senate. The little Democrat was known for his eloquent and fiery tongue. "When he barked at fools or knaves, it was spice to everybody but the victims," a newspaper once wrote. Glass was virulently opposed to Roosevelt's New Deal, calling it "a disgrace to the nation," but he tended to back the president staunchly on defense matters. And like Representative Woodrum in the House, Glass saw Somervell's building as an economic bonanza for his home state. "Carter Glass held the whole thing in the hollow of his hands," a disgusted Harold Ickes wrote in his diary. "With $35,000,000 to be invested in his State this 'grand old man' would not be denied."

Glass easily won the committee's approval, though the Virginian denied any real role in its decision. "Some of you fellows have been writing about my influence with the committee, but I only talked in there about one-tenth of the time some of the other members talked," he told reporters after the vote. Glass did not need to speak much. A mere scowl from the acerbic chairman was enough to cow the more junior members of the committee.

President Roosevelt was still at sea. Just a day earlier, a jaunty dispatch labeled "From USS Potomac" had been distributed to the press in Washington. "All members of party showing effects of sunning," it read in part. "Fishing luck good." In his absence, the Senate ignored Roosevelt's request that the building's size be halved. "The President's hurriedly expressed admonition for caution, written just before he left Washington for a vacation, has been disregarded," the *Star* noted dejectedly.

The opposition had thus far been too divided. Some thought the whole idea of a giant War Department building was ludicrous. Some opposed the size, but not the Arlington Farm site. Others opposed the site, but not the size. Some insisted the building should be put in the District, while others acknowledged that would be impossible and instead favored the quartermaster site. "The Army's blitzkrieg attack on Congress and Washington, with the largest office building in the world as its immediate objective, has been so sudden and so overwhelming that effective resistance has been scattered," the *Star* wrote. "Nothing quite like it has ever happened in Washington before."

But in two days the measure would go to the Senate floor, where there were already signs of a real fight brewing. Senate Majority Leader Alben W. Barkley, the genial and eloquent Democratic warhorse from Kentucky, declared to reporters that he would "infinitely prefer" to see the building placed in Washington rather than Arlington. Somervell's high-speed push had rankled some senators, including Harry Truman and other members of the Public Buildings and Grounds Committee, irritated that the War Department had not consulted them.

On top of that, Ickes publicly split with his absent president, issuing a statement declaring "such a vast structure" at Arlington Farm would "turn our parks into mere traffic ways and spoil the setting of such national symbols as the Arlington Lee Memorial and other monuments." Ickes also sent a letter to Stimson August 12 warning that if the building should be erected "we would all live to regret it. It would be a blackmark against this Administration and a discredit to the Army. And so I, for one, protest." Stimson politely but insistently defended the building. "The plan for Washington cannot be a fixed, inflexible affair which will not meet the needs of the Government," Stimson replied, calling the building an "urgent necessity."

The odds looked in favor of Somervell and his building, but the general complained about the fuss. "It's all gummed up," he groused to a group of reporters. "Well, you newspapers have so many engineers and architects who know better than the Army, you've got us in a hell of a mess with Congress."

Most shockingly extravagant proposal

The Reverend Barney T. Phillips, rector of the Church of the Epiphany in Washington, opened the Senate session on the afternoon of Thursday, August 14, 1941, with a prayer: "In these fateful days, bind us with that bond of earnest devotion which portends freedom and emancipation, that we may yoke life's hostile forces to the loving purposes of God." It was a fateful day, certainly. Senator Barkley took the floor to incorporate momentous news into the Congressional Record: the Atlantic Charter, a joint statement from the president of the United States and the prime minister of Great Britain just released that morning. The secret meeting at sea had been revealed to the world. The charter was a statement of principles whose meaning had only begun to be debated, but the impression left was unmistakable: America and England were bonded in a struggle to end Nazi tyranny.

Discussion on the Senate floor immediately turned to the matter of the day, the $35 million War Department building. Barkley eloquently expressed his reservations. "I cannot divest myself of the feeling that in building up the Capital of the Nation we should have some idea of and some respect for beauty and symmetry as well as utility," he said.

The diminutive senior senator from Virginia rose in defense. The evidence presented to his committee, Carter Glass told the Senate, had demonstrated "that the building is urgently needed immediately [and] that if any other site were selected there would be long delay." The Senate had the assurances of Somervell that the building "would not detract in the slightest degree from the beauty of that section," Glass said.

The floor was not full—many senators were absent from Washington in the middle of August—but the two-hour debate that followed was bruising: "a first-class battle," in the words of the *Star*. A steady stream of senators,

Democrats and Republicans alike, assailed the building. "If we take this step today, because of the argument of haste, we will rue it and regret it for many years to come," warned Senator Abe Murdock, Democrat of Utah.

Frustrations poured out about the cavalier manner in which Somervell and the War Department had proceeded. "It is not so long ago that persons were charging the War Department was without imagination," said Senator Francis Maloney, Democrat of Connecticut. "Someone at the War Department . . . must have heard that and decided that hereafter they would leave nothing to the imagination. . . . Here we have—and heaven knows where it came from—plans already drawn, without consulting the Congress, plans for the world's largest office building."

Arthur Vandenberg, the formidable Republican from Michigan, attacked the "shocking" size. "Unless the war is to be permanent, why must we have permanent accommodations for war facilities of such size? Or"—Vandenberg added to laughter—"is the war to be permanent?"

Senator Pat McCarran, Democrat of Nevada, warned that permitting the War Department to move to Virginia would unleash an exodus of federal agencies moving out of the capital. "Is there any reason why the Department of Agriculture should not be built in Iowa?" asked McCarran. He introduced an amendment requiring that the building be erected in the District of Columbia.

As Representative Woodrum watched nervously from the rear of the chamber, fellow Virginian Glass stood a second time to put down the insurrection. He insisted that thorough investigation had shown there were no adequate sites in the District of Columbia. McCarran's amendment failed 20 to 28. It was the closest call yet for Somervell's plan. A change of five votes would have forced the War Department to build in Washington, a requirement that quite likely would have derailed the whole project.

The fight was not over. Robert A. Taft, the diehard conservative from Ohio and avowed enemy of all things Roosevelt, rose next to lead the sharpest attack of the day. "Mr. Republican," as he was known, pronounced himself staggered by the building's size. "To my mind, there is not any evidence that we shall need such a tremendous building, the largest office building that has ever been built in the entire world . . . ," he said. "It seems to me that in some ways this is the most shockingly extravagant proposal that has been put up to Congress. . . ."

Taft offered an amendment to cut the $35 million appropriation in half, gleefully claiming he was acting in accordance with Roosevelt's own stated desire to halve the building's size. Taft's somewhat disingenuous amendment would effectively kill the proposal, as half the funding would not buy half a building. Taft's amendment failed, 29 to 21. Having weathered the assaults, House Resolution 5412, including authorization to construct the War Department building, finally passed.

Harold Ickes held Carter Glass responsible. "Adams and . . . other senators went along with him like sheep although some senators did make a spirited fight," the secretary wrote in his diary. *The Washington Post* blamed Somervell's rush tactics. "It is impossible to avoid the belief that Congress has been maneuvered into an unwise decision by the emergency circumstances under which this project has been considered," an editorial sadly concluded.

Most important, a majority of senators agreed with Somervell's fundamental argument that the War Department was dangerously scattered. On the morning word of the Atlantic Charter was released, and on the eve of possible war, it was unacceptable.

The matter seemed settled. "The vote apparently assured that the structure would be built at the Virginia end of the Lincoln Memorial Bridge," the *Star* reported on August 15. Roosevelt, still at sea on his homeward journey, could not veto the bill upon his return without delaying the enormous defense appropriation.

Clarke ceded battle too, and awaited the vindication of history. He sent a note to Caemmerer thanking the fine arts commission secretary for his help. "Now that we have been successfully beaten by the Army . . . there is nothing left to do but await public condemnation of this action by Congress," Clarke wrote. "Our record is clear, and we made a fight for what we thought was right."

The new War Department building, it seemed, would be built right where Somervell wanted it.

You've got to build it in a hurry

Somervell's instructions to Captain Clarence Renshaw for constructing the world's largest building were terrifyingly simple. "You've got to build it in a hurry," the general told the rail-thin quartermaster construction officer, who had been chosen to head the project. "I'm not going to tell you how to do it."

Somervell had promised to complete the entire building in one year and start moving people in half that time. Now, the general informed the wide-eyed thirty-four-year-old officer, it would be up to Renshaw to deliver.

Somervell had not waited for the blessing of the Senate to proceed with his plans, but the vote August 14 put matters into overdrive. At the Construction Division staff conference the next morning, Somervell directed his team to gather all the principals—including John McShain, the builder; Edwin Bergstrom, the architect; Colonel Leslie Groves, the deputy chief of the division; and Renshaw—for a meeting in four days officially "starting work on the new War Department building."

Paul Hauck, McShain's job superintendent, gave Groves a lengthy list of pressing business that needed immediate attention. The builder wanted excavation plans, contour maps, foundation drawings, and structural drawings for the first floor. McShain needed to know what part of the building to begin first. McShain had been hard at it for weeks, meeting with Groves to plan the building on July 25, even before his choice as contractor had been officially approved. Within days McShain and Hauck were "working desperately" on the plans for building, setting up a progress schedule, and ordering building material, supplies, and equipment.

Bergstrom and his team had been busy as well, refining the design and layout of their pentagonal building. The project was top priority for the Construction Division, and Somervell gave Bergstrom carte blanche to hire anyone he wanted, inside or outside the Army. Bergstrom turned to his home turf in California to hire top talent. He chose as his chief assistant his friend David J. Witmer, a Los Angeles architect who had become prominent in the 1920s as a designer of Mediterranean-style homes and was considered a pioneer in the field for his expressive use of concrete for exterior work. Bergstrom also persuaded two other well-known California architects to leave their work in Los Angeles and join the project. Robert D. Farquhar, who had designed the California Club, a Los Angeles landmark, and Pierpont Davis, a Baltimore native who had established a successful practice in Los Angeles, were placed in charge of the architectural treatment of the building. All three Californians were considered "particularly conversant" with reinforced concrete, which would be used on a massive scale for the new War Department building. Just as important, Bergstrom had worked with all of them for years in California and could be assured of their competence and loyalty. The core group of architects who would design the Pentagon—a building so closely associated with solid, utilitarian architecture—was thus a group of Southern Californians more experienced at designing breezy hillside villas than dour government buildings.

Renshaw was the most crucial addition to the team. Groves would oversee the project, ensuring everything was properly planned, constructed, and done on time. But as deputy chief of the Construction Division, Groves was responsible for hundreds of war projects around the country, all desperately needed for the mobilizing army. While Groves kept the new War Department headquarters "under my rather close direction," as he later said, the constructing quartermaster would manage the project day to day and was ultimately responsible for its success—or failure.

Renshaw, from Allegheny County in western Pennsylvania, was a happy-go-lucky eldest son thrust into a position of family responsibility at age sixteen, when his father stepped on a nail and died from a tetanus infection. His mother had to prod the boy to leave the family to attend West Point, where he had earned an appointment. Rennie, as he was known, was quite bright but more interested in enjoying life than worrying about grades. He was a track star and a superb tennis player, but he preferred the fun of intramural company football. His *joie de vivre* was mixed with a formidable drive. Fellow cadets knew him as "a fierce competitor who would fight to the death for an extra point, and then give away the farm without a second thought or a backward glance."

In those days, West Point cadets never selected the Quartermaster Corps as their branch of choice upon graduation. Unlike the elite Corps of Engineers, which always drew the cream of the crop, men like Somervell and Groves, the quartermasters were seen as a dead end. Quartermaster General B. Frank Cheatham, determined to change this, made recruiting trips to West Point in 1929, the year Renshaw was to graduate. Rennie and his friend and roommate Elmer Kirkpatrick listened to Cheatham promise rewarding careers in Army construction. The roommates, without telling the other, each applied for a commission in the Quartermaster Corps, and each was accepted. Instructors were not encouraging; one warned that any cadet who joined the quartermasters would likely spend his career issuing shoes and buying groceries.

But Rennie bucked expectations. He loved construction, and the Quartermaster Corps had plenty of that. Throughout his career, Renshaw was happiest when he had mud on his boots. His first project was to help build a memorial to the Wright Brothers atop Big Kill Devil Hill in North Carolina, the sand dune on the Outer Banks where the inventors made their historic first flight on December 17, 1903. A quarter-century of wind had moved Big Kill Devil Hill 450 feet southwest of its 1903 location, and the sand dune was still moving. Rennie's job was to figure out a way to stop it. A mixture of exotic and native grasses planted in the dune along with a wooden mold did the trick. The eighty-ton solid granite memorial, rising sixty feet above the hill, was dedicated in November 1932, and Renshaw was quite proud of it.

Assigned to the Washington, D.C., office, Renshaw assisted in the restoration of the Arlington home Robert E. Lee left on the eve of the Civil War. Congress had approved legislation in 1925 to turn the mansion into a memorial to Lee. The depredations of the Civil War, followed by decades of neglect, vandalism, and casual use as a cemetery office, had left the mansion little more than a shell. The Army was placed in charge of restoring it, a painstaking project that took years; former Lee family slaves still living were consulted to restore the mansion to its antebellum appearance. Renshaw also constructed the formal approaches—walkways and steps—leading up to the nearby Tomb of the Unknown Soldier. From his work in Arlington Cemetery, Renshaw was thus probably more familiar than any officer in the Army with the stirring view from the Lee mansion that he was now supposed to defile.

Renshaw had developed a reputation as a capable and conscientious officer, one who despite his modesty worked with obvious confidence. Renshaw survived the purge when Somervell came over from the Corps of Engineers to head the Construction Division in December 1940. Groves thought highly of Renshaw's organizational skills, relying on him as an expediter to keep construction projects around the country on track. The lanky, chain-smoking Rennie, his head rapidly going bald but with a young and handsome face, somehow managed to be easygoing and efficient at the same time. In the madness of the Construction Division, Renshaw's office was one of the few calm ports. His low-key, nonauthoritarian style won the loyalty and affection of his officers. "He told me immediately he didn't give orders. Just a suggestion was enough," Robert Furman, an officer on Renshaw's staff, remembered more than sixty years later. "He was a prince of a guy."

In August 1941, as Somervell considered whom to place in charge of the enormous War Department project, Groves proposed Captain Renshaw. There were several other candidates, among them Renshaw's friend and former roommate, Elmer Kirkpatrick. Renshaw had a little more project experience than Kirkpatrick and the others. But what Somervell and Groves wanted above all else, Renshaw said years later, was someone they were sure would not fail.

Renshaw added, "I wasn't so sure."

This rape of Washington

Bronzed and refreshed from his two-week adventure at sea, Franklin D. Roosevelt returned to the mainland aboard the *Potomac*, which moored in Rockland, Maine, on August 16. Aboard the yacht, he good-naturedly faced down a pack of reporters "angry as a bunch of bears with sore haunches" about being fooled by the supposed fishing expedition, for which Roosevelt was unapologetic.

An overnight train carried Roosevelt to Union Station in Washington, and he arrived back at the White House on Sunday morning, August 17. The aura of good cheer from his dramatic rendezvous with Churchill did not last long. Roosevelt was quickly brought back to earth by awaiting problems. The Soviets had suffered worrisome reverses in the Caucasus, a major strike had paralyzed a New Jersey shipyard, and there was a headache in the form of the new War Department building in Arlington.

His secretary of the interior was in outright revolt against the project and had written the president "a very vigorous letter . . . begging him not to permit this rape of Washington." A telegram also arrived Sunday from

Frederic Delano, traveling out west. The planning commission chairman told the president he was "greatly concerned" by what had transpired in their absence from Washington. In a follow-up letter sent the same day, Delano urged his nephew to take action, recommending that "you ask Congress . . . to reconsider the decision that has been made so hurriedly by the Appropriations Committee. An examination of the record shows that this decision was in many ways predicated on erroneous assumptions and fallacious conclusions."

The newspapers were pleading with Roosevelt to act. That morning's *Sunday Star* carried a front-page cartoon showing Roosevelt arriving at Union Station, travel bag from the USS *Potomac* in hand, catching Henry Stimson in the act of spiriting the War Department across the river. "I'm glad you're back, Mr. President," Roosevelt is told. "They're about to steal all the furniture."

It all struck a chord with Roosevelt. Unhappy that the Senate had ignored his recommendation that the building's size be halved, the president now was further chagrined that he had agreed to the Arlington Farm site in the first place.

Roosevelt already felt a lingering sense of guilt for his leading role in a previous desecration of Washington. As assistant secretary of the Navy when America declared war on Germany in 1917, Roosevelt had persuaded President Wilson to allow the construction of large temporary buildings on the Mall along Constitution Avenue to house the Navy and Army, then in desperate need of office space. "My plan was . . . to make them of such superlative ugliness that their replacement would have been insisted upon even before now!" Roosevelt later wrote. "However, as on some other occasions, my well-laid plans fell through!"

Nearly a quarter-century after they were built, the barracks-like Navy and Munitions buildings were still there, unsightly but well-constructed, running between the Washington Monument and the Lincoln Memorial. "The one thing which I will always go down on my knees and ask forgiveness for was my plea for the Navy and Munitions building during the war," Roosevelt told reporters in 1934. "I was responsible for it and I am terribly sorry I made them so permanent."

Now, it seemed, Roosevelt's name would forever be linked to a far larger and even more prominent intrusion on the capital plan, and this time it would truly be permanent. For a president who prided himself on his aesthetic sense, permitting this blot was unthinkable, even in an emergency.

On Monday, August 18, the day after his return, Roosevelt sent a copy of Ickes's letter to Harold Smith, the budget director. "Will you speak to me about this?" the president asked.

Smith was only too glad to have another chance to counsel the president against the building. He prepared a memorandum denouncing the proposal, "so hurriedly and incompletely considered that many people are just now beginning to grasp its significance." Without naming him, Smith put the blame on Somervell. "This Administration, which has done more for the national Capital than any other, cannot afford to be party to the prostitution of the Capital plan," he concluded. "The current delinquency seems to have been provoked by a few Army officers on tour of duty in the Capital."

At twenty minutes after noon on August 19, Smith met with the president in the Oval Office and handed him the memo. Roosevelt handed it back; he needed no further persuasion. "The President seemed very much opposed to the construction of such a large building and violently opposed to its location," a pleased Smith recorded in his diary.

Indeed, Roosevelt was so worked up that he told Smith he was considering vetoing the entire $8 billion defense appropriation bill, an act that would throw the mobilization of the Army and Navy into disarray. That would not be advisable, the ever-rational budget director replied. Smith suggested there might be other ways to change the War Department building. The president directed Smith to work out some alternatives and report back.

A mere formality

The mood was euphoric as the principals planning the new War Department building gathered in room 2002d at the Construction Division headquarters at 2 P.M. on Tuesday, August 19. Somervell waved a copy of a $29.5 million construction authorization issued that day by the War Department for a 5.2-million square foot building on the Arlington Farm site.

All that was required now was the president's signature on the defense bill, a mere formality, in Somervell's view.

Groves and Renshaw were there, as was Lieutenant Colonel Pat Casey, chief of the design section, and a handful of other key Construction Division officers. Bergstrom represented the architects, while McShain and his superintendent, Hauck, were present on behalf of the contractors. Somervell opened the meeting. The plans would be presented to the president tomorrow, he announced. With that in mind, Somervell wanted everything ready to go as soon as approval was secured.

Excavation and grading plans were ready, Somervell was told, but plans for the footings were still in the works. There were ample supplies of slate roofing material and asphalt tile, but no gypsum block. As for the huge amounts of concrete that would be needed, cement was not a problem, and the sand and gravel to mix with it would be dredged from the Potomac. A decision had to be made quickly on whether the exterior of the building would be limestone or brick; whichever it was, "an immense quantity" was needed and a supply had to be locked up.

Groves took the floor. In his no-nonsense manner, he ticked off all the basic engineering and design decisions that were "needed at once." They had to determine the exact location of the building on the site. Foundation plans showing footing depths and wall elevations were "necessary for intelligent excavation." Structural drawings for at least the first floor were needed before reinforcing steel and form materials could be secured. Complete drawings of a typical wing were required so McShain could make sure the right material and labor were available. Plans for bringing a water line across the Potomac River and for building a sewage disposal plant had to be provided.

The list was daunting, representing fundamental design work that in normal times could be expected to take months and would certainly have been completed well before any construction began. Not as far as Somervell was concerned. With the president's expected approval, construction would start September 1, he announced. Half a million square feet of office space would be ready for occupancy March 1, and the entire building finished six months later.

The conference broke up at 3:30 P.M. They had their marching orders and were ready to go.

I should be kept out of heaven

Across town at the White House forty minutes later, presidential press spokesman Stephen Early escorted the press corps into the Oval Office, where the reporters gathered expectantly around the president's desk.

It was Roosevelt's first press conference in the White House since returning to Washington two days earlier, and he was in an effusive mood. The president reflected on his historic meeting with Churchill and his own efforts to prepare America for the Nazi threat. He none too subtly tried to evoke comparisons between himself and Abraham Lincoln, shuffling through his papers and finding an excerpt of Carl Sandburg's biography of the sixteenth president that happened to be on his desk. He read to the reporters about Lincoln's frustration in 1862 that "the country hadn't yet waked up to the fact that they had a war to win." There were obvious parallels "in this day and age," Roosevelt said. "I think there are a lot of people who haven't waked up to the danger," he added. "A great many people."

A reporter changed the subject: "Can you say anything about the new War Department building in Arlington?"

Roosevelt certainly could. "Well, that is of interest to not only the Washington papers. I think it ought to be of interest to everybody," he said.

The president then dropped his bombshell. "My present inclination is not to accept that action by Congress," Roosevelt announced.

Before the assembled reporters, the president again prostrated himself before the altar of L'Enfant for having brought the "temporary" buildings to the Mall. "It was a crime—I don't hesitate to say so—it was a crime for which I should be kept out of heaven, for having desecrated the whole plan of, I think, the loveliest city in the world—the capital of the United States," he said. Arlington Cemetery, Roosevelt continued, emotion in his voice, "is known and loved throughout the length and breadth of the land," and its beautiful, unobstructed views treasured by thousands of visitors.

"And here it is—under the name of emergency, it is proposed to put up a permanent building, which will deliberately and definitely, for one hundred years to come, spoil the plan of the national capital," the president said. "Quite aside from any question of access to it, or where people live, how you get across the bridge or anything else, I have had a part in spoiling the national parks and the beautiful waterfront of the District once, and I don't want to do it again."

The best solution, he added, would be for the War Department to stay in Washington and construct additional offices alongside the new building in Foggy Bottom, the long-planned home for the Army and Navy. But his decision was not final. "Tomorrow I am going to see General Somervell, to hear the story on the other side," he said.

News bulletins hit the wires and all sides sprang to action. Representative Cliff Woodrum telephoned the White House and told presidential aide Pa Watson that "he and everybody on the Appropriations Committee are fearful that the President had not obtained the right information about the Army building. All of them want the new building."

"Woodrum is merely asking the President that Somervell present the case before making the decision," Watson reported to Roosevelt.

Gilmore Clarke read the news the next morning in the paper and immediately sent a letter to Roosevelt expressing delight. Newspaper editorialists rejoiced. "President Roosevelt has earned the thanks of Washingtonians of many future generations," *The Washington Post* proclaimed. The *New York Times* beneficently absolved Roosevelt of his past sins. "He has accompanied confession with atonement and the Graces will not only forgive but praise him," the paper editorialized.

The *New York Herald Tribune* was more reserved. "With candor that is all the more engaging because of its comparative rarity President Roosevelt has admitted publicly to a 'crime' which he perpetrated twenty-four years ago and has indicated that his hope of forgiveness at the pearly gates for this offense may prevent him from committing an even more flagrant crime today," the paper wrote. But the *Tribune* was reserving judgment until the president followed through.

Indeed, Roosevelt had not told reporters exactly how he planned to stop the building in Arlington, given it was now authorized by Congress. The *New York Times* reported that Roosevelt was threatening to veto the entire $8 billion defense bill, but *The Washington Post* suggested that the president might ask Congress to make a change by joint resolution. The truth was Roosevelt had not figured out a solution but was confident something would be worked out. Harold Smith, his budget director, had called in a top aide from vacation and was busy studying options, including, at Roosevelt's suggestion, the possibility of simply impounding the $35 million allocated for the building.

Somervell scrambled to salvage the situation. He enlisted the assistance of John J. McCloy, the energetic assistant secretary of war so wise to the ways of Washington. Stimson once said he "sometimes wondered whether anyone in the administration ever acted without 'having a word with Mc-Cloy.' " He was the man to whom everyone in the War Department took their problems, and this certainly qualified. "You've got to take this on, Jack," Somervell told McCloy. "This is getting a little . . . complicated."

Somervell and McCloy reported to the White House on August 20, the morning after the president's press conference. Roosevelt directed them to go back to the drawing board. "The President was unwilling to approve the building as located by us," Somervell reported in a memo after the meeting. But to his relief, Roosevelt retreated from keeping the War Department in Washington. The president said he would support placing the building in Arlington on or near the quartermaster depot site, three-quarters of a mile south of Arlington Farm. Still, Somervell and McCloy put up a fight for Arlington Farm, arguing that a building at the quartermaster site would cost more money because of the poor foundation conditions. Roosevelt assured them he would approve the additional money needed within a year.

Donning his architectural mantle, Roosevelt peppered Somervell with questions about the design of the building. "The President evinced considerable interest in the materials to be used in the façade and other details of the work, asking that Mr. Bergstrom and I present these to him from time to time as the new plans mature," Somervell reported.

Finally, Roosevelt was skeptical that the building needed to be as large as the War Department planned; when Somervell insisted the space was needed, the president indicated he would withhold a final decision until seeing the plans. "Put three shifts on the study and report back as soon as the work is done," Roosevelt directed.

Emerging from the conference, McCloy told reporters that the president had given them "some new ideas." Somervell, irritated, snapped at the reporters' queries. "Why ask me?" he said. "I'm only a bricklayer."

Somervell and McCloy drove across the river to Arlington, where the general gloomily looked over the quartermaster depot site. More than three hundred construction workers were on the job and were preparing to lay the foundation for the depot. Late the following day, August 21, the War Department ordered all work at the site to stop. Worried that it would be seen as a sign he was acquiescing, Somervell ordered that no statement be made to the press. But the newspapers quickly learned of it and reported the news as a signal the Army would build its new headquarters at the depot site. They also reported War Department representatives had approached owners of nearby properties to ascertain sale prices.

"We are proceeding with the work," Somervell reported in a memo delivered by special messenger to Stimson, who was traveling on the West Coast. "About one month will be lost because of change in plans, but the estimated time of completion after we are able to begin work, namely, one year, remains the same."

Somervell waved off the president's skepticism about the size of the building, writing Stimson that Roosevelt "did approve the construction of a building of the same size as originally proposed."

That was news to McCloy; he had heard the president say no such thing. "I did not gather that he gave final approval of the size of the building but told you to work out the plans for the new site and bring them back to him for final approval," McCloy wrote to Somervell, trying to correct the record.

Returning to Washington on Monday, August 25, after a long weekend in Hyde Park, Roosevelt moved to wrap up the controversy. He signed the $8 billion defense spending bill after receiving assurances from Harold Smith that the language in it was flexible enough to allow leeway in locating the new War Department building. The White House released a cryptic statement saying the president did not consider the provisions in the bill relating to the building to be "mandatory."

The following afternoon, when reporters were brought into the Oval Office for a press conference, Roosevelt explained himself. "Start taking this down, Earl," he directed the veteran White House correspondent for the National Broadcasting Corp., Earl Godwin.

The "best solution," Roosevelt announced, would be to put the bulk of the building on the quartermaster site, with a small portion—jutting onto the adjacent Arlington Farm land.

The bill passed by Congress did not specify where on the Arlington Farm site the new building was to be placed. As long as any part of the project was on the Arlington Farm land, the president reasoned, it would technically adhere to the act of Congress. "So that makes it entirely within the bill," the president declared. It was the sort of creative—actually, far-fetched—solution Roosevelt loved.

As for the size, Roosevelt said traffic congestion made a building of 4 million square feet infeasible, and that the building should therefore be no larger than 2.25 million square feet.

Furthermore, Roosevelt said, the new building in Arlington would not be the War Department's permanent headquarters. Ultimately, the department would return to Foggy Bottom in Washington. "Now, my thought is that this new War Department building [in Arlington] would be built on extremely simple lines, and that when this emergency is over, and the War Department . . . reverts to a peacetime status, they will be able to come back here to their regular place," he said.

And when that happened, the temporary buildings that resulted from his transgression a quarter-century earlier would no longer be needed. "I hope before I die to be able to tear down the two excrescences down in Potomac Park, the present Navy Building and the present Munitions Building," he said.

As for the building in Arlington, Roosevelt said, it was perfectly suited for another pet project of his: He wanted a central home for the old files that now used up space in government offices around Washington. He had millions of records in mind, ranging from the individual files of three million Civil War soldiers to the public-land records charting the development of the great West to obscure State Department consular reports on the history of Mongolian ponies. "So I hope that this new building, when this emergency is over, will be used as a records building for the government," Roosevelt said.

The controversy over the new War Department building was settled, the president concluded: "Now this takes care of it entirely."

The whole thing is all up in the air

No one could imagine that Somervell would keep fighting. A round of self-congratulations followed among his opponents. The *Star* called the president's action "highly gratifying," and *The Washington Post* likewise claimed a share of victory. "As one of the institutions which joined heartily in the fight against the erection of a monstrosity on the south shore of the Potomac, The Post hails this compromise as a triumph for rational planning," the paper wrote.

Presumably, Somervell had learned a good lesson, Hans Paul Caemmerer told a colleague. "Since Somervell says he is 'a bricklayer' . . . it seems to me it would have been far better if in the beginning he had come . . . to our Commission or your Committee to ascertain what is appropriate in the way of a building for the National Capital," the Fine Arts secretary wrote.

That was not the lesson Somervell had drawn. The general reported to the White House that he and Bergstrom had new plans ready for the president. Roosevelt's uncle, Frederic Delano, and Harold Smith were likewise anxious to see the president to talk about the building. Roosevelt promptly summoned both sides to the White House on August 27, the morning after his press conference, to hash out the final details. Delano and Bergstrom arrived carrying large packages of blueprints and plans, and all four men assembled with the president in the Oval Office for the 11:30 meeting.

Roosevelt briefly reiterated what he had said the day before, that he wanted to put the building on the quartermaster depot site, and at half the size previously envisioned. Rather than a soldier receiving his president's instructions, Somervell acted as if he were a visiting premier negotiating a treaty. The general staunchly insisted that the War Department should be built on the Arlington Farm site and told Roosevelt that his selection of the quartermaster depot site was unwise. Somervell also argued that the size of the building should not be reduced. Roosevelt seemed amused by Somervell's persistence. "Of course you understand that I am commander-in-chief of the Army and Navy," Roosevelt said, laughing as he spoke.

After a few minutes, Roosevelt instructed the men to adjourn to the adjoining cabinet room and iron out their differences among themselves. An hour's discussion proved fruitless. Somervell would not budge. Somewhat dazed, Fred Delano emerged from the White House and spoke to reporters. "The whole thing is all up in the air," he said. "The Army is holding on to its original proposal both as to size and location."

Somervell at first refused comment, but when told of Delano's statement, he remarked, "That's a proper way of stating it." The general then added his favorite stock reply: "But why talk to me about it—I'm just a bricklayer."

Though the president's declaration had left him with few cards to play, Somervell managed with bulldog stubbornness to carve out some negotiating room. The talks resumed in the afternoon at Delano's office in the Interior Building. Delano drafted an agreement that limited the building to 15,000 people. Somervell strongly objected—he wanted space for 35,000—and both sides exchanged angry crossfire.

Delano persuaded Somervell to make a counteroffer on paper. "What would you insist upon?" Delano asked Somervell. "What is your position?"

Somervell sat down for an hour to write out his stipulations in pencil. He was willing to accept the quartermaster depot site but was holding out for a larger building. After three hours of back and forth, they broke for the day.

Consulting with McCloy the next day, Somervell lamented the avalanche of "unfortunate" publicity that had accompanied his defiance of Roosevelt. The general continued his talks with Delano that afternoon, agreeing to come down from his 35,000 figure. The two negotiated the language of the agreement—practically a treaty—working until late to have it ready for the president the following morning. At first glance, the three-page memorandum looked like a defeat for Somervell, as it provided for a building for twenty thousand workers on the quartermaster depot site.

But the language in the agreement was curious. It said the "general area" of the quartermaster depot site was acceptable as a home for the War Department, leaving Somervell quite a bit of wiggle room as to exactly where he put the building.

As for the size of the building, Somervell arranged even more leeway. The agreement said "the office personnel space should be limited to that for 20,000 persons at 125 square feet per person until it has been demonstrated that traffic facilities are sufficient to handle a greater number of employees." While the language meant that the building would initially have 2.5 million square feet of office space, it did not mean that Somervell could not build a significantly larger building and later convert additional area into office space. Nor did it specify who would determine when the roads and bridges were sufficient to handle more than twenty thousand people.

In deference to Roosevelt's wishes, the agreement stipulated that "the solution proposed is not advanced as a permanent location of the War Department, but one dictated by requirements of space and speed in the present emergency. The solution proposed does not exclude in any way the return of War Department personnel to the District of Columbia after the emergency, in which case the proposed building can be used for other offices, archives and activities if so desired."

The agreement—with spaces awaiting the signatures of Stimson, Delano, and Smith—was presented to Roosevelt the morning of August 29. "It is a compromise," Delano told reporters. "The Army will get some of the things it wanted and we will get some of the things we wanted. It is up to the president."

For his part, the president was exasperated by the drawn-out battle. "I am going out to look at it," Roosevelt announced that morning. He would examine the quartermaster depot site himself later that day, accompanied by the warring parties, and make the final decision.

I'm still commander-in-chief

The president's limousine was waiting behind the White House, its top down. The weather on the late summer day was unseasonably mild, splendid for an open-air afternoon jaunt to Virginia to look over the real estate.

Gilmore Clarke had received a phone call at his office in New York that morning, August 29, asking him to report to the White House by four o'clock that afternoon. The Commission of Fine Arts chairman flew to Washington, hurried to the White House, and was directed to the back, where he found Smith and Somervell waiting.

Clarke introduced himself to Smith and then looked at Somervell, who gazed at his shoes and pointedly offered no greeting. Clarke had the gloating air of a teacher's pet picked to sit at the head of the class. "General, you're acting kind of childish, aren't you?" he said.

Somervell studiously ignored the Fine Arts chairman. "Well, I thank my lucky stars I'm not in uniform, of a rank lower than you are, or I'd probably be behind bars," Clarke continued. Somervell's glowering intensified.

Shortly after finishing a two-hour cabinet meeting, Roosevelt rolled out the back of the White House in his wheelchair. Fala, FDR's black terrier, trotted behind. The president, sporting a new plaid tie, headed toward his waiting open-air car, where two Secret Service agents lifted him from his wheelchair into the back seat in the right-hand corner. Fala hopped into a jump seat in front of the president. Roosevelt beckoned Clarke to sit next to him. Somervell climbed into the back on the other side, while Smith took the front passenger seat. Delano, unable to attend, sent Jay Downer as his representative, and the consultant boarded a second car with Bergstrom and Pa Watson, Roosevelt's military aide.

At 4:25, the party left the White House grounds. Roosevelt, eager to see traffic conditions for himself, had chosen the height of the evening rush hour for the excursion. The limousine passed along the Tidal Basin, where John McShain's crews had almost finished the Jefferson Memorial. Clarke had been steadfast in his biting criticism of the memorial, but Roosevelt could not resist proudly pointing out the pantheon design he had personally approved.

"Gilmore . . . don't you like it?" the president asked.

"No sir," replied Clarke, ever the scold. "I don't like it. It's a disappointment to all of the members of the commission."

"I don't know what we're going to do with you fellows," Roosevelt sighed.

As the entourage took the 14th Street Bridge across the Potomac, Somervell made a final appeal to the president for the Arlington Farm site, speaking across Clarke as if the commissioner were not even in the car. Moving the War Department building from Somervell's favored site would delay the project and add millions to the cost, the general reminded the president.

Roosevelt's face flushed with annoyance as Somervell spoke. "My dear general," he said, leaning in front of Clarke and addressing Somervell. "I'm still commander-in-chief of the Army!"

This time, Roosevelt did not seem to be joking. Somervell retreated into silence.

They arrived at the site. It was known locally as Hell's Bottom, and it looked it, a tawdry neighborhood of shacks, dumps, beat-up factory buildings, railroad yards, and pawnshops. Roosevelt liked it just fine. The car stopped at a spot on the southern edge of the property, and Secret Service agents jumped out and surrounded the car. Roosevelt pointed north to the site. "Gilmore, we're going to put the building over there, aren't we?" the president asked Clarke.

"Yes, Mr. President," Clarke dutifully replied.

"Did you hear that, general?" Roosevelt continued. "We're going to locate the War Department building over there."

Somervell had no choice but to acquiesce.

When Clarke asked about the language in the congressional bill specifying the Arlington Farm site, Roosevelt dismissed the concern, confident his solution legally circumvented the law. "Never mind, we're not going to pay any attention to that, we're going to put it over here," he said.

Inspecting the site at close range, Roosevelt pronounced it excellent. To get a better perspective on the eighty-seven-acre tract, the party continued to a high bluff along Arlington Ridge Road overlooking the site.

Even from up high, it was not a pretty sight. "It was pointed out that the industrial slums along Columbia Pike would mar the environment of the new building, and the President said they ought to be acquired," Downer reported to Delano. Looking to the south of Columbia Pike, Roosevelt asked what could be done about the old brickyards and other properties in that area. Somervell said he was confident the Army could secure the authority for cleaning up the south side to a depth of several hundred feet. It was also agreed that what Downer called "slum dwellings"—actually a respectable black neighborhood known as Queen City—in a triangle of land framed by Columbia Pike and Arlington Ridge Road would be condemned for highway improvements.

Roosevelt wanted to know about the size of the building. Somervell replied that the gross area of the new building would be about four million square feet, or about four-fifths the size originally proposed. But in keeping with the agreement hashed out with Delano and Smith, Somervell promised the president it would hold no more than twenty thousand workers until it was demonstrated that the highways and bridges could handle more.

The entourage rode through Arlington Cemetery, past the Tomb of the Unknown Soldier, and back down toward Memorial Bridge, not even slowing as they passed the stately Arlington Farm site where Somervell had come so close to constructing the building. They drove back onto the

White House grounds about an hour after departing. As the car came to a stop, Roosevelt again addressed Somervell: "General, you're going to show the plans for this proposed building to the Commission of Fine Arts, are you not?"

Somervell had no intention of doing this, and told the president so. The general insisted the new location—certainly not part of L'Enfant's monumental Washington—was outside the commission's jurisdiction.

Irritated, Roosevelt waited until Somervell had finished. "Well, General, you show the plans to the Commission of Fine Arts and, when they've approved of them, show them to me." Clarke listened delightedly. Once that caveat was met, FDR added, the project should "go ahead at full speed."

With that, the president rolled back into the White House for a cocktail.

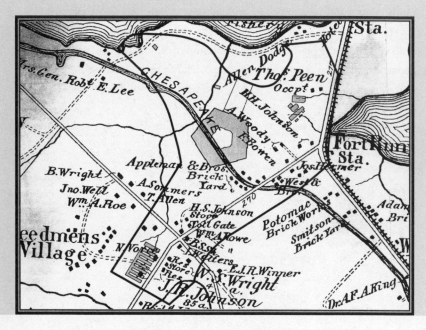

1878–79 Hopkins map showing the Lee mansion and environs, with overlay of modern Pentagon military reservation.

CHAPTER
6

HELL'S BOTTOM

A hot time in the old town

As the southbound train pulled out of Washington's Pennsylvania Station on the afternoon of May 30, 1904, a handsome young mustachioed man with the blazing eyes of a zealot emptied several bags into the aisle. The contents spilled out, revealing a small arsenal of axes, sledgehammers, and sawed-off shotguns. The man distributed the weapons among a party of twenty men accompanying him. Other passengers were terrified, believing it to be a holdup. But the men were not planning to stay aboard for long. By arrangement with the conductor, the train was to slow down for them to jump off immediately after crossing the Potomac River and reaching Virginia.

The man was Crandal Mackey, the newly elected Commonwealth's Attorney for Arlington—then known as Alexandria County—and he was on a mission to restore law and order. In the years since the Civil War, parts of the county formerly under control of Union troops had fallen into disorder and lawlessness. Along the Potomac River, near the bridges connecting Virginia to the District, communities of sin had sprung up. Criminal elements, protected by venal politicians, had set up gambling houses, saloons, brothels, and racetracks serving the citizens of Washington. Two of the very worst areas were Jackson City and nearby Hell's Bottom.

Jackson City, at least, had grand beginnings. Old Hickory himself, Andrew Jackson, laid the cornerstone in 1836. The city was dreamed up by New York speculators who envisioned a bustling port and industrial center across the river from Washington. They chose what was then Alexander's Island, a large tract of land along the Potomac, separated from the Virginia shore by marshland. Its location at the foot of Long Bridge made it a natural setting for commerce, promoters said.

On a raw and blustery January day, President Jackson led a procession of thousands across the bridge. Despite the cold, the old general refused to wear a hat, thrilling those able to capture a glimpse of his famed snow-white head. At the appointed moment, Jackson knocked a ceremonial stone three times with a small gilt hammer, and cannons thundered in celebration. George Washington Parke Custis, owner of the grand Arlington House, gave a speech enthusiastically welcoming the venture, and so many toasts were drunk that police made several arrests.

It was all downhill from there. Facing opposition from Georgetown merchants and lacking support in Congress, the enterprise soon flopped. Jackson City was sold at auction in 1851. The promoters had been right about one thing, though: It was an ideal spot for commerce. A horse track established on the island did a flourishing business. In the 1870s, promoters from New Jersey found it a perfect place for commercial vice after gambling and racing were outlawed in their home state. By 1892, the *Evening Star* referred to Jackson City as "the miniature Monte Carlo on the other side of the river." The neighborhood was particularly raucous late at night and on weekends, when bars in the District closed and the weak-willed strolled across the bridge to quench their various thirsts.

Just inland, occupying low ground off Columbia Pike, sat Hell's Bottom, sprung from the same general atmosphere of lawlessness and vice. There were no streets or sidewalks, just a sordid collection of gambling dens, stills, shacks, and murder traps populated by poor blacks. "Hell's Bottom was described fully and accurately by two words, 'Hell's Bottom' because it was the very bottom of Hell, you couldn't get any lower," Frank Ball, then a young ally of Mackey's, recalled years later. Victims with names like Dusthouse Dan were found with crushed skulls, shot full of bullets, or both after arguments over dice games or disputes over bootlegging territory.

Further up the river, across the Aqueduct Bridge from Georgetown, sat Rosslyn, a village packed with saloons and lewd women servicing visitors from across the bridge. Nearby was Dead Man's Hollow, where at times it was not uncommon to find a body a week. "Some committed suicide, some were killed by the gamblers and liquor people, some got in fights, and a little bit of everything happened," said Ball. "I would not have gone up Dead Man's Hollow after dark for all the money in the world and I was a pretty big boy by that time." Farmers returning to Alexandria County after selling their produce at market in Washington would form armed convoys before crossing the bridges.

By the turn of the century, the respectable citizens among the 6,400 residents of the county were determined to end the lawlessness. They just needed the right man. Mackey, the son of a Confederate officer, had fought in the Spanish-American War, started a law practice in Washington, and established a sterling reputation. Meeting at the home of Frank Ball's father, the Good Citizens' League in 1903 nominated Mackey to run for Commonwealth's Attorney against Dick Johnson, the candidate backed by the gamblers. "They had the doggonest knockdown dragout fight you ever saw in your life," Ball said. In the end, Mackey beat Johnson by two votes.

Taking office on January 1, 1904, Mackey declared war on the gambling interests, vowing to close every saloon in the county. When he had trouble getting the sheriff to cooperate, he took matters into his own hands. Mackey obtained a warrant and quietly formed a posse made up of "the better people of the county."

Jackson City was the prime target. It was easiest to approach from Washington. Mackey's ax party gathered at the train station shortly before 4 P.M. and made its final plans. "After crossing the Long Bridge the train rattled on and the men had a bad moment when it looked as though the conductor had forgotten them," one account related. But the train soon slowed, and the posse hopped off.

The raiders worked their way back to Jackson City. Bursting into the first establishment, they found a healthy contingent of gamblers playing poker and shooting craps. The miscreants quickly scattered. "It did not bother them whether they left through the open doors or the closed windows," the *Star* reported the next day. Most high-tailed it across the bridge back into Washington, leaving the posse to its work.

Mackey's men were nothing if not thorough. They cut garish paintings down from the walls, busted ornate tables, destroyed chairs, and hacked in walls. "Glassware was smashed and the contents of the bottles, demijohns and decanters was allowed to flow, giving the room the appearance of having passed through a Potomac flood," the *Star* reported. A nickel-a-song jukebox was jarred in the ruckus and, by one account, started playing "There'll Be a Hot Time in the Old Town Tonight" repeatedly.

Jackson City never really recovered from Mackey's ax party. Not long afterward, a disgruntled gambler set the place ablaze, and all traces of it disappeared from the earth.

The place where fish are caught

The land where the Pentagon would be built had a long history; it already had been inhabited by Indians for perhaps twelve thousand years when Captain John Smith sailed past it in July 1608. A year after founding Jamestown, Smith had taken fourteen men in an open sailboat to explore the Potomac River, looking for gold and a passage to the South Seas. On the site Franklin Roosevelt would choose 333 years later for Somervell's building, Smith and his men spotted a village consisting of several long-houses constructed of woven grass mats. The inhabitants spoke an Algonquian dialect similar to that of the natives living near Jamestown. The village was called Namoraughquend, a name Smith understood to mean "place where fish are caught."

The plentiful supply of fish had attracted Algonquian tribes to the area, as did abundant waterfowl and deer and nearby quarries of quartzite that could be chipped into weapons and tools. The site was mostly low-lying river bottom, a mixture of sands, silts, and clays, with a long way to bedrock. Farther inland the land started to roll and rise.

Smith received a generally friendly reception from the Indians in the area, but later white settlers faced hostilities. Warfare with Indians prevented the land from being settled until the 1690s, when the natives abandoned the area. Tenant farmers worked pieces of the land in the 1700s, though much of it remained woodland. John Parke Custis, stepson of George Washington, bought the land in 1788, and it was thus part of the estate inherited by George Washington Parke Custis.

In comparison with the noble hilltop where Custis constructed Arlington House, the low-lying ground a mile to the south was scarcely worth noticing. But the land's importance increased markedly in 1808 with the construction of the Long Bridge, a 5,300-foot timber truss span connecting Alexandria County to Washington near the location of the present 14th Street Bridge. Three turnpikes were built around the same time leading out from Long Bridge, converging on the future Pentagon site. The Alexandria Canal, a seven-mile waterway to connect the Virginia port city with westward canal traffic, was begun in 1833, following a route that took it directly through where the Pentagon now stands.

The Civil War transformed the land, turning it into a military reservation, some of it forever. As a strategic transportation hub leading into Washington, the grounds were occupied almost immediately by Union troops and heavily defended with entrenchments, encampments, and two large forts. The land was no longer rural farmland; two busy brickyards made use of the abundant clay in the ground. Union troops took control of the kilns to make bricks for the forts' foundations, chimneys, and wells. After the war, a construction boom in Washington gave birth to more brickyards, and by the 1880s the county was the largest manufacturer of bricks in the country.

A community of escaped slaves, Freedman's Village, had been established on the Arlington estate during the war, and its boundaries reached the present Pentagon grounds. The families lived in a neat horseshoe-shaped village with a hundred homes, two churches, a hospital, a school, and farmland. "The village is quite lively . . . and the place presents a clean and prosperous appearance at all times," *Harper's Weekly* reported in 1864. For the former slaves it was a life almost too good to be true, and in the end it was. The village became increasingly crowded and disease-ridden. The Army, seeking to expand Arlington Cemetery, ordered the residents to leave the grounds in 1887.

Some residents of Freedman's Village resettled nearby and created a new community known as Queen City, on the north side of Columbia Pike. It was a tight-knit neighborhood anchored by two Baptist churches. More than a hundred families lived in well-kept modest frame houses; many of the residents worked at the nearby brickyards. Even Crandal Mackey had no complaints. "The residents of Queen City rarely, if ever, give the county trouble," he said.

That was not the case with Hell's Bottom—down Columbia Pike toward the river from Queen City—which remained home to seamy murders and occasional bootlegger wars. The Ku Klux Klan chose Hell's Bottom to celebrate its sixtieth anniversary on May 6, 1926; more than two thousand members from Virginia, Maryland, and Washington gathered to induct new members amid flaming torches and a burning cross.

Nearby, on the old site of Jackson City and its racetrack, sat the main airfield for the nation's capital. Washington-Hoover Airport, as it was known beginning in 1930, was grossly inadequate even by the standards of the day. A busy road bisected the 2,400-foot runway, with a siren and signal light for alerting automobile drivers to aircraft landing or taking off. The system was hardly foolproof and the sheriff occasionally had to be dispatched to shoo cars off the runway.

Constant burning at a commercial dump in Hell's Bottom left the airfield cloaked in an almost permanent layer of smoke. "I've seen better ones in Siberian wastes," Wiley Post groused upon landing in Washington a year after flying solo around the world in 1933. Navigation was a bit primitive, consisting of a windsock nailed to a pole atop a roller coaster at the neighboring Arlington Beach Amusement Park. The field was flanked by high-tension electrical wires, telephone poles, smokestacks, and an eighty-foot high radio tower. Adding to the hazard was the Airport Pool near the foot of the bridge. By one account, the large pool "played host to frolicsome bathing beauties of the area—their antics providing still one more distraction for the pilot trying to set his plane down between telephone wires on a postage-stamp field." No one even knew if the airport land really belonged to Virginia. The Jackson City site was technically an island and Virginia jurisdiction began at the high-water mark of the Potomac; police from all jurisdictions used the confusion as an excuse not to patrol the area. It was known variously as "The Last Mile" and "No Man's Land."

Legislation for a new airport had been mired in Congress for over a decade while legislators argued where to put it. In 1938, tired of waiting for Congress to act, Roosevelt chose the mud flats along the Potomac at Gravelly Point, about a mile south of Washington-Hoover, as the site for a new airport.

FDR, as usual, could not resist meddling with the design of the terminal and to the horror of the architect added a portico inspired by George Washington's home at Mount Vernon. The builder—once again John Mc-

Shain—moved with typical verve and finished well ahead of schedule. Roosevelt presided when National Airport, the world's most spacious, officially opened on June 16, 1941. There was only one problem, from McShain's standpoint: Dissatisfied that the cornerstone did not bear his name, he sent a crew of eight men to the airport at 3 A.M. one morning to place an aluminum plaque in the terminal carrying the name, "John McShain, Builder."

Hell's Bottom, 1941

Much change was afoot for the land by the summer of 1941. The opening of National Airport spelled the imminent demise of Washington-Hoover, and in July the War Department, covetous of such a large open tract so close to Washington, bought the land for $1 million. Nearly a half million dollars more were spent buying several brickyards and adjoining properties totaling ninety acres.

The latter site—originally planned for the quartermaster depot but by the end of August slated for the new War Department headquarters—was hardly a prime location. Over a century, the brickyards had stripped much of the topsoil for clay, leaving a large marshy area. Two oil refining companies were operating adjacent to the brickyards. A terrible, constant stench arose from a plant east of the brickyards, near the intersection of Columbia Pike and Route 1, where meat scraps and bones were rendered into fertilizer. Further ambience was provided by several flourishing pawnshops, a pickle factory, gas stations, and an igloo—marked by inverted icicles on its parapet—from which frozen custard was sold. The site also included what was left of Hell's Bottom, which had lost most of its aura of danger and was now a pathetic place where squatters lived in tarpaper shacks. "They would put up a shack from old piano boxes and cardboard, anything they could find," a resident of nearby Queen City remembered.

The whole county was in the midst of a great transformation. Arlington had changed its name from Alexandria County in 1920, adopting the name of the mansion on the hill to differentiate itself from the independent city of Alexandria, bordering on the south. Arlington's 1940 population of 57,040 was more than double what it had been a decade earlier. Fueled by the growth of the federal government, Arlington, Alexandria, and neighboring Fairfax County made up the fastest-growing area in the country.

Farms and woodland were giving way to residential developments. The battles between the Arlington Good Citizens' League and the Jackson City gamblers had been replaced by spats between new suburban residents and old-timers raising chickens in their yards.

Faced now with the prospect of hosting the world's largest office building, the leaders of Arlington County were quite bullish. They had recovered from initial dizziness upon learning of the building in July and now hackles were raised over the furious controversy that followed. "We are 100 percent behind anything that the government wishes to do in this regard," Arlington County Board chairman Freeland Chew told a Senate committee. "It is my government, it is our government, and particularly if it is a defense effort . . . we are all the more behind it." The massive influx of jobs, money, and new residents that would accompany the building was not lost on anyone either. Yet county leaders had remarkably little concern about the strains that it might place on a county that had eighteen paid firefighters, forty-two police officers, and an already overloaded sewage system.

Somervell's building would require an enormous amount of land. The ninety-acre quartermaster depot site was not enough. The building alone would need about forty acres, and another twenty-four acres were needed for a separate sewage treatment plant and a power plant. At least fifty-nine acres would be required for two enormous parking lots. Considerably more would be needed for the network of access roads planned for the building.

The engineers and architects puzzled over where exactly to place the building. The first trick was to meet the legal requirements of the bill passed by Congress. In order to make Roosevelt's sleight of hand work, at least some of the building had to be located on Arlington Farm, immediately north of the quartermaster site. Some fifty-seven acres of the four-hundred-acre farm were incorporated into the site. Most of it was slated for parking and roads, but the northern edge of the building was placed within the farm boundary, meeting the letter of the law. The southern and western portions of the building would be located on the quartermaster depot site.

Somervell also ordered the 146 acres of Washington-Hoover Airport added to the project grounds. Much of what was once Jackson City would provide land for parking, sites for the sewage and power plants, and fill for other portions of the project. An eastern sliver of the building would rest on the former airport.

The site as it now stood was 320 acres, bordered on the south by Columbia Pike, on the west by Arlington Ridge Road, on the north by an annex of Fort Myer, and on the east by Boundary Channel, an arm of the Potomac River. Ironically, the building would cover so much land that parts of all three Arlington locations that had been proposed—Arlington Farm, Washington-Hoover Airport, and the quartermaster depot site—would be used to hold it.

A new pentagon

The original rationale for Edwin Bergstrom's pentagonal design was gone. The building no longer would be constructed on the five-sided Arlington Farm site. Yet the chief architect and his team continued with plans for a pentagon at the new location.

Just as the original idea for the five-sided shape was guided by the necessity of fitting the building into the land, the decision to keep the design boiled down to a practical reason: There was no time to change it. Somervell's forced-march pace for constructing the building meant there was no going back to the drawing board.

Besides that practicality, the pentagon design worked. From a purely geometric standpoint, a circle made the most sense for such a large and low building; walking distances within the building would be much shorter than in a square or rectangle. Circular walls would be a nightmare to build, however, and would greatly slow the pace of the construction. A pentagon had many of the benefits of a circle by shortening distances within the building—30 to 50 percent less than in a rectangle, architects calculated—but its lines and walls would be straight and therefore much easier to build.

The architects had been refining the irregular pentagon ever since it was cooked up the weekend of July 18. The original design—two independent five-sided rings with comblike wings—remained awkward. The move from the odd-shaped Arlington Farm site freed the architects from the need to make the building asymmetrical. In August, the architects began experimenting with multiple concentric pentagons placed inside one another, interlaced with corridors and light courts, surrounding a pentagonal courtyard. The advantages gained—a smoother pedestrian flow, better space arrangement, and easier distribution of utilities around the building—"proved startling," the architects concluded, especially compared with a more conventional rectangular design. The inner ring would serve as a quick way around the building, with ten radial corridors leading to destinations in the outer rings.

Somervell liked it. "I believe that what [Bergstrom] has is the answer," he told one of the planning commissioners. The new design "seems to give much the shorter and better circulation," the general added.

The symmetrical design also had a dramatic effect on the look of the building, so ugly in its first permutation. Seen from above, the concentric rings of pentagons, if not beautiful, were at least pleasing to the eye, conveying a sense of coherence.

Something else about a pentagon appealed to Somervell and other Army officers. The five-sided shape recalled a traditional form of fortification. It was reminiscent of a seventeenth-century fortress, or a Civil War battlement; indeed the first shot of that war, a mortar shell that burst with a glare at 4:30 in the morning of April 12, 1861, illuminated the dark, five-sided shape of Fort Sumter.

I should absolutely refuse to live in a building of that type

Roosevelt made the first foray at changing the design. At the end of the cabinet meeting on Friday, August 29, the president proposed a new design for the building, an idea so "bizarre," in Henry Stimson's view, that it made temporary allies of Somervell and Gilmore Clarke. "The president suddenly sprung the plan of having a cubic block of a building in which there would be either no windows or very few and which would be entirely lighted by artificial light and ventilated artificially," Stimson wrote despairingly in his diary.

Stimson, thoroughly a product of the nineteenth century, was dumbfounded by Roosevelt's suggestion. He had no intention of working in a banana warehouse, the secretary remarked out of the president's hearing. "It struck me as so fantastic that I did not express myself to him, but I told Somervell afterwards that he was to stand fast against any such proposition because I should absolutely refuse to live in a building of that type," Stimson wrote.

Roosevelt had picked up the idea from his uncle. Frederic Delano, endlessly interested in new trends in city planning, had reported seeing such buildings on his recent trip out west. Advances in air conditioning and fluorescent lighting had made it feasible to build even large buildings without interior windows and courts, saving space and money.

Roosevelt's vision was for a solid, square building running a fifth of a mile in each direction; the only windows, if any, would be on the exterior. "Suppose it was one thousand feet long, and one thousand feet wide, you would have only four outside walls," he told reporters. "Think of all those rooms on the inside." By his own admission, the idea was "a trial balloon," but the president was enthused about the futuristic possibilities.

Somervell and Bergstrom did their best to dampen the president's enthusiasm, and even Clarke, despite his dislike of the five-sided shape, spoke against the idea. "Well, Mr. President . . . somebody might throw a monkey-wrench into the air-conditioning, and maybe they wouldn't all get out before they suffocated," Clarke told FDR.

"You know, I never thought of that," Roosevelt mused.

By the end of the day, Roosevelt retreated from his suggestion but did not give it up altogether, proposing that perhaps one wing be constructed without windows as an experiment.

I like that pentagon-shaped building

The pentagonal design next came under attack from Clarke and the Commission on Fine Arts. Complying with Roosevelt's instructions, architect Edwin Bergstrom appeared before the commission on the morning of Tuesday, September 2, for a special hearing to review plans for the new building.

Bergstrom arrived for the 11 A.M. hearing at the Fine Arts Commission offices in the Interior Department building with his hair slicked back and a handkerchief peeking out of the pocket of his dark suit. He was accompanied by his Californian coterie—chief deputy David Witmer and top architects Pierpont Davis and Robert Farquhar—who were carrying preliminary drawings of the pentagonal building.

Gesturing to the drawings, Bergstrom explained the plans. The building would be 960 feet long on each of five sides and made of reinforced concrete. The outer ring of the building would be three stories and sixty feet high, while interior wings and corridors would be two stories high. In the middle was an interior pentagonal court measuring 360 feet on each side. Access roads would be built around the building and a plaza constructed in front of the main entrance. Buses would come into the building through a basement entrance on the south side.

The commission's reception was decidedly cool. "A pentagonal has never worked out well and great confusion is apt to result in the circulation of the building," said commission member William H. Lamb, an architect used to loftier plans—he was a partner in the firm that designed the Empire State Building. A rectangular building would be preferable, Lamb said.

His suggestion was endorsed by a most formidable commission member, Paul Philippe Cret. French-born and an internationally renowned practitioner of the Beaux Arts style, Cret was one of America's most distinguished architects. Among many structures to his credit were the Pan-American Union in Washington, D.C., the Valley Forge Memorial Arch in Pennsylvania, and the University of Texas Tower in Austin. Roosevelt considered him one of the century's finest architects and was beholden to him as well; it was Cret who took Roosevelt's rough sketch and designed the president's pet tower at the National Naval Medical Center in Bethesda in 1938. Two years later Roosevelt enthusiastically appointed Cret to the Commission of Fine Arts. His opinions could be expected to carry great weight with the president.

Cret, somewhat deaf from his service in World War I and at sixty-four suffering from ill health that made it difficult for him to speak, nonetheless made it clear he was appalled by the plans. In such a huge building, a pentagonal design would confound visitors. "If one gets into the wrong corridor, he is lost," Cret said. He and Lamb also wanted Bergstrom to rework plans for the façade and "do away with the monotonous appearance."

Bergstrom agreed to make revisions, but made it clear he was determined to keep the pentagon. After the War Department architects left the meeting, Cret declared that the commission should appeal to the president. Roosevelt already had invited Clarke to the White House that afternoon to discuss the plans. Cret drew pencil sketches of a rectangular building to show the president in hopes of persuading him to change the shape.

Somervell beat the commissioners to the punch. At 12:15, the general, nattily dressed in a bow tie and a seersucker suit, strolled into the Oval Office, accompanied by Bergstrom, who was carrying a large sheaf of blueprints. Roosevelt, just back from Hyde Park, reviewed the plans carefully, asking questions and directing a few changes, and approved the design. When he left the Oval Office, Somervell was "smiling affably and appearing in better humor than he has since the President directed him last week to re-study the building plans," the *Star* reported. Everything was "coming along fine," Somervell told reporters.

At 2:15 P.M., it was the commissioners' turn. Clarke, Cret, and Lamb were ushered in to see the president. The mustachioed, dignified old Frenchman presented the case against the pentagonal design, arguing a rectangle made more sense. Cret also appealed to Roosevelt's sensibilities as commander in chief, suggesting that it would be even better to disperse the War Department in several buildings rather than in one single great mass. This pentagon-shaped War Department building, Cret said, would make the world's largest bombing target.

The president listened attentively until the commissioners finished. "You know, gentlemen, I like that pentagon-shaped building," Roosevelt said. "You know why?"

"No," the commissioners replied resignedly.

"I like it because nothing like it has ever been done that way before."

A veil of secrecy falls

Late that afternoon, Roosevelt brought in the press and announced his verdicts about the building to the public. "I have been going over the preliminary plans, and it will be probably a pentagonal building—that means five-sided, if you don't remember your Greek," Roosevelt told reporters, who guffawed appreciatively. One wing would be built as a solid block "to test out this windowless proposition," he added.

The building, the president reiterated with finality, would be constructed on the former quartermaster depot site. "It does not interfere in any way, from any angle, with the view of Arlington," Roosevelt said. As for the size, he said, "It will house not 40,000 people but about 20,000 people."

"Will this building require the full $35 million?" the president was asked.

"I hope not," he said.

All parties in the dispute had signed off on the plans, according to Roosevelt. "I don't know how happy they are—but at least they are together," he said.

Roosevelt insisted that the Arlington building would be only a temporary headquarters for the War Department and that the just-completed structure in Foggy Bottom would become the permanent home. "The War Department, after the emergency is over, can return to it, and the pentagonal building can be used for records," Roosevelt said. The *Washington Post*, for one, was skeptical. "It doesn't seem reasonable to suppose that future officials will agree to turn over the Government's largest and most costly office building for the storage of miscellaneous records," the paper noted in an editorial.

Somervell was cheery, contentedly speaking to reporters after the president's announcement. He radiated confidence and competence, with his gray hair neatly parted, mustache close-clipped, and gray eyes shining, and wearing a gray seersucker suit—"a symphony in gray," as the *Star* described him. "Everybody is going to be as happy about the new War Department building as they are about the Washington National Airport at Gravelly Point," the general said.

The press did not fully appreciate why Somervell was so happy. The *Star*, like other newspapers, reported that the president had approved "a structure half as big as that originally proposed by the Army." Somervell knew better, though he said nothing to reporters. Reducing the occupancy to twenty thousand was a temporary measure and did not mean the building had to be constructed at half the size. By Somervell's reckoning, the agreement authorized him to construct a four-million-square-foot building, or four-fifths the size of what he originally proposed.

Somervell told the press the night of September 2 that construction would start within the next two weeks—an astonishing declaration given that the location, design, and size had only been settled in the previous few days. Somervell did not even have a contract anymore: It would have to be renegotiated with McShain because of the changes to the site and design. Plans still were being furiously revised to accommodate the president's wishes. And Roosevelt was not even finished fiddling. Somervell returned with Bergstrom to the White House the following day, and Roosevelt requested changes to the façade.

Somervell did make one concession to reality: Instead of finishing the building in one year, as he had previously promised, the general told reporters construction would take an additional two months because of the poor ground conditions at the new site. The afternoon of September 4, at a meeting with Groves, Renshaw, Bergstrom, and McShain at his headquarters in the Railroad Retirement Building, Somervell ordered "the mobilization of equipment, materials and personnel necessary for the immediate prosecution of work."

Groves wanted to know which section of the building should be completed first. Even this basic question could not yet be answered. They would have to wait until they knew more about foundation conditions, Somervell said. In keeping with Roosevelt's dream of one day converting the building into a records depot, the general approved a design load of 150 pounds per square foot—a high capacity that would allow the storage of heavy file cabinets throughout the building.

There was one more thing: Somervell's charm offensive with reporters would be short-lived. The general directed that "no further detailed information on the building" be issued to the press "in view of the president's personal interest" in the project. Somervell followed up the next day with a more explicit memo to Brigadier General Alexander D. Surles, chief of the Bureau of Public Relations:

1. In view of the discussion concerning the War Department building, it is considered desirable to limit publicity on our actions to the minimum, and *in no event* should information as to the amount of the contract be given to the press.
2. This information will be seized on by the press as indicative of the amount of work which we are going to do, and will probably start further unfavorable publicity, which we wish to avoid.
3. I am sure my request is in line with what the President would want in the matter.

It was typical Somervell. The money he was requesting—$33.3 million—certainly would have highlighted the fact that the building he intended to construct was not much smaller than the $35-million structure originally planned, so the general simply ordered a cap on the information. The unsubtle reference to the White House made it clear he had Roosevelt's backing.

A veil of secrecy fell over the project.

Architects' rendering of building, October 1941.

CHAPTER
7

UNDER WAY

An army is marshaled

Word was getting around fast at the union hall for the International Brotherhood of Carpenters and Joiners Union, Local 40, in Washington in early September 1941. Hiring was starting for a new project across the river in Arlington. It was no ordinary job—it would be the biggest building in the world.

Stanley "Joe" Nance Allan, an energetic and slender nineteen-year-old carpenter, was interested. His job building an annex at the British Embassy on Massachusetts Avenue had wrapped up in August. Smart and ambitious, Allan had graduated from Western High School in Washington in 1939 but wanted to earn money before going to college. Despite the excitement about the new building, Allan was interested in one thing: the pay. "I knew what the building was and what it was for, but it didn't dawn on me the crisis we were in," he recalled.

Allan promptly drove to the job site and walked into a makeshift office. There was no need for an interview—all he had to do was show his union card. A foreman for John McShain, Inc., hired him on the spot at the standard union wage for carpenters—$1.62½ an hour, or $65 a week. Allan was given badge number six, one of the first of 4,600 carpenters who would eventually be put to work on the project. "There were very few when I started, then the numbers started increasing very, very fast," Allan said. "The word went around that they're hiring, and people just started arriving immediately."

The Great Depression was not yet over in many communities. The pay was good—all union wages. Hundreds, soon thousands, of workers were needed: surveyors, laborers, excavator operators, truck drivers, drilling-rig operators, water boys, cement finishers, and, as time went on, steam fitters, plasterers, electricians, painters, plumbers, and special technicians of all kinds.

Allan had been trained as a carpenter by his father, a builder by trade; the boy had grown up on construction sites and had been working jobs since before high school. But he had never seen anything like the army of construction workers who poured in from all over the region—a mix of men from the rural communities of Virginia and Maryland, hills and valleys of West Virginia, small towns and big cities in southern Pennsylvania, farms of North Carolina, and neighborhoods, black and white, all over Washington. One carpenter from the Eastern Shore of Maryland showed up carrying his tools in a lobster basket.

The man marshaling the growing army of workers was Paul Hauck, McShain's job superintendent. Allan recognized his short and stout figure at the job site. Allan's father was an acquaintance of Hauck's, and the young worker knew his reputation: a veteran construction man, very able and highly respected, and a thoroughly warm and decent man. Hauck had a face as open as a prairie with bright blue eyes behind his wire glasses; he had a tendency to wear fat ties that went halfway down his shirt. He was forty-two but looked older, with thinning gray hair; yet his tremendous will for work remained undiminished.

McShain had developed a stable of first-rate superintendents, men he relied on and kept on the payroll even in slow times. None was better than J. Paul Hauck. As head of McShain's Washington operations, Hauck had overseen many of McShain's most important jobs—the Jefferson Memorial, the Bethesda Naval hospital, and National Airport. When McShain got the contract to build the FDR Library in Hyde Park, Hauck was the man he entrusted with the project.

Hauck was a Pennsylvania-born engineer who moved to Washington in the mid-1930s to join the city's booming construction business. He met John McShain atop a pile of bricks at the builder's first project in Washington, the Internal Revenue Service building. Hauck was soon McShain's indispensable man. He and his wife, Beulah, lived in a modest home in Silver Spring, Maryland, just north of the District border. They had no children, and Hauck was devoted to two things: Beulah and John McShain.

Hauck was different from the effervescent and dynamic McShain. "Paul Hauck was just the opposite," McShain's daughter Polly recalled. "He was quiet, gentle. He was always very sweet in every way. In some ways, he must have suffered more under the pressure than my father, because he was a driver also, but he didn't have the outlets my father had through his personality."

McShain's treatment of Hauck was often rough; he would administer public tongue-lashings at job sites and chide the homey superintendent for looking like a hick. "Why don't you buy a new hat?" McShain once told him. "Certainly I'm paying you enough." Yet McShain could not abide anyone else criticizing Hauck; a new superintendent who followed McShain's lead and was disrespectful to Hauck was nearly fired. Perhaps the fullest measure of the regard McShain held for him is that Hauck was apparently the only employee the builder ever tried to convert to Catholicism. McShain took him to a retreat, but Hauck politely stuck to his Episcopalian faith.

Hauck was a proud man, yet he would absorb McShain's wrath uncomplainingly, even bending down with rags to clean the boss's shoes at job sites. Hauck's respect for McShain boiled down to trust. In all the years he worked for him, Hauck once said, McShain never asked him to do anything dishonest.

The biggest white elephant in creation

Roosevelt, after three weeks of almost daily involvement with the War Department project since his return from the summit at sea with Churchill, was suddenly if temporarily out of the picture, unconcerned with the details of the building or almost anything else. On Friday, September 5, three days after approving the pentagonal shape, Roosevelt traveled to Hyde Park to visit his ailing mother. Sara Roosevelt, eighty-six, a woman of great patrician bearing, brightened at the appearance of Franklin. He spent all Saturday at her side, but that night she fell into a coma. To the great sorrow of the president, she died the next day, in the same bed in which she had given birth to her only child fifty-nine years earlier. "The President, deeply affected by the passing of his mother at noon on Sunday, withdrew at his family home on the Hudson into the deepest seclusion which the demands and responsibilities of his high office would allow, and shut himself off from the world more completely than at any time since he assumed his present post," *The New York Times* reported.

Back in Washington, the first ten days of September passed in a headlong rush. Somervell had ordered work to start the moment the new construction contract was signed and the War Department issued its authorization, which Hauck knew could come any day. The plans and designs were not ready, but that did not matter. They would go with what they had.

In ordinary times, by one estimate made during the war, a year and a half should have been allowed for designing a building the size of the Pentagon. The draftsmen and engineers under Bergstrom's direction—now numbering over a hundred—had had a total of thirty-four days since full-scale work on the design of concentric pentagons had begun on August 8. Drafting at a furious speed in a warehouse basement at nearby Fort Myer, they had produced only a fraction of the necessary plans.

The key to building efficiently, Hauck believed, was timing. It meant getting workers, materials, and plans to the same place at the same time, so not even a minute was wasted. "To build economically and to build fast, you have to know where you're going—just like the quarterback on a football team," Hauck once said. If plans were not ready, Hauck would be quarterbacking the team blindfolded.

As the drafting work continued, McShain and Hauck made a critical decision about how they would organize the labor and construction. It was a way to start the building even in the absence of most of the plans, and it gave them the best—maybe the only—chance of constructing the building in fourteen months, as the contract required, with at least 500,000 square feet ready for occupancy no later than May 1, 1942, less than eight months away.

The pentagonal design of the building lent itself to a division of the construction. On paper, McShain and Hauck split the building into five trapezoid-shaped sections, as if cutting a pentagonal pie. The five sections were labeled A through E. Work would start on the south face of the building, Section A, proceed to Section B to the west, and continue clockwise to the other sections. Construction would soon be under way concurrently in all five sections, but each section would be one stage ahead of the next. This would allow the sequencing of material delivery and scheduling of work crews with specialized skills. The draftsmen could focus their efforts on producing detailed drawings of Section A, and design subsequent sections later.

The assembly-line strategy was simple yet brilliant. "It was broken into five equal pieces, whose main elements were repeatable," one of the Pentagon architects said a half-century later. In effect, McShain would construct five separate buildings. Each would be "erected as though it was a separate and distinct structure independent of any one of the other four," McShain later said. Each section would be occupied as it was completed.

Hauck would have overall charge, but each of the five sections would be built by its own team, each with its own superintendent, assistant superintendents, foremen, labor and carpenter crews, material checkers, clerks, bookkeepers, and so on down the line. It might mean duplication of jobs and higher administrative costs, but McShain knew something else: The five superintendents and their teams would compete, and that could speed the work and ultimately save money.

One danger of such a scheme was that the five buildings might not set together correctly. Mistakes of even inches could have serious consequences. A force of a hundred civil engineers, overseen by Hauck, would be responsible for the overall dimensions of the building and ensure that the different sections were aligned and elevated correctly.

At the site, Hauck oversaw last-minute preparations of the ground. Work had stopped on the quartermaster depot just before the foundation had been poured, but forms laid for the concrete and the beginnings of a long brick wall had to be yanked out. The grading work that had been done was helpful, though, giving them a head start on leveling the ground.

With groundbreaking looming, McShain called a meeting of the contractors' top supervisors. Representatives from all the major subcontractors attended, including those from Potts & Callahan, the Baltimore company that would handle the excavation and grading. McShain addressed the group: There was no time for turf battles or petty disagreements on this job site, either among themselves or with the Army. The watchword for this project, McShain declared, was to be "above and beyond all personalities."

On the eve of construction, the skepticism about the project was palpable. Somervell was an officer "whose judgment is usually right," the *Architectural Forum* wrote in September 1941. "But, there are plenty of planners who think he is wrong this time, that the War Department is about to beget the biggest white elephant in creation."

September 11, 1941

The heat finally broke on September 11, 1941. The mercury had reached a miserable, sultry ninety-six degrees the day before, marking "the hottest September 10 in Washington weather annals," *The Washington Post* noted. Seven cases of heat prostration and one drowning were reported. During the night a wedge of cold air from the Great Lakes reached the region, scattering the tropical front that had broiled Washington. The temperature dropped twenty degrees overnight, and Thursday, September 11, dawned as the sort of perfect late-summer day that sometimes blesses Washington, with a crystal-clear blue sky and a hint of fall in the air.

The cool air sweeping over the dusty job site in Arlington was accompanied by news from the War Department: The new construction contract had been signed and approved by all parties, and a notice to proceed had been granted by letter that day from the secretary of war's office. At 9:45 that morning, Renshaw, McShain, Hauck, and Bergstrom met at Groves's office at Construction Division headquarters. They had approval to begin.

There was no ceremony, no digging of a first spadeful, no recording of the moment. They simply got to work. Steam shovels operated by men from Potts & Callahan dug into the heavy clay and began leveling the ground for Section A, on the south. It was the side farthest away from the river, away from the low airport land, on more or less flat ground—the best part of the site with the least potential of causing problems.

Somervell had eight pile drivers ready to go, but neither the Commission of Fine Arts nor the National Capital Park and Planning Commission had given final approval to the layout of the building. Moreover, foundation plans showing where the piles were to be driven were ready for only twenty of the five thousand pile caps the building would need. "We . . . found ourselves in the sad predicament of starting construction with practically no plans whatever," McShain later said.

Regardless, the general gave orders for workers to start driving piles the following day. "We are starting three pile drivers to work tomorrow on those parts of the building where we feel we can do so without any lost motion," Somervell wrote on September 11 to planning commissioner Frederic Delano. The general wanted quick approval by the commissions "so that we can put all eight of our pile drivers on the job."

Alexander Surles, the Army chief of public relations, had asked permission to issue a press release about the new contract. Somervell approved only on condition that no real information be included, in keeping with his earlier instructions. "The amount of the contract should not be given to the press in view of the fact that plans are not yet developed to the point where the cost of this building can be determined," Somervell told Surles.

The four-sentence press release September 11 was a model of nonspecificity, saying only that a contract to build the new War Department building in Arlington had been awarded that day to McShain and the two Virginia contractors, Doyle & Russell and Wise Contracting. "The contract is on a cost-plus-a-fixed-fee basis, and the amount will be determined by plans for the building as finally approved," the release stated.

In fact, the construction authorization included specific amounts. The construction contract was for $31.1 million, including a fixed fee of $524,000 for McShain and the Virginia contractors. The Army, which would provide all the engineering save mechanical, was allotted $1 million for those services. An additional $265,000 would cover outside architect and engineer fees. The Quartermaster General's office would receive $809,000 for overhead costs, bringing the total to $33.2 million.

Somervell was correct in a larger sense: Those numbers bore no relation to reality. Groves protested to Somervell that the estimates were too low, but the general refused to raise them, pointing out he had already doubled Bergstrom's original estimate of $17.5 million. In any event, Somervell was not about to alert Congress or anyone else that there were doubts as to whether the building could be constructed for even the $35 million he had promised for the original, larger proposal. Army budget officers wanted some of the $35 million back, but Somervell refused to give the money up. He knew he would need every cent. Indeed, the size of the building was creeping upward. The gross area, as recorded September 7 in the personal notebook of David Witmer, the deputy chief architect, was nearly 4.4 million square feet—not a whole lot smaller than the 5.1 million square feet of Somervell's original proposal.

The press release also made no mention of the fact that work at the site had begun, and the papers took no notice. Much was happening in the world on September 11. At his headquarters in the Munitions Building, Stimson received "disturbing news" about the German siege of Leningrad, which had begun three days earlier. At least fifteen Russian divisions were entirely cut off within the city, he was told.

At the White House, a grim Roosevelt was putting the final touches on a much-anticipated fireside chat he would make to the nation that night. The speech, postponed by his mother's funeral, would respond to a September 4 incident southeast of Greenland in the North Atlantic in which a German U-boat had fired several torpedoes at an American destroyer. The U.S. ship, the *Greer*, was not wholly innocent, having aggressively tailed the submarine, but Roosevelt had seized upon the incident as a way of whipping up support for his controversial decision to have the Navy escort British supply vessels in the Atlantic.

At 9 P.M. on the night of September 11, Roosevelt addressed the nation from the White House, his words carried on every radio network in the land and sent around the world by shortwave. The president spoke somberly, a black band of mourning on his left arm. "The Nazi danger to our Western world has long ceased to be a mere possibility," he said. "The danger is here now."

Roosevelt announced he had issued orders to the Navy to shoot on sight any Axis warship found in American defensive waters, a broad definition that included much of the North Atlantic. At Woodley, his eighteen-acre estate in Northwest Washington, Stimson listened to the address, encouraged that after much back and forth Roosevelt was taking such a strong position. "It was the firmest statement and the most forward position yet taken by the President and I heard it with a great sense of relief," he wrote. Roosevelt, as historian James MacGregor Burns observed, "was in effect declaring naval war on Germany. . . . The Atlantic cold war was over. Now it was a hot war." Passions in living rooms around the country were enflamed by Roosevelt's powerful words: "[W]hen you see a rattlesnake poised to strike, you do not wait until he has struck before you crush him."

Across the river in Arlington the next morning, the pile driving began.

Those damn pile drivers

The pounding was incessant and inescapable. Hydraulic hammers struck steel time and time again, driving deep into the ground, and continuing around the clock. The metronomic drumming energized Joe Allan as he hammered together wooden forms. It "created a lively pulsation and rhythm of continuous activity on the job site," he recalled.

Major Gar Davidson, working exhausting hours for Groves in the Construction Division, was less enamored of the racket. At night he would retreat to the Arlington apartment where he lived with his wife and two young boys a mile away from the construction site. Trying to sleep, Davidson found home was no sanctuary from work. "I could hear them all night long, those damn pile drivers," he later said.

The sedimentary soil at the site—layers of loam, silt, sand, gravel, and water-bearing material—was not good for driving piles and would only get worse the closer they got to the river.

The engineers had briefly considered using wood piles, the cheapest option, but quickly rejected the idea when they realized that with variable water conditions in the ground, "their life would be limited and uncertain"; in any event, suppliers would have difficulty providing the huge amount needed. Steel piles were in short supply and could not be used. The Raymond Concrete Pile Company had the answer: cast-in-place concrete piles.

These were corrugated casings of sheet metal with a steel core, or mandrel, fitted inside. The pile drivers, rising high like oil derricks, drove the mandrels to the required depth; then the steel core was pulled out and replaced by concrete poured into the corrugated sheath. The casings, each projecting about a foot above grade, looked like tombstones from a distance. They were driven in clusters of three to twelve piles, depending on the load they would carry; each pile was capable of bearing at least thirty tons.

After concrete was poured into the casings, Allan and other carpenters went to work. Two-man teams assembled four-foot-high wood forms around each cluster. Steel reinforcing grids were put inside, and then concrete was poured into the forms to create pile caps that would serve as the base for building columns. These caps would be the rafts upon which the foundation would be laid. It was a tried and true technique—Renaissance builders in Italy used piled-raft foundations in cities such as Pisa and Florence, where the land was soft, wet, and flat. At the Pentagon, the technique was being applied on a scale never before seen.

After a week they had sunk about a hundred piles, but it was only a start, the equivalent of banging a few dozen nails into a soggy field. This site would need five thousand caps, meaning probably forty thousand piles, the engineers estimated, more than one for every occupant the building was supposed to hold. The first piles had to be driven twenty or thirty feet into the ground before they hit bedrock. Later, workers drilled fifty and even sixty feet down before they met real resistance. Some of the piles disappeared into the muck, never to be seen again.

A week after ground was broken, the National Capital Park and Planning Commission again discussed the building. Planning director John Nolen, unaware that ground had been broken, suggested that commissioners rearrange the layout of the site. The building, Nolen said, should be moved back from the river and oriented "to some important feature on the Washington side."

Brigadier General Reybold, the Army Corps of Engineers representative to the commission, broke the news that Somervell now had eight machines driving piles. "I think he is committed to that location," Reybold said.

This infernal hole

Somervell was indeed committed. A thousand men were on-site, working in a miniature dust bowl. The earth-shattering pounding of pile drivers was accompanied by the grinding of cement mixers and banging of hammers. At night, the spirals of dust, illuminated by flood lights, looked like columns of fire from across the river.

The cool weather that had greeted groundbreaking had been quickly followed by another heat wave. It was the driest September in fifty-seven years—barely half an inch of rain in the entire month and not a drop for nineteen straight days. In his diary, Henry Stimson cursed "this infernal hole they call Washington" and felt his vitality—so remarkable for a seventy-four-year-old man—sapped by the hot weather. "The flatness of the atmosphere is beyond belief," he wrote.

Workers, many wearing overalls and grimy shirts with caps or hats on their heads, had bought into the idea that they were racing the clock. "We'll have government clerks in here in April," a sweating construction worker boasted.

On September 19, Groves ordered crews to work forty-eight hour weeks, which meant plenty of overtime. Construction was under way seven days a week. To keep workers from straying off the site to eat, McShain brought in a lunch cart, a humble start to what would become a vast food operation.

After two weeks, hundreds of thirty-foot piles had been sunk and capped, and atop some of them building columns had been poured. On September 25, concrete was poured for the first part of the floor slab for Section A.

What was left of Hell's Bottom quickly came tumbling down. A handful of wood and cardboard shacks, still sporadically occupied by about fifteen people, were knocked down by Hauck's men. "When I say shacks, these were really, really rough shacks," recalled Lieutenant Bob Furman, Renshaw's executive officer. "There was a lot of low-life down there, prostitution. They just left. I don't think we thought much about their welfare."

Wrecking balls knocked down the brick buildings and smokestacks of the fertilizer plant, the oil refining companies, and other factories along Route 1. The pawnshops were torn down as well, to the shock of their clients. Furman watched people riding the bus from Washington get off at Route 1 and Columbia Pike, clutching items to pawn or tickets to redeem, looking surprised. Washington-Hoover Airport was taken over by the Army, which unceremoniously canceled the leases of all flying organizations. All commercial air traffic had already moved downriver to National Airport, but private aircraft still regularly flew in and out of the old airport, posing a danger to "life and property," Renshaw complained. Furman posted a notice at the airport September 23 ordering flying terminated. Some pilots simply ignored the order, landing and taking off even as heavy equipment tore up the runways.

The airport pool was shut down too. Furman delivered a check to the owners and returned after the place had closed. Water had been drained from the pool and the office was strewn with paper. Furman found a box of season passes for the pool, which he impishly signed and handed out to friends.

By early October, the framework for the first floor of Section A was rising rapidly. Carpenters banged together wooden forms for the columns, which rose like a string of watchtowers. Workers prepared to pour concrete for another section of slab. "It was moving along," said Joe Allan, the young carpenter. "It was kind of a frantic pace, a rhythm."

When construction started, the rolling 320-acre site varied in elevation from as low as eight feet above sea level on the old airport grounds to fifty-five feet farther west. The western two-thirds of the building was to be constructed on ground that averaged forty feet above sea level, while the eastern third was being placed on land only ten feet above sea level. Some six million cubic yards of earth would be required to raise the lower areas above flood stage, as well as to properly grade the land for roads and parking lots. It was more earth than had ever been moved to construct a building. "That is one record that will probably stand for all time," *Popular Mechanics* observed.

The excavation and grading operation grew rapidly from modest beginnings; several horse-drawn excavators helped move dirt during the first weeks of construction due to equipment shortages, to Renshaw's dismay. Potts & Callahan, the subcontractor in charge of excavation and grading, soon built up a fleet of 376 pieces of heavy equipment, including 230 dump trucks, 60 tractors and bulldozers, 19 steam shovels, and 10 cranes, and the horses were retired.

Bulldozers and steam shovels leveled off high ground and trucks carried the earth to lower ground. But more fill was needed than what was available at the site. Some two million cubic yards of earth would have to be trucked in from excavation sites all around Washington. Fill left from the construction of National Airport was used. Tons of earth came from the hills of Rock Creek Park in Washington, where a bridle path was being widened. More fill came from nearby Fort Myer.

Dump trucks lumbering to and from the construction site clogged Washington roads, to the irritation of drivers. Laborers waved red flags to stop traffic on heavily traveled Arlington Ridge Road, backing up cars for a half-mile to make way for trucks coming in and out of the site. "Streams of trucks follow each other on mysterious but purposeful ways, dropping dollops of dirt that flatten out under many wheels and merge with the asphalt," *The Washington Post* reported.

The Army had considered constructing a levee along the west bank of the channel to make the low land safe for building. Somervell elected to instead raise the low ground eight feet or more, to eighteen feet above sea level. Boundary Channel, an arm of the Potomac that ran along the airport and formed a small lagoon, would be dug out and the lagoon enlarged by thirty acres. This would provide fill and improve the looks of the site; but the lagoon had another purpose, critical to the rapid construction of the building. It would serve as a harbor for a concrete batching plant to be built along the waterside. River barges would be able to deliver sand and gravel directly to the site, cutting time and expense.

In the first weeks of construction, the lagoon was attacked from both land and water. Dredges scooped out silt and deepened the channel. Working behind the safety of a clay dike, steam shovels excavated the ground next to the channel. Workers drove well points—hollow pointed rods—into the ground and pumped out water, lowering the water table and further protecting against flooding. The excavators dug fourteen feet below the normal high-tide level of the Potomac. Then a dipper dredge—a floating dredging machine with a machine-operated bucket working on an arm—opened a passage through the dike. The batching plant, constructed simultaneously, was soon ready for deliveries.

More than one million cubic yards of ground was excavated to enlarge the lagoon, and the muck was dumped immediately to the northwest, raising the level of that ground. In effect, more than a hundred acres of marginal land was being converted into seventy acres of usable land. Ironically, tons of dirt that Potts & Callahan trucks had hauled to Washington-Hoover Airport five years earlier to fill low areas had to be dug out to expand the lagoon. "We have accomplished a total of nothing," a worker groused.

We'd better leave town

A month after groundbreaking, a fundamental decision had yet to be made: What material would be used to construct the building's walls?

The original plan was to make the building's exterior brick. Somervell had told a House subcommittee in July that limestone was not being considered. "We did not even dream of getting anything that good," he had said. Yet the tentative plans now called for 150,000 cubic yards of Indiana limestone on the building's exterior.

The light-colored, fine-grained stone was known for its durability and ease of shaping. It had been used in city halls, churches, and statehouses across the land, as well as the National Cathedral in Washington and the Empire State Building in Manhattan. McShain had pushed for limestone on the building's exterior. "I am sure that we all want to be quite proud of this building after it is finished," McShain wrote Groves. "Therefore it is essential that the exterior of the building be very presentable in order to avoid public criticism."

McShain had an ally in the limestone industry, which had fallen on hard times, and, aided by Senator Raymond Willis of Indiana, was lobbying hard for limestone on the new War Department building. "Bricklayers are all extremely busy whereas stone setters are literally walking the streets in every large city," the director of the Indiana Limestone Institute wrote Somervell. The "limestone boys," a War Department official later said, succeeded in making the switch from bricks. Groves thought limestone was a mistake and argued against it repeatedly with Somervell. A brick exterior "would indicate that we were not extravagant," Groves later wrote. But Somervell was persuaded that limestone would lend a dignity to the building at a reasonable cost—$295,000—and if it made the limestone boys and the senator from Indiana happy, all the better. The Commission of Fine Arts approved limestone, but a decision was still needed from Roosevelt, who had reserved final judgment on the exterior.

The limestone debate was only a warm-up to a far more serious disagreement over the rest of the walls. Each of the building's five concentric rings was to have exterior walls on both sides. In essence, ten pentagonal-shaped walls would be constructed around the entire length of the building. The outermost wall would have limestone facing, if Roosevelt approved. The question was what to put on the other nine walls, as well as the walls of the inner-court stairways, bridge passageways, and various approaches to the building. An enormous amount of wall space was at stake—more than 1.1 million square feet.

McShain and Groves thought it easiest and most economical to simply use brick. But Bergstrom, borrowing from designs he had used often in Southern California, wanted to use architectural concrete, a technique that made ornamental use of concrete. Rough-sawn boards would be used as forms, giving the concrete a texture reflecting the pattern of the grain in the boards. A gap would be left between the eight-inch boards, so the concrete would ooze out and form a ridge. The forms had to be stripped with great care to avoid breaking the ridges. Skilled concrete finishers would brush wet grout on the walls to give them the proper color and texture. It would be painstaking work, "a most expensive procedure," as Groves said. The effect was meant to simulate limestone; ironically, it would have been cheaper just to use limestone, Luther Leisenring, the chief of the architects' specifications section, later told Army historians.

McShain was beside himself, predicting disaster. Architectural concrete had been used sparingly on the East Coast, and McShain's crews were unfamiliar with the technique. It would prolong construction by six months or more, he warned, and increase the cost of the walls by $650,000. Groves conceded that architectural concrete would look better than brick but called it "a terrible thing from the cost standpoint and a time standpoint."

Late on the morning of October 10, Somervell slipped into the Oval Office with Bergstrom to decide the controversy with Roosevelt. The general recommended facing the exterior of the building with Indiana limestone. Roosevelt raised no objection, insisting only that the building have no marble, for the sake of appearing thrifty.

Next Bergstrom made the case for using architectural concrete for the other exterior walls, showing the president photographs of a building in Los Angeles he had designed using the technique. Roosevelt was pleased with the look and approved architectural concrete, despite the added cost.

"The president thinks it is swell," Groves glumly told McShain that afternoon.

The fight was not over. Groves ordered three sample walls built, each about twenty feet long by twelve feet high, complete with windowsills. One was to be of an attractive colored faced brick, one of architectural concrete, and one of Indiana limestone, to see how they compared.

Inspecting the concrete wall after it set, McShain was horrified. The concrete was badly honeycombed with voids caused by air. At 8:45 A.M. on October 14, McShain called Groves in a lather. "I went over the sample with Bergstrom and between you and me, Colonel, if they're going to let that go I think we'd better leave town," McShain said.

An appeal had to be made to Somervell and Roosevelt, McShain argued. "I still want the general to see it and if possible we should try to prevail on the President, because what we do here—I don't care whether you and I oppose it—it's going to reflect on us sooner or later," McShain said.

"Of course it's bound to," Groves agreed.

"We are the ones responsible for the job because Bergstrom will be forgotten," McShain said.

Groves pressed Somervell to bring the matter to Roosevelt. "Of course the President decided the way Somervell wanted," Groves later said.

The president was "emphatic in his disapproval of the use of brick, either red or cream colored," Somervell reported. The walls would be made of architectural concrete.

"Well, it's settled," Groves told Somervell. "I won't say anything more but I bet you didn't treat me fair."

McShain, who prided himself on his ability to predict costs, said his estimates for the walls were worthless now. "I was only judging what a good architect would do in designing it," he told Groves. "I didn't anticipate the intentions of a Californian."

It's going to be a whopper

Newspaper and magazine reporters were hounding George Holmes, Somervell's public relations man, for some news—any news—about the new building. Somervell decided progress was far enough along that he could afford to go public with a press release October 7. Reporters were confounded by what they learned.

Each face of the five-side exterior would stretch 921 feet. The pentagonal rings would surround a six-acre landscaped interior court. A large bus terminal would be built in the basement, with two lanes and fourteen loading stations. Two parking lots would accommodate eight thousand automobiles. The whole building would be air-conditioned, and its main concourse lined with a cafeteria, drugstore, barbershop, and other shops and facilities. The 320-acre site, which included separate heating and sewage plants, would be landscaped and beautified. Stepped terraces and plazas would lead up from the lagoon. Access roads would crisscross the property and new highways built to bring employees to work.

It sure did not sound as if the size of the building had been cut in half. Yet the release conspicuously noted that "the size, design and location of the building have received the personal attention of the President and the plans as announced reflect the instructions issued to Brigadier General Brehon B. Somervell, Chief of Construction."

Reporters were further alarmed by the high amount listed in the release for the construction contract, $31.1 million—a figure that did not even include the architectural and engineering costs that raised the total to $33.2 million. "The War Department's new office building in Arlington, Va., will be a dream building after all, costing some 31 million dollars," the *Post* reported suspiciously.

The release described the building as "a three-story building, with basement," but that was a deliberate deception, directed by Somervell. The "so-called basement was above ground," so the building was really four stories. Somervell ordered the basement nomenclature to disguise the inconvenient fact that he had promised a three-story building in his congressional testimony. No mention was made about the sub-basement that was planned, or for that matter, the sub-sub-basement.

Indeed, no information at all had been included in the press release about the total amount of space in the building. Reporters scrambled to find details of the dimensions from closed-mouthed War Department officials but met with little success for several days. An Army press spokesman, employing no little sophistry, told the *Star* that it was impossible as of yet to figure out the size of the building because the plans were not finished.

Finally, leaving the White House around noon on October 10 after a meeting with the president, Somervell was cornered by reporters who demanded answers. "No one is interested in the size of the building except real estate operators and war profiteers," the general insisted. Pressed, Somervell acknowledged the total size of the building would be more than four million square feet, or over four-fifths the size of the original proposal.

Conferring with local architects, the *Star* pieced together the truth. The plans for Somervell's building allotted 125 square feet per employee, a generous amount of space by the standards of the day given the emergency conditions. Some War Department employees were getting by then in as little as forty-five square feet. By halving the space allotment per worker, the building could—with the stroke of a pen—hold forty thousand workers. The building was being constructed with enormous office bays rather than individual suites, so it would be a simple matter of moving in more desks.

The working papers of Witmer, Bergstrom's top assistant, confirm the theory, showing the architects were working with two sets of estimates, one showing capacity of 19,530 workers at 125 square feet per person, the other 37,500 workers at 65 square feet per person.

Speaking to reporters at the White House, Somervell called it "utterly ridiculous" to suggest he had circumvented Roosevelt's directions. "Do you think any government official in his right mind would fail to conform to the President's orders?" he asked. Indeed, despite the press suspicion, Somervell told Roosevelt on August 29 that the building would be four million square feet, and the president raised no objection. Roosevelt, seeking to dampen the public controversy, probably was an accomplice in hiding the true size of the building; Somervell likely spoke the truth a month earlier when he told Surles, the public relations chief, that the president did not want the information released.

As for reporters' doubts that such an elaborate building would ever be used to store records, Somervell insisted it would make a "dandy" archives. Asked if the War Department would ever be willing to give up the building, the general coyly said, "Let's get through the emergency first."

Skeptical reporters consulted with Frederic Delano, who confirmed that Somervell's building adhered to the compromise agreement that he had signed and the president had approved. The commission was "by no means satisfied," Delano told reporters. But, he added, "we treated it as a war emergency and so accepted it."

The newspapers broke the news about the building to the public. The *Times-Herald* sounded bitter about having been duped: "It was finally decided once and for all, positively and definitely yesterday, that the size of the new War Department Building hasn't been cut in half and that it is going to be a whopper."

An aerial view of the site on September 15, 1941, with the Goodyear blimp Enterprise *visible in the background moored to the ground.*

CHAPTER
8

THE VIEW FROM
HIGH AND LOW

Lieutenant Furman's blimp ride

Lieutenant Bob Furman waited for a rare quiet moment to slip away from
the job site. As executive officer for the construction of the new War Department building, he spent his days and often his nights responding to one
crisis after another. But on a clear October morning, Furman walked down
to the grounds of the old Washington-Hoover Airport and headed to the
field where the Goodyear blimp *Enterprise* was tied to a portable mooring
mast.

The blimp was the only aircraft still flying from the old airport, at least
legally. Even in mid-October planes were still buzzing into the airport, pi-
loted mostly by out-of-towners unaware that the airfield had closed down
and somehow oblivious to the heavy equipment tearing up the place. Constructing Quartermaster Clarence Renshaw—newly promoted to major—
publicly appealed for pilots to stop, warning that someone was bound to be
killed soon.

Enterprise, a 148-foot long helium blimp, had been a fixture in Washington skies since 1935, promoting the tire company, carrying thousands of
tourists on sight-seeing tours, and once delivering food and medical supplies

to icebound residents of Tangier Island in the Chesapeake Bay. The War Department granted the ship special dispensation to stay at Washington-Hoover while its enormous hangar was moved, piece by piece, to National Airport. Renshaw soon had cause to regret the benevolence. Every time *Enterprise* launched, a thousand men at the construction site would drop whatever they were doing and turn their heads skyward to watch.

Furman knew time was short to sneak a ride on the blimp. "Nobody knew I was doing it," he said. "I had miscellaneous duties, and I just fit that one in." He plunked down his $3 and boarded the cabin. He had it all to himself.

Tall, bright, and affable, with a pompadour of reddish-brown hair above his angular face and smiling eyes, the twenty-six-year-old Furman had not expected to find his life interrupted by this great construction endeavor. He was the son of the assistant cashier at a small Quaker bank in Trenton, New Jersey. His father, William Amies Furman, had been raised a Quaker in Trenton but was thrown out of the church when he married a Congregationalist. His mother, Lelia Ficht, was the daughter of a Colorado man who built railroad lines through Indian country to copper mines in New Mexico. Bob, born in Trenton in 1915, was raised an Episcopalian along with his two brothers and two sisters. The middle son, Bob was industrious from the start, working for—and soon taking over—a network of neighborhood kids who sold seven hundred *Saturday Evening Posts* around town for a nickel apiece, clearing a penny-and-a-half profit per copy.

He earned enough to pay his first year's tuition at Princeton, where he entered the school of engineering. "I always wanted to build, so civil engineering was naturally the place for training," he said. Furman also joined the ROTC program at the insistence of his older brother, who wanted him to be an officer instead of a draftee if war came. Graduating in 1937, Furman went to work for the Turner Construction Company in New York City.

Furman did not pay much mind to the great mobilization of the Army in 1940 and was quite surprised to find himself called to active duty just before Christmas. With his engineering background, Furman was ordered to report to the Quartermaster Corps Construction Division headquarters in the Railroad Retirement Building in Washington. He was assigned to Renshaw's staff and given a desk next to Colonel Groves's office, the center of the whirling frenzy that was Army construction in 1941.

Groves and Renshaw were impressed with the Princeton boy's smarts and calm competence. When Renshaw was chosen to build the new War Department headquarters in August 1941, he took Furman with him. As executive officer for the construction of what would become the Pentagon, Furman was seeing his dream of building come true on an unsurpassed scale. All the debate about whether the building would be needed after the emergency struck him as irrelevant. "Whether it was useful after the war didn't matter," he later said. "We needed it to win the war."

Now, as *Enterprise* lifted skyward, Furman got his first bird's-eye view of the construction. The blimp's motion had him feeling a tad seasick, but he ignored the queasiness and peered out the window at the ground. Familiar as he was with the project, the scope of what he saw still astonished him. "It was a big site—a hell of a big site," Furman said. "The magnitude of the project was so evident."

Workers swarmed everywhere. Nearly three thousand men were now working three shifts around the clock, the bulk of them during the day. Two sides of the pentagon were clearly visible, joined together like a giant arrow pointing to the southwest. The southern portion, Section A, was further along, the concrete slab for its foundation—some ten thousand cubic yards—already poured. Forms could be seen for part of the second-floor slab. Hundreds of pile cap forms had been placed in Section B, to the west. From the air it looked like a vast punch card riddled with holes. Pile drivers were hammering around the clock, and almost nine thousand piles had been sunk.

The land 1,500 feet below Furman was being reshaped. Steam shovels were excavating earth and bulldozers had already graded a hundred acres of land. Dirt construction roads crisscrossed the site, and dump trucks lumbered along them, raising plumes of dust. In the lagoon adjacent to the site, barges bearing heaps of sand and gravel from the Potomac delivered the aggregate to the concrete batching plant. On the old airport grounds, construction had started on the basement for the new building's power plant. Along the eastern side of the building, workers were nearly finished relocating a mile-long stretch of the Pennsylvania Railroad running north up to Rosslyn.

The blimp ride was short—perhaps ten minutes—but it left a tremendous impression on Furman. Floating down to earth, he marveled that the nation could construct such a great building at the same time it was mobilizing and arming an enormous military. It was a formidable sight. "The size and magnitude and strength of the country was pretty evident," Furman said.

McShain and Bergstrom go to war

Back on the ground, progress was not so evident. The pace of the work was anemic, as far as the builder, John McShain, was concerned. The architects could not supply design plans fast enough. McShain was in a fine fettle: He could have two, three, even ten times as many men on the site constructing the building—if he only knew what he was supposed to build.

McShain had laid down the law that there were to be no personalities and no friction at the job site, but there were personalities—McShain's prominent among them—and there was friction, particularly with Edwin Bergstrom, the chief architect. Though his headquarters and home were in Philadelphia, McShain spent many days in Washington monitoring the work, keeping an apartment at the Hay-Adams House, a luxurious Italian Renaissance-style apartment-hotel on Lafayette Square across from the White House. This project was too important and too big—too magnificent a challenge—to stay away from. He needed to do battle with the architects.

At a meeting the night of October 13 with David Witmer, Bergstrom's deputy, McShain angrily warned he might shut down work on the job if the designers could not provide more plans for the floor slabs. "We're pushing that job frantically to help you and save you any embarrassment rather than close down, which we really should," he told the architect. It was a bluff—McShain would sooner die in anonymity than stop work even temporarily on this project—but the problem was real.

The following morning, a clear and warm fall day more than a month after ground was broken, McShain called Groves to complain. "We haven't got what we really need and what we should have to drive that job the way it's necessary to finish," McShain said. "Now we're losing perfect weather.

Look at a day like today—and, well, we've got about one-tenth of the men we should have out on that job."

By October 28, McShain had only part of the plans for the second floor on Section A, and the situation got worse in each section around the building. He was still waiting for some of the plans for the first floor of Section B, and there were no plans for the piles and foundation in Section C. Bulldozers were ready to start grading Section D but sat idle, waiting for plans. No structural information for the power plant was available save for the basement.

Every day Hauck clamored for more plans from the designers: "What do you have for us to do today, because we finished everything you gave us yesterday."

Further complicating the problem, the project had lost the services of Lieutenant Colonel Pat Casey, the energetic Construction Division design chief who had played a critical role in the early planning for the building. In September Casey received a cable from General Douglas MacArthur, with whom he had previously served in the Philippines, asking Casey to return to Manila as chief engineer with the U.S. Army Forces Far East Command. Casey went to see General Somervell. "Well, you're not going to accept that, are you?" Somervell asked incredulously.

"I definitely am," Casey replied.

Somervell was shocked that Casey would jilt him for a has-been like MacArthur. "Now look, Pat . . . if you do that, you're going to somebody who's reached the top and won't go any further, whereas you should stick with me . . . I'm on the way to the top."

But Casey was not to be dissuaded, even by Somervell, and he departed for Manila in October.

Worried about the growing design crisis, Groves assigned one of his top men, Colonel Thomas F. Farrell, to investigate. Farrell was a widely experienced engineer who had worked on the Panama Canal and served as New York State Commissioner of Canals and Waterways. Farrell knew a mess when he saw one. After he attended a weekly progress meeting on the evening of October 27 with McShain, Bergstrom, and Renshaw, Farrell's assessment was gloomy. "It is apparent that there is no immediate prospect of the Architect-Engineer getting sufficiently ahead of the Contractor as to permit full steam ahead," Farrell reported to Groves the next day. "It would be entirely practicable for the Contractor to employ two or three times his present forces if design information was available."

The design team must be reinforced as rapidly as possible, Farrell concluded. The most pressing need was for first-class concrete structural engineers familiar with modern techniques of calculating how to safely design large reinforced-concrete buildings. It was a specialized and critical skill, especially in a building with miles of concrete walls planned; miscalculations could cause the structure to fail.

Groves telephoned private engineering firms and Army quartermaster depots around the country, desperately trying to find concrete specialists. Price was no object, Groves made plain—he was offering salaries of $125 a week to designers who would normally earn $75. "We're going to pay them twice what they're worth," Groves promised. The colonel was livid when a highly regarded concrete structural engineer who reported from Philadelphia turned around and left when he was mistakenly told his salary would only be $90. "He just laughed at it and came home," Groves was told. A chagrined Renshaw rushed to square things away, but concrete structural engineers remained scarce.

The design bottleneck was not Bergstrom's fault. Yet something had to be done. "It must be recognized that in a construction operation of this character, the Architect would normally have a start of many months on the Contractor," Farrell pointed out to Groves. "Since this start was not available, there will be continuous pressure on the Architect by the Contractor for many months to come. The Architect's present forces are apparently working 'all out' trying to keep ahead."

In the hangar

"All out" was not fast enough. It would be up to Ides van Waterschoot van der Gracht to figure out a way to produce more drawings. Van der Gracht had joined the project soon after ground was broken in September. Somervell had asked William Delano—Frederic's distant cousin—to suggest an architect who could organize the enormous job of producing drawings for the building and oversee the huge force of draftsmen: "Somebody to help operate this mob." Delano, a well-known New York architect, recommended van der Gracht, one of his protégés. As architect for LaGuardia Airport, Delano had formed a lifelong friendship with Somervell during the WPA days, and his recommendation carried great weight with the general. Somervell immediately telephoned van der Gracht in New York; the following day, the thirty-nine-year-old architect, a Dutch man with tousled brown hair, found himself in the general's office in Washington.

"Mr. Delano said you were reasonably competent in those things, and what do you think?" Somervell asked. "Do you think that you can handle it?"

"General, I never even thought of anything as big as this," van der Gracht said.

Somervell was dismissive. "Oh, don't let that worry you, neither have we," he replied.

Ides van der Gracht was thus recruited to be chief of production for the project. He stood a shade under six feet tall and was thin as a rail, with blue eyes that shone like headlamps above his prominent nose and perpetual smile. Van der Gracht had an engaging personality and a cordial, forthright manner that won him friends easily. He was born in Graz, Austria, in 1902 and grew up in Katwijk, Holland, a fishing village on the North Sea; his father was a Dutch businessman and his mother came from a wealthy Austrian family. During World War I, at the age of thirteen, Ides came with his parents to the United States and studied at Jesuit schools. His parents returned to Holland after the war but Ides stayed in America, attending Princeton University. He graduated Phi Beta Kappa in 1923 and stayed on to earn a master's degree at Princeton's School of Architecture, where his professors considered him unusually gifted.

A Princeton friend helped land him a job at the prestigious firm of Delano & Aldrich. William Delano was quite taken with the young Dutchman, treating him as a surrogate son. At a young age van der Gracht was entrusted with the U.S. Post Office project in Washington, part of a group of prominent government buildings constructed in the 1920s and 1930s known as the Federal Triangle. "He has shown exceptional skill and ability in the way he has handled this building, from the beginning to the end," Delano wrote. Van der Gracht became a naturalized U.S. citizen in 1934 and was thoroughly Americanized by his education and work experience. But he retained a European outlook on the world and a European stake in the war. He toured the old country for more than a year on a beautiful British BSA motorcycle beginning in 1937, visiting his mother's family estate in Austria and returning to America just before her homeland was absorbed into the Nazi Reich in March 1938. When Somervell called in September 1941, van der Gracht's parents and sister, living in Roermond in southeastern Holland, were no longer free citizens but living in a Nazi-occupied land. Van der Gracht was eager to sign on.

"Okay, go to work," Somervell said.

The first priority was to bolster the size of the drafting force, already numbering well over a hundred. Van der Gracht was assigned several assistants who "went all over the United States siphoning off the best talent they could lay their hands on to form this team, which grew like topsy," van der Gracht recalled many years later.

More architects and draftsmen of all types were brought in from the Quartermaster Corps headquarters in Washington. Larry Lemmon, a dark-haired and thoughtful thirty-six-year-old bored with his work as a $2,600-a-year assistant landscape architect with the Construction Division, was at work one morning in the drafting office at division headquarters in the Railroad Retirement Building on Capitol Hill when the office chief called for everyone's attention. The supervisor walked down a wide aisle running the length of the room between two parallel rows of drafting tables, tagging every second man on the shoulder, Lemmon among them. Everyone selected was to report the following morning for duty designing the new War Department building. Lemmon's life was about to get much more interesting.

The drafting team was working from the basement of a Fort Myer warehouse previously used to stable horses that drew the caissons at Arlington National Cemetery. To van der Gracht, the warehouse was more like a sweatshop than an architect's drafting room. With the heat wave broiling Washington that fall, the place was miserable. Draftsmen were sweating so much they had to cover their drawings with blotting paper to avoid ruining them. "It was hot as the devil," van der Gracht recalled. "So we sat there, stripped to the waist, some just in their shorts, and with big blotting paper all over the plans with just small holes . . . where you were actually drawing while the perspiration was dripping off your nose onto the drawings."

More problematic, the warehouse was far too small for the burgeoning force of architects. The answer was standing before their eyes on the construction site itself, on the grounds of the old Washington-Hoover Airport: the Eastern Airlines hangar. The large metal-frame building was designed to hold airplanes, not people, but it was hurriedly wired with telephones and outfitted with hundreds of drafting tables and a blueprinting plant. The designers moved in on November 3. A big Eastern Airlines logo remained on the hangar's front, listing the attractive destinations—Miami, Tampa, and New Orleans among them—that the overworked members of the drafting force hadn't a prayer of visiting. The hangar was hardly plush, but compared to the Fort Myer warehouse it seemed luxurious. The architects had sixteen thousand square feet of unobstructed drafting space. Larry Lemmon was astonished at the size—the hangar had "become a huge design factory," he said. "[Yet] large as it was, it was still not large enough."

The design force was approaching its full strength of about 350, including 110 architects, 54 structural engineers, 43 mechanical engineers, 18 electrical engineers, 13 plumbing engineers, various specialists in roads, landscaping, and acoustics, as well as dozens of clerks and messengers. To make room for them all, a large extension was added to the hangar and covered with a shed roof. The expanded hangar had twenty-three thousand square feet, with room for four hundred drafting tables. The draftsmen worked at row after row of the tables, illuminated by lamps hanging from cables strung between the exposed beams of the cavernous hangar.

The drafting force was broken down by specialty—one draftsman might do nothing but detail elements of the façade, another the foundations, another windows, another toilets. They were divided into teams—architectural, structural, highways, mechanical engineering, heating and cooling, and plumbing, among others—each headed by a team chief. Every team in turn was divided into squads, each reporting to a squad leader. Lemmon was assigned to the highway-engineering team and given the job of drawing plans and cross-sections for roads and bridges.

Van der Gracht was a natural organizer—he had a "nit picking mind," by his own description—and he brought order and reason to the chaotic process. Van der Gracht would get orders from Bergstrom as to what was needed, and it was up to him to see that the hundreds of architects and engineers produced it. "My job essentially was to keep everyone drawing in the same direction," he said.

Van der Gracht issued a daily bulletin that kept the entire drafting force up to date on revisions and procedures. He met first thing each morning with the team chiefs, issuing instructions in extremely precise and slightly accented English, liberally sprinkled with corny Americanisms. They tackled the requests that had poured in from the field during the night: The contractor was screaming for foundation plans because a pile driver would be finished by 10:30—where should they move it? Van der Gracht would turn to the section head responsible for the plans—in this case, the structural engineer chief. "It's your baby," he was fond of saying. "So please, get it out, get it duplicated, and get it to the field."

Behind van der Gracht's desk was a long wall that ran along half the length of the hangar, covered with schedules, diagrams, and color-coded progress reports. Assistants constantly updated them with the latest information from the field. Van der Gracht paced up and down the length of the wall, stopping in his tracks when he spotted any sign that a design team was falling behind schedule. "Jeepers creepers!" he would exclaim. "They'd better get off the seat." He would immediately shift priorities and feed reinforcements to the faltering team.

Van der Gracht could tell almost instinctively what was fitting and what was not. "That whole building, in a way, took shape in my mind," he recalled. The thin Dutchman would regularly walk through the aisles between the endless rows of drafting boards, scanning desktops like a proctor monitoring a study hall. His eyes would zero in on anything that looked out of place and he would start asking questions. "Now wait a minute here, this isn't quite right," the offending draftsman would be told.

The draftsmen were using tools that would become antiquated in subsequent years: T-squares, pencils, and carbon copies on typewriters. The Pentagon, van der Gracht later said, "was probably the culmination of the T-square and typewriter way of producing architecture." All drawings were made in pencil on tracing paper; there was no time to ink them.

Drawings were issued nightly in order to record design decisions made during the day and get the information to contractors as fast as possible. At times they were reissued as often as every hour to record near-constant revisions. Two Ozalid machines for copying blueprints ran twenty-four hours a day, operated in three shifts of four men each. The machines, reeking of the ammonia used to produce the blueprints, spit out an average of fifteen thousand yards of print paper per week—at least twelve thousand per week and at times more than thirty thousand. On nights when there was an especially large output, three outside blueprinters would be hired to make copies.

Anywhere from two dozen to five dozen copies of each blueprint were produced, measuring on average three feet by five feet. Some tracings were printed so often that they wore out and had be redrawn two or three times during the night. Every morning a station wagon was loaded with hundreds of prints to be delivered all around the job to Army engineers, contractors, subcontractors, foremen, inspectors, field coordinators, draftsmen, and many others. "The stuff was pushed out by the score," van der Gracht said.

The builders and Army engineers did not always await delivery. "They went in at night and took their plans while they were finishing them and got going," Furman said. "It was that fast." McShain himself would go down to the hangar with Hauck early some mornings to grab the latest plans.

"We were designing just one step ahead of the pile drivers, as it were," van der Gracht recalled. "Construction was always on the heels of design," was the way Renshaw put it. Indeed, construction sometimes got ahead of design, often enough that Luther Leisenring, the architect in charge of the specifications group, took to referring to building specs as "historical records"; by the time they were written, there was often something else already in the building.

"How big should I make that beam across the third floor?" architect Allen Dickey was asked by a colleague.

"I don't know," Dickey replied. "They installed it yesterday."

To curb the design chaos, a separate field force of 117 architects, engineers, and inspectors worked at the construction site; they were divided into six teams, one for each section of the building and another for the grounds. The field architects were granted unusual authority to make decisions on the spot. They served as advisers and interpreters at the construction site, peering at blueprints, gauging the intent of the designers, and trying to reconcile differences between the plans on paper and the realities on the ground. Construction foremen waited impatiently at their elbows for the verdict, ready to relay it to construction gangs, bulldozer operators, or pile drivers. Revisions made in the field were sometimes memorialized in the plans after the fact, and sometimes not.

The architects soon developed an esprit de corps—"it was a tremendously good working gang," van der Gracht said. It helped that they had a common enemy. An unnamed draftsman composed and distributed a bit of doggerel aimed at their primary tormenter, Somervell:

> *Oh the General from the Arkansaw*
> *Has a Jinx for raising H—*
> *And he thinks his Thoughts are the Blooming Law*
> *And Holy Gospel just as well*
>
> *He swears that Things which can't be Done*
> *Are the Things you got to do*
> *And cussed be the Sons of Gun*
> *Who hint that they can't put it through*
>
> *For the General totes a six inch Jaw*
> *And the air around him Reeks*
> *"Get them Jitters out of your Craw*
> *Gimme them Plans in three more weeks"*
>
> *If I had my way, if I had my say,*
> *I'd . . . send that General right way*
> *Straight back to the Arkansaw*

Such verse-mongering was one of the few outlets the draftsmen had—with work days that sometimes stretched to eighteen hours, there was almost no time for a social life. Van der Gracht would make it home around eleven at night to a little white wooden shack in the woods on the crest of a hill on North Nash Street in Arlington Heights, overlooking Arlington National Cemetery. The owner, Bessie Christian, rented it to him for almost nothing—the shack was practically bare and there was no heat and little electricity. Before falling asleep, van der Gracht would relax by working on the design of a little house she hoped to build on the site.

A price to pay

Speed was everything, and there was a price to pay. The lowest laborers paid the most. The morning of October 15 finally brought slightly cooler weather and some scattered showers, though not nearly enough to end the monthlong drought. At the construction site around 11 A.M., Lloyd Brown, an assistant foreman, assigned six men to load a concrete batch hopper into a truck so it could be moved to a new location on the site. Among the workers was Vernon S. Janney, a twenty-nine-year-old laborer from Appeal, a small town in southern Maryland. Janney was black, like many of the laborers.

The hopper was one of eight scattered around the site for mixing and pouring batches of concrete. It weighed a ton, literally, measuring more than six feet high and six feet square at the top. A Moto-Crane on the site could easily have lifted the heavy hopper and was there for such chores, but it was not immediately available and there was no time to wait. Janney and the five other laborers struggled mightily to lift the hopper to the bed of the truck, and then the weight got to be too much. "Six men had it and it slipped halfway up and fell to the ground and when it rolled over, it caught Janney," Brown reported. "It only glanced off the other men."

Janney lay on the ground, grievously hurt. Another man was also injured. An ambulance was called and did not come. A second ambulance was called and both finally arrived at the same time. Janney was taken to Providence Hospital in Washington, where he lingered for a few hours before dying around four that afternoon.

Janney's death was the first fatality on the project, but the accident was hardly unusual. In October alone there were thirty-five accidents serious enough to take men off the job, eight of them with broken bones. By early November labor leaders were publicly warning of an "alarming accident rate" on the job. The rush nature of the job and the War Department's failure to enforce its own safety rules were to blame, said John Locher, secretary of the Building Trades Council.

After *The Washington Post* on November 6 reported a claim by union officials that there had been "several deaths and many injuries, including broken legs and broken backs," the chief of the Construction Division's safety section launched an investigation. The union's claim was wrong as to the specifics—there had been as yet one death and no broken backs—but the truth was hardly comforting.

"Regardless of the exaggerated statement of casualties by union officials, it is a fact that the War Department Building project has had a decidedly bad accident experience since the work began," the safety section chief, Lloyd A. Blanchard, reported to Groves on November 7. The accident rate was four times higher than the average for Army construction projects, and accidents on this job tended to be more serious than on other projects.

"There seems to be an attitude that speed is the only essential and that accidents are an unavoidable by-product thereof," the safety section chief wrote. Blanchard placed much of the blame on McShain. The contractor ignored War Department safety requirements and had refused to hire his own safety engineer and establish a safety program. "Recommendations are not accepted willingly nor adopted promptly," Blanchard told Groves.

Groves ordered Renshaw to reduce the number and severity of accidents. "The accident experience on your project is far worse than" anywhere else in the country, Groves wrote. "The need is obvious for your immediate attention to this problem."

Nobody told Renshaw or McShain to slow down, however.

When push came to shove

Somervell had picked the worst time imaginable to build such an enormous structure on such a fast schedule. With the nation on a war footing, many basic items normally used in construction were in short supply, and the situation was only getting worse. Of all the tremendous problems confronting the Army as it raced to build camps, barracks, munitions plants, training grounds, and a new headquarters, "materials presented the greatest single challenge," in the estimation of Army historians Lenore Fine and Jesse A. Remington. The War Department in August had ordered the Army to take all steps possible to eliminate the use of critical materials in construction projects. At the top of the restricted list were metals such as steel, aluminum, tin, copper, and copper alloys such as brass and bronze, and zinc, used for galvanizing iron and steel.

Industries and citizens across the land had to restrict use of critical materials, and congressmen and reporters were on high alert for any examples of waste, particularly by the War Department. The Office of Production Management, established by Roosevelt to oversee industrial mobilization and holding broad control over critical material, cast a suspicious eye on the new War Department building. The Army and Navy Munitions Board had granted the project the second-highest priority rating—A-1-B— meaning it had greater access to scarce materials than most military construction. But with the public spotlight on the project, the pressure to conserve critical materials was great. "Although we had a high priority, we very seldom used it," said Bob Furman, to whom the task of finding substitute materials often fell.

Steel was most critical of all. In many respects, the design of the building had been dictated by the shortage of steel, which was needed for ships, tanks, munitions, and much else. The main reason Somervell had ordered a low building—even more important than to keep the building in harmony with the low Washington skyline—was that a tall building would require a steel frame. Bergstrom's design for a reinforced concrete frame reduced the amount of steel needed from 65,000 tons to 27,000 tons. The 38,000 tons of steel saved was more than enough to build a battleship, War Department publicists were quick to point out.

Steel was being saved in other ways. There would be virtually no elevators, which would eat up space in the building and require costly equipment and steel. Instead, floors would be connected by stairways and long concrete ramps, wide enough to accommodate trucks. General Marshall approved of the ramps, as much for reasons of physical fitness as saving steel.

To further save on steel, supply ducts for the heating and ventilation were made of prefabricated asbestos tube. Asbestos—also used in the building for pipes, ceilings, and floor coverings—would not be recognized until decades later as a threat to workers' health. The return ducts were of black iron, which was plentiful but tended to rust, and galvanized iron was used only where condensation was expected. Even drainage pipes were concrete instead of cast iron.

It was impossible to build without some metal. Furman was often sent on scavenger hunts to factories around the country. It sometimes took a bit of subterfuge to divert the critical materials. "I went out and made arrangements to steal metal from an [airplane] contract that had high priority, and I did get some metal, but it didn't take more than three weeks for somebody to reverse it," Furman said. "Somebody wrote a letter and next thing you know we were looking somewhere else. We were under instructions not to interfere, although when push came to shove . . . we did use our high priority."

Officials with the Office of Production Management discovered that plans called for two hundred tons of copper to be used, mostly for bronze doors and flagpole trimmings, and demanded a conference with Somervell. To put pressure on the general in advance of the meeting, OPM officials leaked information to the Washington *Star*. "It will perhaps surprise citizens . . . to know that War Department plans, as of today, call for well over 400,000 pounds of copper for ornamental purposes," the *Star* reported November 6.

The OPM leak had its desired effect: Somervell erupted at the negative publicity.

At the conference with OPM officials several days later, Somervell readily agreed to eliminate the bronze doors, and said he would accept substitutes recommended by OPM provided they "did not increase the cost of the building or present a sleazy appearance or result in an unsound structure."

The gold rush

The building's construction had triggered a gold rush among suppliers. The sheer size of the project meant that enormous volumes of materials were at stake, enough to make or break companies and even industries. The biggest battle was over window sashes—with 7,748 windows in the building, no trifling matter. When the War Department chose steel, which was cheaper than wood, manufacturers of wood sashes bitterly complained. Somervell ignored them: "Buy the windows on the bids that you've got now," he ordered Renshaw on November 10.

But OPM chief Donald Nelson, concerned about the use of steel, ordered that the bidding be reopened and reworded to give wood a better chance. The new bids were opened November 18, and steel, again with the lowest price, was selected. Protests from the wood industry again flooded into the White House, Congress, and the War Department, accusing Somervell of everything short of treason. Stimson turned aside the complaints of senators and congressmen from lumber states, telling them steel window sashes would save at least $100,000.

Other members of Congress hounded Somervell and the War Department to hawk their own states' wares. Margaret Chase Smith of Maine sent Somervell a letter to "call your attention to Maine granite." Robert Ramspeck of Georgia wanted specifications rewritten to give granite from Stone Mountain a better chance. Josiah Bailey of North Carolina made a pitch for Mount Airy granite. Francis E. Walter of Pennsylvania told Somervell the nation would be well-served if slate quarried in his home district were used for the baseboards and roof of the building.

Somervell did his best to appease the politicians without caving in outright. Ramspeck was told that while Georgia granite was not the right color for the steps, they would try to find a place for it elsewhere in the building. Somervell assured Walter that "every consideration will be given to slate," and when Bergstrom decided to use slate for the roof, the news was immediately telephoned to Walter's office.

Roosevelt himself was unable to refrain from trying to alter the plans to keep labor happy. On December 4, 1941, Somervell received a confidential note from Pa Watson, the president's military aide:

> The President, after his conversation with Mr. Harry Bates of the Building Trades Union, told me to ask you why you could not use less concrete with steel reinforcement and more brick—and that surely the inside curtain wall could be made of red brick painted white. He was told by Harry Bates that this would save considerable money, and conserve steel.

An exasperated Somervell refused to accept the presidential interference. During the debate over using architectural concrete on the exterior walls in October, Somervell told Watson, the president had so emphatically disapproved of brick "that the plans were entirely redrawn." A substantial number of the curtain—non-load-bearing—walls had already been poured with concrete, Somervell added, and the plans for their design were complete. "The change could not be made except at the expense of considerable delay and money and in addition to this, the use of paint on the exterior would introduce a continuing maintenance cost," he told Watson.

Somervell was, of course, too wise to politics to leave Roosevelt hanging with a powerful labor leader like Bates. He had a suggestion that would mollify everyone. The interior partition walls were supposed to be built from metal lath—sheets of perforated metal serving as a base for plaster. Somervell proposed building them instead with tile, which, happily enough, would require the services of bricklayers. "[W]e can give the bricklayers an amount of work about equivalent to what they would obtain" if the curtain walls were made of brick, Somervell reported to Watson December 5. "I feel sure that Harry Bates will be satisfied with this solution," he added.

Roosevelt was pleased. "Will you tell Harry Bates?" the president asked Watson.

You can kind of out-slicker yourself

It was quite a balancing act for Somervell. Nor was it his only one.

On December 1, 1941, Roosevelt signed legislation that stripped the Quartermaster Corps of its historical role directing Army construction in the United States, giving that responsibility to the Corps of Engineers. The Construction Division was being transferred to the Corps of Engineers. For the Quartermaster Corps, it was a most bitter blow, one that Somervell, as chief of the Construction Division, had surreptitiously helped orchestrate.

The Corps of Engineers played a unique role as a builder of public works in America—canals, river and harbor works, railroads, public buildings, and coastal fortifications, among others. The Corps also had an unusual role in the nation's capital, even helping govern the city. Since 1878, an Engineer had held a seat on the presidentially appointed three-man commission that administered the city. The Corps had helped build many of the monuments, public buildings, parks, and water projects in Washington, most prominently the U.S. Capitol and Library of Congress, and it had completed the Washington Monument. Now it was taking over construction of the Pentagon.

The transfer was the culmination of a decades-long battle that had raged since World War I but had its origins in the Revolutionary War, when Congress assigned the chief engineer the job of building roads, bridges, and fortifications, and the quartermaster general the work of quartering the Army. This division of labor—putting the Corps of Engineers in charge of combat construction and construction overseas and the Quartermasters in charge of building shelter for the troops and facilities for the Army at home—had been largely followed for more than 150 years.

Occasional proposals over the years to consolidate all Army construction under the Engineers had been defeated, but the Quartermaster Corps' poor performance after the emergency was declared in May 1941 had brought the controversy to a full boil. There were calls in Congress to transfer all construction to the Corps of Engineers. Others, including George Marshall, favored making the Construction Division a separate corps, commanded by Somervell.

In mid-1941, Michael J. Madigan, special adviser to Stimson on construction affairs, was directed to resolve the matter once and for all. Madigan was a politically astute New Yorker, a onetime construction water boy who had made a million dollars engineering New York City municipal projects. From the start of his investigation into who should control domestic military construction, Madigan operated on the assumption that the Quartermaster Corps needed to be replaced. Its Construction Division was already being run as a de facto Engineer outfit by Somervell, who had installed many brother Engineer officers in key positions since taking over.

Madigan quietly approached Somervell, who was only too glad to help, regularly advising Madigan, feeding him information, and lending officers to assist in the study. No one else in the Quartermaster Corps was apprised of Madigan's investigation or Somervell's role in it. Even Major General Edmund Gregory, the Quartermaster General and Somervell's ostensible boss, was officially kept in the dark, though he learned of it through the grapevine. After three months' study, Madigan concluded, unsurprisingly, that it would be best to put all construction under the Engineers. Marshall and Stimson approved his recommendation in August, and Congress and the president soon gave their approval.

Somervell was delighted. He fully expected to be the new Chief of Engineers, replacing Major General Julian Schley upon his retirement, and pressed Madigan to use his influence with Stimson to get him the job. Somervell's confidence aside, there were many strikes against him. At age forty-nine he was too young for a job seen as the pinnacle of an Engineer's career. Just as important, Somervell's enemies in the Army were growing in number. It did not help that Schley completely mistrusted him. "Officially, the whereabouts of this man is unknown to me," Schley had written across Somervell's last efficiency-rating form.

Somervell's bid for chief went nowhere. Instead, an Army board recommended Brigadier General Eugene Reybold, the Army chief of supply, a decision ratified by Roosevelt. Calm and collected, with a benign look behind his steel-rimmed glasses, Reybold, fifty-seven, was not a hard-charger. Groves considered him "lazy and confused." Reybold's philosophy seemed to be that what you cannot change, you must endure—and he was not one to bust a gasket trying to change things. Reybold was virtually Somervell's antithesis, which is perhaps why the board chose him. Gregory, for one, took quiet satisfaction in Somervell's failed maneuverings. "You can kind of out-slicker yourself if you go too far with that kind of stuff," he later said.

Somervell was "mad as hell" not to get the job, according to Madigan. Somervell had reason to be upset. The consolidation he had helped engineer effectively eliminated his own job as chief constructing quartermaster. Somervell began scheming to create a new job, proposing that a position be created for a deputy chief of engineers to oversee all military and civilian construction. He suggested the job be filled by a major general, a neat way for Somervell to pick up a second star.

Reybold, though, had no interest in either creating the position or naming Somervell to that or any other job. He viewed Somervell as "a steamroller" and realized if he were deputy, it was Reybold himself who would likely be flattened. Reybold wanted Somervell out of the Construction Division altogether. He chose Brigadier General Thomas M. Robins, a respected veteran engineer, to be the new chief of the division.

General Marshall considered the antipathy toward Somervell a natural reaction to someone who was shaking things up, and he was eager to keep him on hand. Taking a suggestion from Patterson, Marshall on Novem-

ber 25 appointed Somervell to fill Reybold's old position as Army chief of
supply, or G-4. It was a critical position for the gathering Army, with responsibility for preparing plans and supervising supply services.

Yet Somervell was crushed by the turn of events. He considered the
new job a career setback, a position with low visibility and little opportunity to shine. His wife was just as disappointed. "We are right back where
we started from," Anna Somervell said.

Somervell would nonetheless remain, for all practical purposes, the
boss of the War Department headquarters project. Everyone—Renshaw,
McShain, Groves, even Roosevelt—still brought all important matters related to the building to him. The project was so thoroughly identified with
Somervell that it did not seem to matter that he was outside the chain of
command. Just as likely, no one else wanted the headache.

Speed is paramount

By the beginning of December 1941, three thousand men were working the
job during the day. Brilliant flares lit up the work at night, and another
thousand men were pouring concrete and driving piles through the evening
and overnight shifts.

A letter had been delivered at the site recently to Captain Charles
Smith, Renshaw's operations officer. The curious thing was how it had
been addressed: "The Pentagon Building." The project was still known in
the newspapers and Army documents by the clunky term "New War Department Building in Arlington." But some of the construction workers
and Army officers had taken to referring to the place as the "Pentagonal
Building," or sometimes the "Pentagon Building." The letter was the
strongest evidence yet the name was entering the official lexicon. "He got
the letter," Bob Furman recalled. "It was the first time we realized that the
post office recognized something called the Pentagon."

From above, it looked as if the Pentagon was racing along. Aerial photographs in December showed steady progress since the October day Furman took his surreptitious ride aboard the Goodyear blimp. Three sections
of the pentagon were now emerging from the ground, and the crisscross
pattern of pile caps outlined a portion of a fourth. Blocks of limestone
were being hung with steel hangers onto outer brick walls to form the

façade. A forest of cranes, tower hoists, and construction platforms had risen from the ground. Mountains of supplies—cement, lumber, and reinforcing steel—were piling up.

But the numbers told another story. An audit completed November 15 showed only 2 percent of the construction had been completed. At that rate—roughly 1 percent of the work per month—it would take more than eight years to finish the building.

That assessment was obviously too pessimistic, but it was clear changes were needed. When construction had started in September, the Construction Division had restricted how much concrete could be poured to prevent unsightly shrinkage cracks. Similarly, the division guidelines dictated an interval of several days after a slab had been poured before a new slab could be placed adjacent to ensure the first one had cured properly.

By late November, with the project falling further behind schedule, the restrictions were seen as meddlesome niceties. Colonel Farrell—the veteran engineer assigned to find ways to speed the work—urged they be dropped. "It is essential to the progress of the job that pouring be permitted to the maximum extent possible because even moving as rapidly as possible, it will be extremely difficult to meet the scheduled completion date," Farrell reported to Somervell on November 25.

Farrell recommended that workers be allowed to pour concrete slabs continuously from exterior wall to court wall and from expansion joint to expansion joint, enormous pours measuring 210 feet by 210 feet. Likewise, the contractor should be authorized to pour adjacent slabs without waiting. "In view of the urgency for completing the structure, we should take the few cracks and live with them," Farrell said.

Somervell agreed, ordering Renshaw to pour new slabs as big and as fast as possible, cracks be damned. "Speed of construction is paramount," the general told Renshaw.

A new complication had arisen: The Commission of Fine Arts was considering turning the nerve center for the coming war into an artists' colony, complete with the world's largest mural. At its meeting November 14, Commissioner Henry Varnum Poor, an accomplished and exuberant artist who had painted murals in fresco in the Justice and Interior department buildings in Washington, proposed setting aside the new War Department building's five-acre courtyard as a "court of mural painting and sculpture." The five inner courtyard concrete walls, stretching 360 feet in each direction, would be ideal surfaces for murals, Poor said.

"Here would be brought together, working on a carefully harmonized and unified architectural plan, the best mural artists and sculptors of the Nation, and the result of this harmonious but competitive work would bring to this one huge courtyard the finest and most inspired work American artists could give," Poor proposed. The commission intended to take up the matter at its next meeting in December.

Renshaw was also dealing with nitpicking interference from higher-ups in the Construction Division. Rushing to keep up with the high pace at the work site, his office submitted requests for construction materials the moment the need arose. True, it would be more efficient to wait so that orders and delivery dates could be combined. But Renshaw and his men were desperate to get materials to the site as quickly as possible. Working on a Saturday in early December 1941, Renshaw received a memo scolding him about a requisition for delivery of hard green oak bridge timber that day, "which . . . date it is understood, is not a working day," the memo lectured. The date was Saturday, December 6, 1941.

The Pentagon on December 4, 1941, three days before Pearl Harbor.

CHAPTER 9

THEY WOULDN'T DARE ATTACK PEARL HARBOR

Some deviltry

The tails set Bob Furman back $110. For a first lieutenant making about $1,800 a year, that was quite a sum, but the occasion demanded it. John Mc-Shain had invited Furman to attend a formal party the builder hosted in Philadelphia on the evening of December 6. It had been an elegant affair, dinner and dancing, a nice diversion from the pressure of the Pentagon project. The Army lieutenant drove back to Washington in his Ford the following day, a crisp wintry Sunday, listening to the car radio.

In Washington, John McCloy went in early to War Department head-quarters at the Munitions Building. Intercepted communications from Japan had raised uneasy suspicions that something was afoot in the Pacific, but no one knew what. George Marshall went for his regular morning horseback ride on the grounds of the old Arlington Farm next to the construction site, before a scheduled meeting in the afternoon at the White House with Roosevelt. Henry Stimson went to the State Department to confer with Secretary of State Cordell Hull and Secretary of the Navy Frank Knox about the latest disturbing cable intercepts from Tokyo to the Japanese embassy in Washington. Afterward Stimson went home to his estate at Woodley for lunch. "Hull is very certain that the Japs are planning some deviltry and we are all wondering where the blow will strike," Stimson recorded in his diary.

McCloy had read the intelligence intercepts too. "I was sure something was going to happen," he later said. Perhaps the Japanese would attack Singapore or somewhere else in the Far East. But early in the afternoon he was approached by a military aide from the general staff. "Mr. McCloy, there's a report around that they're attacking Pearl Harbor," the aide said.

"Don't kid me, they're not attacking Pearl Harbor," McCloy replied. ". . . They wouldn't dare attack Pearl Harbor."

The Japanese had dared, and succeeded, though the first reports did not convey the full magnitude of the disaster that had struck the U.S. Pacific Fleet and Army in Hawaii. At the White House, presidential press secretary Steve Early announced at 2:22 P.M. that the Japanese had bombed Pearl Harbor. Bulletins went out on the wire services and were aired immediately on the radio, interrupting broadcasts of symphony and swing and drama and sports. The shocking word came over Furman's car radio. There was nothing he could do but keep driving.

The news caught Washington at a placid moment. The winter sun, battling clouds, cast an odd gray light on the marble of the Lincoln Memorial. A sailor and his girlfriend strolled across Dupont Circle. Downtown, parents were lined up with their children in front of theaters awaiting Sunday matinees, little girls gathering their skirts to keep them from flying in the breeze. Across the river, a skeleton Sunday crew was pouring concrete at the Pentagon project.

The largest gathering in Washington was at rickety Griffith Stadium, where a crowd of 27,102 watched the Washington Redskins quarterback, Slingin' Sammy Baugh, rifle a pass downfield as he led the football team against the Philadelphia Eagles in the last game of the season. Word of the attack reached the press box in the first quarter, but Redskins owner George Preston Marshall refused to air the news over the stadium loudspeaker—it was against his policy to announce nonsports news. Nonetheless the crowd stirred at the steady stream of announcements requesting this admiral or that cabinet secretary to report to their offices immediately. Rumors of war spread from row to row through the green grandstands and bleachers, and by the fourth quarter, when Baugh threw two touchdown passes to bring Washington back to a 20–14 win, many seats were vacant.

Helen McShane Bailey had sat down with her housemates in their 16th Street apartment for a Sunday dinner. She had arrived in Washington in April from her home in Colorado Springs, one of thousands of "government girls" who had come from across the country to work for the federal government. The twenty-five-year-old had been assigned to work in Marshall's office at the Munitions Building. The news from Pearl Harbor arrived while Bailey and her housemates were still eating. One of the residents, a young man with a car, broke the stunned silence. He was driving to the Japanese embassy, if anybody wanted to come.

Automobiles choked Massachusetts Avenue in front of the embassy, and the sidewalk was lined with policemen. A crowd of onlookers milled around sullenly. Smoke was rising from the back of the embassy, where Japanese diplomats were burning secret papers in the garden. "We all looked at each other and knew our lives had changed forever," Bailey recalled many years later.

Inside the Munitions Building, McCloy was casting about for some way to respond. "I did not know what you did as assistant secretary of war when Pearl Harbor was attacked, but I thought that we were at war, and that we had to protect the president," he later said. McCloy consulted with Army chief of intelligence Major General Sherman Miles, a descendant of William Tecumseh Sherman, and Brigadier General Ulysses S. Grant III, Somervell's old rival in the Corps of Engineers. The three men went to see Knox to arrange for a cordon of Marines to surround the White House. An aide in the Office of Naval Intelligence, Marine Lieutenant Colonel John W. Thomason, Jr., a Southerner and author of a Civil War history, brought the delegation to see the Secretary of the Navy. "Here's the whole goddamn Union Army," Thomason told Knox.

At the White House, Secretary of the Treasury Henry Morgenthau nervously scanned the skies for German bombers and ordered the Secret Service to sandbag the entrances. Guards patrolled around the building with Thompson submachine guns, and when night fell the grounds were lit up with bright red lanterns. There was talk of putting tanks in front of the White House, but Marshall thought that unnecessary. Special police were dispatched to guard the Washington Aqueduct against sabotage. A partial blackout was ordered for downtown Washington and streetlights were dimmed. Machine guns were placed around the Munitions Building and soldiers took up around-the-clock positions there. By Sunday evening, armed guards were patrolling the Pentagon construction site.

Furman arrived home late in the day to the house where he rented a room in Aurora Hills in Arlington. Orders had been broadcast on the radio for all Army and Navy officers in Washington to report to duty Monday morning—in uniform, the first time in years for many of them. Furman hastily stuffed the formal clothes he had worn to McShain's party into the back of his closet. "I never got to use those tails again," he later said.

Absolute necessity

There was an air of expectancy among the three thousand construction workers reporting to work at the Pentagon project Monday morning, Donald Walker among them.

Walker had been on the job only a week as a rodman for the Kenmar Steel Construction Company, one of McShain's subcontractors. He was a strapping nineteen-year-old with slicked-back blond hair, blind in his right eye since a stone was shot into it from a toy cork gun when he was five. Walker was a journeyman with the job of putting reinforcing steel into concrete beams and columns for $1.62½ per hour. He had graduated from Mount Vernon High School in neighboring Fairfax County and was now working with four hundred other rodmen, many of them experienced steel workers who had come from across the country. Before Sunday, Walker had never heard of Pearl Harbor, and he was only dimly aware of how it was going to "change the lives of everyone."

Shortly after noon, Walker took his lunch break, sitting in his pride and joy, a brand-new light-blue 1941 Ford convertible he had recently bought for $1,125. Walker turned on the radio as he ate his sandwich. A news report was broadcast from the U.S. Capitol, where Franklin Roosevelt, cloaked in his blue Navy cape, had just arrived in a closed black limousine, accompanied by Secret Service men with Tommy guns under their arms. After a stirring welcome in the House chamber, the president addressed a joint session of Congress at 12:31 P.M. Grimly, his patrician voice ringing with indignation, Roosevelt asked for a declaration of war against Japan. "No matter how long it may take us to overcome this premeditated invasion, the American people in their righteous might will win through to absolute victory," the president said, triggering roars of approval from the legislators.

"Glad of it, the dirty rats," Walker thought to himself. He finished lunch and rejoined his crew, sharing the news with the other workers. There were no cheers or bravado at the construction site. Yet the atmosphere at the project was transformed.

The decision was made almost immediately to expand the size of the Pentagon building. The principals—McShain, Bergstrom, and Renshaw among them—were soon huddled in conferences with War Department officials. "It was at once apparent that a maximum of office space in the new building would have to be provided," Somervell eventually explained.

The agreement that Frederic Delano and the White House had painstakingly crafted with Somervell to limit the building to twenty thousand occupants was unceremoniously pitched. "To meet the rapidly developing military requirements our originally announced plans to reduce the size of the building had to be discarded," Groves later wrote.

Somervell had never really reduced the size much anyway, when construction started, it was planned to be 4.4 million square feet, as opposed to the original proposal of 5.1 million square feet. Now, however, all bets were off. The national outcry that accompanied the Japanese attack provided an excellent opportunity to build an even larger headquarters without bothersome consultations with the planning and fine arts commissions, or even Congress.

Congressmen who in November had criticized Somervell about construction costs could not have been more accommodating when Construction Division officers appeared before a House committee on December 8. "We were just given a blank check," an officer later said. "That's how quickly the damn thing changed." The Commission of Fine Arts beat a hasty retreat from the idea of turning the inner courtyard into a training ground for aspiring muralists and sculptors, dropping the plan at its December meeting.

Within days, the War Department approved $3 million to excavate an additional half-million square feet of space in the basement. Renshaw requested and received the funds to pay for it. That was just the start of step-by-step additions over the following weeks and months that would increase the size of the Pentagon beyond what anyone had imagined.

It's not fair to us to expect the impossible

The pressure had been high from the outset, given the building's outlandish size and Somervell's fantastic schedule, but Pearl Harbor had magnified the stakes. "When we began this building it was considered very desirable," Groves wrote not long afterward. With the Japanese attack, he added, "it has become an absolute necessity."

At Somervell's insistence—and over the protests of the architects and builders—the schedule was moved up soon after Pearl Harbor. Somervell wanted twice as much space—one million square feet—ready for occupancy by April 1, a month earlier than the previous deadline. That was little more than three and a half months away.

It seemed an impossible demand, yet Renshaw could not refuse Somervell. The price of speeding construction would be $1.5 million, Renshaw estimated, much of that for overtime. Somervell waved off concerns about extra costs; the only thing that mattered was time. "Instructions were issued to expedite the work in every possible way," Groves reported.

Bergstrom had to be brought along kicking and screaming. "[T]he chief architect is unwilling to commit himself to such a schedule," Renshaw reported to Somervell on December 22. "It will be necessary for me to take more active control of the architect's activities but I can and will do so."

Renshaw told Somervell the new deadline "has the concurrence of the contractors," but that was not exactly true. McShain had only reluctantly agreed to move the date up to April 15 and was beside himself when Groves informed him on December 23 that the deadline was now the beginning of April.

"April first? It's going up," McShain sputtered. "Well, it's almost a physical impossibility, particularly if we have a stretch of bad weather. . . . It's not fair to us to expect the impossible."

"I don't know why not," Groves replied.

"That's quite complimentary [of] you and I appreciate it," McShain said. He paused. "I feel you don't mean it as a compliment."

"No, I don't," Groves said.

Putting the screws to the delegees

Demanding the impossible was not new for Groves; on the Pentagon project, it was becoming routine.

The strategy was simple, as later explained by his son Richard Groves, who followed his father into the Corps of Engineers and retired as a lieutenant general: "If somebody tells you it takes a week, tell them to do it in five days. When he agrees to that, tell him three."

Groves learned it from Somervell, master of the art. Somervell had an uncanny ability to "almost read your mind" and figure out a person's weak points, Major General John Hardin, who worked with both men, told Army historians. "And Groves absorbed a lot of that and his procedures were based on the pressure tactics which Somervell had used to such success." Groves's "philosophy was to delegate wherever he could, and then put the screws to the delegees," said Brigadier General William Wannamaker, another Corps of Engineers officer.

Groves was not a screamer and did not use profanity; instead, he would make infuriatingly sarcastic comments in a quiet, low-key voice. His technique was to make people "awful mad at him," so pride would keep them working. Groves once assigned Bob Furman to take care of a problem, and when Furman came back with his report, Groves pulled from his desk a report by another officer to whom he had assigned the same problem. "That was a typical Groves technique," Furman said. "It made everybody mad." The sardonic humor Groves employed to incite his subordinates was often so dry that many missed the joke. (Physicist Edward Teller, who would work with the Army officer on the Manhattan Project, was shocked decades later when he read Groves's memoir and learned that he enjoyed laughing at himself. "Neither through contact nor through rumor did I ever learn of Groves' sense of humor," Teller wrote.)

"Don't you ever praise anyone for a job well done?" another Construction Division officer once asked Groves. "I don't believe in it," Groves replied. "No matter how well something is being done, it can always be done better and faster."

Groves had stenographers record and type transcripts of all his telephone conversations with subordinates, with a copy then sent "to each officer responsible for the fulfillment of a promise," he later explained. It was

Major Gar Davidson's job to take the transcripts and follow up to ensure "that all commitments were honored." Davidson was Groves's enforcer, his "eyes out in the field," as he put it. "If a guy needed a needle, why, I had to reflect Groves' desires," Davidson later said. Square-jawed and athletic, Davidson was a perfect man for the job. He had been head coach for the West Point football team from 1932 to 1937 and was known for favoring initiative over spit and polish.

Like one of his few heroes, the hard-bitten Union general William Tecumseh Sherman, Groves preferred action to introspection. Groves "drove himself hard, and he drove his subordinates hard, and he was tough, and he didn't take any excuses," Davidson said. "He was demanding, and demanding of results. Not how, but results." If anyone failed him, Groves "could really saw them off at the ankles."

John McShain bore a heavy part of the pressure. The day after his formal party on December 6, the builder had been relaxing with his family at his home on Church Road in Philadelphia when he heard the news of the Japanese attack. "He was absolutely stunned, shocked," recalled his daughter, Polly. McShain knew at once what it meant for the project. "I think the Pentagon was the greatest challenge he ever had, because he was conscious of the desperation of the War Department," Polly McShain said. "To conduct a war when your resources are so scattered was a terrible, terrible situation. . . . It was really a matter of life or death in many ways."

McShain suffered much of his life from depression and was subject to huge mood swings. Normally buoyant and jovial, he would sometimes become deeply morose. In the 1950s, he would be diagnosed as bipolar and would undergo a series of electrical shock treatments. Through it all, his wife, Mary, was his steady rock. "My mother used to say she didn't know which was worse: trying to pull him out of the hole or trying to keep up with him when he was hyper," Polly McShain recalled. Years later, the daughter asked her father what the depression felt like. "It's as though you're in a dark, dark tunnel, and there's no light at the end," he replied.

The tunnel was looking very dark in the days and weeks after Pearl Harbor. "After Pearl Harbor, there was more and more pressure on my father to finish it as fast as possible," said Polly McShain. McShain was frustrated with Groves and Somervell, believing they did not fully appreciate the extraordinary difficulties of trying to marshal such a huge workforce in the face of constantly changing plans.

At least McShain was not in the Army. For Clarence Renshaw, there could be no escaping the wrath of Groves. "It was a very tough time for him," Renshaw's wife, Eileen, recalled more than sixty years later. "There was a sense of hurry, pressure, having to get the job done very quickly. He was dead-tired when he came home because his days were pretty long."

Renshaw found Groves's pressure techniques infuriating and insulting. "There was no love lost between them," Eileen Renshaw said. "They had different ways of thinking and doing." But Renshaw was too cool to rise to Groves's bait. "They got along only because Renshaw was very, very careful," Bob Furman said. "Groves was prickly. Renshaw was smart and careful with Groves. He'd document everything. He was careful how he spoke to Groves. He never gave Groves any reason to bite him."

Groves was often on the road inspecting other Army construction projects around the country, but that was little relief to Renshaw. Given the project's prominence and proximity to Washington—and the fact that Somervell was breathing down his neck—Groves was obsessed with the Pentagon. He assigned a special adviser, Henry S. Thompson—an old construction hand who had shared a tent with Henry Stimson when the two served in the New York National Guard at the time of the Spanish-American War—to spy on Renshaw. "He spent almost all of his time over there just wandering around," Groves recalled. Groves also instructed Gar Davidson to monitor the project. "The two of us kept our fingers on that and watched it," Davidson said. With Stimson's old tentmate and the former West Point football coach looking over his shoulder and reporting back to Groves, Renshaw had no peace.

Edwin Bergstrom, the chief architect, was feeling the pressure too, though not only from the need to hurriedly revise the building plans. On December 17, two letters were sent by registered mail to Bergstrom at his office in the Eastern Airlines hangar. They were from the board of directors for the American Institute of Architects, where Bergstrom had served as president for two terms up to May 1941, and before that as treasurer for six years. Upon Bergstrom's resignation, the board made some uncomfortable discoveries. During the two years of his presidency, the institute had paid $8,610 for Bergstrom's accommodations at the Hay-Adams House near the White House. Bergstrom's suite at the Hay-Adams was "purported to be an additional office" for the institute, a letter stated, though the board had never authorized the expenditure. Bergstrom had also billed the institute for $1,335 in personal expenses, when he was already a full-time salaried employee of the War Department. The board demanded Bergstrom immediately repay the $1,335 and provide a detailed explanation of the $8,610. Bergstrom—whether from the pressing demands of the Pentagon project or for lack of a good answer—did not reply.

Even Somervell, who had always thrived under pressure that had broken other men, was feeling heat. In the weeks after Pearl Harbor, Somervell had many worries beyond the Pentagon project. In his new, unsought job as chief of supply, Somervell was responsible for developing plans to arm and equip an Army that would soon spread across the globe. The news from overseas was unremittingly bad. In the Philippines, Japanese troops had landed in Lingayen Gulf and Lamon Bay on December 22 and were advancing toward Manila from the north and south; U.S. forces—including Pat Casey, Somervell's former design chief—were on the verge of withdrawing into the Bataan Peninsula.

Somervell's three girls were home for Christmas—Mary Anne, twenty-one, and Susan, nineteen, returning from Sweet Briar College in the foothills of Virginia's Blue Ridge Mountains, and Connie, fifteen, back from boarding school at St. Margaret's in Tappahannock, Virginia. But with the pressures of his job, it was not much of a holiday at Somervell's old tobacco farm south of Washington in Welcome, Maryland. Since Pearl Harbor, Somervell had been working late into every night, and rather than going home, he would sleep a few hours at a bachelor apartment in Woodley Park in Washington that he shared with several friends from World War I. On top of everything else, Somervell's wife, Anna, was not feeling well.

McShain went to see Somervell on December 22 to warn him of problems that threatened to delay the entire Pentagon project. McShain was shocked at the general's weary and downcast manner. "I never saw him so worried in my life," McShain said. "He was just sick."

"The whole load has really fallen right on my shoulders," Somervell told the builder.

"I had an awful lot to really go over with him but I didn't have the heart," McShain related to Groves the following day. "I . . . just dropped a couple hints to him that we weren't making the progress we expected to and to sort of give him a warning."

The obstacles they faced were endless. In McShain's view, the architectural concrete walls Bergstrom had insisted upon were holding up work everywhere around the project. Carpenters had built forms for more floor slabs, but concrete could not be poured; no men were available to put steel reinforcement in the slabs. They were all tied up working on Bergstrom's walls. "Now we've got miles of slab forms up there and no steel on them," McShain said. "It's a serious problem and I know it's going to throw us behind."

Despite Somervell's despondency, McShain could not resist making a final, bitter complaint to the general for siding with Bergstrom in the concrete dispute. "I think it's the one mistake you've made on the job," McShain told Somervell.

"Well, that's the only thing I didn't give in to you," Somervell replied.

"Well, that's the most important," McShain said. "I think you should have."

"You die hard, don't you?" Somervell replied.

Remedy this situation

What was really killing McShain was the continuing bottleneck with the plans. Any progress that Ides van der Gracht had made in his industrial-size drafting room was lost by the sudden need to redraw many of the plans after Pearl Harbor.

With fears of a Japanese or German attack on Washington, Somervell instructed engineers to figure out how to protect the building against enemy bombs. "There was an awful lot of scurrying about whether it wouldn't be much too dangerous to have windows because the Japs might come over and bomb it," van der Gracht later recalled. The shape and size of the building—"being such a big target," in Furman's words—compounded the worries.

A team of engineers recommended the building be constructed without any windows, just as Roosevelt had suggested three months earlier.

Large office bays should be crisscrossed with walls to reduce the impact of a blast, and the open light courts running between the rings should be built up, adding stability as well as more office space. The changes would convert "the whole building into an essentially blast and splinterproof structure," the engineers reported, and provide "protection against enemy gas." There was no need even to lose any work time in the event of falling bombs. "The occupants of the building may remain at their desks during raids," the engineers said. General Robins, chief of the Construction Division, estimated the changes would cost a minimum of $2.5 million and delay completion of the building by at least two months.

The engineers also recommended a bomb shelter be built underground about a quarter-mile northwest of the building, connected via tunnel, to serve as a headquarters command post in the event of attack. Somervell agreed to the blast protection and the bomb shelter on December 22, but the decision was being reviewed up the chain of command.

The pace inside the Eastern Airlines hangar was furious. At the order of Groves, Bergstrom put the draftsmen on overtime shifts. Luther Leisenring, the crusty sixty-six-year-old architect in charge of specifications for the Pentagon, suffered a heart attack in December and was carried out "on a slab," in his words. But try as they might, the draftsmen could not draw plans fast enough.

Shortly before Christmas, Paul Hauck, the project superintendent, warned McShain that the plans were falling "far behind the schedule." The lack of plans was not only retarding construction, it was preventing materials from being ordered. Plans for 523 different elements of the building were behind schedule, and specifications had not been issued for "critical portions of the work," Hauck complained.

The decision to excavate a bigger basement meant foundation plans for the last three sections of the building—C, D, and E—were on hold while the design was finalized. By the end of December, three pile rigs had to stop driving piles. The remaining rigs were not driving as many piles as usual, even though only about half of the forty thousand piles needed for the building had been sunk. Moreover, Hauck had been ready to begin interior finish work six weeks earlier, but could not start without plans.

On December 31, Hauck formally notified the Army that the builders were not at fault for the mounting delays. "We cannot assume the responsibility for the progress nor cost of this work because of the lack of necessary plans and specifications continually hampering proper progress and increasing cost beyond our control," Hauck wrote.

Groves received the news with his usual good cheer, which is to say, none at all. After inspecting the project on December 30, he wrote a blistering memo to Renshaw on New Year's Eve ordering the major to solve the problem. "The building will not be done on time, and even more important at the moment, the initial office space promised and vitally necessary cannot possibly be ready on time," Groves wrote. "This situation can and must be corrected promptly. You will report immediately what you propose to do to remedy this situation."

Groves offered no suggestions.

Oh, to hell with it

Yet all was not bleak as the sun rose on the Pentagon construction site on a cold New Year's Day, 1942.

As usual, progress looked better when viewed from above. On the morning of Thursday, January 1, Renshaw sent a messenger to Somervell with some new Army aerial photographs of the site taken on Christmas Eve. The vast amount of structure that had emerged from the bare earth in the three and a half months since construction began was breathtaking, no matter how serious the delays on the ground.

Somervell reviewed the photographs immediately. The sight seemed to lift the cloud hanging over the general's head. "I am encouraged by what I see," Somervell told Renshaw the same day, instructing the major to regularly send him photographs showing the work.

Progress was soon evident from the ground as well. About 12 percent of the building had been completed as of January 15, an Army auditor concluded, a vast improvement over the 2 percent recorded in the first audit two months earlier.

McShain and Hauck had come up with a novel way of building the Pentagon in the absence of plans: They used plans for Section A to build Section B. The drawings apparently served more as a guideline than as a strict road map for the contractors, who often improvised. More than a half-century later, architects and engineers renovating the Pentagon were astonished to find large sections of the building constructed for a while after Pearl Harbor for which drawings either do not exist or bear little relation to reality. "They just started to build without drawings," said Stacie Condrell, an architect for the Pentagon renovation program. "A lot of them they never went back to—and there's just a big area where it's fill-in-the-blank."

Still, there was no hope for the draftsmen to catch up until there was a final decision over whether or not they should try to protect the building against bombs by taking out the windows. Somervell had given quick approval, but the decision was still getting top-level review. Ides van der Gracht and the drafting force were helpless, watching the debate unfold like a tennis match: "The orders came through from on high: 'Cut out the windows.' Then they had second thoughts: 'No, leave them in, at least some of them.' And then the orders: 'Well, no they ought to be out anyway' . . . Then they decided, 'Oh to hell with it, let's have the windows.' "

Renshaw had received word on December 22 that the bomb-protection plan "is going to be approved 100 percent" and that he should "get going on it" immediately. Four days later, the order was revoked—the decision was being reviewed by the secretary of war. On New Year's Eve, word came that Stimson had given approval, and Renshaw was ordered to "proceed at once with construction."

Then Stimson, deciding Roosevelt needed to be informed, sent a memo to the president on January 2 seeking approval, calling the protective measures of "vital importance." But Roosevelt was skeptical, and that was enough to throw the entire matter into doubt again. Renshaw warned a "furious" Bergstrom that he might have to tear up the plans once more.

Each time the order was changed, construction on many parts of the building was suspended. Contracts had to be renegotiated. Materials being fabricated were taken out of production. New architectural, structural, mechanical, and electrical drawings were started. All the while, the clock was ticking and the deadline for occupancy getting closer.

"This indecision has resulted in delay and confusion both to the design forces and to the construction forces and has seriously retarded progress of construction on the building," Brigadier General Robins, chief of the Construction Division, warned Somervell. Lacking definite instructions from above, Robins unilaterally issued orders "to abandon, effective today, January 9, 1942, any attempts to make plans for the splinter proofing and to proceed with the original program." Somervell concurred.

In the end, fear of delay trumped fear of bombs. The proposal for the bomb shelter—a $1.3-million three-story underground building that Stimson told Roosevelt would be "designed to withstand bombs heavier than any known to exist"—was likewise scotched. If the War Department had its own bomb shelter, Roosevelt told Stimson, he would be obliged to provide shelters "for other Departments of the government that are equally vulnerable."

The resolution was a boost to the draftsmen. By January 21, a Corps of Engineers officer reported to Somervell that plans and specifications were no longer delaying construction progress.

Perhaps the biggest measure of progress on the Pentagon project was the money being spent. Construction expenditures in January were $5.1 million, more than three times the roughly $1.5 million that had been spent in December. "If you . . . think it is an easy task to spend a million dollars in a week," John McShain later said, "I would suggest that you try it sometime."

A growing army of workers

Most of the money was being spent on the growing army of workers at the site. More than six thousand men were on the job by mid-January; the number was jumping by the hundreds every week and would reach ten thousand by the beginning of March.

Any skilled laborer who presented himself was hired on the spot. Workers were coming from farther afield to meet the increasing demand. Hundreds of workers with specialty skills—reinforced steel workers in particular—came from around the country, sent by union locals answering the War Department's call for help. Others were simple laborers, both black and white, many from the rural South, looking for a steady job. Some were recent immigrants from Europe. Many of those descending on Arlington had abandoned their homes and uprooted their families because they could not afford to run two households. T. R. Anderson, a sheet metal worker, arrived from Texas pulling his family in a trailer.

Hank Neighbors, a seventeen-year-old Ohio boy whose family had moved to Arlington in search of work, got a job at the site as a payroll witness. He was fascinated by the stream of workers who lined up for their pay at the McShain office in the old factory building on Columbia Pike. Some were hardened and tough construction workers with years of experience under their belts. Others were marginal workers, men well past their prime or never in it to begin with. As more young men enlisted or were drafted into the military, many of the new workers were older: thirty-five, forty, fifty, or even sixty years of age and beyond. "There were so many jobs, so much need for people, that they were digging pretty deep," Neighbors said. "It was maybe not the ideal work bunch."

At the bottom, wielding shovels, were the laborers making eighty-five cents an hour, with an extra nickel an hour if they worked night shifts. Truck drivers made up to a dollar an hour. Cement finishers made $1.50 and bricklayers $1.75, while structural iron workers were fetching $2 an hour. Top workers such as ironworker foremen could make $2.35. "You could almost tell by looking at them, what kind of equipment they had, as to what their job was," Neighbors said.

The workers were paid in cash. The Corps of Engineers regularly sent a Brinks armored truck packed with greenbacks to the McShain payroll office. Two cashiers sat behind a table handing out money stuffed in pay envelopes. "They were operating on three different eight-hour shifts, so the place was busy night and day," Neighbors said. Every Friday afternoon, carpenter Joe Allan would pick up his pay envelope, normally with $65 in cash stuffed inside, minus a dollar and some change for Social Security, but increasingly with extra pay for overtime. In support of the war effort, the unions agreed that workers would be paid time and a half instead of double time, but it still meant costs soared.

As a payroll witness, Neighbors's job was to confirm that the workers received their money. "The key thing I dealt with were the workers who couldn't sign their names—and there were a lot of them," Neighbors said. "When the illiterate guy came up to get his pay, he was given cash, and if he couldn't sign his name, he'd put an X down there on the receipt, and then I would sign for him."

Thousands of men paid in cash spelled trouble. "We have thefts, we have robberies—you can't have [that many] men together without having disturbances," Renshaw complained. Lieutenant Furman was put in charge of a civilian guard force paid for by McShain. Four Arlington police officers who could arrest thieves, drunks, and other lawbreakers were also put on the payroll.

They had their hands full, particularly chasing out liquor salesmen. Men wearing big overcoats prowled the site and discreetly opened up their flaps, revealing fifteen pockets on both sides, each holding a half-pint flask bottle of Calvert's blended whiskey for sale. The booze salesmen were especially active on the night shifts. "We couldn't have liquor on the job," Furman said. "It was the sort of thing you had to beat." But it was impossible to catch them all.

McShain figured he could boost productivity by providing good, cheap meals, and he built an eighteen-thousand-square-foot wood-frame dining hall. It looked like an Army barracks, big enough to accommodate 750 workers at one seating, or 3,000 over the course of a lunch hour. Dining rooms fanned out on the sides. The kitchen and serving counters ran down the middle, and, like everything else on the job, it was an assembly-line setup, serving ten men a minute from each of four food lines. Sandwiches and pieces of pie sold for a dime apiece and coffee, milk, and soft drinks for a nickel. Seven canteens selling drinks and food were scattered across the site, and another twelve to fifteen were planned, enough to serve ten thousand workers. But at the rate the work force was growing, that would not be enough for long.

Even finding the canteens—or anything else—was getting to be a problem on the sprawling site. As the junior man in his steel gang, Donald Walker was sent every morning to get coffee from the canteen. "It was a nightmare," he said. "I used to get lost every day." Reporting for duty one morning, timekeeper Roy B. Pruitt could not find the engineer's shack where he normally worked. A bulldozer had moved it to a new location during the night.

All signifying chaos

The workers descending on the Pentagon project were landing in the midst of a maelstrom. "Washington in wartime has been variously described in numbers of pungent epigrams, all signifying chaos," wrote Dwight D. Eisenhower, a fifty-one-year-old Army brigadier general who arrived in the city a week after Pearl Harbor with orders to report to War Department headquarters.

By 1941, the population of the Washington metropolitan area had exceeded one million, up from 621,000 in 1930. During the ten years before the war, Washington grew far more rapidly than any other city in the nation, jumping by 36 percent, compared to an average increase of 4.7 percent for the ten largest cities in the country.

Yet none of this was preparation for the tumultuous changes brought by the onset of war. "A languid Southern town with a pace so slow that much of it simply closed down for the summer grew almost overnight into a crowded, harried, almost frantic metropolis struggling desperately to assume the mantle of global power," journalist David Brinkley wrote nearly a half-century later.

A war mindset had overtaken life in Washington. Concerned that Washington's white marble buildings made excellent targets, Representative Frederick Bradley of Michigan proposed on the House floor that they be camouflaged with dark-gray paint. Blackout drills were held regularly, with teams of civilian air-raid marshals browbeating homeowners who did not dim their lights.

The most immediate problem for new arrivals was the housing shortage. Terribly overcrowded before the outbreak of war, Washington and its environs were now completely overrun. New government employees were arriving at the rate of more than five thousand per month, and many of them were coming with families. Landlords who already had three or four occupants crammed into single rooms added new bodies. Hallways and porches were converted into sleeping quarters. Families of eight or ten lived in basement apartments. "Newcomers discover private baths went out with Hitler," a *Washington Post* headline reported in January.

Writer John Dos Passos, traveling the country to chronicle the state of the nation, described a typical lodging house in Washington, a mansion that had been partitioned into cubicles housing "a pack" of workers: "The house was clean, but it had the feeling of too many people breathing the same air, of strangers stirring behind flimsy walls, of unseen bedsprings creaking and unseen feet shuffling in cramped space."

Workers turning up for the Pentagon project and hoping to camp out quickly discovered that trailer camps were prohibited in Arlington County. Hundreds of workers and their families, including T. R. Anderson and his family from Texas, had to set up camp miles away in trailer parks along Route 1, south of Alexandria.

The government's need for housing and office space for workers was insatiable. Roosevelt in January even suggested that those living in Washington who were not contributing to the war effort—the president called them "parasites"—move out of town and make room for essential war workers.

Roosevelt's dream of presiding over the demolition of the Munitions Building had evaporated. Instead, the president ordered new temporary buildings to be constructed on the Mall to join the old temporary buildings. A long gray line of two-story barrack-like buildings with rain-streaked cement-asbestos board walls sprouted up on the Mall—almost up to the base of the Washington Monument—"before you could say Franklin Roosevelt," journalist Marquis Childs quipped. The Army and Navy seized buildings, land, and even a college campus in the city to use for military installations and office space. "It was said around town that if the military could seize and occupy enemy lands as quickly as it seized Washington's, the war would be won in a week," Brinkley wrote.

For all the dead seriousness of the situation, the most visible manifestation of war in the Construction Division was comical. Years of peacetime duty had left many of officers so out of shape and overweight that the fabric of their Army uniforms strained mightily against the added girth. "And that was the God-awfulest looking sight you ever saw," recalled Gar Davidson, Groves's aide. Marshall's requirement that officers wear civilian clothes in peacetime Washington meant many had never worn their uniforms outside of rare ceremonial events. Some officers simply did not have uniforms, and long lines formed outside military-apparel shops. "And those that had to dig their uniforms out of mothballs were pretty sorry looking sights," Davidson added.

Somervell, on the other hand, effortlessly made the transition from his seersucker suits and bow ties and looked like "a modern Beau Brummel in uniform," a newspaper columnist wrote. Somervell believed an officer should always be able to fit in the uniform in which he had graduated from

West Point, and he kept himself at a sleek 5' 10" and 150 pounds. Anytime he put on a few pounds, he would drink nothing but water and douse his food with vinegar, a dieting technique he picked up from the Romantic poet Lord Byron.

Renshaw and Furman, both trim, also had no trouble fitting into their uniforms. Groves was another matter altogether; as was often the case, he was on the losing side in his lifelong battle with weight. To disguise his extra pounds, Groves took to wearing a one-size-larger uniform, heavy on the starch. As Groves biographer Robert Norris noted, "Not many were fooled."

All centered here

More than in previous American wars, command would be directed from Washington. In World War I, much of the War Department general staff had been headquartered in France, relatively near the action. This war, with American forces spread around the world, would be different, Marshall told Marvin McIntyre, a White House aide. "Today, due to the fact that we have a number of overseas theatres and are engaged in a colossal program of military material *for our Allies,* all of the responsibilities of the War Department of the first World War . . . have all centered here," Marshall wrote.

"We have got to a point where we are actually impeded in our war effort due to the fact that the offices of the War Department are so widely scattered," assistant secretary of war McCloy warned eight weeks after Pearl Harbor.

In late January, Roosevelt asked White House aide Wayne Coy to check with the War Department about progress of the Pentagon building. Somervell's pre-Christmas demand that one million square feet be ready by April 1 seemed now to be an April fool's joke. The time lost because of the design changes, the debate over bomb-protection—the sheer impossibility of the goal in the first place—led to some recalculations. Renshaw was willing to promise that a larger amount of space—1.3 million square feet—would be ready, but not until June 1. Groves altered the prediction, promising 500,000 square feet by early May, which was what Somervell had originally promised when work started. Word was relayed to the president.

"The first part of the building will be ready for occupancy in early May," Coy reported to Roosevelt. The entire building would be finished by November 15.

It would not be a moment too soon. Predictions were that the War Department, which now numbered 25,000 workers, would have 50,000 employees in Washington by July 1. Big as Somervell was building the Pentagon, it was not going to be big enough.

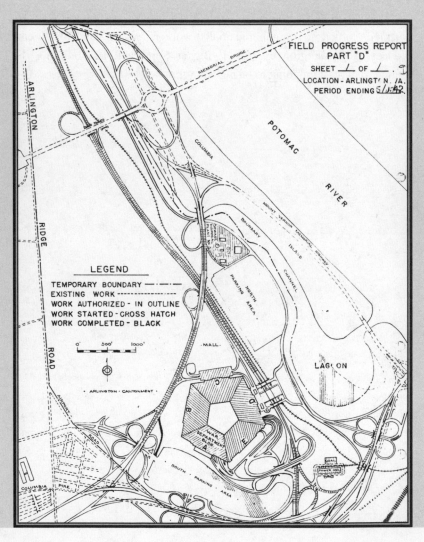

Construction field progress report, May 1942.

CHAPTER 10

THE BIG PUSH

An overwhelming task

The concrete edifice rising from the low ground to the east could be seen plainly through the dreary winter morning light, and the percussion from the pile drivers floated up the hillside to the gravesite at Arlington National Cemetery. Somervell had personally chosen the location, about a hundred yards down the hillside from L'Enfant's tomb and the Lee mansion. It was a lofty spot, benefiting from the magnificent vista that had been spared when Franklin Roosevelt ordered Somervell to build his headquarters downriver. Shortly before noon on Tuesday, January 27, 1942, an Army burial team carried the casket with the remains of his wife, Anna Purnell Somervell, to the grave awaiting in the wet ground.

Connie Somervell, fifteen, watching with her father and two older sisters, tried to stop crying but could not. Down at St. Margaret's, the boarding school she attended in the Tidewater area of Virginia, Connie had known little—only that the illness that had slowed her mother over Christmas had taken a grave turn. First it was thought to be a bad cold. Pinned down with work in January and spending his nights at his apartment in Washington, the general fretted about his wife, suffering with no one to care for her at the tobacco farm in southern Maryland. He arranged to check her into Walter Reed Army Hospital in Washington, where doctors found she was suffering from a staph infection that had developed into blood poisoning. "I used to write her everyday, then my older sister said, 'Don't bother writing mother, she can't read your letters,' " Connie Somervell Matter recalled. "When you're fifteen, you don't believe your parents are going to die. I was distressed, but I presumed she was going to get well." On Sunday night, January 25, Anna Somervell died at Walter Reed at age fifty-seven.

General Marshall was informed the following morning and sent a note to Somervell at the tobacco farm: "I just learned a moment ago that Mrs. Somervell died last night, and I want you to know that you have my deep sympathy. . . . The fact that I have burdened you with an overwhelming task at a time when you were suffering a personal tragedy, makes me feel all the more solicitous of your welfare." A few days later, Henry Stimson personally awarded Somervell the Oak Leaf Cluster for his Distinguished Service Medal, this time honoring his work as chief of the Construction Division. Somervell had overseen "the greatest building program of modern times" and done it in "record-breaking time," the citation noted. "I am very glad that this trifle of encouragement and recognition of his superb services has come to him at this time," Stimson noted in his diary.

The loss of the Red Cross volunteer he had brought home from Germany after World War I, a doting and graceful mother who adored her husband, profoundly saddened Somervell. "He was devastated," Connie Somervell recalled. Yet it slowed him not in the least. In the days before and after his wife's death, Somervell was busy engineering another rise to power. Unlike his machinations the previous summer and fall, this effort would prove more fruitful.

Somervell's rise was perhaps inevitable, once peacetime niceties were cast aside. War had a way of bringing his like to the fore. Four days after Pearl Harbor, Stimson, concerned about the "tremendous burdens" on Marshall's shoulders, privately advised the chief of staff that "it was time to pick out young men [with] outstanding brains and character and bring them forward." Somervell was one of three names Stimson mentioned; Marshall agreed.

Marshall, fed up with an archaic administrative system that divided much of the Army into fiefdoms, already had in mind a radical reorganization to streamline the War Department headquarters. His ability to make quick decisions was crippled by the need to consult with myriad bureaus and commands that tended to jealously guard their prerogatives. Seizing on the opportunity presented by the shock of Pearl Harbor, Marshall moved quickly to do away with much of the headquarters apparatus, cutting the number of officers who had direct access to the chief of staff from more than sixty to six.

Learning in January of Marshall's intention, Somervell immediately got to work influencing developments. He advanced his own plan in February to create a unified supply command, combining disparate bureaus and agencies into one organization that controlled all equipment, construction, supply, and transportation. It fit perfectly with Marshall's vision. Somervell was not shy about suggesting he was the logical choice to head this massive new command. Marshall and Stimson agreed.

On February 28, Roosevelt signed an executive order reorganizing the War Department and dividing the Army into three major commands. Lieutenant General Leslie J. McNair was appointed commander of all Army ground forces, Lieutenant General Henry "Hap" Arnold, commander of all Army air forces, and Somervell, newly promoted to lieutenant general, commander of all Army supply forces. In effect, all of the Army not directly involved with combat now reported to Somervell. Training of troops, communications, military justice, chaplains, quartermasters, engineers, and ordnance, among many other areas, were now part of Somervell's domain. To Somervell fell the task of supplying eight million soldiers scattered across the globe with weapons, bullets, food, shoes, uniforms, medical care, and transportation. "In military annals not even Napoleon's quartermaster could approach the magnitude of the job he had to do," *The New York Times* wrote.

"I will say this for General Somervell," a wary Harry Truman told fellow senators, "he will get the stuff, but it is going to be hell on the taxpayer." Truman was right on both counts.

At the suggestion of Marshall, who wanted him "handy," Somervell moved from his tobacco farm into Quarters Two at Fort Myer, a stately redbrick home next to Quarters One, the home reserved for the chief of staff. Somervell's eldest daughter, Mary Anne, a chemist with the Bureau of Standards, moved in with her father and ran the household, planning menus and seeing that her father's uniforms were pressed. She would breakfast with him at seven o'clock—the eighteenth-century oval mahogany table set with gold-rimmed service plates bearing the Somervell family crest, and a pot of tea at the general's place—before he rushed out the door.

Somervell soared to national prominence. Within weeks, he was on the cover of *Life* magazine, and soon after that, *Time*. He spoke to war workers around the country and with typical flair braced Americans for the sterner realities of war. "Hitler and the Japs aren't interested in the forty-hour, fifty-hour, or sixty-hour week," he told two thousand cheering factory workers in Yonkers.

In little over a year, Somervell had risen from lieutenant colonel to three-star general, a climb surpassed in speed only by a few, among them Eisenhower. In the process, he had leapfrogged in rank over dozens of more senior officers. (He was only forty-nine, but, knowing Marshall's penchant for younger generals, Somervell played it safe and did not tell the chief of staff he would turn fifty in May.) Major General Reybold, who as chief of engineers held the job Somervell had so desperately coveted, was now below Somervell in his new command. Likewise Major General Gregory, the quartermaster general who had taken quiet pleasure at Somervell's comeuppance, now found himself reporting to his former subordinate.

Somervell was again directing all Army construction, now from a much higher level. Hundreds of camps, airfields, and depots needed to be built across the country and around the globe, so many as to make the tremendous $2 billion effort he directed the previous year look like a pittance. From December 7, 1941, until the end of February 1942, the Corps of Engineers was launching construction projects costing an unheard-of $200 million a week. In March, when Somervell assumed his new post, the figure reached $250 million a week.

"The undertaking was truly gigantic, dwarfing those previous great endeavors, the building of the Panama Canal and the emergency construction programs of 1917–18 and 1940–41," Fine and Remington wrote in their official account of Army construction in World War II. "In urgency, complexity, and difficulty, as in size, it surpassed anything of the sort the world had ever seen. The speed demanded, the sums of money involved, the number and variety of projects, the requirements for manpower, materials, and equipment, and the problems of management and organization were unparalleled. So formidable was the enterprise that some questioned whether it was possible." It would be, as Somervell immodestly but perhaps not incorrectly later called it, "the most brilliant chapter in world construction history."

Among many other responsibilities, Somervell was officially back in charge of the Pentagon construction. Of course, he had never really relinquished control of the project, but now the chain again led directly to him, and he wasted no time exercising his authority.

On March 25, Somervell sent a short memo to Reybold that the chief of engineers, knowing Somervell as he did, could only have read as ominous. "The occupancy of the new War Department must be assured at the earliest possible date," Somervell wrote. "I am counting on your personal efforts to see that this is done and in any event that occupancy may be begun on May 1."

The next day, Colonel Frederick Strong, a veteran engineer and trusted aide to Somervell, passed the message on to Groves. "General Somervell and I discussed your 'big building,' " Strong told Groves. There could be no retreat from the deadline: "On account of commitments made to the President and the Chief of Staff, the above schedule will have to be carried out despite all obstacles."

Just when it looked as if winter was over and that McShain and Renshaw could count on some decent weather, a Palm Sunday storm on March 29 dumped eighteen inches of snow on Washington. The blizzard left whole sections of the city blacked out, paralyzed the region's roads, and slowed work at the job site, but it did not stop Somervell from showing up at his office first thing the following morning and sourly looking over his staff with a gimlet eye: "Which one of you sons of bitches remarked that spring was here?"

From the bottom of the Potomac River

Slipping past Alexandria and looking upriver, the captain of the night tug noticed with a start that the dome of the Capitol was blacked out. It had been darkened ever since Pearl Harbor several months earlier, but after fifteen years working the Potomac River, he was still shocked every time he saw the familiar beacon was missing.

Inside the dark pilothouse, the captain gently turned the wheel. A light drizzle began falling, further darkening the night and blurring the remaining lights on the inky shore. Upriver, the captain could see the flashing green buoy at Hains Point, where the Anacostia River flowed into the Potomac. He noted the location with a cross in his mind. "Cross marks spot where the battle begins tonight," the captain muttered.

The tug was pulling two barges, both heavily laden with gravel. The captain wanted to deliver the gravel upriver to a concrete plant in Georgetown, where he knew it would fetch good money. Builders were desperate for concrete to finish half-built apartments, roads, and houses all around Washington. But the War Department was buying almost every ounce of gravel dredged from the Potomac, feeding the insatiable appetite for concrete to build the Pentagon. The captain would have to get past McShain's concrete batching plant in the old airport lagoon, where Army officers kept a keen eye on the river, ready to motor out in a launch to intercept any load of gravel that—by virtue of wartime materiel priorities—they could claim.

The captain had ordered his crew to darken the tug as much as possible. Lanterns were kept off the deck and the portholes blacked out. The doors to the engine room were shut. It was futile, perhaps, since he had to keep his green-and-red navigation lights on. But every little bit might help. This could be the night he slipped past, the captain thought, but then he stopped himself. "Oh, I always think that."

On board the tug listening to the captains was Charles E. Planck, a forty-four-year-old Kentucky native, an aviation writer with a keen eye who had taken a job with the Civil Aeronautics Administration as an information officer. Planck watched as the captain swung wide around the buoy at Hains Point, calculating his turn with an expert eye, and then braced himself for the final run up the river. "All the trip had led up to this one ten minutes," Planck wrote in an account of the unnamed captain's journey.

"He watched the southern shore," Planck continued. "He wished his navigation lights could be doused. He wished his engine would breathe a little more quietly. He even wished that little gray launch which represented defeat to him might suddenly lose a bottom plank from stem to stern and sink in two minutes."

The tug slipped under the 14th Street Bridge, just below the lagoon. There was no sign yet of the launch, and for a moment the captain again had hope. Then he spotted a small, dark-gray vessel nosing out from the mouth of the lagoon. "He could see the faint white plume of its wake as it headed straight for him," Planck wrote. "Soon he heard the little bump as it came alongside and then the officer's shoes hit the deck. He gritted his teeth as he heard the man's feet on the ladder rungs and saw his face dimly as it came up into the pilot house."

The officer's genial greeting broke the silence. "Howdy, captain," the officer said. "Guess we can use these two loads."

The War Department could indeed use it. The need was inexhaustible. Concrete was being poured on a scale never seen for a building—410,000 cubic yards would be required for the Pentagon compared to 62,000 for the Empire State Building.

The location chosen to construct such a building was a wise one, from the standpoint of the basic ingredients needed. Just south of the site, beneath the waters of the Potomac and below a layer of soft mud, lay a boundless supply of sand and gravel. The melting of glaciers when the Ice Age ended fifteen thousand years ago had turned the Potomac into a vast waterway carrying enormous volumes of both materials. The glacier melt left gravel deposits up to eighty feet deep beneath the bed of the Potomac near where National Airport was built, giving the area its name, Gravelly Point.

The Pentagon was being built out of the Potomac—some 680,000 tons of river sand and gravel when all was said and done. "It is interesting that more than one-half the weight of the building . . . came out of the bottom of the Potomac River," Renshaw later observed.

Though the supply of sand and gravel was inexhaustible, the amount dredged was not. The Smoot Sand & Gravel Company, the main supplier, struggled to meet the demand, particularly in January, when two of its river dredges broke down and some of the company's most experienced dredge operators were drafted by the Army. Many area construction jobs suffered, yet Smoot managed to supply enough for the Pentagon project, which had priority.

Floating dredges scooped up sand and gravel from various beds in the river. The stones were sand-colored, rounded and smooth from the force of water, their coarseness varying with which river bar was being worked. The dredges loaded the sand and gravel onto barges—including the ones delivered by the unnamed and unwilling captain. Shipping the aggregate directly to the construction site saved not only time but also money—about thirty-five cents per cubic yard of concrete.

On the bank of the expanded lagoon, the concrete batching plant run by the Howat Concrete Company of Maryland received barges twenty-four hours a day. Two stiff-legged derricks, equipped with big clamshell buckets, scooped the aggregate off the barges and swung it over into an enormous receiving hopper. The aggregate was dropped from the hopper onto a radial stacker, a 185-foot-long conveyor belt that carried the material to the top of a mountainous stockpile. From there it was drawn as needed through a buried timber tunnel to more conveyor belts that carried the aggregate to one of two batchers, where it was weighed and measured to reach a proportion of roughly two parts sand to three parts gravel. Portland cement, brought to the plant via a rail spur, was added to the mix, along with precise amounts of water.

The massive operation produced as much as 3,500 cubic yards of concrete daily, requiring about 5,500 tons of sand and gravel, 937 tons of cement, and 115,000 gallons of water every day. When concrete was being poured, which was most of the time, mixing trucks lined up beneath the batchers to fill up. Each truck carried four cubic yards of concrete, mixing it as they hauled to save time. Often twenty or thirty trucks made runs back and forth, along dirt roadways laid out to speed passage directly to the foot of tower hoists next to the building and other locations where concrete was needed.

Steam-powered hoists lifted it in one-cubic-yard buckets. Reaching the proper level, the concrete was dumped into chutes that carried it into small hoppers. With cries of "Concrete!" workers rushed it in wheelbarrows and concrete buggies over planks to its final destination. To speed up the pouring, Renshaw tried using concrete pumps, a new technology. Pumps were set up in the courtyard with pipes attached to carry the concrete up into the building. "When the pumps worked they could really put a hell of a lot of concrete in the building," Bob Furman recalled. But they sometimes broke down, creating an unholy mess and slowing the work. "Then the pipe would be full of concrete setting up—it'd be a bitch," he said. Most of the concrete ended up being hoisted to the deck hoppers and distributed in buggies.

It was a freewheeling operation, so much so that other military projects lacking the same priority were filching concrete from the site. "Apparently we didn't supervise them too carefully," Furman said. "Later we learned that the Army bases that were being built or renovated in the area were sending trucks over and lining up with our trucks."

The pouring continued nonstop in good weather and bad, many times simultaneously in different sections of the building. Big pours were scheduled every Friday, often lasting well into the night, giving the concrete time to cure relatively undisturbed over the weekend, when smaller crews were at work. "We built so damn quickly, I remember one column wasn't even poured," Furman said. "We stripped the [forms], and there wasn't any column there."

The constant pouring of concrete meant the carpenters, Joe Allan among them, had to race to keep up. "There was always concrete going in," Allan said. "Every morning some of the forms were ready to be poured. There were concrete trucks all over the place every morning, pouring, and then in the afternoon and the evening too. They didn't waste any time."

The carpenters set up assembly-line operations to build the forms. Each of the building's five sections had its own mill, manned by large crews of carpenters with power saws who cut and assembled lumber into modular forms for the columns, beams, slabs, and walls. Allan was assigned to the mill for Section D, where he used an electric skill saw to cut the lumber to the proper lengths—three-quarter-inch-thick boards, a foot wide and six to eight feet long. The forms were assembled using tongue-and-groove joints and secured with battens.

"It was like a mimeograph," Allan said. "It was designed so it could be done easily."

The mass-production techniques, rough at the start of construction, were constantly refined by Paul Hauck and his foremen, and by spring the pace of work was rapidly accelerating. New workers quickly picked up the simple and repetitive assignments. "Coming from different backgrounds and different unions and different experiences, they were able to comprehend immediately what to do and how to do it," Allan said.

So much wood was being cut that several carpenters at each mill did nothing all day but sharpen and set the teeth on saws. A sudden and unexpected lumber shortage in the spring left the Army scrambling to get enough. The forms were broken up and the boards reused, but the job still required enormous amounts of lumber—more than twenty-three million board-feet in the end.

After a spectacular fire at a hotel under construction in Washington in February, it suddenly dawned on Groves that the War Department site might erupt into the world's largest construction fire. He ordered Renshaw to immediately rid the site of fire hazards. Renshaw decided that an officer on his staff must be at the site at all times to respond to any emergency. In the middle of a huge office bay in Section A, McShain's men walled off a small bedroom, which was outfitted with three beds, a bathroom, shower, and telephone. Furman, rotating duty with four other officers, spent every fifth night there. He would get up every three or four hours and walk around the entire site, looking for trouble. "I can tell you right now there are 921 and a half feet to a side," Furman recalled more than sixty years later.

Their emergency preparedness was soon tested when a large toolshed used by construction workers caught fire one night. The next day, the construction site security chief presented Furman with a report proudly listing how quickly firefighters responded to the blaze. "His report read to that point as the most efficient call to put out a fire you could ever imagine," Furman recalled. "Then the bottom line read, 'The building burnt to the ground.' "

Are there really guys buried down there?

Given the vast size and fast pace of the concrete pours, it did not take long for rumors to start spreading about workers who had fallen into wet concrete and perished. Sometimes the worker disappeared without a trace, the story went; other times the body had to be removed with jackhammers. "That was the scuttlebutt," recalled Donald Walker. In the version he and his steel crew heard, workers had stripped the forms off a beam and found a body embedded in the concrete. Walker had no trouble believing it. "Oh, yeah, it was very feasible," he said.

Working as usual on a weekend, Clarence Renshaw brought along his eight-year-old son, Alan, to see the work one morning. They went to the top of the building, where from up high the boy marveled at the sights: cranes swinging about with supplies, fleets of trucks moving on the roads below, and mountains of material. As his father conferred with McShain, Alan walked over to watch concrete being poured. A rough-looking worker stopped him. "Hey, kid, don't get too close," the worker barked. "We lost two guys down one of these holes last week."

Such stories spread around town. John Brockwell's parents, like many families in the area, opened their house in the Del Ray neighborhood of Alexandria to war workers needing room and board. One of the boarders was a worker on the Pentagon project, a mixing truck driver nicknamed "Concrete." He would come home covered in it. Concrete told a story about a worker who fell into a deep pool of freshly poured concrete when the long pole he was using to stir the mix snapped. "He said they started to stop the concrete pour, but the foreman told them to keep going because the worker would be dead before they could get to him, and the effort wasn't worth stopping the concrete job," Brockwell recalled years later. "So on they went, leaving the worker's body inside the concrete foundation. Whether that actually happened, I don't know, but it made a good story for 'Concrete' at the time and was a great story for a kid like me."

The stories only multiplied with time. An unnamed construction supervisor told the *Army-Navy-Air Force Register* in 1961 about a worker who failed to show up for work the day after he had been assigned to oversee the pouring of a column. "The construction section boss ordered the molding to be stripped from the pillar and, as was feared, workers found a body embedded in the drying cement," the *Register* reported. "Jack-hammers were needed to release the deceased from his concrete tomb."

The tales have never stopped; a recycled version was reported as fact by the Pentagon's official newspaper in 1984. Marian Bailey, who started working in the Pentagon as a telephone operator in 1942 and stayed six decades, relished taking visitors on building tours and speaking mysteriously of workers buried in the concrete. Sometimes she would dramatically point to spots in walls or floors where some unfortunate was said to be entombed.

The stories, as Bob Furman put it, are "myths." There is no evidence in any records that anyone died in such a manner. The most definitive answer came from Clarence Renshaw himself. Many years after Alan Renshaw's visit to the Pentagon roof—after he himself had attended West Point and been commissioned as an officer in the Air Force—the son asked his father about the stories. "Are there really guys buried down there under that concrete?" Alan Renshaw asked.

Clarence Renshaw had to laugh. Nobody had been lost that way, he told his son. He would have known.

Don't slip on it

Workers were dying in plenty of other ways, though, and not necessarily in more pleasant manners. Two workers were killed in early February operating a mechanical hoist, including one who stuck his head into a hoist shaft to see if the hoist was coming. It was, and he was decapitated. A few days later, on February 13, Guy R. Milliken, an electrician who came down from New York for the job, was fetching his lunch when he walked into the path of a concrete truck. His death brought the number of fatalities on the job to four.

Inspecting the site before the spate of deaths, Lloyd Blanchard, chief of the safety section, was dismayed to find that none of the urgent safety improvements he had recommended after Vernon Janney was crushed in October had been implemented. "It is still necessary for the general contractor to show a radical change in attitude toward providing safe working conditions," Blanchard wrote.

Renshaw was unapologetic when queried by a reporter about the deaths. "We are lucky that we have not had 20 deaths," he said. "We cannot have 13,000 men together on one job working at the rate we are going and not have some accidents. Considering that a normal job would take two years, our accident rate is very low." Renshaw put the blame for the deaths on "human failure," which was another way of saying it was the workers' fault. "Real safety actually only comes from the men themselves," he said.

"At times, we have had trouble impressing that on them, particularly those who are new on the job."

Labor leaders thought otherwise, and, given the cavalier attitude toward safety at the site, they had good reason to. At the demand of the unions, McShain and Army representatives met with labor leaders to review safety procedures. "They have been promising to institute proper methods, but we are very doubtful that they will," C. F. Preller, president of the Washington Building and Construction Trades Council, told *The Washington Post*. The Virginia labor commissioner, John Hopkins Hall, Jr., wrote a letter to Stimson later in the spring expressing concern about the accidents. Stimson promised that "every effort is being made to keep preventable accidents at a minimum." Some improvements were made and the accident rate fell as the months passed. After the two hoist deaths, a signal system was installed and an additional watcher was placed at the shaft. But the job site remained dangerous.

Further aggrieved by a wage dispute with the government, union leaders in March threatened to pull thousands of workers from the Pentagon job site to testify at a Department of Labor hearing. The threat was not carried out, but the labor-government truce that had ruled since Pearl Harbor was fraying.

There were racial tensions as well among the construction workers. About 40 percent of the work force was black; many of them worked as laborers, but because of wartime manpower shortages, others were given jobs as skilled workers. The prominent role of black workers bred resentment among some whites. The construction cafeterias had separate sections for black and white workers in accordance with the "Virginia Separation of Races" law. Out on the construction site, brawls broke out several times between groups of white and black workers; on one occasion, Furman arrived at the scene to find a large group of black and white workers facing off, hurling angry words at each other. "They were drawing lines, and I walked between the lines," Furman said. "Whether it did any good or not I don't know." The standoff broke up but the tensions remained.

Discrimination created an absurd new concern for Renshaw: He was supposed to build a segregated Pentagon. The word came in a telephone call March 7 from one of Groves's aides, Major Donald Antes. "Colonel

Groves just asked me to call you and find out whether you have made any provisions for separate design for the different classes of people in the War Department Building," said Antes, who then clarified his euphemism. "By that I mean separate toilet rooms for black and white as required by the Virginia law, and if you haven't taken such precautions that you are to do so immediately."

This was news to Renshaw. "Separate design of toilet rooms?" he asked. Yes, replied Antes, who added this coda from Groves: "He said don't slip on it." Renshaw promised to take care of it.

The matter was not as simple as Groves believed, however. While Virginia law required whites and blacks to be segregated in public places, Franklin Roosevelt had signed Executive Order 8802 the previous June, which forbade discrimination against government workers on the basis of race, creed, color, or national origin. Moreover, on March 11 Virginia governor Colgate W. Darden granted a request from Stimson to give the War Department exclusive jurisdiction over the land on which the Pentagon was being built. Still, whether out of ignorance or deliberate discrimination, the Army made preparations for separate bathrooms.

The road network

Renshaw's biggest worry now was building the roads to the Pentagon. It would do no good to have the building ready for occupancy if no one could get there. An enormous road network was to be constructed, second only to the building itself in cost and scope.

When he had sold the building to Congress and the commissions the previous summer, Somervell had played down the need for roads, describing the problem as "perhaps less serious than getting people to and away from a ball game." The reality was quite different. "It is almost like providing highways for a city of 100,000," Thomas H. MacDonald, the longtime director of the federal Bureau of Public Roads, warned a congressional committee in December.

Planners for the War Department and the roads bureau designed a futuristic swirl of roads, ramps, and access lanes emanating from a triangle of highways surrounding the building. The idea was to speed cars and buses from Washington by building the roads without crossroads or traffic lights.

Counting access roads and ramps, the equivalent of forty-seven miles of twenty-four-foot-wide roadway were to be constructed. In all, twenty-one bridges needed to be built, most of them overpasses carrying ramps and roads across one another. The design included three freeway-scale cloverleaf interchanges, among the first to be constructed in the United States and a concept still foreign to most American drivers.

The basic plan for the main highways had been on the books since long before the Pentagon was conceived. In 1934, Frederic Delano's National Capital Parks and Planning Commission had approved a system of roads that would provide approaches from Virginia to the three main bridges leading into Washington. But no money had been allocated to build the roads; they existed only on planning maps.

Roosevelt took care of that problem, giving the War Department and the roads bureau the green light to spend millions acquiring the needed land. Somervell and MacDonald negotiated who would build and pay for which roads; the roads bureau director was delighted when Somervell offered to pay not only for the circulatory access roads immediately around the building, but also $6.3 million for the portion of the highways that went through War Department land—roads that the bureau would have been expected to fund.

To speed the work, Somervell further promised the roads bureau up to $4 million in War Department funding "to assure the early initiation of actual construction," he told MacDonald. Somervell added one condition, though. He had a score to settle with Gilmore Clarke, the Commission of Fine Arts chairman who had been so nettlesome during the battle over the building's location. As an accomplished landscape architect who often worked on parkways, Clarke regularly served as a consultant to the roads bureau and had helped design the Mount Vernon Memorial Highway running along the Potomac shore to George Washington's estate. According to the story later related by Clarke—quite believable, given Somervell's lust for revenge—the general promised to give MacDonald the money on condition that the bureau not allow Clarke to have anything to do with planning the roads for the new headquarters. "I need hardly add that I was not employed by the Bureau of Public Roads for this project," Clarke recalled. Instead, William S. Chapin, a New York highway engineer, was hired at $50 a day plus expenses to design the road system.

Colonel Edmond Leavey, one of Somervell's top engineers, was worried the initial plans for access roads were impractical. Leavey assembled a sand-table model of the headquarters with the access roads built to scale in an old building near the construction site; he sent an aide, Captain Bob Colglazier, to a five-and-dime store in downtown Washington to buy a fleet of small toy cars and trucks. "I brought these little vehicles back to all these high-powered engineers so they could sit around and start from here and take a coal truck and see how you got to the power plant," Colglazier recalled. "[W]ith the sand table model, and these little trucks, we were able to spend all afternoon making the necessary changes to make it very practical."

By normal standards, the roads program moved rapidly through the fall and winter. Groves had steamrolled objections raised by the War Production Board against demolishing the West Brothers Brick Company to make way for a cloverleaf interchange; bricks were needed for construction of war plants, and the board recommended that the road plans be altered to spare the brick plant. Board member Herbert J. Weber personally appealed to Groves, but the colonel refused to consider any change that might delay the roads. "I might just as well have talked to a brick wall," Weber later complained.

But the roads program was not keeping up with the pace of the work on the Pentagon. The Federal Works Agency, which oversaw the roads bureau and was in charge of acquiring land for the highways, did not feel the same urgency as the War Department. "The real estate people have not moved at all on the land to be occupied," Renshaw reported to Somervell in February. "They still have not condemned it, but are wasting time appraising it." Renshaw predicted disaster if something were not done: "The probability of having the road construction schedule meet the building occupancy dates is decidedly in jeopardy, and further delays will have serious consequences. To meet our schedules everything must click."

This was a nice little neighborhood

To make it click, the Army needed Queen City. About 150 black families lived at the southeastern edge of the construction site in a cluster of houses in the area known as East Arlington, which included the Queen City neighborhood.

It was a small collection of homes, many rundown, and some lacking toilets. Yet Queen City was still the strong community that the man who cleaned up Arlington, Crandal Mackey, had praised thirty years earlier. It had stores and a barbershop, two Baptist churches, and a feeling of shared history among proud residents, many of them descendants of the freed slaves evicted by the Army from Freedmen's Village a half-century earlier. Now, the Army again needed their land. East Arlington sat on the north side of Columbia Pike on twenty-five acres needed for a highway and an interchange near the building's south parking lot. All the residents would have to leave.

This was not seen as a problem by the men planning the roads. Quite the contrary. Jay Downer, the highway consultant who had played such a critical role in selecting the former quartermaster depot site as the location for the headquarters, saw it as a nice bonus to uproot the black families. The road network "takes out some troublesome darkey slave cabins," Downer told the National Capital Planning Commission in October 1941. "This cleans up that strip." No one raised any objections. Roosevelt had approved the plan when he surveyed the site in August. Plans went forward to raze the community, though no one bothered to consult or even inform the residents.

Construction had been scheduled to begin around Queen City the week of January 19, but notices were not sent to the more than 150 families until early February, telling them they had to leave by March 1. Most residents had no idea the Army headquarters being constructed a quarter-mile away meant the end to Queen City. "We just thought they were going to build a building over in the field, but we had no idea it was going to be as big as it was," George Vollin, Jr., who grew up in Queen City and was then thirty-nine years old, recalled decades later. "Then they came to building the roads, and that's when they took all the houses."

"It was a predicament," Gertrude Jeffress, then nineteen and living in Queen City with her mother and sister, later said. "Where in the world where we going to find a place to live?"

The desperate residents bound together and had an attorney send a letter to Eleanor Roosevelt, the great champion of the disadvantaged. Lifelong residents of Arlington had been given only thirty days' notice to leave their homes, the president's wife was told. Moreover, the letter said, the amount the government was paying for their homes was paltry, certainly not enough to exchange for new homes—not that any were available in wartime Washington anyway. The First Lady forwarded the letter to the House Military Affairs Committee, which held a hearing on February 13.

Thomas MacDonald was unapologetic about the short notice. "It is a matter of split-second timing," the roads bureau chief told the committee. "Any delay would be very serious." The congressmen did not pursue the matter. Complaints about the low sums being paid to the residents likewise went nowhere.

There was little public outcry over the plight of 150 black families losing their homes. The Arlington County Board expressed sympathy that lifelong residents were losing their homes for little recompense, but raised no objections. The federal government—perhaps because Eleanor Roosevelt had poked her head into the matter—promised in court papers to put the residents up in trailers until permanent housing could be found. The U.S. District Court in Richmond granted the government possession of the land as of March 1, contingent upon trailers being provided. The government deposited a check for $369,427 to be divided among about 180 property owners, which worked out to about $2,052 per owner. On March 6, condemnation notices began to be served on the residents. Albert Shanklin, a lifelong resident of Queen City, was in agony when he was served. "I remember his going crazy almost because they were taking his home," his daughter-in-law, Ruth Shanklin, recounted.

Renshaw was not concerned with historical injustices, not with Somervell and Groves breathing down his neck. He fumed all through a three-week delay while the trailer camp was set up. "Nobody has moved," Renshaw said on March 23. "That little spot is going to throw the whole road program out. Everything, if they don't come to life."

At the end of the month, the Queen City residents began moving into a camp set up nearby in a muddy lot off of Columbia Pike. In court papers, the government had promised "accommodations practically as comfortable as those from which persons will be required to move." The residents found themselves living in cramped trailers with stoves and convertible couch-beds, meant to accommodate four persons but often holding more. There was no running water—the trailer occupants had to walk over to a water-dispensing station inside a lattice-metal shack to get water. Some of the residents were still living in the trailers when the war ended.

With the families out of Queen City and the rest of East Arlington, workers quickly fired the frame houses, while bulldozers knocked down brick homes. Grading equipment soon reshaped the land into something unrecognizable. Not a trace of the neighborhood was left. Queen City was nothing but a memory, and not much of one at that. Fact sheets handed out to visitors to the Pentagon a half-century later describe the building location as "nothing more than wasteland, swamps and dumps."

"Whoever said it was nothing but shacks, well, that ain't true," Gertrude Jeffress said more than sixty years after leaving her Queen City home. "This was a nice little neighborhood, I'll say that."

Some change, eh?

With the arrival of spring, it was possible to stand at the site of Queen City and imagine what the Pentagon would look like once it was finished. Long limestone façades now covered much of the southern and western walls, each of which would stretch a fifth of a mile when completed.

So much limestone was needed that it was being quarried from multiple locations in Indiana's limestone belt, a twenty-five-mile-long deposit in the southern part of the state formed by remnants of shellfish and other particles that collected on the bottom of a shallow sea covering much of the Midwest more than three hundred million years ago. Unlike monumental Washington landmarks such as the National Cathedral, which was built with pristine, tightly grained Indiana limestone blocks, the Pentagon was using rougher, less expensive grades of limestone known as rustic buff and variegated, with gray and tan shades. The limestone ran from the ground to the roofline; a course of hard stone—which would have served as a base for the limestone and provided a more finished appearance—was omitted to save time and money. On the roof, a thin strip of light-green slate was visible, merging the limestone with blue sky. It was not beautiful, but the limestone lent a properly imposing and dignified look to what was to be the nation's war headquarters.

Each of the façades was dominated by a central colonnade of sixteen columns, bordered by smaller four-column pavilions. The columns, purely ornamental, ran flush along the façade's middle section, which projected about ten feet from the rest of the exterior wall to break up what would otherwise be a long, flat, monotonous surface. The middle façade included a parapet, Bergstrom's answer to an optical illusion known to architects at least since the Greeks placed a slight arching curve on the roof ridge line of the Parthenon in Athens. If built perfectly level, the 960-foot-long roofline of the Pentagon would appear to sag; the parapets broke the line.

The *Washington Daily News* ran a photograph on March 23 showing the two long, low façades, stretching seemingly forever across eight columns of the newspaper. "This is how the New War Department Building is coming along, in case you've been staying home saving gas and rubber," the caption read. "Some change, eh?"

It was indeed. The building was 40 percent complete, Renshaw reported in March. More than thirteen thousand workers were now on the job, and their numbers would soon peak at fifteen thousand, more than four times the number that built the Empire State Building. It was "a scene that could have been remindful of the construction of the pyramids," Department of Defense chief historian Alfred Goldberg later wrote. A reporter for the *Star* who visited the site in early April was amazed. "In one of the swiftest construction jobs on record, an army of workers seemingly imbued with a spirit of accomplishment is nearing completion of the first sections of the enormous War Department office building in nearby Arlington—less than seven months since ground was first broken," he wrote.

Renshaw—now a lieutenant colonel, his second promotion since construction began—had a new set of aerial photographs for Somervell showing the progress as of March. Two of five sections, A and B to the south and west, were largely built to their roofs, while Section C was well on its way. The framework was rising for the second and third stories in Section D, facing the lagoon. Piles were still being driven for Section E, the fifth and final one, but the building's entire layout was now apparent. Before sending the photographs, Renshaw used a black pen to outline a chevron-shaped wedge in the building that included about half of Section A and half of Section B—about 500,000 square feet in all. "The section outlined in ink is for May occupancy," Renshaw wrote to Somervell. "We are running a close race with the architect and with our appropriations."

The architect, at least, was running relatively well. The designers in the Eastern Airlines hangar were still lagging 5 percent behind schedule in February but by March had largely caught up, and by the beginning of April, they had actually moved 6 percent ahead of schedule—though still not fast enough to satisfy McShain.

The appropriations race was another matter altogether. Through the winter, the Army clung to the convenient fiction that the building was going to cost $35 million, the amount appropriated by Congress. Official construction documents listed this amount even after Bergstrom estimated in February that the cost would be $45 million, what with the space added to the building after Pearl Harbor, the roads Somervell promised, and all the changes to the design. The news just got worse. On April 3, McShain reported the project was more than $13 million over budget. Overtime wages alone accounted for $2 million. Conditions at the swampy site were responsible for $2 million in extra earth excavation and fill and $1.4 million in additional pile driving. Added space in the building accounted for $2.7 million. Beyond that, as McShain's job superintendent, Paul Hauck, dryly remarked, "it is noted that the type of building which was originally planned differed greatly from the one which is now being built."

Somervell blew up when McShain told him the news. Chagrined, McShain reworked the numbers. "Since seeing you last week I have been very much concerned about your reaction towards the rising cost," the builder wrote him on April 10, adding, "I am ever mindful of the fact that you awarded this job to me." McShain reported that he had found an error in the estimates for concrete that reduced the overrun to $10 million over the original estimate. Somervell replied that this was "hearty news," adding cautiously, "I hope that your predictions will be borne out."

They would not. The predictions would soon prove hopelessly optimistic. Just a week later, Renshaw reported that he was short $15.7 million, and more overruns were possible. Ultimately, it was not Bergstrom's, McShain's, or Renshaw's fault. The problem was with the $35 million estimate itself. Somervell did not, however, feel it necessary to notify Congress just yet. He would wait until the building was occupied, probably figuring he would wrap bad news with good to soften the blow. Somervell's PR man, George Holmes, told Renshaw that any information released to reporters about the building should have "nothing to do with the actual details."

Renshaw had reported on March 28 that he was on track to meet the

May 1 deadline. But it was not going to be pretty. The limestone was being hung outside, but the arriving employees would not find a finished building inside. There would be no heat or air conditioning; with a little luck nobody would freeze or boil to death, though either was possible, given Washington's fickle May weather. No one was sure they would be able to feed the employees. "It is hoped the temporary cafeteria will be ready and operate somehow," Renshaw reported.

The Chesapeake and Potomac Telephone Company would rig up a temporary switchboard, and the Potomac Electric Company would bring in temporary electricity, since the power plant was not finished. With all the delays acquiring land, most of the road network would not be finished until the fall, though two lanes of a new highway leading from the Memorial Bridge were expected to be ready. Office employees would have to delay their arrival in the morning so as to not create a jam with the thousands of construction workers arriving for the day shift at 7:30 A.M. Once at the building, it was not yet clear how the employees would enter, as there was no guarantee entrances would be ready. Plaster in the building would not be thoroughly dry, and leaks and other "incidentals" should be expected. "Naturally it must be expected that the occupants of the building will be more or less dissatisfied with these existing conditions, which may result in unfavorable comments to outside sources," Renshaw observed. That was to prove quite an understatement.

At War Department headquarters, Brigadier General Wilhelm "Fat" Styer, chief of staff for Somervell's Services of Supply, was having doubts about the wisdom of rushing in employees. Heavyset and easygoing, Styer was the polar opposite of Somervell in both looks and temperament, yet was a loyal and effective deputy to the general. With cool reason and a knack for seeing both sides of an argument, Styer was often able to rein Somervell back from his more impulsive decisions. Meeting with Renshaw on the morning of April 20 about the expected working conditions in the building, Styer raised the possibility of delaying occupancy. He did not want the first employees working amid clouds of dust.

Groves was infuriated when he learned of Styer's suggestion. Less than two weeks earlier, on April 9, an army of 35,000 American and Filipino troops, wasted by hunger and disease, capitulated to the Japanese on the Bataan Peninsula in the Philippines. It was the largest surrender in American history. Here in Washington, the War Department was desperately short of space, and an army of thirteen thousand workers was racing to get the building ready. Now the higher-ups were worried about a little dust? Groves sent Styer an impassioned note April 21 warning of a disastrous let-down in morale if the move did not take place by May 1. "Everyone connected with the building has been driven to make this date," Groves wrote. "If the War Department now hesitates there is no question in my mind but that the efficiency of the construction forces will be permanently impaired and that the building will fall behind schedule and the cost will be increased substantially."

If dust was a problem, Groves added with a touch of sarcasm, then they might as well not move in at all until the building was finished in November. "There will be dust in this building from now until the completion of all construction," he said. Styer brought the issue to Somervell, who immediately reiterated that he wanted employees in the building and working by May 1, regardless of discomfort.

On April 22, Fat Styer issued the orders. The first employees—several hundred from the Ordnance Department—would begin moving in to the Pentagon at 8 A.M. on Thursday, April 30, and must be at their desks working the following day, May 1.

Gathered in haste from the four winds

Edwin Bergstrom, the man most responsible for the Pentagon's design, would not see that day.

On the evening of April 11, the chief architect composed a letter addressed to the 350 members of the design team working in the Eastern Airlines hangar. "Fellow Workers," he began. "I am leaving this job tonight."

It was a sudden and shocking departure, brought about by personal scandal, though his letter made no mention of it. Bergstrom had never replied to the American Institute of Architects' demand in December that he reimburse the institute for his questionable expenses and justify his expensive suite at the Hay-Adams House while he was president. At 10 A.M. on March 20, 1942, R. Harold Shreve, Bergstrom's successor as president of the institute, convened a special meeting of the board of directors at the Commodore Hotel next to Grand Central Terminal in New York City. Charges of unprofessional conduct against Bergstrom were on the agenda.

No one knew if Bergstrom would show up for the hearing, but he did, accompanied by Pierpont Davis, one of his assistants from the Pentagon project. Proud and imperious, Bergstrom read from a prepared statement and denied all charges. He declared that "he was entitled as President to live in a manner to which he was accustomed and which the head of the Institute should command." Because he drew no salary from the Institute, he argued that he was fully entitled to have his expenses paid even after he accepted a full-time position with the War Department. His entertainment expenses had not been excessive, he added, and in any event were "a necessity in Washington."

J. Frazer Smith, a board member from Tennessee, was uncomfortable with suggestions that the board had not known of Bergstrom's expenditures. "Everybody understood that President Bergstrom was accustomed to an expense account that looked like a month's salary to some architects," Smith said. Another sympathetic board member, St. Louis architect Kenneth E. Wischmeyer, suggested the charges against Bergstrom were being pursued because of the enmity that a group of institute members from the east bore against the Californian over an old funding dispute. Shreve, an eminent New York architect who helped design the Empire State Building, agreed some eastern members were driving the case against Bergstrom. "But they are not alone," Shreve added; protests of Bergstrom's conduct had been registered from members across the country.

Whether it was based upon geography or not, a majority of the board was clearly lined up against Bergstrom. When the board recessed at eight o'clock that evening, Bergstrom approached treasurer John R. Fugard and offered to cut a deal: He would make restitution on at least some expenses and offer an accounting of others as best he could—provided the board drop the charges of unprofessional conduct. Informed of the offer, Shreve turned it down on the spot.

The board deliberated the following day until late in the afternoon. When a motion was forwarded to censure Bergstrom for improper and unprofessional conduct, twelve members voted in favor, two against, and one abstained. On March 28, the institute sent out a confidential notice of disciplinary action to all its chapters and members around the country: "The Board terminates the corporate membership of George Edwin Bergstrom effective March 21, 1942, for improper and unprofessional conduct."

It was a humiliating rebuke, and, for a man of his position and reputation, the damage was perhaps irreparable. Whether Bergstrom decided to leave the Pentagon project of his own volition, or whether Somervell, fearing any taint of scandal, forced him to resign is not known. David Witmer, Bergstrom's friend and deputy, was immediately appointed to replace Bergstrom as chief architect; Witmer had directed much of the exterior detailing of the building and was unquestionably qualified to take over.

The farewell letter Bergstrom wrote the night of April 11 left no doubt of the pride he felt:

> Gathered in haste from the four winds and from eight professions, you have worked together so completely and earnestly and so loyally as a unit that we have accomplished everything we were set to do, in the utmost harmony and without confusion.
>
> The building, the project, are yours far more than they are mine. No one realizes that more than I do and I hope you will treasure as I will the happiness of our working together and that each of you will be intensely proud of your part in the creation of this building and its environs.
>
> . . . Whatever may come in the future, the association with you all will always be the happiest memory I have, and the most treasured one for what remains to me of life.

Bergstrom left the project that night, never to return.

Army soldiers ponder a Pentagon corridor map in 1949.

CHAPTER 11

THE PLANK WALKERS

Justifiable pride

Joe Allan knew he could forget about going home. The foreman had given orders that everybody would work straight through. The first employees were due to report to the Pentagon early the next day, April 30, 1942, and that meant Allan and the other carpenters in his crew would work all through the day and night. The building was not quite ready.

Crews had worked frantic overtime hours through April trying to get 600,000 square feet of Sections A and B ready for occupancy. Teams of workers raced to lath and plaster the interior walls and put up suspended ceilings of acoustic tile. Plumbers hooked up water and sewage lines to the washrooms and electricians installed power outlets in offices. Asphalt tile was laid in office bays and corridors. Painters slapped thousands of gallons of alkaline, flat oil, and lead paint on interior walls, corridors, and stairways. A joke later told was that if a carpenter was moving too slowly, he got his hammer painted. With a few days to go, there was nothing but scaffolding and building material scattered around a large section of the ground floor in Section A where a temporary cafeteria with seating for 1,800 was to go. "Bingo, and it was done," the *Star* reported. "They were setting up tables as fast as the floor was laid."

Finishing work was a misnomer—there was always more to be done. All through the last night Allan and the others worked, hanging doors, finishing trim work, and putting up partitions. When the sun came up, they were still at it, operating mainly on adrenaline. "Excitement was in the air," Allan recalled. "We were all in the spirit of the thing." Finally, at 8 A.M. the foreman told them to stop, pick up their tools, and go home. It was over. It was for Allan. After seven months on the job, he had saved enough money to begin summer school at the University of North Carolina at Chapel Hill. His final twenty-four-hour shift had left him exhausted, but giddy with enthusiasm about what the crews had accomplished.

Walking outside into a warm spring morning, Allan saw Army officers and secretaries lined up outside the south entrance, waiting to move in. "They were excited and ready to get to work," Allan recalled.

More were arriving from Washington. Military police directed cars coming across the 14th Street Bridge onto Columbia Pike and into the south parking lot, still mostly dirt but with spaces paved for eight hundred cars. "The MPs did such a good job that all the cars that came across the bridge went into the parking lot, including lots of people heading to Richmond," Bob Furman recalled. Furman—newly promoted to captain—had to redirect the southbound vehicles, including at least one bus on its way to the Virginia state capital, a hundred miles to the south.

Several hundred employees from the Army's Ordnance Department had been chosen as guinea pigs to move in over the first few days. Marjorie Hanshaw, a twenty-three-year-old secretary from Iowa assigned to the supply section for the Chief of Ordnance, rode a bus from her home in Arlington with two other young women who worked in the office. Dropped off at a temporary bus-and-taxi terminal in the south parking lot, they entered the building without a clue where their office was.

Hanshaw and her friends wandered down long corridors, looking fruitlessly for a familiar face. They roamed about enormous office bays, amid scattered piles of desks, boxes, file cabinets, and building materials. "These things were just stacked up sky-high," she recalled. "It took us about an hour to wind our way through that to find anybody we knew." Finally, in the midst of a vast, largely empty office bay on the outermost E Ring, they saw their section chief, known to them only as Mrs. Wright, an eccentric Kansan who was trying to regain the red hair of her youth by popping a daily dose of alfalfa pills.

Hanshaw and the other Ordnance workers were moving from the Social Security Building at 4th Street and Independence Avenue on Capitol Hill, an elegant building with escalators, marble halls, and a fine cafeteria. Their new home was something altogether different. Water and sawdust were collected on the floor, and telephone wires dangled like seaweed from the ceiling. From her desk, Hanshaw could see the bright-blue sky a short distance away, but not through a window—it was an unfinished, open section of the building leading outside. Hanshaw and her companions could only laugh. "We couldn't imagine why they'd move anybody in there, but at that age we weren't too upset about it," she recalled. "We found it rather amusing. . . . We were the pioneers. It was an adventure."

The two dozen workers in Hanshaw's section—under the direction of Wright, who kept her overcoat on despite the warm May weather—set up an island of desks within their big bay, trying to make order out of chaos. "You couldn't really tell where the office started and where it finished," Hanshaw said. "We were all just in there." By the weekend, about three hundred workers from Ordnance had moved into the building, but it was a mere drop in the bucket. The employees "rattle about in the immensity like a small sewing circle in Madison Square Garden," an observer wrote.

Yet the building was officially open for business. Renshaw, McShain, and Hauck took reporters and photographers on a tour May 2 to see the completed section of the building and watch new employees at work. McShain, wearing a double-breasted suit and a fedora, glowed with pride. Even the normally dowdy Hauck was turned out for the event.

The newspapers exhausted themselves with superlatives. "The pentagonal nest of buildings . . . dwarfs the great pyramid of Cheops," the *Times-Herald* enthused. Its construction, the paper added, "was a story-making achievement without parallel outside the pages of the Arabian Nights' tales or the annals of Paul Bunyan." *The Washington Post* called it "a breath-taking study in immensity."

A War Department press release trumpeted the event as being "six months ahead of the schedule originally planned for the occupancy of the New War Department Office Building." All the newspapers highlighted the claim, and it has entered the litany of standard facts recited about the Pentagon. Yet it is entirely untrue. From the day he proposed his building, Somervell had promised that half a million square feet would be ready six months after construction began; the contract signed by McShain in September stipulated that at least 500,000 square feet of the building was to be "ready for occupancy" no later than May 1, 1942, which was under eight months. They had met that deadline—indeed, with 100,000 square feet to spare—and were opening the building right on time.

Ahead of schedule or not, the opening of the Pentagon for business on April 30, 1942, was an extraordinary achievement. It needed no embellishment. Barely more than nine months from the July evening when Somervell launched his idea, and seven and a half months after ground was broken, employees were moving into the world's largest office building. Somervell's promise had been fantastic, but its fulfillment was even more so. "It is almost inconceivable that any part of such a colossal structure . . . should now be occupied," the *Post* noted in an editorial saluting the "remarkable feat."

Somervell was exhilarated, sending rare words of praise to Renshaw's office the day occupancy began. "This is, I believe, a record-breaking accomplishment in which all concerned can take justifiable pride," Somervell said.

Somervell also sent a note on April 30 to Harry Hopkins, his old friend at the White House. Hopkins had made a bet—more than likely with Roosevelt—that the general would succeed in getting employees into the building by May 1. "This is merely to advise you that the Ordnance Department began moving into the new Army Building today," Somervell wrote. "I believe this information will make it possible for you to collect a two-bit bet which I understand you have with a certain distinguished person."

Roosevelt and Hopkins came over to see the building for themselves on Saturday, May 2. The president told Renshaw he was delighted with the progress. Touring the interior, however, Roosevelt and Hopkins were puzzled to find four large washrooms on each of the main hallways leading from the outer ring of the building to the inner, according to an account related by historian Constance M. Green in *Washington, A History of the Capital, 1800–1950*. The president, "upon inquiring the reason for such prodigality of lavatory space," was informed that this was to comply with Virginia segregation laws requiring separate facilities. But signs marking "colored" or "white" were never painted on the doors, possibly at the insistence of Roosevelt, who had signed the executive order banning discrimination in the federal government the previous summer. A War Department employee used chalk to mark the women's restroom doors on one corridor as "white" and "colored," but the markings were erased after complaints.

Another confusing matter needed to be cleared up—the building's name. The Army was still officially calling it the "New War Department Building in Arlington," which was a mouthful. The situation was confounding, considering that another "New War Department Building" had opened a year earlier at 21st Street and Virginia Avenue in Washington. People would ask, "Which New War Department Building? The one on Virginia Avenue or the one in Virginia?" Some had taken to calling the first one the "Old New War Department Building" and the second the "New New War Department Building."

Nine days after occupation began, the Army threw in the towel and decided to call the building by the name many workers and officers had been using informally for months. On May 9, 1942, Major General James A. Ulio, who as adjutant general was in charge of all administrative matters for the Army and reported to Somervell, issued a curt one-paragraph memorandum: "For the information of all concerned, the building at 21st and Va. Ave. NW., is correctly designated as the 'War Department Building'; the building in Arlington, now under construction for the War Department, is the 'Pentagon Building.' "

Preserving the War Department name for the building in Foggy Bottom was in keeping with Roosevelt's insistence that, after the war, the Army headquarters would move back to Washington. The building in Arlington was somewhat second-class, an aberration of war. But it was now official: It was the Pentagon.

The plank walkers

Even as the Pentagon's first occupants moved in, piles for the building's foundation were being pounded into the ground in the final section. The last of 41,492 concrete piles—which if lined up would stretch two hundred miles—were still being driven well into May. The new employees were vastly outnumbered by the army of construction workers, whose strength had dropped temporarily from thirteen to eleven thousand with the completion of the first part but would soon rise again as a new push began to finish the building.

Indeed, as much construction remained to be done as had been accomplished. When occupation began, the building was 50 percent finished, by Renshaw's estimate. Marjorie Hanshaw and her co-workers certainly needed no reminder. On top of the pile driving, they coped with the hammering and sawing of carpenters and the rumbling of concrete trucks. Officers shouted on telephones to be heard over the thunderous percussion of jackhammers. The tapping of typewriter keys and clicking of calculating machines were drowned out by the continuous clamor of construction.

Groves ordered Renshaw to make sure the higher-ups in the Ordnance Department were treated well. "I want them to have a good taste in their mouth towards the Engineers," he told Renshaw.

The overriding taste anybody in the building had was of dirt. Bulldozers grading the earth for roads raised enormous clouds of dust, which floated freely into the building and coated everything: water fountains, typewriters, the food in the cafeteria. It was thick enough to write with on any desk in the building.

When there wasn't dust, there was mud. "You just had to work your way through this muck, mud, water, and everything," recalled payroll witness Hank Neighbors. "It was just a combination between a marsh and a moor." Boards of lumber snaked around the grounds as walkways through the mud and puddles. In the Navy, the original crew members of a newly commissioned ship are called the "plank holders." The first occupants of the Pentagon came up with a variation—they were the "plank walkers."

Reporting to the building for a job interview, Lucille Ramale, a nineteen-year-old newly arrived in Washington from Brick Church in western Pennsylvania, was instructed to follow a rifle-toting soldier into the building. "It was a mess," she recalled. "The front entrance, it was so muddy, they had a plank down. You walked it. If anybody came towards you, they had to swing around you, or else put one foot in the mud."

Hanshaw and her office mates soon learned to keep lumber under their desks as well. "Oftentimes when it rained, we had our feet up on two-by-fours to keep them out of the water," she recalled. Other times streams of water from restrooms flowed down corridors. Field mice and occasionally frogs roamed the building.

"You know, today, environmentally, they wouldn't let anybody in a place like that," Marjorie Hanshaw Downey reflected more than sixty years later. "First of all, it was a hazard just walking among that stuff. We just worked in that condition and accepted it."

The ranks of War Department employees were growing steadily, about two hundred moving in every day. The entire Ordnance Department was soon in the building, followed quickly by other portions of Somervell's Services of Supply (the general stayed in the Munitions Building for the time being with Stimson and Marshall). By June 7, more than seven thousand War Department employees were working in the building, with thousands more from the Signal Corps and Adjutant General's office due to move in shortly. Already, the exodus of war workers from Washington to Arlington was noticeably relieving pressure on office space in the capital.

Moving crews carried desks, file cabinets, and other furniture into the Pentagon twenty-four hours a day, though not always with the greatest of care. One night in May, movers dumped the contents of an Army office from the trucks onto the loading platform, leaving desks broken, bookcases with glass shattered, and cabinets scratched. "The actual handling of furniture was done by very unskilled workmen who did not have much regard for government property," Major Bayard Schintelin, one of the victimized officers, complained to superiors.

The employees were packed into the Pentagon, with only eighty-five square feet of office space allotted per worker, a tight ratio that would allow 37,000 people to fit in the building if maintained. The biggest office bays were crammed with as many as 450 desks.

Senior officers wanted no part of such conditions and demanded partitions to wall off private office space. They wanted big, executive-style hardwood desks, too, complete with dentil molding around the edges. "If you gave a general an itty-bitty desk you'd be out of a job the next day," recalled Allen Dickey, an architect overseeing the furnishing. Moreover, the generals were choosing the prime real estate, the offices on the outer E ring with windows looking out. It meant most employees were walled off from the outside. Renshaw, feeling a certain proprietary interest in the Pentagon, wanted to preserve what little ambience the building had. "They're spoiling the outer ring in a lot of respects," he complained to Groves in a telephone conversation May 14.

Groves was incredulous. "You aren't getting esthetic, are you?" he asked.

"Almost," Renshaw replied. "There are so few nice places in the building that I hate to ruin the nicest one by putting partitions there." They should save the view for the masses.

Groves was having difficulty understanding Renshaw's point. This was a military headquarters, not an experiment in egalitarianism. "You want the big shots to have the view, don't you?" Groves said.

"I think the clerks would appreciate it more," Renshaw persisted. In the same three hundred square feet needed to accommodate a private office for a general, he said, eight or ten clerks could have desks with a nice view.

Renshaw was fighting a losing battle. The comforts for the privileged outweighed the accommodation of the masses. The big shots would always get the private, walled-off offices at the Pentagon, as well as the nice views.

Overshooting the mark

Somervell finally notified Congressional leaders by letter in May that his building was $14.2 million over budget. He also mentioned, almost as an aside, that due to the outbreak of war, it had become "necessary to abandon any plan to reduce the originally contemplated size of the building," and that he had in fact increased it by 650,000 square feet. To stifle any outcry, Somervell assured the chairmen of the Senate and House appropriations committees in his letter that he would not ask Congress for the money and would instead cover the overrun with unexpended balances from other construction projects. The Army "constantly expanded the size of the building yet Somervell never once went up and asked for more money," Groves later marveled.

Groves offered no apologies himself about the additional cost when he appeared before a House Appropriations subcommittee on June 15 to brief members on the building's progress. (Groves always took an aggressive approach with Congress. "I'm in favor of asking for a lot and letting them turn you down if they have the nerve—they won't have the nerve," he once explained to a fellow officer.)

"You have overshot the mark by a pretty big margin," remarked the subcommittee chairman, J. Buell Snyder of Pennsylvania.

"The building has overshot the original conception both as to size and speed of completion," Groves retorted. The building, he added, would total four million square feet. Asked how many workers it would hold, Groves offered no specifics. "It will have all of the capacity that was originally contemplated, and a great deal more," he said.

No protest was raised at the increased size or cost. Instead, much of the hearing dealt with complaints that the floors of the Pentagon were dusty. "We can get rid of the dust inside the building, but we cannot get rid of the dust outside, and it keeps coming in," Groves explained.

Renshaw was incredulous; they had been dreading Congress's reaction to the overrun, and all the members cared about was the dust. "They listened to a $15 million deficit, and swallowed it without a comment," he afterward told George Holmes, Somervell's PR man. "When somebody said there was dust on the floors, they sent for me to come up and explain it."

"Well, I'll be darned," said Holmes.

Nothing is usual

Like everyone else, Marjorie Hanshaw was still having trouble locating her desk—every day a new office had sprung up or a corridor was blocked with construction materials. Another employee, Robert Sanders, tried identifying visual landmarks to mark his way. Almost inevitably, by the time he made a second trip, the landmark had disappeared. Returning to their office from a meeting about manufacturing small arms, two Ordnance workers soon realized they were hopelessly lost but were too embarrassed to admit it; finally they followed exit signs outside to regain their bearings. It was happening all the time.

Adding to the confusion was the jumble of numbers and letters marking room numbers—2D-489, for example. Renshaw had come up with the numbering system on the fly shortly before occupancy started. Ordered one day to quickly develop a scheme, Renshaw sat down at an empty desk and drew a sketch of the building. It showed the five rings, labeled A for the inner ring through E for the outer ring, and the ten radial corridors, labeled 1 through 10 in clockwise order. Each office was numbered according to its floor, its ring, the nearest corridor, and then the specific office bay, in that order. Thus 2D-489 was on the second floor, on the D ring, off of corridor 4, in bay 89.

Groves was skeptical. "It already sounds like a procurement authority," he complained to Renshaw. Actually, once mastered, Renshaw's numbering system would prove a reliable guide to finding an office no matter where it was in the building. The interior setup of offices would change considerably over the years, but Renshaw's method—drawn up in about ten minutes—has stayed intact.

Yet to newcomers, it was like reading Greek. Nobody could remember which number referred to what.

"Nothing is usual about your thing over there," Groves told Renshaw. "Nobody can find his way around."

My people are Americans

The cafeteria, at least, was well-marked. Henry E. Bennett followed the signs directing him through the maze of hallways and down to the first floor. Bennett, a clerk in the Ordnance Department, had moved into the Pentagon that morning, Thursday, May 14, part of the vanguard. Like about 10 percent of War Department employees, Bennett was black. He joined a group of Ordnance staff—several secretaries and another man, all black—for lunch. Entering the cafeteria, they got in line but were immediately intercepted by a cafeteria supervisor: Colored employees were to eat in a separate dining room in the back. Bennett started to object, but one of the secretaries grabbed him by the arm. Don't make a scene, she said.

They went to the rear as directed, where a smaller, dustier, and shabbier dining room awaited, occupied and operated solely by blacks. Bennett got the lamb stew but was unable to take a bite. He had lost his appetite. A modest and serious-minded twenty-nine-year-old, Bennett had overcome a hardscrabble youth in Texas and Indiana—helping to raise his younger siblings by shining shoes—to graduate with honors from high school. He had interrupted his studies of mathematics and commerce at Indiana State

Teachers College in Terre Haute to serve his country. Bennett sat at the table, seething, ignoring his companions' pleas to eat. As the group prepared to leave, a cafeteria worker passed on some news: There was a young colored man who had refused to go to the back and was eating in the white section.

Bennett wanted to meet this man. He was easy to spot in the white section, sitting alone at a table, a slight young man, 5'7" and 140 pounds, wearing glasses. Bennett walked over and introduced himself. The young man was Jimmy Harold, a well-spoken, bright twenty-one-year-old who had come from Detroit six months earlier to join the war effort and had taken a job as an assistant engineer and draftsman with the Ordnance field service. This was his first day in the Pentagon too. Harold's polite and mild manner could not disguise the inner steel of a man whose upbringing would not allow him to accept second-class citizenship. Bennett liked him instantly. If anything happens, he told Harold, come find me.

Roosevelt's executive order barring discrimination in the federal government had succeeded in keeping the Pentagon's restrooms from being segregated. The cafeteria was different. The Public Buildings Administration, which normally operated cafeterias in federal buildings, had refused to do so in the Pentagon until the building was finished; it was still a construction site. Yet some way had to be found to feed the employees; isolated as the Pentagon was, there were few places nearby where they could eat.

The Army had turned to McShain for help. The builder's food subcontractor was already feeding thirteen thousand–plus construction workers every day. Renshaw asked the subcontractor, Industrial Food Systems Inc. of Washington, to operate a temporary cafeteria inside the Pentagon for War Department employees until the building was finished. The contractor set up the Pentagon employees' cafeteria with separate sections for black and white workers, the same as the construction cafeteria. The building had not been officially turned over to the Army, the contractors reasoned, and thus remained subject to Virginia law. However, Virginia had ceded the entire site to the federal government in March.

Whatever the legal rationales to justify the discrimination, Jimmy Harold was not going to stand for it. On Friday, he and Bennett, accompanied by two other black Ordnance employees, went back to the cafeteria for lunch. A white woman supervising the line approached them. "I'm very sorry, she said, but we don't serve people in here." Bennett looked around the vast dining room, filled with white employees eating lunch. "Apparently you are mistaken," he said in a deadpan manner. "There are quite a few people in here." The woman's demeanor hardened. "You know what I mean," she said coldly, and asked for the men's names. Harold took off his badge and showed it to her. The four men got their food, sat down at a table in the white dining room, and ate.

The rebellion of the black Ordnance employees was creating a stir. Walter P. McFarland, president of Industrial Food, called for help, and a guard from McShain's building security force, Officer Horace W. Crump, arrived shortly before noon. Instructions came from Renshaw's office—relayed by Captain Bob Furman—to make no move to evict the black employees, but to warn them not to eat in the white section again. Crump stationed himself outside the entrance and warned black employees as they left: "Tomorrow, you'll eat in the place provided for you." There was a hint of menace in his tone.

The chief of the Pentagon police force, Sumner Dodge, called McShain Saturday morning for instructions. McShain was no more but no less prejudiced than most men of his day; he considered separate facilities for whites and blacks critical for healthy relations with the labor unions. McShain told the police chief to back McFarland. When the cafeteria opened for lunch that day, Crump and a second officer were stationed at the entrance. Signs had been put up directing black employees to a separate entrance leading to the "colored cafeteria." Harold came down, accompanied by Bennett and two women. When Harold stepped in the line for white employees, Crump told him he was in the wrong cafeteria and should leave. Harold refused. "No, I am eating in here today," he said, walking past the guard, and the others followed. Laurel Carson and her friends did the same. The black Ordnance workers ate in the white section, ignoring hostile stares.

On Monday, the line was drawn. McShain notified Renshaw in the morning that he intended to have the security guards enforce segregation. "We see no reason whatever, since the colored people have equal facilities and conveniences as the white people, why they should not use their own dining room exclusively," McShain wrote. Guards were given orders to block any blacks from entering the white dining room and take the badge numbers of any trying to get in.

Gladys Lancaster, a black messenger in Ordnance, was one of the first to go down for lunch that day. Unnerved by the guards, she turned back, afraid even to go into the colored section. Back in the office, she begged the others not to go to the white dining room. Ruth Bush, for one, was not cowed. Bush, a junior clerk typist from New York, went down around 11:30 A.M. with a half dozen others for lunch. A guard stuck a nightstick in front of the door and said they could not enter.

"This is America, not Germany," Bush angrily told the guard. Her three brothers were in the Army, and she would not back down. "I am an American; I'll die for America, therefore I have every right that any other American has," Bush said. "Just think, I have brothers in the war now, fighting." She started to cry. "We are just as good as they are," she told her companions.

At 11:35, Harold stopped by Bennett's desk and said he was going to lunch. Bennett followed a few minutes later. They arrived to find the entrance blocked by a crowd. Ruth Bush was angrily giving the guards an earful. Harold worked his way to the front.

McFarland had arrived and pleaded with the black employees to use the colored dining room, insisting it was "just as good, with the same food and same furniture, same everything." Harold, polite but determined, pressed for an explanation. McFarland said it was a McShain cafeteria, not a federal cafeteria.

The backup grew to over a hundred people. White employees trying to get into the cafeteria found their way blocked, and others who had finished their lunch were stuck. Crump telephoned Chief Dodge, asking for reinforcements.

Four officers rushed to the cafeteria at 11:45, and they ordered blacks to stand back and let white people through. One of the guards, Theodore Lee, Jr., a stocky, 190-pound forty-year-old, decided to resolve the matter quickly. "There were white people and niggers all ganged around there at the door trying to go in," he told an investigator several days later.

Lee and another officer barreled through the crowd, yelling "Break it up" and roughly shoving black men and women aside. Lee pushed Harold in the back, knocking him off balance. Harold threw his arms up reflexively to protect himself, possibly grabbing at Lee's nightstick. Lee drew his gun, and some of the women screamed. The crowd scattered, white and black; some ran and others backed against the walls. Everyone moved away except Jimmy Harold. He took one step back, but then stood still and kept his eyes on the gun until Lee put it back in his belt. Then Harold turned his back to Lee and, without a word, started to slowly walk away. He had taken one step when Lee's stick sank into his head with a sickening thud, sending blood from his scalp spurting into the air. "Some of the girls screamed and the blood was flowing on the floor furiously," Bush said. "The floor was saturated with blood and my dress was full of blood and another girl's dress was full of blood."

Harold was staggering. Laurel Carson tried to stop the blood with her hand but it gushed through her fingers. Others put handkerchiefs on the cut but they were quickly sopping. None of the fifty or more white employees who witnessed the episode offered help. Co-workers brought Harold out of the cafeteria and half-carried him upstairs to a restroom. Charles Brown, an office mate, washed Harold's wound with a handkerchief and cold water, but it was a long time before the bleeding was stanched.

Henry Bennett stayed at the scene until he was able to comfort several crying women, one hysterical. He easily found Harold and the others by following the trail of blood that led from the cafeteria up to the second floor to the men's washroom. Bennett and the others took Harold to the first-aid room, where an Army nurse cleaned the wound with alcohol and put a pressure bandage on it. It was a very nasty cut, the nurse told Bennett; she sent Harold to a public health clinic in Washington where doctors could stitch his wound.

Back at the cafeteria, Theodore Lee twirled his baton, pleased with his work. "The niggers started going in their dining room and white people started to go in their dining room and the whole thing was quiet from then on out," he said.

Integrating the Pentagon

Judge William H. Hastie was in his office in the Munitions Building that afternoon when a contingent of five black women, all Ordnance employees, came to his office, too upset to return to work at the Pentagon.

They had heard Hastie, a civilian aide to Secretary of War Stimson, was the man to come to for such matters. At age thirty-seven, Hastie was one of the most distinguished black men in the country, a man of moral certitude. Raised on a chicken farm on the outskirts of Knoxville, he studied law at Harvard and eventually won appointment by Roosevelt as the first black federal trial court judge in American history. In 1941, Hastie joined the War Department and went to work combating rampant discrimination in the Army. Despite his respect for Stimson, Hastie was under no illusions. On one occasion, he spoke to Stimson about integration in the Army Air Forces, an area where Hastie was optimistic he was making progress. Then Stimson spoke: "Mr. Hastie, is it not true that your people are basically agriculturists?"

Stimson, Hastie later said, "was a most honest and dedicated man, a patriot in the best and highest sense of the word, but he was a man whose whole life in his practice of law, in his social contacts, his whole background, had isolated him from the areas, the problems, of which I was basically concerned." As for General Marshall, his attitude was that it was not the responsibility of an Army in wartime to right social wrongs.

In his office, Hastie listened with alarm to the women's story about what had transpired at the Pentagon that day. Then a telephone call came from Henry Bennett, who was with Jimmy Harold at the public health clinic downtown. Hastie immediately drove over to pick them up in his car and brought Harold to his room at the YMCA for colored men on 12th Street, where he and Bennett saw him to his bed. The next morning, the judge sat down with Bennett and heard the full story. Dismayed, Hastie won approval that day from Stimson for an investigation by the War Department's inspector general.

The resulting investigation was almost as disgraceful as the incident. The Army attorney appointed to perform the inquiry, Colonel Carl L. Ristine, adopted an accusatory and condescending tone with all black witnesses, referring to Harold, a draftsman and engineer, as "that colored boy." "You are rather an innocent looking person to cause a riot down there," he told Ruth Bush.

"Riot? Did they call it a riot?" Bush replied. "If it was a riot it was their causing; they are the ones who started fighting and pushing our women around like they were dogs."

Ristine suggested the black employees had a premeditated plot to block the cafeteria entrance, and he accused Harold of "subterfuge." Most infuriating of all was Ristine's insistence—repeated to almost every black witness—that segregation was not discrimination. "If the whites were segregated in one room as the colored in another, it is just as much segregation for the whites as it is for the colored, isn't it?" he asked one employee.

In their testimony, Theodore Lee and the other security guards stuck to a story that Harold was about to assault Lee and that the guard had clubbed him in self-defense. Their account was corroborated by several white witnesses. Yet not a single Ordnance Department witness—including many who did not know Jimmy Harold and others who were clearly intimidated by the questioning of a white Army colonel—agreed that Harold had threatened Lee, despite constant prodding from Ristine.

Moreover, Charles Meisel, a white retired Army master sergeant disturbed by what he had seen, testified that Lee had swung "almost indiscriminately. . . . That is what really shocked me, it was handled so crudely. . . . There was no occasion to use the club."

Reporting his findings May 25, Ristine concluded that the guards were "justified" in using force. The "colored employees" were at fault for blocking the entrance, he wrote, and "their failure to . . . disperse constituted an unlawful assembly." Ristine ignored the fact that it was the guards themselves who had blocked the door.

Hastie had to fight for permission to review the testimony; reading it, he was appalled at the conduct of the investigation. In a memorandum to Under Secretary of War Robert Patterson, Hastie pointed to the "singularly unjudicial attitude of the investigating officer." While dismissing the testimony of black witnesses, Ristine had accepted without reservation all the testimony of the white guards and contractor employees, all of whom had "a clear interest . . . either in protecting a fellow guard or in protecting their employer."

An aide to Patterson, agreeing that Ristine "was clearly not an objective investigator," asked the inspector general to review the report. Examining his own office's findings, Major General Virgil Peterson, the inspector general of the Army, backed Ristine's investigation, and the matter was dropped. It was yet another dispiriting case for Hastie and his allies; around the country, physical violence and insults had been directed at blacks entering the Army.

Yet the rebellion of the Ordnance employees at the Pentagon succeeded. Immediately upon hearing of the cafeteria disturbance on May 18, Somervell that day issued orders to Groves "to insure the discontinuance of any enforced segregation of negro employees in the cafeterias in the Pentagon building." McShain, backed by Renshaw, protested that he had to comply with Virginia law and warned that allowing blacks and whites to eat together could cause labor disturbances among construction workers. But Somervell's order stood.

McFarland kept the colored dining room open in case black employees decided to eat in there voluntarily, but it was to no avail. "Not one of them would enter that room," McFarland reported several days later. Henry Bennett, Ruth Bush, Laurel Carson, and, most of all, Jimmy Harold, had integrated the Pentagon.

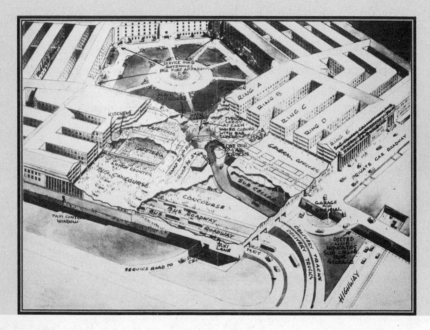

Popular Science *schematic from 1943 showing interior of Pentagon.*

CHAPTER
12

HELL-AN-GONE

Miss Ten Thousand

Opal Sheets did her best to ignore the parade of officials walking past her desk, but they would not go away. The twenty-four-year-old from Parsons, West Virginia, an administrative assistant to a colonel in the Services of Supply, had just moved into the Pentagon on that hot July day in 1942. "She's the one," she heard someone whisper.

Before she could protest, Sheets was whisked away from her desk and brought outside the building to pose before waiting newspaper photographers. Next she was feted at a luncheon, given the seat of honor next to Lieutenant Colonel Renshaw. War Department PR men had decided it would be good publicity to make a big deal about the ten-thousandth employee to report to work at the Pentagon, and they made sure they picked an attractive woman. "Officially she is 'Miss Ten Thousand,' but off the record she is typical of the thousands of girls who keep the wheels moving in the War Department's new building," the *Washington Daily News* reported.

Off the record, Miss Ten Thousand was impatient with the frivolity. Her brother Cecil—the youngest of the four Sheets boys from Parsons, a kid who joined the Army to see the world—had been in the Philippines when the Japanese landed and had surrendered with the rest of the U.S. and Filipino force in April on the Bataan Peninsula. He was now officially listed as missing in action. It would be years before she learned of the hell he went through on the Bataan Death March and his eventual death of malaria as a prisoner at Camp O'Donnell. Right now, Opal Sheets wanted to help her brother the best way she knew how, which was to get back to work.

Yet she represented another remarkable milestone. It had been exactly a year since Somervell dreamed up the project, and already there were ten thousand employees working in the Pentagon, more than in any building in Washington. McShain's workers had finished a million and a quarter square feet, and the Pentagon was two-thirds complete.

By the time Opal Sheets posed for the cameras, it was obvious to Assistant Secretary of War John J. McCloy that the Pentagon needed to be bigger. McCloy was in charge of allocating space in the building, and by July, every inch—including in the sections still under construction—had been assigned. Army departments clamoring for offices were told there was no more room in the Pentagon.

Critical days were at hand for the War Department. After months of debate about where the Army should launch its war to liberate Europe, a decision was close. At the order of Roosevelt—and despite the misgivings of Henry Stimson and George Marshall—secret preparations would begin by the end of the month for Operation Torch, the invasion of North Africa. Stimson and Marshall were still in the Munitions Building, but the plan was to bring the high command into the Pentagon in the fall and guide the course of the war from there. The more of the War Department that could fit in the Pentagon, the better. "Without some cohesion there, without some center, we would have been in a bad way in the war," McCloy later said.

McCloy had an idea how to wring out more space. The building as designed included a fifth floor atop only the inner and outermost rings, A and E. This area, designed primarily as an attic to hold machinery and equipment, included space for storage but not much for people. On July 13, 1942, McCloy dashed off a memorandum to Somervell: Why not build a fifth floor atop all five rings of the Pentagon, and use as much of the space as possible for more offices? "In view of our growing need for space, I am wondering if it would not be wise to do this while the contractor is on the ground," McCloy wrote. "It could be done much cheaper now while his equipment and personnel are on the job.

"I am aware of the fact that we are short about $12,000,000 to complete the building as now planned, but since we are going to concentrate, why not do a good job of it?"

Reviewing McCloy's suggestion, Somervell's deputy, "Fat" Styer, agreed with the reasoning. "A decision should be made immediately if we are to go ahead with this," he told Somervell. The latter's reaction was succinct: "Okay. Where is money coming from?" Somervell wrote back. That was a good question. Nor was it the only one.

Without a doubt, adding a full fifth floor at this late stage would delay the Pentagon's completion. About 40 percent of the roof had already been put on the three intermediate rings, and roofers were hard at work building more. All that effort would be for naught. The building's heating and cooling system, designed for four floors, would be thrown out of kilter. Areas of the building that had already been occupied by Army workers would become construction zones again. On top of all their other tribulations, the plank walkers would have to cope with construction workers building a new story over their heads.

Groves notified Renshaw the next day that he might have to build a bigger Pentagon. Renshaw, likely numb to the prospect, raised no protest, but he begged for a quick decision. Memories were still fresh of the debacle after Pearl Harbor, when construction was paralyzed by the debate over whether to bombproof the building. Renshaw reported July 17 that adding a full fifth floor would provide 340,000 square feet of additional office space, room enough for another four thousand employees at the rate they were cramming them in.

As he awaited a decision, Renshaw ordered a stop to all roofing work. "Each day we go ahead is going to cost us about $5,000 a day to rip out," he said. But stopping the work meant finished areas of the building would be exposed to the elements. A powerful thunderstorm hit the site the night of July 20, accompanied by lightning that struck two Fort Myer soldiers on sentry duty and nearby flash floods that swept a three-year-old girl to her death. The storm dumped more than an inch of rain in less than a half hour onto the open building. "We had a gang—a couple hundred men—doing nothing but stopping leaks last night on those roofs that aren't covered," Renshaw complained the next day to Gar Davidson, Groves's aide.

Somervell soon issued instructions to build a fifth floor. It had never really been in doubt. Whatever problems the fifth floor was going to cause, and whatever the cost, Somervell was not going to turn down an invitation to make his building bigger. While he was at it, Somervell also approved converting more than 300,000 square feet of storage space in the basement into offices for more than a thousand employees, including the world's biggest reproduction plant, where the War Department could do its own offset printing, mimeographing, and photo printing.

No public announcement was made about the additions. Army documents submitted to Congress and published in the *Congressional Record* described the new space on the fifth floor as "Fourth floor—intermediate." It was not unlike Somervell's subterfuge of describing the first floor as the basement and the basement as the sub-basement.

Nor was it the only subterfuge. The War Production Board, which oversaw the allocation of critical materials, "started to raise thunder" about steel window sashes ordered to build the fifth floor. Groves, suffering a case of "the jitters," directed that Renshaw deceive the board by pretending the material was for the lower floors. "The only thing we want to be damn sure of is we get the material, and don't make it look as though it's being ordered for the top floor," his aide, Lieutenant Colonel Donald Antes, told Renshaw on July 25.

To further cover their tracks, they concocted a fiction that the War Department had always intended to include a fifth floor. "Here's the story, as I see it: This story has been planned from the beginning and just deferred," Renshaw suggested. He was sick of struggling with the board every time he needed materials for the building. "The War Department is having a hell of a time functioning over here," Renshaw told Antes. "[T]hey'd better leave us alone if they want [us] to run this war."

Groves wanted Renshaw to get started on the new floor before anybody changed his mind. No plans had been drawn yet, but that was just a nicety. The builders would use schematic designs based on the construction of the lower floors while the actual plans were drawn. Without plans, it was impossible to say realistically how much the work would cost. "We can fake it, certainly, but we won't have that design for two and a half months, although we're going to start to build tomorrow," Renshaw said.

When they started construction of the new floor on July 25, workers did not even bother to rip out the old roof in some sections. To their surprise, crews renovating the Pentagon sixty years later discovered roofing tiles between the fourth and fifth floors. Even given this haste, the additional work meant that completion of the building would be pushed back six weeks, to January 1, 1943. "To get the whole thing in November 15th is more of a miracle than I want to bargain for," Renshaw said.

McCloy, you blackmailer

One problem remained. Revised blueprints had been sent to Roosevelt, and the president was taking his fine time with them, exercising his architectural fancies, McCloy later recalled. Weeks passed, and construction of the fifth floor continued unabated, but eventually the president's approval would have to be secured. Somervell enlisted McCloy's aid to get the plans back from Roosevelt, but the assistant secretary had no luck. "Every time I tried it, the president would snap me over the fingers and say, 'I've got some other ideas,' " McCloy recalled.

Help came from an unlikely source: an unsavory, half-American Nazi named Ernst "Putzi" Hanfstaengl. Educated at Harvard, where his acquaintances included Roosevelt and T. S. Eliot, Putzi had been a member of Hitler's inner circle from the days of the Beer Hall Putsch. He served as Hitler's personal foreign press chief from 1933 to 1937. Fleeing Germany after falling out with the Nazis, Putzi was taken into British custody in 1939 and eventually moved to Canada. Roosevelt had personally arranged for his old Harvard classmate to be flown secretly to Washington on June 30, 1942, and put to work as an intelligence operative. He was taken to Fort Belvoir in Northern Virginia and began providing the White House with his assessments of the Nazi leadership. The British warned that Putzi was "an adventurer, untrustworthy and a liar," and his intelligence estimates quickly proved to be of dubious value, but Roosevelt remained intrigued. Nonetheless, the president wanted to distance the White House from the project and asked for the War Department's help. A White House aide spoke to McCloy. "Can't you take Mr. Hanfstaengl . . . off the president's budget?" the aide asked him.

McCloy, ever the wheeler-dealer, saw an opportunity. "So I sent back word if we get those Pentagon blueprints okayed by FDR, I'll take care of Mr. Hanfstaengl," McCloy later said. "And that's how we got them."

McCloy recalled that he helped arrange for a "safe sinecure" from which Putzi could continue his intelligence reports, and the revised Pentagon plans were approved. At the next cabinet meeting, Roosevelt saw the assistant secretary. "McCloy," the president said, "you blackmailer!"

Great strain

Even as War Department employees moved into the Pentagon, the site remained a dangerous place. On the morning of June 20, James D. Mitchell, a fifty-seven-year-old ironworker from Washington, was directing the movement of a giant hoisting crane when it struck a high-tension wire. The cable broke and fell across wooden concrete forms, setting them afire. Mitchell pulled the wire away from the forms and was electrocuted. George R. Love heroically but foolishly tried to pull Mitchell away from the wire. The twenty-six-year-old laborer from Glen Burnie, Maryland, also died from the shock. A few weeks later, Percy Bailey, a thirty-five-year-old worker from Washington, was changing a tire on a concrete truck when the tire exploded and the rim flew off, hitting him in the throat and leg. He died at the hospital.

A heat wave settled over the region in July, tormenting the workers with high temperatures and stupefying humidity. Thomas Lauria, a fifty-five-year-old cement finisher from Staten Island, collapsed on the job late on the afternoon of July 17 and died soon afterward of prostration. Thousands of Washingtonians, desperate for a breeze, abandoned their homes at night to sleep in Rock Creek Park or other open areas. Wilting in the heat, Henry Stimson fled to the cool climes of the Adirondacks at the end of the month. Escaping the city regularly was a necessity for him—Stimson considered the climate in Washington to be "designed for the destruction of the sanity of government officials."

Even Paul Hauck, the great rock of the Pentagon construction, was starting to crack. With the job more than half done, McShain's job superintendent had yet to take a day off, sometimes working twenty-two hours straight, and never less than fifteen hours a day. Hauck, McShain noticed, "was beginning to show the great strain he was under in driving the project."

Against Hauck's will, McShain ordered his superintendent to take a two-week vacation. McShain would personally supervise the Pentagon construction during his absence. It was a typical McShain gesture—the generous solicitousness toward his loyal employees. But also typically, McShain could not resist turning his stint into a competition. McShain raced all over the site night and day, coaxing and prodding workers to pick up speed and outdo Hauck's pace. His target was Hauck's record of 2,250 cubic yards of concrete poured in one day.

Hauck, too wound up to relax, spent his vacation traveling to different parts of the country to expedite shipment of building materials to the Pentagon. The day before Hauck returned to work, McShain and Lew Edwards, one of the section supervisors, were on their feet eighteen hours supervising a new record concrete pour, 2,875 cubic yards. Hauck came back to the job only to hear McShain's endless boasting about how the boss had set a new record for the job. The record stood, too.

One day I'll be famous

The job and the weather were taking their toll on McShain as well—he had lost eight pounds in the heat subbing for Hauck, and he punctured his foot walking around the site. McShain had to answer to a higher authority. His wife, Mary, watching her husband for signs of a physical or mental breakdown, ordered him on vacation. "Mother would use these words: 'John, go upstairs and get the suitcases. We have to go away,' " Polly McShain recalled. "She knew it was either sickness, death, or a vacation, and she would not let him kill himself."

Yet there was little time for McShain to relax. Building a bigger Pentagon, McShain wanted assurances he would be paid accordingly. By the terms of the contract, the builders were to be paid a fixed fee of $524,000. The contract had provisions for increasing the fee, but the amount depended on how much space was added, a figure open to interpretation given a building as vast as the Pentagon. "There's loads of tricks to this figuring on this building," Renshaw observed.

The Army put McShain off, insisting in August that the matter be settled only after the building was finished. "We'll have one grand fight instead of a lot of little ones," a budget official explained. McShain—"a pretty hard customer," in Renshaw's words—yelled long and hard, but to no avail. Groves, as usual, was entirely unsympathetic. "If he'd been as much interested in doing the job cheaply as he is in fighting for this little amount of fee, why, we'd have saved a lot of dollars," he told Renshaw.

Meanwhile, open warfare broke out among the contractors over the wording of a dedication plaque naming the principals in the building's creation that was to be placed at the Pentagon's Mall entrance. The inscription approved by Renshaw in late July listed John McShain, Inc., as the contractor, and the two Virginia firms, Doyle & Russell and Wise Contracting Company, Inc., as "associated contractors." The Virginia firms objected, insisting that the wording on the panel match the language of the contract, which listed all three companies as contractors.

Contract or not, it was a presumptuous complaint. The Virginia firms had served primarily as underwriters for the project, each contributing 20 percent of the financing and each receiving 20 percent of the fee. Except for one man—John F. O'Grady of Doyle & Russell, chief accountant for the job—the two Virginia firms supplied managers only in minor supervisory roles. "There is no question but that Mr. McShain has received little assistance from the other firms in this venture," Groves noted. ". . . They have taken little if any part in the management of operations, or in the solution of the many difficult construction problems."

Indeed, the first time Hobart E. Doyle, president of Doyle & Russell, visited the Pentagon site was when he came to complain about the wording on the plaque. "Whoever it was, it was the first time I'd ever seen him," said Groves.

The contrast with McShain was obvious. Arguments about fees were one thing, but to McShain the plaque was sacrosanct. It represented the recognition of the ages that he, John McShain, had built the Pentagon.

Renshaw and Groves backed McShain, but the argument raged through August. Lee Paschall, the president of Wise, visited Renshaw's office on August 29 and was so abusive that Renshaw threatened to call the Pentagon police to escort him out of the office. Paschall apologized and Renshaw accepted it, but Groves was unforgiving, considering the contractor's behavior "disgraceful and disrespectful." Groves dismissed the Virginia firms' demands. "We can force them to accept anything," Groves told Renshaw.

However, the Virginia firms had an important benefactor—Representative Clifton Woodrum, the Virginia congressman largely responsible for getting them the contract. Woodrum called Somervell August 31, and during their chummy conversation they settled the matter in less than a minute. "These people, the Virginia contractors, they're just a little bit upset," Woodrum explained. "They have a little pride of authorship in that building." Would it be all right to list all the contractors equally?

"Oh absolutely," Somervell said. "I'll have it done right away."

That was that. The limestone plaque was installed on the Mall entrance not long afterward. There was no ceremony and no photographs; the date was not even recorded. The job was "too rushed to take the time," Hauck recalled. The stone had Franklin D. Roosevelt's name at the top, followed by Henry L. Stimson, Under Secretary of War Robert P. Patterson, and General George C. Marshall. (Patterson's middle initial was mistakenly carved as "B" and later corrected, but the change remains obvious.) Below were the officers directly responsible, including Somervell, Groves, and Renshaw. Next were the chief architects, Edwin Bergstrom and his replacement, David Witmer. (There had been debate about including Witmer, but Renshaw insisted; Witmer had solved numerous design conundrums after Bergstrom's departure.) Next were the contractors; as consolation, McShain was listed above Doyle & Russell and Wise, a first among equals, at least. Last was the builders' manager, J. Paul Hauck.

Just before the rectangular panel was placed in the wall, two more names were added, unbeknownst to almost all. Captain Bob Furman and Major Charles H. Smith, Renshaw's operations officer, took some tar and impishly wrote their names on the back of the stone. "Roosevelt's on the front, and we're on the back," Furman later said. "One day, I'll be famous."

Hell-an-gone

Why anyone would want his name on the building in the first place was beyond the comprehension of the plank walkers. As summer wore on, the good-natured patience of Marjorie Hanshaw and the other government girls was wearing thin. "Hell-an-gone" was one of the nicer nicknames they came up with for the place. Some employees claimed that the architect had gone insane after his design was completed; others insisted he was insane before he started.

The more people moved in, the more chaotic the place got. The question of racial segregation in the cafeteria had been settled, but the food operation was still an endless headache for McShain and Renshaw. Between the construction workers and the War Department employees, they were feeding as many as 25,000 people, going through two tons of meat, four tons of vegetables, and 625 gallons of coffee every day. "I am inclined to believe that the task was even greater than that of erecting the building," McShain later remarked.

There was no kitchen in the building nor would there be one until the end of the year, when the permanent cafeteria was built. Groves deemed temporary stoves a fire risk, so food was prepared in the construction workers' cafeteria in a big frame building with a kitchen the size of a football field. Hot food was loaded into vacuum containers and delivered by truck several hundred yards to the Pentagon.

Two temporary dining rooms now operated in huge unoccupied office bays, and together with the construction cafeteria, there was seating for ten thousand people—if only employees could get through the long lines. The thirty minutes that war workers were allowed for lunch simply was not enough. "It takes that much time to walk to the cafeteria and stand in line to wait your turn," complained J. H. Beswick of Washington. "If you are too long waiting you make a dash for the beverage bar only to learn that the things they call sandwiches are all gone. There is no other place to eat, no time to go elsewhere. You have to eat this outfit's food or do without."

Those eating in the Pentagon dining rooms complained of flies and dust or worse. In June a young Ordnance clerk reported to first-aid carrying a "filthy, lousy" sandwich he said he had bought at the cafeteria and had made him ill. Simultaneously, an anonymous caller telephoned the newspapers to report the sandwich was infested with maggots. The story unraveled like a dimestore detective novel. Renshaw ordered the first-aid nurse "to hold the person and the sandwich" and rushed over officers to investigate. "The first thing we found out were the bread and the meat were entirely different brands than we used," Renshaw told Groves. Under interrogation by Furman and two other officers, the kid admitted the sandwich was planted, but said he "wasn't going to squeal on anybody." Renshaw suspected a union operation aimed at embarrassing the contractors.

Nonetheless, most complaints were coming from employees who needed no instruction from the unions or anyone else. "If the city has an epidemic, it will be a safe bet where it started," wrote the *Times-Herald*.

Groves worried obsessively about the complaints, convinced that as much as any other feature, food service would determine whether people considered the building a success. He ordered Renshaw to inspect the cafeteria regularly for cleanliness and to make sure the silverware was polished. "I think until I stop getting complaints, you'd better eat there about every other day," Groves told Renshaw on July 30.

"That's a permanent assignment, Colonel," Renshaw protested. "Because they're never going to stop complaining."

Groves was particularly worried about conditions in several dining rooms reserved for Army officers. "Have you got some good-looking hostesses in those other rooms?" he asked Renshaw.

"Beautiful, Colonel," Renshaw replied.

"How many have you got?"

"One in each room."

"Well, you better double that number, and get them better-looking," Groves ordered.

Still dissatisfied, Groves took to sending an officer on undercover missions to inspect conditions in the cafeteria. After receiving the spy's reports, Groves sent Renshaw a memorandum on August 6 complaining of "a considerable fly problem" and critiquing in detail the condition of the butter patties: "The individual butter pats were piled six deep, separated by layers of oil paper but were in an unsightly condition and had a strong scent inasmuch as no ice had been placed around or underneath the butter."

Renshaw was infuriated. Here he was trying to construct the world's largest office building in record time and Groves was sending spies to examine the butter patties? Renshaw reported the butter was now being iced, and as for the flies, workers were spending three hours every morning spraying. "Instead of starting at 5 A.M. we come in there at 3 A.M. and spray everything," Renshaw said. "If we spray anymore we'll be poisoning the people."

Renshaw had proudly displayed a gold star that had been awarded the cafeteria by the Arlington County Health Department. The undercover officer recommended that it "be removed entirely, or placed in an obscure location, inasmuch as this undeserved trophy is regarded with manifest scorn by the diners."

The plank walkers reserved their greatest scorn for the sweltering conditions inside the Pentagon. Air-conditioning was still a novelty for many Washington workers, but in most buildings they could at least open windows and doors to get a draft. In the Pentagon, most workers were stationed far from any openings. Those close to the windows, like Lucille Ramale, were not necessarily better off—the construction was right outside. "When the noise got so bad, and the dust got so bad, we couldn't even open the windows," she said. "So I remember getting combs to put my hair up off my neck, because it was so hot. You'd just ruin your clothes because you'd just sweat them completely wet every day. It was miserable."

Air-conditioning the Pentagon was an unprecedented challenge for the relatively young technology. Not only was the building far bigger than anything previously air-conditioned, its seven-thousand-plus windows and low, spread-out design left it extremely vulnerable to changes in outdoor temperature.

Charles S. Leopold, a renowned Philadelphia mechanical engineer who had air-conditioned big buildings such as the New York Stock Exchange and Madison Square Garden, had been hired by Somervell for $85,600 to design the heating and cooling for the Pentagon. Leopold set up the largest air-conditioning system of its kind, with twelve centrifugal compressors manufactured by the Carrier Corporation of Syracuse, New York. They operated on huge amounts of water—46,600 gallons of water were pumped per minute from the Pentagon lagoon and carried to the building through a 1,200-foot tunnel, where it was chilled by the compressors to forty-three degrees and used to cool the air. The system may have been impressive, but in the hot summer of 1942, with temperatures soaring and more than ten thousand employees in the building, the air-conditioning was simply not working.

It was impossible to cool the building, given it was still a construction site with large sections open to the sweltering humidity. More than three thousand employees were working in areas with no air-conditioning, and there was little hope of getting it to them before the end of August. Huge fans were installed to improve air circulation in the building, but the plank walkers remained thoroughly unimpressed.

The situation here is tragic

The final insult was the commute. Epic traffic jams were being reported with only a fraction of the employees in the building. "The afternoon outbound trip is something like a retreat from Singapore," the *Washington Daily News* wrote May 27.

The maze of roads around the building was not even half completed. All around the building, roadbeds were being graded, bridges built, pavement poured, and overpasses constructed. The trip was a nightmare for drivers—routes to the building seemed to change every day. Hundreds of cars would end up lost every day, "their drivers completely confused and befuddled, not knowing whether they were going toward the building or in the opposite direction," McShain later said.

Military police directed the traffic, but it seemed to make little difference. "We're putting on more MPs, and they run them around in more circles," Renshaw complained.

Drivers who did make it to the building found parking saturated. By June, spaces had been paved for three thousand cars, but with nearly twenty thousand construction workers and War Department employees, they went fast. Those who were able to find a spot often would have trouble finding their cars after work. A layer of fine Virginia clay dust stirred up by the construction coated every vehicle in the lot, giving them all the same orange-red color. Robert Sanders, a Services of Supply employee, took to tying a colored ribbon to his radio antenna so he could spot his car.

Traveling by bus was not a pleasant option. Nelson Clayton, an eighteen-year-old from the foothills of Virginia's Blue Ridge Mountains working as a telephone installer, paid a nickel every morning for an adventurous bus ride from his sister's home in Arlington. "You'd ride the bus in, if they could find a way in," Clayton recalled. "But they'd get lost, the roads would change, they'd stop out in the middle of the fields and you'd have to walk in through the mud. 'There's the building, we don't know how to get there.' You'd hike in half a mile maybe."

In the evening, employees swarmed out of the building and into long lines to cram onto scarce buses. "Girls would smack each other over the head with their purses to get into the buses," secretary Marie Dowling Owen later said. Most were left behind, coated with dust.

The Capital Transit Company, the largest of three private companies that served the building, had thirty-five buses, about two hundred short of what they would need once the building was finished. There was little immediate prospect of getting more, since the War Production Board had frozen the manufacture of buses. Those that existed were mostly wheezing old heaps. The ancient red bus Hanshaw rode home one day was unable to even climb up Columbia Pike. She and the other passengers got off and walked so the bus could make it up the hill.

Getting to and from the building was such a nightmare that a War Department official suggested the top two floors be converted into dormitories. Numerous war workers demanded transfers to other agencies to escape the Pentagon; others resigned from the government altogether. Plank walkers were going public with their criticisms. "Some may reproach us, and some do, for complaining about working conditions when our boys are dying in fox-holes," an anonymous war worker wrote in a letter to the *Times-Herald* published September 5.

> However we would like to inform the general public about our working conditions. Primarily we spend approximately three hours daily traveling to and from work.
>
> We don't mind the crowded conditions of the transportation vehicles, for we have already completed our course in the sardine stance. We don't mind the poor air conditioning that causes one to perspire during the hot weather. . . . We don't mind catching a permanent cold or dying of rheumatism. We wouldn't mind the devil himself if we might be able to buy a decent lunch during our half hour recreation period.
>
> The situation here is tragic. When this building is completed forty thousand people will be employed within this geometric castle. Forty thousand people ill-housed and ill-fed. The Army marches on its stomach—what about the War Department?

The most fantastic operation

General George Marshall, at least, did not think the situation entirely tragic. Throughout the construction, Marshall had been a frequent visitor to the Pentagon, often trotting down from Fort Myer during his evening horseback ride on Prepare, his chestnut gelding, to watch the progress. He and Somervell toured the building in August, and Marshall declared himself impressed with the cafeteria. On a September morning a few weeks later, Renshaw warned Paul Hauck that Marshall would be arriving in thirty minutes to inspect the Pentagon with a visitor. Marshall wanted to show off the building to British Field Marshal Sir John Dill, chief of the British military delegation in Washington. Personable and forthright, Dill had forged a close relationship with the Americans, particularly the Army chief of staff, and he had single-handedly improved the tenor of British–U.S. military cooperation.

Hauck took Marshall and Dill up to the roof, where they could see the entire project. Reaching the edge, the generals looked over a vast panorama of men and bulldozers, trucks and steam shovels moving in every direction, raising spirals of dust. The building was more than 80 percent complete and now home to about seventeen thousand war workers. Concrete was being poured for the upper floors of Section E, the last of the five sections. Workers were constructing the fifth floor atop the interior rings. All around the Pentagon, they could see a bewildering mix of half-built roads, intersections, and overpasses—many of them standing incongruously alone, like bridges in a desert.

Marshall and Dill surveyed the scene without speaking. The longer they looked, the more nervous Hauck grew. Finally Marshall asked Dill for his impressions. After a pause, Dill replied. "George, I'm speechless," he said. "This is the most fantastic operation I have ever witnessed. It's unbelievable." The Pentagon, he told Marshall, was one of the most amazing buildings in the world. The building made a further impression on the visitors when Marshall and Dill wandered down a corridor with David Witmer, the chief architect, and were soon entirely lost. Hauck managed to track down the party and rescue the heart of the Anglo-American military alliance.

Even before its completion, the Pentagon was entering the national consciousness as a vast, unfathomable maze. A soon-to-be-famous joke made its first known appearance in print on August 17 in the *Washington Post:* "And have you heard this one? About the War Department messenger who got lost in the Pentagon Building in Arlington and came out a lieutenant colonel." Almost everyone had heard it before long. It was told on the radio and in wire service accounts appearing across the United States. With time, the joke evolved and generally involved a freckled-faced Western Union messenger boy who went into the Pentagon to deliver a telegram on Monday and walked out Friday a full colonel; others insisted he came out a major. Another popular story told of a visitor who was hopelessly lost in the Pentagon. Sitting down at an empty desk to rest his feet, he was promptly outfitted with a phone, blotter, desk set, and secretary.

Soon after Marshall and Dill went missing, large wooden pentagonal-shaped maps showing the building floor plans were put up in all corridors, with arrows identifying the viewer's location. They only helped a little. Lieutenant Katharine Stull, a Women's Auxiliary Army Corps officer from Muskogee, Oklahoma, was striding down a Pentagon corridor when she noticed an Army captain staring uncomprehendingly at a wall map.

"Sir, may I help you?" Stull asked.

"Lady, I'm lost," the captain responded. "But don't tell me where to go. Lead me by the hand!"

Among all the visitors to the Pentagon that summer, perhaps none was more bewildered than an investigator sent by the Bureau of the Budget, the White House agency headed by Harold Smith, who had been so skeptical of Somervell's project in the first place. The unnamed investigator was not lost, but he did spend five days in August inspecting the project, reviewing plans, specifications, and official records, and interviewing McShain, Renshaw, and others. What he learned shocked him. By his calculations, the building would reach an estimated size of 6.6 million gross square feet, which was far bigger than what had been initially proposed. Groves had told the congressional committee in June that the building was four million gross square feet, a figure the War Department repeated in a press release in July. Even Somervell's original, grandiose proposal a year earlier had encompassed only 5.1 million gross square feet, before it was cut back under pressure.

Moreover, the investigator figured, the Pentagon's cost was far beyond the $35 million approved by Congress a year earlier. It was far beyond the $49 million cost that Somervell had reported to Congress in May. It was $25 million beyond that, in fact.

"This project, with its building, access roads, parking areas, landscaping, terraces, utilities, all estimated to cost in excess of $74,000,000 . . . is an entirely different project than that which was placed before Congress during the summer of 1941," the investigator wrote in his August 31, 1942, report, which was not made public.

> The only similarity between the building, as proposed, and that now being constructed is its intended use. The location of the site, the design and architecture of the building, and the cost of the project or building is in no way similar to that which was presented to Congress.

> Information as to who was directly responsible for the radical change is very meagre.

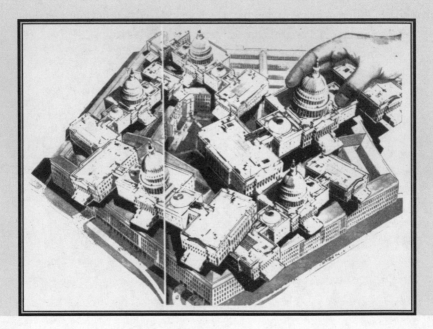

1943 illustration from Popular Mechanics *showing how many Capitol buildings could fit into the Pentagon.*

CHAPTER
13

ONE OF THE WORST
BLUNDERS OF THE WAR

Washington's demon investigator

Albert Engel had a pretty good idea who might be responsible. Like the anonymous investigator from the Bureau of the Budget, Engel, a Republican congressman from Michigan, had been poking around the Pentagon construction site over the summer of 1942. As fall approached, Engel was taking dead aim at Lieutenant General Brehon B. Somervell.

Engel was "Washington's demon one-man investigating committee," in the words of the *Saturday Evening Post*. The "mop-haired, jug-shaped" congressman specialized in dropping in unexpectedly on Army camps, munitions plants, and other military installations under construction around the country. Engel would cram his 5′ 7″ 235-pound body behind the steering wheel of his car and take off for days or weeks, his stuffed briefcase and a paper sack with sandwiches and an apple on the seat next to him. To avoid tipping off his presence, Engel would arrive in town around dusk and find accommodations in a rooming house or a fleabag hotel. More often than not, workers at the plant he was investigating would be staying there too, and they would be quizzed by the visitor. By midnight, Engel would station himself at a neighborhood hamburger joint, pumping workers coming off the evening shift for more intelligence. After a few hours' sleep, he would be up at dawn and report to work with the morning shift.

By the time authorities learned of his presence, it would be too late. Armed with his findings, Engel would interrogate the project's officers and contractors, taking voluminous notes with a stubby pencil on ruled yellow paper and typing them up at night. By sundown he would be on his way to the next project on his list. "Usually, they fire off a sixteen-gun salute, wine and dine you and then say 'Goodbye and God bless you,' but I went in as a worker and talked with everyone—a time-keeper here, a carpenter there, and I took a picture here and there," he proudly said.

Engel was nothing if not dogged. During one extended tour of defense plants, his car broke down and he left it at a repair shop in Detroit. Engel continued to Ohio in a new automobile, but was struck by a train as he crossed railroad tracks. The car was destroyed and Engel was rushed to a hospital in Akron suffering lacerations to his scalp and two black eyes.

"No anesthetic," Engel told the emergency room physician. "I'm in sort of a hurry." An hour and twenty-two stitches later, Engel was on his way in a taxicab to the train station, ready to resume his journey.

In early 1941, after discovering that the Army was running a deficit of more than $300 million in its construction program, Engel launched his most ambitious tour yet. Somervell, then head of the Construction Division, solicitously offered to arrange the trip for Engel and provide an Army officer to serve as his guide (and doubtless as a spy for Somervell), but the congressman would have none of it. Over the course of several weeks, driving alone through snow and weather as cold as fifteen degrees below zero, Engel covered fourteen thousand miles and made unannounced visits to thirteen construction projects from upstate New York to northern Florida. "He had four generals backed into a corner, peppering them with questions," said a fellow congressman who happened to be visiting Fort Bragg, North Carolina, at the same time as Engel in mid-February. "They looked as if they would rather have been facing a firing squad." An officer at Fort Bragg telephoned Groves to warn that Engel planned to attack the Construction Division when he returned to Washington. "Encourage him to go further away," Groves replied.

Engel did make it back to Washington and presented his findings on the floor of the House on April 3, 1941, mincing no words. "I say here and now that the officers in the United States Army who . . . are responsible for this willful, extravagant and outrageous waste of the taxpayers' money, ought to be court-martialed and kicked out of the Army," he declared.

Somervell was irritated, considering an attack on his methods to be tantamount to an attack on the United States. "I have been speculating, without being able to get an answer in my own mind, as to just what help these speeches are going to be to national defense," he remarked to his staff the morning after the congressman's speech. Engel, he told Groves, should be "very carefully watched" from then on.

Engel's investigation made a big splash, but then died away. Especially after Pearl Harbor, Congress and the public were not in the mood to curb military spending. But by mid-1942, after the shock of war had worn off, Engel was quietly at it again, this time investigating the project being built right under his nose across the river from Washington.

The man on horseback

Somervell by then was reaching new heights of fame and notoriety. Since taking command of the Services of Supply in March 1942, he had created a vast global logistical empire and was now one of the most powerful figures in Washington. Rumors were circulating that summer that George Marshall would be sent to England as commander in chief of Allied forces and that Somervell would replace him as chief of staff of the Army. It was "brilliant, dashing" Somervell, wrote *Time* magazine, who "beyond all others in the Army except Douglas MacArthur has caught the public eye."

Somervell's rise inspired loathing from both sides of the political spectrum. The conservative radio commentator Fulton Lewis, Jr., railed against Somervell as a Roosevelt stooge and political appointee, describing him on the air as "a sort of personal protégé of that mystic figure who lives at the White House, Mr. Harry Hopkins."

Roosevelt's own liberal secretary of the interior did not entirely disagree. "There is more and more talk about Somervell supplanting Marshall and everyone seems to agree that he has the active backing of Harry Hopkins," Harold Ickes wrote in his diary on June 21. The secretary, still aggrieved that the Pentagon was being built, was now smarting that Somervell had launched an astonishingly bold—and ultimately foolhardy—project to build an oil field, pipeline, and refinery for military use in uncharted mountainous terrain in Canada and had done it without so much as consulting the Interior Department, which was ostensibly in charge of oil concerns. Ickes seemed to believe Somervell was on the verge of launching a coup. "He gets things done but he is arbitrary and dictatorial—just the kind of a man who could become a danger in certain situations," he wrote.

Lunching with Roosevelt at the White House several months later, Ickes warned the president that two Army generals were potential "men on horseback," military strongmen who might seize power: MacArthur and Somervell. "He agreed as to MacArthur but said that he had not thought of Somervell," Ickes recorded in his diary. "I told him that he would bear watching, pointing out that he was ambitious, ruthless and vindictive." Roosevelt—more than likely to appease his volatile interior secretary— replied mildly that it would be "perfectly easy to shift a lieutenant general if necessary."

Many in Washington "would gleefully have seen [Somervell] boiled in oil," Roosevelt adviser Rexford Tugwell later wrote. "But he was just what Marshall needed, and so long as Marshall and the President were behind him he could not be reached." Somervell occasionally needed to be "curbed," Stimson later wrote, but his "driving energy was an enormous asset to the Army." Those who accused Somervell of being an empire builder were absolutely right, but they missed a larger, more important truth—that the centralized and efficient empire he had established over mobilization, production, and supply of the U.S. Army would be absolutely critical in winning a global war.

Somervell was "one of the few Americans who really understand total war," said Bernard Baruch, financier and adviser to many U.S. presidents. It was Somervell, perhaps more than any other leader, who made the case that America's situation was desperate, and that sacrifice was required from all citizens. "We must face the truth, no matter how bitter the truth may be—we're not winning the war," he thundered in a speech in July to Detroit industrialists. To another audience in St. Louis he warned, "We've lost ships by the hundreds, men by the thousands. We've lost the freedom of the seas. We've lost everything except a smug sense of complacency. And that's one thing we've got to lose, and lose fast, or we'll lose our independence." If American industry could out-produce the Axis, Somervell promised, "we'll kick the living hell out of Hitler and the Japs."

Somervell was driven by what one subordinate described as an "abiding sense of urgency," one so compelling that he stopped signing his middle initial once the war broke out. The same techniques that had marked the Somervell Blitz in Army construction were now applied to logistics. Somervell declared war on what he called the Army's "muzzle-loading" mentality. Officers who did not move fast enough were shuffled to obscure posts or forced into retirement. He fired or demoted more than a dozen generals "not to mention whole squads of colonels," *Life* magazine noted.

"For cutting red tape and getting things done there had never been anyone like him," Tugwell wrote.

A request for munitions was not paperwork to be pushed around on a desk, Somervell told his staff. "That is no piece of paper," he said. "It is life or death, victory or defeat, for hundreds of our men in some stinking jungle." With the Army in need of a good antitank weapon, Somervell went out to a range to observe a new shoulder-launched rocket-propelled weapon that had been fired only a few times and ordinarily would need much more development and testing before it was put in production. Somervell watched it fire and on the spot ordered ten thousand of them for the Army. "That damn thing looks just like Bob Burns' bazooka," an officer watching the demonstration remarked, referring to a popular radio comedian known for playing a crude wind instrument made out of gas pipes. The bazooka, as the weapon was soon also known, proved very effective in the hands of American soldiers.

None of it came cheaply. Somervell was going through phenomenal amounts of money—on weapons, on pipelines, on buildings—but complaints had been stifled since the outbreak of war. The muted response Somervell received in May when he belatedly notified the appropriations committees about the $14 million overrun at the Pentagon was typical. Renshaw marveled at Somervell's ability to keep Congress in line, later describing the general's methods: "Prominent members of the Appropriations Committee were invited to the Somervell home for a quiet evening of talk and a few drinks," according to a summary of Renshaw's remarks written by Army historians. "When the right glow of good fellowship was evident, he would casually mention a problem he was trying to solve and let it be known that the cost would probably be a little higher than had been anticipated. Things like this were difficult to estimate with dead accuracy. Thus, there was no shock when the bill reached them officially. Somervell liked it that way."

The obstacle course

The glow of good fellowship was not going to work with Albert Engel, however. Groves would later say that Somervell had deceived Congress about the true cost of the Pentagon, and that this had provided good grounds for opponents such as Engel to attack him. Yet Groves himself was at least as guilty of deception.

In July 1942, Renshaw informed Groves that the Pentagon project had exceeded the $49 million figure Somervell had reported as the amended total cost for the project.

"And there's no way to cover it up?" Groves asked Renshaw.

There was, though the idea Groves and his aides came up with was hardly foolproof. Lieutenant Colonel Gar Davidson, the former West Point football coach, telephoned Renshaw on the afternoon of July 10 with details of Groves's plan. "He wanted the report on the building not to show any amount in excess of $49,250,000," Davidson told Renshaw. "And then, he wanted a supplementary report on the roads and the parking area."

"In other words, handle it like two projects," Renshaw said.

"That's the idea," Davidson replied.

Never mind that Somervell had expressly promised Congress that his estimate would cover everything but parking. They would subtract the $8.6 million the War Department was paying for roads from the project total, and thereby keep the cost at $49 million. The only problem was Engel was hardly as stupid as Groves believed. (Groves later conceded that Engel "was stupid in a lot of ways but sharp in others.")

Ironically, it had been Groves's idea to bring Engel to the Pentagon in the first place. Groves had nothing but disdain for the congressman, considering Engel's ballyhooed inspection tours "silly and at times almost idiotic." Engel had been a consistent opponent of Construction Division projects on the House Appropriations Committee, yet Groves thought he could woo him with a personal tour of the Pentagon. "Groves had the idea he was going to make a friendly speech for us," a rueful Renshaw later explained to another officer.

The congressman fancied himself an amateur builder, having recently borrowed some masonry books from the Library of Congress. When he was not on the road, Engel would get up at 4:30 in the morning and lay bricks for a six-foot-high wall around his house in suburban Washington, meticulously recording the number of bricks laid each day in a notebook he carried in his vest pocket. (The total had reached 14,391 by 1943.) To Groves, it was just proof that Engel was a dilettante who knew nothing about construction.

Groves's strategy was to set up a construction playpen at the Pentagon and give Engel free run, figuring this would delight the congressman while wasting his energy. Before the tour, Groves directed McShain to put up an "obstacle course of scaffolding, plasterers and the like" in the area they would visit. When Groves brought Engel over to the Pentagon at 10 A.M. on June 24, "I saw to it that he had everything to climb under and over that he could," Groves later chortled. By 2 P.M., he returned to his office and left Engel to continue his visit. Groves was quite pleased with himself, thinking he had enlisted the congressman's support.

Groves had certainly succeeded in piquing Engel's interest in the Pentagon. As soon as Groves left, Engel sat down with Renshaw and requested numerous confidential documents about the project. Renshaw, under the impression he was to cooperate fully with Engel, dutifully handed over everything, including weekly field reports and monthly progress reports packed with interesting details.

In the days and weeks that followed, Engel flooded Renshaw with requests for more information: lists of subcontractors, utility costs, wage scales, construction equipment, maps of the site, and updated progress reports. He also wanted a breakdown on the amount of space in the Pentagon, a figure that Somervell, eager to conceal the true size of the building, had recently ordered not be made public. Renshaw complied, but he implored Engel to keep the information confidential.

When Groves finally learned all that Engel had acquired he was horrified. "Groves is very much interested in finding out how Engel got hold of those field reports," his aide, Major Franklin Matthias, told Renshaw.

"Groves brought him over here and gave him the house," Renshaw protested.

It was too late to point fingers. Engel was busy piecing together the truth and getting angrier by the day.

A building unique in Washington

Groves grew paranoid as Engel's investigation continued. Inspecting the building on the morning of August 24, the colonel froze in his tracks at the Mall entrance. There, at the base and risers of the staircase leading up to the next floor, was marble. It was unmistakable.

Groves erupted. In his testimony to Congress in June two months earlier, he had expressly vowed that the Pentagon had "no marble, no marble floors, no marble walls, nothing of that character." Yet here it was at his feet. He dispatched Matthias to search for more. "Walk down every corridor and make a note of every bit of marble that there is in the building," he ordered.

Lieutenant Colonel Antes, another aide, called Renshaw that afternoon with orders from Groves to remove the marble. "Oh, that's ridiculous," Renshaw protested. "He wants the marble risers cut out?"

"He wants all the marble taken out," Antes said.

It would cost as much as $100,000 to pull all the marble out of the building, Renshaw said. In the name of appearing economical, they would waste even more money.

"That's his orders," Antes insisted.

Marble had been used sparingly in the building. Chief Architect David Witmer envisioned the Mall entrance, on the Pentagon's north face looking toward the Lincoln Memorial, as the principal entry to be used by high-ranking officials and distinguished visitors. As such, he included a formal staircase, and that meant marble risers and stringers. "There was no other way to treat it that wouldn't look like hell, or be more expensive," Renshaw said. The marble had been in the building for months, since well before Groves testified to Congress, but he had only now noticed it. Renshaw debated painting or plastering the marble rather than cutting it out, but that hardly seemed a good option. Not only would it look terrible, it would be even more embarrassing if someone discovered that marble at the Pentagon had been covered up.

Somervell looked it over and said if anything, there was not enough marble. Groves relented after a week and said the marble already in the building could stay, but he ordered that not one more piece be installed without "my personal approval."

Witmer had also developed grandiose plans to sprinkle the grounds around the building with fountains, paved circles, and plantings. The Mall entrance was again given elaborate treatment in the plans, with cannons and a statue at the top and a series of terraces dropping down to a long grassy mall screened with trees. The idea, Witmer wrote, was that the Pentagon "will prove in appearance symbolic of not just a neighbor strong and protective, but rather that of a powerful but friendly neighbor."

Groves cared not a whit whether the Pentagon looked friendly. He had promised Congress that "there would be no fountains and no circles. We will have a building unique in the city of Washington." Accordingly, Groves assigned Matthias to scrub the plans of all niceties. Statues, circles, fountains, cannons, and most of the trees—"all that crap," as Matthias later referred to it—were cut out. Witmer was crushed and fought to reinstate his plans. "He wanted every fountain and every blade of grass and every gorgeous walk," Renshaw said. It was to no avail, and Witmer was left to hope that improvements would be made down the road.

On September 11, Renshaw telephoned Groves with an update on the landscaping. "I find when we decipher the names of the trees in the center court, there are thirteen Japanese cherry trees," Renshaw reported. "Do you think there's any chance of criticism if we put them in?"

Groves was aghast, if slightly amused. "Good night," he exclaimed. "We don't want a Japanese cherry on the whole lot." The Japanese cherry trees were summarily yanked from the courtyard, victims of war, and replaced with more acceptable American varieties.

Oddly, despite his paranoia about marble and trees, Groves fervently pushed to add recreational facilities to the Pentagon, believing Army officers manning desks in the building needed exercise. His girth notwithstanding, Groves considered himself to be in "top-notch physical condition" and indeed he was a terror on tennis courts, using a combination of cunning, physical stamina, surprising nimbleness, and a wicked slice shot to regularly defeat younger and slimmer opponents, Renshaw and Furman among them. Groves wanted to install a gymnasium with lockers and showers, squash and handball courts, even a golf driving range. "Maybe the next time we have a war we won't have all these unfit officers that can't do the proper amount of duty without breaking down," he griped.

Somervell had quashed all such proposals from the beginning. For one thing, he had promised Congress the building would have no frills, but beyond that, Somervell considered athletics a waste of time for Army officers in a nation at war. It could be a public relations disaster. Groves thought Somervell's position "a terrible mistake." Early in the construction, apparently unbeknownst to Somervell, Groves selected a site for a gymnasium in an undeveloped basement area below a terrace approach to the building on the lagoon side. He had engineers design the space with pilings and columns spread out far enough that it could eventually accommodate "a full sized squash court or two" or even a swimming pool. Groves would get his gymnasium, but it would have to wait until the war was over.

Groves seeks peace

The job, it seemed, was burning out the indestructible Groves. By September, he was desperate to get overseas. Many of his colleagues and West Point classmates had been given combat assignments, the obvious road to promotion. "I was hoping to get to a war theater so I could find a little peace," Groves wrote.

He had been particularly annoying on the Pentagon job in recent weeks. Even Renshaw, so adept at handling Groves, was reaching the end of his patience. When Groves issued orders September 3 to immediately remove a huge, unsightly pile of lumber from the roof, Renshaw blew up. The lumber was being used for shoring and as forms for concrete pours. If they took it down from the roof today, they would have to put it back tomorrow. Groves's micromanagement—on everything from butter patties to marble to piles of lumber—was driving Renshaw and job superintendent Paul Hauck crazy. "What I want to get over to Groves is that he cannot interfere with the operations, or we're going to lose the job just as sure as hell," Renshaw told Groves's aide, Major Matthias. Hauck was so fed up he offered to quit and let Groves take over his job.

Groves backed down on the lumber in the face of the rebellion, but he was not through. Several days later, when a walkout by carpenter foremen over wages threatened to delay the Pentagon's completion, Groves blamed

Hauck. "If we had competent management over there, maybe they'd take care of these things," Groves told Hauck. "If you really earned your fee, in other words."

Hauck was stunned and hurt. He was one of the best construction men in the business, and for nearly a year he had poured his heart and soul into the project. "The colonel says if there were competent management— we've done everything in God's world we know to do," Hauck said bitterly.

Harsh as he was, Groves had not asked for anything of anyone that he was not delivering himself. Most mornings he would wake up at 5:30 at his home in the Cleveland Park neighborhood of Washington and be out the door of his yellow brick duplex by 6:15, driving himself to work in his green Dodge sedan. When not on the road he often stayed late at the office, missing dinner. He was gone so much of the time that communication with his wife, Grace, and thirteen-year-old daughter, Gwen, was often through written messages left on the hall table.

Groves fueled himself with sweets and was particularly unable to resist mints and chocolate. On those occasions when he did make it home for dinner, Grace Groves would often put him on diets of boiled food without butter and salt, but it seemed to have little effect on his waistline. His wife and daughter surmised, usually correctly, that he was hitting the candy again. "He was so amiable in the face of these meager, uninteresting groceries and so persistent in gaining weight, that we were naturally suspicious," Gwen later wrote.

The job of constructing the domestic camps and training facilities for the mobilizing U.S. Army had peaked in July 1942, and the action was shifting overseas. Groves believed he had "most of the headaches of directing ten billion dollars' worth of military construction in this country behind me—for good, I hoped," he later wrote. "I wanted to get out of Washington, and quickly."

Groves was not alone in that sentiment. Many of his colleagues wanted him shipped on the first train out of town. His rapid rise, his arrogant manner, and the roughshod way he treated other officers had made him many enemies within the Corps of Engineers. Several Construction Division engineers asked Major General Reybold, the chief of engineers, to remove Groves from the job, but Reybold declined. However, Somervell's deputy,

Major General Wilhelm "Fat" Styer, hearing the complaints, concluded it would in the best interest of Groves—and everyone else—to get him as far away from Washington as possible.

If you do the job right, it will win the war

Groves was feeling uncommonly sprightly on the morning of September 17, 1942, despite the hot, muggy late-summer weather. He was scheduled to give routine testimony before the House Military Affairs Committee on a military housing bill, but that had nothing to do with his good mood.

The day before, Groves had received what he considered "an extremely attractive" offer for duty overseas. He was elated; it was exactly what he wanted. He was already making plans to move Grace and Gwen to a farm in Delaware for the duration of the war. The only thing he needed now was Somervell's approval. Leaving the hearing room in the House office building after his testimony, Groves ran into Somervell in the corridor outside.

"About that duty overseas," Somervell said, "you can tell them no."

Groves was stunned. "Why?" he asked.

Somervell guided Groves to a quiet corner of the hall and spoke in a lowered voice. "The Secretary of War has selected you for a very important assignment, and the President has approved the selection," Somervell said.

"Where?"

"Washington."

"I don't want to stay in Washington," Groves protested.

Somervell spoke carefully. "If you do the job right," he said, "it will win the war."

Groves's spirits sank. "Oh," he replied, "that thing."

Groves knew a bit about "that thing": a secret project that the Army had taken over earlier in the summer to use uranium to build an atomic bomb of unprecedented power. From what he could tell, the project was a backwater assignment with little prospect of success.

Somervell read his mind. "You can do it if it can be done," Somervell said. "See Styer and he will give you the details."

Seething, Groves went straight to Styer, who formally notified him that he had been selected to head the Manhattan Project. "That's impossible," Groves replied heatedly. "I won't take it. I was assured that I could go overseas where I have been promised a good job."

In Groves's mind, not only was he being prevented from going overseas, he had been given an assignment that was a distinct comedown from his job overseeing domestic construction in the United States, including the Pentagon. The whole Manhattan Project was not expected to total more than $100 million—an amount Groves typically went through in one week.

"Who on earth recommended me to the Secretary of War?" Groves demanded of Styer.

The answer, ultimately, was Somervell. There were Machiavellian considerations, of course, and Groves often speculated about Somervell's true motives. Groves suspected Somervell was trying to distance himself from the Manhattan Project in case it failed by assigning an officer who was not a "Somervell stooge." He also theorized Somervell wanted someone who would fall on his sword rather than pass around blame in the event Congress held hearings into the potential debacle.

In the summer of 1942, the program was unfocused and unguided, mostly theory with few concrete steps taken toward the production of an atomic bomb. Dr. Vannevar Bush, who as director of the Office of Scientific Research and Development was leading the push to develop an atomic bomb, was dissatisfied with the progress. In June, the Army had taken over the program from civilian control, but the man chosen to command it, Colonel James C. Marshall, had not provided the needed vigor and urgency. Bush decided a more aggressive officer was necessary.

Bush wanted Somervell himself—who better than the Army's miracle logistics man to drive the Manhattan Project to success?—but that idea went nowhere. Even had Somervell wanted the job, which he did not, Stimson and George Marshall were opposed to losing the services of their dynamic supply chief, particularly with furious preparations under way for the invasion of North Africa.

Bush's second choice was Fat Styer, already serving as Bush's liaison with the Army. Marshall approved, telling Styer that he would have to take the job. But Styer balked at the prospect of leaving his powerful position as Somervell's deputy to head up a project that was such a long shot. Somervell likewise did not want to lose Styer and tried to talk Marshall out of it. The chief of staff told Somervell he would either have to give up Styer or come up with someone who was "entirely suitable" for the Manhattan Project.

Styer had a suggestion, having already concluded that Groves was ripe to leave the Construction Division. Styer admired Groves for "the fearlessness with which he tackled difficult jobs." The Manhattan Project, though headquartered in Washington, would keep Groves on the road much of the time, away from the division engineers. It would be a perfect outlet for his forceful energy. "Somervell and I discussed the matter and decided you would be the victim," Styer told Groves years later.

Yet Groves was not selected simply as a convenient way for Somervell to keep Styer and get rid of a talented but overly brusque officer. Somervell respected Groves's quick mind, telling Stimson and Marshall that if Groves were assigned to the project, within a matter of weeks he would "understand and have a thorough knowledge of all the scientific and technical matters involved."

Despite all his speculation, Groves later identified the most important reason Somervell selected him. "Somervell did feel that I was probably more capable than almost anyone he could think of, with respect to seizing hold of new ideas and carrying them forward," Groves wrote. "[H]e knew that I was one person who would drive the thing forward."

The Machiavellian considerations Groves identified likely influenced Somervell's decision. But ultimately, the reason Groves was chosen to build the atomic bomb was precisely what Somervell whispered to him in their hallway conference on September 17, 1942: If it could be done, Groves would do it.

Political dynamite

Groves left Styer's office, his venom spent. He was resigned to his fate and never looked back. With typical nerve, he wrangled a promise of quick promotion to brigadier general, and he rushed to work.

Formally taking over the Manhattan Project on September 23, 1942, Groves met that afternoon in Stimson's office with the secretary of war, George Marshall, Vannevar Bush, Somervell, Styer, and other senior officials. Despite being easily the lowest-ranking man in the room, Groves

Lt. Gen. Brehon Burke Somervell, the "father" of the Pentagon, after assuming command of the Army Services of Supply in 1943. His eyes— "the keenest, shrewdest, most piercing eyes one is likely to meet"—were said to be able to spot red tape before it turned pink. (U.S. Army)

(Right) Col. Leslie R. Groves in 1941. The man who would be chosen to head the Manhattan Project to build an atomic bomb would first oversee the construction of the world's largest office building. (U.S. Army)

Builder John McShain with Franklin D. Roosevelt at the president's home in Hyde Park, N.Y., on August 30, 1941, twelve days before ground was broken on the Pentagon. Roosevelt fancied himself an architect and played a key role in the project, selecting the site and fiddling with the design. (AP, reprinted by permission.)

The project as seen from th[e] air on October 22, 1941, [a] little over a month after breaking ground. In Section A (left), the first floor form[s] are in place. In Section B (adjoining), the pile cap forms are ready. (U.S. Army)

G. Edwin Bergstrom. The chief architect was the man most responsible for the shape of the Pentagon, but he would have to leave before the job was done. (U.S. Army)

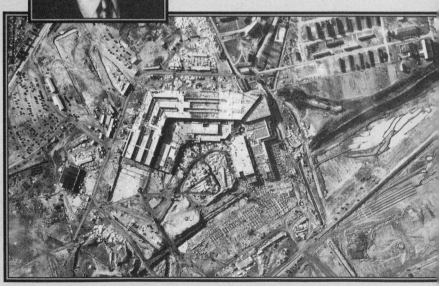

The project seen from overhead on Christmas Eve, 1941. Work on all five sides is visible. (U.S. Army)

Lt. Col. Clarence Renshaw. Somervell and Groves picked the army officer to head the project because they wanted someone who would not fail. "I wasn't so sure," Renshaw later said. (OSD files)

Maj. Bob Furman in October 1942. The young officer who had dreamed of becoming a builder suddenly found himself in the midst of the largest building construction project in the world. (OSD files)

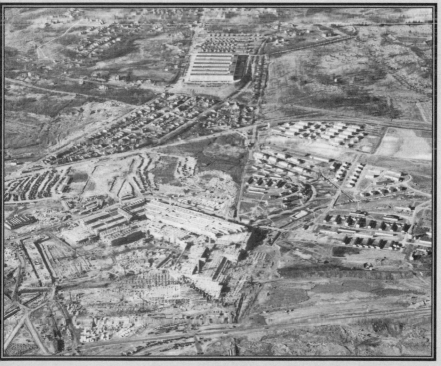

The project seen from above the Potomac River on January 29, 1942. (U.S. Army)

David Witmer, Bergstrom's chief assistant; Bergstrom; Somervell; J. Paul Groves, job superintendent; Renshaw; and Hauck looking over plans for the building at a design conference after Pearl Harbor. The restrictions on the building's size were jettisoned after the attack. (U.S. Army)

Renshaw sent Somervell this aerial shot taken March 5, 1942, showing the structure 40 percent complete. "The section outlined in ink is for May occupancy," Renshaw wrote Somervell. "We are running a close race with the architect and with our appropriations." (U.S. Army)

John McShain, Clarence Renshaw and construction adviser Henry Thompson atop the building during construction. (U.S. Army)

With cries of "Concrete!" workers on the roof rushed to deliver with wheelbarrows and buggies for a roof pour. (U.S. Army)

A view of second floor construction. (U.S. Army)

The limestone facing is erected on the Section E façade. (U.S. Army)

Gen. George C. Marshall and Secretary of War Henry L. Stimson conferring over a map of Europe soon after moving into the Pentagon in November 1942. (U.S. Army)

Ides van der Gracht (right), was recruited by Somervell to bring order to the massive design operation. "General, I never even thought of anything as big as this," van der Gracht told Somervell. "Oh, don't let that worry you, neither have we," the general replied. (AOC Archives)

The Pentagon, as seen from a hill overlooking the black community of Queen City, in April 1942. Within days, the church, businesses, and homes in the foreground would be razed to make way for the building's road network. (U.S. Army)

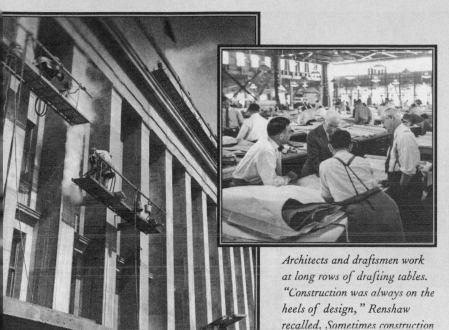

Architects and draftsmen work at long rows of drafting tables. "Construction was always on the heels of design," Renshaw recalled. Sometimes construction was even ahead of design. (U.S. Army)

Columns being steam cleaned during construction in April 1942. (U.S. Army)

An aerial photo from 1944 shows the finished Pentagon. (U.S. Army)

Hundreds of soldiers sort through Army personnel records in one large basement office in this 1950 photograph. (U.S. Army)

Messengers use special tricycle carts to navigate the seventeen miles of Pentagon corridors. (U.S. Army)

Visitors check in with receptionists at big desks in the concourse. "The girls are selected for their good looks, brains, tact, and just ordinary horse sense, and many a male lingers at the counter," a newspaper reported. (U.S. Army)

forcefully and frequently voiced his opinions. Then, abruptly, he rose to his feet, looked at his watch, and asked to be excused; Groves told the startled officials he had to catch a train to Tennessee to inspect a possible site for an atomic plant at a place called Oak Ridge. Somervell and Styer exchanged a grin as Groves left. "You made me look like a million dollars," a delighted Somervell told Groves upon his return. "I'd told them that if you were put in charge, things would really start moving!"

Groves was moving fast with the Manhattan Project, yet he was not done with the Pentagon. At their meeting September 17, he and Styer agreed that Groves would retain personal control of the Pentagon's construction until the building was finished. The Pentagon project had such a high profile and "was of such great importance" to the Army that he could not drop it, Groves later wrote. "The impact on the reputation of the War Department and of the Corps of Engineers was tremendous."

In part, keeping Groves in charge of the Pentagon was a security measure to avoid drawing attention to his assignment to the secret Manhattan Project. "My sudden disappearance from the work on the Pentagon would attract much more notice than would my absence from other Army construction activities," Groves wrote.

The second reason was that the Pentagon project was "full of political dynamite," and Groves was needed to handle Congress. "It would be better for me to continue to carry the responsibility for that job than to pass it on to someone else who was unfamiliar with its past problems and their many political ramifications," Groves wrote. Another way of putting it is that Groves knew better than anyone where the skeletons lay at the Pentagon.

Somervell "very heartily approved" of keeping Groves in charge of the project. "I just told him bluntly that there was nobody there that I thought could handle Congress as well as I could, which he knew," Groves later said.

They would not have to wait long to put Groves's services to work.

One of the worst blunders of the war

The whole Pentagon project looked fishy to Albert Engel. He summoned Renshaw to his office on Capitol Hill on the morning of September 22 to explain various discrepancies he had uncovered, including how the $8.6 million for access roads and parking included in earlier progress reports had mysteriously disappeared by August. That figure, Engel calculated, should be added to the $49.2 million for the building proper, the $9.5 million being spent by the Public Roads Administration on access highways and bridges to reach the building, and $2.4 million being spent on landscaping. The public should be advised that they were pouring $70 million into a project of "doubtful value" instead of the $35 million initially promised, Engel told Renshaw. He was further incensed that the reports were all stamped confidential.

Engel had also homed in on the sweetheart deal with the two Virginia contractors. McShain was supplying more than 90 percent of the manpower for the job while Doyle & Russell and Wise had insignificant roles. It was obvious, Engel told Renshaw, that the Virginia contractors were on the project "purely for political reasons."

Renshaw could barely get a word in edgewise. "Engel talked at me for two hours this morning," Renshaw complained after the meeting. He raised the alarm at Construction Division headquarters that Engel was on a rampage.

For some reason, Groves had seemed "sort of disinterested" in construction business over the last few days, noted his aide, Major Matthias, who, like most officers in the Construction Division, knew nothing yet of the Manhattan Project assignment. However, the news about Engel got Groves's attention in a hurry. "Groves is very much concerned about this," Matthias told Renshaw that afternoon.

Renshaw replied that it would do no good to cover up the costs anymore. Engel, he had concluded, was "smart enough to know if you're trying to withhold anything."

Groves thought differently. He wanted the money being paid for outside architects and engineers—now about $1.6 million, or six times higher than estimated—deducted from the next Pentagon progress report. "He doesn't think anybody will pick that up," Matthias told Renshaw.

But it was too late for Groves's number games. Representative Lane Powers, a New Jersey Republican Appropriations Committee member and Somervell confidant, spoke with Engel on the afternoon of September 22, trying to head off disaster. "Why don't you give Bill Somervell a ring and sit down with him?" Powers suggested.

"I don't owe Somervell a goddamned thing," Engel replied.

Immediately after his conversation with Engel, Powers warned Renshaw that Engel was going to go public on the floor of the House with his investigation. "I think he's going to probably get a half hour some day, and get up and just blow the whole thing," Powers told Renshaw over the telephone. "[O]f course he can yank the thing around where it'll make a hell of a good newspaper story."

He was right about that. On Thursday, October 1, the congressman took the floor of the House, a shock of gray hair standing on end. In grim tones over the next forty minutes he outlined his findings: The Pentagon project would cost $70 million, twice what Congress had authorized, and the building had grown to a staggering six million gross square feet. The Virginia contractors, he continued, had done little to earn their fee of more than $200,000. The War Department had used censorship to cover up a "shameful squandering" of money.

Engel ridiculed the War Department's claim that the amount of office space in the building was a military secret. "If there is going to be any bombing, the Japs certainly are not going to come over here and measure a building that covers 42 acres of ground before they start any bombing," he said. "They are going to bomb it whenever they can and wherever they can."

Engel placed the blame for the whole matter squarely on two men: Franklin D. Roosevelt and Brehon B. Somervell. "There is no evidence that the President has taken one step . . . to prevent some of the shameful waste of the taxpayers' and bondbuyers' money," Engel declared. As for Somervell, Engel said, the general had "violated the mandate" of Congress by ignoring the cost limits.

Somervell's reliable ally, Clifton Woodrum of Virginia, rose to defend the general and the president, as well as the Virginia contractors. But Engel gave no quarter. "He is known as a two-fisted, forthright debater, and yesterday he was unsparing in his denunciation of the Administration for the expenditures in connection with the War Department Building," the *Washington Times-Herald* reported.

At Somervell's order, Groves coordinated the response to Engel's attack. Groves conferred with Renshaw and McShain to figure ways of refuting the claims. To his relief and amusement, Engel had not criticized him; indeed his speech praised Groves for his management of the project and said the building was well-constructed. Engel had figured out a lot but never realized Groves's role in trying to hide the costs of the Pentagon.

Groves monitored the newspaper coverage, a key barometer of how much damage they had sustained. On the bright side, the New York papers largely ignored the affair. "The 'New York Times' gave but scant attention to the matter, on an inside page," Groves informed Somervell. But all the Washington newspapers gave Engel prominent, front-page coverage, some with screaming headlines that the War Department had squandered millions of dollars and tried to squelch Engel's investigation.

The day after Engel's speech, Somervell—aided by Groves—composed a letter stoutly refuting the charges. It was quickly delivered to Woodrum, who rose in the House that afternoon brandishing the letter, declaring that it vindicated Somervell.

"I cannot agree that the War Department failed to keep faith with the Congress in respect to this building," Somervell wrote. The letter noted that the general had warned from the start that moving the building from his preferred site at Arlington Farm would increase the $35 million cost. Further, Pearl Harbor had necessitated a bigger building. Somervell had informed the Appropriations Committee in May that the price of the building would be $49 million. Including the Virginia contractors had been necessary owing to the "size and complexity of the undertaking." As for the secrecy that had surrounded the project, Somervell wrapped himself in a cloak of national security. "An alert enemy, and our enemies are alert, gains valuable information from the disclosure of facts not generally recognized as military secrets," he wrote.

Finally, no one could now argue that the Pentagon was unnecessary. "The wisdom of the Congress in providing this building has been proven by the events of the past year," Somervell concluded. "The efficiency of the War Department has been tremendously increased."

Engel declared himself unimpressed. "He'll have to do better than that to convince me I'm wrong," he said. Somervell, Engel said, had displayed "an utter disregard" and "contempt" for Congress.

Yet there was no demand in Congress for further inquiry, nor did Engel request any action—for the time being, at least. Engel, Groves later wrote, "was a peculiar man. He enjoyed the respect of his colleagues in the House as a man of complete honesty, but he was also known as a man who started many things with a flourish and then abandoned them once his publicity had been achieved."

Somervell's response to Engel's charges, also given front-page play, muted some but not all the public criticism. "It is to be doubted if Congress would have approved the building, had these costs been known then," the *Evening Star* commented.

It was not just the price tag that was shocking. Everyone had known the Pentagon was big, of course. But until now, few had understood that Somervell had built a headquarters even larger than what had been proposed a year earlier. "The public was led to believe that the size of the building had been scaled down," *The Washington Post* lamented in an editorial. ". . . Actually, however, the size of the building was enlarged even beyond its inflated proportions. . . . Congress was not asked to authorize this enlargement of the project. It has merely been informed of a *fait accompli.*"

This was entirely true. The newspapers were further shocked when Engel announced a few days after his speech that a fifth floor was being added to the Pentagon. Though that work had been under way since July and was now nearing completion, this was the first the press or public had heard of it. The War Department, after all, had labeled the space "fourth floor intermediate."

It was all cause for heartburn. "Washington has many reasons to regret the construction of the gigantic War Department Building," the *Post* editorialized. ". . . All our enemies know, of course, that the War Department has located a magnificent target just south of the Potomac." The editorial included this prediction: "If the finished project is now to cost 70 million dollars, as Representative Engel charges, it may easily stand out as one of the worst blunders of the war period."

Clifford Berryman cartoon from the Washington Evening Star, *April 1944.*

THE RACE TO MOVE IN
THE HIGH COMMAND

By command of General Somervell

The race was on to get Henry Stimson and George Marshall into the Pentagon, and as far as Groves was concerned, an act of God would not suffice as reason for delay. The invasion of North Africa—Operation Torch—was imminent, and it was vital to have the command post ready for the secretary of war and the chief of staff of the Army. More than nine thousand construction workers were still on the job. Groves had issued orders that the offices for Stimson, Marshall, and the rest of the high command be ready by November 1, 1942.

"If unfavorable weather occurs it will not be accepted by me or offered by you or any of your personnel as an excuse for failure," Groves informed Renshaw on October 22. "I am not interested in excuses or explanations, only in the accomplishment of the desired results."

Renshaw had cause to worry. Acts of God were not out of the question, though it helped to have Somervell on your side. Just a few days earlier, on Friday, October 16, word arrived that a massive flood was coming down the Potomac River toward Washington. Days of soaking rain in the Shenandoah Valley had raised the river to record levels. At 1:15 P.M., the Army's Military District of Washington launched emergency preparations. Informed later that afternoon that the impending flood might be the gravest in Washington history, Roosevelt telephoned Somervell from the White House seeking his help to protect federal buildings in low-lying areas. "The Potomac will be over Constitution Avenue before morning unless you stop it," the president told Somervell. "Stop it."

Somervell was at the scene within two hours with 1,100 soldiers and a battery of heavy equipment—a half-dozen bulldozers, four large steam shovels, five cranes, eight fire pumps, and 130 trucks hauling dirt for sandbags. Laboring under floodlights, soldiers and civilian crews had six hours to reinforce a half-mile-long levee and fill in a gap at 17th Street before the waters crested. Somervell's emergency aide for the night—Major Munro Leaf, a gentle soul who before the war had written *The Story of Ferdinand,* a lovely fable about a peace-loving bull—watched in astonishment as the general leaped into the breach. Somervell joyfully sloshed through the rising water to direct operations in the soaking rain, wearing a floppy old hat, a rumpled raincoat with no stars on the shoulders, trousers rolled up above his knees, and galoshes, which unaccountably could not be fastened. It was the happiest anyone had seen Somervell since before the war and before Anna Somervell died.

The flood proved as dangerous as feared. The Potomac crested Saturday morning at the Wisconsin Avenue gauge in Georgetown at 17.7 feet, or more than 10.5 feet above flood stage, the highest recorded before or since. Hundreds of families were evacuated from their homes and five people in the region were swept to their deaths. Residents of Georgetown were rescued by boat from their rooftops. The newly completed Jefferson Memorial was an island. But the dike protecting the federal buildings held. "By command of General Somervell, the water stopped short of Constitution Avenue," *Newsweek* reported.

The waters spared the Pentagon as well. Despite the Army's own warnings against constructing any permanent buildings on the low ground of the former Washington-Hoover Airport, the easternmost portion of the Pentagon—including the area where Stimson and Marshall were to go— jutted onto that land. Construction crews had filled the area, raising the water table from ten to eighteen feet above sea level, and engineers were confident the building was safe, but no one had wanted the flood of the ages to be the first test. Some roads to the building were cut off, the concrete plant was inundated, and hangars on the old airport grounds used to repair construction vehicles were halfway underwater, but the building itself remained unscathed. Those War Department employees able to make it to the Pentagon worked on uninterrupted. The engineers had raised the ground just enough, as it turned out. Still, the water was so high that there were fears a German U-Boat plying the waters off the East Coast might wend its way up the Potomac and deliver a torpedo directly into the Pentagon's doors. Wags responded that not even a bomb could enter the building without an appointment.

Our lives depend on that

The Pentagon had survived the flood of 1942, but Renshaw was hardly in the clear. From outside, the Pentagon hardly looked like a finished product. Limestone was up on only about half the building; stone setters were still hanging the stone on Section C and had not even begun Section D, where Stimson and Marshall would go. Atop the building, crews were still pouring sections of the new fifth floor. The fifth and final section of the building, Section E, remained under construction, including an enormous terminal on the ground floor where buses and taxis would disgorge passengers within the building. An armada of heavy equipment was filling, surfacing, and grading the grounds for roads and landscaping. Mounds of concrete debris, wood forms, and trash were scattered about, particularly in the inner courtyard, which construction crews used as a dumping ground. The rains left the courtyard such a muddy mess that a concrete truck sank to its belly.

Somervell had made sure Stimson had the best view in the house, doubtless mindful of the secretary's warning the previous year that he would refuse to move into a windowless office of the type Roosevelt had briefly contemplated for the Pentagon. Facing toward the Jefferson Memorial, the secretary's suite on the third floor of the outer E Ring in Section D had a panoramic vista overlooking the lagoon and river, with the Capitol and Washington Monument in the background. Stimson would also be overlooking a dump until construction was finished and the mess cleaned up.

Much exacting work was needed to finish the suites for Marshall and

Stimson, which could hardly be thrown together like the average office bay. Groves wanted everything in pristine working order, including the heating and ventilation. It would not do to have the secretary of war freezing or sweating, like many Pentagon employees. Stimson's spacious suite would include paneled walls and thick scarlet carpeting, with an adjacent wardrobe room. Directly next to Stimson, connected by a door, was Marshall's office, smaller but similarly plush. A private elevator—the only passenger lift in the building—would serve both Stimson and Marshall's suites, and a moving escalator would carry visitors to their floor. Stimson's office included a map alcove, with twelve-by-eight-foot panels that would slide out on tracks and push back into a wall recess when not needed. Across the hallway, workers were finishing an elegant private dining room with seating for twenty-four and an adjacent serving pantry.

Groves had been unsure what to use on the walls lining the entrance to Stimson's office. Groves thought marble would look nice, but that was impossible—he himself had strictly forbidden its use. He consulted with Stephen Voorhees, a member of the War Department's Construction Advisory Committee. "Why don't you use wood?" Voorhees suggested.

Groves objected that this would cost even more than marble.

"Who said anything about cost?" Voorhees replied. They used wood.

Inspecting the building, Somervell was particularly interested in the accommodations for Stimson. He instructed Renshaw and Hauck that before the secretary moved in, he wanted "everything pretty near right for the big boy."

Renshaw told Somervell that with Engel on the hunt for extravagance, they were striving to make the building "less ornate."

"Well, don't do it for the Secretary," Somervell replied. "Our lives depend on that."

The same was true for the various assistant secretaries of war and top generals. An officer representing Lieutenant General Henry H. "Hap" Arnold, commander of the Army Air Forces, and Robert Lovett, the assistant secretary of war for air, demanded his bosses get the same kind of paneled suite that Somervell and Assistant Secretary of War John J. McCloy were getting, including a private bathroom with a shower. Renshaw hesitated—their suites had already been plastered and adding special features now would cost at least $15,000. "I don't see any sense in it," Groves agreed.

Somervell certainly saw the sense in it. The general was "much put out that we even questioned it," Renshaw reported a few days later. The private bathrooms went in. Renshaw took to calling the Army Air Forces area "the Gold Coast suites."

Most irritating of all were the demands for special treatment from Colonel Edward F. French, a pompous Signal Corps officer in charge of the Signal Center being built on the fifth-floor inner ring of the Pentagon. This was to be the largest and most modern military communication facility in the world, with state-of-the-art equipment that would allow for the transmission and reception of five million words a day between the Pentagon and U.S. forces around the globe. It would be the modern equivalent of the War Department telegraph office that Lincoln haunted during the Civil War. French was also determined to make it the fanciest communications facility in the world.

For months, French badgered Renshaw with one special request after another, demanding additional stairways and walkways leading to the Signal Center, all of which threatened to throw off the schedule. In late October, as Renshaw scurried to meet Groves's looming deadline, French had a new demand:

> In the firm belief that not only the morale but also the efficiency, accuracy, and all-around performance of personnel is affected to a very great degree by the character, quality and appropriateness of their immediate surroundings, the Chief Signal Officer and the Director of Army Communications Division desire that special treatment be given the main entrance and the interior of the new Signal Center. Accordingly, the services of the architectural firm of Eggers and Higgins, New York, have been engaged, with Mr. Otto R. Eggers personally planning the design.

French submitted Eggers's plans for fluorescent lighting, clock outlets, special paneling, and floor tiling to Renshaw. The architect had recommended that the Signal Center entrance space and the code room be "tiled with a random field of Morocco Brown, No. 104, and Quarry Red, No. 106, with a border of Black, No. 102." The walls of the classified message center were to be painted "lettuce green (Pratt Lambert color card No. 233)."

This was beyond the pale, as far as Renshaw was concerned. They were racing the clock to move the Army's high command into the Pentagon, American troops were preparing for ground combat against the Axis powers, and Colonel French had hired a fancy-pants New York interior designer to make sure the colors and lighting were properly soothing for the teletype operators?

Renshaw appealed for help from superiors. Major General Thomas M. Robins, the Construction Division chief, informed French that Otto Eggers's "decorative features," however desirable, would not be approved, and he directed the colonel to work with Renshaw to figure out "the minimum essential" features needed for the Signal Center.

Renshaw had a measure of revenge with the Signal Corps, though it was purely accidental. The first Signal Corps workers to move into the Pentagon—the Organization and Procedures Branch—found that their third-floor offices on the outer E Ring were deafening due to construction noise outside and above their heads. Signal Corps Second Lieutenant George W. Good, Jr.—a young officer "green as the grass in Kentucky," in his words—was constantly distracted by the temptation to peer out the window and watch. He need not have looked far.

Good was working at his desk on October 1 when a hunk of plaster suddenly burst from the wall next to him, followed by a cascade of wet concrete. Construction crews above them were pouring the new top deck but had neglected to properly block off a heating duct leading to the floors below. The concrete came pouring down the duct and out the wall. Good's desk was swept across the room like a small boat in a flood. "All the women started to scream, and very quickly, the whole floor was a huge pool of concrete," Good recalled.

"We were all sitting at our desks and the wall behind us caved in—the fresh cement poured down like molten lava," recalled Daphne Webb, a secretary in the office. "We jumped over our desks and ran for our lives." All escaped, though the office was entirely uninhabitable. Good, Webb, and the rest of the office packed up equipment and belongings that had survived and moved back to Washington.

Renshaw roared with laughter when he heard the news. Amid all the pressure of finishing the building, it was the funniest story he had heard in months. Relating the incident to Groves's aide, Major Matthias, the following day, Renshaw could barely contain himself describing the Signal Corps employees "minding their own business" when they were inundated by bucket loads of concrete.

"It couldn't have been Colonel French's office, could it?" Matthias asked.

Renshaw was wistful. "I wish it had have been," he said.

This is the War Department

The Pentagon had to be fully functioning before the high command moved in, and, as much as anything else, that meant working telephones. To meet the War Department's fantastic need for telephone service—likened to providing a system from scratch for a city the size of Trenton, New Jersey—an ambitious plan had been devised to lay a dozen submarine cables one-third of a mile across the bottom of the Potomac River. These would connect the switchboard with the Chesapeake and Potomac Telephone Company's central office in Washington.

Frank E. Watts, a twenty-six-year-old telephone company employee from Alexandria, reported with other workers to the Arlington bank of the Potomac near the Pentagon on a rainy and chilly morning. Two barges awaited, heavily laden with the cables, along with tugboats and a diver. The cables had been manufactured at Western Electric's Point Breeze Works near Baltimore on the biggest cable-armoring machine ever constructed. Telephone wire had been sheathed with layers of lead, jute, and steel armoring. The cables, each weighing more than twenty tons and stretching two thousand feet, were rolled up onto twelve huge reels and shipped on the barges from Baltimore down the Chesapeake Bay and up the Potomac.

The workers were to lay all twelve cables across the river—the most that had ever been attempted in one operation. The diver would follow the barge and guide the cables into a trench that had been dredged across to the Washington side. Two brakemen—Watts among them—were assigned to each reel, with the task of making sure the cable did not pay out too fast as a tugboat towed each barge across the river. It was a forlorn hope. The heavy cable splashing into the water quickly built up a momentum of its own, pushing Watts's barge forward with alarming speed and forcing the tugboat out of the way. "The sliding cable was pushing the barge and we, as brakemen, could do nothing to slow it down," Watts recalled. "The barge wound up jammed up against the north bank, luckily where it was supposed to be." Somehow, no one was injured and the job was done.

Just before midnight on September 12, the massive Pentagon switchboard was plugged into service. Like seemingly everything in the building, it was the world's largest. The switchboard, especially designed for the Pentagon by Bell Telephone Laboratories, filled 32,000 feet on the first floor of the building, four times larger than the temporary board that had been in use. Hundreds of telephone installers working in teams spent seventeen weeks stringing 68,600 miles of trunk lines through the Pentagon and connecting 27,000 telephones.

In the somnolent years before the war, ten operators had been able to handle the War Department switchboard at the Munitions Building. The Pentagon switchboard required three hundred operators and twenty-two supervisors, most of them women. They sat in long rows stretching dozens of yards, shoulder to shoulder on high stools with backs, headsets over coiffed hair. Some handled calls to, from, and within the building, others placed long-distance calls, and a smaller number provided information. The operators were soon answering 90,000 calls a day—and later over 100,000 a day, each caller hearing the same greeting with a recitation of the Pentagon telephone number: "This is the War Department—RE 6700." Every call, even those within the building, had to be connected manually; the operators would plug a jack in the proper line group and dial the last two digits of the individual extension.

"It really was the eighth wonder of the world," recalled Marian J. Bailey. Twenty years old, with long chestnut-brown hair, Bailey was a government girl who had arrived in Washington in January 1942 from Chadron, Nebraska. She was hired by the War Department in March and put to work training operators for the Pentagon switchboard. Bailey, who had a bossy streak, was in heaven in the Pentagon. The operators "were very important, very prestigious," she recalled. "You couldn't do anything without us."

Indeed, the switchboard was so vital that officials considered building an eighteen-inch-thick concrete wall fortified with sandbags to protect the telephone room. Ultimately they decided against it, using faultless Army logic: "[S]hould we experience an air raid causing great damage to the building and should there be very little of the building left, there will be little need for telephone communications," a report noted.

The whip

The men leading the project, Renshaw, McShain, and Hauck, had not failed yet, and by late October there was no reason to expect they would. But that was not good enough for Groves. "Certainly, even the greatest racehorses have to have the whip applied in the home stretch," he once wrote.

Groves had been consumed in recent weeks with the Manhattan Project, trying to establish an enormous production facility at Oak Ridge and attempting to assert control over the unruly scientists. He wanted to imprison Leo Szilard, the brilliant Hungarian physicist who had an important role in initiating the project. Groves considered him a dishonorable troublemaker who might delay the whole project. On October 28, Groves drafted a letter for the secretary of war proposing that Szilard be confined as an enemy alien for the rest of the war. (Stimson declined to sign the letter, reasoning that as far as he knew the Constitution was still in effect. "This was the answer I expected but I thought that there was no harm in trying," Groves later said.)

After writing the letter, Groves devoted much of the next three days to ensuring that everything at the Pentagon was ready for Marshall and Stimson. He inspected the site each day, ready to apply the whip. What bothered Groves most was the mess. The inner courtyard in particular was a shambles, filled with construction debris and mounds of dirt. "There's got to be more effort shown on cleaning up around there," he told Renshaw. "There's a tremendous amount of stuff still to move out, and I'm afraid you're going to get caught."

There were not enough trucks to haul out debris—every one that Renshaw could scrape up was hauling fill for the roads, which also had to be finished by November. The Army had taken to "recapturing" many of the trucks and excavators that had been rented for the job, using a federal seizure law that allowed the government to purchase the equipment, applying rent that had already been paid. The companies that owned the trucks and excavators pleaded they would be driven out of business if the government seized their equipment, but the Army was unsympathetic. The owner of a 1941 International dump truck recaptured by the Army took matters into his own hands, sneaking into the Pentagon job site on the night of September 21 and repossessing his truck while the driver was eating dinner. The owner hightailed it to the hills of central Maryland and hid the truck in the woods, using a welding torch to disguise it. Maryland State Police found the truck a month later, and it was brought back to the Pentagon the night of October 20. Despite all this, Renshaw was still short—he was trying to find twenty-five more trucks to haul out debris, thus far without success.

Fortunately for Renshaw, he had some leeway. On October 24, the largest war fleet ever to sail from America had weighed anchor from Hampton Roads with a secret destination: the shores of North Africa. Stimson and Marshall would wait until the troops were ashore before moving into the Pentagon. It would be too dangerous to be moving in the midst of a landing, particularly if things went badly. The invasion—three separate landings in French Morocco and Algeria—was set for Sunday, November 8, 1942; the high command would move into the Pentagon the following weekend.

The timing of the move was kept quiet for security reasons. Indeed, until recently the press had been confused as to whether Stimson would even relocate to the Pentagon. Over the summer the War Department had insisted that no decision had been made. As late as September 17, the *Washington Post* confidently reported that Stimson would not move into the Pentagon but would either stay in the Munitions Building or move into the other New War Department Building in Foggy Bottom.

But in Stimson's own office, there was never any doubt that the secretary of war was going to the Pentagon. Stimson, it was true, was not eager to abandon Washington for the wilds of Virginia, and he was personally content to stay in the Munitions Building. But he had long since decided that the most efficient prosecution of the war lay in consolidating the high command with as much of the War Department as possible.

Reporters were appalled to learn in late September that the Bureau of Public Relations—their lifeline for war news—would be moving shortly to the Pentagon, meaning news organizations already left shorthanded by the war would have to regularly send correspondents on time-consuming trips across the river. The executive committee for the Radio Correspondents' Galleries at the U.S. Congress—a young reporter for CBS named Eric Sevareid among them—unanimously objected to the move and wrote Stimson asking him to reconsider. Other press organizations, including the National Press Club, also appealed to the secretary to save them from the Pentagon.

In reply, Stimson sympathized that the move to "the Pentagon Building does not seem to make the day's work any easier for my good friends of The National Press Club.

"Since my own antipathy to moving across the river is well known," the secretary continued, "it must be assumed that the movement of the Bureau of Public Relations would not have been approved had I believed that it could save time or provide adequate service for the Press by remaining at or near its present location, isolated from its sources of information and of policy rulings." Stimson's reply made it clear that the War Department's center of gravity—most important, he himself—was moving to the Pentagon, and if reporters wanted to cover it, they had better adjust.

Carry me back to Old Virginny

No organization was more aghast at the thought of moving into the Pentagon than the United States Navy. Yet Admiral Ernest King, commander in chief of the U.S. Fleet, approached George Marshall in October with the suggestion that King move his office into the Pentagon alongside the Army chief of staff so that the two men could work in closer harmony.

That such a proposal would come from Ernie King was, at first glance, startling. The cantankerous and blunt admiral was a fierce Navy partisan with a legendary temper. "He is the most even-tempered man in the Navy," his daughter once said. "He is always in a rage." King and Marshall, so unlike in temperament, had little fondness for each other. Since the war began, King had constantly pushed for greater priority to be placed on defeating Japan, a stance that often put him at odds with the War Department and the official U.S. strategy to defeat Germany first. Yet King, for all his intemperance, believed it his duty to improve relations with Marshall and the Army.

In recent weeks, moreover, the Navy had suffered a series of setbacks in the Solomon Islands in the South West Pacific Area. A spate of news stories suggested that the Navy was holding back the war effort by refusing to join a unified command under General Douglas MacArthur.

Stimson was often dismayed by the Navy's selfish and anachronistic ways. Many problems between the Army and Navy were inevitable, Stimson wrote in his memoirs, but some "grew mainly from the peculiar psychology of the Navy Department, which frequently seemed to retire from the realm of logic into a dim religious world in which Neptune was God, Mahan his prophet and the United States Navy the only true Church." The high priests of this church were a group Stimson referred to as "the Admirals"—the powerful chiefs of various Navy bureaus who were not accountable to King or Admiral Harold Stark, chief of naval operations, but instead reported to the secretary of the Navy and Congress. Faced with the same situation at the turn of the century, Secretary of War Elihu Root, Stimson's mentor, had cleaned house of the bureaucratic service officers who then dominated the Army. That had not happened in the Navy. " 'The Admirals' had never been given their comeuppance," Stimson wrote.

The secretary of war was pleased to find a change in King's tone in late October, noting in his diary that the admiral "is now in a very humble frame of mind on account of the pounding he is getting from the press in respect to Navy command matters." Perhaps this new attitude helped account for King's proposal to move into the Pentagon. It also probably did not hurt that conditions in the Navy Building—another so-called "temporary" World War I structure—were at least as bad as in the Munitions Building next door on Constitution Avenue; one admiral described King's broken-down, filthy headquarters as "the most disreputable office I have ever seen."

Marshall, even more than King, had long sought deeper cooperation between the services, but the admirals had rebuffed his past efforts. Mulling King's request, the Army chief of staff decided to go much further. He proposed that the entire Navy high command, including Secretary of the Navy Frank Knox, move into the Pentagon, along with as much of the Department of the Navy as would fit. In the name of unity, Marshall would keep a large part of the War Department out of the Pentagon and give 800,000 square feet of office space to the Navy. Knox and King would be placed in suites on the floor directly above those of Stimson and Marshall. The displaced War Department workers would either stay in the Munitions Building or move into the Navy Building. It was a bold and magnanimous proposal, one that might bring about a revolution in Army-Navy relations.

Marshall sounded out the idea with Stimson on the morning of Saturday, October 31. The secretary was delighted. "I told him at once that I thought it was a magnificent idea at this time when there is so much discontent over the alleged lack of unity of command between the Army and the Navy," Stimson wrote.

Stimson invited Knox to his office the following Monday, November 2, to discuss the proposition. Open-faced and affable, the sixty-eight-year-old Knox had energetically rebuilt the Navy since Pearl Harbor but, no great naval mind, deferred to the admirals on most matters. As Stimson outlined the proposal, Knox responded warmly, calling it "very generous." King was pleased too, envisioning the Navy and Army headquarters consolidating much of their work—the Army staff taking over some jobs entirely and the Navy staff other assignments.

After their meeting, Stimson and Knox made separate trips to inspect the Pentagon—it was the first time Stimson, who was wedded to Washington, had even laid eyes on the building—and both were well satisfied with the arrangements. Knox timed the trip by limousine from the Navy Building to the Pentagon and was pleased to find it took only five minutes. Captain Bob Furman trotted behind as Knox and his entourage toured the building. Reaching Stimson's suite, the secretary of the Navy covetously looked the plush surroundings up and down. "I want the same damn thing on my floor," Knox announced. After his visit, Knox spoke with Stimson and formally accepted the Army invitation. Stimson telephoned Roosevelt at Hyde Park at the end of the day November 2 to report on the proposition and get the president's approval. "He was very much pleased with it and told us to go ahead," Stimson reported.

At a press conference the next day, Knox announced the Navy would move into the Pentagon. It was shocking news, coming as a surprise to most ranking Army and Navy officers. As many as ten thousand Navy employees would move into the Army building by December 1, occupying one entire floor and parts of two others. "It gives the two departments the closest possible contact physically and lends itself to the closest possible liaison and cooperation and coordination between the two," Knox told reporters. As Stimson had predicted, the press hailed the decision as an important step toward a unified command.

The admirals were less pleased, seeing their independent fiefdoms threatened by the move; Navy workers themselves were absolutely distressed at the news. Why would they not be? Everything they had read in the newspapers or heard from war workers about the Pentagon told of horrific transportation problems, crowded cafeterias, dusty offices, and utter confusion in the vast, unfathomable network of corridors. "On the other hand it's a swell break for several thousand War Department employes," a columnist for the *Washington Daily News* wrote. "Most of them have taken it for granted they would have to move to the unpopular Pentagon sooner or later. Now they get a reprieve. Lucky people!"

Some Navy employees distributed a impeccably official-looking memorandum addressed to all personnel of the Navy Department moving to the Pentagon. According to paragraph 2, subsection b,

All personnel being moved will provide themselves with a sleeping bag, food and water for one week, clothing for one week, iron rations, three extra pairs of shoes, a compass, a scout knife, a pistol and roller skates or a scooter. No motorized equipment or collapsible boats will be permitted. . . . Cow bells will also be issued as emergency equipment.

A Navy officer wrote a parody based on the Virginia state song and sent it to the newspapers:

Carry me back to Old Virginny
That's where the Army and Navy have to go;
That's where the roads are a mess in springtime,
That's where the tombstones are heavy with the snow.
Carry me back to the Pentagon Building,
Five sides instead of the four that make a square;
Carry me back to Old Virginny
'Cause that's the only way
You'll ever get me there.

The real opening of the Pentagon

The convoys started rolling from the Munitions Building on the morning of Saturday, November 14, 1942. All classified papers had been locked in safes and placed on Army trucks, along with the desks and furniture. Armed soldiers were positioned along the route leading from Constitution Avenue across Memorial Bridge and down to the Pentagon. The secretary of war was moving in.

The invasion of North Africa had begun exactly a week earlier, on the morning of Sunday, November 8—Saturday evening in Washington. Stimson had awaited reports on the landings at Woodley, his estate in Northwest Washington, together with his wife, Mabel, and Beatrice Patton, the wife of General George Patton, commanding the western assault force that was to land in French Morocco. Around 9 P.M. they received word that all three landings were under way. "This was a great relief in the case of Patton's force because we had been troubled by prophesies of bad weather which might prevent the landing and disjoint the whole performance and, as Patton is impulsive and brave, I was very much afraid he might take off in an impossible sea and suffer great losses," Stimson wrote in his diary.

Once the troops were reported ashore, Stimson's fears were hardly assuaged. He had not shaken his "very grave misgivings" about the wisdom of the whole North African excursion, and in the coming days he fretted about the Germans moving through Spain across the Strait of Gibraltar and cutting off the American forces. "But now when we get it out on maps, the hazard of it seems to be more dangerous than ever," he wrote. By the end of the week, Stimson was exhausted and for a change he felt like the seventy-five-year-old man he was. He flew north with Mabel to relax over the weekend at Highhold, his country estate on Long Island, riding his horse while his office was relocated.

The move to the Pentagon, personally overseen by Major General John T. Lewis, commander of the Military District of Washington, went without a hitch. Unlike the desks of many hapless Pentagon employees, the secretary's elegant furniture was carried gingerly into the building. Marshall's office came in on the heels of Stimson's.

At 4 P.M. Saturday afternoon, the secretary of war's office was declared established in the Pentagon. The Army chief of staff's office was ready on Sunday. The move of Stimson and Marshall's offices, Marshall biographer Forrest C. Pogue noted, "marked the real opening of the Pentagon." It was no longer merely a very large, very curious office for war workers. It was now the Army's command post for the global war.

Inspecting his new headquarters, Marshall found his dark mahogany desk with carved lion heads and brass ring drawer pulls in place. Unlike Stimson, Marshall dispensed with the elaborate map alcove, contenting himself with a large globe and a few simple relief maps. Behind his desk was a tall grandfather clock and an oil painting of Pershing, whom Marshall revered. But the chief of staff raised Cain when he discovered his telephones were not working correctly.

Marshall already had a crisis to manage. Washington was in an uproar over the deal that General Dwight Eisenhower, the Allied commander in North Africa, had struck with the reptilian Admiral Jean-François Darlan, commander of Vichy French military forces, allowing Darlan to retain power in exchange for the surrender of all French forces.

Stimson arrived the next day from Long Island, coming straight from National Airport with his wife. "Mabel and I drove to the Pentagon Building where I found my new office all beautifully prepared and ready for me and Mabel inspected it," he wrote in his diary. Stimson—probably oblivious to all the blood, sweat, and toil that had gone into making his office just so—seemed pleased with his new surroundings in Room 3E-884.

Stimson sat behind the massive carved mahogany desk used by every secretary of war since Robert Todd Lincoln in 1883. At his right was a telephone with a direct, secure line to the White House. An electronic squawk box—which Stimson would never learn to operate properly—could be used to summon McCloy or other key aides. To his left was a small oval table used by Jefferson Davis when he was secretary of war under Franklin Pierce. Hanging on the wall behind his desk, flanked by the flags of the United States and the secretary of war, was a portrait of former secretary of war Elihu Root, Stimson's hero. The windows, framed with Venetian blinds and drapes, overlooked the river; most of the construction debris was out of his immediate sight. It was a spacious office, more than twice the size of his office in the Munitions Building. Overstuffed leather chairs in green-

and-tan tones were positioned about the suite. Across the hall was the private dining room, walls paneled with solid light oak and four mahogany dining tables covered with white linen. The serving pantry was equipped with Army cooks, a refrigerator, and an electric steam table. Stimson was most pleased with the map alcove in his office, upon which Army cartographers had prepared maps with positions of American troops in all theaters around the world, including the latest updates from North Africa.

As soon as his wife left, Stimson called in Marshall and Hap Arnold to discuss his thoughts on how to defend the North African landing force against the attack he feared the Germans might launch from Gibraltar. Then McCloy came in to update Stimson on the uproar over the Darlan affair, which was only intensifying. There was moral outrage in what Stimson called "starry-eyed circles" about dealing with the Nazi collaborator in North Africa. It was all mystifying to Stimson, who considered the arrangement a necessary evil that had saved American lives, but he went to work trying to calm the furor.

The high command settled quickly into the Pentagon. Two days after Marshall's arrival, Colonel William T. Sexton, an aide to the chief of staff, heard a commotion in the hallway and instinctively reached for his pistol. Hap Arnold had commandeered a bicycle, and, accompanied by an aide on roller skates, rolled into Marshall's office, where the chief of staff was in the midst of a conference. Marshall looked up to see his tall, white-haired air forces chief perched on a bicycle. Arnold saluted. "New carrier service, sir," he announced, and then pedaled out. Marshall "roared with laughter," Sexton recalled.

The chief of staff was satisfied with the Pentagon, once his phone was fixed. He and Stimson found it an effective command post, particularly as the rest of the high command moved in. It would be even more effective once the Navy arrived.

These damned admirals

Stimson was hoping to make an early escape from work on the afternoon of November 19 and get some rest. He was still fatigued from overseeing North Africa operations and had been unable to sleep for several nights, lying awake with worry. But Somervell caught the secretary as he was heading home with some bad news: The admirals were agitating for more space in the Pentagon and threatening to sabotage the whole deal.

The Army had already increased the amount of office space offered to the Navy from 800,000 to one million square feet, roughly 40 percent of the building. Stimson had reluctantly agreed to kick the chief of ordnance office out of the Pentagon to give the Navy extra room. If the Army lost any further space, half the intelligence section would have to go elsewhere. But Assistant Secretary of the Navy Ralph A. Bard, who was "violently against" the deal agreed to by his chief, insisted the Navy needed more space. All eight Navy bureau chiefs were objecting to the move. "Incidentally these admirals are trying to use their power over Knox to extort a good deal of further space from us," Stimson fumed in his diary. "We have already given them 200,000 feet more than we originally offered and I shall set my face against any further concession."

Stimson telephoned Knox and complained "pretty freely" about the Navy's behavior. Knox told Stimson he was trying to work it out with the admirals, but he wanted to do so "without a row."

Stimson knew what that meant—the genial secretary of the Navy lacked the steel to break the admirals' blockade. Knox was no Elihu Root. "The Bureau admirals are holding Knox up and he is as helpless as a child in their hands," Stimson wrote. "As a result, it seems as if this really important improvement of having the Navy come into our building and share it with us in such a way as to assist united command will break down simply from the crusty selfishness of some Bureau officers which their chief has not force enough to command."

The press was starting to wonder what was going on. The Navy was supposed to be in the Pentagon by December 1, and on November 20 Knox was forced to publicly admit the move would be delayed until at least Christmas. At the White House later that day, Knox gingerly approached Stimson at the end of the Cabinet meeting and asked for another 200,000 square feet of space.

Stimson responded icily. Conferring afterward with McCloy and Marshall, Stimson found them equally adamant that the Army make no further concession. The Army now had 63,000 workers in Washington, and the Navy 27,000. As it stood now, each service would be able to fit about one-third of its Washington workforce into the Pentagon. If the Army conceded another 200,000 feet, the Navy would have 40 percent of its Washington force in the Pentagon, and the Army less than 30 percent—and this in a building the Army had moved heaven and earth to build.

The beleaguered Renshaw—his dreams of soon completing the command section dashed by the decision to move in the Navy—had been working since November 3 to prepare the suites for Knox, King, and other top Navy officials. Renshaw warned Groves that the construction crews were in dark moods about ripping out much of their finished work to accommodate the Navy. It was going to be expensive—Renshaw estimated it would cost $8.3 million. Navy representatives insisted that the offices of every Navy officer with the rank of captain or above be fitted with private bathrooms, leather chairs, and wainscoted walls. Marshall turned visibly angry when he heard the demand. "They'll get exactly what the Army gets—nothing more, and nothing less," he ordered. Meanwhile, while the Navy dithered for more space, large sections of the Army's Ordnance, Signal, Intelligence, and Air Forces that were supposed to move into the Pentagon were in limbo.

Marshall told Stimson he was so disgusted with the Navy's actions he would rather withdraw the whole offer. At a tense meeting on Tuesday, November 24, Stimson told Knox that one million square feet was his final offer; otherwise, the Army would occupy the entire building.

Knox promised to get back to Stimson within an hour. The day passed, and two more, with no word from the secretary of the Navy. After a thoroughly unrelaxing Thanksgiving Day—much of it spent in the Pentagon working with Marshall on the Darlan affair—Stimson called Knox on Friday, November 27, and found the secretary of the Navy "still in the same helpless condition." Knox explained that Rear Admiral Samuel Robinson, chief of the Bureau of Ships, insisted he needed more space.

That was it, Stimson decided. "I told him then that I was afraid that we would have to withdraw the offer and call the thing off," Stimson wrote. "He said he was afraid that was so."

The whole matter left Stimson depressed. "It seems to me a frightful condemnation of the ability of men that we can't settle a matter which had so much good in it because of such a trivial objection by one bureau head," he wrote in his diary.

Stimson set to writing a letter to Roosevelt informing him that the plan had collapsed—"a rather difficult letter to write because I did not wish to have it sound provocative and yet I wished the President to know the justifying facts," he noted. After conferring with Somervell on the wording and reading a draft to Marshall, Stimson sent it by courier to Roosevelt at Hyde Park on Saturday, November 28.

Stimson's word's to the president were restrained but left no doubt that he and Marshall blamed the Navy for making unreasonable demands. "We believe that the harmonious cooperation which we have sought to obtain by this union of the two services might be entirely frustrated by such an unequal division," Stimson wrote. He asked Roosevelt's permission to start moving War Department units into the space reserved for the Navy. They had lost nearly four weeks waiting, noted Stimson, adding, "we must begin at once with the work of getting our people moved in the building."

Roosevelt sent his regrets to Stimson and approved of the Army taking the space. The president did not seem particularly surprised at the breakdown; indeed, he probably had been well aware of the admirals' protests against the move. Knox announced to the press November 30 that the Navy had abandoned plans to move into the Pentagon, explaining that "careful investigation" had revealed the building was not big enough for both the Army and Navy.

The Navy had legitimate concerns about moving into the Pentagon. Without more space, some bureaus would have to be split up. The Navy's sophisticated communications system needed considerable space, and the time needed to get it up and running in the Pentagon might upset ongoing military operations. But the benefits—the sharing of resources and intelligence, consolidating work, the close working proximity of the high command, not only of Marshall and King but also of their staffs, creating greater cooperation—would have outweighed the inconveniences. Less than a year into the war, a great opportunity had been lost. Unity of command would have to wait.

Lost perpendicularly and horizontally

Few tears were shed among Navy workers over the news they would not move across the Potomac. It seemed particularly fortuitous on the afternoon of December 1, the day Knox's announcement hit the newspapers, when dozens of Army officers and civilian personnel at the Pentagon began collapsing shortly after eating at one of the cafeterias. More than seventy Army workers were felled, victims of food poisoning. Ambulances descended on the building. "The halls of the Pentagon Building resembled a base hospital as workers who had collapsed were carried to the emergency infirmary on stretchers," the *Star* reported. Employees blamed the corned beef hash, but an investigation supervised by the ubiquitous McCloy quickly pinpointed the salad dressing. No one died, but the incident certainly confirmed the suspicions of relieved Navy workers that the Pentagon was a hellhole.

Accounts from war workers—some twenty thousand were in the building now—further cemented the image. Dorothy Potter Benedict, an author of children's books who worked as a translator for the Army Air Forces, sent a letter to *The Washington Post* in November describing her experiences in the building:

> We are in the Pentagon now, that maze across the river, surrounded by noise, dust, the debris of hastened construction and overcrowded, precipitant buses. But these minor hazards are as nothing as compared to the obstacles to be overcome between the entrance and the office to which one may be assigned.
>
> Since the Army's Dream Building is made in a series of pentagonal rings, like misshapen doughnuts placed one inside the other, one loses one's sense of direction the moment one leaves the outer ring. In answer to the question, "Where am I?" The guard will answer cheerily: "Can't say, Madam. This is my first day," or, "Couldn't tell you. I've just been transferred from the other side of the building."
>
> This is discouraging news for a worker due in the outer ring at a certain hour and vaguely aware that she is somewhere in the inner ring—lost. But not alone. Far from it. Weary colonels, bleak-faced majors, haggard captains and lieutenants pass and repass trying to find their respective destinations. They get lost perpendicularly as well as horizontally.

Newspapers reported that a hundred people a day were getting lost. New arrivals to the Pentagon were described by *Life* magazine as being "as confused as a fresh rat in a psychologist's maze." Even Under Secretary of War Patterson admitted to getting lost "every time I get three doors away from my own office."

Psychologists debated whether Pentagon employees were suffering from a fear of being shut in or a fear of being in the midst of open spaces. "I suspect that an overpowering delusion that the building is dangerously different is the basic cause of complaint—but time will cure that in the case of permanent employees," a doctor told *Newsweek*. "They will get to love the Pentagon."

One letter-writer saw a bright side to the Pentagon's working conditions. "The generals are right—there is not yet enough hate in this war," G. Dorrance of Washington wrote the *Post*. War workers, he said, "may feel a growing dislike for the Fuehrer when they arise each morning an hour or two before daylight, swallow breakfast without chewing, join the battle of transportation outside, and work in the Pentagon all day without benefit of sunlight or fresh air. . . ."

The press made much of Stimson's luxurious accommodations in comparison with the rest of the building. *Life* followed this theme with particular zest, running a two-page photo spread showing Stimson's spacious suite: "Looming across the Potomac like a Cecil B. DeMille backdrop, the War Department's new $85,000,000 Pentagon Building is just a colossal pain-in-the-neck to thousands of bewildered Washington visitors and harassed employees. They resent the . . . miles of barren corridors, the jammed ramps, the pile-up at entrances and exits, the parking and transportation problems, the six overcrowded cafeterias, the staggered working hours. The only really happy person in the War Department's whopping new reinforced-concrete 'home' is the Army's civilian chief, Henry L. Stimson."

Somervell was impervious to the constant stream of complaints and jabs directed his way—indeed, he was quite proud of the Pentagon. "The building is very dear to my heart," he wrote Ides van der Gracht in September. The general assured the press in November that all the problems would soon be ironed out. "I think it's a magnificent building," Somervell said.

Those least impressed with life in the Pentagon included the black

Americans assigned to the building and given continued treatment as second-class citizens in it. The cafeterias had been integrated; now much of the trouble centered on the buses. At the end of a wearisome day at work in the Aircraft Radio Branch of the Signal Corps, Masie Ashby and Florence Cole boarded a bus in front of the Pentagon at 5:15 on the evening of October 27 to begin their journey home to Washington. They sat together in the third seat from the front. Several military policemen were standing near the bus and one of them, a Sergeant Clark, tapped the window next to the women with his baton and motioned for them to move to the back of the bus. The women ignored him. Clark boarded the bus and when the women refused to go to the rear, he ordered them off.

It was not an isolated incident. Judge William Hastie, Stimson's civilian aide, pressed each time for an investigation. Every time, Army officials would respond that they could not confirm the details, or that the bus company was at fault and the Army was not responsible, or that the black employee had somehow provoked the incident, or that the problem had been corrected and would not happen again. But it would happen again, and it was not just the buses. The Pentagon cafeteria manager advertised for "competent white female help" in the dining rooms; black employees were targets of racial epithets. Hastie was frustrated. In January, he would resign from the War Department in protest of the Army's plans to establish a separate Officer Candidate School for blacks. The betrayal black employees felt was reflected in a letter that Dorothy J. Williams, an Ordnance employee, wrote to her superior after she was forced to the back of her bus: "It is ironic that our Nation will wage war to guarantee an end to human persecution of individuals, based solely on race, color, or creed, and remain impervious to a similar plight of approximately one-tenth of its citizens."

The glorious chords of free men singing

By Christmas Eve, there were 22,000 war workers in the Pentagon, and all were invited to gather in the interior courtyard late that afternoon for a holiday celebration. Stimson spent quite a bit of time during the day "fussing over the speech" he was to deliver at the ceremony. Initially the secretary of war had given the matter little thought and intended to simply read remarks drafted by the Public Relations Bureau. "I had not taken it very much to heart at first . . .," he wrote on his diary, "but the closer I got to it the more important I felt it was to make the thing more in my own language and personal to myself." At 4 P.M. Stimson, accompanied by his wife, took his place at a pavilion set by the north face of the courtyard wall, where he was joined by Somervell and several other top Army commanders. The stage was brightened by a large Christmas tree decorated with bells and evergreen garlands wrapped around the railings.

A vast crowd of Pentagon employees had gathered in the five-acre courtyard on the gray and chilly afternoon—fifteen thousand, by one esti-mate. Many others looked on from the five floors of windows surrounding the courtyard. Renshaw had succeeded in cleaning out all the debris, but it was hardly a garden spot, with a few scraggly trees, none of them Japanese cherries. The courtyard was surrounded by towering five-story concrete walls, with bastion-like landings at each corner, reminiscent of a medieval castle. Most employees stood on the walkways that crisscrossed the court-yard, trying to avoid the puddles and mud, like the veteran plank walkers they were. Yet the scene had an air of grace and beauty. Looking down from a window, one observer noted, the thousands of Army officers and civilian employees standing on the intersecting walks "unconsciously formed a huge star."

The audience—whites standing shoulder to shoulder with blacks—sang as the Army Air Forces Band played "Jingle Bells" and "Joy to the World," and a choir made up of some two hundred black War Department employees sang spirituals. An NBC microphone was on the stage to broad-cast the event by radio around the country. "It was a very impressive and pleasant occasion," Stimson wrote in his diary. "A very large crowd was there, filling up all the standing room that there was in the courtyard and the speeches went off very well and the music was very good."

Somervell spoke first, addressing the throng in the place he had dreamed up seventeen months before. He was hatless but bundled against the cold in a heavy gray Army overcoat with three stars on the shoulders. The general was gracious in his praise of the work being done in the Pen-tagon, but, of course, he asked for more. "Much of the blackness is back of us," Somervell said. "A year ago we were a stunned people. We had not asked for war. It was thrust upon us. We faced what seemed an impossible task. Today it is different. We have done the impossible. Now we must perform the miraculous."

The choir sang more spirituals and the audience joined in carols, and then Stimson spoke, addressing his words to his fellow Pentagon workers in the most personal terms his austere Eastern establishment makeup would allow. "[Y]ou and I have been obliged under the pressure of our work to hurry past each other in crowded corridors without any full realization of our real comradeship," he said. "Today we are able to celebrate our Christmas face to face and all together, and it is very fitting that we should do so."

Stimson was relieved to find his voice in good shape and carrying well over the loudspeakers. ("I felt that it was reaching the people that I spoke to although the audience covered an enormous piece of ground," he later wrote.) Stimson continued, telling the employees that every worker in the building had a vital, "personal share in the task before us." During the past year, the War Department had taken no holidays, even working through the Fourth of July. "But Christmas we could not ignore," Stimson said. "Although all necessary operations of the War Department must continue as usual, those of you who can be spared will have tomorrow to spend with your families in customary enjoyment of the most important holiday in the Christian world. In the midst of total war, Christmas has a very special significance to us all."

There had been no ceremony when ground was broken for the Pentagon in September 1941, nor when the plaque was installed at the mall entrance a year later, nor would any note be taken when construction was finished in early 1943. The Christmas Eve 1942 gathering was the dedication ceremony the Pentagon never had. As darkness approached following Stimson's speech, the music continued and everyone sang "Silent Night," and then to close the evening, "The Star Spangled Banner." A newspaper account described it this way: "The huge court, bounded by the five interior faces of the world's largest building, echoed again and again the glorious chords of free men singing."

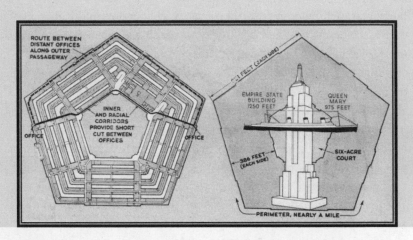

Popular Science *graphic from 1943 showing the shortest route between offices and comparing the relative sizes of the Empire State Building, an ocean liner and the Pentagon.*

CHAPTER
15

HEADQUARTERS
FOR THE WAR

Able and fearless constructors

The Pentagon was still not finished in the New Year. Some five thousand construction workers remained on the job. They rushed to get the fifth floor ready for occupancy, and they tiled, painted, and plastered the basement. Outside, crews poured the last of the road network, battling cold weather. John McShain had a theory as to why it always seemed impossible to finish a job: Construction crews had a built-in bias against completing the work and losing their jobs. "If you want to finish on time, fire everybody, and bring a whole new crew in," he told Bob Furman. McShain was joking, but only just.

The goal of completing the building by November 15 had long since been abandoned, pushed back to January 1, 1943, because of the additional fifth-floor work. Following a visit to the Pentagon on New Year's Day, Groves reported to Fat Styer, Somervell's deputy, that work would be completed by January 15. Official construction progress reports record the building as "substantially complete" by January 15. This has been adopted as the Pentagon's official completion date, recited in fact sheets, and used to mark the building's anniversary.

Yet "substantially complete" was not the same as finished; records show the building was not quite done by January 15, and thousands of employees had yet to move in. The main holdup was installing pipes for the heating and air-conditioning on the fifth floor; War Department employees could not move in until it was done. Steam fitters and mechanics needed for the job were in such short supply that McShain was scouring other cities for available workers. By January 9 Groves had postponed completion to February 1; on January 14 McShain told Groves they would not meet this date either. "While we have every desire to meet your request and complete the building by February 1st, we are of the opinion that it is a physical impossibility to accomplish this date," McShain wrote. He promised they would finish by February 15. This they did.

Whether the official completion date is considered to be January 15—some sixteen months after ground was broken, or February 15, seventeen months after—is of little import. Either way, it was a stunning accomplishment.

The auditor from Harold Smith's Bureau of the Budget, so appalled at the design, scale, and cost of the building, nonetheless tipped his hat to the builders. The speed with which the Pentagon was built "unmistakably indicates that the men responsible for this project were able and fearless constructors possessed of a large fund of amicability and common sense," he wrote.

Able and fearless they had been—Somervell, Groves, Renshaw, McShain, and Hauck chief among them.

The Pentagon

In the Pentagon, the War Department now had a headquarters that was four times the size of the British War Office at Whitehall, the German Kriegsministerium in Berlin, and the Japanese General Staff headquarters building in Tokyo—combined.

Originally proposed to have 5.1 million gross square feet, cut to 4 million square feet by groundbreaking, the official tally as 1943 dawned was calculated to be 6.24 million gross square feet. The Pentagon also included more office space than previously thought. Instead of the 2.3 million net square feet of office space figured the previous fall, the engineers calculated that 3.6 million net square feet could be occupied, once the fifth floor, the conversion of the basement from storage to offices, and other alterations were included. Its massive size told of the vast scale of the American war mobilization, as well as the U.S. Army's reliance on a huge staff—not to mention the overwhelming force of Somervell's personality.

In short order, Somervell had conceived and built an institution that would rank with the White House, the Vatican, Buckingham Palace, and a handful of others as symbols recognized around the world, a building in whose name pronouncements were made and declarations issued. At a price of about $75 million, more than twice what Somervell promised, the building also represented the Pentagon's first cost overrun.

Upon its creation, the massive concrete building assumed an aura of permanence that made it seem as if it had always been there—"a large geometrical form existing almost beyond time or place," in the words of architectural historian Richard Guy Wilson.

On February 12, 1943, Major General Alexander D. Surles, chief of the Army's Bureau of Public Relations, sent a memorandum to Marshall's office concerning the official designation of the new War Department headquarters:

1. As time goes on the permanent home of the War Department will occupy a place of increasing dignity and distinction in the Nation's history. The building will be world-famous and its name a household word.
2. It has been suggested that the designation, "The Pentagon," would be more in keeping with this historical character than the one now in use, "The Pentagon *Building*."
3. It is recommended that the building officially be designated as "*The Pentagon*."

Not everyone was taking the building's name so seriously; Roosevelt, ever the punster, had taken to calling it "the Pentateuchal Building," a reference to the first five books of the Old Testament. The president's quips notwithstanding, Stimson's office approved Surles's recommendation on February 15, and "The Pentagon" was made the official name by a general order signed by Marshall on February 19.

Surles's memorandum was striking for saying the Pentagon would be the permanent home of the War Department. This was entirely contrary to official policy, which was that the War Department would move back to Washington after the war. Surles had recognized a truth that nobody in the Army was saying publicly: They would never abandon the Pentagon.

The miraculous takes a little longer

The focal point of the Pentagon was above the River entrance of the building, on the third floor of the E Ring, where Stimson and Marshall's suites lay and where momentous decisions would soon be made. At the Casablanca conference in January 1943, Roosevelt—to Churchill's surprise—had publicly declared that the Allies were fighting a war that would end only in the "unconditional surrender" of Germany, Italy, and Japan. Returning from Casablanca on January 29, Marshall set to work with Stimson to chart the path. Of immediate concern, operations in North Africa were at a standstill and tough fighting lay ahead in Tunisia. Marshall was determined to find ways to help Eisenhower deal with mounting military and political crises. At the same time, preparations were needed for the next step, advancing on Italy via an invasion of Sicily, which Marshall had agreed to despite his misgivings about getting bogged down in the Mediterranean. Plans were also in the works to recapture Burma, overrun by the Japanese in the spring of 1942. Overriding everything else were decisions to be made about the cross-Channel invasion of western Europe from England—Operation Overlord, now set for 1944.

Marshall's routine at the Pentagon was already well established. He was picked up from Quarters One at Fort Myer at 7:15 A.M. in an Army Plymouth for the short drive around Arlington Cemetery to the Pentagon. At Marshall's order, the driver often would stop to pick up young Army officers or other war workers left stranded by overcrowded buses; the shocked riders would be quizzed about their jobs by the chief of staff during the rest of the trip to the Pentagon. At the River entrance, the driver would take Marshall down a ramp leading into a garage beneath the building, pulling up to a door that led to the private elevator he and Stimson shared. (One predawn morning, when Marshall stopped by without his building pass on his way to go duck hunting, the guard at the elevator would not let him in, failing to recognize the man in the hunter's garb.) Marshall preferred taking the private elevator up from the garage directly to his office to avoid wasting time with hallway chatter. This drove Marshall's staff to distraction, as they could never be quite sure when the general had arrived.

Early on the agenda every morning was a briefing on the situation with U.S. forces around the globe, with much of the emphasis these days on operations in North Africa. There was a minimum of ceremony; Marshall was usually joined by Hap Arnold, commander of air forces, Major General Thomas T. Handy, head of the operations division, and often Somervell. The briefing officers, who had been at the Pentagon all night reviewing the message traffic coming into the Signal Center and communicating with all the theaters, would speak for ten or fifteen minutes. Marshall would often make decisions on the spot. "A question would come up and you could get the general's thinking on it right then and go on and do something about it," Handy recalled. Even if there was no immediate answer, the policy was to get back to the theater within twenty-four hours with some kind of reply while the issue was further investigated.

Stimson often would come visiting soon afterward. The door connecting his office to Marshall's was never locked—one measure of the enormous respect and trust the two men had for each other—and the secretary would walk in two or three times over the course of the morning to consult. Two other doors led into the chief of staff's office, further complicating the task of keeping track of who was in the room.

Marshall's office, Room 3E-921, served as a de facto conference room, with a half-dozen leather chairs spread about. A succession of officers came in and out, sometimes stacking up in the tiny anteroom outside Marshall's office as they awaited a chance to go in. Peering into Marshall's office to see if the general was available was a serious mistake. Marshall hated being spied upon, and anyone poking his head in would be met with a stern order to enter the room. A junior officer might find himself stating his business before Marshall and a half-dozen generals. Marshall soon pasted a three-by-five card on the door leading from the anteroom with a warning: "Once you open this door, walk in regardless of what is going on inside." That eliminated most of the peeking.

Somervell was a frequent visitor to the command suites, enjoying close if formal relations with Marshall and Stimson. He had, of course, ensured that the headquarters for his Services of Supply (SOS) was not far from the seat of power. Somervell's office, Room 3E-672, set grandly atop the Mall entrance to the building, was in the next section of the E Ring, on the same floor as Marshall and Stimson. Somervell kept two telephones on a side table within arm's reach of his desk, and a door in his office led to a sound-proof room with four secure, direct-line telephones, including one to the White House. In many respects the Pentagon was Somervell's building, and not just because he was responsible for its creation: His enormous Army services organization occupied just over half of the Pentagon's office space. By comparison, the Office of the Secretary of War and the Office of the Chief of Staff, including the entire general staff, occupied 22 percent of the building, and the Army Air Forces 11 percent.

There was no downtime in Somervell's office. "He streaks through the day like a Lockheed Lightning," recounted a reporter who spent a day with the general. Within five minutes of arriving in his office, Somervell had "pressed down every buzzer in sight" to summon aides. His top officers—among them his deputy, Fat Styer, and a talented brigadier general named Lucius D. Clay—came in frequently to confer and study oversize wall maps in Somervell's office. One showed the United States, the other the world, and they were covered with a forest of yellow, blue, and white pins, each representing a different SOS project.

When Somervell's temper flared—generally a dozen times a day—he would jettison his gracious manner, drop his voice even lower than normal, and tug agitatedly at his neatly clipped mustache. His latest method to try to control his temper was to go into another room, walk violently back and forth, and return with an unconvincing smile on his face. Somervell had given up cigarettes in the summer of 1942 and preached against smoking with the zeal of a convert, but on stressful days his secretary, Katherine King, would find billowing clouds of smoke in his office. As Somervell figured out the logistics for supplying the North Africa campaign, he hurled invectives about "bathtub admirals" and "knotty-pine powder-room strategists" or anyone else slowing him down. Occasionally Somervell had reason to regret his outbursts—he publicly raged about "golf-playing industrialists" after being unable reach one on the telephone the previous summer and since then had been forced to give up his favorite sport, fearing it would be unseemly if he were spotted on a golf course.

On the wall of Somervell's office was a framed photograph of his hero, Teddy Roosevelt, and a sign bearing the words that Somervell had popu-

larized as the Services of Supply motto: "We Do the Impossible Immediately. The Miraculous Takes a Little Longer." Somervell and the SOS were
proving it to be more than a slogan.

Attending the Casablanca conference in January with Marshall, Somervell
learned that Eisenhower desperately needed more trucks and other equipment. Somervell quickly contacted Styer at the Pentagon, dispatching a ca-
blegram "as long as a book" listing equipment to be sent immediately to
North Africa: trucks, locomotives, boxcars, tank engines, carbines, artillery
sights, machine guns, tractors, and road equipment, among other items. The
staff in Somervell's office, well versed in their master's ways, "settled down
to furious days and sleepless nights." Across America, wires hummed, orders were typed, trains rolled, and cargo planes flew. Somervell told Eisenhower he would have 5,400 trucks at U.S. ports in three days, ready to be
shipped. The arrival of the trucks three weeks later—"which by the way
won the Africa campaign," Eisenhower later said—enabled the commander
to keep his battlefront supplied and to transfer troops rapidly around Tunisia
to fight the forces of German Field Marshal Erwin Rommel. When all the
trucks and equipment had been sent, an exhausted Styer sent a plaintive message to Somervell, still in Casablanca: "If you should happen to want the
Pentagon shipped over there, please try to give us about a week's notice."

A foretaste of the future

Just arriving at the Pentagon in the first days of 1943 was like stepping forward in time. There was a sense of excitement about the whole building
that even the lowliest clerks shared. The nearly completed road network
leading to the building, with its cloverleaf interchanges, ramps, and overpasses, was quite unlike anything most Americans had seen. *Architectural
Forum*, a respected magazine in the field, enthusiastically described the
overall vision of the project. "For miles around the results of building the
Pentagon are visible: the reclaimed slums, the broad roads, and the new, integrated approaches to the capital," the magazine wrote in January 1943.
"Perhaps the greatest lesson of the Pentagon is here: as building approaches the scale technically feasible, the distinction between architecture
and city planning vanishes. Despite its shortcomings, the Pentagon gives a
real foretaste of the future."

Most people came into the building via the massive bus terminal, which had opened in November. Leading up to it was a looping access road, its turns utterly confounding to riders. "The highway began to contort itself into weird geometrical figures so that now the building was on our starboard, now on our port, now immediately in front of us and now directly behind," a taxi passenger wrote. "There can be no doubt that the chief of army engineers collaborated with the landscape architect so that army headquarters could not be taken in a frontal assault." After a final loop, the buses and taxis swooped into the Pentagon through a thousand-foot tunnel running the entire length of the first floor on the building's southeast face. Parallel rows of neon lights lined the whole route, forming a continuous streak to passengers aboard the rushing vehicles.

"Here is the picture of a future architecture in which buildings will be linked to their users by smooth-flowing traffic networks," *Architectural Forum* reported. "To the visitor who has just been exposed to the vast and boring expanse of windows, cornices and columns, nothing comes as a greater surprise than this sleek tunnel, for its entrances have been almost hidden in the corners of the building. The buses glide in between low walls of smooth gray brick, their engines muffled by a ceiling of acoustic tile."

The terminal, the largest that had ever been incorporated into a building, could handle 25,000 persons an hour. At peak hours, buses rushed through at the rate of one every eight seconds, pulling up in two lanes to one of fourteen loading platforms. A third lane served taxis. Passengers pouring off the buses and taxis complained of near-asphyxiation from gas and dust, but engineers promised conditions would improve as more roads around the building were paved and eight huge exhaust fans were properly adjusted. The passengers moved from the platforms through doors leading toward twenty-one stairways, feeling a rush of cool air coming down the steps from the building.

At the top of the stairways, they dropped a nickel for the bus ride into fare boxes manned by conductors and strode into the Pentagon Concourse on the second floor. This was a vast and bustling expanse 690 feet long and 135 feet wide, almost the width of a football field and more than twice as long. A long row of round columns, painted a glistening red, ran down the middle almost as far as the eye could see. The concourse—larger than that of New York's Pennsylvania Station—"seemed to me to be big enough for tank maneuvers," one visitor wrote. "If you waited around there long enough you'd see every American general you'd ever heard of and more second lieutenants than you dreamed existed." It was a futuristic scene—a precursor to an indoor shopping mall. There were no windows, just diffused light. The walls were lined with neon signs identifying various facilities. Already there was a bank, a sixteen-chair barbershop, a checkroom, newsstands and shoeshine stands, and there were plans for shops, a post office, and more. It was a self-contained community, designed that way because the Pentagon was considered in the hinterlands, with few services nearby.

A reception desk was centered at each end of the concourse—one for government employees, the second for other visitors. Eight women—all of them "comely young ladies," according to the *Star*—presided behind the counters. "The girls are selected for their good looks, brains, tact, and just ordinary horse sense, and many a male lingers at the counter," the newspaper reported.

Visitors—those not asking for dates—stated their business. Receptionists checked identifications and verified appointments. Military and government visitors receiving clearance were given badges. All others had to wait—often for lengthy periods—for an escort, usually an officer or employee from the office to be visited.

Once past security, the visitor moved into the abyss. A writer for *Popular Science* likened it to "something of the sensation of a tourist viewing Niagara Falls for the first time. . . . Torrents of humanity swirl through its corridors—Army officers and men, civilian specialists, stenographers, cafeteria waitresses, switchboard operators, messengers."

Broad ramps of polished black terrazzo led out from the concourse; one carried pedestrians farther into the second floor, another led up a 10 percent slope to the third floor, a third with two switchbacks rose to the fourth floor. The corridors had the feel of a circus, as messengers rolled by on bicycles, roller skates, and oversize tricycle carts tinkling their bells to avoid running over pedestrians. Message centers on each floor served as hubs, linked by fifteen miles of pneumatic tubes that whisked files and correspondence throughout the building inside plastic containers.

The quickest way to any far-off point in the building—even if it was on the same ring where one started—generally was to go toward the center of the building to the inner A Ring and follow signs leading to the proper radial corridor. Hugging the inside track of the A Ring, an employee could circle the building in 1,800 feet, while sticking to the E Ring was a journey of 4,605 feet, not much short of a mile.

Travelers gauged their location by color-coded corridor walls—the first floor was tan, the second green, the third red, the fourth gray, and the fifth blue. The upstairs floors, in theory, had a bit more natural light. The rings on the top three floors were divided by light courts—open space allowing sunlight and fresh air to reach the thousands of steel casement windows lining both sides of each ring. Seen from the air, the light courts gave the building its distinctive look of five parallel rings circling the center court, rather than one solid block of concrete.

The fifth floor was packed with oddities, most born of the hasty decision in July to add another story atop the three middle rings. There was less headroom in the hallways and fewer toilets, stairways, and fire escapes. The exterior façade outside the fifth floor was covered with a slablike entablature that wrapped around the building. It gave the Pentagon a classical look, but it meant none of the fifth floor had windows out front.

The first floor was darker and danker still, with narrower corridors and less light—even on the E Ring, many offices lacked windows. First-floor employees also had to watch out for trucks, cars, and carts: An interior truck road, forty feet in width, ran between the B and C rings through four of the Pentagon's five sections, giving supply trucks and firefighters a route to the inner courtyard.

Most unnatural were the basement and sub-basement, a maze of mezzanines, corridors, and gangways. Much of this netherworld was built into the low ground on the eastern side of the building, but there were pockets of space all around. The basement extended beneath the Mall and River terraces, well beyond the Pentagon's confine creating an F and even a G Ring below some of the building. Utility pipes, ducts, and pneumatic tubing snaked through the narrow corridors.

The basement had a Byzantine quality that would only grow over the years, as various mysterious offices took up residence in the Pentagon's lower reaches. Yet its design had more to do with engineering than secrecy. Since the Pentagon had been built on both low ground and high ground— the western two-thirds forty feet above sea level, and the eastern third ten feet above—the low ground had been raised with eight feet of fill. A retaining wall had been needed along the line where the forty-foot and eighteen-foot levels came together. Rather than build a long, twenty-two-foot-high retaining wall—a difficult and expensive proposition—engineers constructed one eleven-foot retaining wall stepping down to a second eleven-foot retaining wall. The result was the Pentagon had a mezzanine floor and a smaller basement.

The building's low setting in what was once Hell's Bottom placed it well below the surrounding high ground of Arlington Ridge and the commanding ground of the Arlington mansion. Moreover, the building was so low in relation to its width—71 feet, 3½ inches high, with outer walls each 921 feet long—that its mass was dispersed. It was impossible from the ground to see more than two sides at a time, which disguised the building's size. Large as the Pentagon was, it barely made a ripple on the landscape.

Likewise, from an architectural standpoint, the Pentagon blended surprisingly well into the evolving design of Pierre L'Enfant's Washington. The Pentagon's façades carried the story of twentieth-century architecture in federal Washington until that point. In the early 1900s, as L'Enfant's plan was resuscitated from the dead, Beaux-Arts classicism enjoyed a revival. By the 1920s, reaction against such elaborate and monumental design helped spawn the rise of the modern style, with an emphasis on simple design and functionality over ornamentation. Stripped classicism—a synthesis of classical and modern—became the dominant style in 1930s federal Washington. The Pentagon was stripped classicism writ large. With it, the style reached a pinnacle—certainly in size, but also in effectiveness, in the view of some later critics. Stripped classicism "may never have been so gainfully employed as on those long Pentagon walls," wrote *Washington Post* critic Benjamin Forgey.

The façades followed a traditional classical form. The colonnades, with tall, narrow, rectangular columns, were clearly delineated on the top by the entablature and on the bottom by a pediment molding line. On two sides facing Washington—the River and Mall, the building's official entrances—the colonnades projected out to form central porticos with steps. The two official entrances were decorated with simple cornices and friezes. Yet all the building's exterior features, including the columns and the entablature, were stripped and smooth, with little ornamentation.

The limestone of the façades was an excellent match for the stripped classicism, not shining like marble yet conveying a timeless look. On the rest of the exterior walls, the architectural concrete Edwin Bergstrom had insisted be used—for all the headache it caused McShain—lent a coherence that brick could not have provided. A sloping roof of unfading green Vermont slate stood atop the inner and outer rings and the radial corridors of the building. The slate—pooled from many quarries because of the great amount needed—had a variegated gray-green hue that one observer found pleasingly reminiscent of the old copper roof on part of the U.S. Capitol.

None of this was to say the Pentagon was beautiful. Public reprobation was swift and severe. "About the building's exterior, the less said the better," wrote *Architectural Forum*, which, despite its enthusiasm about the road network and bus tunnel, found the endless stripped classical walls dreadfully unimaginative: "In essence it is the official Washington front, stretched thin to cover 4,600 running feet of façade." *Newsweek* condemned its "simple, penitentiary-like exterior." The *New York Times* described it as a "great, concrete doughnut of a building." "Monstrosity" was a word frequently heard.

Yet the first judgments were perhaps too harsh. David Witmer, chief architect after Edwin Bergstrom's departure, observed that "the design is far from, yet reminiscent of, the classic tradition. Withal, while it is harmonious with the public buildings of the national capital, it offers a [sheer] quality which sets it apart."

Major William Frierson, an Army historian assigned to write a booklet about the building soon after its completion, elaborated on Witmer's words and eloquently captured what set the Pentagon apart: "The world's largest office building was designed in a race against time and was planned for efficiency, not beauty," he wrote.

Yet of all Washington's public buildings reminiscent of the classic style, The Pentagon is least imitative; and of all the structures modern in conception, it is the least self-consciously startling. Its massive, fortress-like outline suggests at once its military function. There is a quiet dignity in the symmetrical facades with square columns recessed in projection which break the long flat expanses and give both order and variety to the pattern. This is reflected on all of the five sides, each displaying . . . nicely proportioned stone facing. The effect is Hellenic in its simplicity and harmony; modern in its lack of curves, its rigid formality, and its vastness.

A little chiseling

The building was completed before winter's end, but the project was not. The 320-acre Pentagon grounds remained an enormous work zone as crews hurried to finish reshaping the land. Through February and March, more than 40 bulldozers and 125 dump trucks rumbled about, moving tons of fill, rocks, and grass seed. A thousand men were at work, some operating heavy equipment, others swinging picks and wielding shovels. The work was being planned and directed by famed Cleveland landscape architect Albert D. Taylor—a follower of the Frederick Law Olmsted school of American landscaping and another one of the big, pricey names Somervell had brought to the Construction Division.

The landscaping was not primarily a beautification project, although Taylor's goal was to integrate the Pentagon grounds with the abutting Arlington National Cemetery and National Park Service land along the Potomac. The ground had to be covered with topsoil and planted with grass, trees, and shrubs to prevent serious erosion and possible damage to the highway network. Already there had been erosion in uncovered areas, and drains were clogging with mud. The landscaping had been vastly pared down from what was originally contemplated. Taylor and Witmer had hoped to plant some six thousand trees, but the number was cut in half. To further save money, Groves ordered that they plant only scrawny trees with diameters less than three inches.

The whirl of activity nonetheless raised the curiosity of *Time* magazine, which began asking why the War Department was spending so much time, money, and effort landscaping the Pentagon. Groves resorted to his old tricks, juggling figures to hide costs. "The General figures we ought to do a little chiseling on *Time* magazine . . . and define landscaping as planting of trees and bushes and shrubs," Groves's aide, Franklin Matthias, told Renshaw February 17.

"And leave out the topsoil?" Renshaw asked.

"Yeah."

"Well that's one way of handling it alright," Renshaw said.

That accounting trick, together with the actual cuts, reduced the amount ostensibly being spent on landscaping from $2.3 million to $385,000. But it did nothing to stop *Time* from running a story denouncing the landscaping as a senseless beautification project. The likely explanation, the magazine theorized, was that Somervell and Roosevelt wanted it, and "now, even with the manpower pinch here, no one had the time nor strength to stop its course."

Groves responded to the criticism by banning the word "landscaping" from any documents related to the Pentagon. He erupted in fury in April when cost estimates from Renshaw's office violated this edict. "How long is it going to take to eliminate the word 'landscaping' from the writings and droolings, and I mean droolings, (good soldiers keep their mouths shut) of your personnel," Groves wrote in a memorandum to Renshaw on April 9. He also ordered Renshaw to return the memo "so that I can destroy it," but a copy survived.

By whatever name, the landscaping continued. Once the grading was finished, planting continued well into the spring, performed "almost entirely by squads of Negro women, who all wear straw hats, cotton blouses and blue dungaree trousers, giving the countryside something of a plantation aspect," *The New York Times* reported.

I prefer not mentioning our fee

Constructing a building that was more than half again bigger than the one they had begun did not translate to a similar bigger profit for McShain and the Virginia contractors. The original contract setting their fee at $524,000 was based on a building of four million gross square feet. McShain argued that the contractors' fee should be raised by at least $200,000.

Groves mercilessly drove down the figure. "Successive negotiations have brought him to the point where I think he is ready to accept an amount in the neighborhood of $110,000, although he appears none too happy about it," Groves reported on March 16. McShain was even less pleased when the War Department's Construction Contract Board reduced the amount to $90,000, making the total fee $614,000. By the terms of the 60-40 split in the contract, McShain would get $368,400 and the Virginia contrac-

tors $245,600. McShain would claim it was one of the lowest fees the War Department ever paid to any firm in proportion to the size of the building. "Contrary to the opinion of many, the profits on the job were not too attractive considering the great responsibility," he said.

Perhaps to soften the blow, the War Department promptly chose McShain to receive the Army-Navy "E" Award for war construction. Major General Thomas Robins, the Construction Division chief, presented the builder with a large "E" burgee at a ceremony in Arlington on April 17. "Fly it proudly, for it is the visible symbol of what your country thinks of your efforts," Robins told McShain. "It is Uncle Sam's version of 'Well done, thou good and faithful servant.' "

McShain did fly it proudly, trumpeting the award in a full-page ad in the *Washington Post*. But it did not quite erase the sting of his fee, which rankled McShain to the end of his days. "I prefer not mentioning our fee, as it will constantly be a source of embarrassment to the Government," he wrote in a 1978 letter. "They considered it was such a great privilege for me to build the Pentagon that the fee should be very low."

Yet the Pentagon project had cemented McShain's reputation. Before long, it was being said in Washington that Pierre L'Enfant may have designed the city, but it was John McShain who built it. That was not much of an exaggeration. So many construction projects in Washington were adorned with the McShain name that a radio commentator would later joke that signs at the city line reading "Welcome to Washington, the Nation's Capital" should be changed to "Welcome to Washington—John McShain, Builder."

A Herculean enterprise

By late spring 1943, it was time to close down the job and disband Renshaw's office. Groves approached the matter with his usual sentimentality: "[Y]ou should be liquidated," he informed Renshaw.

Various odds and ends needed to be wrapped up, but they were increasingly picayune. The Army would create the position of building engineer to replace Renshaw; the building engineer would supervise all further work, which would be treated as additions, alterations, and improvements rather than as part of the cost of the original construction. The handover was set for June 30.

As the project wound down, there was a growing realization that something remarkable had been accomplished. Already the previous fall, some of the leading project architects and engineers had created the Society of the Pentagon, an organization of 129 members celebrating the "foresightedness . . . and boundless energy" of the building's creators—to wit, themselves.

The whole thing smacked of self-celebration, but it was understandable: There had been few public kudos for their work. "In the years to come, the mere mention of the word Pentagon will connote just one thing: the Pentagon Building of the War Department, across the Potomac in Arlington," the society's secretary, landscape architect B. Ashburton Tripp, told the *Star* in May. "A Herculean enterprise, done in the manner of Hercules himself."

Roosevelt and Stimson were given honorary memberships, as well as most of the key Army officers involved, Marshall, Somervell, Groves, and Renshaw among them. Curiously, McShain and Hauck were left off the list, a sign of lingering enmity between the architects and builders.

The society founders did not forget to include a now-absent figure: Edwin Bergstrom, the disgraced former chief architect. Ides van der Gracht, the design team production chief, sent Bergstrom's certificate of membership to California, where the latter was working on War Department projects. "He was being kicked around quite a lot," recalled van der Gracht, who included a letter to Bergstrom saluting the "marvelous job" he had done. Bergstrom sent back a note saying he was "exceedingly" grateful for the kind words. "He apparently didn't get very many of those," van der Gracht said.

Van der Gracht, who had played such a crucial role organizing the drafting force in the Eastern Airlines hangar, had already left the job, and so had many others. The war was only beginning for many of them, from the lowest workers to the top project leaders.

Van der Gracht had been commissioned as a captain in the Army Air Forces in September 1942, after most of the drafting work was completed. "You are due a large part of the credit which we may receive," Renshaw told him upon his departure. Van der Gracht was sent to the Libyan desert, serving as intelligence officer for a squadron of Liberator bombers. When the squadron was wiped out attacking the Ploiesti oil fields in Romania in

1943, van der Gracht had the "curious experience" of being assigned to the Pentagon he had helped design, this time to brief officers on lessons learned from the bombing raids. In September 1944, after being assigned to the Office of Strategic Services, he parachuted into Nazi-occupied Holland to gather intelligence on German forces; when Allied forces swept into Roermond, van der Gracht rode with the troops and personally liberated his mother and sister.

McShain's performance directing men and machinery building the Pentagon had so impressed Somervell that the general tried to enlist the McShain organization into the Army. Soon after the Pentagon was completed, McShain recalled, Somervell called the builder into his office with a proposition: He would create an engineer construction regiment overseas with McShain in command as a brigadier general, and various key men in the McShain organization would be commissioned as officers. "General McShain" had a pleasing ring to the contractor; he accepted on the spot. His wife and daughter were appalled. More details soon emerged. Somervell did not actually have the power to commission McShain as a general; that would be subject to Senate confirmation. But Somervell assured McShain he could begin immediately as a full colonel. McShain began to suspect, not without cause, that Somervell was trying "to get the work of construction done at the minimum price rather than pay me as a general contractor." Heeding his wife's pleas, McShain passed on the offer.

Renshaw, to his disappointment, was not sent overseas because he lacked experience as a combat engineer. He was promoted to colonel and served successively as District Engineer for Washington and Philadelphia, prestigious posts in the Corps of Engineers. The War Department would award Renshaw the Legion of Merit in 1945; the citation noted that "his leadership, technical ability and sound judgement made possible the early occupancy of the Pentagon."

Groves had his eye on a sharp officer in Renshaw's office: Major Bob Furman. Playing tennis a few months after the Pentagon was completed, Groves ran into Furman at the Army Navy Country Club in Arlington, and he asked the twenty-eight-year-old major what he would work on next. "I told him I didn't have anything," Furman recalled. Groves directed that Furman report to his office the following Monday morning: He had some work of a highly classified nature for him.

Furman consulted Renshaw, unsure what to do. Renshaw's answer was simple: "If Groves wants you, you better go." Furman was sworn into the Manhattan Project and given a heavy responsibility: Find out what the Germans were up to in terms of building an atomic bomb. Furman was soon traveling the world on missions as Groves's chief aide for foreign intelligence. He worked in Italy and Germany with agents for the Office of Strategic Services to track the whereabouts of Axis scientists who might be working on an atomic bomb. He dodged sniper fire in Belgium to help recover uranium ore. He helped plan the capture of Werner Heisenberg, Germany's leading physicist, in the Bavarian Alps, and later escorted Heisenberg and other German scientists to safe locations in France, Belgium, and England.

For a while, Major Furman had the most convenient apartment around whenever he returned to Washington. The bedroom and shower in the Pentagon where Furman and the other officers would spend the night while keeping an eye on construction had never been dismantled. It was now in the middle of a large Ordnance Department office bay. "The bedroom was still there, and I had the keys," Furman recalled. "And I was the only one left."

Furman would stay there whenever work brought him to Washington, inevitably getting odd looks when he emerged into the midst of "a clerical beehive" carrying a suitcase. "I'd walk out in the middle of the morning into the Ordnance Department," he said. "They all wondered what was in that room." Building administrators eventually wised up, confiscating Furman's key and later demolishing the bedroom. He had to find new accommodations.

We take 'em back

The end of April 1943 brought the first anniversary of the occupation of the Pentagon, and the occasion was marked by another incident of food poisoning. More than a hundred Army officers and employees were left white-faced and weak-kneed on April 27; three dozen were rushed to hospitals. The culprit this time was found to be the butterscotch cream pie. The assessment of the cafeteria director was not reassuring: "The place seems to be jinxed."

Yet conditions in the Pentagon were a far cry from those that had greeted the plank walkers on April 30, 1942. The building was no longer a construction site; the mud and dust and noise that had accompanied everyday life had largely disappeared, replaced by an existence that was relatively clean and efficient—even comfortable, once the air-conditioning worked.

Indeed, compared to most Washingtonians, Pentagon employees had it very good. By July, when a wicked heat wave struck the area, there was a distinct change of tone in some of the press coverage of the building. "Pentagon's Lucky 30,814 Toil in Air Conditioned Beatitude," read a *Washington Post* headline, and the article continued in the same vein:

> Dear War Department: We take 'em back—all of those barbed remarks about the Pentagon that Washington's civilian populace made between late 1941 and early 1943. Those days, friends, are gone forever; today your happy lot has the rest of the Capital green with envy. . . . Word has got about that life at the Pentagon is closely akin to heaven, in comparison with the nonair-conditioned existence required of employes in less swank office buildings.

Even the Pentagon's six cafeterias—serving up to 55,000 meals a day—were getting swank. The Army would soon coax master chef Otto Gentsch, president of the Société Culinaire Philanthropique in New York and former chief chef at the Hotel Astor, out of retirement to become production manager for the Pentagon cafeteria system. At the Pentagon, Gentsch forsook dishes such as paté de foie gras and breast of guinea hen under glass for more standard fare, but he cooked with no less passion. "Within the labyrinth of the vast Pentagon culinary department he whisks about the experimental kitchens concocting corn fritters with the air of a great master preparing an epicurean delight," the *Post* reported. "And when Gentsch makes corn fritters, they are no less than that."

The layers of dust that had coated the Pentagon had been replaced by a bit of luster, applied by a force of seven hundred janitors and charwomen who mopped the miles of corridors, cleaned the two hundred restrooms, and tidied up around the 21,000 desks and 140,000 chairs. Among those who now found themselves cleaning the Pentagon were former residents of Queen City, the neighborhood destroyed to make way for the building's road network. Gertrude Jeffress, who had lost the home where she lived with her mother and sister and was now living in a trailer, was too glad to have a job—and too tired from the work—to reflect much on the irony. She worked from "the sub-basement, mezzanine all the way up to the fifth floor," scrubbing, waxing, and buffing endless corridors, cleaning eight bathrooms a night, and emptying countless waste cans.

Mockery of the labyrinth design was now leavened by a general recognition of the efficiency of the rings and corridors that run like spokes through the building. Despite the Pentagon's size, it took no more than seven minutes to walk between any two points in the building—if one did not get lost on the way.

The road network around the building was finished and traffic flowed reasonably well. Construction was also under way for a seventeen-mile "superhighway" running through northern Virginia and leading directly to the Pentagon. The road—the Shirley Memorial Highway—was the first limited-access highway to be built in Virginia and the beginning of what would become the commonwealth's interstate system.

Even the once-ugly courtyard was looking good, with grass growing on former mud patches and trees blooming. In the center of the courtyard, the Army erected a large tent purchased from a Coney Island resort. A lunch bar served sandwiches, and tables shaded by gaily colored beach umbrellas were scattered about. Secretaries spent their lunch breaks sunning their legs on the grass. Military bands and singing groups put on occasional concerts. The *Star* likened the scene to a Riviera resort.

Movie stars came calling, promoting war bonds or other patriotic endeavors. Actor Clark Gable, then a captain in the Army Air Forces, nearly brought the Pentagon to a standstill. "His appearance upset the work of hundreds of War Department women workers who swarmed out of their offices, ignored the shouts of federal policemen to 'keep moving,' and sighed as the former actor hurried through the halls," *The New York Times* reported. Famous faces—Bob Hope, Cary Grant, and Charles Lindbergh among them—were spotted coming through the River entrance. Eleanor Roosevelt had a special pass allowing her to enter without challenge, but Vienna-born Supreme Court Justice Felix Frankfurter, late for an appointment with Stimson, was given the treatment by a suspicious receptionist. "That man was born in Austria," the receptionist remarked to the next visitor. "You can't be too careful these days."

On the concourse, a large Walgreen's drugstore opened in May, followed a few months later by a Brentano's bookstore. Most astonishing of all, from the standpoint of the plank walkers, was the Pentagon Shopping Service, which opened in June, promising to purchase whatever employees needed in their lives, from lingerie to lawnmowers. War Department personnel officers, worried about absenteeism among Pentagon employees, teamed up with merchants to provide the shopping service, billed as the first of its kind in the country. A curtained window display, changed weekly, showed off the latest wares from Washington's shops. A staff of five trained shoppers—all attractive, smartly dressed women, it seemed—were at the ready. Employees would describe what they needed or leaf through stacks of fashion magazines and newspaper ads kept at the counter; the women would telephone shops around town to find the item and have it delivered to the Pentagon. The item could be picked up the following day, with no service charge.

Pentagon employees flocked to the center, gathering in groups to admire the dresses and hats on the display-window mannequins, and they placed hundreds of orders each day. Baby equipment topped the list, with underwear a close second. Almost anything could be requested, except gasoline, groceries, and other rationed items. The best customer was an Army major who visited every day to order classical music records. At least ten orders for black chiffon nightgowns were placed each month, always by men. One man asked the shoppers to find him an "economical" engagement ring; another asked for a marriage license.

Tall and erect, General Henri Honoré Giraud, the French hero who had escaped Nazi captivity and replaced Admiral Darlan as high commissioner of French forces in North and West Africa, was taken on a tour of the Pentagon during his visit to Washington in July. An officer escorting him boasted that an office girl could buy both a wedding ring and a baby carriage within the Pentagon walls. "Which do they buy first?" the Frenchman asked.

Somervell's Folly

In the spring of 1943, Albert Engel began poking around the Pentagon again. The crusading Michigan congressman had taken a hiatus after his initial attack on Somervell and the War Department in October 1942. But his interest was piqued by the news accounts of the Pentagon landscaping. When Engel demanded more information about expenses in April, Groves sounded the alarm, ordering Renshaw to compile data "for explanation and defense against any new charges which might be made by Congressman Engel."

Equally alarming, Somervell's old foe, Senator Harry Truman, began investigating the Pentagon in June. The chief counsel of Truman's special committee investigating national defense peppered the War Department with requests for information about construction costs and the disposition of surplus material from the job, but Truman's inquiry petered out after several months. "I was watching you," a smiling Truman later told McShain, adding his investigators found no grounds for criticism of the Pentagon job. Engel, however, kept up his investigation, and by early 1944 it was coming to a head.

On Capitol Hill, representatives Clifton Woodrum of Virginia and Lane Powers of New Jersey, Somervell's loyal allies, passed on intelligence about a pending attack by Engel. Groves recalled Renshaw to Washington from Philadelphia, where he was then stationed. At 3 P.M. on the afternoon of February 29, 1944, Engel took the floor of the House, condemning the Pentagon project during a thirty-minute speech in language even more strident than he had used in 1942. Government funds had been "juggled in a wholesale flouting of the will of Congress," Engel said. "Anyone must be a wizard to follow the ouija board methods that the War Department must have followed."

Engel mocked the accounting machinations that kept the building cost at $49 million—a "charmed figure," as the congressman put it. Yet Engel's proclaimed cost of $86 million in the ten-thousand-word report he submitted to the House was as dubious as the War Department's claims. In addition to the $6 million the War Department spent on access roads and parking on the Pentagon grounds, Engel included $16.9 million spent on highway construction for miles around the building by the Public Roads Administration.

Somervell telephoned Renshaw from the Pentagon after the speech, asking about the reaction "our friend" Engel had received. "Did he get any attention or any hand or anything?" Somervell asked.

"He got a little applause at the end," Renshaw reported.

"He did?" Somervell was disappointed. "I suppose the newspapers will be over here and they'll goad the hell out of us and we will have to say something," he sighed. Renshaw tactfully suggested that they not incite Engel, and Somervell held his fire.

Engel nonetheless kept up his assault. A week later he gave a second speech with a new litany of outrages. The Pentagon was costing $3.8 million a year to maintain and operate. In 1943 alone, Engel reported, the War Department had spent $87,360 to replace 249,600 burned-out lightbulbs, $75,000 to mow the lawn, and $337,260 to heat and cool the building. The War Department did not challenge the numbers but complained in an internal report that the criticism was unfair. "The figures for operating costs are impressive only because the size of the building is impressive—there is none like it anywhere in the world," the report said.

Once again, Engel's attacks generated headlines. Wire service stories reporting his charges of "outrageous waste" were carried in newspapers around the country. "The rotund (225 pounds) and ripsnorting Al Engel landed on the Pentagon Building like a financial blockbuster," *Newsweek* reported.

Even the German press took note. A Berlin newspaper labeled the Pentagon "*Das Somervell-Narrenhaus*"—the Somervell Madhouse—and identified the general as the "ruler" of the building. "The corridors are said to be so long that the messengers had to use bicycles," the *Berliner Börsenzeitung* reported. "It has already cost the American taxpayers the tiny sum of 80 million dollars, and there is still no end in sight," the paper happily added. "Appearances seem to indicate that another Army scandal may be imminent."

Other congressmen took up the cry against the Pentagon. "Fabulous spending, waste and skullduggery," charged Representative Dewey Short, Republican of Missouri. "A shameful waste of the taxpayers' money," said Harold Knutson, Republican of Minnesota.

Representative John D. Dingell of Michigan, a Democratic member of the Ways and Means Committee, harshly criticized Somervell. "I am convinced from the record that Somervell, among other top officers, has spent the public funds with extreme recklessness," he told the United Press. "Someone should be penalized. The Pentagon should be investigated."

The Pentagon's reputation as outrageously expensive had been confirmed. There was even a new nickname for the building, coined by Dingell, and it caught on: "Somervell's Folly."

Architect's drawing showing proposed Pentagon tower, August 1945.

CHAPTER 16

WHAT TO DO WITH THE PENTAGON

I no longer consider the Pentagon a safe shelter

As the clock counted down to Trinity, Groves lowered his considerable bulk down onto the New Mexico desert, his feet pointing toward ground zero and his eyes covered by a welder's mask. The thoughts of some of the men waiting to witness the first test of a nuclear weapon in the early morning of July 16, 1945, turned to God. Groves could think of only one thing: What if the bomb failed to explode?

In the nearly three years since Somervell had selected him to head the Manhattan Project, Groves had spent $2 billion overseeing the work of almost 200,000 people at eighty-seven secret plants and laboratories. "If our gadget proves to be a dud, I and all of the principal Army officers of the project . . . will spend the rest of our lives so far back in a Fort Leavenworth dungeon that they'll have to pipe sunlight in to us," Groves sardonically predicted to another Manhattan Project officer nine months earlier.

Somervell was no more sanguine, telling Groves he was thinking of buying a house about a block from the Capitol. "The one next door is for sale and you had better buy it," Somervell added with a straight face. "It will be convenient because you and I are going to live out our lives before Congressional committees."

No one could be sure what would happen when the plutonium bomb set at the top of a hundred-foot-high steel tower was detonated. During the tense hours the evening before the test—code-named Trinity—in the flat, scrub desert of the Alamogordo Bombing Range in New Mexico, Groves's mood was darkened by wind and rain heralding an approaching storm. He was anxious not to postpone the test. The Big Three—Churchill, Stalin, and now, with FDR's death in April, Harry Truman—were then gathering outside Berlin in preparation for the Potsdam Conference, where plans were to be laid for the defeat of Japan. The outcome of Trinity would be of utmost importance, particularly for the wording of an ultimatum to be delivered to Japan.

The weather worsened after midnight, with fierce thunderstorms, drenching rain, and wind gusts of thirty miles per hour. At the Trinity control center, Groves angrily confronted the project's weather forecaster, Jack Hubbard, and complained about the weather. The storms would disappear by dawn, Hubbard insisted. "You better be right on this or I will hang you," Groves said. It seemed he might.

Groves pushed back the time for the test from 4 A.M. to 5:30 A.M. He and project director Robert Oppenheimer spent the remaining time trying to calm each other's nerves. "During most of these hours the two of us journeyed from the control house out into the darkness to look at the stars and to assure each other that the one or two visible stars were becoming brighter," Groves later wrote.

Accompanied by Vannevar Bush and James Conant, the top two civilians overseeing atomic development, Groves returned to the base camp ten miles from ground zero to observe the test. When two minutes remained, the three men took their protective positions on the ground, lying down next to one another on a tarpaulin. Except for the countdown broadcast over a loudspeaker, the silence was total. "As I lay there, in the final seconds, I thought only of what I would do if, when the countdown got to zero, nothing happened," Groves wrote.

Groves, as he said, "was spared this embarrassment." His first impression was of a tremendous flash, "this burst of light of a brilliance beyond any comparison." Groves and the others rolled over. Through the smoked glass of their welder's masks, they could see a great ball of fire rising ten thousand feet in the sky, then mushrooming. Sitting on the ground, the three men silently clasped hands.

Groves felt enormous relief. "I personally thought of Blondin crossing Niagara Falls on his tight rope, only to me this tight rope had lasted for almost three years," he wrote. Still, he kept his exuberance in check. Brigadier General Thomas Farrell, the veteran engineer who had helped troubleshoot the early days of the Pentagon construction and later joined the Manhattan Project as deputy director, came over to congratulate Groves. "The war is over," Farrell told him.

"Yes," Groves replied, "after we drop two bombs on Japan."

Groves boarded a plane that afternoon to fly back to Washington, arriving at noon the next day and reporting to the Pentagon. With Stimson in Potsdam, Groves briefed George L. Harrison, the secretary's representative for atomic affairs. Cables had been sent to Stimson informing him of the successful test, but the curt and coded language—describing the bomb as a "husky" newborn baby—provided few details. Groves wrote a thirteen-page top-secret report to be taken by courier to the secretary of war in Potsdam.

In graphic and, for Groves, ebullient language, he tried to convey to Stimson the full magnitude of what he had witnessed. By conservative estimate, Groves reported, the bomb was as powerful as fifteen to twenty thousand tons of TNT. Light from the explosion had been seen as far away as Albuquerque, 180 miles to the north. The explosion created a 1,200-foot-wide crater from which all vegetation had disappeared. A forty-ton steel tower a half-mile from the test site had been torn from its concrete foundation, twisted, ripped apart, and left flat on the ground.

The results of Trinity prompted Groves to include this observation: "I no longer consider the Pentagon a safe shelter from such a bomb."

I just plum forgot

On the morning of August 6, 1945, Groves was at the Pentagon before seven, waiting for General Marshall to arrive. The previous evening, just before midnight Washington time, Groves had received word from the Pacific that the mission to drop an atomic bomb on the Japanese city of Hiroshima had been "successful in all respects." Groves had stayed in his office in the New War Department Building in Foggy Bottom all night, preparing a report for Marshall and sleeping on a cot before hurrying to the Pentagon in the morning.

When Marshall arrived, Groves handed him the two-page report. Reconnaissance aircraft had not yet returned with photographs, but the preliminary reports from observers on the mission indicated the bomb had set off a massive explosion. General Hap Arnold, commander of the Army Air Forces, quickly joined the discussion. On a secure telephone, Marshall updated Stimson at his Long Island estate. The secretary of war, exhausted from the Potsdam trip, spoke to Groves and sent "very warm congratulations." It was clear to all of them "that our hope of ending the war through the development of atomic energy was close to realization," Groves later wrote.

Yet after the conversation, Marshall was somber. He cautioned against too much exultation, saying the bombing undoubtedly involved a large number of Japanese casualties.

Groves felt no such compunction. "I replied that I was not thinking so much about those casualties as I was about the men who had made the Bataan death march," Groves later wrote.

Out in the hallway, Arnold slapped Groves on the back. "I am glad you said that—it's just the way I feel."

Marshall wanted Groves to stay close at hand and installed him in Stimson's vacant office. The main issue now was announcing to the world that an atomic bomb had been dropped on Japan. A statement had been prepared in advance and approved by Truman. Groves was eager to put out the announcement as quickly as possible, part of a strategy to shock Japan into surrender. Others urged caution, suggesting that the announcement be delayed or the language softened until more details were known of the damage to Hiroshima. Bob Lovett, assistant secretary of war for air, reminded Groves that the Army Air Forces several times had claimed to have destroyed Berlin in bombing raids, only to be proven wrong. "It becomes rather embarrassing after about the third time," Lovett said.

Groves agreed and urgently tried to get more information from Major General Curtis E. LeMay, commander of the 21st Bomber Command, who had overseen the mission from a B-29 bomber base on the Pacific island of

Tinian. Groves finally reached LeMay at 10 A.M. via teletype. LeMay said they still had no damage estimates, but he reported "the target completely covered with smoke and a column of dense white smoke rising to about 30,000 feet."

Groves felt this was strong enough evidence to declare to the world that an atomic bomb had been successfully dropped over Japan. At 11 A.M., the announcement was released by the White House. It declared that a new weapon—"a harnessing of the basic power of the universe"—had been dropped on Hiroshima, and that if the Japanese did not surrender, "they may expect a rain of ruin from the air, the like of which has never been seen on this earth."

Groves soon ran into Somervell, who had "this most pained look on his face," Groves recalled. Somervell had been given no advance word of the attack on Hiroshima. "Why didn't you tell me?" Somervell asked.

"I just plum forgot," Groves replied. He later described it as "the perfect answer for Somervell because it was absolutely honest." It also bespoke a change in their normal roles: Groves was the man of the hour.

How did you know Truman was going to be president?

Somervell waited in his office all day August 14, 1945, for official word of the Japanese surrender. He had arrived early, as usual. Somervell rose religiously at 5:45 A.M., no matter how late he had worked the previous night, and was out the door of Quarters Two at Fort Myer soon after seven. Usually he walked briskly through neighboring Arlington National Cemetery, an aide trotting at his heels as he occasionally veered off to hunt down historic graves. His driver, a square-jawed master sergeant, would be waiting at the cemetery gate to bring the general the rest of the way to the Pentagon.

His hours on the job were as long as ever, though he was again a married man. In 1943, a little over a year after Anna Somervell's death, the general wed an old acquaintance, Louise Hampton Wartmann. She was from Arkansas and as a girl attended Belcourt Seminary, the finishing school Somervell's mother had operated in Washington all those years ago.

Though only fifty-three, Somervell had aged visibly during the course of the war. His silver hair was now whiter, and the once-smooth skin on his face and neck was wrinkled. He was troubled by a hernia he had nursed through the war and never taken the time to mend. Just a few months earlier, in March, he had received his fourth star, despite concerns from Marshall's staff that his promotion would "undoubtedly create a ruckus on the Hill."

At 7 P.M., the announcement that Somervell had expected came. President Truman, speaking to reporters in the Oval Office, said he had received a message from the Japanese government agreeing to "unconditional surrender." The news flashed around the world. Somervell immediately signed a paper on his desk ordering his command—now known as the Army Service Forces, or ASF—to put its demobilization plans into action.

The vast supply empire he created and commanded had backed the landings in North Africa, Sicily, and mainland Italy, and made possible the greatest amphibious invasion in the history of the world, the D-Day landings in Normandy. In 109 days, they landed a million men and 100,000 vehicles onto the beaches of France. His supply lines—including the famed Red Ball Express—kept the U.S. Army rolling all the way to the Elbe River. "The only question we were ever asked was, 'What do you want, and when do you want it?'" Eisenhower later said. In Asia, the ASF was a lifeline for American troops in New Guinea, New Britain, the Aleutians, China, India, Australia, and many way stations in between. After Germany's surrender, the command had shipped 1.2 million men and five million tons of supplies from Europe to the Pacific, where they were still gathering for an invasion of Japan, which was no longer necessary.

Somervell signed a second paper that day, addressed to Marshall. "I feel I have discharged my obligations to the country and Army," Somervell had written. Marshall himself planned to retire shortly, and Somervell requested permission to resign from the Army the same day as the chief of staff. He handed the memo to Marshall in person on August 18.

Miracle man or not, Somervell's days in the Army were numbered. He had known it for months, since Roosevelt died of a cerebral hemorrhage while in Warm Springs, Georgia, on April 12, 1945. The next day, Somervell had called Groves into his office. Somervell "looked very sorrowful," Groves recalled, but it was not simply because he was mourning FDR.

"Dick, how did you know that Truman was going to be president?" Somervell asked Groves.

The man Somervell told to "go piss up a rope" in 1941 was now his commander in chief. Somervell and Truman had continued battling through much of the war, and, if anything, their relations had grown worse.

Truman's investigations of Somervell's work—from his criticism of the camp-construction program in 1941 through his inquiry in 1943 and 1944 into Canol, a spectacularly ill-advised and expensive oil project in the Arctic wilderness—helped bring the senator to national prominence, changing his reputation from that of a run-of-the-mill Pendergast-machine politician to a respected and objective voice on national defense. His name was placed in contention to be Roosevelt's running mate in 1944. In the Somervell family, it was an article of faith that Truman made his name with cheap second-guessing of decisions made by the general in the heat of war.

Despite all the criticism—over the Pentagon, over his management style, over Canol—rumors of Somervell replacing Marshall as chief of staff had persisted through much of the war. Somervell would have dearly loved to become chief of staff when Marshall stepped down. With the war ending, no other job in the Army offered remotely the same challenges as his current post. But any hope of becoming chief of staff was already slim after Canol, and died altogether with Roosevelt.

Two weeks after Roosevelt's death, newspaper columnist Drew Pearson wrote that Somervell was among the public figures who had lost the most standing when Truman became president; others included Winston Churchill and Harry Hopkins. "Somervell will never become Chief of Staff, or rise any higher in the Army," Pearson wrote.

It was obvious by then that when Marshall retired, he would be replaced as Army chief of staff by Eisenhower. Ike was feted as a conquering hero when he returned to Washington on June 18, 1945, a little over a month after Germany's surrender. A crowd of close to a million—bigger than those for presidential inaugurations—turned out to greet Eisenhower on a hot and humid morning. It was described in the newspapers as "the greatest welcome in Washington's history," and it was at least on a par with the ones that greeted Grant and Sherman in 1865 and Pershing in 1919. Arriving at National Airport aboard the *Sacred Cow*, the presidential airplane, Eisenhower rode directly to the Pentagon standing in a three-quarter-ton command car, trailed by an entourage of jeeps. They took the interior road into the Pentagon's courtyard, which was packed with thousands of cheering Army officers and war workers. The train of vehicles took a victory lap around the courtyard—Ike charming all with flashes of his huge grin—before reaching the pavilion stage, where Stimson stood, waiting to greet him. Somervell was part of the welcoming committee.

It was no great surprise to him. "So strategist and tactician get into today's headline and tomorrow's history books," Somervell dryly remarked in 1944, "and the logistician gets into a congressional investigation."

We can only leave with the greatest feeling of pride

On September 20, 1945, the War Department announced that Marshall and Somervell would retire shortly and simultaneously. "With their departure, the Army's Washington wartime high command will be about wiped out," *The Washington Post* noted.

Henry Stimson was leaving too. Two days after Hiroshima, he felt sharp pains in his chest; doctors offered assurances, but soon after Japan's surrender Stimson informed Truman that he intended to resign. His departure was set for September 21, and though it was an affirmation that the war was over, it was a bittersweet moment at the Pentagon. Stimson had never spent much time roaming the corridors, shaking hands or chatting with war workers, but nonetheless he had left a firm imprint on the building, one of integrity and selfless service. "He gave it tone which all who worked there could sense," John McCloy later said.

On his final morning at the Pentagon, Stimson met for an hour with George Marshall in his office. "The termination of our more than five years of service together was a very deep emotional experience for me and I think also for him," Stimson wrote in his diary. When he left the Pentagon the last time that afternoon and arrived at National Airport for his flight home, he found every general officer in Washington lined in two rows, waiting to bid him farewell. A nineteen-gun salute was fired. The day, Stimson later wrote, "was full of tension and emotion and, though I did not feel it, I was on the eve of an emotional and coronary breakdown." Stimson, now in his fourth decade of high office and serving his fourth president, had very nearly given the last full measure of himself to his country. A month after returning to Highhold, Stimson suffered a serious heart attack and was confined to bed for months.

The Pentagon bade farewell to Marshall at noon on November 27, 1945, and his departure was even more momentous. Some twenty thousand people packed the inner courtyard and lined hundreds of windows. Truman presented the general with the Oak Leaf Cluster, equivalent to a second Distinguished Service Medal. It was the only American military decoration he received for the war—Marshall had refused all previous ones, saying it would be improper while his soldiers were dying overseas. "To him, as much to any individual, the United States owes its future," Truman told the Pentagon audience. "He takes his place at the head of the great commanders of history." The Army band played "Auld Lang Syne" as Marshall—no emotion betrayed on his stern face or in his piercing blue eyes—walked off the platform.

The chief of staff was the most trusted American military man since George Washington, *Time* magazine wrote. Command of the invasion of Europe—and the glory that fell on Eisenhower's shoulders—could have been his for the asking, but Marshall was of too superb and self-sacrificing character to put his wishes above the country's needs. "I didn't feel I could sleep at ease if you were out of Washington," Roosevelt told Marshall. Churchill called him "the true organizer of victory." To Stimson, Marshall was simply "the finest soldier I have ever known."

Somervell's departure was delayed until December while he recovered from surgery on his hernia. Back on duty, he testified before Congress one last time to support a War Department proposal for unification of the armed services.

Marshall was disappointed by Somervell's decision to retire, believing that, at fifty-three, Somervell could still do much for the Army. Demobilization was itself going to be an enormous job. Yet Marshall did not try to change Somervell's mind, or, if he did, he did not succeed. His faith in the man who had put a roof over his Army and then supplied it around the globe was undiminished by Canol or anything else. Somervell "shook the cobwebs out of their pants," Marshall later said. "What he did was a miracle," he added. "I depended on him very, very heavily."

From Highhold, still recuperating from his heart attack, Stimson wrote

Somervell a personal letter in November. "I send to you not only my warmest thanks but my congratulations on your magnificent accomplishments during the war," Stimson wrote. "You know without my trying to put it now in words how much I depended on you in every big problem which has come up."

Patterson, who had succeeded Stimson as secretary of war, presented Somervell with a second Oak Leaf Cluster, following the Distinguished Service Medal he had been awarded in World War I and the first Oak Leaf Cluster he had received in 1942 for his performance directing Army construction. "In organizing and directing the world-wide supply lines on which our troops depended for their offensive power, General Somervell performed a service without parallel in military history," Patterson said.

There were rumors that he would seek political office, perhaps even run for president, but Somervell quashed them. "I have ambitions, but none is political," he told reporters. Private industry beckoned, but that could wait.

"I'm going to rest," Somervell told a friend. "For six weeks, I'm going to just sit on the porch. After that, I'm going to start rocking—slowly."

After they were all gone, Katherine King, Somervell's longtime secretary, still at the Pentagon, wrote him a letter. "[N]ow that the play is over and all of the actors have left the stage and the curtain is about to fall on the most gigantic performance in the history of the world, we can only leave with the greatest feeling of pride. . . ."

Hell in a handbasket

It was well into October before Major Bob Furman returned from overseas. After Germany's surrender, Furman, now thirty, had been sent by Groves to escort uranium components of "Little Boy"—the first atomic bomb to be dropped on Japan—from Los Alamos to the B-29 base at Tinian, a speck of land in the northern Marianas. Furman had taken grim satisfaction in watching the *Enola Gay* take off from Tinian and disappear from view, destination Hiroshima. "I was pretty much fed up with the war," he said. After the bombings of Hiroshima and Nagasaki, he had been sent to Japan to tour universities and corporations with a Manhattan Project scientist, trying to discover what progress the Japanese had made toward building an atomic bomb. Back in Washington, he found no one cared where he had been or what he had been doing. "Everybody had quit and gone home," he said.

Furman was eager to do the same—he wanted to start his own construction business—and he put in his papers to get out of the Army. "The war was just an interruption for most of us," Furman recalled nearly sixty years later. "We all went to war. We all went back to our dreams and ambitions. We lived through the war to get life going again."

The Pentagon was put on what was called a "partial peacetime basis" in September. The number of guards was cut in half, and visitors no longer needed escorts. "Instructions will be given visitors on how to find offices with the hope they do not get lost," the *Star* reported. Soon even the requirement for building passes was dropped.

Before long, Lieutenant General Thomas T. Handy, Eisenhower's deputy chief of staff, was complaining of the "slovenly appearance" of military personnel in the building. "During the war days, stenographers clicked along the corridors bearing trays of coffee and sandwiches for officers who had neither the time nor the inclination to walk the distance of several city blocks," the *Star* reported. "Now it is rather a common sight to see a colonel in shirtsleeves marching down the corridor bearing his own tray, and even an occasional coatless general has been seen outside his office." Handy ordered inspectors to patrol Pentagon corridors, beverage bars, and cafeterias to look for dress-code violators.

The population of the building was about 25,000, considerably less than its wartime peaks. The Pentagon had never been able to accommodate forty thousand people, as planned, a projection based on allowing about eighty square feet per worker. The big offices given to senior War Department officials and the many general officers in the Pentagon far exceeded that average; even many junior officers grabbed extra space. Areas meant for workers were used as storage or meeting rooms; in some offices, partitions divided the big bays into smaller fiefdoms, further decreasing the amount of usable space. Still, the number of workers in the building had been generally well over 30,000 and may at times have reached 35,000, including building maintenance workers, guards, and janitors.

Navigating the Pentagon remained a puzzle; a favored nickname now was "the concrete cobweb." Even Eisenhower was disoriented the first time he tried to return to his office by himself from the general officers' mess. "So, hands in pockets and trying to look as if I were out for a carefree stroll around the building, I walked," Eisenhower later wrote. "I walked and walked, encountering neither landmarks nor people who looked familiar. One had to give the building his grudging admiration; it had apparently been designed to confuse any enemy who might infiltrate it."

Eisenhower finally approached a group of female stenographers and quietly asked one, "Can you tell me where the office of the Chief of Staff is?"

"You just passed it about a hundred feet back, General Eisenhower," she replied.

As Eisenhower noted with chagrin, "By grapevine, the Army's astoundingly efficient bush telegraph, the word got around the Pentagon quickly."

What to do with the Pentagon

The question now was what to do with the Pentagon. The belief was still common in many quarters that, once the war ended, the War Department would have no possible need for a building so large. There had been no shortage of suggestions, most of them sardonic, of what to do with the place. The Pentagon could shelter a second bonus army; the government could rent out the space to all the generals who wanted to write their wartime memoirs; six-day bicycle races could be staged in the building's outer ring. *Life* magazine reported, tongue in cheek, that the Pentagon might host peace talks after the war because it was "the only building in the world large enough to hold all the factions that will have a say-so on the treaty."

Other suggestions were more serious. A Maryland congressman proposed that the Pentagon be converted into the world's largest hospital—with a projected capacity of fifteen thousand beds—serving both disabled veterans and the general population. The ramps connecting the different floors made the building well-suited to be a hospital, proponents argued. Truman considered a proposal to move the Veterans Administration into the Pentagon. Others envisioned the Pentagon as an enormous university.

A congressman from Massachusetts introduced a bill to convert the Pentagon into a national college for war veterans, arguing that the building was a white elephant and that the cost to the government "will assume fantastic proportions unless we find some good use for it."

As far as the Army was concerned, it was keeping the Pentagon. Postwar plans were being made on this assumption. Whatever the price had been—the $63.6 million the War Department insisted was a fair figure for the whole project, including roads; the $86 million Albert Engel claimed was the true cost; or the $75.2 million that the War Department actually spent on construction and is probably the best estimate—the value of the building was obvious, at least to the Army.

"It is probable that when the history of the present war is written and the full value of the Pentagon in the prosecution of the war is disclosed, those who had even the smallest responsibility for its construction will be prouder than ever of their part in this work," the Office of the Chief of Engineers wrote in an internal forty-one-page rebuttal to Engel, refuting the congressman's accusations line by line.

However, notes compiled in preparing the report admitted that the Army had not been above board in revealing the Pentagon's cost. The notes, written by an unknown War Department official, listed a series of "Problems Related to Pentagon Project," among them:

> Failure to tell Congress true extent of exceeding original appropriation in summer of 1942.

> Original plan of building was conceived too hurriedly (July 17–22, 1941); hence original estimate of $35 million was too low even for the first site. . . .

> The juggling of figures around to show a desired cost figure instead of listing true cost of each main item separately and giving true total . . .

No such admission was made publicly, of course. The War Department produced several confidential reports in the later years of the war justifying the Pentagon—including one ordered by Somervell when Senator Truman had been sniffing around the project. Together the reports made a strong case for the building's effectiveness, and they argued the cost overruns were unavoidable due to changes to the site and size of the building. Ironically, Somervell and Groves were so defensive about the Pentagon that these reports were never released to the public, out of fear that they would merely stir up more controversy.

"Imagine what the War Department's situation would have been—today in the midst of grueling war—if the Pentagon had not been built," read a draft of one of the reports presented by Renshaw to Somervell in January 1944. "It is the nerve center of the military effort. . . . The Army does not have to imagine the handicaps resulting from being scattered in many different buildings in different locations. It remembers the days before the Pentagon was built. The speed and efficiency it has helped to produce has saved and will save the lives of many of our soldiers."

It was a claim impossible to prove, yet entirely justifiable. The top echelons of the War Department's command, control, and communications were concentrated at the Pentagon in a manner that previously had been impossible. It is hard to imagine that the days, hours, and even minutes shaved off decisions—from putting new weapons into the hands of soldiers to the formulation of broad strategy—did not make a difference and did not save American lives.

Still, the Pentagon had failed miserably in one goal: putting the Army headquarters under one roof. While the high command and the administrative and staff activities requiring the most interaction and centralization were housed in the Pentagon, the War Department had grown even beyond the scope of Somervell's ample imagination. The Pentagon was able to provide only about half the seven million square feet of office space the War Department needed in Washington in 1945. At war's end, the Army was scattered in more than thirty buildings around town.

The eighth wonder of the world

Little more than two weeks after Japan's surrender, a new suggestion for what to do with the Pentagon was unveiled by the building's commandant, Colonel Henry W. Isbell. On August 31, 1945, *War Times,* the Pentagon's weekly newspaper, published the commandant's proposal to make the building "the eighth wonder of the world."

An enormous five-sided, twenty-four-story office tower would be built in the Pentagon courtyard. It would add as much as two million square feet of space, room for another ten to twelve thousand workers. The tower would "solve the government's space problems for the next 50 years," boasted Isbell, who included a familiar pitch: With the tower, the Pentagon could house the War Department "under one roof."

Washington newspapers picked up the story, publishing preliminary sketches prepared by a War Department architect that showed the massive tower rising improbably to the sky from the Pentagon's courtyard. A dome would sit atop the building, holding an eternal light that would burn as a memorial to Americans killed in the war. "What Washington's skyline needs is something that sticks up," Isbell told reporters. "Why, the Washington Monument is nothing but a needle and a towering skyline is practically an American symbol."

The town was aghast. For one thing, the proposal carried the implicit suggestion that the War Department would remain so large after the war that the Pentagon needed to be expanded rather than shut down. Then there was the tower itself. "The Pentagon as it stands is pretty bad and a tower wouldn't make it any better," Louis Justement, a prominent Washington architect, told the *Star*. Frederic Delano had retired three years earlier, but his old board, the National Capital Park and Planning Commission, went on record as being horrified by the idea. After a few weeks of public ridicule, the tower idea faded away. The proposals to convert the Pentagon into a hospital or university fared no better.

It was George Marshall who had the best sense of what direction the Pentagon might take after the war. Marshall had never given up his belief that the Army and Navy should be together under one roof. In May 1944, two weeks before D-Day, he and Admiral Ernest King, commander in chief of the U.S. Fleet, who shared Marshall's conviction of the need to bring the services together, decided to give it another go.

"Following up on our conversation of Tuesday last—and apropos of our endeavors which came to naught to get together in the Pentagon Building in the autumn of 1942, I wish to confirm that I am agreeable to make another try at it," King wrote Marshall on May 26, 1944. "I still think—as I did then—that it is worth while to consider whether one service cannot, in some lines, do everything that the other service requires."

Marshall's staff, still bitter about the 1942 episode, was not as magnanimous as their chief. Some thought they were being set up. "I believe the Navy is bluffing and has no intention of moving," Major General Otto L. Nelson told Marshall's deputy, Lieutenant General Joseph McNarney. Even Stimson, so enthusiastic a proponent at the time, bowed out, declining comment when Marshall showed him King's letter. The 1944 effort died because of staff inertia.

Now, with the war over, the time seemed ripe to try yet again. In November 1945, during his last days at the Pentagon, Marshall once more pushed the idea. "I think it would be a tragic mistake if we do not make every positive effort to put the Army [and] Navy under one roof," he wrote. Patterson, now secretary of war, picked up the effort and took it a step further, inviting both the Navy and the State Department to move into the Pentagon.

Secretary of the Navy James Forrestal, who had taken office after Frank Knox died in April 1944, was cool to the idea, telling Patterson it made little sense for the Navy to move people into the Pentagon at a time both services were cutting jobs. The State Department likewise declined the offer. For now, the Pentagon remained the exclusive province of the Army.

If we get a decent peace

Franklin D. Roosevelt had also left behind his wishes for the Pentagon. One month before he traveled to Yalta—where, ill and exhausted, he met with Churchill and Stalin for a final conference on the fate of Europe—and three months before his death at Warm Springs, the president reiterated his vision for the building. "It has been my thought that after the war is ended all the personnel records of the Armed Forces should be placed in the Pentagon Building," Roosevelt instructed Harold Smith, his budget director, in a memorandum written on January 8, 1945.

Roosevelt had never given up his pet scheme to convert the Pentagon into an archives after the war. The War Department, as he had insisted in the past, would then move into the New War Department Building in Foggy Bottom, which would be expanded. The Navy Department would move into a similar building to be constructed next door. "The plans are ready to go ahead with," the president told Smith.

"The War Department will doubtless object to giving up the Pentagon Building, but it is much too large for them," Roosevelt added, "if we get a decent peace."

PART II

THE REMAKING OF
THE PENTAGON

*An officer shows Brazilian visitors a model of the Pentagon
in the concourse during a post-war tour of the building in 1946.*

CHAPTER
17

NO DECENT PEACE

I want to take the oath

At 9:45 A.M. on the morning of September 17, 1947, James V. Forrestal decided he could wait no longer. "Get the Chief Justice down here at noon," the secretary of Navy directed his staff. "I want to take the oath." Aides rushed to round up senior military commanders, senators, and the press. An assistant scrambled to find a Bible. Forrestal, a lapsed Catholic, did not have one in his office at the Navy Building on Constitution Avenue.

President Harry Truman had hoped to officiate at the historic occasion, and an elaborate White House ceremony marking the swearing-in of the nation's first secretary of defense was set for the following week, upon the president's return from an inter-American conference in Brazil. But as the battleship USS *Missouri* steamed back from Rio de Janerio on September 15, carrying the president, Truman received a cable from his trusted aide, Clark Clifford. Sent at the behest of Forrestal, it warned of a burgeoning international crisis at a time of deep tension between the United States and the Soviet Union. The communist government of Yugoslavia, locked in a territorial dispute with Italy, was threatening to seize the Adriatic city of Trieste, which was occupied by a small force of American and British troops. Forrestal was concerned that his ambiguous status—confirmed by the Senate but not sworn in—"might signal indecision to Moscow," Clifford reported.

Truman, alarmed by Clifford's message, scrapped plans for the full-dress ceremony. "The President responded during the night with instructions that I should be sworn in immediately and take action to see that all available reinforcements were provided" for the allied force in Trieste, Forrestal recorded in his diary on September 16.

Forrestal and Clifford went ahead with the plan on September 17. Minutes before noon, Chief Justice Fred Vinson arrived in Forrestal's office. The military service chiefs—General Dwight Eisenhower, Admiral Chester Nimitz, General Alexander Vandergrift, and General Carl Spaatz, formidable war heroes all—looked on as Forrestal, grim-faced and wearing a gray business suit with a polka-dot tie, prepared to take the oath. A broken nose from a Princeton boxing match gave the wiry Irishman the perpetual look of a tough middleweight—"rather pugnacious," Eisenhower thought. It was not just the nose, though. "He has the bearing given to goodhearted gangsters in the movies," one observer wrote. "There is the suggestion of the possibility of violence and the surface of perfectly constrained restraint."

Amid "an atmosphere of urgency, drama, and tension," as Clifford later wrote, Forrestal raised his right arm and placed his left hand on the Bible held by Vinson. With that act, the provisions of the landmark 1947 National Security Act would go into effect at midnight. It was the most sweeping military reorganization in American history, creating the National Military Establishment, which would be renamed the Department of Defense two years later. The Air Force was split off from the Army as a separate service. The War Department was renamed the Department of the Army. The act formally established the Joint Chiefs of Staff, and it created the Central Intelligence Agency and the National Security Council.

Forrestal crossed the Potomac River the next day to inspect his new headquarters—the Pentagon. Though it seemed an obvious choice, there had been uncertainty about where the secretary of defense would set up. A Forrestal aide recommended that the headquarters be established close to the White House and that the Pentagon be left to the Army. After his nomination in July, Forrestal told reporters that no decision had been made about the location of his headquarters, and no announcement that the Pentagon had been chosen was made until August 28. But Truman told Forrestal in July he was to move into the Pentagon. Angered by the Navy's continued resistance to unification, Truman did not want the first secretary of defense to be seen as a Navy partisan; the move into the Army building would be symbolic of unification. Even so, Forrestal's advisers treated the decision as tentative for a week before concluding that the president would not change his mind.

A Navy band gave Forrestal a fond farewell when he left the Navy Building, striking up "For He's a Jolly Good Fellow" as he drove off. No band was on hand to greet Forrestal at the Pentagon when the secretary of defense officially moved in on the morning of September 22, 1947. The Army viewed Forrestal suspiciously. During his seven years with the Navy, Forrestal had battled the Army on many issues, most prominently unification. Yet Forrestal—a deferential man, his pugnacious looks aside—was taking pains to be accommodating and to keep his arrival low-key.

Forrestal's advisers wanted to change the Pentagon's name to the "National Defense Building," and they consulted with the Public Buildings Administration on officially making the switch. On the morning of September 22, Marian Bailey and the other telephone operators dropped their traditional "This is the War Department" greeting, and callers instead heard, "This is National Defense." Road signs went up directing drivers to the "National Defense Building." But when reporters asked if this was to be the building's new name, Forrestal balked. The Pentagon would remain the Pentagon.

Most noteworthy of all, Forrestal did not presume to evict the secretary of the Army, Kenneth Royall, from the suite above the River entrance formerly belonging to the secretary of war. Instead, he opted to take the offices Somervell and Under Secretary of War Robert Patterson had occupied on the Mall side during the war. He left the grander suites once home to Stimson and Marshall—with the private elevator, dining room, and dressing room—to his ostensible Army subordinates.

It was a gracious gesture. Yet there was no mistaking that a new era had begun. After five years as the domain of the War Department and the Army, the Pentagon was now home to the secretary of defense and the new American military establishment.

The biggest cemetery for dead cats in the world

There had been no decent peace. Just two years after his death, Franklin D. Roosevelt's vision of converting the Pentagon into an archives seemed hopelessly quaint in the burgeoning Cold War atmosphere. The New War Department Building on Virginia Avenue in Foggy Bottom, long envisioned by FDR as the Army's future home, was turned over to the State Department in 1947.

Accidental and ad hoc though its construction was, the Pentagon had come to represent the new global role the United States had assumed. The Pentagon's very size hinted that the nation would no longer be bound by the Founding Fathers' warnings against a large standing army. Even the iconic pentagonal shape—the five concentric rings—seemed a deliberate statement meant to convey unity and strength, rather than a design born of chance.

The Pentagon's postwar role as the command center for the Department of Defense and the military services, which it keeps to this day, was born amid an atmosphere of Cold War tensions and new security commitments. The tenuous wartime alliance with the Soviet Union quickly disintegrated after the defeat of Germany and Japan, replaced by a tense rivalry that had raised fears of a third world war. The flare-up over Trieste in September 1947 settled back to a simmer, but tensions remained across Eastern Europe. Ignoring agreements made at Yalta promising self-determination, Stalin had installed pro-Soviet regimes in Warsaw, Budapest, and Bucharest. Looming over the continent was the threatening presence of the Red Army, larger than any in the West. In May 1947, at the request of Truman, Congress approved military and economic aid for Greece and Turkey, filling a breach left by Britain's near-bankruptcy. The president coupled this aid with a declaration, soon known as the Truman Doctrine, to assist free people against totalitarian aggression.

It was a sweeping commitment, made all the more remarkable by the sorry state of the American armed forces. Enormous cuts since the end of the war had left the services a shell of the fighting force that had rolled through western Europe and island-hopped across the Pacific. When Forrestal took office, fewer than 1.6 million of the more than 12 million American troops in the service at the end of World War II were still under arms.

Only ten of the Army's ninety-one combat-ready divisions on V-J Day remained, just two of them ready to fight. Truman's cabled instructions for Forrestal to reinforce Trieste had proven moot, but the order "left behind it an obvious and embarrassing question," noted Walter Millis, editor of Forrestal's diaries. "What reinforcements, in fact, did the United States possess against menaces which were now apparent in nearly every quarter of the globe?"

The atmosphere lent urgency to a renewed drive to reorganize the armed services for better efficiency and command. Marshall and Stimson's wartime push for unification—including their fruitless effort to bring the Navy into the Pentagon in 1942—had finally gained traction as the fighting came to an end. It would be unconscionable to fight another such war with the same divided military organization, they believed; the nation might not survive. Based on his experiences in Europe, Eisenhower felt the same way. They found a ready ally in Truman, who had been appalled at the waste and duplication he found while leading his Senate investigative committee. "I have the feeling that if the Army and the Navy had fought our enemies as hard as they fought each other, the war would have ended much earlier," Truman told Clifford. In a message to Congress on December 20, 1945, Truman had proposed the most fundamental reorganization of the military in American history, building on the proposals of Marshall and Stimson and calling for a single department of national defense unified under a civilian secretary.

Again, it was the Navy that refused to go along, viewing unification as a threat to its independence. The Army—and the towering figure of Eisenhower—would dominate a single military department, and the Navy would find itself relegated to secondary tasks, Navy partisans feared. The Marine Corps was even more strident in its opposition, seeing its entire existence in question—a not-unfounded fear. Truman regarded the Marines as a naval police force and, were it not for the political backing the Marines enjoyed, would have been happy to see the Corps disbanded. ("They have a propaganda machine that is almost equal to Stalin's," Truman complained.)

The most formidable opponent to unification was James Forrestal, an irony that would not be lost on anyone when he was named secretary of defense. The son of an immigrant from County Cork in Ireland, Forrestal possessed enormous vigor and drive within his 150-pound frame. Dropping out of Princeton six weeks before graduation, he took a job selling cigarettes before drifting into the investment business. He made his fortune and name on Wall Street, eventually coming to the attention of Roosevelt, who brought him to Washington in 1940.

After seven years with the Navy, Forrestal had adopted Navy mystique and tradition as his own and felt a keen sense of duty to protect it against Truman's proposal. "We are fighting for the very life of the Navy," he told Clifford. Forrestal pushed an alternative plan that called for broader coordination of foreign and military policy but preserved the independence of the Navy and Marine Corps. Forrestal's campaign against the president's unification plan was bold—some said it bordered on insubordination—and he half-expected the White House to fire him. Meeting with Truman on June 19, 1946, a tight-lipped Forrestal accused the Army of "steamroller tactics" and threatened to resign rather than accept unification.

Truman may have been tempted to take him up on the offer, but he recognized that Forrestal's resignation would turn him into a naval martyr and doom any hope of unification. Truman ordered Forrestal and Patterson, Stimson's successor as secretary of war, to negotiate a compromise. They did, though Patterson did most of the compromising, preferring that to seeing the whole effort fall apart. The resulting agreement—creating a weak confederacy of the military departments with little power given to the secretary of defense—was much along the lines of what the Navy had proposed. "They fought a bitter, intelligent, artful and skillful battle, and they won," Clifford recalled.

Forrestal was not Truman's first choice to be secretary of defense. The president tried to persuade Patterson to take the job, but the judge's wife insisted that he earn some money in the private sector. Despite his fight against unification, Forrestal, as a well-respected veteran of Roosevelt's war cabinet with enormous public stature, was an obvious second choice. It had been Forrestal who had raised early warnings about Soviet intentions and had urged a get-tough policy at a time when many in Washington—including Truman—had taken a more benevolent view. Forrestal was a key architect of the containment strategy then evolving as a way to counter Soviet hegemony. He was a leading advocate of rebuilding military strength as a way of preserving peace.

Beyond that, Truman realized that Forrestal, with his keen sense of duty, would do his best to make the new entity work. It brought Forrestal into the tent. "I believe the President thought the way to get this job done is to put Forrestal in, because if anybody else takes that job, Forrestal is going to sit back and carve him to ribbons," Clifford later said.

Forrestal, for his part, was not eager for the job. Years of helping build and oversee the largest naval force ever assembled—tackled in his characteristic frenetic manner—had left him exhausted and, though no one realized it, on the brink of a mental breakdown. Forrestal took the post, feeling an obligation both to the country and to the Navy, which he believed he could safeguard as secretary of defense. The job, after all, "was fashioned in his own image," as *New York Times* military correspondent Hanson Baldwin, a friend of Forrestal's, wrote. This was to prove a problem. "The man who had done the most to weaken the unification law was charged with making it function," writer Carl Borklund observed.

Forrestal had his own doubts. "This office will probably be the biggest cemetery for dead cats in history," he wrote to his friend, playwright Robert Sherwood, shortly before moving into the Pentagon.

Forrestal quickly set about trying to prove himself wrong.

When the soul's life is gone

Forrestal brought forty-five employees from the Navy Department, most of them secretaries, clerks, and the like—a tiny drop in the ocean that was the Pentagon. That was the way Forrestal wanted it. The legislation he had framed left him with no deputy and just three special assistants. Large staffs, he believed, "begin to gather the attribute of God to themselves very fast."

It was immediately clear that Forrestal had greatly underestimated the job; he was trying to manage the new defense entity—representing roughly one-third of the U.S. budget, and thus by far the largest government agency—with a staff equivalent to that of a midsized law firm. Undaunted by the challenge, Forrestal threw himself into the work, but he and his staff were quickly overwhelmed by technical and administrative chores they had not anticipated. Leaving the office one Sunday night at 10:30 after working his staff seven straight days, Forrestal bade farewell without a trace of irony: "Well, have a nice weekend." The long hours could not disguise that his young aides, though smart and dedicated, lacked the experience and standing to challenge senior generals and admirals.

Forrestal lacked authority too. The secretary of defense was little more than a coordinator; real power remained with the individual services and *their* secretaries. Forrestal had an idyllic vision of running the Pentagon by consensus, seeing his role in relation to the three service secretaries as first among equals. Instead, he found deadlock. With Truman demanding a pared-down defense budget, the services turned on one another, bitterly fighting for a larger share of the shrinking pie. The Navy and Air Force squabbled over everything, especially control of aviation. The Joint Chiefs of Staff—which lacked a chairman, at the Navy's insistence—were similarly paralyzed. Forrestal would consult the chiefs on issues but get divided replies or sometimes no replies at all.

Even getting the Navy to move into the Pentagon was a challenge, as in the past. Truman proved to be the strongest champion in adopting a new role for the building; the president told Forrestal that he wanted the Army, Air Force, and Navy headquarters at the Pentagon. But to opponents of unification, the Pentagon was the symbol of their threatened independence. Nimitz, then chief of naval operations, was not eager to move into the Pentagon, and the admirals dragged their feet, arguing that the move would be cumbersome and that putting all the service commanders in one building would leave "all our eggs in one basket," as one Navy official complained.

Forrestal saw the Navy's absence as a drag on unification and insisted the service make the move. "This action will undoubtedly facilitate my own work and will make possible a greater degree of day-to-day contact among personnel of the three services," Forrestal reported to Truman on February 28, 1948. After months of negotiations, Secretary of the Navy John L. Sullivan and Admiral Louis E. Denfield, Nimitz's successor, finally moved into the Pentagon in August 1948, along with the rest of the Navy high command and 2,500 workers. To free up 300,000 square feet of office space, the Army kicked out a like number of its workers from the Pentagon and sent them to the Navy building in Washington. Like the Air Force high command, the Navy secretary and military chiefs were given offices on the fourth floor of the E Ring, while the Army headquarters stayed on the third floor, a general arrangement that would last a half-century.

Of all the military services, only the Marine Corps held out, stoutly asserting its independence by maintaining its headquarters in the Navy Annex atop Arlington Ridge, overlooking the Pentagon a half-mile away. A Marine officer kept an artillery sight at his window and every morning worked out firing problems using the Pentagon as a target. "I've got the whole place zeroed in," he told a visitor. "With a battery of 155s, I could level the place to the ground in two days." The Corps would successfully stay out of the Pentagon for another half-century, until 1996, when General Charles Krulak, the Marine Corps commandant, decided the self-imposed exile had isolated the Marines from the rest of the armed services.

Getting the Navy into the Pentagon was one of the few concessions Forrestal would receive from the service. He turned to old Navy colleagues, but to his shock found that not only would they not help, they worked actively to sabotage unification. Forrestal found himself treated as a pariah by the Navy, and he came to see the Army as the only service making a genuine effort at unification. Forrestal confided to Eisenhower, who was serving as his adviser, that while "in the army there are many that I trust," there were only two or three admirals in whom he still had confidence. "It must have cost him a lot to come to such a conclusion," Eisenhower noted in his diary.

As Forrestal's frustration grew, he realized that his brand of unification was a failure and that the system needed to be changed. In the summer of 1948 he approached Clifford: "Clark, I was wrong. I cannot make this work. No one can make it work." Forrestal subsequently told Truman much the same, and, with the president's approval, he went to work framing changes to strengthen the office.

Clifford later called Forrestal's transformation the most "dramatic metamorphosis" he saw in forty-five years in Washington. "To put it simply, he realized that he had been wrong, and publicly admitted it. It was a brave but enormously costly decision for him, alienating many of his closest friends in the Navy, and it added enormously to the strain under which he was already working."

By the latter part of 1948, Forrestal was exhausted and behaving in ways that, in retrospect, would be seen as signs of mental illness. His aides knew he was having difficulty concentrating and was unable to make even simple decisions. Sitting behind Forrestal at a Cabinet meeting, Clifford watched with alarm as the secretary constantly scratched at a raw spot on the back of his head. "He had opened an open sore there, and yet still couldn't stay away from it," Clifford recalled. "It was a nervous manifestation that I found very disquieting, and you could sense something was going on within the man." Every time Clifford saw Forrestal, the sore was larger.

Forrestal's anxiety was compounded by uncertainty over his status with the White House. In the months following Truman's stunning upset victory in the 1948 presidential election, the president had grown frustrated with Forrestal's increasing indecisiveness and odd behavior and came to the conclusion that he should replace his secretary of defense. Moreover, Truman had a most important benefactor he needed to satisfy: Louis Johnson, the chief fundraiser for his presidential campaign.

Shortly before his inauguration in January 1949, Truman informed Forrestal that he intended to replace him with Johnson. Forrestal went into a confused denial; while at times he expressed eagerness to leave office, in his frantic, debilitated mental state, he became convinced that he needed to stay at the Pentagon to unravel the mess he had helped create. With Forrestal making no real motion to leave office and his behavior becoming more eccentric, Truman summoned him to the White House on March 1 and asked for his resignation "at once." The dismissal seemed to throw Forrestal over the edge. He had nothing but contempt for Johnson. "It just galled him to think that an office he had created to be above and beyond politics would become a spoil of the 1948 campaign," Najeeb Halaby, then a young Forrestal aide, later said.

The ceremony to swear in Johnson was set for March 28 at the Pentagon. That morning, Eisenhower, laid up in bed with severe stomach cramps, got an urgent call from Forrestal. "Ike, I simply can't turn over this job to Louie Johnson," Forrestal said. "He knows nothing about the problems involved and things will go to pot. I'll have to go to the President and withdraw my resignation immediately."

Eisenhower later recounted, "I replied with all my strength, urging him not to do anything so foolish."

Johnson was sworn in as the new secretary of defense before an audience of eleven thousand packed into the Pentagon courtyard; the ceremony, complete with marching bands and a thundering Air Force flyover, was so grandiose it was dubbed an inauguration. At the White House shortly afterward, Forrestal was led away speechless when Truman pinned the Distinguished Service Medal on his lapel. Forrestal was accorded further honors at a special House Armed Services Committee meeting held the next day. Afterwards, Forrestal went back to the Pentagon and retreated to a small office that had been set aside for his use in answering correspondence. His aide Marx Leva found him a little later, still wearing his hat, sitting entirely rigid, staring at a blank wall. Leva asked if there was anything he could do. "Yes," Forrestal replied. "Call for my car. I want to go home." Forrestal had no car—the secretary's official limousine had passed on to Johnson. Leva "ran like hell" and found another official car to take Forrestal to his Georgetown home. The first secretary of defense, leaving the Pentagon for the last time, was bundled into the commandeered car and driven away.

Alarmed friends arranged for an Air Force plane to take him that evening to Florida, where his wife, Josephine, and his old friend Bob Lovett, assistant secretary of war for air under Stimson, were vacationing. Lovett met him at the airfield and was shocked at Forrestal's haggard appearance. His sunken eyes darted about and his mouth was so tightly drawn that his lips had disappeared. Lovett tried to be jovial, suggesting they play some golf. Forrestal stared at his friend with a desperate look in his eyes. "Bob, they're after me," he replied. Walking the beach in subsequent days, Forrestal became convinced that metal sockets in the sand for holding beach umbrellas had been wired to monitor his conversations. The Kremlin had marked him for liquidation, he said. After at least one suicide attempt, Forrestal was admitted to the Bethesda naval hospital on April 2. Despite his suicidal tendencies, Forrestal was put in a VIP suite on the sixteenth floor, where he could be more easily isolated from the press.

Forrestal was diagnosed as suffering from severe reactive depression, not unlike combat fatigue, caused by intense pressures that had overwhelmed his mind and nervous system. Forrestal told a Navy psychiatrist he had failed at the Pentagon; instead of "banging heads together" as he should have, Forrestal blamed himself for naively believing the military services would bow to the common good to work together.

On the night of May 21, Forrestal stayed up late reading. A Navy corpsman stationed outside his room looked in on Forrestal around 1:45 A.M. and found him writing on sheets of hospital paper, copying a poem from a red leatherbound anthology of world poetry. About 3 A.M., while the corpsman was on an errand—possibly sent by Forrestal himself—the former defense secretary left his room and slipped across the corridor to a kitchen. Forrestal removed the unsecured screen from the window and tied one end of his bathrobe sash around a radiator below the window and the other end around his neck. He climbed out the window and was perhaps suspended for a few moments before the sash slipped off the radiator. The soaring granite tower conceived by Franklin Roosevelt and built by John McShain nearly a decade earlier proved to be a more than adequate platform for Forrestal to end his life. His broken body was discovered on the roof of a third-floor passageway connecting to another wing of the hospital.

On the bedside table in Forrestal's room, his book was found open to the poem he had been copying, "The Chorus from Ajax" by Sophocles. It included these lines:

> *When Reason's day*
> *Sets rayless—joyless—quenched in cold decay,*
> *Better to die, and sleep*
> *The never-waking sleep, than linger on*
> *And dare to live, when the soul's life is gone*

I want that office

It had not been an auspicious start. Nor did it not soon get better.

Big, bluff, backslapping Louis Johnson, a savvy and nakedly ambitious West Virginian, was the virtual antithesis of the introverted Forrestal. Johnson had served as assistant secretary of war under Harry Woodring, working assiduously to undermine him. When the president replaced Woodring in 1940, Johnson had fully expected Roosevelt to name him to the job. Instead, FDR chose Henry Stimson. Nine years later, Johnson viewed his arrival at the Pentagon as sweet vindication, and, many suspected, a springboard to the presidency.

Moving into Forrestal's office on the Mall side, Johnson found the accommodations not grand enough for his taste. Brigadier General Louis H. Renfrow, a bumptious Truman crony from Missouri serving as Johnson's assistant, covetously eyed the suites above the River entrance occupied by the secretary of the army and the chief of staff, with the private elevator, dining room, and larger offices. Things were going to change. "I want that office," Johnson declared. Forrestal's "postage stamp"–sized desk was also deemed inadequate. The biggest desk in the Pentagon sat in an office set aside for General Pershing, but never occupied by the World War I commander before he died in 1948. The desk, a nineteenth-century, nine-by-five-foot solid walnut antique, had been used for years by Black Jack in the old State, War and Navy Building. Johnson claimed it.

Renfrow informed Army Secretary Kenneth Royall, who was planning to resign, that he was being "dispossessed" of his office a little early. Army Chief of Staff Omar Bradley, a five-star general and one of the greatest of American soldiers, was likewise evicted. In April, movers packed up Royall and Bradley's offices, including the Victorian grandfather clock and enormous globe on a carved wooden pedestal that Marshall had used. In came the Pershing desk and Johnson's belongings, including a television set and a Buddha statuette with a bulging tummy, its hands upflung and roaring with silent mirth.

Room 3E-880 became and would remain the office of the secretary of defense. Bradley's office would go to Johnson's deputy. However ungracious, it was a shrewd move. In the hierarchical Pentagon, office size spoke volumes. "He wanted to establish his preeminence in the Pentagon," Marx Leva, Forrestal's aide, who stayed on to work for Johnson, later said. ". . . That was a symbol, but that symbol permeated at various echelons and he also wanted this to be known to the Joint Chiefs of Staff as well as to the civilian military establishment, the Army, the Navy, and the Air Force."

Johnson did not stop at switching a few offices. Construction crews had been working night and day for months to remodel a pie-shaped ninety-thousand-square-foot slice of the Pentagon into a secure and soundproof area that would be home to the Joint Chiefs of Staff. Walls were knocked down, and a huge map room, conference rooms, and rooms within rooms were built. Expensive acoustic tile went up. Thick doors with steel reinforcement were installed, and iron bars placed over windows. The $100,000 project was impressive, but there was one problem: It had been built near Forrestal's office.

The carpenters and painters had just about finished, and the electricians were starting to install sophisticated communications systems, when Johnson declared in April he wanted the Joint Chiefs near his new office. Building superintendent Carl Muvehill, a testy, enormous man—almost five-sided himself, it was said—felt like weeping when the stop order came. Johnson ordered a new, identical hideout built for the Joint Chiefs, this time on the floor below his office. The area the workers had nearly completed would have to be turned back into regular offices.

The secretary of defense and his staff were taking over all the second and third floors along the E Ring on the River entrance side. Army offices would be concentrated on the first, second, and third floors on the Mall and on the southeast-facing side of the building. The Navy would be concentrated on the fourth and fifth floors along the Mall and west sides of the building. The Air Force would be on the fourth and fifth floors along the River and southeast sides. In all, 12,500 Pentagon workers were moved in "a gigantic game of musical chairs," as one reporter put it.

Disruptive as it all was, the Pentagon was being converted into the nation's command post for a unified military in the nuclear age. The Joint Chiefs' area—once Muvehill's men rebuilt it near Johnson's office—was soon bustling with senior officers from all three services and was the most closely guarded area of the Pentagon. The Joint War Room lay behind double steel doors, its walls covered with large maps of the world. The area also included "The Tank," the conference room where the Joint Chiefs— Bradley, Denfield, and General Hoyt S. Vandenberg, the Air Force chief of staff—regularly met. Nearby were "telecon" rooms, where the chiefs held secure conferences with commanders in Tokyo, London, or Berlin. Incoming messages were decoded and projected on a glass screen; outgoing messages were displayed on an adjacent screen.

The most important command post—even more critical than the Joint War Room—was the Air Force command post in the Pentagon basement.

It was here, behind steel-shielded walls, that word of an enemy air attack would likely first come. A battery of direct-line telephones gave the command post instant contact with radar warning networks in the Arctic and on the North American coastlines, as well as with Air Force fighter and bomber bases around the world. The command post was manned twenty-four hours a day, with an Air Force general always on duty and empowered to make immediate decisions in the event of a crisis. Orders could be given to scramble fighters to intercept enemy aircraft, and—should Truman give the command—to launch long-range strategic bombers bearing atomic weapons on retaliatory strikes against Russian targets.

The threat of a nuclear attack on America took on real meaning about five months into Johnson's tenure, on August 29, 1949, when the Soviet Union exploded a nuclear bomb in Siberia. It was a shocking development, coming three years before U.S. intelligence had predicted. (Before the news was released in September, retired Lieutenant General Dick Groves confidently predicted the Soviets were "ten to twenty years" away from exploding a bomb.)

The news immediately rekindled questions that had been heard after Pearl Harbor about the wisdom of concentrating the military command in the Pentagon. Senator Alexander Wiley of Wisconsin called on the military to immediately abandon the Pentagon, saying it was "suicidal" to keep the defense headquarters there. "We would be a sucker for a solar plexus blow which could knock our country out of an atomic war a few minutes after such a war started," he said. Johnson, in response, announced a study to create an alternative command post in the event the Pentagon was attacked. By the spring of 1951, locals were buzzing about the construction crews excavating around the clock in secrecy underneath Raven Rock Mountain in Pennsylvania near the Maryland border in the scenic Catoctin Mountains. Some 500,000 cubic yards of the hardest rock on the East Coast was blasted from the mountain's core and hauled away, and a three-story, 220,000-square-foot building erected underground, its entrance protected by two heavy steel blast doors. It was designated Site R, the nation's alternate military headquarters in the event of nuclear war.

George Marshall eventually admitted to second thoughts about the Pentagon. "If we'd known there'd be an A-Bomb, the Pentagon would probably never have been built," he later said.

Pentagonians—as employees were generally referred to in those days—used gallows humor to deal with the anxiety. "No enemy would be stupid enough to bomb the Pentagon, because that would end the confusion in Washington," a common joke went. Employees would eventually come up with a nickname for the hot dog stand in the middle of the Pentagon courtyard: The Ground Zero Cafe.

We weren't ready to fight

Louis Johnson was in a dramatically stronger position at the Pentagon than Forrestal, yet he proved unable to capitalize on it. The Pentagon was in chaos. The fighting among the services grew worse; the generals and admirals were united only in how much they despised Johnson. In Omar Bradley's view, "Truman had replaced one mental case with another."

Taking the opposite approach from Forrestal, Johnson vowed "to crack a few heads together." The changes Forrestal had sought were passed by Congress and signed into law by Truman on August 10, 1949, giving the secretary of defense unequivocal power over the armed forces. The unwieldy National Military Establishment was converted into an executive department known as the Department of Defense. The Army, Navy, and Air Force secretaries were removed from the president's cabinet and their power diminished. The position of chairman was created to preside over the Joint Chiefs.

Johnson launched a crusade against defense spending, but it came to a sudden halt on June 25, 1950, when the Soviet-supplied North Korean People's Army rolled over the South Korea border and quickly captured Seoul. Poorly trained and poorly equipped U.S. 8th Army troops—living the high life of an occupation army in Japan—were rushed in to support the crumbling South Korean army. The first troops, Task Force Smith, were positioned on the highway north of Osan to stop the advancing North Korean tanks. But the 2.36-inch bazooka rockets fired by the U.S. troops could not penetrate the heavy armor of the T-34 tanks. The American force was overrun. The task force commander, Lieutenant Colonel Brad Smith, could see more tanks approaching, and behind them, stretching for miles, a line of infantry marching four abreast. "We had a pretty good idea right then that we had something that was going to cause us a hell of a lot of woe," Smith recalled a half-century later. "We weren't ready to fight, there's no question about it." After one week, three thousand U.S. soldiers were dead, wounded, captured, or missing.

The pathetic state of the American military had been revealed. Johnson received much of the blame for the debacle, even though he had been following Truman's guidance to cut defense spending. The president, already angered by Johnson's "inordinate egotistical desire to run the whole government," soon fired his second secretary of defense. Before delivering the news to Johnson, Truman had picked his third.

George C. Marshall had been vacationing in Michigan at the Huron Mountain Resort in August when he was called to the telephone at a nearby country store. It was the president, asking Marshall to come to the White House when he got back to Washington. Truman had already called Marshall back to service twice since he retired from the Army, once as an envoy to China, and then for a momentous two years as secretary of state, overseeing the creation of a recovery plan for Europe. Now, with the nation again at war, Truman turned to Marshall a final time, asking him to become secretary of defense. Marshall had been hoping to retire for five years, but his sense of duty made that impossible. He told Truman he would serve no more than a year.

On September 21, the day he was confirmed by the Senate, Marshall rode to the Pentagon in an old Studebaker and reported to Stimson's old office, next door to the suite he had occupied as Army chief of staff. "Guess we have to go through the oath business," he muttered. Ten minutes after being sworn in, Marshall called the Joint Chiefs in for a conference and they went to work. For Marshall, it was a familiar position, reminiscent of when he had been given charge of the Army in the dire days of 1939. "I was getting rather hardened to coming in when everything had gone to pot and there was nothing you could get your hands on, and darned if I didn't find the same thing when I came into the Korean War," Marshall later said. "There wasn't anything."

Marshall went to work rebuilding the U.S. armed forces. Three months shy of his seventieth birthday when he took office, Marshall did not have the same vigor as in his younger years, and he left much of the detail to his deputy, Bob Lovett. Yet his commanding presence restored order and had an electrifying effect on morale in the building.

Inside the Pentagon, the population of workers in the building soared. By December 1950, six months after the war began, it had jumped 6,000 to 31,000, and would later reach 33,000. Security posters, unseen since World War II, reappeared on corridor walls. In their secure war room, the Joint Chiefs held regular 2 A.M. "telecon" conferences with MacArthur in Japan. From outside, long rows of lights could be seen burning from windows until late in the night. The wartime Pentagon was back.

He served America magnificently

Marshall was not the only giant of World War II to whom Truman turned. The war in Korea took a desperate turn in November 1950, when more than 300,000 Chinese soldiers launched a massive offensive across the Yalu River, striking a devastating blow at advancing American troops. In the spring of 1951, with the war settling into a long and brutal fight, Truman, through an intermediary, asked Brehon Burke Somervell to take over leadership of the Defense Production Administration, an agency set up to marshal U.S. industry behind military production.

Somervell was astonished. "In view of my experience with the gentleman, this came, to put it mildly, as a complete surprise," Somervell later wrote to Marshall. Just in January, he had given a speech criticizing Truman's foreign policy as "vacillating" and "nebulous." The years had done little to erase the bitterness he felt at Truman's criticism of Army construction and the Canol oil project. Still, Somervell gave the request serious thought before turning it down, saying he would reconsider if full-scale war broke out between the world powers.

To Somervell's further amazement, Truman then wrote him a gracious personal letter saying he was "greatly disappointed" by the decision and asking him to reconsider. "[I]t is an assignment for which your previous experience and magnificent contributions have proved you are so eminently fitted," Truman wrote Somervell on April 23, 1951. "You said you would accept the assignment in the event of all out war. The emergency conditions facing us today are as serious as they would be in that eventuality. The Korean difficulty is enlarging in scope and is obviously very serious."

Somervell agonized over the decision and came close to accepting before writing Truman a polite note declining the post. His sense of duty—though great—was not as unconditional as Marshall's. Somervell was entirely a creature of total war, and he doubted that Truman—who had termed Korea a "police action"—was willing to follow through with the commitment Somervell would want. Further, skeptical of Truman's motives, Somervell thought that the president might be setting him up to take the fall if the mobilization failed.

"He wished to make me 'Czar of the Pacific' to clean up the mess left in the wake of the war and otherwise take a terrific beating on all fronts," Somervell wrote Marshall. ". . . Though it was very embarrassing at the time, I managed to talk myself out of it and now it seems very funny."

After his retirement from the Army, Somervell had been recruited by Richard K. Mellon in March 1946 to take over Koppers Company, a Pittsburgh manufacturing conglomerate owned by the Mellon family. Koppers was considered "the dog" of the family's vast holdings, but Mellon knew from wartime experience that Somervell was just the "scorcher" he needed. In short order Somervell streamlined the company's management, diversified its operations, and more than tripled its profits.

Somervell, belying his reputation as a publicity hound, had made no effort to stay in the public eye since retiring from the Army. He told a friend that he had "made up my mind that I am going to be the only commander [from World War II] who does not write a book." Somervell had largely stayed out of the great postwar debates on military organization and strategy.

Somervell did take satisfaction in a growing if grudging public acknowledgment that the Pentagon had been worth building. "Gen. Somervell's 'Folly' Proves Itself Despite Jeers of Critics," a headline in the *Washington Post* declared in 1954. The accompanying article noted "mounting evidence that the general might even have known what he was doing when he poured something like 83 million dollars into one man's conviction that the military minds of this nation could best plot for its defense under a single roof—no matter how big the roof had to be." The *Star* noted that the Pentagon had "become in the short span of less than 10 years as familiar a world institution as the centuries-old Tower of London."

After a friend sent him a magazine article entitled "The Pentagon

Makes Sense," Somervell replied that ". . . it would have satisfied my soul to see an article such as the one you forwarded signed by our buddy Al Engle (sic) or one H.S.T. [Harry S. Truman.]"

To an artist who painted his portrait and suggested that it hang in the Pentagon, Somervell in August 1954 happily acknowledged that "the Pentagon is my brain-child," and he agreed that "the river entrance of the Pentagon would be a fine place indeed" for the portrait to hang. That never happened.

Several weeks later, Somervell suffered a severe heart attack and went to Florida with his wife, Louise, to recuperate. Fat Styer, visiting him in Ocala that fall, found that while his old boss had slowed physically, "the same old time sparkle shot from his flashing eyes, the humor and gaiety of spirit were undiminished." By January, Somervell was complaining bitterly to his longtime friend William Delano of the boredom caused by enforced rest. After breakfast on the morning of February 13, 1955, Somervell handed his wife a cartoon he had torn from the morning newspaper and then slumped over in his living room chair. A doctor was summoned from next door but it was too late. Somervell was dead of a heart attack at age sixty-two.

Newspapers were filled with tributes. "Gen. Brehon B. Somervell was one of the ablest officers the United States Army has produced," *The Washington Post* said. "Atomic bombs and Alcan Highway—Pentagon Building and Red Ball Express—name any of the great achievements of World War II and somewhere the hand of Somervell was in it," wrote the Memphis *Commercial Appeal*. "Thrift is admirable, and so are tactfulness and gentleness," said the Baltimore *Sun*. "But when the guns are roaring, certain other qualities are needed. Somervell knew what they were, and he had them to a superlative degree. He served America magnificently."

Somervell would soon fade from memory, the fate of most logisticians. Yet he was a towering figure among American military leaders in World War II, one who deserved to be remembered in the front rank of Allied architects of victory. George Marshall later described what he would do if he were placed in charge of another global war: "I would start out looking for another General Somervell the very first thing I did, and so would anybody else who went through that struggle on this side."

On February 17, 1955, Somervell was buried at Arlington National Cemetery. Marshall—who kept his word and retired in September 1951 after one year as secretary of defense—was there to salute the man who had housed and supplied his great army. A caparisoned horse with reversed boots in the stirrups followed the horse-drawn caisson bearing Somervell's casket from the Fort Myer Chapel to the gravesite. The general was buried next to his first wife, Anna, at the spot he had chosen thirteen years earlier, below Pierre L'Enfant's tomb. From there, noted the *Post*, Somervell was "overlooking the ponderous Pentagon which stands as a memorial to him."

Water flowed like money

Somervell's folly had by then become a tourist attraction. Visitors would sometimes wander into the Pentagon, gawking in the concourse, strolling in the corridors, and enjoying the now-lovely courtyard. The building had entered the realm of legend, its statistics cited like rote: It had three times the office space of the Empire State Building. The U.S. Capitol could slide into any one of its five wedges. Covering thirty-four acres, the Pentagon had the largest ground area of any office building in the world; a walk around its exterior walls was a journey of almost a mile. There were seventeen and one-half miles of corridors and seven acres of windows.

There were no organized tours of the Pentagon, and no passes were required to enter the building. The light security was odd; the Korean War had ended with an armistice in 1953 that left that country divided in two, but Cold War tensions were higher than ever. Among the most appreciative of the easy access was Pawel Monat. "Anyone, from a four-star general to a fifteen-year-old boy, can get *into* the Pentagon," Monat later wrote.

Monat was no ordinary tourist, though. From 1955 to 1958, he was the military attaché to the Polish Embassy in Washington and a Communist spy. "One of our best sources of loose talk about military subjects was—of all places—the Pentagon," Monat wrote after he defected to the United States.

Monat and his aides, as well as military attachés of other countries, would visit the Pentagon frequently. They would browse in the concourse shops, buy stamps at the post office, roam contentedly among stacks of books in the Army library, and line up for food at the snack bars. All the while they would eavesdrop. Monat wrote:

> Two officers meeting in a hall confirmed a rumor we had heard that an infantry regiment was undergoing special nuclear training. A colonel told a friend that he had just been ordered to evaluate a new weapon that we had never heard of. We got our first real hint about the reorganization of the Army into new, stream- lined 'pentomic' divisions in the Pentagon concourse. And one of my assistants first heard about the new B-70 airplane from an Air Force colonel who mentioned it to a colleague of his as the two of them stood waiting for hamburgers at a Pentagon snack bar.

The information "gave Warsaw—and Moscow—an incredibly intimate insight into the daily workings of the American high command," he added. It was so easy to work at the Pentagon that Monat wanted to set up a secret drop in the building where classified material could be left for the spies. He found an ideal spot in a crack in the wall near the bus tunnel. But his supe- riors in Warsaw refused to approve the operation, finding it inconceivable that the Pentagon would be so lax. "Warsaw was wrong, of course," Monat wrote. "It would have been a snap."

It was not just spies who found the Pentagon a convenient place to do business. In the early 1950s, an insurance salesman found an unlocked room in the Pentagon that was used at night by the cleaning crews but was empty during the daytime. He set up an office inside and operated for two years before being detected by the authorities. There was a desk, telephone, and a ready supply of stationery. "That was all he needed to organize a very prosperous little business, convenient to his Pentagon clients," Charles B. Overman, Carl Muvehill's successor as Pentagon superintendent, later said. Overman got wind of the scam and ordered the room locked.

Building supervisors had more serious concerns than rogue insurance salesmen. They discovered in the 1950s that the Pentagon was sinking. More precisely, the wet fill that McShain's crews had used to raise the low ground on the east side of the building was settling below the concrete slab, causing occasional breaks in the sewer lines, water mains, and electrical ca- bles running through the basement. Crews reinforced the pilings along a seventy-five-foot strip under the River entrance in 1958, but it did not seem to help. A burst water pipe in April 1959 flooded the basement and first floor with up to three inches of water, routing two thousand Pentagonians from the building. "Water flowed like money at the big building," wrote a wag at United Press International.

Three months later, the Pentagon was struck by its most serious calamity since opening. On July 2, 1959, beneath the concourse in a first floor storage room in the D Ring, a lightbulb ignited a stack of acetate magnetic tapes. Some seven thousand computer tapes—many containing classified Air Force information—went up in flames, creating a dense, acrid smoke. A five-alarm fire was soon raging, and more than seventy fire trucks and some three hundred firefighters from Virginia, Washington, and Maryland descended on the Pentagon.

Just getting to the fire was a tremendous problem. Firefighters dragged hoses down long corridors against "smoke so thick it was hard to walk against," Arlington Fire Chief Joseph H. Clements told reporters. It took so long to get to the fire that they had little oxygen left to fight the blaze. Choking firefighters were driven back time and again; some were overcome and had to be carried out. Security guards had been unable to tell the firefighters how to even get to the blaze.

When the Pentagon had been completed sixteen years earlier, its enormous bays and concrete slab construction made it "about as fireproof as a building can be made," Clements said. Since then, at the insistence of defense officials and military officers who wanted private offices, the building had been honeycombed with wood partitions, and floors and ceiling covered with combustible material. Corridors that had been sealed off to limit access or increase office space acted as dead-end chimneys, confining smoke and gasses. False ceilings screened the blaze from firemen, forcing them to jackhammer manhole-sized holes in the concourse floor so they could snake hoses down to douse the heart of the fire. With firemen desperate for more pressure in their hose lines, Secretary of Defense Neil McElroy ordered the building's entire water supply put at their disposal.

After four hours, the fire was brought under control. Some thirty thousand workers had been evacuated, although the most essential   including those operating the command centers—stayed on duty. The damaged area, equivalent to four city blocks, looked like a collapsed mine shaft, with blackened beams, twisted steel, and wet, hip-deep debris. Some $6 million worth of brand-new IBM computing machines—some of the first computers installed in the Pentagon—were destroyed or buried under charred partitions. Smoke, heat exhaustion, and poisonous fumes sent thirty-two firefighters to the hospital, and dozens more were treated at the scene.

The fire of 1959 had given a chilling first taste of what it would be like to fight a major inferno in the Pentagon.

I don't give a damn what John Paul Jones would have done

By October 24, 1962, Secretary of Defense Robert McNamara, red-eyed and hoarse, was grabbing catnaps on a cot in his office dressing room. It had been nine days since the United States had learned from U-2 surveillance photographs that the Soviet Union had placed nuclear missiles in Cuba, ninety miles from the American mainland. U.S. forces were on maximum alert, with ballistic missiles and bombers targeting the Soviet Union and Cuba. Squadrons of destroyers, aircraft carriers, antisubmarine ships, and picket planes had placed a naval quarantine around Cuba. McNamara felt the weight of history on his shoulders as he sat at the giant Pershing desk in Room 3E-880. Directly behind his chair hung a portrait of Jim Forrestal, tight-lipped and intense, seemingly watching his every move.

A private elevator took McNamara down to the National Military Command Center, which had opened only three weeks earlier; it was an initiative he and his team of analytical "whiz kids" had taken to establish worldwide command and control at the Pentagon. The Joint War Room had been rebuilt and combined with reconnaissance, intelligence, and communications facilities. The timing had proven fortuitous.

A fanciful version of the Pentagon war room, depicted two years later in Stanley Kubrick's film *Dr. Strangelove, or: How I Learned to Stop Worrying and Love the Bomb,* would cement a crazed image of the place in the minds of millions around the world. The reality was strange enough. Sitting at a large oval-shaped brown table in the green-carpeted main conference room, McNamara and the joint chiefs could routinely speak by secure telephone with major field commanders. Intelligence photographs, maps, and status reports were projected onto a large screen covering one wall. Screens in the corner showed updated information from the Strategic Air

Command, or the latest images from missile-warning radar systems in Alaska, Greenland, and Scotland.

Yet the National Military Command Center did not have the answers McNamara wanted on the evening of October 24. He was infuriated that the Navy had not immediately alerted him about National Security Agency reports that some of the cargo ships in a Soviet flotilla sailing toward Cuba had mysteriously altered course. Moreover, McNamara was worried the Navy was acting too aggressively. In an address to the nation two days earlier, President John F. Kennedy had called the operation a quarantine, aimed at only stopping ships suspected of carrying military cargo, rather than a full-scale blockade. The difference was more than semantics. "It was a means of telling [Soviet leader Nikita] Khrushchev we had to get the missiles out of there without going to war," McNamara later said. The secretary thought the chief of naval operations, Admiral George Anderson, did not fully appreciate the difference.

At 9:45 that evening, McNamara and the deputy defense secretary, Roswell Gilpatric, went up to the fourth floor and marched down the corridor to the Navy's command center, known as Flag Plot, which was crowded with senior Navy officers monitoring the quarantine. One wall was covered with a large chart that plotted the positions of Navy ships along the quarantine line. Studying the chart, McNamara spotted a marker showing one ship off by itself, far from the line. "What's it doing there?" he asked. McNamara was stunned when Anderson told him the ship was trailing a Soviet F-class submarine and holding it down at that location. To the secretary, this was exactly the kind of action that could start an incident that might spin out of control. Anderson insisted the submarines represented a potential threat to Navy warships and had to be trailed. Struggling to control his temper, McNamara quizzed Anderson on the exact details of how the ships would respond to different scenarios.

Anderson—at fifty-five, a tall and proper man regarded in the Navy as a sailor's sailor and a first-rate strategist—viewed McNamara's adversarial questioning as improper civilian interference in a military operation. "Mr. Secretary, the Navy has been handling blockades successfully since John Paul Jones," the admiral finally said, according to McNamara. "If you let us handle this, we'll do it successfully."

To McNamara, Anderson was a fine tactical commander who understood nothing of the geopolitics involved. "I don't give a damn what John Paul Jones would have done," McNamara replied. "I want to know what you are going to do now."

Anderson, red-faced, waved a copy of the Manual of Naval Regulations in McNamara's face and told him the procedures were explained within. "Now, Mr. Secretary, if you and your deputy will go back to your offices, the Navy will run the blockade," Anderson said.

The confrontation—along with several others McNamara and Anderson would have in the Flag Plot over the course of the crisis—made for the tensest moments in the building's twenty-year history, and quite possibly the most significant. McNamara angrily returned to his office, but at his insistence, the next day the Navy issued a public warning that described its procedures for the Soviets, explaining that U.S. ships trailing submarines would drop four or five harmless explosives in the water as a signal for the vessels to surface and identify themselves.

It did not help. Navy destroyers continued in subsequent days to aggressively track Soviet submarines, whose commanders ignored the explosive signals. They stayed submerged until forced to surface to get air and recharge their batteries, where they were surrounded and spotlighted by Navy ships and surveillance planes. McNamara—and the rest of the world—only learned at a conference in Moscow in 2002 that the Russian submarines had been armed with nuclear-tipped torpedoes. Moreover, the commander of one submarine had mistaken the explosive signals for depth charges, and, angry and exhausted after four days of chase, ordered his nuclear torpedo brought to battle readiness on October 27. "Maybe the war has already started up there, while we are doing somersaults here," the captain said, according to a Soviet document released in 2002. "We are going to blast them now! We will die, but we will sink them all. We will not disgrace our navy." More level-headed officers were able to talk the captain back from the brink and prevent an explosion that almost certainly would have led to a nuclear exchange between the United States and the Soviet Union.

For all the marvel and pride in the McNamara-era command and control that could now be exercised from the Pentagon, the sobering truth was that it had been chance, and the decisions of men at sea, that prevented the deaths of millions and the destruction of countries.

On October 28, Khrushchev ordered the removal of the missiles from Cuba. The crisis diffused, the National Military Command Center, the Flag Plot, and the other command centers in the Pentagon could go back to more routine business, including monitoring the status of a small force of American military advisers and Army helicopters that was operating now in South Vietnam.

Antiwar marchers congregate in front of the Pentagon,
October 21, 1967.

CHAPTER 18

THE BATTLE OF
THE PENTAGON

You had to be scared

Under the cover of darkness through that Friday night, dozens of Army trucks packed with soldiers riding in the back behind tarps rumbled into the Pentagon bus tunnel. By 6 A.M. Saturday, October 21, 1967, nearly 2,400 troops were hidden inside the Pentagon, stationed strategically in corridors near building entrances. Soldiers sat on the floors and chatted with secretaries. Others dozed on their packs and helmets, lying amid their M-14 rifles, field kits, and cases of C rations. The courtyard had the air of an encampment, with field kitchens cooking breakfast and radios crackling at command posts. By afternoon, the final defenses were being readied. Troops installed thirteen tear-gas launchers on the roof, covering various approaches to the building. Throughout the building, a "defender-of-the-castle feeling" prevailed, as one participant described it.

Inside the green-carpeted Army Operations Center conference room, Robert McNamara joined General Harold K. Johnson, the Army chief of staff, and other senior officials around a huge T-shaped table for a final briefing on preparations for a massive antiwar protest meant to shut down the Pentagon that day. Closed-circuit television sets lined one wall, each showing live pictures from seven television cameras that had been mounted on the Pentagon roof to monitor the demonstration from every angle. The overheated operations center was packed with so many officers in full crisis mode that the air-conditioning could not keep up. A map showing Washington and Arlington had replaced the one of Vietnam normally displayed in the war room. Switchboards and teletype machines in adjoining rooms were humming. The ops center, usually monitoring combat half a world away, would on this day be right at the frontline, just ninety feet from the Mall entrance targeted by the demonstrators.

All day, minute-by-minute updates had come in from Army intelligence agents who had infiltrated the marchers assembling at the Lincoln Memorial. Operatives reported seeing militant demonstrators carrying everything from water pistols and walkie-talkies to canisters of tear gas and billy clubs. Other agents reported on the whereabouts of Abbie Hoffman and H. Rap Brown, two of the most notorious protest organizers. Overhead, military reconnaissance aircraft circled the demonstrators. Meanwhile, from twenty-three listening posts set up inside the Pentagon, Army agents with earphones on their heads sat hunched over radio equipment, eavesdropping on citizens' radios. It was an unprecedented—and illegal—surveillance operation by the Army against Americans.

As the first demonstrators trickled onto the Pentagon grounds, a thin line of military police stood in front of the building's Mall and River entrances. Despite the overwhelming force hidden in the building and the intelligence flowing into the operations center warning of impending violence, the perimeter of the building had been deliberately left lightly defended.

Colonel Ernie Graves felt uneasy about it. He was the son of Pot Graves, the legendary Corps of Engineers officer and West Point football coach who had commanded Somervell in Mexico and France and served as mentor to Dick Groves. Ernie Graves had grown up at the feet of those larger-than-life Army men and felt a palpable connection to them.

Personable but tough-minded like his father, Graves was the executive assistant to the secretary of the Army, Stanley Resor. In the weeks leading up to the march, Graves sat in on endless debates about what kind of barricades to place in front of the building. Major General Charles S. O'Malley,

Jr., commander of the troops defending the Pentagon—Task Force Inside—wanted to ring the building with triple concertina wire or, failing that, a six-foot fence. That idea went nowhere. Drawing on his experience as an engineer, Graves proposed fashioning long, triangular-shaped barriers using four-inch pipes. The barriers would not hurt anybody who pressed against them, yet would remain stable even if protesters flipped them over. But this suggestion was rejected too.

McNamara and Under Secretary of the Army David McGiffert, who was in charge of the building's defensive preparations, were determined to present an image of a tolerant and beneficent Pentagon. They did not want many troops outside, and they did not want barricades. "They didn't want to put up any kind of barrier because they felt the media would interpret that as a fortress mentality, and I think probably they're right," Graves recalled. "I wasn't thinking about it in those terms. I was thinking, 'These poor soldiers needed something between them and those guys.' "

A line of MPs—575 in all—were standing ten feet apart, protecting the two long flanks of the building facing the demonstrators. The soldiers wore plastic helmet liners, without the steel covers, and were dressed in their Class As—jacket-and-tie uniforms appropriate for office duty, not a riot. They were armed with pistols and nightsticks. Behind them, spread out in five-man teams, stood 236 U.S. federal marshals, white helmets on their heads and batons in their hands. A strand of rope, held by rickety wooden stands, protected the government line.

A northeast wind was rippling the trees and shrubs around the Pentagon; after a quarter-century, the plants had matured and softened the edges of the great building. It was a spectacular Indian-summer day, with cool temperatures in the morning warming by afternoon to sixty-eight degrees.

McNamara went to the Pentagon roof to get a better view, scampering near the low parapet like a mountain goat. His bodyguard, Army Chief Warrant Officer Reis Kash, tailed nervously behind, wondering how he would explain if he let the secretary of defense fall off the Pentagon.

From his sweeping vantage point atop the Mall entrance, McNamara was oblivious to the concern. Instead, he stared at the tens of thousands of marchers approaching the Pentagon. "Christ, yes, I was scared," McNamara later said. "You had to be scared. A mob is an uncontrollable force."

The true and high church

It had been almost exactly twenty-five years since George Marshall and Henry Stimson had moved into the Pentagon in November 1942, but no celebrations were planned in the fall of 1967. In the five years since the Cuban Missile Crisis, the tiny American presence in Vietnam had escalated with the introduction of ground forces in 1965 and would soon reach 500,000 troops, with no end in sight. By October, more than 13,000 Americans had been killed and 86,000 wounded. Public opinion was turning against the war, fired both by the growing number of casualties and by reports on great suffering in Vietnam. By mid-1967, for the first time, a near-majority of Americans believed the war was a mistake.

The targeting of the Pentagon by antiwar demonstrators reflected the sinister image that it had assumed in the minds of many Americans. The building had come to personify the "military-industrial complex" that President Dwight D. Eisenhower had warned of six years earlier. The building's very size and shape made it the perfect outlet for hostility. Norman Mailer, who would march with the demonstrators and win the Pulitzer Prize for his account of the event, *The Armies of the Night*, wrote that the protesters ". . . were going to face the symbol, the embodiment, no, call it the true and high church of the military-industrial complex, the Pentagon, blind five-sided eye of a subtle oppression which had come to America out of the very air of the century . . ."

There had been previous demonstrations at the Pentagon, the most shocking two years earlier, in the twilight of a November evening in 1965. Standing near a wall on the River terrace outside the building, within sight of the secretary of defense's office, a thirty-one-year-old Quaker from Baltimore named Norman R. Morrison doused himself with fuel and burned himself to death. He had been holding his one-year-old daughter in his arms, but at some point—whether before or after flames shot up his body is uncertain—the child ended up on the ground, uninjured. Horrified Pentagon workers ran toward them. An Air Force sergeant and an officer tried beating out the flames that were consuming Morrison, but it was too late. McNamara, called to his window by an aide, saw the aftermath and was deeply shaken.

By 1967, protests had became a regular feature of life in the Pentagon.

In February, some 2,500 well-dressed women—most carrying large blue shopping bags emblazoned with "Mothers Say Stop the War in Vietnam" in bold green letters—angrily descended on the building. The "shopping-bag brigade," as *The Washington Post* called them, shouted antiwar slogans at the River entrance, and several women heatedly banged on the doors of the Pentagon with the heels of their shoes in a futile attempt to meet with McNamara.

The march on the Pentagon on October 21, 1967, was shaping up to be something entirely different. The National Mobilization Committee to End the War in Vietnam—the Mobe, as it was known—had vowed to "shut down the Pentagon" in what it promised would be the greatest antiwar protest in history. The Mobe included a vast array of peace groups and radical organizations with conflicting agendas under its umbrella—"Ghandi and Guerrilla" and most everything in between, as Mobe chairman David Dellinger said.

A healthy dose of comic absurdity was thrown in. Abbie Hoffman, cofounder of the radical Youth International Party (Yippies) and a showman in the tradition of P. T. Barnum, announced plans to use the psychic energy of thousands of protesters to levitate the Pentagon three hundred feet in the air, where it would turn orange and vibrate until all evil spirits spilled out. Several hundred hippies in New York City's East Village practiced on a table-size cardboard model, chanting ecstatically as wires raised the model Pentagon—illuminated by psychedelic lights—into the air. Hoffman and cohort Marty Carey also made a reconnaissance of the Pentagon to calculate how many "witches" would be needed to encircle the building. "Marty brought some incense and Tibetian bells, we improvised an Apache war dance and proceeded to measure at arm's length the distance from one corner to the next," Hoffman later wrote. They measured off 103 lengths before MPs took them into custody.

Not everyone was amused. The White House complained that antiwar protests were aiding Communist forces in Vietnam. The Army, to which McNamara assigned the responsibility for defending the Pentagon, viewed the pending march through the prism of deadly race riots that had flared in the summer of 1967, including one in Detroit that left forty-three people dead. In a speech from the pulpit of a Washington church on July 27, the militant black leader H. Rap Brown advised black residents to "get you some guns" and "burn this town down." Violence, he told reporters that day, "is as American as cherry pie."

When the Mobe held a press conference in August describing its plans to block entrances to the Pentagon and disrupt its activities, Brown was among the organizers who spoke, setting off alarms within the Army. "I may bring a bomb, sucker," Brown announced. Moreover, Mobe organizers described plans for simultaneous rallies in black neighborhoods in Washington. Army planners envisioned a nightmare scenario in which tens of thousands of demonstrators intent on attacking the Pentagon might spill over and ignite a race riot in Washington.

"This confrontation was no ordinary one," said an Army report written two weeks after the march. ". . . The government's response thus had to be extraordinary, if it were to deal with all aspects of the challenge—physical, psychological, political and international—in a manner worthy of the nation."

This "extraordinary" response included spying on Americans. Following the lead of President Lyndon B. Johnson, who had instructed the CIA and FBI to begin surveillance of antiwar leaders, General Johnson on October 14 approved electronic eavesdropping on the Pentagon demonstrators, despite a congressional prohibition against it. The Army Security Agency was authorized to monitor citizens, police, taxi, and amateur radio during the march, something never previously done. The agency was also told to jam radio transmissions if necessary. The National Security Agency hunted for evidence of "foreign influence" among march organizers, another unprecedented measure.

In the days before the march, soldiers flew in from around the country, including contingents of military police from the Presidio in San Francisco, Fort Hood in Texas, and Fort Dix in New Jersey. Troops were also sent from ten Army installations in Virginia, Maryland, North Carolina, and Georgia, among them elements of the 3rd Infantry Regiment, the 6th Armored Cavalry Regiment, and the 91st Engineer Battalion.

The Army also wanted to bring up a brigade of paratroopers from the elite 82nd Airborne Division in Fort Bragg, North Carolina, and hold it in reserve at Andrews Air Force Base outside Washington in case of riots. Attorney General Ramsey Clark opposed the move, but the Army hotly protested. "I can appreciate the image implications associated with the At-

torney General's decision, but from a military standpoint I regard it impru-
dent and, indeed, dangerous not to pre-position this brigade," Brigadier
General Harris W. Hollis, director of operations for the chief of staff, told
superiors. At the last minute, shortly before 11 P.M. Friday night, President
Johnson approved the deployment. C-130 transports flew into Andrews
through the night and all 2,900 paratroopers were in position at the base by
shortly after noon on Saturday. Some forty Army helicopters, forty-five
buses, and sixty-four trucks were staged at Andrews, ready to move the
brigade to the Pentagon or wherever needed around Washington. In all,
more than 12,000 soldiers, National Guard troops, federal marshals, and
civilian police officers were available in the Washington area; another
25,000 troops around the country had their weekend passes denied and
were on alert in case needed.

For all the extraordinary measures, an overriding concern was that it all
be hidden from public view. It was a cynical deception, of course, yet in part
also a sincere effort to demonstrate tolerance. McGiffert, the under secretary of the Army, argued that this stance would give the Pentagon the moral
high ground. One of the Army's goals for the march, he told McNamara
on the morning of October 21, was "to show the world that in troubled
times this nation is strong enough and confident enough to permit expres-
sions of criticism which few other governments would dare tolerate."

The zeal to show tolerance, however admirable, had created an atmosphere in which appearances were more important than practicality. Most
troubling was the convoluted command structure. General O'Malley was
the operational commander, but in name only. General Johnson retained
overall military command, including any decision to load weapons, fix bayonets, or use tear gas. Yet Johnson had little authority himself. McNamara
retained the final decision on the use of force. "I told the president no rifle
would be loaded without my permission, and I did not intend to give it,"
McNamara later wrote. At the insistence of the White House, the attorney
general's approval was needed not only for making arrests but also for
committing the reserves hidden in the building. Civilian direction was supposed to be shared by McGiffert and Deputy Attorney General Warren
Christopher, who would be positioned at the Pentagon, but decisions on
the use of force and reinforcements would have to be cleared by Attorney
General Clark, the overall coordinator of the federal response, over a hot-

line connecting the operations center to the Department of Justice command post in Washington. O'Malley had less power than a traffic cop.

The day before the march, at 4:45 on Friday afternoon, General Johnson brought all the military commanders together in the Army Operations Center. Johnson was a tough, spare North Dakota native, a West Point graduate with little political tact. Taken prisoner by the Japanese in the Philippines in 1942, Johnson survived the Bataan Death March, weighing ninety pounds upon his liberation in 1945. He had seen some of the toughest fighting in Korea, from the Pusan breakout on, and had been awarded the Distinguished Service Cross for extraordinary heroism. Johnson was not particularly worried about the demonstrators descending on the Pentagon.

The Army chief of staff told his commanders that he had met with McNamara and the service secretaries, and the message was clear: "This is looked upon as fundamentally a public relations problem," Johnson said.

The situation became extremely fluid

A vast cross-section of America came marching across Memorial Bridge toward the Pentagon on the afternoon of Saturday, October 21. More than fifty thousand people had rallied late in the morning at the Lincoln Memorial for speeches and songs, though not all continued to the Pentagon. Claims by organizers of 100,000 or more marchers notwithstanding, counts made by two intelligence agencies of the number of protesters crossing the bridge—and corroborated by analysis of high-resolution photographs made by a Navy Skywarrior reconnaissance plane—put the figure closer to 35,000. It was by any measure an impressive and powerful showing, far exceeding any Pentagon demonstration before or since.

The great majority of marchers were intent on a peaceful demonstration; for many it was an act of conscience against a war they deeply opposed; for others it was simply a lark, a chance to join in the excitement of a youth movement challenging authority and promising free love. A much smaller but not insignificant number of marchers were intent on destruction. Army intelligence concluded after the march that there had been "probably fewer than 500 violent demonstrators; however these violent types were backed by from 2,000 to 2,500 ardent sympathizers." The actions of this hardcore minority would dominate the day and form the lasting impressions of the march.

Marching at the front, arms linked, were prominent antiwar demonstrators including Dave Dellinger, Jerry Rubin, Norman Mailer, the poet Robert Lowell, and Benjamin Spock, the beloved pediatrician and author of books on raising babies (an Army report noted with suspicion that he advocated "permissive child rearing"). Great cheers greeted a contingent of veterans of the Lincoln Brigade, who had fought the fascists in Spain and now marched carrying a sign reading "No More Guernicas." The crowd was mostly young, with sizable contingents of middle-aged and older protesters. Many of the college students looked as if they were dressed for a homecoming football game, the men in tweed jackets and flannels, the women in stylish skirts and stockings. Long-haired hippies wearing love beads and leather bells lent a colorful shade to the crowd.

High on spirit but low on organization, the marchers started and stopped their way across the bridge with excruciating slowness beginning about 1:45. Arriving in Virginia, Mailer got his first glimpse of the Pentagon, which he likened to the five-sided nozzle on a can of antiperspirant, "spraying the deodorant of its presence all over the fields of Virginia." The demonstrators marched through the fields of the old Arlington Farm and on to the concrete fortress. The route marked by police channeled marchers into the North parking lot, where a platform had been set up for speeches at a spot more than a thousand feet from the Pentagon, separated from the building by an eight-foot chain-link fence, a four-lane roadway, an abandoned railroad line, and an embankment. Protesters were also allowed to assemble on a large grassy triangle much closer to the building, directly below the raised Pentagon Mall plaza. But access to the grassy area was not clearly marked, and many arriving marchers were under the impression they were fenced off from the building. Demonstrators, Mailer among them, milled about in confusion, unsure of where to go or what to do. "No enemy was visible, nor much organization," he wrote. "[T]he parking lot was so large and so empty that any army would have felt small in its expanse."

Walter Teague and several hundred militants from a group known as the Revolutionary Contingent had a distinct purpose in mind. After crossing the bridge, they tore off from the main body and raced toward the building. Teague, a thirty-one-year-old New Yorker and tough veteran of the radical movement, wearing a white crash helmet on his head and a gas mask strapped to his side, ran at the forefront, flanked by two demonstrators carrying fifteen-foot staffs with the red, blue, and gold flag of the Viet Cong. "Our specific goal was to create a confrontation—a nonviolent one, because they were military and we were not—and make a physical effort to get into the Pentagon," Teague recalled nearly forty years later. Scouts dispatched by Teague found—or created—a gap in the roadway fence that separated the North parking lot from the Pentagon, and they ran for it. At 3:59, a call came in to the Army operations center warning that at least two hundred demonstrators, some armed with ax handles and gas masks, had broken through the fence and were charging the River entrance, which had been left even more lightly guarded than the Mall.

Chanting "Viva Che!"—Guevara, the Latin American revolutionary, had been captured and executed in Bolivia two weeks earlier—the shock troops rushed toward a line of a dozen MPs, who waited with their riot sticks held high. Teague called for his colleagues to slow down and link arms. The first row of demonstrators slammed into the soldiers, and the Battle of the Pentagon was on. A protester swung a picket sign at a soldier, a U.S. marshal grabbed a Viet Cong flag, and an MP clubbed a protester in the back. More demonstrators followed the lead of Teague's shock troops and rushed through gaps in the fence; as the crowd grew, it flowed toward the Mall entrance and was soon pressing at the rope barrier.

It was quickly apparent that the whole low-profile strategy had backfired. Rather than somehow mollifying the advancing protesters, the sight of the Pentagon guarded by a thin green line seemed only to encourage those intent on attacking the building. "The low visibility philosophy may have developed an air of over confidence on the part of demonstrators and encouraged violence," an Army report written soon after the march concluded. Teague, for one, was both surprised and relieved there were not more soldiers protecting the Pentagon.

O'Malley, the operational commander, recognized instantly that his men were in trouble, and at 3:59 requested reinforcements from the building to block the demonstrators. Minutes later, Johnson, McGiffert, and Christopher agreed to send troops to the River entrance and the Mall plaza. But the reinforcements could not be dispatched until approved by Attorney

General Clark across the river in Washington. The call was made and they waited.

From his office window, Deputy Secretary of Defense Paul Nitze watched with alarm as demonstrators advanced below on the River entrance. At 4:03 he called McGiffert. "What gives?" Nitze asked. "Are you going to let them come up there?"

The crowd at the Mall plaza was likewise surging, and at 4:12 demonstrators on one side broke through the useless rope barrier and began shoving MPs. Still no approval had come from Clark, and no reinforcements were allowed out of the building, despite the rapidly deteriorating situation. Five minutes later, at 4:17, the operations center received Clark's O.K. A minute later—nearly twenty minutes after O'Malley had initially requested them—soldiers came running out of the building, some with sheathed bayonets fixed to their M-14 rifles. They were able to contain the crowd, and demonstrators who did not fall back were arrested by U.S. marshals.

Soldiers were not supposed to fix bayonets without Johnson's authorization, which the chief of staff had not given; subordinates later blamed the confusion on the stress of the moment but did not pretend to be apologetic about it. "The vision of the fixed bayonets by the incendiary demonstrators was regarded by many as a psychological plus in containing the restive crowd," an Army report said. McGiffert, though, was unhappy when he saw the sheathed bayonets on television monitors. "This is not in accordance with instructions," McGiffert complained to Johnson. At 4:25, Johnson ordered the bayonets removed.

The violence was kept momentarily at bay, but the twenty-minute free-for-all had emboldened the crowd and encouraged a sense of anarchy. "From this point on, the situation became extremely fluid," an Army report said. More protesters moved up, many not looking for trouble but soon caught up in the chaos.

At the rope barriers, a small but vocal group of demonstrators— usually those hiding several rows back—taunted and abused the troops. "They spat on some of the soldiers in the front line at the Pentagon and goaded them with the most vicious personal slander," James Reston of the *New York Times* reported. Others pelted troops with eggs, overripe tomatoes, fish, and plastic bags filled with beef liver. The soldiers, under orders to hold the line but left without masks or protective shields, made easy targets.

Captain Phil Entrekin, the commander of the 6th Cavalry's 1st Squadron, C Troop and a Vietnam veteran, considered the lack of protection afforded his soldiers the "dumbest decision" he would see in more than twenty years with the Army. "Our kids were standing there and having all kinds of things thrown at them, to include feces," he recalled.

Ernie Graves, accompanying Secretary of the Army Resor and other senior Army officials inside the Pentagon as they monitored the demonstration, was burned up by what he saw. "My own personal reaction was that it was somewhat of a travesty to put these soldiers out there in what I saw as a disadvantageous position and let these people abuse them," Graves said. "I frankly thought it was cowardly."

Out, demons, out!

Elsewhere, the crowd was more entertaining than ugly. Abbie Hoffman, wearing a tall Uncle Sam hat, went about his effort to levitate the Pentagon, but did not get far. He and his wife, Anita, split their last tab of LSD, held hands, and approached the building until they were stopped by MPs. "We're Mr. and Mrs. America, and we declare this liberated territory," Hoffman cried.

Nearby in the North parking lot, from atop a flatbed truck equipped with a sound system, musicians sounded an Indian triangle and a cymbal. They were "The Fugs," an underground music group from New York assisting with the levitation. Coming upon the scene, Mailer described them in their orange, yellow, and rose capes, as looking "at once like Hindu gurus, French musketeers, and Southern cavalry captains." The Fugs offered a sing-song litany of exorcism, chanting "Out, demons, out!" for a full fifteen minutes. A supporting cast of flower children sang their own hopeful incantations.

The Pentagon, by most accounts, did not move.

Hippies danced up to the lines of soldiers and placed flowers in the muzzles of their rifles. Some soldiers shook out the flowers, but one young soldier stayed motionless, unsure what to do. His sergeant solved the prob-

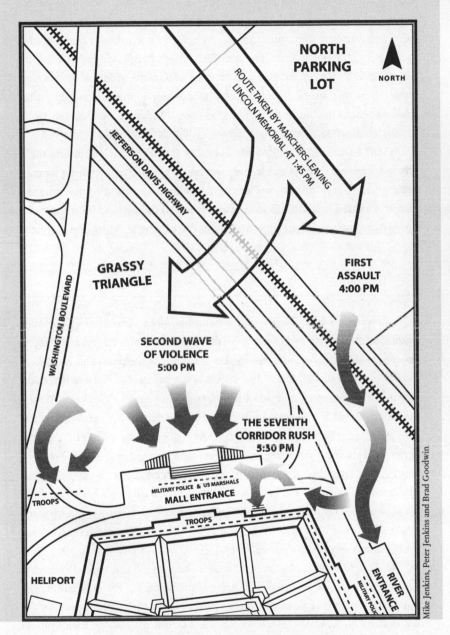

The following text labels appear within the map image:

NORTH PARKING LOT

NORTH

ROUTE TAKEN BY MARCHERS LEAVING LINCOLN MEMORIAL AT 1:45 PM

JEFFERSON DAVIS HIGHWAY

GRASSY TRIANGLE

FIRST ASSAULT 4:00 PM

WASHINGTON BOULEVARD

SECOND WAVE OF VIOLENCE 5:00 PM

THE SEVENTH CORRIDOR RUSH 5:30 PM

MILITARY POLICE & US MARSHALS
MALL ENTRANCE

TROOPS

TROOPS

HELIPORT

RIVER ENTRANCE

MILITARY POLICE

The march on the Pentagon, October 21, 1967.

lem. "Jones, get that fucking flower out of your muzzle," the sergeant ordered.

Some women went about trying to convert the soldiers, flirting with them or making impassioned if ponderous antiwar arguments. Others were simply crude and mocking. Some women tested the soldiers' resolve by trying to unzip their flies; one coarsely propositioned the troops, promising to take them to the bushes if they would drop their rifles. "Of course, none of the soldiers said anything," wrote Allen Woode, who witnessed the episode. "So, after trying this with several of the boys, she left, calling them all machines and fascists and fairies, and feeling smug." One young woman grabbed the groin of one of Captain Entrekin's C Troop soldiers; he reflexively butted her with his rifle, and she fell to the ground bleeding from her head. It was a violent sight that shocked soldiers and protestors alike.

The holy of holies

The first round of trouble at 4 P.M. was only a precursor for a second, more violent wave an hour later. Angry demonstrators surrounding the Mall plaza launched a three-pronged assault on the building. About a thousand protestors swarmed around the northeast corner of the plaza and moved on the River entrance, while another group broke off in the opposite direction toward the heliport and battled with troops manning roadblocks on Washington Boulevard. The main body of the crowd surged forward against the line of MPs at the Mall plaza, many of them cursing, throwing bottles and rocks, and slashing at soldiers with picket signs.

Frank Naughton, an Army military intelligence special agent posing as a reporter wearing slacks, a sports shirt, and a silly camera around his neck, saw a demonstrator kicking an MP who had fallen to the ground. Naughton, a big man, waded into the crowd and walloped the demonstrator. "I blew my cover," he recalled.

A platoon of MPs ran out to reinforce the sagging line at the front edge of the Mall plaza, where steps led up from the lawn, but they were immediately overwhelmed by demonstrators who overran the rope barriers. In the ensuing struggle, many MPs were knocked to the ground, an Army report said, and thirteen tear-gas grenades "were seized by the demonstrators who proceeded to employ them against the troops." As clouds of gas drifted about the Mall and River entrances, demonstrators, soldiers, and reporters alike gagged and felt their eyes burning; a female demonstrator fainted and at least one MP was overcome. Protest leaders later accused the Army of using tear gas; the Army indignantly blamed the demonstrators, and there is no evidence in the official record that the high command approved using tear gas. Based on eyewitness accounts and circumstantial evidence, it is fair to conclude that in the wild melee, both soldiers and demonstrators threw tear gas.

The protesters who had reached the Mall plaza also made good use of the worthless rope barriers. Knots were tied in the ropes and they were tossed down high walls that protected the plaza from the bulk of the demonstrators on the grassy triangle below. With the lines secured at the top, protesters below scaled the walls like mountain climbers to reach the plaza. Bill Ayers, a mop-haired, twenty-one-year-old militant from Michigan, watched the first wave of protesters climb the wall and then went up himself. The scene on the Mall plaza, with troops rushing about and tear gas floating in the air, felt to him like *Ten Days That Shook the World*.

Inside, McGiffert watched the disintegrating scene with disquietude. "No reason to hold back now," he told Christopher. More reinforcements were brought out of the building. At 5:05, 6th Cavalry troops burst out of the Mall entrance and ran down the steps with M-14 rifles and tried to restore order, and others were sent to the River and heliport sides.

It was not enough to stop the surging crowd. At 5:30, thirty demonstrators who had climbed a hill to the left of the Mall steps spotted an opening in the Army's flank. They rushed through it and ran for an open door to the left of the main Mall entrance. The Army's perimeter crumbled. Soon about two thousand demonstrators had broken through the Mall security line and pressed toward the building. The first thirty demonstrators, meanwhile, made it up the steps and victoriously stormed through the outer door. "The line was too thin and we just began pressing forward," twenty-four-year-old Leonard Brody of New York later said. "We were so surprised we made it through, we kept looking around to see if it was true." It was. The Pentagon—"the Holy of Holies," Mailer called it—had been breached.

The "Seventh-Corridor Rush," as it became known in Army reports, was the high-water mark of the march, but it did not last long. As soon as the protesters entered the door, a company of soldiers from the 91st Engineer Battalion waiting just inside the corridor came rushing out, smashing violently into the demonstrators. McNamara happened to be in the corridor and was nearly caught between the protesters and rushing soldiers. Kash, his bodyguard, pushed McNamara into the nearest office and held the door shut as the soldiers rushed by. The intruders were hit with rifle butts and driven back, leaving the steps spattered with blood. Four demonstrators made it past the inner door and into the building before they were pounced on by soldiers and roughly ejected. The entrance was secured by a thick wall of soldiers.

The Mall plaza remained in chaos. "They were closing ranks in front of the building, but by that time, hundreds and then thousands of people were up there," Ayers recalled. Hundreds of protesters ran up to the Pentagon walls, chased through the bushes by soldiers and marshals. Some of the demonstrators hurled rocks at the building, breaking five windows, including two in the press room. Others scrawled obscenities onto the limestone façade. "Crush Imperialism with Sex," someone wrote. Many took advantage of the opportunity to urinate on the building. Calling through bullhorns, protest leaders directed demonstrators to sit on the pavement and occupy the captured space.

In the operations center, General Johnson was fed up and urged force to clear out the intruders. "I think we ought to get some cold steel and start using some gas," the Army chief of staff told Christopher at 5:44. Christopher did not rule out unsheathing bayonets and using tear gas but told Johnson they should wait. "We should first attempt to move the people back with troops," the deputy attorney general said.

Yet the demonstration had peaked. As darkness fell, the crowd thinned, many boarding buses that were due to leave for distant cities, others trudging off on foot in search of something to eat. But several thousand hardcore protesters remained, including hundreds still occupying the Mall plaza. Johnson still wanted to use bayonets and gas to move them back. McNamara, after making another reconnaissance from the roof, turned him down. "Let boredom, hunger and cold take their course," the secretary said.

Most protesters managed to stay warm. Numerous bonfires sprung up, fed by the placards, pamphlets, and debris. "[W]hat prehistoric forms the dark bulk of the Pentagon must have taken from its spark, how the figures studying them with field glasses must have looked—how much like gargoyles on the ridge of a cathedral," Mailer wrote. Indeed, an intelligence report was soon sent to the Army operations center reporting on ten bonfires on the pavement and grass near the Mall entrance: "All are presently sitting around singing. . . . People appear to be cooking."

Boredom and hunger did not seem to be much of a problem either. Teams of protesters were dispatched to get food and drink from stores. "Beer came in, sandwiches, it was Saturday night—Saturnalia came in: couples began to neck on the grass, some awed by their audacity, some stimulated by the proximity of the Pentagon," Mailer wrote. The sweet smell of marijuana was everywhere.

Ayers celebrated on the Mall plaza with his girlfriend, Diana Oughton. "We sang and chanted, feeling jubilant to have gotten this close," he later wrote. "I peed on the Pentagon. I burned my draft card a foot from the line of troops, threw the ash on the ground and spit on it." A rumor—false, an investigation later established—swept the crowd that several soldiers had thrown down their weapons and defected, prompting wild cheers.

A three-quarters harvest moon rose over the Washington Monument. Around one fire in the middle of a road where the Mall and River sides meet, a group of young demonstrators sang "Down by the Riverside." Soldiers standing nearby removed their sheathed bayonets from their rifles and fastened them to their waists.

McNamara, Resor, and McGiffert silently surveyed the scene from the secretary of the Army's office overlooking the Mall. Colonel Graves stood behind them. The landscape around the Pentagon was lit by bonfires, illuminating the faces of the congregated demonstrators.

"Isn't it beautiful?" McGiffert remarked.

Graves struggled to contain himself. "I had to bite my tongue," he recalled. "I didn't think it was very beautiful."

Swept away

Whatever beauty there had been was quickly swept away. As the night wore on, Army commanders remained uneasy about the demonstrators still in the Mall plaza. McNamara, however, insisted "it would be a mistake to use force" unless the demonstrators were threatening the safety of others or damaging the building. Shortly before leaving the operations center around 11 P.M., McNamara reiterated that the demonstrators should be left where they were.

Trouble flared shortly before midnight when the marshals moved to evict demonstrators from a press trailer they had occupied on the plaza. Protesters around the trailer threw empty liquor bottles and kicked at soldiers and marshals. Chief U.S. Marshal James J. P. McShane—a burly former New York City policeman and onetime bodyguard for JFK—decided it was time to crack down. Soldiers from the 3rd Infantry Regiment at Fort Myer, in battle-dress uniforms, moved forward in a wedge, using rifle butts and boots to clear a path through the protesters, hitting them more indiscriminately than had the MPs who previously manned the line. Behind the wedge came the marshals, who clubbed dozens of demonstrators, even some lying passively, and dragged them off to be arrested. The restraint the government forces had shown most of the day disappeared. About three hundred were arrested during the sweep, more than had been during the day.

The absurdity was inescapable. In the critical first hours at the Pentagon, when a show of strength might have discouraged violence, the commanders' hands were tied. Then, late at night, at a time when the situation was largely under control and the top command had gone home or was paying little attention, heads were bashed. The coveted image of restraint sought by McNamara and McGiffert—bought at the cost of the soldiers left without barricades and reinforcement when they were needed—was washed away.

By dawn, only about two hundred demonstrators remained on the cold pavement, Bill Ayers among them. Hundreds more returned during the day, and there were flurries of arrests when protesters tried to push through the lines. At midnight Sunday, when the Mobe's forty-eight-hour demonstration permit expired, 150 remaining protesters sang "The Battle Hymn of the Republic" as they were arrested, put in vans, and hauled away.

Within minutes, crews began cleaning up the grounds. Workers carted away truckloads of debris, including beer cans, milk bottles, shoes, shirts, sweaters, and an unusual number of bras and panties. The last of the obscenities and slogans painted on the Pentagon walls were being cleaned off as employees arrived to work Monday morning. Official figures showed forty-five persons injured, seventeen of them seriously enough to be hospitalized. Injuries suffered by protesters included ten head wounds, a broken arm, and assorted hand, leg, and rib injuries; soldiers and marshals received eye and chest injuries. In all, 683 protesters were arrested, resulting in fifty-one jail terms of up to thirty-five days and $8,000 in fines.

O'Malley was seething, telling General Johnson and other senior Army commanders that his line at the Mall had been left too thin with no backup, and that his troops had taken "extreme physical and oral abuse" from the crowd. The delay caused by the need to get authority to use reserve troops "gravely hampered" the reaction to the violence, he said.

Nobody could argue with that. "Light military presence was directed in order to avoid bad press and to avoid inciting demonstrators," Colonel George M. Bush, McGiffert's military aide, told the under secretary. "I think that was fuzzy thinking. . . . I think we encouraged them to violation by not showing sufficient force." McGiffert agreed the restrictions had been a mistake, and two subsequent after-action reports, by the Military District of Washington and the chief of staff's office, reached the same conclusion.

Yet for all the missteps and miscalculations, the Army's defense of the Pentagon could not be called a failure. No one had been killed, and not a shot had been fired, something McNamara remained proud of nearly four decades later. There had been no race riot; a black nationalist rally in Washington had been peaceful. Some three thousand Pentagon employees had been at work during the demonstration—not much less than on a normal Saturday—and all critical operations were manned. The Pentagon had not been shut down.

The antiwar movement itself won few hearts and minds that weekend, as the acts of a violent and abusive minority of protesters dominated press coverage and overshadowed the respectful message of peace that most demonstrators sought to convey. The 1967 march on the Pentagon would prove a defining moment of division in the country, one that hardened attitudes on both sides.

A full load

Robert McNamara was waiting when the limousine carrying President Lyndon B. Johnson pulled into the Pentagon garage beneath the River entrance. It was shortly before noon on February 29, 1968, McNamara's last day at the Pentagon. Johnson, increasingly at odds with McNamara over how to handle the war, had nominated him several weeks after the Pentagon march to be president of the World Bank. McNamara would later say that he did not know whether he had been fired. ("The answer was that he had been," David Halberstam wrote in *The Best and the Brightest*.)

Out on the River terrace parade ground, a military honor guard and an audience of a thousand dignitaries and Pentagon workers waited under a leaden sky for the farewell ceremony to "the man known as the most efficient secretary in history," as the *Star* called him. A hard, cold rain began to fall.

Johnson and McNamara, accompanied by a retinue of aides, climbed into the elevator to ride up to the second floor, where they would descend the steps leading from the River entrance to join the ceremony. Master Sergeant Clifford Potter, the elevator operator, worked the controls. The elevator, packed with thirteen passengers, lurched and began rising, and then came to a quiet stop. At first no one suspected there was a problem, and then the reality set in: The president of the United States, the secretary of defense, and a host of aides were stuck on an elevator inside the Pentagon. Presidential aide Lawrence Levinson, one of those crammed into the elevator, wondered if a coup were underway.

McNamara, as always, tried to seize control of the situation. "Let me see if I can't get this to work," he said, reaching past the sergeant and pushing buttons on the panel. Nothing happened. McNamara directed Potter to turn the switch from manual to automatic. The elevator did not budge.

"You better use the telephone," McNamara said.

Potter opened the elevator's telephone box and got a maintenance man on the line. He told him the elevator was stuck.

"Do you have a full load?" the maintenance man asked.

"We sure do," the sergeant replied.

Johnson kept calm, even as a Secret Service agent wedged next to him made frantic radio calls. LBJ jokingly told McNamara he was going to take a line out of his speech saluting the efficiency the secretary had brought to the Pentagon.

Waiting outside in the rain—it was starting to sleet—Clark Clifford wondered where everybody was. Clifford had been on hand the dramatic day more than twenty years earlier when Jim Forrestal had been sworn in as the nation's first secretary of defense, and in two days it would be his turn. Since his days as a young naval aide to Truman, Clifford—tall, elegant, perpetually unruffled—had established himself as the premier Wise Man of Washington, and he was Johnson's choice to succeed McNamara.

Watching McNamara's last months in office, Clifford could not help but draw comparisons to Forrestal. He was not the only one. "We mustn't have another Forrestal," LBJ said privately in the summer of 1967. McNamara would later deny that he had been on the verge of an emotional collapse, but, he acknowledged, "I was tense as hell." Late one afternoon during his last year, pacing back and forth in his office as he considered a request to ship more ammunition to Vietnam, McNamara suddenly stopped and stared at the Forrestal portrait. As an aide looked on, McNamara's body shuddered with silent sobs. At the White House the day before the Pentagon retirement ceremony, McNamara had choked up and been unable to speak when the president awarded him the Medal of Freedom. Johnson had put his arm around him and led the secretary out of the room. To Clifford, silently watching, "it was an eerie echo of what Jim Forrestal had gone through nineteen years earlier."

Inside the Pentagon elevator, the air was getting stuffy. They had been stuck for ten minutes. Johnson told aide Will Sparks to wedge a notebook between the outer doors to get more air. Sparks managed to pry the doors open an inch, and, through the crack, they could see a landing, but no one knew which floor. Clint Hill, the exasperated head of the Secret Service detail, radioed his agents to go to every floor and "open the damn doors." Within two minutes they could see several people on the landing, including a maintenance man who promptly pried the doors open.

The elevator was still three feet below the landing, so someone grabbed a leather chair and put it inside the elevator, allowing LBJ and the others to climb out. The party found itself on the fourth floor, in the outer office of the under secretary of the Army. With McNamara in the lead, they raced down two flights of steps and came bursting out the River entrance. "At least this one didn't happen on your watch," someone quipped to Clifford.

The ordeal was not over. McNamara, wearing a blue suit with no hat or coat, stood in the driving rain as four 105 mm howitzers fired a nineteen-gun salute. A young aide held an umbrella over Johnson, but all it did was channel water onto McNamara's glasses, leaving the secretary "standing at attention going blind," as Johnson later recounted. The president took the podium: "I have heard this building referred to as the puzzle palace," he said. "Bob McNamara may be the only man who ever found the solution to the puzzle, and he is taking it with him." It was a nice tribute, but nobody could hear it: The rain short-circuited the public-address system. The climax of the ceremony, a scheduled flyover featuring the new Air Force F-111 all-weather fighter—a controversial McNamara initiative—was canceled due to the rain. Thoroughly soaked and chilled, McNamara saw Johnson off, went inside, and cleared his belongings out of the Pershing desk.

McNamara had served longer, and with more consequence, than any other secretary of defense. In the view of Clifford, one of the authors of unification, no one had done more to move the Pentagon "toward what we had intended it to be during the battle for military reform." Applying systems analysis—breaking complex issues down into their component parts for better understanding—to every problem he faced at the Pentagon, McNamara brought order to budget planning, curtailed duplication in weapons development, and contained the rivalry among the services. (Even the Pentagon march came in for the McNamara treatment: The protest leaders had not properly organized the demonstrators, McNamara later said; had he been in charge, "I absolutely guarantee you I could have shut down the whole goddamn place.") He applied the same techniques to Vietnam, Clifford wrote, failing to recognize that "Vietnam was not a management problem, it was a war, and war is about life and death, filled with intangibles that defy analysis."

McNamara had come to the building believing no problem could withstand rational analysis, and, at the end, he found himself imprisoned in a Pentagon elevator. Even McNamara appreciated the irony, though he could not quite put his finger on it. "God, it was symbolic of something," he later told writer Paul Hendrickson.

The bastards were going to get it

Much had happened in the more than four years since Bill Ayers jubilantly danced on the Pentagon Mall plaza during the 1967 march. Ayers followed an increasingly radical course, taking to the streets of Chicago for violent protest during the 1968 Democratic convention and the "Days of Rage" the following year. In 1969, he was among those who broke off from Students for a Democratic Society to form a more radical group, the Weathermen, taking their name from a Bob Dylan line: "You don't need a weatherman to know which way the wind blows."

The Weathermen wanted to use bombs to bring the Vietnam War home to what they called "Amerikan" soil, but their efforts did not begin well. In May 1970, Ayers's girlfriend, Diana Oughton, who had celebrated with him at the Pentagon, was among three Weathermen blown to bits when a homemade bomb meant for an Army dance at Fort Dix instead accidentally detonated in their Greenwich Village townhouse. Devastated by the loss, Ayers and other Weathermen went underground. A photograph of Ayers, head tilted and smirking, was on FBI wanted posters hanging on every post office wall in the country. Also featured on the posters was his new girlfriend and fellow Weatherman, Bernardine Dohrn, a black-leather and mini-skirt-wearing firebrand whom FBI Director J. Edgar Hoover labeled "the most dangerous woman in America."

The Weathermen retreated from bombing people after the Greenwich Village disaster and instead targeted government buildings. The group bombed the New York City police headquarters building in 1970 and a marble-lined bathroom in the U.S. Capitol building in 1971, both times with no casualties. By early 1972, the Weathermen—now variously also known as the Weather Underground or Weather People, after objections from female members—focused on a familiar target. "The Pentagon was ground zero for war and conquest, organizing headquarters of a gang of murdering thieves, a colossal stain on the planet, a hated symbol everywhere around the world," Ayers later wrote. In April 1972, when President Richard Nixon launched Operation Linebacker—a major bombing campaign against North Vietnam in response to a Communist offensive—the Weather Underground decided it was time to strike.

A team of three Weathermen—Ayers identified them only as "Anna and Aaron and Zeke"—was sent to the Washington area, where they rented a cheap apartment and scouted the Pentagon. The team learned what Pawel Monat and his fellow spies had discovered nearly two decades earlier: Despite the climate of the times, the Pentagon remained a remarkably open building. Anna, wearing office clothes, a dark wig, and thick glasses, her fingertips covered with clear nail polish to hide her fingerprints, entered the Pentagon every morning with hundreds of workers, walked the corridors, and ate breakfast in the cafeteria. No one ever challenged her. "Their reconnaissance led them deep into the bowels of the Leviathan, and they soon knew every hall and stairway, every cul-de-sac and office and bathroom," Ayers wrote.

In an Air Force section of the building, on the fourth floor, Corridor 10, Anna found a women's restroom that seemed isolated and had a floor drain in a toilet stall. On a subsequent visit, she measured the drain. Back in the apartment, Aaron fashioned a twelve-by-three-inch sausage-shaped bomb, tailored for the drain, with a timing device at one end. On the morning of May 18, Anna entered the Pentagon carrying a briefcase with the two-pound bomb hidden underneath papers and personal effects. She went to the selected restroom—4-E10W—and locked herself in the toilet stall. Anna took the screws out of the drain, popped off the cover, placed the bomb inside, and replaced the cover. She immediately left the building and linked up with Zeke at a prearranged meeting place. They were soon on a train out of town while Aaron closed down the operation, cleaning out their apartment. The bomb was set to go off at 1 A.M. the next morning, Friday, May 19, 1972—the date had been picked to honor Ho Chi Minh, the North Vietnamese leader who had died in 1969, on what would have been his eighty-second birthday.

Ayers awaited word on the operation from a safe house in another city where he lived with Dohrn. "Everything was absolutely ideal on the day I bombed the Pentagon," he later wrote. "The sky was blue. The birds were singing. And the bastards were finally going to get what was coming to them."

The bastards, in this case, were Rita Campbell and her cleaning ladies who scrubbed floors and toilets, picked up the trash, and dusted the offices on the Pentagon's fourth floor. The crack Weathermen reconnaissance had somehow missed the fact that custodians cleaned the Pentagon bathrooms at night. It was not a state secret, nor was it even surprising. Moreover, the Weathermen had chosen one of the busier locations in the building at that hour; just down Corridor 10 was a bustling mailroom filled all night with workers, many of them women.

At 12:42 A.M. on the morning of May 19, *Washington Post* operator Bernadine Gibson answered a telephone call from a man who identified himself as a "weatherman" and warned that a bomb would explode on the Pentagon's "eighth floor." Gibson immediately telephoned police in Washington to report the threat. The police department informed a night-duty officer at the Pentagon at 12:53, and the Pentagon officer quickly called the *Post* for more information. According to Ayers, Aaron also called the Pentagon from a telephone booth in Washington to warn that a bomb would explode in twenty-five minutes in the Air Force section of the building. No evacuation was ordered, probably because the information was too sketchy and there was little time to respond; the Pentagon often received bomb threats that turned out to be hoaxes.

In her office on the fourth-floor A Ring, Rita Campbell, the custodial foreman for the floor's cleaning force, looked at the clock on the wall. It was almost 1 A.M. The "zone ladies"—Mrs. Wilcox, Mrs. Delaney, Mrs. Colbert, and one other woman, all black and in their forties and fifties, friends who had cleaned the same zone together for years—would just about be finishing up in restroom 4-E10W, always their last stop before going to the locker room to change when their shift ended at 1:15 A.M.

Campbell was chatting with a colleague at 12:59 A.M. when the building shook and she heard an enormous boom. She rushed down the A Ring and around the corner to Corridor 10, where she saw a billowing cloud of black smoke. The mailroom people said the explosion had come from the far end of the corridor, where the restroom was.

"Oh, no, not the bathroom," Campbell called. "I hope not the bathroom."

She tried to get closer but somebody stopped her: "You can't go down there, Mrs. Campbell, because whatever was down there is gone."

The explosion had blown out a twenty-five-foot section of wall separating the restroom from the corridor. The lavatory was entirely destroyed, its ceiling buckled, its toilet stalls smashed, and a two-foot-wide hole blown in the concrete slab. Water was shooting in the air as thousands of gallons of water poured from broken pipes.

Campbell was frantic. "Where are the ladies?" she yelled. "Where are the ladies?" A voice finally called to her: "Here they are, Mrs. Campbell, they were in the locker room!" The ladies had finished early and sneaked off to change. Campbell recalled: "They were crying, we were all crying, they were apologizing for going to the locker room early, and I said, 'No, I'm glad you went to the locker room early, because if you hadn't, we would have lost four women.' "

Later that day, the Weather Underground issued a communiqué boasting that "today we attacked the Pentagon, the center of the American military command." No one had been hurt, though the explosion caused $75,000 in damage. The water gushing from the pipes soaked offices on the floors below, disabling an Air Force computer center and damaging the department store and Pentagon bookstore on the concourse. The cleaning ladies were terrified to return to work but all did; none could afford to lose their jobs.

At his safe house, Ayers found himself in "deepening shades of delight." He and Dohrn took time "to rejoice and congratulate ourselves and laugh some more." When interviewed in 2006, Ayers said he was unaware that cleaning crews had been working in the area. "I didn't know about it, and definitely had no intention of hurting anybody, and didn't hurt anybody," he said.

Terrorism had struck the Pentagon, though Ayers rejected the term. The Weathermen's surgical operation, he boasted, ensured no one would be hurt: "Terrorists destroy randomly, while our actions bore, we hoped, the precise stamp of a cut diamond." Rita Campbell had a different understanding of why no one was killed: "By the grace of God."

Does anyone know what really exists down here?

Air Force Lieutenant Colonel Alan Renshaw, assigned to the Pentagon in 1973, had a fourth-floor office just around the corner from the restroom blown up by the Weather Underground. His E-Ring office window gave him a bird's-eye view whenever the Berrigan brothers or other protesters came by to splatter goat's blood on the River entrance columns, which was pretty frequently. Security was tighter since the bombing; guards now checked identification for anyone entering the building, though the concourse shops remained open to the public. Some days, employees were told not to use the River entrance because of demonstrations. To keep a low profile, military personnel were discouraged from wearing their uniforms to work.

That was just life in the Pentagon these days, Renshaw figured. Still, after two tours overseas—one flying B-52 bombing missions over Vietnam out of Guam, and another planning the missions from Thailand—Renshaw enjoyed life in the building. Every now and then, when visitors expressed curiosity about the Pentagon, Renshaw would take them to the Mall entrance and show them the plaque. The ninth name down, after Roosevelt, Stimson, Somervell, Groves, and the others, was that of the engineer in charge of construction, his father.

Clarence Renshaw had gone on from the Pentagon to build Thule Air Force Base in Greenland, one of the toughest Arctic engineering jobs ever undertaken, and had retired in 1960 as a brigadier general in charge of all military construction for the Corps of Engineers. Living on Long Island, he was a convenient font of information for his son about the Pentagon's oddities. On an earlier assignment to the building, Alan Renshaw worked out of the Air Force operations center in the basement, and he noticed the floor was often wet after heavy rain. "The water would actually squirt up through the floor from below," he recalled. Clarence Renshaw was not surprised in the least. He blamed it on the decision to put the Pentagon in Hell's Bottom, telling his son, "it was almost like a boat, on that swampy, no-good piece of property."

It did not help that the basement slab had been poured directly on top of the wet, organic fill dredged from the lagoon. Over the years, the building's weight had compressed the soil, forcing out water. "As the building gets older, it's going to find ways to get inside the building," Clarence Renshaw told his son. As usual, he was right.

The Pentagon was aging badly. As the symbol of American national security, the Pentagon seemed invincible, the nerve center of the mightiest military power in the world. Inside the building, the truth was more prosaic. By the 1970s, decades of neglect and shoddy maintenance had left the Pentagon a dump, with broken plumbing and wheezing ventilation. After Vietnam, the hollow condition of the American military seemed reflected in the deteriorating corridors of the Pentagon. Windows were rusting, walls shifting and settling, and cornices disintegrating. In the light courts and center courtyard, the concrete walls were spalling, exposing rusted re-inforcing bars. Cracks and water stains were visible everywhere. Inside, the corridors were awash with vehicles; the old bicycle carts had been largely replaced by fleets of gas- or electric-powered carts, which gouged holes in the walls, demolished hallway corners, and occasionally ran over pedestrians (among them Eugene Zuckert, secretary of the Air Force under McNamara, felled at an intersection near his office).

The great office bays where Marjorie Hanshaw and her fellow plank walkers once worked had been divided up into rabbit warrens. The building's mechanical systems, designed for the large spaces, could not operate properly. Some parts of the building would be roasting while in other parts people wore sweaters year-round. Corridors had been walled off with cin-derblocks to make more space for the ever-increasing secretary of defense staff, putting further stress on the building.

Soon after taking office in 1975, the new secretary of defense explored the outer reaches of the building. Donald Rumsfeld—at forty-three the youngest man ever to serve in the position—was appalled at the general shabbiness. "It was dreary and bleak and the corridors were bare," Rums-feld recalled more than thirty years later. Many corridors were dim, a ves-tige of an LBJ-inspired campaign to save power by keeping some lights off. Rumsfeld ordered the lights back on, and a campaign was launched—tied to the American Bicentennial in 1976—to decorate the corridors. Paintings that had been sitting for years in basement storage rooms were hauled out and put on walls. Corridors were designated to honor George Marshall, Douglas MacArthur, and Hap Arnold—accompanied by photographs, paintings, and displays—joining ones previously created for Dwight Eisenhower and Omar Bradley. Dozens more followed over the years—featuring presidents, recipients of the Medal of Honor, wars and events—turning the Pentagon into something of a military museum. Rumsfeld ordered the Pentagon opened for tours in an effort "to demystify" the place. Tourists once again wandered the building, albeit with escorts.

The corridors were spruced up, but the rot within the building contin-ued unabated. The General Services Administration took a penny-wise, pound-foolish approach to caring for the building, routinely deferring im-portant repairs and maintenance. GSA administrators were intimidated by its sheer bulk. Renovating most federal buildings was one thing, but the

Pentagon might eat up the entire GSA budget. The twenty-nine-acre coal-tar roof regularly leaked but had never been replaced. Nothing was done about deteriorating pipes throughout the building. To Walt Freeman, the Defense Department's facilities manager, it was like dealing with an absentee landlord. Freeman warned that the Pentagon's ancient coal-fired boilers would not last much longer and needed to be replaced. GSA officials said they would study it, and they kept their word: They studied it.

In 1984, Steve Carter took a job in the operations and maintenance shop at the Pentagon. He had retired from the Navy as a machinist's mate first class after fourteen years in ships' engine rooms; looking for a little income, he figured the Pentagon assignment would be a no-headaches, no-pressure type of job. Surely the headquarters of the American military would be in tip-top shape. Carter was quite shocked by the reality. "I expected to come in here and see a state-of-the-art facility, all the gee-whiz stuff," he recalled. "When I reported aboard it was mainly a manually operated building with mostly 1940s technology." The building manager's office did not have a single computer. Service tickets were written on paper and stored in cardboard boxes. If somebody wanted to know how many power outages there had been in the last year they would have to take out the boxes and sort through the tickets.

Even more worrisome was the condition of the building's infrastructure. The basement was worse than ever. The construction of the Metro subway line to the Pentagon in the mid-1970s aggravated the problem; water was pumped out of the ground and the soil compressed further, leaving voids under the building. The basement slab had bellied down a foot or more in places and groundwater came in through the cracks. "We joked about it being tied to the tides," said Carter. "It seemed that way. We'd get a good rain outside and the water level would pick up for the next two or three days." The basement floor was so warped that forklifts in the Pentagon printing office sometimes toppled over. The ancient air handlers in the basement were rusted out. Carter found he could take a ballpoint pen and poke a hole in the big sewer pipes that ran through the basement.

Carter started asking a question: "Does anyone know what really exists down here?"

Logo for the Pentagon renovation program.

CHAPTER 19

THE REMAKING OF
THE PENTAGON

If we're lucky the floods will be shallow

The Pentagon was bustling on the evening of Tuesday, August 7, 1990. It was C-Day—commencement day—the start of Operation Desert Shield, what would become the largest U.S. military deployment since the Vietnam War. The first elements of the 82nd Airborne's ready brigade were aboard C-141s, just a few hours from landing at Dhahran Air Base in Saudi Arabia. Two squadrons of F-15 Eagles had flown from Langley Air Force Base in Virginia—refueling in the air from flying tankers—and the first fighters were now starting combat air patrols over northern Saudi Arabia. At U.S. bases around the world, a vast armada was being mobilized.

Five days earlier, the Iraqi Army had rolled over the Kuwaiti border and captured the tiny oil-rich nation. Late on August 6, Secretary of Defense Dick Cheney telephoned General Colin Powell, chairman of the Joint Chiefs of Staff, from Saudi Arabia to report that King Fahd had accepted an offer of American troops to defend his kingdom against a feared further incursion by Iraqi forces.

The Army and Air Force operations centers in the Pentagon basement were packed; the temperature inside the Army facility—the air-conditioning inadequate as always—was approaching ninety degrees. It was a nerve-racking time. The fledgling American force was at its most vulnerable, arriving in Saudi Arabia with little combat power. Lead elements of two Iraqi Republican Guard divisions were staged within a mile of the Saudi border. If Iraqi leader Saddam Hussein chose to seize the vast Saudi oil fields twenty-five miles to the south—which the CIA was predicting—the lightly armed paratroopers of the 82nd would be little more than "speed bumps," as Powell put it. "We were going into a combat zone with a very small force initially, with no idea whether the Iraqi army would continue south or not," he recalled.

The coffee was flowing freely in all the operations centers, as usual during a crisis. In a small, secure room in the Joint Chiefs' area, somebody filled a cup and stuck the nearly empty pot back on the coffeemaker burner. At 7:30 P.M., the untended coffeepot started smoking profusely. The smoke was sucked into the ventilation system and began pouring out of ducts into pressurized command-center rooms. No one knew where the smoke was coming from. Arlington County firefighters rushed to the Pentagon for a two-alarm fire and hooked up a fire truck to a standpipe near the River entrance. As soon as they pressurized the system, a four-foot section of a deteriorated ten-inch water pipe blew out on the south side of the building. A torrent of muddy water began pouring into the Pentagon basement.

Steve Carter, the building engineer on watch that night, raced out of the Building Operations Center. The fire was now the least of the worries. Water was cascading down the hallways and spraying violently out of a crawlspace between corridors 9 and 10. Carter poked his head inside, trying fruitlessly to find the source of the leak, accomplishing little but getting soaked.

The pipe had burst in a steam tunnel that connected the Pentagon to the heating and refrigeration plant a thousand feet southeast of the building. The rupture was just outside the Pentagon, but close enough that it was blowing a tremendous volume of water and thick mud through the tunnel into the basement. Hundreds of thousands of gallons of water—eventually millions of gallons—poured into the building.

Inside the Air Force operations center—a good five hundred feet away from the rupture—the water was rising: two inches, four, eight, and count-

ing. Harried Air Force officers waded out in the hallways, pleading for someone to make the water stop. "They were rather excited," Carter recalled.
" 'This was a most inconvenient time,' was how it was explained to me."

Carter was most concerned by the rising water in a high-voltage electrical vault located in the building near the rupture. If the water reached the
current-bearing bus bars, there was imminent danger of electrocution.
Electricians Bobby McCloud and Reimund Schuster, called from their
homes to assist with the crisis, measured the distance of the rising water to
the bottom of the bus bars. The deluge had been pouring into the building
nonstop for more than an hour now and was over a foot high, within a few
inches of the bus bars. They had the power plant on standby, ready to shut
down the electrical feed to the vault. That would mean killing power to half
the building right as U.S. forces were moving into Saudi Arabia.

Schuster found a manhole outside the building leading to a shutoff
valve. The water rushing through the pipe was making an awful roar, like
a missile firing, and he feared it would blow up in his face if he shut off the
valve. "I finally decided, 'Ah, the hell with it,' " Schuster recalled. He shut
the valve and the water finally stopped rising, just in time. "It probably
only needed another two or three inches and we would have had to kill the
power," McCloud later said.

The smoky fire was long since contained, extinguished in twenty-five
minutes. The flood was another matter. The basement was a disaster zone.
A vast area—350,000 square feet—was under up to a foot and a half of
water, some three million gallons. Once it was pumped out, it took several
days to shovel out the deposit of thick mud left behind. The water inside
the Air Force operations center had reached fourteen inches. The heating
and refrigeration plant, lying at the other end of the steam tunnel on lower
ground than the Pentagon, was in even worse shape; its basement under
seven feet of water, and it was knocked out of service for two days. All
told, the flood had done about $1 million in damage.

Mechanical engineers were dispatched to find the cause of the flood. It
was no great mystery. The problem, they soon reported, was the old, deteriorated pipes. It could happen again anytime the system was pressurized.
"If we're lucky," said John Irby, one of the building supervisors, "the
floods will be shallow."

The horror board

Doc Cooke would later say he knew it was time to renovate the Pentagon when he saw fungus on the wall taking the shape of Elvis. By the time of the flooding fiasco during Desert Shield in August 1990, the sixty-nine-year-old Cooke had been sounding the alarm about the building for years. Just in March, he had described the Pentagon to a House subcommittee as "a chamber of horrors." As proof, he lugged along what had become known as "the horror board." It was a two-by-three-foot panel upon which Steve Carter had mounted evidence of the Pentagon's decay: chunks of loose wire, a rusted pipe with a pencil shoved through a soft spot, loose asbestos. The horror board was an effective prop, much better than any charts or figures.

David O. Cooke had many titles—presently it was Director of Administration and Management for the Secretary of Defense—but he was known universally as the "Mayor of the Pentagon." Doc—the nickname came from his initials—was the keeper of the keys, the man who dispensed the prime offices and kept everything working. Bald and cherub-faced, with the twinkling eyes of a man privy to secrets, Cooke knew every inch of the Pentagon's corridors.

Colin Powell had learned early on of the power Cooke wielded. When he was assigned to the Pentagon in 1984 as an aide to Secretary of Defense Caspar Weinberger, Powell took a colleague down to the parking lot one day to show him an old Japanese army rifle he had in the trunk of his car. From the fourth floor, an Air Force secretary spotted two men in the parking lot handling a rifle and called Pentagon police. A Defense Protective Services officer quickly arrived on the scene to take Powell into custody.

Powell tried to explain. "Look, I'm Major General Powell," he said. "I'm Secretary Weinberger's military assistant."

"Please come with me sir," the officer insisted. Powell was in the Pentagon basement waiting to be processed for arrest when Cooke got wind of what was happening and ordered him released. Cooke, as Powell later wrote, was "the chief fixer" for the Pentagon: "Want a private bathroom worthy of your rank as assistant secretary? Doc can install it. Can't get a parking place in the prestigious River Entrance lot? Try Doc. Need to spring a major general who is about to get busted? Doc's your man. His power was formidable, this Godfather of the Pentagon."

Defense secretaries and their staffs came and went like summer help, but Cooke stayed on as the building's chief administrator and trusted confidante to the powerful. Cheney was his twelfth secretary, and he had sworn in every one since Melvin Laird in 1969. Each secretary learned to depend on him. When they asked for something inappropriate, Cooke would turn them down, but he usually did it so gently they did not even realize they had been rejected.

Generations of Pentagon employees viewed Doc as a father figure, and he was always looking out for them. Steve Carter would often see him ambling around the hallways, talking to one and all, so approachable that many junior workers called him Doc. It was one reason why, unlike many powerful Defense officials, Cooke knew the situation on the ground, or in this case, the Pentagon basement.

The Pentagon did not meet any fire, safety, or health codes, nor had it for decades. There were no sprinklers, except in some computer rooms. The fire alarms were outdated and inadequate; it often took twenty minutes to locate a sounding alarm. There were no dampers in air, pipe, and cable shafts to stop the flow of smoke through the building, meaning corridors would draw smoke and turn into deathtraps in a fire.

The building had not met National Electrical Code standards since 1953. Electrical panel boards were overloaded and the building suffered twenty to thirty power outages a day, almost every time somebody plugged in a laser printer. Offices were poorly lit and gloomy. Disabled employees were relegated to using the building's twelve freight elevators, which had doors that closed from ceiling to floor, causing more than forty head injuries in one three-year period.

The asbestos used to save steel during World II threatened the health of Pentagon employees; research had established that airborne asbestos was a dangerous carcinogen. Constant leaks in the plumbing and roof had deteriorated the asbestos-laden ceiling plaster. Tests showed harmful fibers were being released into the air from ceilings, pipe insulation, and asbestos-lined air ducts throughout the building. Thousands of lighting fixtures contained highly toxic polychlorinated biphenyls (PCBs), windows had lead paint, and there was mercury in the ground.

Throughout the building, a sense of decay prevailed. The Pentagon was home to an estimated two million cockroaches, and the ones in the basement were said to have reached fearsome proportions, big enough to "put saddles on." Rats were enjoying a population boom, with an average of four a week caught in the food-service areas. The rats had no respect for rank, showing up in E-Ring offices as well as inner corridors with equal alacrity.

The General Services Administration had never replaced the boilers, though they were of a design dating back to the construction of the Panama Canal; only one of the five was still operating and the Pentagon was renting temporary boilers parked on flatbed trucks at a cost of $1.2 million a year.

With GSA showing little interest in renovating the Pentagon, Cooke decided in 1987 that the Defense Department should wrest control of the building from the agency. It was a risk, because the GSA made a convenient scapegoat. If the Defense Department took over, "you could no longer point a finger and say GSA is responsible," recalled Paul Haselbush, a Cooke deputy. But Cooke was convinced that the deteriorating conditions in the building left him no choice, and he went about staging a coup. The GSA was only too happy to rid itself of responsibility for the Pentagon and delegated day-to-day maintenance to the Defense Department. But GSA retained ownership, collecting hundreds of millions of dollars in rent from the Defense Department each year, but balking at renovation.

That had to change, and the basement flood was proof. An investigation by the General Accounting Office would soon report that among the 1,600 federally owned buildings nationwide, the Pentagon represented one of the two worst cases of neglect. The Pentagon had been left "seriously deteriorated and functionally obsolete" because of the GSA's repeated failures to repair and upgrade the building, the report concluded.

Cooke requested that Congress give the Defense Department ownership of the Pentagon in 1989 and was narrowly turned down, out of fear that every federal agency would then want a divorce from GSA. But in November 1990, largely based on the authority and respect Cooke had earned in all corners of Washington over the years, Congress passed legislation transferring ownership of the Pentagon from the GSA to the Department of Defense. The legislation allowed the Defense Department to deposit money that would have been paid in rent to the GSA into a fund that would not only operate and maintain the Pentagon but also pay for the renovation. Cooke moved forward on a ten-year, $1 billion renovation plan.

The timing turned out to be exceedingly poor. As the plans were final-ized, the Cold War suddenly and inconveniently ended, and with it much of the *raison d'être* for an enormous American military establishment. The So-viet Union collapsed in 1991, just two years after the fall of the Berlin Wall, and the threat that the Warsaw Pact posed to Western Europe evaporated. Iraq had been forcibly ejected from Kuwait in February 1991, and the Gulf War was now seen as an aberration, perhaps the last American conven-tional war. A painful drawdown of the military began, with dozens of bases to close and the size of the force to shrink 25 percent by 1995. The question was soon being asked in Congress and the press: Why was the Defense De-partment spending $1 billion to renovate the Pentagon at a time the fighting forces were being gutted? Politically, it did not look good, members of Congress told Cooke. The Pentagon, military affairs columnist David Hackworth wrote, "shouldn't be rebuilt. It should be blown up."

Several months before the renovation was set to begin in the summer of 1992, Congress put the plan on hold. Cooke did not give up. The horror board was updated with new exhibits, and for another year Cooke hauled it around town for all to see. "These hazards, if not corrected, could threaten the lives and health of the 25,000 employees in the Pentagon," Cooke told a Senate subcommittee in May 1993. Cooke was able to convince enough people on Capitol Hill of the urgent need for renovation. He soon had ap-proval to start, although one congressman made him promise that he would never again bring the horror board to Capitol Hill.

A certain respectability

It would have been cheaper—not to mention quicker and easier—to build a new Pentagon. The planned renovation would not only cost more than a billion dollars, it would be "one of the most complex construction projects ever undertaken," a consultant hired by the program predicted.

The plan began with an ambitious scheme to double the size of the basement. The ground slab would be jackhammered out, and in some parts the ground below excavated another three feet. Dropping the floor would leave room for both a basement and a mezzanine in a much larger area than previously existed. The plan called for adding some 1.1 million square feet of usable space, including room for a sophisticated new National Military Command Center and operations centers for all the services.

The rest of the Pentagon would be divided into five equal chevron-shaped wedges to be renovated in sequence. Renovation crews would follow the original path of construction, starting in the southwest wedge—the first section to be built and occupied—and working their way clockwise. The five thousand workers in the first wedge would be evicted, most of them going to rented office space in Northern Virginia; the rented offices would have to be upgraded and made secure for military use. Once vacated, the wedge would be entirely gutted, stripped down to concrete columns and slabs. Thousands of tons of hazardous materials would be removed. Then the wedge would be rebuilt from scratch, with state-of-the-art technology and new infrastructure. When it was finished, the employees in the second wedge would be moved into the newly renovated wedge, and the whole process repeated in the next wedge. The renovation was to take ten years. All the while, the work of the Pentagon would have to continue uninterrupted, twenty-four hours a day, seven days a week.

Later, when it was all going poorly, renovation program officials would study building a new defense headquarters at Fort Belvoir, the large Army post sixteen miles down the Potomac River in Fairfax County, Virginia. A five-story low-rise building—in the shape of a rectangle, but similar in size, with 6.5 million square feet and big enough for thirty thousand people—could be built for less than the $1 billion-plus estimated for renovating the Pentagon.

But there would be extra costs, perhaps including hundreds of millions of dollars to extend a subway line and expand the road network to Fort Belvoir. Moreover, the government could not simply lock up the Pentagon and leave, tempting as it might be. Demolishing the building would be a mammoth and expensive undertaking. If it were left open in some new capacity, all the asbestos, lead paint, mercury, and PCBs in the building would still have to be removed. It all added up to being at least as expensive as renovating the building.

More fundamentally, the idea of the military abandoning the Pentagon had become unthinkable, not unlike Congress moving out of the Capitol or the president leaving the White House. The Pentagon had none of the grace or beauty of those buildings, but it was every bit the American institution.

Though the building was reaching the depths physically, age had bestowed a certain respectability on the Pentagon. The fiftieth anniversary of its completion was marked on May 12, 1993—the date chosen to avoid winter weather—and, for the first time, the Pentagon itself was celebrated. On the warm spring morning, hundreds of dignitaries, old-timers, and Pentagon employees gathered for a grand ceremony on the River terrace lawn. Four howitzers fired in salute, an honor guard presented the colors, the Army band played, and an enormous American flag suspended from a crane waved over the lawn. General Colin Powell, now chairman of the Joint Chiefs of Staff, paid affectionate tribute to the Pentagon:

> The Eiffel Tower may be more impressive, the Taj Mahal more exotic, the pyramids more mysterious, and St. Peter and St. Paul's basilicas more sublime. But the Pentagon has stood . . . for half a century as a powerful and renowned symbol of America's convictions, America's power, and of America's willingly accepted obligation to the world. In its somber and unpretentious way, it has weathered time, it has weathered wars, it has weathered innumerable crises, and it has weathered the storm of politics.

The building so reviled by so many had been deemed a national treasure. Secretary of the Interior Bruce Babbitt presented a bronze plaque declaring the Pentagon to be a National Historic Landmark. The Pentagon was now considered an integral part of the grand vision that the defenders of L'Enfant had battled to protect five decades earlier. "Its configuration, role, and location have combined to make the Pentagon an essential and important physical and symbolic element of the Monumental Core of the Nation's Capital," the National Park Service nomination proclaimed.

Even the much-mocked design was found worthy of preservation; the building was saluted as an important example of stripped classical style. "Architecturally, the Pentagon is a remarkable example of complex, yet highly efficient, design," the nomination said. "It is virtually a small urban center under one roof, containing all the functions normally associated with a municipality." The building's unparalleled size and the "monumental effort in design and construction" made it further unique. Five elements of the building were given historic status: the five outer façades; the center courtyard and surrounding façades; the Mall terrace; the River terrace; and the distinctive five-sided shape.

Finally, the figures who had strode along its corridors—from Marshall and Stimson, to Forrestal, Eisenhower, McNamara, Powell, and many others—and the decisions they made, for better or worse, in its command centers and executive suites—about the atomic bomb, the Cuban Missile Crisis, Vietnam, and beyond—pointed irrefutably to the extraordinary role the building had played in American history since World War II. The Pentagon, the nomination concluded, "is of an exceptional level of historic significance."

The Pentagon was now officially a landmark. There was no choice but to fix it.

They wanted the noise to stop

It was shades of 1942. The "rata-tat-tat" of jackhammers always seemed to be followed by the "whomp-whomp" of impact drills. Pentagon employees soon were complaining of incessant noise, clouds of dust, black sootlike residue that coated desks, and various unpleasant odors emanating from the basement.

Construction of a new heating and refrigeration plant had begun the previous year, but the beginning of the basement work on October 17, 1994, marked the real start of the Pentagon renovation. Cooke had been eager to begin before Congress again changed its mind. His office—Washington Headquarters Service—had overall management of the renovation, but as was the case a half-century earlier, the U.S. Army Corps of Engineers was in charge of design and construction, overseeing the work done by the prime contractor—the Clark Construction Group, headquartered in Bethesda, Maryland.

The first work involved one-third of the basement, a 200,000-square-foot segment beneath the corner of the Mall and River sides. Workers in protective clothing removed all asbestos-bearing material in the ceiling plaster, floor tiles, insulation, and elsewhere. Next, demolition crews gutted the interior down to the columns. Then workers jackhammered the basement slab, and Mini Diggers excavated the first of 45,000 cubic yards of soil that would be hauled from the basement. It was chaotic work. Crews jackhammered one slab unaware that they were atop a top-secret Air Force communications room. Shocked Air Force workers below watched helplessly as concrete fell from the ceiling.

It was not long before other problems were uncovered. The renovators learned to their surprise that some of the fifty-year-old drawings—the ones Ides van der Gracht and his army of draftsmen had churned out in the old Eastern Airlines hangar—often had little connection with reality. "What we thought was in the foundation and what was there were actually quite different," said Ken Catlow, a Corps of Engineers supervisor. Moreover, conditions were much worse than anyone had imagined. Spectral analysis indicated the soil would continue to sink for another fifty years, depending on the height of the water table. Much of it was contaminated with fuel and other pollutants. "We even found a few buried cars," said Catlow. "Lots of debris and trash. Nobody knew what was down under there."

The real trouble began when the basement work snaked its way under Secretary of Defense William Perry's office during the first months of 1995. Perry, a gentle professorial type who spoke in a quiet voice, found the noise upsetting. Steve Carter soon got a call from the secretary of defense's office. "They wanted the noise to stop," Carter recalled. "I went down there and told [Corps on-site project engineer Ed] Mullins that the Secretary of Defense wanted the noise to stop. He told me to take the message back that there was a renovation project going on, and people were going to have to get used to some of this. I took the message up."

The message was not well received. At a press conference on March 16, 1995, Pentagon spokesman Kenneth Bacon announced that much of the renovation work was being frozen, and that work in the first wedge, due to start later that year, was being put on hold for at least one year. The whole plan was being reviewed by a steering committee overseen by Deputy Secretary of Defense John Deutch. Perry and his staff were hardly aware of the Pentagon renovation until they were disturbed by the noise. "In a sense, that was the genesis of it," Bacon said. "People began complaining about the noise. A group of people sat down one day and said, 'What's going on here? What is this plan?' When we looked at the plan, we saw that it was a huge plan, and it seemed prudent to review the plan and decide whether that's the way we want to go."

The work already under contract in the basement and center courtyard was allowed to continue, but with tight restrictions limiting the noisiest work to nights and weekends. Perry's daily schedule was sent to the renovation office, with various times marked "quiet, quiet, quiet." Likewise, the jackhammers and pile drivers came to a stop whenever the Joint Chiefs met in the Tank. Crews still had to be paid, and the delays were adding $30,000 a day to the cost of the basement construction. Even an insistent bandmaster, upset to find his musicians competing against construction noise, forced work in the courtyard to cease during a summertime lunch concert in 1995 at a cost of $16,000.

Doc Cooke had a new generation of Defense Department leaders to educate about the horrors of the Pentagon. He arranged for Steve Carter to take Deutch on what was dubbed "the Armpit Tour," a voyage to the bowels of the building. Carter met Deutch and his entourage in the deputy secretary's office. Before they started out, Deutch took Carter by the elbow and gestured to his well-appointed office. "You've got exactly thirty seconds to show me why we need to renovate," Deutch told him. Carter walked him sixty feet from the front door of his suite to a small utility closet, opening the door to expose a chilled water riser. The large pipe was rusted, scarred with welds from top to bottom, and covered with a jelly from years of condensation. "That's behind every wall of the Pentagon," Carter said.

Deutch stared at the pipe. "Let's walk," he said. They saw the seeping sewer lines and rusted air handlers, visited the decrepit steam and mechanical rooms, and pondered broken concrete ramps and walls. "I was impressed by the deterioration in the building's infrastructure," Deutch later recalled. But he remained skeptical about embarking on a $1.2 billion renovation when needs for the military in the field were going unmet.

The review continued. John Hamre, then serving as comptroller under Perry, was astonished as he began to realize how enormous—and expensive—the renovation would be. "The whole renovation was typical Doc Cooke—pulling off a much bigger deal than he was telling people he was really doing," Hamre recalled. "Gradually the full scope of it started to appear, but you never, ever saw it in any displays. Doc was just getting every-body pregnant, and then once you get into it, you got to keep working it." In the end, the need for renovation was too great, and they were too far down the road to cancel it. On December 26, 1996, Deputy Secretary of Defense John White, Deutch's successor, signed papers directing that the renovation of the first wedge finally begin in January 1998. To keep support on Capitol Hill, the Defense Department certified to Congress that the total cost of the renovation would not exceed $1.118 billion. "That turned out to be an entirely fake number," Hamre later said.

At the rate the program was spending money, Cooke was informed in January 1997, the entire $1.118 billion would be consumed with only a portion of the work done. But that was not the worst news. On November 7, 1996, the Corps reported a leak in one of the new sewer pipes in the base-ment, beneath a concrete floor slab that had already been poured. The Corps described it as "a local, isolated problem." Pentagon building engi-neers inspected the area with television cameras and discovered it was far worse. There were three dozen areas with breaks, some deep in the ground. The sewer lines had been laid without proper insulation from the ground subsiding beneath them. Lines had settled and disconnected from vertical risers. Others had been installed with incorrect slope or had been left with low points, or bellies. The Corps lacked any real quality control beyond ac-cepting the contractor's assurances that everything was fine. To make it worse, the sewer lines had been laid in trenches, affording little access to the piping. The new slab atop the pipes would have to be jackhammered out, the ground excavated, and the pipes relaid.

The renovation was in shambles. Throughout the building, the pro-gram was seen at best as a nuisance and more often as a joke. Frank Probst, a retired Army officer who joined the renovation program as a communi-cations contractor, found spirits low among his colleagues. "The program wasn't looked upon as doing great and wondrous things, so the morale was not real high," he recalled. There was talk again on Capitol Hill of cancel-ing the renovation.

Hamre, who had succeeded White as deputy secretary, blew his top at the cost overruns and told Cooke things had to change. "Look," Hamre said. "We're going to find somebody else to build this."

The psychology major

Walker Lee Evey knew nothing about construction—he was a psychology major, as he often pointed out. The cheerful Air Force contracts specialist, a short, mustachioed man with wire-rim glasses and an avuncular manner—did not seem particularly imposing. But he was a master of human nature and motivation. More than anything, Evey was a troubleshooter.

Evey was from St. Petersburg, Florida—his psychology degree was from the University of South Florida in Tampa—but what he usually did not mention was that before he got his degree, he had served in combat as an infantry platoon leader and later a company commander with the 1st Infantry Division—the Big Red One—in Quan Loi in Vietnam during 1968 and 1969. After leaving the Army and earning his degree, he started with the Air Force as a contracting officer in 1974 and rose to become one of the top procurement officials for the Air Force Systems Command. He left in 1987 and spent nine years with the National Aeronautics and Space Administration, serving as NASA's lead negotiator on the contracts for the Mir Space Station and the International Space Station. After successfully dealing with the Russians, he had come back to the Air Force as a high-ranking acquisition official in 1996, his reputation firmly established as a negotiator extraordinaire.

On November 17, 1997, Evey was called in to meet with his boss, Darleen Druyun, the Air Force's chief acquisition official, in her fourth-floor Pentagon office. Evey had just returned from another successful rescue—this time a top-secret Air Force "black project" in California, a satellite program that had been mired in a contract dispute. Druyun was a demanding and powerful boss, usually up to some scheme. (Seven years later, she would be sent to federal prison for funneling work to Boeing, her future employer.) Druyun told Evey she had a new assignment for him. "I'd like you to volunteer to do a really special major project," Druyun said.

"What is it?" Evey asked.

"Actually I would prefer that you agree to do it first and then I'll tell you," she said. Evey warily agreed.

"I want you to become program manager for the Pentagon renovation," Druyun said.

Hamre and Cooke had decided to create the position of Pentagon Renovation Program Manager and to make it a slot for a high-ranking official, either a general officer or the civil-service equivalent from the Senior Executive Service (SES). At Hamre's insistence, the program manager would report directly to the deputy secretary of defense, giving the renovation chief unquestioned clout in the building. The first choice, a one-star Corps of Engineers general, backed out after discovering the full extent of the program's disarray. Hamre had turned to the Air Force, the service he believed most competent at handling complicated contracts.

Hamre "asked Air Force to put up a program manager to run the program, and I'm asking you," Druyun told Evey.

Evey tried to beg off. Like everyone in the building, he knew the renovation by its reputation. "The program is a loser, and I don't know how to do construction," he told Druyun.

"I've got faith in you," Druyun said. "Go see Dr. Hamre."

Back in his office, somewhat dazed, Evey waited to be summoned by Hamre. He recalled a front-page story in *The Washington Post* he had glanced at that morning before leaving his suburban Virginia home. It detailed enormous cost overruns and delays in the construction of the new Ronald Reagan Building in Washington, at 3.1 million square feet second in size only to the Pentagon among all federal buildings. "I started thinking, 'Gee, if I'm going to do design and construction, I better start learning about this stuff—here's one that seems to have gone bad,'" Evey recalled.

Evey found the article in the office and had just finished copying it when he was told Hamre wanted to see him right away. Evey stuffed the article into a manila folder and hurried to the deputy secretary's office. Hamre warmly ushered Evey into his third-floor suite overlooking the River entrance. After they took seats around a coffee table, Hamre, "in his very best Interview 101 voice," began the questions: "Now, Lee, could you tell me, what are your goals for the Pentagon renovation program?"

Evey froze. "I didn't know jack about the renovation program," he later said. "I'm thinking, 'What the hell kind of answer do I give to that?'" After a moment, Evey opened up his manila folder, took out the newspaper article, leaned over and put it in Hamre's lap.

"My goal for the Pentagon renovation program is not to end up on the front page of the *Washington Post*," Evey said.

Hamre looked at the article and then at Evey. "That seems like an *excellent* goal," Hamre said. "I really like that goal. I think you're my guy."

"Dr. Hamre, I've got a confession to make," Evey said. "I'm not an architect, I'm not an engineer. I don't know anything about construction. I'm a psychology major."

Hamre waved him off. "I've talked to people about you, and they say you'll do just fine," he said. "I'm sure you'll do just fine."

Whistling in the dark

On his first morning on the job, Lee Evey toured the basement renovation. It was November 27, 1997, the day before Thanksgiving. At first glance, the basement looked beautiful. In one area, carpeting was on the floor, lights were on, furniture was in place, and telephones were on the desks. But twenty feet away, the floor had been jackhammered away, and big mounds of dirt and concrete were piled up. Another leaking sewer line was being replaced.

Evey went to the edge and peered over. The hole went twenty feet down into the wet, dark earth, to the very depths of the Pentagon. Shoring beams held the dirt from collapsing. Down at the bottom of the hole, raw sewage flowed around chunks of broken concrete. A little yellow rubber ducky was bobbing in the fetid water. The renovation team had a sense of humor, at least.

After the tour, Evey went to his new office, shut the door, sat at his desk, and put his head in his hands. In subsequent days, Evey wandered around the renovation headquarters—set in a modular office complex at the far end of the North parking lot—talking to people. Few were willing to speak about the program's problems. "Everybody was whistling in the dark, walking past the graveyard," Evey recalled.

At one of his first staff meetings, Evey asked a key question: Who was in charge of the basement renovation? "Everybody got real interested in their feet," Evey recalled. It turned out one person was responsible for determining requirements, someone else for planning, another person for design, someone else for construction, another person for information technology, and so on. The various departments were organized like silos, with little or no interaction. The typical problem—how to make sure sewer lines did not subside in poor soil, for example—could take six months to work its way through the system. "Six months just to decide we need to put crushed rock underneath the goddamn sewer line—give me a break," Evey recalled.

Within days of taking over, Evey gathered all three hundred people in the renovation program in the fifth-floor Pentagon auditorium. It was the first time the entire team had ever been together. In preparation, Evey spent hours thinking about how to capture the renovation program goals in a few words. Up on the stage, he unveiled a single chart with one phrase: "On Cost, On Schedule, Built for the Next 50 Years."

"We're going to practice right now saying what our goals are, and you're all going to say it with me," Evey announced. "Our goals are, 'On cost, on schedule, built for the next fifty years.'" Evey repeated it rhythmically.

The employees looked at Evey as if he were insane. "This guy's lost it," thought Frank Probst, the communications contractor. But a sprinkling of Army officers in the audience finally picked up the chant: On Cost, On Schedule, Built for the Next Fifty Years. It started to build, louder and louder. Before long three hundred people were screaming "On Cost, On Schedule, Built for the Next Fifty Years!"

The first sign that anything had taken hold was visible as soon as Evey arrived at work the next morning. One of the secretaries had stayed late the night before pasting the slogan all over the program offices: on doors, next to light switches, even above the urinals in the men's room. Then, when Evey held a second program-wide meeting in the auditorium several weeks later, he was interrupted by Jack Matthewman, one of the contractors, who stood up holding two big poles. "Sir, before you even get started, there's something we want to say to you," he announced. Matthewman handed one pole to another employee and they unfurled a banner between them. It had taken hours to print out on an old dot-matrix printer: On Cost, On Schedule, Built for the Next 50 Years. The whole room erupted in the now-familiar chant.

At that point, Evey felt it was going to work: "I knew there were answers there and we were going to find them. People had this internal drive that they were sick and tired of being unsuccessful, tired of being the butt of everybody's joke. . . . They were tired of failing."

The Big Bash

The Big Bash was set for February 12, 1998. With his unerring instinct for showmanship, Evey made the start of demolition in Wedge 1 a big production, complete with a VIP wall-bashing ceremony. Pentagon dignitaries showed up in coats and ties or skirts, and were given mini-sledgehammers to pound against targets on the fourth-floor E Ring walls. Doc Cooke, wearing safety glasses and a hard hat perched atop his bald head, could not stop grinning.

Wedge 1 would be the test. The basement work had been sharply curtailed; plans to put all the command centers there had been scrapped for being too costly and time-consuming. The basement represented "a Pyrrhic victory at best," Evey recalled. "So we needed to make Wedge 1 work and work right."

It was easier said than done. Once again demolition brought surprises. Some were just historical curiosities, like the newspapers from 1942 with headlines about Hitler or the old whiskey bottles stuffed in the walls—Bob Furman had been unable to chase off all the liquor salesmen. The biggest problem was that the asbestos was far more prevalent than expected—crews would remove twenty-eight million pounds of asbestos-contaminated material from Wedge 1 alone, all of which had to be triple-wrapped and trucked to landfills in Pennsylvania. The demolition was soon behind schedule.

As the work continued, Evey mulled how to turn the program around. Motivation and slogans were great, but by themselves were not going to change much. Evey wanted to change the fundamental nature of contracts for the Pentagon renovation program. His biggest brainstorm—once again—came from the newspaper, a story in the home section giving advice to readers who wanted to have new houses built. The worst thing to do, the article said, was to hire an architect to design a house, and then hire an unrelated construction contractor to build the plans. It was buying trouble, a situation where the architect and builder constantly squabbled over plans and costs. (Bergstrom and McShain were proof of that.) The best approach was to hire a construction contractor and architect who worked as a team. Evey, the construction novice, was intrigued: "Gee, that would probably make sense on our program too."

Evey unembarrassedly brought up the newspaper article at the next staff meeting. Soon he was convinced that this design-build concept then gaining popularity in industry circles was the path the Pentagon program should take. Evey also wanted to experiment with incentives. Most contracts assume failure and set up rules by which the government and the contractors could argue when things went wrong. He wanted to award fees based on performance, including quality of construction, ability to communicate, and problem-solving. To encourage cutting costs, the contractor would get a share of any savings.

Evey soon hit a brick wall with the U.S. Army Corps of Engineers. The Corps—the organization of giants like Somervell and Groves—was the constructor of the Pentagon. Now they were supposed to take construction advice from a contracts guy who was getting his ideas from the home-improvement section of the newspaper? This was not what the Corps had in mind from the program manager. The Corps had liked the idea of having someone with clout in the building but had expected construction would remain its bailiwick.

It was a battle of egos, in which Evey had no shortage of self-confidence. The chief of engineers, Lieutenant General Joe N. Ballard, a traditional-minded officer with two combat tours in Vietnam, refused to change the way the Corps did business. The divorce was done as civilly as possible. Evey did not put sole blame on the Corps for what had gone wrong, saying there was plenty of fault to go around. He offered Corps civilian employees a chance to stay, and many did, resigning from the Corps and forming the heart of the new Pentagon renovation team. The Corps described its departure from the renovation as "a business decision."

But there was no disguising the reality: The Corps of Engineers was out of the job of renovating the Pentagon.

Terrorists don't arrive on buses

At about 10:30 A.M. local time on August 7, 1998, a 3.5-ton Mitsubishi Canter truck took an abrupt left turn off of Haile Selassie Avenue in downtown Nairobi, Kenya, and barreled toward the American embassy. The truck's path was slowed by an oncoming car and then blocked by a barricade, but when the bomb in the rear of the truck—a concoction of TNT and aluminum nitrate weighing several hundred pounds—detonated moments later, it sheared off the façade of the embassy and caused a nearby building to collapse. Nine minutes later, another truck pulled into the parking lot of the American embassy in Dar es Salaam in neighboring Tanzania and exploded. The two bombs killed 224 people, including 12 Americans, and wounded more than 4,000, many of them horribly maimed.

Intelligence quickly pointed to a Saudi Arabian multimillionaire named Osama bin Laden, leader of an Islamic terrorist group known as al Qaeda. At the Pentagon, military planners prepared for an attempt—ultimately futile—to kill bin Laden by firing seventy-five Tomahawk cruise missiles at an al Qaeda camp in eastern Afghanistan.

In his office, Doc Cooke made his own assessment: The Pentagon remained shockingly vulnerable to a truck bomb. Indeed, a suicide bomber would probably find it easier to get to the Pentagon than the embassies. Every day, some two hundred delivery trucks backed into the Pentagon to the loading docks on the south side of the building; there was no practical way to secure the docks or inspect trucks at the Pentagon before they got close to the building.

Cooke had been pushing for years to build an annex on the Mall side of the building to house loading docks. In May 1993—three months after a bomb intended to destroy the World Trade Center in New York City had exploded in an underground garage and killed six people—Cooke told Congress that moving the loading docks to a remote facility "dramatically improves" the Pentagon's security and "diminishes the possibility of a World Trade Center type incident." It was to no avail. The Mall annex was deleted from the plans later that year to gain Congress's approval to start renovation; there was little support to expand the Pentagon at a time of military cuts elsewhere.

Cooke did not give up. He and the head of the Pentagon police force, John Jester, raised alarms after the Oklahoma City bombing in 1995 that killed 168 people in the Alfred P. Murrah Federal Center, the deadliest terrorist attack yet on American soil. They did so again after an enormous truck bomb exploded in front of the Khobar Towers housing complex in Dhahran in 1996, killing nineteen U.S. servicemen. Still no funding was available, and eighteen-wheelers backed into the Pentagon every day.

The embassy bombings in Africa brought the issue to a tipping point. In the fall of 1998, Cooke got signals from Capitol Hill that he was likely to get money for his Mall annex. Cooke called Lee Evey into his office. "I want you to take a project on," Cooke said. The mall extension needed to be built, and fast. Construction of the Remote Delivery Facility was soon under way. In the interim, Pentagon police began using a warehouse in nearby Crystal City to screen truck deliveries.

The loading docks were hardly the Pentagon's only vulnerability. Before the embassy bombings, Wedge 1 project leaders warned Evey that the planned renovation did not adequately protect the building against potential threats. The demolition had revealed an unwelcome surprise. The renovation team had anticipated that the backup walls behind the limestone façade would be made of the same reinforced concrete seen everywhere else in the building. But when crews pulled down the wallboard on the outer E Ring walls, they discovered the façade was backed with brick inside a concrete frame.

Brick was simply not as strong as reinforced concrete. To make it worse, the hurry with which McShain's crews had thrown up the brick walls was plain to see. Bricklayers had taken some shortcuts; rather than putting mortar between each layer of brick, they put down two layers of brick in some places before applying mortar.

Before departing the program, the Corps of Engineers performed classified simulations at a research center in Mississippi measuring the damage the Pentagon would suffer from a truck bomb. Depending on the amount of explosive and its proximity, it could be catastrophic.

Putting blast-resistant, two-inch-thick windows on the outer walls of the Pentagon would be expensive. In Wedge 1 alone, there were 312 outer windows, plus another 70 facing the inner courtyard, and the windows cost $10,000 apiece. But it was an easy decision. Evey, with Cooke's approval, agreed to buy the windows.

The tougher problem was figuring out how to strengthen the walls. One recommendation was that the limestone be temporarily removed, the brick torn down, and the wall recast with reinforced concrete, but the cost was prohibitive. Project engineers came up with a plan to reinforce the brick walls with steel. They would frame the windows with six-inch-thick steel beams. It would all be bolted together, floor by floor, creating a steel web backing the wall. To further protect occupants, a Kevlar-type ballistic cloth would be hung between the steel beams, almost as if the building were being dressed in a bullet-resistant vest. The cloth was designed to catch shards of masonry, which analysis showed had killed many of the victims in the Africa bombings.

The Pentagon's bus-and-subway system was another vulnerability. The old bus tunnel—considered such a marvel of mass transit when the Pentagon opened—was replaced by a surface-level bus station in 1977 and closed off altogether in December 1983, a few months after a terrorist bombing killed 260 Marines in Beirut. (The tunnel was converted in 1987 into the headquarters for the Strategic Defense Initiative Organization—President Ronald Reagan's "Star Wars" program.) But the surface-level bus station allowed buses to drive within nine feet of the building. Moreover, an escalator from the Metro subway station below carried passengers directly into the building—Pentagon security officials dubbed it the "terrorist delivery tube." The 1995 sarin-gas attack on the Tokyo subway only heightened their concerns.

In the spring of 2000, the renovation program revealed plans to close the escalator and build a new subway entrance away from the Pentagon. The bus station would be moved three hundred feet from the building. The plan brought howls of protests from local politicians and bus passengers angry at the long walk exposed to the elements. "We were severely criticized, and in fact even to some extent ridiculed," Evey later said. "One particular quote that sticks with me is somebody thought that this was kind of a stupid thing to do, and made the comment that, 'Don't you know that terrorists don't arrive on buses?' "

From an old VW Bug to a big Cadillac

The Arleigh Burke Bell was about the only reminder of the old Navy Command Center to make it to the new one. The eight-inch-diameter bronze ship's bell had been given to the Navy as a gift by the legendary "31 Knot" Burke, the hard-charging World War II destroyer squadron commander who later served three tours in the Pentagon as chief of naval operations, longer than anyone in the building's history.

Everything else in the Navy Command Center in Wedge 1 was new—the furniture, floors, lighting, and computers. To Lieutenant Kevin Shaeffer, a junior action officer in the Navy's Strategy and Warfighting Concepts

Branch, even the odor was different—everything smelled fresh. The old command center on the fourth floor had been stale, bursting at the seams with equipment and personnel.

When Shaeffer and his colleagues moved into the new command center on August 15, 2001, it was "like stepping from an old VW Bug to a big Cadillac," recalled Lieutenant William Wertz. Officers went about putting up home touches in their cubicles, pinning family photographs and "Beat Army" stickers into the light gray fabric. Shaeffer, a twenty-nine-year-old from Peters Township, Pennsylvania, put up a photograph of his wife, Blanca, a fellow Naval Academy graduate. Navy Commander Patrick Dunn, who shared a four-person cubicle with Shaeffer and two other officers in their branch, set up a big jar of candy on his desk where everybody helped themselves to sweets, accompanied by a few of Dunn's trademark jokes. The new command center was in business, monitoring the whereabouts of the Navy's 317 ships.

Wedge 1 was on cost and on schedule, as Lee Evey had promised. The first employees—a group of a hundred Air Force personnel—had begun occupying the renovated section six months earlier, and people were moving in at the rate of almost 150 per week.

In some respects, it was like a brand-new building. The corridors were bright and modern, painted in light colors and well-lit, with polished terrazzo floors. At the apex of corridors 3 and 4 at the inner courtyard, a gleaming bank of escalators with glass balustrades traversed all five floors. There were even passenger elevators, a revolution in Pentagon travel. In the restrooms, modern fixtures with electronic sensors had replaced the ancient toilets and sinks. A new cafeteria, lit by a skylight, was bright and airy.

Other changes were barely noticeable, like the sprinklers installed in the ceilings overhead, the blast-resistant windows, and the interlocking steel tubes and geotechnical mesh hidden behind the drywall. The windows did not open like the old ones, but included faux handles to replicate the historically certified look.

The Pentagon was a markedly safer building. The Remote Delivery Facility had opened on schedule in August 2000. The triangle of lawn where demonstrators had frolicked thirty years earlier during the 1967 march on the Pentagon was now home to the 250,000-square-foot annex, which housed loading docks, thirty truck bays, maintenance shops, and offices. Deliveries were screened by dogs and X-ray machines and then carried on carts through a tunnel underneath the Mall plaza that connected to the first floor of the Pentagon; in effect the annex was part of the building, with its hallways accordingly marked as the J and K rings. At the dedication ceremony, Evey read a proclamation naming it the David O. Cooke Delivery Facility; it was less formally known as Doc's Dock.

Evey, for his part, was making plans to retire in January after thirty years of government service. He was ready to slow down after a quadruple heart bypass the previous year. He had been in charge of the Pentagon renovation for nearly four years, and the program was firmly set on a new course. Wedge 1 was scheduled to be fully occupied by the end of October, and they were days away from signing a contract for renovating the rest of the building.

By September 10, 2001, fewer than a hundred renovation workers were still on the job. They were down to punch-list items, checking the floor tiles for cracks and hooking up computers and telephones. Frank Probst, the retired Army officer overseeing quality assurance for the communications facilities, was having trouble with some computer-room air-conditioning units. They kept shutting off when they were not supposed to. He would go check on them again the following morning.

The Pentagon, September 11, 2001.

CHAPTER
20

SEPTEMBER 11, 2001

I'm never going to see my boys again

Frank Probst checked the new computer rooms on the morning of September 11, 2001, and found the air-conditioning was working fine. Finishing up his inspection in a first-floor telephone closet on the E Ring, Probst looked at his watch. It was 9:25 A.M. He had a ten o'clock meeting at the renovation headquarters, a good hike away at the far end of the North parking lot.

Thin and taciturn, Probst had left his home of Altoona, Pennsylvania, at eighteen for West Point and had never gone back. He arrived in Vietnam in June 1966, serving as a platoon leader with the 173rd Airborne Brigade until he was wounded the following January when a Viet Cong tunnel he was clearing exploded during search-and-destroy operations in the "Iron Triangle," a Communist stronghold in the rural provinces near Saigon. Probst returned for a second tour in 1969 with the 1st Cavalry Division. He burned out on the infantry and in 1973 transferred to the Signal Corps, an assignment that gave him a chance to raise two young boys with his wife, and the expertise for his present job overseeing the installation of new communications equipment in the Pentagon.

Leaving the building, Probst stopped in a construction trailer in front of the renovated wedge. On a little black-and-white television in the break area, Probst looked in disbelief at a news report showing the second of two planes crashing into the World Trade Center in New York earlier that morning. "You know what would be a good target?" another worker remarked. "This building would be a good target."

"Yeah, I guess it would," Probst thought. He picked up his notebook and left the trailer at 9:35 for his meeting, walking along a sidewalk toward the heliport in front of the Pentagon's west wall. The day was spectacular, that same pristine late-summer weather that had greeted the construction crews when they broke ground that day exactly sixty years earlier, just a few dozen yards from where Probst was walking.

Probst did not notice the jet until he looked up and saw it heading right at him. The aircraft had just come over the hill at the south end of the Navy Annex overlooking the Pentagon. Probst had not heard a thing until he saw the plane, and then all he could hear were the engines cranking, as if the pilot were flying full bore. The nose was dropped, no lights were on, and the wheels were up. The plane seemed impossibly low—its wings clipped off several light poles and the antenna on a Jeep Grand Cherokee as the jet crossed over Washington Boulevard, flying toward the Pentagon. Probst did not even notice that—his eyes were focused on the engine on the plane's right wing, heading straight at his face. "I'm dead," he thought.

Probst dove to the pavement—the quick reactions honed in Vietnam had not abandoned him. A fleeting, sad thought passed through his head as he fell: "I'm never going to see my boys again."

It's headed toward the Pentagon

American Airlines Flight 77 had departed Washington Dulles International Airport at 8:20 A.M. that morning bound for Los Angeles. Pilot Charles "Chic" Burlingame III, a former naval aviator who had spent years assigned to the Pentagon, brought the jet up to its assigned cruising altitude of 35,000 feet twenty-five minutes later.

The Boeing 757, more than fifty yards long and with a wingspan of 124 feet, could accommodate two hundred people, but the Tuesday morning flight was unusually light, with fifty-nine passengers and five crew members. A mix of businesspeople and tourists were aboard. Among them were

Leslie Whittington and Charles Falkenberg, starting a two-month adventure to Australia with their daughters Zoe, eight, and curly-headed Dana, three. Whittington, a popular and sharp-witted associate professor of public policy at Georgetown University, had been appointed a visiting fellow at the Australian National University, and the whole family was accompanying her, hoping to explore the land.

Three more children were on board: eleven-year-olds Bernard Brown, Rodney Dickens, and Asia Cottom, all sixth-graders from Washington public schools who were traveling with their teachers to a marine sanctuary near Santa Barbara, California. The children had been selected for the National Geographic Society–sponsored trip because of their good grades and potential. Navy Chief Petty Officer Bernard Brown, Sr.—who worked in the newly renovated Wedge 1 but was taking the day off—was proud of his mischievous, basketball-loving son, but could not help feeling nervous as the boy set off on the journey.

Barbara Olson, a former federal prosecutor who had come to prominence as a television commentator in the late 1990s with her fiery skewering of President Bill Clinton, sat in first class. She had been booked on a flight to Los Angeles the day before but had delayed her departure to have breakfast that morning with her husband, Theodore Olson, the solicitor general of the United States. It was his birthday.

Hani Hanjour was also sitting in first class, in Seat 1B. He was a devout Muslim from Taif, Saudi Arabia, with a thin face and an ascetic manner. In the spring of 2000, at an al Qaeda camp in Afghanistan, Hanjour's prior training as a pilot came to the attention of Osama bin Laden and the al Qaeda chief of operations, Mohammed Atef. Hanjour was selected to be one of the pilots for a plot to fly hijacked airliners into prominent American buildings. The idea had been proposed to bin Laden in mid-1996 by Khalid Sheikh Mohammed, and bin Laden had approved the plan in the months following the August 1998 African embassy bombings. At a series of meetings at a camp outside Kandahar, Afghanistan, in the spring of 1999, bin Laden, Atef, and Mohammed selected an initial list of targets, among them the White House, the U.S. Capitol, and the World Trade Center. It was bin Laden himself who insisted the Pentagon be included.

Hanjour was joined in the first-class section by two Saudi accomplices,

Nawaf and Salem al Hazmi, baby-faced brothers from Mecca. Two more hijackers, Majed Moqed, also a Saudi, and Khalid al Mindhar, a Yemeni, sat in seats 12A and 12B in the coach section.

The Hazmi brothers had attracted some scrutiny during check-in at Dulles because one of the brothers lacked a photo ID, but they were nonetheless given boarding passes. Moqed and Nawaf al Hazmi both set off metal detectors and were checked with a hand wand by a screener, who allowed them through without bothering to resolve what had set off the alarm. It may have been the box cutters and knives they were carrying.

The hijackers made their move shortly after 8:51 A.M., probably around the time the plane crossed out of West Virginia and into southern Ohio. They took control of the cockpit and herded the passengers and possibly the crew to the rear of the plane. At 8:54, with Hanjour likely at the controls, the plane turned south toward Kentucky; radar contact with the aircraft was lost minutes later. The plane was soon streaking eastward back over West Virginia toward Washington, its transponder turned off, its whereabouts unknown to authorities.

In the back of the plane, Barbara Olson used her cell phone to call her husband at his office, reaching him sometime after 9:16 A.M. "Our plane has been hijacked," she told him. As Ted Olson listened, the line went dead. Then she called again. "What can I tell the pilot to do?" she asked. Then the phone cut off, and there were no more calls.

At 9:32, air traffic controllers at Dulles spotted an aircraft on the radar "tracking eastbound at a high rate of speed" toward Washington. A minute later, as the plane crossed the Capital Beltway about five miles west of the Pentagon, a tower supervisor at Reagan National Airport telephoned the Secret Service to warn that the aircraft posed a threat to the White House. At 9:34, the plane turned south away from the White House and flew over Alexandria, continuing for a minute before turning to the west and circling back. Two minutes later, Secret Service agents at the White House grabbed Vice President Dick Cheney from his chair and hustled him down to a basement bunker.

But the aircraft was heading to a different target. At the end of its tight 330-degree turn, the plane was down to 2,200 feet and still descending rapidly, so low it disappeared from controllers' radar screens. It was by then over Arlington, flying east, following Columbia Pike toward the Pentagon. Arlington County motorcycle patrol officer Richard B. Cox, standing near Bob and Edith's Diner on Columbia Pike less than a mile from the Pentagon, heard a sudden roar, turned, and was astonished to see a plane directly overhead, trees and buildings and cars reflected on its belly. It was no more than a hundred feet off the ground. Cox rushed to his radio to call in a warning: "It's an American Airlines plane and it's headed toward the Pentagon, I think."

In the last seconds, as the jet plunged toward the Pentagon's west wall, its two Rolls Royce engines screaming with 44,000 pounds of combined thrust at full throttle, witnesses could see the silhouettes of passengers huddled in the rear.

Something can happen in this world

"My God! What's happened?" Petty Officer Michael Allen Noeth jumped out of his chair in the Navy Command Center and pointed to a bank of large televisions that framed one side of the watch section. News broadcasts from New York City showed a plume of black smoke rising from the North Tower of the World Trade Center. An airplane had crashed into the building at 8:46 A.M.

It was the first inkling of trouble in what had been a routine morning in the command center. Coats were slung over chairs and briefcases sat beside desks. The daily briefing for the Navy leadership—"Around the World in Fifteen Pages" as the staff liked to call it—was already over. Lieutenant Kevin Shaeffer had reviewed his e-mail and digested *The Early Bird,* the compilation of military-related news stories put out every weekday morning by the Defense Department. The lead item reported plans by the new secretary of defense to cut the Pentagon bureaucracy by 15 percent. "I have no desire to attack the Pentagon," Donald Rumsfeld was quoted as saying. "I want to liberate it. We need to save it from itself." *The Early Bird* had missed one of the more interesting stories of the day—a centerpiece feature on the front of *The New York Times* Arts section about Bill Ayers, now a distinguished professor of education at the University of Illinois at Chicago. He had just published a memoir on his life with the Weather Underground in which he described, among other acts, the 1972 bombing of the Pentagon. "I don't regret setting bombs," Ayers was quoted as saying in the first paragraph of the story. "I feel we didn't do enough."

Shaeffer and his branch office mates—Commander Pat Dunn, Commander Bill Donovan, and Lieutenant Commander Dave Williams—had finished their morning meeting with their branch head, Captain Bob Dolan, at 8:30, and were settling down to the tasks of the day when the images from New York stopped everything. Then, at 9:03 A.M., "a tense, audible gasp erupted throughout the space," Shaeffer recalled. A second aircraft had flown into the Trade Center's South Tower.

On the opposite side of the Pentagon, Rumsfeld was hosting a breakfast in his private dining room with Deputy Secretary of Defense Paul Wolfowitz for a group of congressmen to talk about defense budget proposals. In his second tour of the Pentagon, Rumsfeld was not noticeably lacking in confidence, and he had ruffled the feathers of many senior officers with his aggressive push to "transform" the military. Some of the congressmen expressed doubt about the wisdom of supporting an expensive missile-defense program, saying the public was more concerned with issues such as Social Security. Rumsfeld leaned forward across the table and forcefully lectured the congressmen. He predicted that before the 2002 election, some crisis would bring the voters' focus back to national security. "Something can happen in this world that can jar people, and they're going to start looking at who understood that," Rumsfeld warned. Wolfowitz said much the same, predicting an "ugly surprise," like Iran testing a nuclear bomb or North Korea firing a long-range missile.

An aide came into the dining room and handed Rumsfeld a note reporting that a plane had hit the World Trade Center. "Everyone assumed it was an accident, the way it was described," Rumsfeld recalled. "We went on with our breakfast." Soon afterward, the secretary returned to his office for his morning CIA intelligence briefing. Right before it began, his assistant, Larry Di Rita, stuck his head in the office with an update: A second plane had hit the World Trade Center.

Below Rumsfeld's office, in the National Military Command Center, the senior watch commander, Navy Captain Charles J. Leidig, Jr., realized upon the second crash that the nation was under attack. He decided to convene a "significant event" teleconference meant to establish the chain of command between the national leadership—the president and the secretary of defense—and the relevant combatant commanders, in this case, the North American Aerospace Defense Command, NORAD, responsible for protecting American airspace.

In the Building Operations Center, assistant building manager Steve Carter watched on television as the second plane flew into the South Tower. "That's not an accident," he told his assistant, Cathy Greenwell. "We have an event going." He ordered an immediate lockdown of all mechanical and electrical rooms in the building. At the same time, John Jester, chief of the Pentagon police force, raised the building's security posture one level from normal to alpha, which meant spot checks of vehicles and additional outside patrols. The National Military Command Center learned at 9:31 A.M. that a hijacked airplane was reported to be Washington-bound. But no steps were taken to alert Pentagon employees or evacuate the building.

Despite the flurry of activity and the thousands of televisions and computers in the building, some in the Pentagon were entirely unaware of what was happening at the World Trade Center. In room 2E483, an Army conference room on the second floor in the newly renovated section, Colonel Phil McNair had been holed up with a dozen members of his staff since 9 A.M. The lively staff meeting, held every second Tuesday, was the day the low-key Texan cracked the whip on behalf of his boss, Army personnel chief Lieutenant General Timothy Maude, making sure projects were on schedule.

In other offices, the news from New York caused a stir; if there were more attacks, the Pentagon was an obvious target. Workers in the Defense Intelligence Agency comptroller's office in Room 1C535, across from the Navy Command Center, were uneasy. Office supervisor Paul Gonzales, a cheerful retired Navy commander, reassured his colleagues: The Pentagon is probably the safest building in the world. By 9:30, most people had settled back to business.

I didn't want to get burnt again

Frank Probst—on the ground, surprised to be alive—felt the plane pass a few feet over his body and watched as it continued toward the Pentagon a hundred yards away. It seemed to be going in slow motion. First, he watched the right wingtip slice through a trailer holding a backup generator "like it was butter." Almost simultaneously, Probst saw a cloud of dust exploding in the air as the plane's left engine struck a concrete steam vent outside the building. The pilot seemed to be aiming for a window on the first floor, almost exactly where Probst had been checking the air-conditioning ten minutes earlier. "And then the fire—a big fireball, and the plane just disappearing into the fireball." The burnt-orange fireball was enormous, rising high in the air and exploding out from the building. It seemed to be coming right at him.

"Well, the plane didn't hit you," Probst thought. "Now you're going to roast." Probst had a special fear of fire that went back to Vietnam, when the tunnel explosion in the Iron Triangle had badly burned his arms, neck, and ears. "I didn't want to get burnt again," Probst said. "So I wasn't real brave. I didn't run toward the fire. I ran the other damn way." He stumbled and fell twice as he ran, tearing his pants and ripping the skin on his hands. Fine bits of metal and concrete floated around him like a gray confetti shower.

Alan Wallace, fifty-five, a firefighter manning the small fire station at the Pentagon heliport, had just finished adjusting a valve on a new red foam truck when the jet suddenly appeared, twenty-five feet off the ground. He sprinted until he heard the plane hit the building, and then dove underneath a big Ford van parked next to the station to escape the blast and burning metal. Wallace felt a terrible heat—"I got to get farther away than this," he thought—but it was too late.

When he emerged, everything seemed to be on fire—the grass, the building, the firehouse. Two big magnolia trees were ablaze. Even the foam truck was burning. Wallace climbed in the cab anyway, thinking he could pull it to the building and use its 1,500 gallons of water and 200 gallons of liquid foam. He punched the ignition buttons and the engine fired up. "Oh, my Lord, thank you!" he exclaimed. Wallace took off the emergency brake and floored the accelerator, but the truck did not move; instead, the flames in the back of the truck flared up. Another fireman yelled at him to kill the engine and get out. Wallace grabbed a couple of breathing apparatuses and his helmet and jumped out. He heard someone calling from the Pentagon: "We need help over here." People inside were at the windows, trying to get out.

A rapidly moving avalanche

Army Specialist Chin Sun "Sunny" Pak—her nickname matched her disposition—was chatting on the phone with a friend at 9:37 A.M. when she glanced up and gasped. The twenty-four-year-old personnel specialist from Oklahoma sat at her desk facing the window on the second-floor E Ring, Room 2E462 in the newly renovated Office of the Deputy Chief of Staff for Personnel. "Oh my God," Pak said. She let out a long, terrified scream before the phone went dead.

The Boeing 757, weighing approximately 181,520 pounds, was traveling at 460 knots—about 780 feet per second—when its nose struck the first-floor west wall of the Pentagon. It crashed through the windows of rooms 1E462 and 1E466, right below Pak's office, just north of Corridor 4. The front of the aircraft largely disintegrated on impact, but it blew open a hole in the limestone-faced exterior between the first- and second-floor slabs that allowed the rest of the fuselage to pass into the building. While the nose came to an almost immediate stop, the midsection of the plane was still moving at 775 feet per second. These portions, disintegrating as they pushed through the building, cleared a path for the trailing sections. "[T]he debris from the aircraft and building most likely resembled a rapidly moving avalanche through the first floor of the building," an engineering study later said.

The avalanche burst through Army accounting offices on the first floor of the E Ring, continued through the Navy Command Center on the D Ring, and slammed into a Defense Intelligence Agency office in the C Ring. The plane was flying east-northeast at a forty-degree angle to the face of the building when it struck. The destruction followed the same path, traveling diagonally through the building for 310 feet toward the fifth corridor, out of the renovated Wedge 1 and into the non-renovated Wedge 2. The concussion broke a nine-foot-diameter hole through the back wall of the C Ring, and debris spilled out onto AE Drive, the service road that circles the Pentagon between the B and C rings. The blast force escaped out AE Drive into the air, leaving the B and A rings virtually untouched.

The outer three rings were utterly devastated, both by the force of the impact and the resulting fuel explosion. The plane was carrying 36,200 pounds of jet fuel in three tanks on both wings and the fuselage. A relatively small portion of the fuel—less than five thousand pounds—exploded against the façade, feeding the huge fireball Frank Probst witnessed. But an enormous amount—more than thirty thousand pounds—passed into the Pentagon. Some of the fuel detonated seconds after impact, sending fireballs through the interior and blowing a hole through the second-floor slab. More fuel cascaded through the area, soaking occupants and offices.

The wings of the plane were most likely severed as it burst into the façade. Likewise, much of the plane's forty-five-foot-high tail appears to have been destroyed by the fireball before hitting the building; damage from the impact went only twenty-five feet up the outer wall.

The fuselage in essence turned inside out as it passed through the Pentagon. The bodies of the hijackers, who were in the front of the plane, were deposited near the front of the building. Almost all the remains of the passengers, who had been in the back, ended up deep in the C Ring. Such was the brutal force of the impact and the intensity of the fire that no identifiable remains would ever be found of five of those on board, including the tiniest passenger, three-year-old Dana Falkenberg.

Hail Mary full of grace. Help me out of this place

In the Navy Command Center, Lieutenant Kevin Shaeffer was slammed to the floor by a thunderous shock wave, and the room around him exploded in orange. He had been standing by his desk, peering over the shoulder-high cubicles at the burning towers on the television screens. Commanders Dunn, Donovan, and Williams had been seated at their desks a few feet away. Now they were gone.

The room was pitch-black, and for a few seconds the silence was absolute. Lying on the ground, Shaeffer felt his head and back on fire. He ran his fingers through his hair and face and rolled his body on the floor, trying to put out the flames. He managed to stand and tried to get his bearings. He could see little but could tell the ceiling had collapsed and that he was surrounded by rubble. The space—1D535 was no longer a room—was rapidly filling with thick, caustic smoke, and through it he caught glimpses of carnage. He called for help but no one answered. His mouth and throat were burning and he struggled to breathe. He thought of his wife Blanca and was sickened at the thought of never seeing her again. Shaeffer began crawling through the darkness, climbing over piles of rubble. He yelled out: "Keep moving, Kevin! Keep moving!"

In the adjacent DIA comptroller's office, Paul Gonzales had just dropped a memo on the desk of Patty Mickley, one of his budget analysts, when he heard a rushing sound: "Things started to go flying by me, there was a wind, and I started to fly with it." The room felt like an oven. Co-worker Aaron Cooper, facing the explosion, saw two streams of fire roaring through the room, as if from a fire-breathing dragon.

Landing on the ground, Gonzales looked at his hands. The skin was peeled back from his palms, curled like carrot peels from a vegetable scraper. He heard someone screaming. It was Kathy Cordero, one of the office workers, swatting helplessly at a burning ceiling tile that had fallen on her head like a hat. Gonzales crawled to her and batted the tile off with the back of his hand. Smoke filled the room, lowering the ceiling of breathable air closer to the ground. He and Cordero found three office mates— Dave Lanagan, Patty Pague, and Christine Morrison—clustered on the floor. The room was unrecognizable, its fire exits blocked by furniture and rubble. Gonzales did a roll call and realized a half-dozen workers were missing. They called back to Gonzales's office, where Mickley and others had been. There was no answer. Gonzales climbed on a desk, feeling the temperature soar as his head rose, and looked over a seven-foot partition. "I saw what I believe was hell," he said. Black smoke billowed around the space, illuminated by eerie islands of fire.

Gonzales crawled back to the others. The room was baking hot. Lanagan had taken off his shirt and the women their blouses, trying to cool off. They lapped up water that had collected on the floor from broken pipes. "This doesn't look real good," Lanagan told Gonzales. "I don't know if we're going to get out of here."

His words sparked new desperation in Gonzales, and he crawled off again to the back of the room, trying to find a way out. He kicked at partitions and tossed furniture, pulling on anything that could move. The others could no longer see him and were losing hope. Lanagan prayed aloud: *Hail Mary, full of grace. Help me out of this place.*

Then they heard Gonzales's voice, coming through the thick smoke like a foghorn: "There's a hole!"

There are people behind me

In the Building Operations Center on the first-floor A Ring, Steve Carter heard a big boom and felt his knees buckling. A strange crinkling sound rippled through the ceiling tiles overhead. He looked at the command-system computers and saw all the screens going red, the signal for an emergency. The fire-system screen showed how many alarms had been triggered, and the numbers were spinning like a gasoline pump. After a few seconds it had reached 352 and showed no signs of slowing. "I think we just got hit by a bomb," Carter told his assistant. "I'm going to grab my radio and go check it out."

Out in the corridor, Carter saw drywall dust and smoke rolling down the hallways like tumbleweeds. He rounded a corner and ran into several military officers who screamed that they needed fire extinguishers. Carter calmly told them they should evacuate the building and let the fire department respond. One of the officers looked at Carter: "You don't understand," he said.

Carter followed them out to AE Drive, the service road that circled the Pentagon between the B and C rings. The double doors to an electrical vault on the service road had been blown off, and the back wall inside it had been blown out too. Looking through the vault into the building, Carter could see a deep red inferno; the vault had become the escape route. Pentagon employees stood in ankle-deep water in the electrical vault—braving electrocution—and had formed a chain to pull survivors out. Carter understood now. He joined the rescuers.

Nearby, confusion reigned in the corridors close to the impact but spared a direct hit. Some thought a bomb had exploded; almost no one understood the building had been hit by a plane. Army Lieutenant Colonel Paul "Ted" Anderson boomed out instructions and took command of stragglers milling in the hallways; he led dozens of employees down Corridor 6 to the Mall entrance. "People, we are moving!" he barked. The guards refused to open the doors, saying the building was under attack from outside. The crowd in the corridor was growing, two hundred people or more; some turned back, looking for another way out. Anderson ignored the guards and kicked open an emergency door with his dress shoes. He looked around the Mall entrance, saw no threat, and directed people to follow him out. Most of them streamed toward the North parking lot, away from the smoke. Running down the Mall steps, Anderson looked in the opposite direction, to his left toward the heliport, and sprinted toward the smoke.

Wearing civilian clothes—suspenders, striped shirt, and tie—and with his wire-rim glasses, the forty-two-year-old Anderson looked like an unlikely warrior; yet he was, to the core. After sixteen years in the field as a paratrooper and with combat experience in the Gulf War, the Ohio native had been mortified when he was assigned to a cushy staff job in the Army congressional liaison office at the Pentagon. He did not want his peers to find out. Now, approaching the west wall, he found a battleground.

Anderson saw flames coming from blown-out windows and tremendous flash explosions inside. Victims were staggering out of the building, some terribly injured, and people inside were screaming. As he ran through the grass, Anderson saw gray debris strewn about, pieces of a disintegrated aircraft. Army Staff Sergeant Christopher D. Braman fell in stride with Anderson. Braman, a chef for the general officers' mess, was a strapping Army Ranger of the same pedigree as Anderson. The two formed an ad hoc rescue team.

Two women had jumped out of a window and were on the ground in front of the burning building, unable to move any farther. Anderson and Braman dragged them to the far side of the heliport, away from the blast and fire. They ran back to the building a few dozens yards north of where the plane had hit, broke jagged shards of glass from a blown-out window, and boosted themselves through. The two soldiers crawled blindly through a smoke-filled hallway. "Is there anybody in here?" Braman called. Sheila Mooney—an Army civilian employee on her second day on the job—lay on the floor, overcome by smoke and saying prayers. Mooney heard them calling but had sucked in so much smoke she was unable to call out. She clapped her burned hands together to get their attention. They dragged her out the emergency exit and passed her off to other rescuers.

Reentering the door, Anderson was stunned by nearby secondary explosions and instinctively dove to the floor. As he pushed himself back up, he saw a brilliant glow out of the corner of his eye. Anderson thought the ceiling was collapsing and threw himself back on the ground, covering his head. Then he realized the glow was moving. It was a man on fire. He was a human torch, trying to get out of the building, but he ran into a window and bounced back. Anderson had seen horrible sights in combat, but never anything like this. The man's nose and lips had been burned off. Anderson could tell he was a civilian because the man's suit coat was still affixed to his arms and a white shirt stuck out of his cuff. But everything else had burned away. Anderson and Braman grabbed him and smothered the flames. The whole time the man was screaming: "There are people behind me! You have to get the people behind me out of the corridor!"

Anderson and Braman carried him out and headed back. They paused for a moment outside the building to plan their search for the people in the corridor. Anderson figured he would crawl to the corridor with Braman holding his foot so they would not be separated in the smoke. As they readied themselves to go in, they were grabbed by firefighters. Arlington County fire commanders, arriving and taking charge of the scene, had ordered military rescuers to stay out of the building. The soldiers did not have the training or equipment, and it was too dangerous.

The soldiers and firemen angrily confronted one another. Anderson was incredulous: *Who are you to tell me I can't go in to get my men out? You don't leave anybody behind in combat. Ever. If you have to give your life, give your life.* Two firefighters physically restrained Anderson. He felt as if he were losing his mind. *Here we are at war*—he knew the country was at war—*and we're not going to mount a rescue attempt?*

I'm alive

Colonel Phil McNair felt as if he was trapped in a maze. For those still in the impact zone, the time for escape was rapidly vanishing. The area was getting hotter, the smoke thicker, and the floors in danger of collapse. Though he had no idea what had happened, the plane had hit the building one floor below, passing within twenty feet of the conference room—2E483—where McNair had been sitting at a table with ten members of his staff. McNair had heard a tremendous explosion and seen ripples of flame licking out from the ceiling. Then everything was inky-black. McNair leapt to his feet. "What the hell was that?" he called.

Smoke filled the room and everyone crawled out, separating into several groups in the darkness and confusion. McNair at first figured they should go out to the nearby E Ring and escape out the front of the building. But, coming to a corner, McNair felt the heat growing and saw flames under the door ahead. "If you open that door, we'll get toasted," McNair told his group. They crawled in the opposite direction. Two other officers from the conference room—Lieutenant Colonel Dennis Johnson and Major Steven Long, apparently unaware of the turn taken by their colleagues—went through the door into the E Ring and collapsed almost immediately, perishing in the furnace-like heat.

McNair's group crawled through the enormous office bay toward the C Ring. There were few ways out of the thirty-thousand-square-foot space; the closest exits were blocked by fire, and others lay a hundred yards across the bay through an unfathomable darkness. They kept hitting dead ends beneath desks or at locked doors. They continued moving, holding onto one another's shoes to stay together. The smoke dropped like a curtain to within a foot of the floor, and it was getting harder to breathe. Water from sprinklers soaked Lieutenant Colonel Marilyn Wills's black Army sweater; she breathed through the moist fabric to cool her mouth and throat, and then stripped off the sweater to share it with McNair and other gagging colleagues. Flaming pieces of ceiling fell around them. McNair figured they would probably die, and it struck him as a lousy way to go.

Unlike Ted Anderson, McNair was no warrior in disguise. He had never jumped out of airplanes or been in combat. McNair had been an administrative officer for his entire twenty-five-year Army career and looked like one, with thinning hair and wire-rim glasses. He was stoic and even-tempered, the son of a newspaper man from Midland, Texas. McNair's wife, Nancy, always said she had married the nicest man she had ever met. Yet he had an inner steel.

McNair heard a voice calling from inside an office at the back of the bay: "Come over here, there's a window." Through the smoke, Army Specialist Michael Petrovich had spotted a window overlooking the service road, AE Drive. The concussion had partially blown the window frame away from the wall but not far enough for anyone to escape. Petrovich threw a laser printer at the window, but it bounced off the industrial-strength glass. McNair joined him. Using their feet, the two pushed the window frame back far enough to create an opening. They dropped their co-workers out, one by one. Twenty feet below, sailors who had escaped from the Navy area on the first floor caught them. Petrovich leapt out and soon only McNair and Wills remained. Wills was distraught—people from the conference room were still missing. Without a word, McNair turned back and disappeared into the black smoke.

On the first floor, the DIA comptroller employees crawled toward the sound of Paul Gonzales's voice. The hole that Gonzales had discovered was a tight tunnel running for six feet beneath a mountain of furniture and debris. Gonzales, a stocky fellow, had barely fit through, losing a shoe in the process. Coming up behind Gonzales, Kathy Cordero found the opening, but Chris Martinez was sure that the tiny tunnel could not be the right way out. "This isn't the hole," she said. "Paul couldn't get through that hole."

"Get your skinny ass through the hole now," Cordero told her. They all made it through. Gonzales kept crawling—the others following—until he saw daylight. They had reached Corridor 5 and walked out to AE Drive.

In the adjacent Navy Command Center, Lieutenant Kevin Shaeffer kept moving, crawling over rubble piles. He slipped past frayed electrical cables dangling from the ceiling, fearing electrocution, and then found himself outside the command center, having unknowingly followed the plane's path through the building. Toward the back of the C Ring, through the smoke, he caught glimpses of sunlight. A hole had been punched through the brick wall, reaching AE Drive. A surge of adrenaline carried him over a dozen desks to the opening.

Shaeffer staggered onto the service road, skin dangling from his outstretched arms. His hair was burned off, his khakis melted into his flesh. His left side was still burning. People looked at him in disbelief. Shaeffer called out: "I'm alive!"

It was just a smoking, burning mess

Rumsfeld had been in the midst of his CIA briefing on the opposite side of the Pentagon when he felt the building shake and the round antique table where he was sitting jump. Many Pentagon workers on the far side of the building—especially those far from windows—did not feel anything, and they ignored evacuation alarms until forced to leave by insistent guards. In parts of the building, no alarms even sounded. But in his office on the E Ring overlooking the river, Rumsfeld had no doubt something was wrong. The defense secretary rushed to the window. Unable to see anything, he hurried from his office and down the third-floor E Ring "to see what the hell had happened."

Rumsfeld found his way blocked at Corridor 6 by smoke. He ran down the steps and out the Mall exit, chased by an anxious bodyguard. Outside, Rumsfeld spotted a cloud of black smoke and rushed toward it. "It was a funny thing for me to do, I suppose, and unusual, but I just felt I had to see what it was and what had happened, because no one knew," Rumsfeld recalled. "There were no eyewitnesses running around the halls telling me. You couldn't call up somebody and ask."

Reaching the heliport, he saw pieces of metal sprayed across the grass and flames coming out of the building. "It was just a smoking, burning mess," he recalled. "There were people struggling out of the building." The first rescue workers—civilian as well as military personnel with medical training—were arriving. Rumsfeld helped lift several victims onto stretchers.

Hundreds of employees were running from the building, some panicked, most confused. Alan Wallace, the heliport firefighter, was catching office workers as they came out a first-floor window headfirst. People collapsed on the grass, crying. Rumsfeld saw people standing and watching from a distance, and he impatiently gestured for them to come help. Others sprang into action. People adopted roles irrespective of rank—some took charge, setting up triage areas; others ran for supplies or carried stretchers. Army colonels, Marines, Navy petty officers, and civilian contractors joined in. Generals took orders from nurses. Rumsfeld's eyes fixed on a young woman sitting in the grass, bleeding, disheveled. "If I can help, bring someone here," she said. "I can hold an IV or something."

Carl Mahnken, an Army public affairs specialist who had been blown through a wall and narrowly escaped with his life, cared for victims despite a welt the size of a baseball on his forehead where his computer had struck him. Mahnken was holding an IV bag for a burn victim when he looked up and saw Rumsfeld helping other injured workers, a sight he found reassuring.

Rumsfeld was stunned when a colonel told him that a plane had flown into the building. After a few minutes at the scene, the secretary realized he needed to get back to his office and the command center. "I decided I had done what I could, there were enough people there, and came in," he later said.

Rumsfeld's instinctive rush to the scene was courageous, an inspiring act for Pentagon employees at a dark hour. Vice President Cheney later said the act remade Rumsfeld in the eyes of the military. But it also took the secretary out of the chain of command while critical decisions were being made about shooting down passenger jets to prevent further terrorist strikes.

Rumsfeld made it back to his office by about 10 A.M. and hurriedly conferred by telephone with President George W. Bush, but the two did not discuss the possibility of military jets taking out hijacked planes. At 10:15 A.M., Rumsfeld walked into Executive Support Center—informally known as "Cables"—a secure communications hub with a video teleconference facility near his third-floor office. Rumsfeld smelled of smoke, and he had sweat and ashes on his face and clothes. His aides were still uncertain what had happened to the Pentagon. "Rumsfeld was our first eyewitness," his spokeswoman, Torie Clarke, later wrote.

"I'm quite sure it was a plane and I'm pretty sure it's a large plane," the secretary said.

Fifteen minutes later, Rumsfeld moved downstairs to the National Military Command Center. The maze of offices, cubicles, and conference rooms was crowded and hectic. More than a hundred people were in the command center, seemingly all of them talking on telephones and radios or bustling about with papers. The staff had not even felt the plane's impact but saw the aftermath on television screens. Captain Leidig, the senior watch commander, had convened an "air threat" conference with the White House and NORAD two minutes after the plane hit; they wanted to include Rumsfeld but he had been out of the building. Operators were also frantically trying to get the FAA on the secure connection; the lapse was causing serious confusion on the critical question of whether more hijacked planes were in the air.

At 10:39, Rumsfeld used a secure red telephone in a corner to speak with Cheney, learning for the first time that the vice president had more than twenty minutes earlier authorized fighter aircraft to shoot down hijacked civilian airliners. Rumsfeld later said his absence from the command center during the first minutes after the attack made little difference. "I don't think so—who knows?" he said. "My deputy was here. The chain of command was complete."

As Rumsfeld conferred with the vice president and gained "situational awareness," William J. Haynes, II, the Defense Department counsel, noticed smoke infiltrating the command center. He was surprised—he had been under the impression that it would be protected against such hazards. It was getting hazy and people were coughing, and somebody worried aloud that the smoke could be poisonous. Aides suggested Rumsfeld get out of the building, but the secretary paid little attention. They tried again about ten minutes later, warning the smoke might be toxic, but he again ignored them. Finally, after another ten minutes, Deputy Secretary Wolfowitz approached Rumsfeld and told him he ought to leave. To his deputy's chagrin, Rumsfeld responded by ordering Wolfowitz to fly to Site R, the alternate command center in Pennsylvania. That was contrary to the established continuity of government plan, which called for the secretary of defense to relocate to the alternate command center. "That's life," Rumsfeld later said. "That's what deputies are for." The secretary figured the forty-five minutes to an hour it would take to evacuate to Site R would leave him out of touch for too long.

Rumsfeld stayed, but the smoke was getting worse.

That's when I saw real fear

The first Arlington County firefighters were on the scene within two minutes of the crash. Many had not waited to be dispatched, but, hearing the radio calls, followed the plume of smoke to the Pentagon's west wall. Arlington Fire Department Captain Mike Smith, a thirty-year-veteran, arrived with Engine Company 108 and was the first fire captain into the building. His crew hooked up a fire hose to a hydrant and raced into Corridor 5, brushing past workers escaping the building. They turned right into the C Ring, working their way to the impact zone.

Smith, who had responded to the Pentagon many times over the years for calls small and large, was astonished by the devastation. "There was a tremendous amount of fire all around us," he later said. "I was actually totally unprepared for the physical destruction of the building." Smith had a construction background and was immediately wary about a building collapse. He could see areas in the corridor where walls had shifted out into the hallways. Smith did not want to commit his firefighters too deeply until they had assessed the structure's stability.

Outside, Arlington County Fire Captain Chuck Gibbs, directing search-and-rescue efforts from the front of the building, was uneasy as well. At 9:55 A.M., he spotted cracks spreading on the façade wall near where the plane hit. Gibbs immediately ordered all rescue workers out of the building. An evacuation tone, with a distinctive high-low pitch, sounded over all radios. Dozens of firefighters abandoned their hoses and rushed out. A team of paramedics came running out an emergency door carrying two injured survivors. Firefighters spotted a disoriented woman inside the building, rushed in, and pulled her out.

At 10:15 A.M.—about forty minutes after the plane struck the building—the Pentagon collapsed around the impact point. Firefighters sprinted back as debris fell and the fire surged. The collapse of the E Ring started on the fifth floor and continued down, each floor falling on those below. It was over in a few seconds. An enormous cloud of dust and smoke shrouded the collapse zone. When it cleared, a great gash in the limestone was exposed, opening the Pentagon from top to bottom.

All the rescue workers escaped, including several dozen who had been in the collapse area. Gibbs's quick and decisive action almost certainly saved them from death or serious injury. Ted Anderson, who had been kept out of the building minutes earlier, realized the firefighters had probably saved his life.

Fifteen minutes after rescue efforts resumed, FBI Special Agent Chris Combs, on the scene as a liaison between the FBI and the Arlington fire department, got alarming news from the bureau's Washington Field Office headquarters. Combs was a former New York City firefighter—two of his cousins would die in the collapse of the twin towers—and on his own initiative had established a close working relationship with Washington-area fire departments. At 10:15, the FBI headquarters informed Combs that another hijacked plane was on its way, twenty minutes from Washington. Combs borrowed a radio from an airport firefighter and confirmed the information directly with the control tower at National Airport. Combs then told Arlington Assistant Fire Chief James Schwartz, the incident commander.

Schwartz immediately ordered the entire site—not just the building—evacuated. Firefighters and rescue workers in full gear ran the equivalent of five football fields for cover under a highway overpass. Word quickly spread that a plane was inbound. Though there was no information that it was headed for the Pentagon, everyone assumed it was; the towers had been hit by two jets. Police officers and FBI agents screamed at military officers and civilians to move away from the building. People sprinted in panic across the South parking lot. It was terrifying, the most hopeless moment of the day, recalled John Jester, chief of the Pentagon police: "That's when I saw real fear in people's eyes."

The plane is five minutes out

Inside the Pentagon, Steve Carter heard the report of the inbound plane on his handheld radio. Carter was fighting his own battle to keep the Pentagon open. He had just learned that the building's chilled water plant was out of commission because of low water pressure. A million gallons of water were flowing through the building from broken pipes. Without chilled water, the computer and communication systems would overheat and shut down. If that happened, the National Military Command Center and all the other Pentagon command centers would shut down—this on top of the Navy Command Center, which was already out of action.

Carter made a quick decision. He would stay with five other building mechanics—half his team—and rebuild water pressure by shutting off valves to isolate pipes in the damaged areas. The rest of his team would evacuate the building. That way, if a second plane hit and Carter and the others were lost, there would still be mechanics left to save the building. Carter assigned engineers to close valves in various basement tunnels. One of the men was an electrical engineer who knew little about water pipes. "All the big valves that are colored green, close," Carter told him.

Carter climbed down into his tunnel. The smoke was so thick it felt like a sponge in his mouth. All the while he heard updates on his radio. *The plane is fifteen minutes out. . . . The plane is ten minutes out. . . . The plane is five minutes out.* Carter struggled to close the valves, breathing through the sleeve of his suit jacket. One by one, the valves were shut off. Water pressure soon built up to fifty pounds per square inch, enough to support firefighters. Carter then got a call that the chillers were back up. He figured he had just enough time to make it to the center courtyard before the next plane hit.

Let me know in case I picked the wrong side

Colonel Phil McNair made it fifty feet back into the black smoke on the second floor Army personnel office and realized he would likely die if he went any farther. Unable to find anyone else in the office bay, he retraced his steps and escaped out the second-floor window to AE Drive, the service road. McNair landed on the ground near a smoking hole in the C Ring wall. It led to what had been the Navy Command Center. He and Sergeant Major Tony Rose, a career counselor from the Army personnel office, could hear voices from behind the rubble calling for help. McNair, Rose, and others formed a chain, tossing computers, desks and ceiling tiles aside, the debris growing hotter and the smoke thicker the further they tunneled. Then an arm appeared through the rubble. It was a female sailor, trying to dig her way out. The rescuers pulled her out, and six other sailors behind her.

They were still digging when a fireman yelled for them to leave: "There's another one coming in!"

McNair was puzzled: "What do you mean, there's another one coming in?" he asked.

"Another airplane," the fireman told him. McNair was dumbfounded. All this time he thought it had been a bomb. McNair followed others to the center courtyard.

Some three hundred employees and rescue workers had gathered in the courtyard, and the scene was chaotic. Doctors and nurses from the Pentagon medical clinic had set up two triage stations and were treating patients on the grass, Paul Gonzales among them. After leading his band of DIA employees out of the building, Gonzales had collapsed and gone into shock—hot, chemicals-laden air had damaged his lungs.

Arlington Fire Battalion Chief Jerome Smith, commanding fire units in the courtyard, ignored the evacuation order, fearing the sight of fleeing rescuers would add to the victims' trauma. But word spread and much of the crowd streamed out, heading through the undamaged portions of the building to the parking lots. Gonzales, on his back sucking in oxygen through a mask, heard people around him yelling: "A plane is coming! We've got to get him out." Gonzales was put on a cart and driven to the North parking lot.

McNair saw doctors kneeling over a badly burned victim lying beneath a courtyard tree and overheard the man give his name—it was John Yates, the security manager from his office. McNair would never have recognized him—Yates had been directly in the path of a fireball and now had burns over 38 percent of his body, his hair burned off and his skin raw. "I walked over and knelt down and put my face next to his, let him know there was a friendly face there, and tried to hold his hand," McNair recalled. Yates screamed in pain. McNair looked and realized Yates' skin was coming off his hand. They took Yates away on a gurney, leaving McNair standing alone. Then someone yelled for him to leave before the plane hit.

Steve Carter, reaching the courtyard, decided to stay, breaking up his maintenance team into three groups of two. Each headed to different parts of the five-acre courtyard. Carter radioed his team members outside: "If anybody sees what side the plane is coming from, let me know, in case I picked the wrong side."

I guess that will be us doing the shooting

At Andrews Air Force Base outside Washington, Brigadier General David F. Wherley, Jr., commander of the D.C. Air National Guard, learned the Pentagon had been hit when one of his officers screamed while watching the news on the office television. Wherley took a moment to calm the woman, whose husband worked at the Pentagon. "You've got to be strong," he told her. Then he raced out of his office and ran several hundred yards to the headquarters of the D.C. Guard's 121st Fighter Squadron.

Unlike other National Guard units, the D.C. Guard reported to the president, not a state governor. Squadron officers—who had a close relationship with the Secret Service agents who worked across the runway in the Air Force One hangar—had already heard from their contacts that the White House wanted fighters in the air. Wherley wanted more explicit authorization. "We have to get instructions," he told the squadron officers. "We can't just fly off half-cocked."

Wherley called the Secret Service. An agent got the White House bunker on another line and began relaying instructions that Wherley was told were coming from the vice president. Within a half-hour, Wherley had received oral instructions giving his pilots extraordinary discretion. The White House authorized them to shoot down any aircraft—including passenger airliners—threatening Washington. "They said challenge them, try to turn them away; if they don't turn away, use whatever force is necessary to keep them from hitting buildings downtown," Wherley recalled.

Three of the squadron's F-16 jets had just returned from a training mission to North Carolina. Only one of the aircraft had enough fuel to keep flying. Major Billy Hutchison, who had just landed and was still in his cockpit, was told to take off again. He launched at 10:38, carrying no ammunition and with little idea of his mission. His F-16 roared up and down the Potomac and over the Pentagon. Two other pilots, Lieutenant Colonel Marc Sasseville and Lieutenant Heather Penney, were given a cursory briefing at the headquarters. "There wasn't a whole hell of a lot to talk about, because we didn't know what was going on," Sasseville recalled.

They ran to the tarmac, but their jets had not yet been armed with missiles. "Just give me an airplane," Sasseville demanded. They took off at 10:42, carrying 20-mm training rounds for their Gatling guns. On the radio, the squadron relayed instructions to look for a hijacked aircraft approaching from the northwest, in the direction of Georgetown. "We didn't know what we were looking for—how high he was coming, or low, or where he was going," Sasseville recalled. He wondered how to take down a passenger jet with training rounds and thought he might be able to saw off a wing. Penney—whose call sign was "Lucky"—planned to fly her F-16 into the passenger plane to bring it down, calculating she might have time to eject before the collision.

Two more jets were launched ten minutes later carrying AIM-9 air-to-air missiles. Monitoring radios in the operations room, Wherley heard the FAA broadcast orders closing airspace across the country and directing all planes to land, concluding with a warning that violators would be shot down. The words chilled the general. "I guess that will be us doing the shooting," he thought.

Well, a little too late

In the Pentagon courtyard, Steve Carter heard the roar of a jet growing louder, echoing around the walls. Carter anxiously scanned the sky. Then Hutchison's F-16 soared over the Pentagon, less than a thousand feet over the building. "That's the point when I felt nothing else bad was going to happen," Carter recalled. In front of the building, through a break in the smoke, Ted Anderson saw F-16s orbiting low over the city and was shocked. He had never thought he would be looking up through a burning Pentagon at jets flying fighter protection over the nation's capital. Arlington Police Lieutenant Bruce Hackert, who served with the Army in Vietnam, had a different reaction when he saw the jets: "Well, a little too late," he thought.

It was too late, on several counts. United Airlines Flight 93 had crashed in a field at Shanksville, Pennsylvania, at 10:03 A.M., thirty-five minutes before the first F-16 was launched from Andrews. Moreover, the hijacked plane had gone down twelve minutes before fire and rescue workers were ordered to evacuate the Pentagon.

The false information reporting the plane's continued approach to Washington apparently came from FAA displays showing the plane's projected path to Washington, not its actual radar track. The information was relayed to the Secret Service and the FBI. Combs, the FBI special agent at the Pentagon, had stayed at Chief Schwartz's side, giving him updates on the plane's supposed path, all of which were broadcast on the emergency network, spreading great alarm. At 10:37, Combs reported to Schwartz that the hijacked plane had crashed, supposedly at Camp David, the presidential retreat in the mountains of Maryland—one more bad piece of information.

At 10:38 A.M., Schwartz sounded the all-clear, ending the evacuation twenty-five minutes after it started. Between the two evacuations, rescue workers had had little time to fight the fire or look for survivors in the one hour since the plane had hit the building. Combs and Schwartz—who would perform heroically through the ordeal—were blameless. They had acted responsibly on information Combs had confirmed from a second source. The evacuation for the phantom plane—and two more false alarms over the next twenty-four hours—"extracted a serious toll in terms of the physical and psychological well-being of responders," a federal after-action report on the emergency response concluded. "These evacuations also interrupted the fire attack and changed on-site medical treatment of in-jured victims during the crucial early stages." Whether the evacuations cost any lives is unknown. "I really can't say if there was anybody in there whose life hung in the balance," Schwartz later said.

The evacuation was just one of several grave miscommunications in-volving United Flight 93. Air Force F-16s under command of NORAD had scrambled from Langley Air Force Base in southeast Virginia at 9:30 A.M. and were high over the Washington area by 10:10 A.M., but the pilots had been told they did not have shootdown authority. Meanwhile, no one in the National Military Command Center at the Pentagon or at NORAD head-quarters was even aware that the D.C. Guard F-16s from Andrews were over Washington with authorization to shoot down passenger jets. Cheney apparently thought his shootdown instructions were being relayed to the NORAD jets and later told the 9/11 Commission he did not know that fighters had been scrambled from Andrews.

Had brave passengers aboard United 93 not staged a revolt against the hijackers that ended with the crash in Pennsylvania, the plane would likely have reached Washington by 10:23 A.M. At that time, the F-16s from Lang-ley lacked authority to shoot down the plane, and the F-16s from Andrews were not yet in the air. The 9/11 Commission wrote, "We are sure the na-tion owes a debt to the passengers of United 93."

Tell me exactly where it hit

Lee Evey pulled into the Wendy's on I-81 just south of the Virginia-Tennessee border for lunch on September 11. His brother-in-law had died the day before, and the Pentagon renovation chief had been on the road for six hours with his car radio and his two cell phones turned off, driving to North Carolina for the funeral.

No one was at the counter at first, but then ashen-faced employees came from the backroom and told him the news. Evey raced back north, talking into both cell phones at once. "Tell me exactly where it hit," he instructed his deputy, Michael Sullivan. The jet had cut diagonally through the newly renovated wedge and then continued into Wedge 2, Sullivan told him.

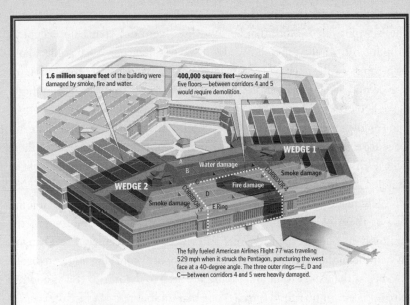

1.6 million square feet of the building were damaged by smoke, fire and water.

400,000 square feet—covering all five floors—between corridors 4 and 5 would require demolition.

WEDGE 1

WEDGE 2

A

B   Water damage

Smoke damage

CORRIDOR 4

Fire damage

CORRIDOR 5

D

Smoke damage

E Ring

The fully fueled American Airlines Flight 77 was traveling 529 mph when it struck the Pentagon, puncturing the west face at a 40-degree angle. The three outer rings—E, D and C—between corridors 4 and 5 were heavily damaged.

Impact on
The First Floor

The plane's path on the first floor carried through Army accounting offices on the E Ring, continued into the Navy Command Center on the D Ring, and into the Defense Intelligence Agency's comptroller's office on the C Ring. The Amy Deputy Chief for Personnel offices sat on the second floor E Ring directly above the plane's path.

CORRIDOR 4

Damaged column

Army

Navy Command Center

Defense Intelligence Agency

C Ring   D Ring   E Ring

CORRIDOR 5

The plane's path.

From a purely analytical perspective, the plane had hit the building in the best possible place. First, both wedges were only partially occupied. About a fifth of the offices in Wedge 1 were still vacant. Meanwhile, about two-thirds of the occupants of Wedge 2 had moved out in preparation for the next phase of renovation. Instead of the 9,500 employees who might have been there, about 4,600 employees occupied the two wedges at the time of the terrorist strike. Of those, about 2,600 were in the immediate impact area. Moreover, the plane had hit an area with no basement. If there had been one under the first floor, its occupants could easily have been trapped by fire and killed when the upper floors collapsed.

The plane struck the Pentagon just to the right of an expansion joint, one of the gaps left in the concrete work from the original design of the building to allow expansion or contraction from temperature changes. When the building collapsed around the impact point, the concrete broke cleanly at the expansion joint, saving the area to the north. It was another stroke of enormous good fortune, one that undoubtedly saved lives.

The hijackers had not hit the River or Mall sides, where the senior military leadership had been concentrated since 1942. Rumsfeld had been sitting in the same third-floor office above the River entrance as every secretary of defense since Louis Johnson in 1949, a location that had been a matter of public record all that time. The joint chiefs and all the service secretaries were arrayed in various prime E-Ring offices on the River and Mall sides. All the command centers save the Navy's were on the River or Mall sides; the National Military Command Center could have been decimated as the Navy Command Center was, a disaster that could have effectively shut down the Pentagon as the first American war of the twenty-first century began.

The plane, ironically, had struck the first section of the Pentagon occupied in the spring of 1942. Marjorie Hanshaw Downey, the Iowa girl who had moved in then with her fellow War Department plank walkers, wept in her suburban Maryland apartment as she watched television that day and realized the area she had occupied nearly sixty years earlier been hit. "It really hurt when I saw that," she recalled. "Not only for the people, but what it did to our country."

Most remarkably, the plane had hit the only renovated wedge. The renovators had started their work in the same place as the original constructors. The plane had hit the only place where the exterior wall had been re-inforced with steel; the only place ballistic cloth had been hung to catch blast shards; the only walls with blast-resistant exterior windows; the only wedge with sprinklers.

Years of work had gone up in flames, but Evey felt overwhelming re-lief when Sullivan told him where the plane had hit. The costly improve-ments had bought priceless protection and time for the thousands who managed to escape.

I'm not running anymore

The plane's path did not strike Phil McNair as good fortune. Leaving the center courtyard, he had walked out a corridor to the South parking lot. He was soaking wet and black with soot, unable to talk from the smoke he had inhaled. McNair walked around the building until he came to the smoking hole where his office had been. The plane had hit almost directly below the office of his commander, Lieutenant General Tim Maude, the Army's chief of personnel. One look, and McNair knew there was no hope for most of his people. He knew where he had been, and, seeing the devastation, he knew that anyone who had been closer than he had been had to be dead.

A nurse saw McNair, standing unsteadily, gazing at the wreckage. She grabbed him. "Are you okay?" she asked.

"Yeah," McNair croaked. "I could use a little oxygen." Within minutes he was in an ambulance on his way to Arlington Hospital with dangerous levels of carbon monoxide in his blood. Ambulances had already rushed Paul Gonzales and Kevin Shaeffer to Walter Reed Army Medical Center in Washington, their drivers swearing and driving off-road to get around hor-rendous traffic. Gonzales would soon be on life support after his lungs failed. Shaeffer had burns over 42 percent of his body, and in the emer-gency room he overheard a nurse assessing his chances as fifty-fifty. Shaef-fer grabbed her and pulled her close. "No! I'm alive!" he gasped. "I'm going to live!"

They had made it out alive, but by then it was obvious to Arlington Fire Captain Mike Smith that no one else would. Firefighters had re-grouped after the evacuation for the phantom airplane and were making a new assault on the blaze, which had intensified in their absence. The young firefighters in Smith's crew were taken aback by what they saw. Smith was one of the anchors of the fire department, solid and even-keeled, a captain whom other firefighters would follow anywhere. "Listen, the key is we're going to stay together and we'll stay safe," Smith told them. But he was worried too.

It was unlike any fire Smith had fought in thirty years. Jet fuel had splashed deep into the building and ignited raging fires. Later measurements indicated the fire reached 1,740 degrees Fahrenheit, a temperature similar to that in the twin towers. The intensity of the fire was forcing crews out of some areas. Protective clothing shielded the firefighters from the fire, but Smith felt as if he was in an oven.

Smith looked up through a ventilation shaft and could see big fires burning through the second and third floors. They were spreading up into the fourth and fifth floors and then the roof. A thick layer of roofing wood beneath the slate was soon burning out of control, protected by the concrete below it and the slate atop it. Up on the roof, exhausted firefighters cut trenches across the slate roof to break the path of the flames, guessing where to breach ahead of a fire they could not see.

Those watching the scene on television and those standing in front of the building had a deceptive view of the scope of the disaster. The Pentagon's very size distorted the perception, even among emergency officials, at first. The 80-foot gash on the building's face was a relatively short gap in the 921-foot wall. But the rescue workers inside found an entirely different reality. "Huge heaps of rubble and burning debris littered with the bodies and body parts . . . covered an area the size of a modern shopping mall," the federal after-action study said. Smith knew from training that a high-impact airline crash decimated a body, but that was no preparation for seeing it on this scale. "It was just a horrible, horrible scene."

The five-story collapse zone in the E Ring was surrounded by damaged areas extending hundreds of feet, where columns and supports had been blown out and floors were sagging and in danger of further collapse. Structural specialists dispatched by the Federal Emergency Management Agency feared the collapsed two-foot thick concrete roof was poised to slide onto rescue workers. As Smith's crew moved deeper into the building, there were dead zones where his radio was not picking up any traffic. "I didn't have the safety of feeling like someone really knew where we were," he recalled.

At 2 P.M. the evacuation tone sounded and all rescue workers were pulled out again; the control tower at National Airport warned of an "inbound unidentified aircraft." Smith heard the tone and left the building but sat down on the back of his fire truck and refused to go farther. "Well, if they're going to crash something, they're just going to get Mike today," he said. "I'm not running anymore." It turned out to be a plane carrying Attorney General John Ashcroft. Firefighters were furious.

After the all-clear, Smith and his crew attacked the fire, but the exhausted firefighters were replaced at 4 P.M. by fresh teams. They had each gone through four bottles of oxygen—one was usually enough even for a big fire—and the fire was still out of control. Smith and his dehydrated crew were put on IVs and taken to the hospital.

As Smith had feared, rescuers were not finding anybody alive. A FEMA urban search-and-rescue unit had been hunting through the rubble with dogs since early afternoon, with no success. Everybody the dogs found was dead.

Out front, Lieutenant Colonel Ted Anderson had given up hope. "There were hundreds of us just waiting with backboards, because we figured at some point we were just going to start dragging the dead out," he said. Late in the day, Anderson overheard fire commanders talking. A group of bodies—five, according to a later FBI evidence report—had been found clustered in the first-floor E Ring corridor, about forty feet from the emergency exit where Anderson had tried to go back to pull more people out. Whether they were the ones the man in flames had screamed were looking for a way out, no one knew.

They would have won

Inside the National Military Command Center, the smoke continued to build. The Arlington County Fire Department was pressing for everyone—Rumsfeld included—to evacuate the NMCC. Rumsfeld still refused to go to Site R, but he did consider moving his headquarters to one of three close-by locations: the White House, the Defense Intelligence Agency headquarters across the river at Bolling Air Force Base, or a third classified alternate command center nearby. Rumsfeld's eyes were smarting and his throat was raw. "The smoke was a problem, but it was not killing people in the part of the building we were in at that moment," he later said.

Rumsfeld decided the Pentagon would not be abandoned. Even on fire, the Pentagon was the best place from which to run the new war. "We had things to do and business to conduct and problems to solve, and we had the necessary people and capacity here to do it, and I decided we'd do it," he later said. Beyond that, the decision was completely in keeping with the secretary's personality. For better and for worse, Rumsfeld had a long stubborn streak; he was a former naval aviator and had the swagger to match. "I also didn't like the idea of evacuating," he said. "They would have won, the terrorists."

Fire commanders decided to send a team to evaluate the smoke and knock down any fire threatening the command center. Firefighters assembled gear, chalked out a plan, and were ready to go, but then realized nobody knew where the command center was. Ted Anderson, hovering nearby, volunteered to take them in.

A battalion chief threw an oxygen tank on Anderson's back and a mask on his face. A bus drove them around to the River entrance, and Anderson—wearing his oxygen tank atop his striped shirt and tie—led the firefighters to the command center. The entrance was guarded by machine-gun–toting Pentagon police officers wearing black uniforms and helmets. Inside, it was packed and hazy, and many were wearing medical masks. The firefighters measured the air quality and deemed it survivable. Exhaust fans were set up to improve the air flow. They checked the area and found no fire near the command center; instead, it was smoke from the crash scene that was wrapping around the building and getting in the intake vents. Steve Carter got a call on the radio and came up with a low-tech solution. When the smoke wrapped around to the vents, workers on the roof closed the dampers, and when it blew away, they opened them.

The smoke did not entirely dissipate, and communications remained unreliable, but the command center stayed open. Rumsfeld and Air Force General Richard Myers, vice chairman of the Joint Chiefs, shuttled back and forth between the command center and the Cables communication

James Forrestal leaving his office on September 22, 1947, the day the first secretary of defense moved into the Pentagon. "He has the bearing given to good-hearted gangsters in the movies," one observer wrote. "There is the suggestion of the possibility of violence and the surface of perfectly constrained restraint." (H&E)

With Forrestal looking over his shoulder, Robert McNamara welcomes his successor, Clark Clifford, to the secretary's office in February 1968. "We mustn't have another Forrestal," LBJ said before ousting McNamara. (Washington Post, Wally McNamee)

The view of the Pentagon Mall plaza from the roof as marchers congregate on October 21, 1967. (CMH)

Military police try to hold back protesters during the chaos on the Mall plaza. "The situation became extremely fluid," an Army report said. (Washington Post, Wally McNamee)

he Pentagon in the minutes after it was struck by a hijacked jet at 9:30 A.M. on September
, 2001, before the building collapsed. (PENREN)

he fire surged after the collapse. (DoD)

Patty Pague, one of the Defense Intelligence Agency workers who escaped from the comptroller's office by following Paul Gonzales, is treated at the scene. (Washington Post, Juana Arias)

Lt. Col. Ted Anderson, who pulled victims from the building before being restrained by firefighters, at the Pentagon River entrance. (Washington Post, Michael Williamson)

An enormous cloud of smoke rose over the building, seen from the opposite side of the Pentagon. (PENREN)

Firefighters on the roof investigate the collapse zone on September 11. (Washington Post, Michael Lutzky)

Firefighters and soldiers unfurl an American flag from the roof of the Pentagon on September 12, 2001. (DoD)

Lee Evey, head of the Pentagon renovation, tours the damage on September 21, cataloging the work that lay ahead. Evey knew nothing about construction but was a master of human nature and motivation. (Washington Post, Bill O'Leary)

Col. Phil McNair led colleagues from a burning office bay on September 11 and then pulled others out of the wreckage. (Washington Post, Michael Williamson)

Allyn Kilsheimer, with pink hard hat. "You make it happen at the construction site," Evey told him. (Washington Post, Michael Williamson)

Doc Cooke, Director of Administration and Management for the Secretary of Defense, during the Phoenix Project reconstruction. "His power was formidable, this Godfather of the Pentagon." (PENREN)

A Phoenix Project worker prepares a column in February 2002. (Washington Post, Carol Guzy)

The "T-Rex" excavator, on the right, joined by other demolition equipment, tears down destroyed portions of the Pentagon on October 25, 2001. (PENREN)

Peter Murphy, counsel for the commandant of the Marine Corps, on August 15, 2002, the day he moved back into his rebuilt E Ring office near the point where the plane hit the building. Behind him is the window where Murphy was standing when the plane hit. (Washington Post, Michael Lutzky)

The restored wall of the Pentagon, seen shortly before sunrise in September 2002, nearly one year after the attack. (Washington Post, Bill O'Leary)

hubs upstairs, depending on how bad the smoke was, and with whom they needed to speak.

Despite the problems, Rumsfeld had another surprise for the fire department. In mid-afternoon, he ordered that the Pentagon open for business the next day. The secretary did not bother to consult with Chief Schwartz or building supervisors before making his decision. "Having it open for business the next day seemed to me to be important," Rumsfeld later said.

To make the point crystal-clear, Rumsfeld agreed to hold a press conference that evening inside the burning Pentagon. Reporters would be bussed to the press briefing room on the Mall side to hear a defiant statement that the Pentagon was still functioning.

Schwartz was astonished at the news. They were battling a big and dangerous fire, an unknown number of dead were in the rubble, and there was danger of further collapse. Rumsfeld's decision "placed additional burdens" on the fire department as well as the FBI evidence-recovery team, the federal after-action report concluded, although Schwartz later said it caused few problems.

Steve Carter was likewise flabbergasted. By early afternoon he believed the building was past the worst and was stabilizing; that, however, was a far cry from making tomorrow a regular workday. But as Carter thought about it, he could understand the rationale. The Pentagon had never closed its doors.

Nobody left

Lee Evey had driven back from Tennessee in record time and showed up late in the afternoon with a car trunk filled with forty orders of hamburgers, french fries, and sodas for the renovation team. He was not prepared when he saw the destruction at the Pentagon. The news reports could not convey the smell of the smoke, the way it grabbed his throat when the wind shifted. It was virulent.

In Evey's absence, the renovation office set up a command center on the heliport landing pad, assuming the role of logistics center by bringing in any supplies requested by the fire department, FBI, and other agencies at the scene. "If they needed it, we wanted it to be there," Mike Sullivan, Evey's deputy, recalled. AMEC, the Wedge 1 prime contractor, brought in shoring timber and steel. Facchina Construction, a major subcontractor, sent a fleet of backhoes, front-end loaders, dump trucks, and cranes, escorted to the site by state police. Construction managers brought in large, clean refuse containers the FBI could use to store evidence; they trucked in gravel for a road to support the heavy equipment in front of the building. When the fire worsened, they ordered generators and floodlights, knowing operations would be going around the clock. Sullivan made verbal contracts with construction companies to support the rescue, and within a few hours had assigned $400,000 worth of work. "I sure hoped the money would follow at some point," he later said.

Jack Kelly and Les Hunkele, two of the most experienced construction hands at the site, recommended a first-rate structural engineer be brought in immediately to assess the building's condition and advise fire and rescue teams on what areas were safe. They were in agreement: The guy they really needed at the scene was Allyn Kilsheimer.

When the call came from the Pentagon late in the morning, Kilsheimer already had a request from New York asking him to help at the World Trade Center. The calls were not surprising. Kilsheimer, founder and president of KCE Structural Engineers, was often called when disaster struck; he had worked the 1985 Mexico City earthquake, the 1993 World Trade Center bombing, and the 1995 Oklahoma City bombing. He was expert at quickly assessing a damaged building, figuring out what had to be demolished, what could be saved, and how to fix it. Kilsheimer was a maverick, a profane sixty-one-year-old with a reputation for enormous energy. He summed up his management style simply: "I take charge of shit."

At his office near Dupont Circle in Washington, Kilsheimer debated briefly whether he should go to New York or to the Pentagon. The latter was practically his back yard, so he had his office call New York to say he would help as he could but was on his way to the Pentagon.

Kilsheimer drove as close as he could to the building, but with the security and confusion, it took him two more hours on foot to work his way to the security barriers. Hunkele retrieved him—Kilsheimer was easy to spot, with his thick black and white beard and hair in a ponytail.

Evey had never heard of Kilsheimer, but he liked what his construction people told him. The two spoke at the heliport. "What do you want me to do?" Kilsheimer asked.

"Help these emergency people do what has to be done," Evey replied. That was the extent of the meeting.

That evening, Kilsheimer spoke with Brigadier General Carl A. Strock, the senior Corps of Engineers officer at the site, to assess the building's stability. Strock told Kilsheimer a team of structural engineers was on the way, but Kilsheimer did not want to wait. "Let's just go take a look," he told the general. The two borrowed firefighters' uniforms and worked their way deep into the building, trying to gauge the conditions of the columns. Kilsheimer's fireman pants were too big and he tripped and broke his toe, but kept going. They found terrible devastation, everything blackened and small fires still burning. Some areas were dangerously unstable, the columns destroyed or severely distorted. But it was clear that many areas of the building were holding up well, despite the damage.

Kilsheimer and Strock sloshed through water to reach the Navy Command Center. It was hot and horrible, filled with a terrible acrid smoke. Scalding water cascaded down from the floors above. The bright new renovated space where Lieutenant Kevin Shaeffer had begun his morning had served as a funeral pyre for two dozen people. To Kilsheimer's right lay the remains of several victims, completely charred by fire. At his feet were two more bodies, oddly untouched by the flames. One victim—his face waxy and mouth bloody—seemed to be looking at Kilsheimer. "I wish we could do something for these people," the general said.

"I don't know what you can do, but we can fix it so you have people back here within a year," Kilsheimer replied.

That night, Evey addressed about sixty renovation program workers gathered around him on the heliport. "Life, as we know it, has changed," Evey said. ". . . If any one of you wants out, now is the time to do it. No questions will be asked."

Nobody left.

Aerial view of the Phoenix Project, March 2002.

CHAPTER 21

THE PHOENIX PROJECT

The Pentagon had held

The orange glow on the horizon grew brighter as Lieutenant Colonel Ted Anderson drew closer. Shortly after 3 A.M. on September 12, 2001, Anderson was riding up Interstate 395 through Northern Virginia, heading back to the Pentagon. Late the night before, he had made it home to his Alexandria apartment, sleeping for several hours before bolting awake. He tossed aside his soot-and-blood-covered suspenders and tie and put on his green Army battle-dress uniform. Another Army officer picked him up and they drove to the Pentagon, carrying flashlights, water, and breathing masks. At first they could not see the building—the low ground of Hell's Bottom was shielded from sight until they crested the hill at Arlington Ridge. Then the Pentagon burst into view. Flames were shooting from the roof, and the enormous building glowed like a harvest moon. Firefighters in front of the gash pumped long streams of water into the blaze.

At 3:30 A.M., Anderson walked into the building to report to duty. He was not alone. Some ten thousand colleagues showed up for work that morning at the Pentagon. The building was burning and the hallways were dark with a smoky haze. An unknown number of their colleagues lay dead in the rubble. Anderson was distraught, but the defiant scene in the Pentagon that morning revitalized him. He now understood what it must have been like to be in Washington on December 8, 1941. "The thing I'm most proud of is that I was part of ten thousand people who reported to work in a blazing building," he later said. "Ten thousand people instinctively knew we were at war now and knew their place of duty was here, regardless of the fact that we had no electricity, we had no water, we had no communications."

Donald Rumsfeld, back in his office at 5:30 A.M., went to a Pentagon studio to tape a message that was broadcast during the day to U.S. troops and Defense Department employees around the world. "This building is a place dedicated to the ethos of heroism," Rumsfeld told them. "Heroes have gone before us. At the Pentagon yesterday, heroes were here again."

The building itself proved heroic on September 11, holding up long enough to allow thousands of people to escape. The ones most impressed were those who knew its warts best, among them assistant building manager Steve Carter. "The plane went through three rings, but it stopped it," he said. "The building held." Through it all, most of the building had not even lost power. The only reason many areas were dark was because electricity was turned off to protect rescuers from arcing and sparking. To Carter, the Pentagon was like an aging battleship, an old bucket of bolts, hit by a kamikaze attack but refusing to go down.

It was hardly business as usual. Half the building was closed off; many corridors were blocked by yellow crime-scene tape and guarded by soldiers with M-16 rifles. Employees stood at windows looking onto the center courtyard, watching firefighters on the roof struggle with the blaze; the fire underneath the slate had grown during the night. Inside the crash zone, pools of fuel from the jet had ignited and firefighters were attacking the fire with foam.

Military officers walked down hallways filled with the stench of smoke, greeting one another with relieved handshakes or commiserating over missing colleagues. Down in the Army Operations Center, where Anderson reported, plans were being formed to pursue the al Qaeda network in Afghanistan.

An American flag, put on the roof during the night by firefighters, flew over the collapse zone. Major General James T. Jackson, commander of the

Army's Military District of Washington, spotted it and wanted a much larger one put up. "If I can get a flag to drape off the side of the building, can you put it up?" he asked Arlington assistant fire chief Jim Schwartz, the incident commander. The roof was still burning, but Schwartz agreed. Soldiers from Fort Myer arrived in the afternoon with the U.S. Army Band's twenty-by-thirty-eight-foot garrison flag. With the help of firefighters, the soldiers brought the big flag up an aerial ladder to the roof and moved to a point twenty-five yards south of the collapse zone. Yellow-helmeted firefighters, red suspenders over their blue T-shirts, attached it to the limestone entablature atop the fifth floor. Under a brilliant blue sky, the soldiers stood at attention and saluted as the flag unfurled three stories down the side of the building.

The Pentagon had held, and so had its people.

Hell's kitchen

By the afternoon of September 12, the fire in the building was largely under control, and the bodies were coming out. By mid-afternoon the next day, seventy bodies had been recovered, but at least a hundred people were missing.

The chaos of the first hours had been replaced by order, and a tent city supporting recovery operations had sprung up in front of the crash site. Arlington police detective Don Fortunato volunteered for a body recovery team and steeled himself for the job. "You know you're going into hell's kitchen, and you're going to get a guided tour," he recalled. "And you don't want to see it, but you know you got to do it."

Fortunato donned a hooded white protective suit along with a helmet and respirator. His four-man team was guided into the building by FBI agents, entering the crash zone through a hole in the wall. The blackness seemed to swallow up the light inside. Fortunato shone his flashlight, but it was still hard to see. Space was tight; in some spots there was room only for one person to get through at a time. Pieces of tangled aircraft metal were scattered about, and wires and ceiling tile frames hung from above. It was like walking through a metal jungle that had sharp edges everywhere.

Fortunato missed the first body they came to, but he was working with an arson investigator with a sharp eye. "I never would have seen it, because it was just char," Fortunato recalled. "And as soon as you started recovering it, then you saw human flesh. You know, it was that bright pink burn. And he was not intact, to put it nicely." He was a lieutenant colonel, according to the insignia on his beret. Half his uniform was burned off, and the other half had been burned into his body.

Fortunato combed through the debris with his hands, looking for anything that might have been part of the man, part of his life, anything that might help his family. Even with masks, the odor was powerful. They put him in a body bag, along with the beret, epaulets, and a pair of tennis shoes. When they had found everything they could, they put the bag onto a stretcher and carried him out. The rule was that no body bag ever touched the ground until they made it out.

Rescuers had not officially given up on finding survivors, although as Wednesday turned into Thursday, what little optimism remained was disappearing. Inside the building, Allyn Kilsheimer thought he heard something overhead, but when he reached the spot, it was another body. More than likely, the sound had been in his head. That had happened to him when he was searching for earthquake survivors in Mexico City: "You wanted to hear something, you wanted to hear somebody alive."

Kilsheimer accompanied Army soldiers using sophisticated listening equipment to search for any sign of life. They heard cell phones ringing, but nobody was calling out. Thousands of square feet on all five floors were piled chest-high with incinerated debris. Someone could be alive, pinned under debris or trapped in a pocket; they would not know until search teams could shore up all the damaged areas.

Shoring had begun around midnight on September 11. Crews first knocked down loose limestone panels hanging on the façade—widowmakers, as they were known. The most critical point in need of support was at the edge of the collapse zone, where the building had broken at the expansion joint, and five stories were standing despite missing first-floor columns. Workers gingerly set the first crib shore in place at 1 A.M.; by dawn the exterior column line had been supported, and the building was significantly safer.

Rescuers methodically worked their way in from shored areas into danger zones, looking for survivors. They used pneumatic pipes for temporary shoring and painstakingly dug with hands and tools to clear the area. Tons of debris were cut and carried out of the building bucket-brigade–style. Thousands of pieces of shoring timber came in the same way, already cut to specified dimensions at a makeshift lumberyard out front.

Whenever a body was found in the debris, work in that area would stop. An FBI evidence team would photograph the spot, document the location, and gather any evidence. A rescue team would remove or cut away any debris pinning the body. Then a mortuary team—usually soldiers from the Army's Old Guard regiment at Fort Myer—would reverentially carry out the remains.

A large area near where the plane struck remained too dangerous to shore up and search. The two-foot-thick collapsed roof hung precariously over the area, and engineers were unsure what was even holding it up. Nobody could rule out the possibility that survivors might be trapped below.

Search-and-rescue team leaders decided to break the concrete roof into manageable pieces and lift them off the building. An engineer recalled a particularly awesome piece of heavy machinery that could do this job almost by itself. It was a huge excavator with a long, articulating boom, with a combination concrete pulverizer and shear—like a giant thumb and forefinger—able to cut, crush, and remove concrete slab. The Caterpillar hydraulic excavator, informally known as T-Rex, was quickly located at a construction site in Baltimore. It was owned by Potts & Callahan—the same excavation company that broke ground on the Pentagon on September 11, 1941. The excavator was soon on its way, escorted by state police. By the afternoon of September 13, T-Rex was sitting in front of the Pentagon.

Kilsheimer asked the operator if he had ever done anything like this before. "No," the man replied. Kilsheimer asked if the man was uncomfortable doing it. "Yes," the operator replied.

They were honest answers, but the operator proved extraordinarily nimble—the best Kilsheimer had ever seen. On the evening of September 14, T-Rex began dissecting the roof, cutting up the two-foot-thick reinforced concrete slab and bringing each piece to the ground. Layer by layer, the collapse zone was pulled apart. Overhead, a lookout crew in a basket suspended by a two-hundred-foot crane scanned the wreckage for any signs of life. As hoped, rescuers found pockets in the rubble big enough to hold survivors, and search teams checked them with cameras and dogs, or crawled in themselves, if possible.

But all they found were more bodies, now coated with concrete dust. The fire that raged for thirty-six hours had been so intense that no one survived.

You make it happen

Unlike in New York, which was dealing with the total collapse of two towers and death on a far greater scale, there was no debate about what would happen with the destroyed section of the Pentagon. Doc Cooke—his teeth gritted—made it clear within hours of the attack. "We'll rebuild it," Cooke declared.

Even as search-and-rescue operations continued, Lee Evey was planning the reconstruction. But the Corps of Engineers wanted the job. They had formally left the renovation in 2000, half pushed, half of their own volition. But the reconstruction of the Pentagon would be a project of national importance, carrying enormous prestige. The Corps, after all, had built the Pentagon, and it asked to be given responsibility for the reconstruction.

Cooke refused. The Pentagon Renovation program had proven itself, as far as he was concerned. "Lee Evey and PENREN have the situation under control," he told the Corps on September 13. "We will call you if you are needed." The Corps was asked to analyze ways to improve the building's structural safety and was put in charge of planning a Pentagon memorial on the building grounds.

Evey quickly selected AMEC—the British conglomerate that had just finished renovating Wedge 1—to demolish and rebuild the destroyed areas. Nobody knew Wedge 1 better, he reasoned. He also signed a contract with Colorado-based Hensel Phelps Construction Company, which right before the attack had won the design-build competition to renovate the rest of the Pentagon, wedges 2 through 5. Hensel Phelps would do the interior work in damaged portions of Wedge 2. Pentagon attorneys concluded that because of the urgent circumstances, they could modify the existing contracts with AMEC and Hensel Phelps without opening the process to outside bids. Evey thus had two major contractors ready to begin work immediately.

The main question was who would lead the effort. The answer was right before his eyes. For three days, Evey had watched Allyn Kilsheimer taking charge and working like a madman.

Anyone going into the impact zone was required to wear white Tyvek suits with respirators for protection from hazardous materials, but Kilsheimer refused to wear the "bunny suits," as he derisively called them. He also refused to wear a hard hat, even when darting under leaning slabs of concrete to rescue classified computer hard drives for the Navy and Army. Kilsheimer had no patience with formalities and was soon infuriating fire and law enforcement officials by traipsing into the crash zone without permission. More than once, FBI agents threateningly took out their handcuffs. Chief Schwartz wanted him thrown off the site. "You're not only about to be removed from the scene, you may find yourself being hauled off to jail," Schwartz warned him.

Kilsheimer was exactly what Evey wanted: someone to propel the reconstruction forward. If it needed to be done, Kilsheimer would get it done—right now. Having a structural engineer in charge of the project's design and construction was unorthodox—typically, that was a construction contractor's job. Yet for all his outlandish behavior, Kilsheimer was known as a conservative engineer who would ensure that whatever was built had ample support. It would not fall down after Kilsheimer was through designing it.

On Friday, September 14, Evey asked Kilsheimer to take charge of the demolition and redesign and to work with AMEC to rebuild the Pentagon. Kilsheimer was reluctant—he did not like the bureaucracy that typically came with government projects. He told Evey he would take the job, but only under these conditions: "I follow no rules but my own rules; I won't deal with anybody wearing white shirts, except for you; and I won't deal with any lawyers or any military people, except at my choice."

Kilsheimer's part of the bargain, Evey said, was this. "You make it happen at the construction site."

Only by the grace of God

That Sunday night, they signed a contract. Then they had to wait. The site remained under control of the Arlington County Fire Department while recovery operations continued, and next it would be turned over to the FBI as a crime scene.

After five days at the site, operating on nothing but catnaps, Kilsheimer decided to go to his home in Northwest Washington. He hobbled on his broken toe toward the car he had abandoned on September 11. When he reached Route 110, he found that a chain-link fence had been erected. As he climbed it, an MP challenged him. Kilsheimer looked down at the MP. "So go ahead and kill me," he said. The soldier helped Kilsheimer over the fence. He made it home, took a shower, and changed his clothes. Then he headed back to the Pentagon to figure out the work that lay ahead.

The first step was to find out if the pile caps in the impact zone were strong enough to rebuild on. Load-bearing tests soon showed the sixty-year-old piles were fantastically strong—three to eight times the thirty tons-per-pile specified in the original drawings. Those footings would support almost anything, and no pile driving was needed, a major relief. However, ground-penetrating radar showed that while the first-floor slab was four inches thick in some places, it was as little as one inch in others. Moreover, the ground had settled in some areas. They would need to pump concrete under the slab in spots to fill the hollows.

Next they had to determine how much of the building would have to be demolished. About fifty concrete columns had been destroyed or seriously damaged, some by the plane's impact, others by the blast and gases that went ahead of the fireball. Kilsheimer ordered tests on surrounding columns in the fire zone that appeared relatively undamaged. Calibrated devices measuring the strength of the concrete showed many columns had been weakened, and that much more of the building would have to come down than they originally thought.

Core samples were drilled from columns and sent to American Petrography Services in St. Paul, Minnesota, for further analysis. The geologists there were incredulous. The concrete—the sand and gravel that had been dredged from the Potomac River sixty years earlier and mixed with cement and water—had been exposed to the most extreme conditions they had ever seen. The heat of the fire had been so intense it had driven out the water attached to the cement molecules, disintegrating the paste and turning it to mush. Saw-cut cross sections of the concrete showed some of the stones had taken on a reddish, even bright orange tint. The extreme heat had caused tiny amounts of iron in the gravel to oxidize, leaving microfractures in the rock.

It meant many of the columns were no longer capable of bearing a load. On paper, there was no way the columns still standing in the fire zone should be holding up four stories. "They are working only because of the grace of God," Kilsheimer said after seeing the test results.

Kilsheimer figured they would have to tear down 400,000 square feet, an enormous rectangular-shaped area encompassing all of rings C, D, and E between corridors 4 and 5. It was a far larger area than what had collapsed, but Kilsheimer concluded it would all have to go, right down to the ground slab.

It was surprising that more of the Pentagon had not collapsed. Paul Mlakar, a blast-resistance expert with the Corps of Engineers, was among those intrigued. Mlakar, lead investigator for a team dispatched to the Pentagon by the American Society of Civil Engineers, walked through the rubble a few days after the attack, slipping chunks of concrete and steel into his pocket. Mlakar, who conducted a similar inquiry after the 1995 Oklahoma City bombing, had found that the damage caused there by the bomb was somewhat small compared to how much of the building actually collapsed. Here was just the opposite: The collapse did not extend beyond the area hit by the airplane. It was clear to Mlakar that the Pentagon had survived an extraordinary event far better than might have been expected. It was certainly worthy of further study.

The remains

At 8:45 in the morning on September 21, all activity outside the Pentagon halted. After ten days, search-and-rescue operations were ceasing. Hundreds of firefighters, FBI agents, and Old Guard soldiers gathered at the crash site for a moment of silence. The Arlington County Fire Department turned command of the scene over to the FBI. It was a sad moment, reflecting official recognition that there was no hope for the 125 people from the building assumed dead.

The Army had lost the most, seventy-four people, twenty-one of them military. One office alone—Resource Services Washington, located directly in the plane's path on the first floor—had thirty-four killed, more than half its workforce. Most of the office's victims were budget analysts and accountants, not soldiers, yet they suffered a casualty rate rarely seen by American combat forces, one comparable to that suffered by a few companies landing on D-Day at Omaha Beach. Despite the devastating losses, the survivors had banded together with volunteers and were working eighteen-hour days in the Pentagon to close out the fiscal 2002 budget by September 30 and keep cash flowing for Army agencies around the world— critical for a nation facing a new war.

The Navy lost forty-two workers, thirty-three of them in the service; most of the dead had been in the command center. The survivors had likewise reconstituted and were now temporarily working in the Marine Corps command center in the nearby Navy Annex, where they were tracking the movement of aircraft carrier groups to the Indian Ocean in preparation for possible strikes against al Qaeda and its Taliban regime protectors in Afghanistan. Nine others in the building were killed, including seven from the Defense Intelligence Agency. All sixty-four people on the plane died, including five crew members and five hijackers. In all, 189 people had died at the Pentagon, though only 116 had thus far been identified.

The search for remains was now focused on a large pile at the far end of the North parking lot, behind a fence patrolled by military police and marked with signs warning against photography. Tons of debris from the crash site had been loaded into dump trucks and carried to the parking lot. Front-end loaders spread it out as flatly as possible. Police cadaver dogs sniffed through the pile first, and searchers painstakingly raked through the debris, looking for remains, personal items, or evidence. The work continued around the clock, with bright lights trained on the debris at night. There were two hundred or more people on each shift—federal agents, police officers, firefighters, and soldiers, most of them volunteers. It was gruesome work—veteran homicide detectives described it as the grimmest of their lives. In their white protective suits and respirators, the searchers looked like astronauts exploring an otherworldly terrain. In these dreadful piles, 70 percent of all the body parts recovered would be found.

I would certainly be dead now

The same day the FBI took control, Lee Evey walked through the damaged areas of the building, cataloguing the work that lay ahead. Blackened cables dangled from ceilings. Windows were shattered, and walls were greasy with soot and covered with markings left by rescue workers and FBI agents. "19 at the least D.O.A.s," was painted in fluorescent orange on the wall by one doorway. Nothing had been done to dry out the soggy building and toxic, psychedelic-colored mold was growing on walls, computers—almost everything. "Doggone," said Evey. "It's all shot now."

The damage caused by smoke and water extended far beyond the 400,000 square feet that would be demolished. Roughly one-third of the building had been affected, and 4,600 Pentagon employees displaced. Industrial fans hummed in hallways, trying to blow out the smell of smoke hanging in the air. Workers wearing hard hats and surgical masks moved down corridors, visible only by the flashlights they held. It was as if time had stopped in some rooms. A soot-covered newspaper from Tuesday, September 11, was neatly arranged on the coffee table in one Navy office.

It was a mess, but Evey kept finding bright spots. He walked into a cafeteria, so new it had not even opened, his feet crunching on shattered glass. Someone had written in the soot in the salad bar: "We will build anew." Evey looked at the skylight overhead. "Isn't that amazing?" he said. "It's not even cracked."

Two days earlier, on September 19, Evey had received an e-mail from Peter M. Murphy, counsel for the commandant of the Marine Corps, whose office in Room 4E468 was in the renovated fourth-floor E Ring overlooking the heliport. On September 11, Murphy had been standing less than a foot from the window watching television when the plane hit. The fireball flashed across the window, the ceiling fell, and the floor buckled. But the blast-resistant windows held. Murphy and the others in the office fought smoke and jammed doors to escape. After they got out, the building collapsed directly behind Murphy's office, leaving the scarlet-and-gold Marine Corps flag in his office exposed to the world but still standing.

"If you had allowed lesser quality windows, I would certainly be dead now, as would other members of my staff," Murphy wrote to Evey. Many had similar stories—the windows and other improvements had saved their lives. Blast-resistant windows as close as ten feet from where the plane hit were not cracked, while many windows farther away in non-renovated sections had shattered. Almost everyone on the third, fourth, or fifth floors escaped—even those directly above where the aircraft hit. Of 2,600 people in the impact area, 125 had died, and all but two of the victims were from the first or second floor.

The sprinklers in the renovated wedge had clearly made a difference. The fire damage in Wedge 1 was markedly less than in Wedge 2, where the fire spread after the impact. Though the sprinklers were useless in extinguishing the hottest areas of fire, the water cooled and wetted those trying to escape.

But there were other stories, disturbing ones, about what had gone wrong. Georgine Glatz, the renovation program chief engineer, assembled a task force of engineering and fire experts to interview survivors and make quick recommendations on how to improve safety. Many survivors, still raw from the experience, simulated their escapes from the building, showing how chaotic and difficult it had been to get out. Exit signs above the doors had proven largely useless. The smoke had descended so rapidly that workers in office bays were unable to see any signs and had been completely disoriented.

The blast-resistant windows, for all the lives they saved, were not entirely a blessing. When the plane and fuel exploded into the Pentagon, the rigid windows and structure helped contain the force of the blast within the building. The blast was channeled with tremendous energy through the D and C rings before exiting through stairwells and elevator shafts and out the C-Ring windows—which were not blast-resistant—into AE Drive, where it dissipated in the open air.

The big open-bay Pentagon offices—in particular the one housing McNair and the Army personnel office—had proven to be terribly difficult to escape. Structurally, the Army office was one room, making it easy for

the blast and fire to spread. The wallboard partitions that divided conference rooms and offices went up only to the suspended ceiling. The space
above served as a superhighway for the blast, dispersing fire and fuel over
a vast area.

Most disturbing were complaints about fire-suppression doors. The
smoke doors, as they were commonly known, had been installed in Wedge 1
corridors as part of the renovation. The heavy, accordion-type doors, hidden in pockets and driven by electric motors, had worked the way they
were supposed to. As soon as smoke alarms detected the fire, the doors slid
shut, blocking off corridors to stop the spread of smoke.

Few of the Wedge 1 occupants had known anything about the doors.
There had been no fire drills yet. People trying to evacuate found their
paths blocked by doors they did not know existed. There were handles to
open the doors, but they kept forcing themselves shut. Building workers finally managed to jam the doors open. Had they not, Glatz later said, "many
more would have died." People were supposed to use stairwells to get
around the doors and leave through designated exits. But the blast, drawn
toward the path of least resistance, had blown through all the staircases,
and they were smoking like chimneys.

The main problem was on the second floor at the foot of Corridor 4,
where people trying to escape the smoke and reach the inner courtyard
found their path blocked at the A Ring. The fire door had closed and people were trapped behind it, caught by the smoke. "All the stairways were
compromised and there was no way out," Glatz said. Two Army officers
used their electronic keys to open B-Ring doors and create an escape route
out a rear door, and then led a chain of their trapped colleagues to safety.
Others, including McNair and his group, jumped out windows. But some
workers turned back toward the fire into danger. Glatz's study was unable
to establish that any of the dead included people whose path was blocked
by the fire-suppression doors. "Some people went back, and I cannot today
tell you if these were the people who died," she later said.

The task force study—and another one by the Corps of Engineers—
exposed underlying safety flaws that had to be addressed. The hard truth
was that, just as some aspects of the renovation had saved lives, other aspects had made it harder to escape. The renovation had not been designed

to protect the building against a hijacked airliner, nor could it be expected to have done so. Now Evey and his team knew differently. Lives might depend on how well and how quickly they could rebuild.

Somebody could fly into the doughnut hole

Evey's initial reaction was to do away with the fire-suppression doors, the cause of so much grief and confusion. But fire-safety experts persuaded him that the doors were needed. They had prevented the fast-moving smoke from reaching areas where it could have endangered more lives. The answer was to mark the doors with luminescent signs and instructions and, most important, to drill occupants on how to use them.

Some of the fixes were easy. Luminescent exit signs would be installed low to the ground, where they would be visible even if smoke were filling up a room. More exits would be added. The sprinkler system would get a backup feed, ensuring two sources of water in case pipes were severed. More fire escapes would be added, especially for the fifth floor; many stairwells went up only four floors because of the last-minute decision in the summer of 1942 to build out the fifth floor.

Corridors that had been blocked off over the years would be reopened, giving workers in the cubicle farms a quicker route out. The building's interior would be hardened with concrete masonry unit walls—cinderblocks filled with concrete and steel rebar. Fire-resistant wallboard would go up in the corridors. Partitions would be put up in big office bays to prevent fire and blast traveling across large areas so easily.

Ironically, though no one realized it, the safety upgrades were similar in some ways to the recommendations—ultimately rejected because they would slow construction—to protect the building after Pearl Harbor by crisscrossing the big office bays with walls.

As was the case after Pearl Harbor, the terrorist attack opened up the cash coffers. The renovation was not scheduled to be finished until 2014 because of congressional funding restraints, but money was no longer a problem. Representative John Murtha of Pennsylvania, the senior Democrat on the House Appropriations defense subcommittee, toured the building in October and declared thirteen years was too long to leave major portions of the building unprotected. Congress soon appropriated $300 million to accelerate the renovation to 2010; offices for senior officials would be completed by 2007. Even as the renovation program geared up to rebuild the destroyed portion of the building, work raced along in Wedge 2.

Security officials decided the time was ripe to fix a threat long posed by the triangle of major roads surrounding the Pentagon. One of the roads, Route 110, ran directly in front of the River entrance, passing within about forty yards of some of the most sensitive places in the building. The idea of moving the road had been dismissed in the past as too expensive, but $40 million was soon found to cover that and other road-security improvements.

The original renovation plan to move all command centers to the basement—scrapped after the disastrous cost overruns—was revisited. Some security officials wanted all the command centers in the basement; others argued they should be dispersed throughout the building. As debate continued, Evey ordered his top staff to design plans for basement command centers, correctly guessing that this would be the ultimate decision.

In October, Wolfowitz approved a $15 million package of chemical, biological, and radiological protection for the most critical parts of the building, including the offices of senior leaders and all command centers. The plan called for filtered air systems, biological, chemical, and radiological detectors, and a quick reaction team to respond to attacks.

To Evey's astonishment, there was even a willingness to reconsider moving the top command out of the E Ring and into more protected positions on the A and B rings. "Recent events have shaken up complacency and there is unprecedented willingness" among the services to do whatever Rumsfeld and Wolfowitz wanted, Evey wrote in an e-mail on October 1. There was a window of opportunity after September 11 to make changes. "That window will not last long," Evey predicted.

Evey asked to brief Wolfowitz about the security proposals. Brigadier General John Batiste, the deputy secretary's senior military adviser, wanted the recommendations "fully coordinated" among all parties before he would set up an appointment with Wolfowitz. Evey exploded with frustration. "I can easily get conscnous by *not changing anything that high rank ing people already want to do,*" he wrote Batiste October 2.

Three years ago I could have made everyone in this building lots happier if I had agreed to take the money I spent on blast resistant windows and steel reinforcement in the walls and spent it instead on walnut paneling and private bathrooms. Believe me, there WERE such discussions.

Batiste scheduled the meeting, but the proposal did not get far. The "magnetism of the E ring was a little too powerful," Wolfowitz later observed. Rumsfeld was later dismissive of the idea, saying the A Ring was no safer than the E Ring: "You don't think somebody could fly into the doughnut hole?"

Are you nuts?

The crash scene was turned over to Evey and the renovation program on October 2. Evey had intended to begin demolition the moment he gained control, but he had second thoughts. A memorial service was to be held on the opposite side of the building on the River terrace on October 11, the one-month anniversary of the attack. Evey talked it over with team leaders. "What's it going to be like for the families to be on that side of the building, and we're over on this side of the building just ripping the hell out of it?" Evey asked.

They delayed demolition, but crews kept working inside the building, cleaning out water- and smoke-damaged areas. It was miserable wearing protective suits in the unseasonably warm autumn weather, but the workers moved quickly. Thousands of displaced employees were soon moving back into the periphery of the demolition zone.

Kilsheimer was worried about getting limestone for the exterior wall; the quarries in Indiana, where the original Pentagon limestone had come from, would be closing for the winter. His initial plans called for substituting concrete for the hundred yards of limestone wall that would have to be replaced. But the Bybee Stone Co. in Indiana immediately sent an estimator to the Pentagon to determine the proper finish and color of the existing limestone, then made sure enough of the right blocks were quarried before operations shut down.

Evey and his team found that attitude almost everywhere. All they had to say was, "I'm calling from the Pentagon reconstruction," and people instantly wanted to help. Home Depot sent truckloads of material, never charging a cent. Small companies that could afford it less were doing the same.

All around the site, there was an undercurrent among the construction workers, an eagerness to respond to the terrorist attack by quickly rebuilding the Pentagon. In early October, Evey was walking through the damaged area when a group of construction workers stopped him and said they wanted a goal established for the program. "We've all been talking about it, and we think the goal ought to be that you move people back within a year," one of the workers said.

Evey considered the idea. The worst thing he could do was set an unachievable goal. He wanted a target that was a stretch but at least possible. The early estimates had been that it would take two years to rebuild. The physical shell alone—the reconstruction of columns, floors, outer wall, roof—was expected to take eighteen months. But Kilsheimer said it could be done quicker.

On October 5, Evey publicly declared the goal: By September 11, 2002, the outer ring of the Pentagon now lying in ruins would be rebuilt and inhabited by office workers. "Not a made-for-TV sham where people sit there with little plastic computer simulations that aren't hooked up to anything and a phone that doesn't work," Evey later said. "Real computers hooked up to real networks doing real work with real phones, everything functional."

As Evey walked around the building in subsequent days, more construction workers came up to him.

"Are you nuts?" one asked.

The view from Arlington

Demolition began first thing Thursday morning, October 18. Heavy-equipment operators climbed into the cabs of their front-end loaders and worked their way into the debris. Bucket cranes carried rubble to waiting dump trucks, while workers riding high in baskets sprayed water from hoses to cut down the dust. An acrid odor—the same one present in the days after the attack—arose from the pile.

Employees inside the Pentagon could hear the thunderous collapse of concrete as the huge yellow excavators ate away at the building. The demolition went on twenty-four hours a day, with 450 workers at the site six days a week and a smaller crew on Sundays, and it continued at night under the glare of generator-powered stadium lighting. Dump trucks streamed in and out of the site, carrying 56,000 tons of debris to landfills.

Early on, the stoneworkers taking limestone off the building were not moving fast enough for Kilsheimer. He ordered the T-Rex operator to start biting into the concrete near them to give them a nudge. Then he did the same thing to encourage the teams removing hazardous material. "All of a sudden they started moving much faster," he said. It had a ripple effect.

Most estimates of how long demolition would take varied from three to eight months. Kilsheimer was the most optimistic, predicting it could be done in six to eight weeks. Whatever the prediction, it was soon apparent that the work was moving fast. In two weeks, workers had cleared half the area.

From the gravesites at Arlington National Cemetery, Colonel McNair could see the work progressing. The funerals for his Army personnel office were in full swing by mid-October. Most of his people were being buried in the same section at Arlington, almost in a line, directly across the road from the devastated section of the Pentagon. The funerals—there were twenty-four of them—continued into December, and the survivors each went to as many as they could handle emotionally.

Seeing his friends and colleagues buried within sight of the place they died was depressing for McNair. During the first funerals, the building looked so stark, with its charred wall and the black gash. As autumn progressed and the leaves fell from the trees, McNair could see more clearly. Cranes and tents were set up, and bustling crews were scraping out the collapsed area. McNair felt something. It was a sense of urgency.

I'm not leaving until this damn place is rebuilt

Kilsheimer felt it too. The one-year goal—"Butts in chairs by September 11, 2002," as he called it—had taken on a life of its own. The more people bought into it, the fewer obstacles there were. "In the beginning everybody thought that I was a crazy son-of-a-bitch and that there was no way that we

could pull this off," he boasted at the end of October. "Now they know that
I am crazier than they thought I was, but it can be pulled off."

Demolition was completed on November 19, one month and a day
after it began. All that remained of the area was the original concrete slab,
swept clean. From the air, it looked as if a huge rectangular slice had been
neatly cut from the Pentagon.

The quick demolition did more than save time, Kilsheimer thought.
The fact that it was so fast meant that the workers for each subsequent
phase would try to beat the schedule. Indeed, reconstruction had already
begun on the far right corner of the slab. Workers drilled one-and-one-
quarter-inch thick, high-strength stainless-steel dowel rods into the old pile
caps. Spiral steel rebar was set around the dowels, and then prefabricated
formwork assembled around the steel. The initial concrete pour was on
November 7, and the first columns were rising.

It was time that the reconstruction got a name. Les Hunkele, one of the
project managers, sent a note to Evey. There had been a terrible fire, and
now the Pentagon would rise from the ashes. They should call it the
Phoenix Project. Not everyone liked the name; some feared people would
associate it with the Phoenix Program, the notorious covert U.S. operation
during the Vietnam War to assassinate Viet Cong cadres. But Hunkele persisted, and the name started to catch. As demolition finished, Evey signed
off on the name.

Thousands of Phoenix Project stickers and patches were given to
workers, all emblazoned with a drawing showing the mythical bird rising
from a smoking Pentagon. Below it was the slogan the project had adopted,
"Let's Roll"—words attributed to one of the passengers who had revolted
against the hijackers aboard United 93. Kilsheimer ordered four thousand
Phoenix Project jackets for workers, these bearing his own favorite saying:
"Lead, follow, or get the hell out of the way."

The momentum built through the holidays. More than a thousand
workers were now on the job. They worked straight through Thanksgiving, but at Evey's insistence—and over the protests of the workers—they
stopped for two days at Christmas.

As was the case sixty years earlier, workers came from near and far for
the job. The morning after the attack, two hundred laborers had lined up
outside the construction gates, and as the weeks passed, tradesmen arrived

from around the country, many sharing hotel rooms or apartments. Phillip Sykora left his home in Cleveland over his wife's protests to join the project and went to work each night with a small American flag clipped to his hard hat. Samuel Mauck, a twenty-eight-year-old carpenter from Front Royal, Virginia, was working twelve-hour days, six days a week, on top of a three-hour daily commute. For him, and many others, the Phoenix Project was "a smack in the face of bin Laden. He tried to take us out, and here we are just putting it right back up."

About 40 percent of the workers were Hispanic, most of them immigrants. The largest contingent was Salvadoran, part of a large population that had come to the Washington area during the 1980s to escape the civil war in their country. Contractor Douglas Ortiz, a native Salvadoran, had waded across the Rio Grande as a seventeen-year-old in 1989 and eventually became a legal permanent resident. Others came from Mexico, Honduras, Nicaragua, Bolivia, and virtually every other Latin American country. Spanish was heard all around the job site, and many signs were bilingual. A lunch truck sold hot tamales and Salvadoran pupusas.

Whatever the nationality or job, nobody was leaning on a shovel or taking cigarette breaks. Workers chipped in wherever they were needed, no matter their trade. Highly skilled tradesmen would pick up brooms and sweep. Sheet-metal workers helped electricians. Union workers helped non-union workers. If someone on a ladder needed a tool, he didn't have to climb down—someone passing by would get it.

Workers were putting in days as long as twenty hours. Many day-shift workers would arrive at five or six in the morning, an hour or two ahead of schedule. Stephen Ludden, a construction foreman from Virginia, would tell them they did not have to start that early, but it did no good. "They didn't want to let up," he recalled. Sometimes the emotion of the job would get to Ludden and he would walk over to an impromptu memorial on a grassy hill overlooking the west wall, where thousands of people had left flowers, notes, ribbons, and teddy bears, and regain his composure.

Everyone worked with purpose, perhaps no one more than Michael Flocco, a fifty-three-year-old third-generation sheet-metal worker from Delaware. Two nights before September 11, he had dropped off his son, Matthew, at the train station in Wilmington. The twenty-one-year-old petty officer was reporting back to duty at the Pentagon, where he analyzed weather patterns for the Navy.

Navy Aerographer's Mate 2nd Class Matthew Flocco died in the Navy Command Center. For months Michael Flocco was flooded with grief for his only child. Nothing helped until he asked his union to transfer him to Local 100 in Maryland, which was providing workers for the Pentagon job. He drove his Winnebago south in January and joined the Phoenix Project. The workers embraced him, joked with him, and shared his grief.

On his first day on the job, he was taken to the spot where his son had died. "How ya doin', kid?" Flocco said. "I'm here. And I'm not leaving until this damn place is rebuilt."

The odd couple

Evey and Kilsheimer had formed a close bond, though they made an odd couple. Evey was polite and perpetually chipper, a short man who strolled around the construction site in a tie, giving pep talks. Kilsheimer, with his full beard and long hair, looked like a disheveled bear and had a temperament to match. For months, safety officials complained that Kilsheimer was not wearing a construction helmet. He finally got a pink hard hat plastered with Mary Kay cosmetics stickers. "My way of saying, 'Fuck you,' " he explained.

Kilsheimer would go to sleep about 10 P.M. and sometimes be awake by midnight. A half-hour later, he would be at his office and work until 4:20 A.M., when he would drive to the Pentagon for the day's first meeting at 4:30 A.M. He would eat an apple on the way for breakfast. Working seven days a week, Kilsheimer had never taken time to see a doctor about the toe he had broken the night of September 11. It had abscessed and gangrene had set in. Over Thanksgiving, he had part of his big toe amputated. He relied on a John Deere electric cart to get around the sprawling Pentagon grounds. He kept veering onto Route 27—a busy road with cars whizzing by—because the sidewalk was blocked. Pentagon police threatened him with arrest, but Evey pled for mercy and arranged for the sidewalk to be cleared.

Kilsheimer's work ethic came from his parents, Jews who left Nazi Germany after the outbreak of war in Europe. They escaped from their home near Baden-Baden in southwest Germany with the help of an American reporter who, according to family lore, intervened when his mother was about to be taken off a train by guards at the French border. The family settled in Washington, and his father went to work as a butcher. Kilsheimer worked construction jobs and earned an engineering degree from George Washington University. He had four decades in the field, but the Pentagon was the event of a lifetime. "It's like I've been in training my whole life for this," Kilsheimer told his wife. "I just didn't know it."

Evey told Kilsheimer he was the program's hired gun. "That's fine," Kilsheimer said. "Just tell them my guns are loaded and to stay out of my way." Evey did keep people away from Kilsheimer, especially reporters; the engineer figured it was so he could do his job, but later learned that Evey was afraid of what he might say.

Whenever questions were raised about Kilsheimer's methods or decisions, Evey stood by him. Kilsheimer himself could not always understand the blind faith Evey showed in him. "How come you let me do all this?" he once asked Evey.

The answer was that Evey had confidence—not so much in Kilsheimer, although he had that, but in himself. After a lifetime of high-stress jobs—including making life-and-death decisions for his soldiers in Vietnam—Evey was not afraid that he had made the wrong call.

Evey considered himself different from the men who built the Pentagon. He was a modern manager using motivational and organizational skills, not a general issuing orders. "I wasn't a Somervell," he later said. Yet there were more similarities than he recognized. Both men demanded the impossible, each with a Southern charm that masked an iron will. Their force of personality drove people to accomplish more than they, or anyone else, thought possible. They shared the same willingness to delegate authority to those they believed could do the job. Evey, like Somervell, was an adept politician, skilled at keeping superiors happy. He was hardly a martinet in the style of Somervell, yet he could make hard decisions about people who failed him. At times, Evey seemed less like a mild-mannered program manager and more like the infantry platoon leader and company commander who led soldiers in combat with the 1st Infantry Division at Quan Loi in Vietnam in 1968 and 1969.

Steve Carter, serving as a liaison between the building management and the renovation program, considered the one-year goal a nice motivational tool but wholly unrealistic. At a meeting soon after the goal was announced, he was shocked at Evey's reaction when someone raised the need to make contingency plans in case they missed the date. Evey's face reddened and he slammed his hand on the table. "The question at the table is not whether it's going to get done, it's what we have to do to get it done," he said. "Whether it will be, there's no question. It will be." Anyone who felt differently needed to find a new job.

Of course, it was easy for Evey to say. He could not even read the construction drawings. Even though he was the boss, Evey often felt like a kid brother to the engineers and construction managers, poking his head over their shoulders as they studied plans. He would ask questions, and they would patiently explain. "I couldn't understand half what they were doing," he later said.

But Evey understood enough. "He convinced everybody that it could be done," Carter said. "If you'd seen what I'd seen, it was an impossible dream."

Out of the ground

In the new year, the building started emerging from the ground. The exterior wall was going up, the second-floor slab had been poured, and columns were rising for the third floor. It was high enough that it was visible above all the trailers and clutter on the ground. Lieutenant Colonel Ted Anderson watched it rising every morning in the dark as he zipped up Interstate 395 in his black Mazda Miata, aiming to get from his Alexandria apartment to the Army Operations Center by 5 A.M. Approaching the turnoff for the Pentagon, Anderson could see the crash site illuminated by construction floodlights, lit up as brightly as the monuments of Washington. For Anderson, the drive was therapeutic. The black scar was gone.

By mid-January, the reconstruction was three weeks ahead of schedule. Construction managers divided the project into three zones, running from north to south. The work progressed wedding-cake fashion, each zone several steps ahead of the next. The strategy allowed them to sequence the work like an assembly line. Though Kilsheimer and the construction team did not realize it, the strategy was strikingly similar to that devised by John McShain and his construction supervisor, Paul Hauck. And it had similar results—the work raced forward.

As had happened sixty years earlier, design and construction were moving concurrently; drawings were frequently updated several times a day. Fabrication drawings for the reinforcing steel would be turned around in one day, and the steel delivered the next. If that were not quick enough, stock steel and a hydraulic bender were kept at hand to meet immediate needs. Every day, confronted with potential snags, Kilsheimer would make decisions on the spot to keep the work moving. "He'd say, 'Drill here. Move this over there,' " recalled Ludden, the construction foreman. "He would know exactly what to do."

Nothing was allowed to slow the work. When concrete trucks were hung up at security checkpoints, Evey assigned badge-carrying renovation workers to ride shotgun on each truck, making sure they got through police lines. Tower cranes swung big hoppers of concrete for a deck pour through high winds, despite fears the stress might burn out the cranes' motors. When snow was forecast for Saturday, January 19, the day a major deck pour was scheduled, the concrete subcontractor, Facchina Construction, brought in extra workers the day before, and they poured six hundred cubic yards, double the normal volume, to keep the project ahead. (Still, that was less than a quarter of the record 2,875-cubic-yard Pentagon pour overseen by McShain in the summer of 1942.)

The goal of having the E Ring ready by September 11, 2002, meant the building had to be constructed from the outside in. It was not the most efficient way to sequence the project—the E Ring would be a barrier blocking easy access to the interior—yet the work did not slow. Contractors brought a surplus twenty-eight-ton hydraulic crane into the interior, and it swung twenty-four hours a day; the crane would be scrapped once the walls were up because there was no way to get it out. To get concrete past the rising E-Ring walls and into the D and C rings, two concrete pumps were set up inside on the slab. Trucks dumped concrete into a hopper in front of the building, and a pipeline carried it to the pumps.

Modern construction techniques allowed shortcuts in building the concrete exterior walls. The old architectural concrete walls built at the insistence of architect Edwin Bergstrom had been painstakingly created with ridges left by gaps in the wooden forms. Ironically, reconstruction managers assumed the ridges were imperfections born of haste sixty years earlier, not a carefully nurtured look. Still, they needed to be replicated, now that the Pentagon was a National Historic Landmark. This time, crews fabricated custom-made plastic liners made from molds of the existing walls. The liners were attached inside formwork and concrete poured in. After the concrete cured, the plastic liners were stripped to reveal new walls that replicated the ridges and even the grain of the sixty-year-old wooden forms.

By late February, the exterior blast wall—this time made of reinforced concrete instead of brick—was ready for limestone panels to be hung. Bybee Stone, the Indiana limestone company, had recreated the original rough, shot-sawn finish of the Pentagon's limestone. Studying the original walls, Patrick Riley, Bybee's drafting supervisor, recognized that the rough finish had been created by an older, horizontal gang saw. Most limestone companies had tossed the old gang saws in favor of modern saws tipped with industrial-grade diamond that made a much finer cut, but Bybee had hung on to theirs.

A crew of a hundred Bybee workers toiled through the winter, milling, carving, and planing nearly eighteen thousand cubic feet of limestone. Bybee's fifty-thousand-square-foot mill next to Jack's Defeat Creek in Ellettsville, Indiana, was filled with clouds of limestone dust and the sounds of buzzing saws and hammering chisels. The gang saw's twelve-foot blades cut through twelve-ton raw limestone blocks, while water and pebble-size bits of buckshot were sprayed across the stone's surface, replicating the look of the original stone. The first truckload of limestone had left Ellettsville with an honorary state police escort in December, and more arrived every week.

On February 25, Evey presided as the first piece of limestone was placed on the exterior. It was a major milestone, and, as usual, Evey made a big production out of it, waving his fist triumphantly as he helped guide the stone into place. After the VIPs and cameras departed, masonry workers discreetly flipped the stone over. It had been installed upside down. "We had a fifty-fifty chance, and we guessed wrong," Evey later said.

5544

The countdown clock

Evey changed the schedule several times to reflect the faster pace, but workers kept gaining on it. A display clock had been set up in the foremen's trailer counting down the days until the September 11, 2002, deadline. Construction workers demanded their own. A second clock, topped with a sign bearing the "Let's Roll" battle cry, was installed atop posts in front of the construction site in early March. Construction workers and passing drivers alike could see the large red digital display clock counting the days, hours, minutes, and seconds until September 11.

At mid-morning on March 11, the six-month anniversary of the attack, the clock registered the time left: 183 days, 22 hours, 35 minutes, and 43 seconds. In the Pentagon's center courtyard, 184 red roses were placed in memory of each of the victims. At the River entrance, Secretary Rumsfeld paid tribute to allies in the war on terrorism; fierce fighting was under way in Operation Anaconda in eastern Afghanistan, where the Army's 10th Mountain Division was battling al Qaeda and Taliban fighters holed up in the Shah-i-Kot Valley. At the job site, the cranes kept swinging and the workers did not pause.

On April 5, the last of the concrete was poured for the roof. The Pentagon was now weathertight and all five floors complete; the concrete frame had been completed three months ahead of the original schedule. The occasion was marked by a traditional "topping off" ceremony. A Marine Corps country-and-western band played amid the concrete pillars and duct work on the second floor. Barbecue sandwiches were served for 1,800 workers, Pentagon employees, and fire and rescue crews that had responded on September 11. Rumsfeld toured the site and razzed construction workers attending the festivities. "I was told you never stopped working—what's going on?" Rumsfeld joked. The workers gave no ground—above their heads, they told the secretary, the final concrete was being poured.

On June 11, the nine-month anniversary of the attack, the last of 3,996 limestone panels was to be placed into the wall. A piece of the original wall—still blackened by the fire but otherwise undamaged—had been chosen. A simple inscription was carved in the stone: "September 11, 2001." Evey was shocked when he first saw the limestone. He had forgotten how dark and damaged the building had been that day.

Hundreds of workers in hard hats formed a semicircle around the building for the ceremony. Others stood atop heavy equipment and building supplies. Evey knelt and placed a steel time capsule into an opening in the wall near the ground, where the limestone would go. Inside were photos, letters from schoolchildren, badges from police and firefighters, and a bronze box with the names of the 184 Pentagon victims. The intent was that the capsule never be opened. A crane lifted the limestone off the ground, and Paul Wolfowitz, the deputy secretary, guided the stone to its place, a few dozen yards from where the plane hit. The charred stone stood in stark contrast to the surrounding new panels.

That evening, after 273 nights, spotlights that had been trained on the damaged wall were turned off. The outside work was essentially complete, and now the main effort would be inside. There, too, the work was ahead of schedule. Workers were already running wires, hanging drywall, and laying carpet. The countdown clock showed ninety-two days left and nobody doubted that they would finish on time.

People needed to remember

Peter Murphy's knees felt weak as he walked into his office on August 15, 2002. Murphy, counsel for the commandant of the Marine Corps, was moving back in that day with twenty-one colleagues, the first employees to return to the E Ring. Murphy was apprehensive and awestruck at the same time. "It's kind of a twilight zone, almost," he said. "It's a strange sensation, coming back to an office you could have been killed in."

His fourth-floor office had been demolished in the terrorist attack, and the building had collapsed directly beyond his desk. The whole area had been razed, but less than a year later, the office had been recreated. A scarlet-and-gold Marine Corps flag again stood in the corner, and the blue drapes and the blue-and-red carpet were immaculate. Movers wheeled in Murphy's antique desk—a gift from a former commandant—which had somehow survived. The desk was placed in the same spot it had occupied before. It was as if the clock had been turned back to 9:37 A.M. September 11, just before the plane hit.

In the hallway outside Murphy's office, workers adjusted fluorescent lights. Others hooked up computers and telephones in neighboring suites. The muffled sounds of hammering and drilling drifted down the corridor.

Murphy, tall and lean and dressed in a blue suit, walked over to where he had been standing at that moment, in front of a blast-resistant window that had saved his life. He opened the shades and looked out the new window. The Pentagon heliport below was now a staging area filled with construction equipment and workers. "We used to consider this place so incredibly safe," he mused.

"Welcome back" signs emblazoned with American flags hung on the walls of the offices, and Rumsfeld came by to shake hands. But the sense of celebration was muted. Everyone felt a bit uneasy about moving back, remembering those who had died and would not be returning.

Murphy needed no reminders. But some Pentagon employees had been far from where the plane hit and had never seen the damage. Earlier, Evey overheard some of them talking in the corridors. "They see it looking exactly like it did before, and they think there was no damage here, maybe they came through and spritzed it a little," he said.

That bothered Evey. It was almost as if September 11, 2001, had never happened. He ordered photographs put up on the bulletin boards in the corridor near the escalators. They showed the twisted shards of metal hanging from ceilings, the smashed doors, the burnt-out offices. People needed to remember.

Murphy had been astonished when he was told he would reoccupy his office before a year had passed. He had gone back to the scene a few days after September 11, accompanied by Kilsheimer. It was an unsettling experience. His desk was near the open edge of the four-story abyss. Had the plane hit ten feet to the left, he and everyone in his office would have perished, Kilsheimer told him. "The idea of getting back in seemed so unrealistic," Murphy said. "It was god-awful in there."

Outside, the countdown clock was stopped at 10:51 that morning, the exact time Murphy's desk was delivered. The 3,000 workers of the Phoenix Project, led by Evey and Kilsheimer, had made good on their promise, and beaten the deadline by more than three weeks.

"They felt they had been watched," Evey later said. "Not just by the eyes of an anxious nation, but by the spirit of the workforce that first wrestled the Pentagon out of the quagmire of Hell's Bottom."

The common wisdom was that the World War II esprit and national purpose that built the Pentagon in seventeen months would be impossible to recreate sixty years later. It seemed all the more unlikely, given the problems the Pentagon renovation had faced. Yet the doubts had been proven wrong. The damaged building had been restored in a manner that echoed its creation.

Artist's rendering of the Pentagon memorial shaded with maple trees, with 184 benches representing the victims.

EPILOGUE

September 11, 2002

Except for the wind, the morning of September 11, 2002, was much like that of a year earlier, a pleasant, warm day under a brilliant blue sky. A crowd of thirteen thousand filled the grounds in front of the Pentagon's healed west wall to mark the one-year anniversary of the attack. Soldiers, sailors, airmen, Marines, rescue workers, airline pilots, and construction workers were packed into bleachers, their uniforms, dark-blue suits, and hard hats reflecting the great scope of the disaster that brought them together. The victims' relatives sat in front of a bunting-decked stage, their faces telling of the enormous loss suffered September 11, 2001.

Dozens of flags flapped furiously on their poles. Clouds of dust swirled around the construction site and blew above the crowd, over husbands without wives, wives without husbands, and children missing parents. As the national anthem played, soldiers atop the Pentagon unfurled the same American flag that hung from the side of the building after the attack. But the wind kept blowing it back to the roof. At 9:37 A.M.—the time the plane struck the building—the crowd fell silent for a long moment. When Secretary of Defense Donald Rumsfeld spoke, he chose words meant to echo those spoken 137 years earlier by Abraham Lincoln at Gettysburg. "In a sense, we meet on a battlefield," Rumsfeld said.

> If it does not appear so today, that is because of the singular devotion of the men and women who worked day and night to fulfill a solemn vow that not one stone of this building would be out of place on this anniversary. . . . But one year ago, this was a battle zone, a scene of billowing smoke, towering flames, broken rock, and twisted metal. It says much about our nation and the fierceness and resilience of the American people that were we not here now in this solemn ceremony, a visitor passing would see no hint of the terrible events that took place here but one year ago today.

All around the Pentagon that day, a sense of change was in the air. The focus inside the building was already moving away from hunting al Qaeda terrorists in Afghanistan and toward a new conflict with unclear connections to September 11. Speaking after Rumsfeld, President George W. Bush made a veiled reference to Iraqi leader Saddam Hussein, whom the president had accused of harboring weapons of mass destruction. "As long as terrorists and dictators plot against our lives and our liberty, they will be opposed by the United States Army, Navy, Coast Guard, Air Force and Marines," Bush said. In the audience, Cory Holland, the nephew of Pentagon victim Rhonda Rasmussen, thought there was no mistaking the intent of those words, and he felt uneasy. "It was prepping for what's going to happen in Iraq," he told a reporter after Bush spoke.

Doc Cooke was conspicuous in his absence from the ceremony. After forty-five years and fifteen secretaries of defense, the mayor of the Pentagon was gone. Three months earlier, driving to a conference in Charlottesville, Virginia, Cooke was severely injured when his car veered off the road. He died on June 22, 2002, at age eighty-two. Hundreds had attended a memorial service for Cooke in the Pentagon courtyard, among them Secretary of State Colin Powell, honoring the man who had bailed him out of the Pentagon hoosegow almost two decades earlier. Rumsfeld noted that without the renovation championed by Cooke, "many more than 184 lives would have been lost" on September 11. Cooke had been a towering figure at the Pentagon for four decades—"not only its operational brains but its spiritual ballast," Rumsfeld observed—and his loss still hung heavy at the one-year anniversary of the attack.

The Phoenix Project was winding down, its leaders departing. Lee Evey would retire from government service in a few weeks, having put off retirement after the attack. But by June 2003—three months after the U.S. invasion of Iraq that toppled Hussein—he would be sent to Baghdad by the U.S. government to serve as the senior adviser to the Iraqi Ministry of Housing and Construction. Insurgents attacked Evey's convoy on the day he arrived, forcing the caravan to hightail it back across the Kuwaiti border temporarily, setting the tone for a frustrating four-month stint.

Allyn Kilsheimer was leaving the program, his work largely done. In the final weeks before the ceremony, Kilsheimer visited the cemetery where his parents, refugees from Nazi Germany, were buried, near Washington in Prince George's County, Maryland. It was the first time he had been able to make it since the terrorist attack. He told his parents he had been able to pay back a debt the family owed to America.

The Pentagon ceremony on the morning of September 11 was somber and sad, and properly so, honoring those lost in the attack. But in the afternoon, there was a second gathering honoring the construction workers— the "hard-hat patriots of the Phoenix Project," as General Richard Myers, chairman of the Joint Chiefs of Staff, called them. It was a more casual, celebratory affair. Construction workers, their hard hats covered with patriotic stickers, whooped and cheered and waved American flags. They sat with their families, along with Pentagon employees, military officers, and victims' relatives who had come to thank the workers.

They had dedicated a year to the project, putting their own lives and families on hold in pursuit of something greater than themselves, and the thanks they received were heartfelt: "The honor at this moment is ours, as we stand among those of you who represent the very best of America, to be among men and women who have demonstrated once again that America is a land where dreams are large, where hearts hunger to build a better world, where ordinary people achieve extraordinary things," Paul Wolfowitz, the deputy secretary, told them.

Evey, emotional and ebullient, addressed the crowd of six thousand: "We promised, with the eyes of the nation on us, that we would rebuild the damaged portions of the Pentagon faster than anyone has a right to expect.

Today we are delivering on that promise. We are back in business with a building stronger and more capable than ever before. . . . America, we give you back your Pentagon."

A $5 billion affair

The work on the Pentagon was far from done. There were no countdown clocks ticking toward deadlines, and no media glare on the construction, yet more than a thousand workers remained on the job, the largest reconstruction project in the world. Indeed, the renovation and add-on projects soon ballooned into a $5 billion affair. It was a figure that dwarfed the estimated $75 million cost of building the Pentagon and surrounding roads and facilities when it was finished in 1943; even converted to 2006 dollars, Somervell's Folly had cost approximately $925 million.

Upon the official completion of the Phoenix Project in February 2003—with the restoration of all Wedge 1 areas damaged by the attack—the main effort turned to renovating the remaining four Pentagon sections, led by the Colorado-based contractor Hensel Phelps. The old $1.1 billion congressionally mandated cap had been dropped to speed the work. New legislation provided more than $1 billion for wedges 2 through 5 alone, with adjustments allowed for inflation. That cost did not include the complete transformation of the Pentagon's information-technology infrastructure, itself a $1 billion-plus project overseen by General Dynamics. Another $50 million was being spent to replace the 1.3-million-square-foot roof, which had proved such a fire hazard on September 11.

Further adding to the tally were the security upgrades ordered after September 11—the rerouting of roads, the chemical, biological, and radiological safeguards, the stronger building. A $300 million Command Communications Survivability Project added backup communications throughout the building and elsewhere around Washington; it came from the realization that, had the plane destroyed the building's telephone or classified messaging centers, the Pentagon could have been forced to close.

As Evey had predicted after September 11, the Pentagon's command centers were being moved to the basement. An additional $175 million was appropriated to create another 200,000 square feet of space in the basement, put the command centers under the building, and finish the work by

2007. Crews were digging again in the basement, picking up where they had left off after the costly excavation in the 1990s was canceled. Workers spent months in 2003 welding together a huge steel-plate box to house sensitive portions of the new National Military Command Center.

Rumsfeld had seized the opportunity to overhaul and create a more unified command infrastructure. He was dissatisfied with the chaos on September 11, with command and communications spread in different locations. "The question came up as you redid the Pentagon . . . can we merge them in ways that are useful and create a more joint approach?" he later said. Rumsfeld wanted command more centralized in the National Military Command Center, with better collaboration among the services and the Joint Chiefs. The services would retain their individual centers, but Rumsfeld wanted them to serve as operations centers, not command centers. When the new NMCC opened in early 2005, it included a unified command center watch cell, with all four services always represented. The destroyed Navy Command Center was replaced with a Navy Operations Center in the basement, with a plaque dedicating it to the memory of the forty-two Navy victims and with the Arleigh Burke Bell, which survived the inferno, back on display.

Various extras were thrown into the Pentagon renovation. A new $25 million Pentagon Athletic Center was constructed with features that Dick Groves, the original Pentagon gym advocate, could only have dreamed about. The athletic center—built outside the building, partially underground, between the Mall terrace and Doc Cooke's delivery facility—had an Olympic-sized pool, basketball, squash, and racquetball courts, a weight room, whirlpools, and a suspended jogging track. The space included a $15 million Pentagon auditorium, complete with a television studio where the Defense Department could produce its own programming. Meanwhile, the old gym that Groves had created six decades earlier underneath the River terrace was expanded and converted into a $38 million Pentagon Library and Conference Center, a state-of-the-art meeting facility for banquets, performances, and lectures; the once-gloomy underground space was illuminated with large skylights and a glass wall. Even the Ground Zero Cafe in the courtyard was to be rebuilt and quadrupled in size.

By 2007, the renovation was on pace for completion by 2011. Wedge 2, the second of the five Pentagon wedges, was finished in the fall of 2005, four years after it began. Demolition of Wedge 3, home to the most senior Pentagon officials and including the space once occupied by Henry Stimson and George Marshall, proceeded apace. In November 2005, Rumsfeld was evicted from Room 3E880, the first secretary of defense forced out of the prime space atop the River entrance since Louis Johnson commandeered it in 1949. Movers wheeled out the great Pershing desk. The office was shifted to the newly renovated third-floor offices in Wedge 2, above the Mall entrance, the area once home to James Forrestal and, before him, Brehon Somervell. Rumsfeld groused about leaving and complained the new space was not to his liking, but he had no choice. To save money and the trouble of moving again, renovation officials wanted to keep future secretaries in the Mall offices. But, at Rumsfeld's insistence, his successors will be back in the old location after the renovation of the area is finished in 2007.

Ironically, despite the billions of dollars spent and more than fifteen years of work, the Pentagon will in the end hold many fewer employees than when the renovation started. Office space is being swallowed up to bring the Pentagon into compliance with handicapped-access laws and fire-safety codes; more space is being lost to senior officials insisting on private offices. "When we get done, the whole Pentagon will hold approximately 20 percent fewer people than it held at the beginning," said Ken Catlow, who took over as director of the Pentagon renovation in 2004. "But it wasn't safe when we started. It will be safe when we finish." When completed, the Pentagon will hold just under twenty thousand people—five thousand fewer than before the renovation started, and less than half the forty thousand Somervell once envisioned.

Despite the safety upgrades, a palpable uneasiness lingered among many Pentagon employees, an inescapable realization that the building remained a target in the new age of terrorism. As time passed, workers— especially those who had narrow escapes—worried that the lessons of September 11 were being forgotten. They complained that exits were once more being blocked off as Army colonels and Navy captains rearranged their spaces. They feared that people could be trapped again behind fire suppression doors. Their fatalistic notions were not unlike those of Pentagon workers from the Cold War generation, sitting at ground zero in the center courtyard, munching a hot dog.

Perhaps inevitably, the renovation drew carping from some employees. Partly this was because the new construction did not always seem as solid as the original; the new walls were soon gouged with holes and scuff-marks, bathrooms with fancy modern sensors fell out of order, and con-crete steps crumbled. And partly it was intangible nostalgia about the original building, with its design quirks, World War II–era decor and signs on the walls, and ancient fixtures. Somehow, they liked the old Pentagon better.

We claim this ground

The aspect of the Pentagon renovation program that now held the greatest emotional resonance was the construction of a memorial to the victims of September 11.

The project moved swiftly at first; the Corps of Engineers began plan-ning it within days of the attack. In spring 2002, Doc Cooke—in one of his final acts before his death—chose a two-acre memorial site on land outside the west wall near the point of the plane's impact, on the ground over which the jet flew in the last split-seconds before hitting the building. An open design competition held soon afterward generated more than 1,100 entries from around the world. A panel of jurists, including family mem-bers of victims, chose a design submitted by two young New York archi-tects, Julie Beckman and Keith Kaseman.

It would be a peaceful, tree-shaded memorial with 184 illuminated benches, each representing a victim. The benches—cantilevered, stainless-steel structures—would be set above individual reflecting pools of water and lit from beneath. They would be oriented along a timeline set to the age of each victim, from the youngest, three-year-old Dana Falkenberg, to the oldest, seventy-one-year-old Joseph Yamnicky. Some eighty paperbark maples—their bark cinnamon-brown and their leaves brilliant red in the fall—would shade the site. "The memorial had to be like no other memor-ial, because September 11 was like no other day," Beckman said.

When the design was revealed on March 3, 2003, renovation officials said they expected to break ground that June and finish the memorial by September 11, 2004. This prediction soon proved wildly over-optimistic, and the initial cost estimate of between $4.9 million and $7.4 million far under the mark. Groundbreaking was pushed back. By 2005, the cost was estimated at $22 million, with another $10 million for an endowment to maintain the memorial. The federal government contributed $1 million, but most of the money would have to come from private contributions. Family members led the fund drive, but raising that much money proved challenging. Donations came from many sources—Pentagon employees, defense corporations, newspapers, churches, and construction companies, among others. Rumsfeld and his wife gave $100,000. Sixth-grader Kelsey Donovan—whose father, Commander Bill Donovan, was among those killed in the Navy Command Center—held a bake sale and set up a drink stand along a bike trail in Northern Virginia. Slowly but surely, the money was raised.

On June 15, 2006—another brilliant, sunny day at the Pentagon—some 300 families members, joined by the Joint Chiefs of Staff, cabinet members, and other dignitaries, gathered at the memorial site. Ground was being broken at long last. Crews were already removing utilities from the site, and the new goal was to dedicate the monument in the fall of 2008.

It had been a long haul to get to this day—longer than expected, nearly five years since the attack. Yet Lisa Dolan, whose husband, Navy Captain Bob Dolan, died in the attack, was at peace with the time it had taken, as were other family members at the ceremony. "The families have always felt it didn't matter how long it took, as long as it was done right," she said.

Rumsfeld came striding from the building, accompanied by the official party. The secretary had been determined to see this day before he left office. The days of September 11—when Rumsfeld had captured the nation's imagination with his heroic rush to the crash site and his bravura performances in the Pentagon press briefing room as American forces overthrew the Taliban in Afghanistan—seemed a distant memory. The Iraq war had been a long and difficult slog. Many failures had been laid at Rumsfeld's door. The secretary and his top aides were accused of ignoring warnings and not preparing for the long Iraqi insurgency that followed the invasion. More than 2,400 American soldiers had died in Iraq, and no exit seemed apparent. Rumsfeld's tenure had seen the torture of Iraqi prisoners at Abu Ghraib prison and similar incidents that marked the erosion of long-held standards of American conduct in war. The secretary of defense with whom he was most often compared was the only one who, as of that date, had had more time in office than Rumsfeld—Robert McNamara. Calls for Rumsfeld's resignation were routine, and he would be ousted before the year was over amid deteriorating public support for the war. Rumsfeld had dismissed the criticism, an attitude that further infuriated his critics and fostered regular accusations that he was coldly insensitive to the costs of the war.

Yet when Rumsfeld spoke on this day about those lost on September 11 and all that had followed, his voice seemed to catch, and he spoke with real emotion. "He still feels it in his heart," thought Kris Fisher, whose husband, Gerald, an Army employee, died in the attack.

Rumsfeld and a family member pulled off a black cloth unveiling a piece of limestone—one of the original pieces of the Pentagon, salvaged after September 11—that would serve as a memorial marker. The secretary read aloud the words carved on it: "We claim this ground in remembrance of the events of September 11, 2001." Afterward, Rumsfeld stayed for over an hour at the dusty site, talking to dozens of family members, anyone who wanted a word with him.

Nearby, Abraham Scott lingered too, standing not far from the spot where a bench would one day bear the name of his wife, Janice, an Army budget analyst. He was proud of the families for driving the memorial forward, and he felt sure his wife would have been too. It was hard to be back on this ground. They had worked together at the Pentagon for many happy years, and though he could no longer bring himself to walk into the building where Janice had died, he knew this spot was the right place for the memorial. It was little more than windswept ground with gravel and withered grass. But he could see it, a place where they would be at peace.

For the ages

On January 23, 2003, Army Corps of Engineers blast expert Paul Mlakar appeared at the Pentagon to release the American Society of Civil Engineers' study on how the building had performed on September 11, 2001. The six-man investigation team, including specialists in structural, fire, and forensic engineering, had finished their work in April 2002, but the Pentagon Force Protection Agency, responsible for the building's security, balked at releasing the report out of fear that it might provide a blueprint to terrorists seeking to strike again. Engineers argued that the report held important lessons on how to construct safer buildings. After months of debate, the security agency finally agreed to release it.

The report affirmed that the blast-resistant windows added by the Pentagon renovation had saved lives on September 11, and that the new steel framework had strengthened the exterior walls. But the real credit for why the Pentagon performed as well as it did—and why so many escaped—belonged to its builders. "There was a lot about the way the building was originally constructed that contributed to its resilience," Mlakar later said.

The building had held up so strongly in the face of extreme forces that the engineering team recommended that "the features of the Pentagon's design that contributed to its resiliency in the crash—that is, continuity, redundancy, and energy-absorbing capacity—be incorporated in the future into the designs of buildings and other structures in which resistance to progressive collapse is deemed important." These features were fairly typical of reinforced-concrete construction in the 1940s but are not as common today, having been jettisoned in favor of streamlined construction methods that meet safety codes but do not provide the extra protection given the Pentagon.

The building's structural redundancy came from the robust beam-and-girder system that held up its floors. Floor slabs were supported by beams that in turn were supported by girders, in a crisscross pattern interlocking with the columns. "That two-dimensional network was very forgiving, in that if you removed a column, the load could go in two different directions without collapsing," Mlakar later said.

Reinforcement bars in the beams and girders extended into adjoining sections, providing continuity that further strengthened the floor. The structure acted as a whole, rather than as individual pieces. Thus—even though about thirty columns were destroyed by the plane's impact, another twenty were significantly damaged, and dozens more were weakened by the fire—the building bridged the gaps. The built-in redundancy and continuity enabled the structure to transfer the load to stronger columns and remain standing.

Moreover, the Pentagon had an unusual measure of strength thanks to a curious, almost forgotten oddity: Franklin D. Roosevelt's quixotic hope to turn it into an archive after the war. FDR had insisted that Somervell build the floors strong enough to hold heavy file cabinets; the general ordered them designed to support 150 pounds per square foot, twice the norm. Sixty years later, Roosevelt's tinkering paid off. The extra steel and concrete and the close spacing of the columns—generally ten, fifteen, or twenty feet apart—gave the building reserve strength that helped it withstand the blow. The plane disintegrated against the "forest of columns" on the first floor, the report noted.

The Pentagon's columns were particularly strong because the builders used spiral rebar—circular coils of reinforcement steel that wound through the columns like a rib cage. Spiral rebar tends to be used more often in seismic zones, because of the added strength it provides when an earthquake shakes a building. Most modern buildings are constructed with straight reinforcement rods, which require less labor. Spiral rebar was more common in the 1940s, and it is not surprising that architect Edwin Bergstrom and his design team, coming from earthquake-prone California, would favor it.

"It makes a strong column—strong as the dickens," recalled Donald Walker, the steel rodman who put rebar into the Pentagon's beams and columns. On September 11, the spiral-reinforced columns acted like shock absorbers against the tremendous lateral forces created when the aircraft slammed into the Pentagon. The plane's impact and subsequent explosion scoured the cover off about thirty columns, but the core of concrete within the spirals stayed whole. Columns were twisted with dramatic curves— some bent like a bow shooting an arrow—but they remained standing, still bearing their loads.

Two columns in particular made a difference. They stood next to each other along the D Ring, labeled 9 and 11 F, and were directly in the path taken by the plane. They had been hit by the avalanche of aircraft and building debris and were subjected to terrific heat. The two columns were bowed and burned yet continued to support the building at its most critical point, bordering the expansion joint where the collapse broke off. "The spiral reinforcement in those two columns must have been a key factor in preventing a widespread collapse," the report concluded.

Six decades earlier, Ides van der Gracht might have paced the aisle beside the sweating draftsmen who drew the plans for those columns. Joe Allan and his fellow carpenters could have put the wood forms for the columns together, hammering to the rhythm of the pile drivers. Perhaps Donald Walker's steel crew rushed to put up the spiral rebar. The concrete for the columns may have been poured under the watchful gaze of the ever-present job supervisor, Paul Hauck, or perhaps the indomitable John McShain himself. Captain Clarence Renshaw and Lieutenant Bob Furman might have roamed the dusty site as the columns went up, looking for any problem before their great taskmaster, Colonel Dick Groves, discovered it. The two columns were built right, and they held, and they made a difference.

The Pentagon had been conceived over a long weekend. Its design had been one step ahead—and sometimes one behind—its construction. The pentagonal shape, like so many aspects of the building, was essentially an accident, born of the speed in which the project was pursued. The construction had been slapdash; columns were missing, concrete pours uneven, drawings wrong or missing altogether. Yet somehow the Pentagon was designed wisely and constructed well. Somervell's building had proven itself one for the ages.

ACKNOWLEDGMENTS

In trying to reconstruct the creation of the Pentagon from a distance of sixty years, I was fortunate to be able to rely on the groundwork laid by many Army historians. In particular, thanks are owed to Lenore Fine and Jesse Remington, authors of the Army's official history of construction by the Corps of Engineers in the United States during World War II. While the Pentagon occupies only a small portion of their 1972 book, their research over more than two decades was of enormous value to this book. The interviews they conducted with figures large and small and the documents they left with the Corps of Engineers' history office are a treasure trove of records on the Pentagon's construction.

Alfred Goldberg, the Defense Department's chief historian, first laid eyes on the Pentagon in 1943. His pictorial history of the Pentagon, published in 1992 to mark the building's first fifty years, is an invaluable resource and served as a road map for many avenues of research I pursued. He and his staff were unfailingly supportive of this endeavor and gave me access to the history office's many important records. Stuart Rochester, the department's deputy historian, was a great source of encouragement and assistance. Goldberg and Rochester graciously read early chapters and made helpful suggestions. Their colleague Ed Drea pointed me to important papers gathered by the late Army historian Paul Scheips on the 1967 march on the Pentagon, and he offered much valued comments on portions of the manuscript.

Retired Brigadier General John S. Brown, chief of military history, opened doors for me at the U.S. Army Center of Military History and other superb Army history facilities. Thanks also to CMH archivist Frank Shirer for his assistance. Richard Sommers graciously led me to valuable papers and oral histories at the U.S. Army Military History Institute. At the Corps of Engineers' history office, archivist Mike Brodhead good-naturedly helped me track down numerous documents and interviews, and Paul Walker and Bill Baldwin also were helpful.

Tim Nenninger was a friendly and exceptionally knowledgeable guide through the modern military records collection at the National Archives; he and his staff, including Ken Schlessinger and Wil Mahoney, pointed me toward many avenues of pursuit. Thanks also to the staff, in particular Robert Parks, at the Franklin D. Roosevelt Library. I also appreciate the assistance of researcher Doris Kinney. At the United States Military Academy, archivist Alan Aimone was very helpful.

I am indebted to Linda Castle for her hospitality and assistance during my research at the George C. Marshall Library, where archivist Joanne Hartog was also of great help. I am grateful to Nancy Hadley at the American Institute of Architects, Andria Fields at the Architect of the Capitol, and Lynn Catanese and the staff at the Hagley Library and Museum for their assistance. Thanks to Adwoa Bart-Plange, who conducted research on my behalf in the John J. McCloy papers at Amherst College.

At the Pentagon itself, I am grateful for much help over the years from Glenn Flood and Bryan Whitman. Brett Eaton with Washington Headquarter Services and Bill Hopper at the Pentagon Renovation Program set up many tours and interviews, and Bill also assisted in finding photographs. Lee Evey graciously allowed me to review his personal papers from the Pentagon renovation, a collection that included many important documents from the aftermath of the 9/11 attack. I am grateful to the staff at the Pentagon Library, a tremendous source of military histories. Special thanks to the many Pentagon denizens—a hardy and good-humored bunch—who told me tales and accompanied me on tours. John Ware took me on a trek to visit the Pentagon's legendary purple water fountain, now in the mezzanine; alas, the age-old mystery behind its color remains unsolved.

It is impossible to individually thank all the people I interviewed for the book, but I am especially grateful to Bob Furman, a wonderful man who was witness to much history. Alan Renshaw, Ernest Graves, Jr., Richard Groves, Connie Somervell Matter, and Sister Polly McShain graciously shared many stories about their fathers. Thanks also to my friends Lee and Amy Trainer, who put me in touch with Sister Polly and then put up with me during my research through the McShain papers at the Hagley Museum.

I am deeply grateful to the survivors, rescuers, and family members who shared painful recollections of the 9/11 attack.

Like many reporters before me, I am fortunate to work at *The Washington Post*, where chairman of the board Donald Graham is well-known for his generous support of book projects. Former Metro editor Jo-Ann Armao was very supportive, as was Steve Coll, the former managing editor, who offered invaluable tips on how to organize my material and writing. I appreciate the patience of my editor, Phyllis Jordan. Many colleagues offered encouraging words and good counsel along the way, and I am especially indebted to Rick Atkinson in this regard. As reflected in the bibliography and notes, I also benefited from the fine reporting of dozens of *Post* journalists over sixty years, covering the birth of the "Dream Building" in 1941 through the 1967 march on the Pentagon to 9/11 and its aftermath.

Post colleagues Brenna Maloney and Laris Karklis gamely agreed to put together the maps in the front of the book, and I deeply appreciate their fine work. I am also grateful to Mike Keegan for preparing *Post* graphics for use. Thanks also to Mike Jenkins, a longtime friend and talented cartoonist, who enlisted the aid of his brother Pete and their friend Brad Goodwin to create the map of the 1967 march.

Margaret Roth, a longtime colleague, graciously volunteered to give me transcribed interviews she made with firefighters and police officers who responded to the 9/11 attack. Peggy compounded her kindness by going through the manuscript line by line to make innumerable fixes. I owe special thanks to the indefatigable Bobbye Pratt, a now-retired *Post* researcher, who enthusiastically tracked down people and articles. Eddy Palanzo was also helpful in locating photographs. Thanks also to Russell James for his help.

Rafe Sagalyn, my agent, was enthusiastic about the idea from the start, helping to define the scope of the book and guiding me through every step of the process. I am also grateful to Eben Gilfenbaum for his careful reading and suggestions. Will Murphy, my editor at Random House, shared my vision for the book and was unfailingly upbeat. His assistant, Matt Kellogg, was a voice of calm, while Lea Beresford and Jennifer Rodriguez cheerily kept things moving. Thanks also to Richard Elman, Marc Romano, London King, Carol Russo, and Beck Stvan.

Many friends took turns reading parts or all of the manuscript. Sean Callahan had many thoughtful observations. Ferdinand Protzman gave it a rigorous reading and offered many improvements. Gina DiNicolo saved me from many mistakes, small and large. Jim Auchter offered important perspective. Special thanks to Benjamin Pepper and Becky Sinkler for their encouraging support.

Thanks also to brothers Peter and Stuart Vogel and sister Jennifer Davisson for helping their technologically challenged sibling through various conundrums. My mother, Joan Vogel, was a great inspiration, as was my late father, Donald Vogel.

More than anyone, I am grateful to my wife and life partner, Tiffany Ayers, who walked every step of this journey with me. Every night, she put her editing skills to work on the pages I wrote that day, greatly improving that first draft and every subsequent one. Beyond that, she was the rock of support for this project, picking up the slack left at home while I worked on the book. My love and thanks also go to my young children, Donald and Charlotte, who offered cheer, encouragement, and company during long hours in our attic office. For a long time, they knew me as the guy who lived in the attic. The happiest part of this project for me was being there to watch them grow.

Steve Vogel
Washington, D.C.
December 2006

NOTES

To save space, references for one or more paragraphs are often grouped together in a single note. The order of the citations in each note generally corresponds to the information or quotation being referenced. The following abbreviations are used in the endnotes and bibliography:

AAR—After Action Report

ACL—Arlington Central Library, Virginia Room

AIA—American Institute of Architects

ACOHP—Arlington County Oral History Project

AOC—Architect of the Capitol

AP—Associated Press

CEHO—U.S. Army Corps of Engineers Office of History, Fort Belvoir, Va.

CFA—Commission of Fine Arts

CMH—U.S. Army Center of Military History, Fort McNair, Washington, D.C.

CU—Columbia University Oral History Research Office

DoD—Department of Defense

ENR—Engineering News-Record

FDR Lib—Franklin D. Roosevelt Library, Hyde Park, New York

F&R—Army Corps of Engineers historians Lenore Fine and Jesse Remington

GCM Lib—George C. Marshall Library, Lexington, Va.

HML—Hagley Museum and Library, Wilmington, Del.

HST Lib.—Harry S. Truman Library
LOC—Library of Congress
MDW—U.S. Army Military District of Washington
MHI—U.S. Army Military History Institute, Carlisle, Pa.
MLK Lib—Martin Luther King Library, Washingtoniana Division
NARA—National Archives and Records Administration, College Park, Md.
NARA DC—National Archives and Records Administration, Washington, D.C.
NCPPC—National Capital Park and Planning Commission
NYT—The New York Times
OSD—Office of the Secretary of Defense
OSD HO—Office of the Secretary of Defense Historical Office
OUSA—Office of the Under Secretary of the Army
PENREN—Pentagon Renovation Program
RG—record group
SDF—Somervell Desk File, NARA RG 160
Star—Washington *Evening Star*
USMA—United States Military Academy Archives, West Point
WP—The Washington Post
WT-H—Washington Times-Herald

PRELUDE

A pentagon

xv **On a warm** Planning memorandum, 30 Sept. 1942, David Witmer papers, box 1306, OSD HO (hereafter known as Witmer planning memorandum); "The Pentagon Project," Control Division, Army Service Forces, 25 June 1944, box 15, file 4, SDF, NARA RG 160 (hereafter known as "The Pentagon Project—ASF"); Alfred Goldberg, *The Pentagon: The First Fifty Years*, 16–20; Steve Vogel, "The Battle of Arlington," *WP*, 26 Apr. 1999.

xv **The general spoke** Maxwell Taylor, oral history with Forrest C. Pogue, 1959, GCM Lib.; George C. Marshall, oral history with Pogue, 14 Feb. 1957, GCM Lib.; Forrest Pogue, *Ordeal and Hope*, 297; "The S.O.S." *Fortune*, Sept. 1942.

xv **"Pat, we're going"** *Engineer Memoirs—Major General Hugh J. Casey*, 1993, 137–140; Casey letter to Lt. Col. David Matheson, 11 July 1955, vii, CEHO.

xvi **Yet it must be no** Witmer planning memorandum, OSD HO; Somervell notes on the building July 1941, I, CEHO.

xvi **"Now, don't question"** Robert Colglazier, oral history, 1984, MHI.

xvi **"That," Casey later** *Engineer Memoirs—Casey*, p. 137.

xvi **Washington was consumed** *The Papers of George C. Marshall,* vol. 2, 547; "The Pentagon Project," Engineer Historical Division, 1, I, box 16, CEHO (hereafter known as "The Pentagon Project—EHD"); "Report of the Secretary of War to the President, 1939," 33.

xvii **Working around the clock** *Engineer Memoirs—Casey,* 137–140.

CHAPTER 1: DYNAMITE IN A TIFFANY BOX

Stimson looks for the right man

3 **To his staff** T.T. Handy, oral history, 1959, GCM Lib; Lucius Clay, oral history, 1972, MHI.

3 **The largest peacetime** Lenore Fine and Jesse A. Remington, *The Corps of Engineers: Construction in the United States,* 152–153, 519–520; "Report of the Secretary of War to the President, 1941," 55.

4 **"They had gotten into"** Henry L. Stimson diary, 7 Feb. 1942 (hereafter Stimson diary); F&R, *The Corps of Engineers,* 239–41; *Time,* 23 Dec. 1940.

4 **Back then, he had seemingly** *NYT,* Stimson obituary, 21 Oct. 1950.

4 **"I am not satisfied"** Stimson diary, 20 Aug. 1940; John J. McCloy, memorandum to Jesse Remington, circa 1957, VII, box 32, CEHO.

5 **"Have him assigned"** George C. Marshall to Gen. Bryden, GCM Papers, box 85, Somervell folder, GCM Lib.

I suppose the fellow who built the Pyramids was efficient, too

5 **None of Brehon** L. D. Dunbar, "Army Man at Work," *New Yorker,* 10 and 17 Feb. 1940.

6 **Somervell found the idea** *NYT,* 8 July 1939.

6 **Somervell imposed** Stephen Voorhees, F&R interview, 1958, VII, box 33, CEHO; *NYT,* 8 Feb. 1940

6 **"I suppose the fellow"** Dunbar, "Army Man at Work."

7 **"Well, girls"** *New York World-Telegram,* Nov. 1937; Dunbar, "Army Man at Work."

7 **"Dynamite in a Tiffany box"** Charles J. V. Murphy, "Somervell of the S.O.S.," *Life,* 8 May 1943.

7 **Somervell was one of the only** *Ibid.*

7 **Somervell "went up like a torch"** Florence Kerr, oral history, 1963, Smithsonian.

7 **A furor arose** John Kennedy Ohl, *Supplying the Troops: General Somervell and American Logistics in World War II,* 35.

7 **"The day before yesterday"** William A. Delano, letter, *New York Herald Tribune,* 16 Feb. 1955.

7 **Much of the $45-million** Ohl, *Supplying the Troops*, 32–3; "New York Municipal Airport" brochure, undated, Somervell papers, MHI; *NYT*, 16 Oct. 1939, 8 Nov. 1940.

8 **"I was much impressed"** Ohl, *Supplying the Troops*, 33.

Just a country boy from Arkansas

8 **"I'm just a country boy"** Address at University of Arkansas, 7 June 1943, "General Brehon B. Somervell Public Addresses," v. 2, Somervell papers, MHI (hereafter Somervell addresses); *Kansas City Star*, 30 Dec. 1943.

8 **He had been born** Biographical papers, Somervell papers, MHI; Ohl, *Supplying the Troops*, 9–10.

8 **There Brehon was raised** Murphy, "Somervell of the S.O.S." Connie Somervell Matter, author interview, 25 Feb. 2004.

9 **Brehon had a wild streak** John Janney, "The Man Behind the Invasion," *American Magazine*, June 1944; *The Brecky* 1909 Central High School yearbook, Somervell papers, MHI; Murphy, "Somervell of the S.O.S."

9 **Somervell won** West Point academic records, Somervell papers, MHI; Ohl, *Supplying the Troops*, 10; Janney, "The Man Behind the Invasion"; Murphy, "Somervell of the S.O.S."; Dunbar, "Army Man at Work."

9 **Touring Europe** "Service Reminiscences of Lt. Gen. John C.H. Lee," MHI; Janney, "The Man Behind the Invasion"; Murphy, "Somervell of the S.O.S."

10 **"I was hard at work"** Dunbar, "Army Man at Work."

10 **The Pershing expedition** "Recollections of General Brehon Somervell," memorandum to author, Lt. Gen. (Ret.) Ernest Graves, Jr., 12 Feb. 2004; Ernest Graves, Jr., author interview, 12 Feb. 2004; "Investigation of National Defense Program," Statement of Lt. General Brehon B. Somervell to U.S. Senate Special Committee Investigating the National Defense Program, 20 Dec. 1943, Somervell papers, MHI; Ohl, *Supplying the Troops*, 11.

10 **Motoring down** Dunbar, "Army Man at Work"; Janney, "The Man Behind the Invasion."

11 **Somervell's performance** Murphy, "Somervell of the S.O.S."; Lee, "Service Reminiscences," MHI; John M. Carlisle, "Somervell," *Detroit News*, 7 May 1944; Distinguished Service Medal citation, Somervell papers, MHI.

11 **"I have yet to hear"** Murphy, "Somervell of the S.O.S."

11 **"What do you know"** Dunbar, "Army Man at Work."

12 **"truly an answer to prayer"** Lee, "Service Reminiscences," MHI.

12 **For his exploits** Somervell service record, Somervell papers, MHI; Ohl, *Supplying the Troops*, 13–14.

12 **"This is the best officer"** Janney, "The Man Behind the Invasion"; Ernest Graves letter to Roy Finch, 31 Dec. 1936, Somervell papers, MHI.

12 "He called himself a mean" *Engineer Memoirs—General William M. Hoge*, 1993, 97.

12 "Watch Somervell" *Time*, 8 Dec. 1941.

13 His reputation Murphy, "Somervell of the S.O.S."; Matter, author's interview; Lee, "Service Reminiscences," MHI.

Magnitude never seemed to bother him

13 In 1929, Somervell pondered Maj. Brehon Somervell, "Report to the Chief of Engineers, United States Army on the Potomac River and Its Tributaries," 1 Sept. 1930, Records of the Washington, D.C., District, NARA RG 77; *WP*, 29 Dec. 1929; *Chesapeake and Ohio Canal*, National Park Service, 1991, 30.

13 Somervell was pitted *Washington Daily News*, 3 Apr. 1930; *Star*, 3 Apr. 1930; *WP*, 6 Apr. 1930; Albert E. Cowdrey, *A City for the Nation*, 1979, 50.

14 He saw himself Ohl, *Supplying the Troops*, 18; *Engineer Memoirs—Major General John R. Hardin*, 1981, 107, CEHO.

14 In 1934, President Roosevelt Ohl, *Supplying the Troops*, 22–24.

15 "He got his orders" Hugh S. Johnson, *New York World-Telegram*, 15 Mar. 1941.

15 Attracted by the grand scope Ernie Pyle, "44 Year-Old War Hero is Boss of the Florida Canal Job," *Washington Daily News*, 3 Mar. 1936.

15 Congress cut off Ohl, *Supplying the Troops*, 22–24. The canal project would be periodically revived, including during World War II and again in the 1960s. Work was again shut down in 1971, and the project officially canceled in 1991. Today the canal right-of-way is a 110-mile-long environmental "greenway" across central Florida.

A gleam of light on the horizon

16 Among those he met F&R, *The Corps of Engineers*, 256; Doris Kearns Goodwin, *No Ordinary Time: Franklin & Eleanor Roosevelt: The Home Front in World War II*, 87; *NYT*, Harry Hopkins obituary, 30 Jan. 1946, Leslie R. Groves, F&R interview, 1956, VII, box 32, CEHO; Voorhees, F&R interview, VII, box 33, CEHO.

16 "If I hadn't" Murphy, "Somervell of the S.O.S."; Richard C. Moore, memo to F&R, 1955, VII, box 32, CEHO.

16 La Guardia, by now *NYT*, 8 Nov. 1940; Ohl, *Supplying the Troops*, 36; *Current Biography 1942*, 777.

16 Leaving New York "Comments of Lt. Gen. Leslie R. Groves on MS, Construction in the United States," 1955, 51, VII, box 34, CEHO (hereafter Groves comments); John D. Millett, *The Army Service Forces*, 5; Julian Schley, F&R interview, 1955, VII, box 33, CEHO; George C. Marshall to Major Smith, 25 October 1940, GCM Papers, box 85, folder 17, GCM Lib.

17 Arriving in Washington Ohl, *Supplying the Troops*, 38; Stimson diary, 19 Dec. 1940.

Waiting in the wings

17 **Brigadier General** Charles Hartman, memo to F&R, 1955, CEHO; Mary Pagan, F&R interview, 1955, CEHO.

17 **Being chief** Winnie Cox, F&R interview, 1956, CEHO; *NYT,* 28 Dec. 1940; Michael Madigan, F&R interview, CEHO.

18 **"It is a pathetic situation"** Stimson diary, 11 Dec. 1940.

18 **The White House had threatened** McCloy memorandum to Remington, VII, box 33, CEHO.

18 **Gregory, who was the Army's** Edmund Gregory, F&R interview, 1955, VII, box 32, CEHO; R. C. Moore memo to history office, 1953, VII, CEHO. Gregory disputed this account, telling Army historians the decision to sack Hartman was his.

18 **Gregory finally saw** Hartman memo to F&R, VII, CEHO; Pagan interview, VII, CEHO; F&R, *The Corps of Engineers,* 256–7; James Burns, F&R interview, 1956, CEHO.

19 **Somervell's appointment** AP article, in *NYT,* 14 Dec. 1942; Stimson diary, 19 Dec. 1940; Cox interview, VII, CEHO; Pagan interview, VII, CEHO.

19 **"Somervell was like"** Stimson diary, 19 Dec. 1940.

CHAPTER 2: THE SOMERVELL BLITZ

I will just move

21 **The officers of the Army's** "Conference on the Organization of the Construction Division," 22 Feb. 1941, Otto L. Nelson Papers, box 6, folder 6, GCM Lib.

21 **Since taking command** F&R, *The Corps of Engineers,* 265.

22 **The new construction chief** Christian Dreyer, F&R interview, 1959, VII, box 32, CEHO; F&R, *The Corps of Engineers,* 265.

22 **The Somervell Blitz** Brehon Somervell, "The Engineer and Defense Construction," *Engineer Society Magazine,* 2 Feb. 1942, Somervell addresses, MHI; Gar Davidson, "Grandpa Gar—The Saga of One Soldier as told to his Grandchildren," 1974, CEHO (hereafter Grandpa Gar).

22 **The first battle** Somervell, "The Engineer and Defense Construction," MHI; F&R, *The Corps of Engineers,* 293–94; Brehon Somervell, "Housing an Army Overnight," *Army and Navy Journal,* 28 June 1941, Somervell addresses, MHI.

22 **A new story emerged** F&R, *The Corps of Engineers,* 373–74; Somervell memo to Construction Division, 14 Jan. 1941, Office of the Quartermaster General, entry 2102, boxes 1–4, NARA RG 92.

23 **Somervell handled** Clarence Renshaw, F&R interview, 1959, VII, box 33, CEHO; Voorhees interview, CEHO; Gregory interview, CEHO.

23 **For Somervell, it was** "Conference on the Organization of the Construction Division," GCM Lib.; Ohl, *Supplying the Troops*, 41; *WT-H*, 4 July 1941.

24 **Truman considered** Harry S. Truman, F&R interview, 1958, VII, CEHO; Ohl, *Supplying the Troops*, 46–47.

24 **Somervell did despise** Somervell letter to Groves, 24 July 1952, Papers of Lt. Gen. Leslie R. Groves, box 9, NARA RG 200; W. D. Styer letter to Somervell, 26 July 1952, Somervell papers, Correspondence S-Z, MHI. Leslie R. Groves, oral history with Forrest C. Pogue, second interview, 14 May 1970, GCM Lib.; Truman declined to discuss the matter in his 1958 interview with Fine and Remington.

24 **"Mr. Senator,"** Garrison H. Davidson, oral history, 17–19 Nov. 1980, 151–52, CEHO; "Grandpa Gar," 71, CEHO.

24 **The committee was established** David McCullough, *Truman*, 261–2; Ohl, *Supplying the Troops*, 46; *WP*, 15 Aug. 1941.

25 **Truman's slings** Henry L. Stimson and McGeorge Bundy, *On Active Service in Peace and War*, 452; *WP*, 15 Aug. 1941.

Who is this stinker?

25 **Groves was bemused** Groves, F&R interview, 1956, CEHO.

26 **Beneath his thick** Robert S. Norris, *Racing for the Bomb*, 347; Stephane Groueff, *Manhattan Project*, 3; War Department press release, background information on Major General Leslie R. Groves, 6 Aug. 1945, NARA RG 200.

26 **Somervell "was a gentleman"** *Engineer Memoirs—Hardin*, 107; Norris, "Racing for the Bomb," 150.

26 **"When you looked at"** *Ibid.*, 135.

26 **Captain Donald Antes** Donald Antes, F&R interview, 1958, VII, box 32, CEHO.

26 **Hartman had been forced** Leslie Groves, F&R interview, 1956, VII, CEHO; Groves, oral history with Forrest C. Pogue, first interview, 7 May 1970, GCM Lib.

26 **Groves could not** Groves comments, 108, CEHO; Groves, oral history with Pogue, second interview, GCM Lib.

27 **Groves, know as Dick** Vincent C. Jones, *Manhattan: The Army and the Atomic Bomb*, 73; Norris, *Racing for the Bomb*, 41, 57–59, 79, 83, 97.

27 **They shared a mentor** Ibid., 117–120; Richard Groves, author interview, 9 Feb. 2004.

27 **Graves's protégés** *Engineer Memoirs—Casey*, 97; Groves, assessment of Somervell, entry 7530, Comments, Interviews and Reviews, 1949–1970, box 5, NARA RG 200; Groves memo to file, "Somervell," 30 Mar. 1967, Groves collection, USMA (Copies courtesy Stan Norris).

28 **He had no complaints** Groves comments, 51–52, CEHO; Groves dictation on Manhattan Project associates, 19 Nov. 1958, Groves collection, USMA; Groves,

F&R interview, 1956, CEHO; Norris, *Racing for the Bomb*, 601; Groves, Somervell assessment, NARA RG 200.

A new headquarters

29 **Henry Stimson was not** Goldberg, *The Pentagon*, 9–10; David Brinkley, *Washington Goes to War*, 70.

29 **Through much of the 1930s** Malin Craig memo to Secretary of War, 1 Feb. 1938, NARA RG 107.

29 **"That is a small office"** Gilmore Clarke, "Reminiscences of Gilmore David Clarke," 1960, 162–3, CU (hereafter Clarke oral history); *NYT,* 23 June 1946; William B. Rhoads, "Franklin Roosevelt and Washington Architecture," *Records of the Columbia Historical Society of Washington, D.C.*

29 **"It is a most wasteful building"** Stimson diary, 25 Apr. 1941.

30 **The 24,30 War Department workers** "The Pentagon Project—ASF," 1, NARA RG 160; Norris, *Racing for the Bomb*, 155.

30 **It was a far cry** *War Times,* 31 Dec. 1943; Chalmer M. Roberts, *Washington, Past and Present* 138–140; *St. Louis Post-Dispatch,* 21 Jan. 1993; Goldberg, *The Pentagon,* 4–9; White House Web site, www.whitehouse.gov/history/eeobtour/historicalview-1800.html; John Clagett Proctor, "When War Department Had 18 Employees," *Star,* 24 Aug. 1941.

31 **When World War II** Goldberg, *The Pentagon*, 5; Marshall to General Malin Craig, 21 Aug. 1939, and speech to the Chamber of Commerce of the United States, 29 Apr. 1941, *The Papers of George Catlett Marshall*, vol. 2, 37, 489.

31 **"The matter of office space"** Patterson to Secretary of War, 29 Nov. 1940, NARA RG 107; Marshall to Adm. Harold R. Stark, 10 Sept. 1940, *The Papers of George Catlett Marshall*, vol. 2, 301–2.

31 **Even with the New** U.S. House Committee on Appropriations, Subcommittee on Deficiencies, 77th Congress, 1st sess., Hearings on the First Supplemental National Defense Appropriations Bill for 1942, 17 July 1941, 488 (hereafter House hearing 17 July 1941); Stimson diary, 22 July 1941; Col. E. H. Householder to Under Secretary of War, 6 May 1941, NARA RG 107.

32 **To help house** Goldberg, *The Pentagon,* 14; *WP,* 16 March 1941 and 5 June 1941; *The Papers of George Catlett Marshall,* vol. 2, 531–2.

The overall solution

32 **Woodrum, a powerful** James E. Sargent, "Clifton A. Woodrum of Virginia," *The Virginia Magazine of History and Biography,* July 1981.

33 **The proposal before** Historical background of Pentagon prepared by architects, entry 5, Groves files and correspondence related to Pentagon, box 1, NARA RG 200 (hereafter architects' historical memo); House hearing 17 July 1941; U.S. Senate Subcommittee of the Committee on Appropriations, 77th Congress, 1st sess.,

Hearings on the First Supplemental National Defense Appropriations Bill for 1942, 8 Aug. 1941, 181 (hereafter Senate hearing 8 Aug. 1941); "The Pentagon Project— EHD," 1–3, CEHO.

33 **The bespectacled Reybold** *WP*, 21 May 1943; *Current Biography*, June 1945.

33 **With typical brio** Ohl, *Supplying the Troops*, 47; Goldberg, *The Pentagon*, 12–14.

CHAPTER 3: DREAM BUILDING

Incidentally, the largest office building in the world

35 **The first problem** Casey letter to Matheson, CEHO; *Engineer Memoirs—Casey*, vii–viii, 137–140; House hearing, 17 July 1941, 491; U.S. House Committee on Appropriations, Subcommittee on Deficiencies, 77th Congress, 1st sess., Hearings on the First Supplemental National Defense Appropriations Bill for 1942, 22 July 1941, 500 (hereafter House hearing, 22 July 1941).

36 **But the foundation** Minutes of staff conference, Construction Division, July 1941, NARA RG 92; House hearing, 22 July 1941, 500. *Engineer Memoirs—Casey*, 138–39.

36 **Like the adjacent cemetery** Arlington County Visitors Center exhibit, author's visit; Tom Sherlock, "Arlington National Cemetery, Historic Background Southern Portion," Arlington Cemetery historian's office.

37 **Marshall wanted to use** Marshall to Secretary of War, 17 Sept. 1940, GCM papers, box 84, folder 2, GCM Lib. The experimental farm was relocated north of Washington to Beltsville, Maryland, where it remains.

37 **In approving the site** House hearing, 22 July 1941; "The Pentagon Project— EHD," 3, CEHO.

Bergstrom gets to work

37 **A formal man** Socrates Thomas Stathes, author interview, 21 Aug. 2004; Bob Furman, author interviews, 2004–06.

37 **Bergstrom—known** George Edwin Bergstrom membership file, AIA; Bergstrom biographical sketch, I, box 16, CEHO; Christina J. Hammond, "Chapter III, The Architect, George Edwin Bergstrom," from "The Italian-style Garden at Kimberly Crest" manuscript, Baldwin Memorial Files, AIA. Among many others Parkinson and Bergstrom designed in the Los Angeles area were the original California Club, the Crocker Bank Building, the Mason Opera House, and the Alexandria Hotel.

38 **In the same vein,** Somervell F&R, *The Corps of Engineers*, 266–67; Somervell, *Army Navy Journal*, 23 Aug. 1941, Somervell addresses, vol. I, MHI. Groves comments, 52, CEHO, Dreyer, F&R interview, CEHO; Luther Leisenring, F&R interview, 1957, VII, box 32, CEHO.

38 **Bergstrom, at least** "AIA Convention," *Architectural Record*, June 1941; F&R,

The Corps of Engineers, 347; Colglazier, oral history, MHI; "The Pentagon," 4, Witmer collection, OSD History Office.

It fit

39 **The Arlington Farm** "The Arlington Office Building," Witmer notebook, Witmer Collection, OSD HO; "New War Department Building," undated report circa 1942, Witmer papers, OSD HO; architects' historical memo, NARA RG 200.

39 **Stathes was known** Stathes, author interview.

40 **Despite the layout** *Engineer Memoirs—Casey,* 137–39; "The Pentagon Project-EHD," 3–4, CEHO; Groves, "Notes on the Pentagon," June 1969, entry 5, box 1, NARA RG 200; "Personnel principally responsible for design and construction," Oct. 1943, Hadden notebook, I, CEHO.

41 **There were many problems** Maj. William Frierson, Office of the Chief of Military History, *The Pentagon,* 10, 1944, box 1311, OSD HO (hereafter Frierson, *The Pentagon*); Stathes, author interview.

It should not ever come to pieces

41 **The whole idea** Stimson diary, 22 July 1941; U.S. Senate, Subcommittee of the Committee on Appropriations, 77th Congress, 1st sess., Hearings on the First Supplemental National Defense Appropriations Bill for 1942, 31 July 1941, 60 (hereafter Senate hearing 31 July 1941); House hearing, 22 July 1941, 505–511.

42 **At the suggestion of Moore** F&R, *The Corps of Engineers,* 415; Ohl, *Supplying the Troops,* 47.

42 **At the hearing** House hearing, 22 July 1941, 500–13.

44 **The War Department building as proposed** "The Pentagon Project-EHD," 7, CEHO; 22 July 1941 memorandum for the Secretary of War, NARA RG 107.

44 **Stimson decided** Edwin Watson memorandum for the president, 24 July 1941, Papers as President, Official File (OF) 25, War Department files, FDR Lib.

44 **Earlier that month the president** James MacGregor Burns, *The Soldier of Freedom, 1940–1945,* 105.

45 **When the proposal was raised** Stimson diary, 24 July 1941; Stimson letter to Woodrum, 24 July 1941, I, CEHO.

Lebensraum

45 **On July 24, 1941** *Cong. Rec.,* 24 July 1941, 6303–04, 6322–23; architects' historical memo, NARA RG 200.

46 **The cat was now** "War Building 'Blitz' Leaves Capital Stunned and Confused," *Star,* 13 Aug. 1941; War Department press release, 24 July 1941, entry 5, box 1, NARA RG 200; *Star,* 24 and 25 July 1941; *WP,* 25 and 26 July 1941; *Washington Daily News,* 26 July 1941.

47 **On Friday morning, Woodrum** *Cong. Rec.* 28 July 1941, 6363–6375; Minutes of

the Special Meeting of the National Capital Park and Planning Commission, 29 July 1941, 4, RG 328, NARA DC (hereafter NCPPC minutes, 29 July 1941); architects' historical memo, NARA RG 200.

49 **Sensitive to appearances** Senate hearing, 8 Aug. 1941, 234; Harold L. Ickes diary, Personal Papers, Manuscript Division, LOC, 5840–41 (hereafter Ickes diary); NCPPC minutes, 29 July 1941, 6.

A grand fellow

50 **Across the Potomac** Carl M. Brauer, *The Man Who Built Washington*, 63.

50 **Viewing the progress** Mary McShain letter to President George H.W. Bush, 6 Dec. 1989, series VII, personal papers, subseries 2, Papers of John McShain, HML (hereafter McShain papers); Adm. J. J. Manning, memo to McShain, 10 Jan. 1950, personal papers, McShain papers, HML.

50 **Roosevelt was a greater admirer** Rhoads, "Franklin D. Roosevelt and Washington Architecture"; *WT-H*, 4 July 1943; *WP*, 10 Dec. 1943; John McShain, "Hyde Park Diary 1939–1940," chapter 3, 3, series VII, subseries 1, McShain papers, HML (hereafter McShain, "Hyde Park diary").

51 **McShain stood only** J. Lacey Reynolds, "John McShain, Builder," undated draft of article circa 1949 in VII, subseries 1, McShain papers, HML; Brauer, *The Man Who Built Washington*, 50, 184; L. Stuart Ditzen, "Billion Dollar Builder—Philadelphia's John McShain," *Philadelphia Bulletin*, 8 Aug. 1976.

51 **McShain's parents** Sister Pauline "Polly" McShain, author interview, 8 Mar., 2004; Brauer, *The Man Who Built Washington*, 1–23; McShain autobiographical notes, 1970s–1980s, VII, subseries 1, McShain papers, HML.

52 **What set McShain apart** John Gerrity, "He Changed the Face of Washington," *Nation's Business*, Jan. 1952; Brauer, *The Man Who Built Washington*, 40–1; McShain autobiographical notes, "The Pentagon," VII, subseries 1, McShain papers, HML.

52 **It was glory** *Time*, 14 Nov. 1949; Polly McShain, author interview; McShain comments in 1984 video, courtesy Polly McShain; Brauer, *The Man Who Built Washington*, 61–2.

53 **McShain was just a few months** McShain, "Hyde Park diary," chapter 1, 1–4; Cynthia M. Koch and Lynn A. Bassanese, "Roosevelt and His Library," *Prologue*, Summer 2001.

54 **McShain's Republican leanings** Polly McShain, author interview; Gerrity, "He Changed the Face of Washington"; McShain, interview with Harold Wiegand, 1979, VII, McShain papers, HML.

54 **Roosevelt treated McShain** McShain, "Hyde Park diary," chapters 3–4; *NYT*, 5 July 1940.

55 **"After viewing the Library"** McShain letter to FDR, 8 July 1941; Roosevelt letter to McShain, 12 July 1941, VII, subseries 1, McShain Papers, HML; Roosevelt, *The Public Papers and Addresses of Franklin D. Roosevelt*, 1941 vol., 361.

55 As work commenced FDR: Day by Day—The Pare Lorentz Chronology, 24–25, July 1941, FDR Lib.; McShain autobiographical notes, 12, VII, McShain papers, HML. The conversation most likely took place July 25, 1941.

No greater worlds to conquer

56 **Somervell had started** Styer memo to Construction Advisory Committee, 22 July 1941, I, CEHO.

56 **McShain, well plugged** McShain autobiographical notes, 12, VII, 1, McShain papers, HML.

57 **"The board was in Somervell's way"** Ferdinand J.C. Dresser, F&R interview, VII, box 32, CEHO; F&R, *The Corps of Engineers,* 184, 188.

57 **On July 24** F&R, *The Corps of Engineers,* 433; Benjamin Forgey, "The Master Builder; John McShain's Monumental Legacy to Washington," *WP,* 15 Feb. 1997. McShain autobiographical notes, 17, VII, 1, McShain papers, HML.

57 **Somervell heartily endorsed** Somervell memo to Under Secretary of War, 25 July 1941, I, CEHO; Dresser, F&R interview, CEHO.

58 **As to why Somervell chose** McShain autobiographical notes, 13, VII, 1, McShain papers, HML; Groves, F&R interview, 1956, CEHO; Richard Groves, author interview; architects' historical memo, NARA RG 200; McShain, memo to Groves, 2 Oct. 1942, I, CEHO; McShain autobiographical notes, "The Pentagon," 1, VII, 1, McShain papers; Brauer, *The Man Who Built Washington,* 78; Thomas Munyan, author interview, 24 Mar. 2004.

CHAPTER 4: CARRYING L'ENFANT'S BANNER

The resurrection of Pierre L'Enfant

61 **The men digging** *WP,* 23 and 29 Apr. 1909; Cowdrey, *A City for the Nation,* 1–10, 35; National Capital Planning Commission, *Worthy of the Nation,* 13–36, 133–146.

63 **Arlington Cemetery by then** Author tour and interviews with Arlington House site manager Kendell Thompson and Arlington Cemetery historian Tom Sherlock, 26 Jan. 2005; Philip Bigler, *In Honored Glory,* 20–35, C. B. Rose, Jr., *Arlington County, Virginia: A History,* 99, 108–9; National Park Service Web site, http://www.nps.gov/archive/arho/tour/history.html

64 **So many thousands** *WP,* 12 Nov. 1921 and 5 June 2002; Cowdrey, *A City for the Nation,* 48–9.

L'Enfant rolls in his grave

65 **In July 1941** Clarke, letter to Senate, 2 Aug. 1941, Records of the Commission of Fine Arts, NARA DC RG 66; Senate hearing, 8 Aug. 1941, 139; Sue A. Kohler, *The*

Commission of Fine Arts: A Brief History; Constance McLaughlin Green, *Washington: A History of the Capital, 1800–1950,* vol. II, 140–2.

66 **Clarke, a New York City** Moore, letter to FDR, 9 Apr. 1936, NARA DC RG 66; Clarke oral history, 42, 182–84, 282; *NYT,* Clarke obituary, 10 Aug. 1982; *WP,* Clarke obituary, 11 Aug. 1982; Rhoads, "Franklin Roosevelt and Washington Architecture"; Clarke would not be reappointed to the commission by Harry Truman in 1949 after objecting that a balcony the president added to the White House did not fit the design.

66 **But Somervell had not bothered** House hearing, 22 July 1941, 504; Senate hearing, 8 Aug. 1941, 186; Clarke, letter to Senate, 2 Aug 1941, NARA DC RG 66.

If Hitler would postpone his war

66 **Somervell had also ignored** Senate hearing, 8 Aug. 1941; House hearing, 22 July 1941.

67 **Delano, younger brother** *NYT,* Delano obituary, 29 Mar. 1953; *WP,* Delano obituary, 29 Mar. 1953; *Worthy of the Nation,* 161, 186.

67 **When the meeting began** NCPPC minutes, 29 July 1941.

My God, what will that boy do next?

68 **In 1938, the Navy** Clarke oral history, 126–130, CU; Rhoads, "Franklin D. Roosevelt and Washington Architecture"; *WP,* 7 May 1982; M. A. LeHand to Henry K. Toombs, 17 Nov. 1939, OF 1380, FDR Lib.; Richard Guy Wilson, author interview, Aug. 2004. The neoclassical look of the Jefferson memorial was the same favored by Hitler, the chief architect, Albert Speer, later noted.

69 **Roosevelt had been itching** Rhoads, "Franklin D. Roosevelt and Washington Architecture"; author visit to National Naval Medical Center, 2 Feb. 2005; *WP,* 12 Nov. 1940.

Uncle Fred goes to bat

71 **At 3 P.M. Wednesday** Conferences with the President, 1941, Harold Smith papers, FDR Lib.; NCPPC minutes, 31 July–1 Aug. 1941; Lee Carson, International News Service, 14 Feb. 1943; Pare Lorentz Chronology, 24–30 July 1941, FDR Lib.; *WP,* 31 July 1941. Delano, who served with the Army in France during World War I, was wiser than Smith on this score, understanding instinctively that the military was not going to shrink once it had such a building. "Well one thing, the Army will be, on a permanent basis, much larger than it has ever been before and that will mean larger headquarters staff and everything else that goes with it," he told his commission colleagues.

72 **Delano sent the Senate** Delano, letter to Committee on Appropriations, 31 July 1941, OF 25, FDR Lib.; Clarke, memorandum for the press, 1 Aug. 1941, NARA DC RG 66; NCPPC minutes, 1 Aug. 1941.

Roosevelt's fishing expedition

73 **Two days later** Theodore Wilson, *The First Summit: Roosevelt and Churchill at Placentia Bay, 1941*, 1–6.

73 **Before leaving town** FDR letter to Senator Adams, 1 Aug. 1941, OF 25, FDR Lib.; Conferences with the President, 1941, Harold Smith papers, FDR Lib.

74 **With all final business** Wilson, *The First Summit*, 4.

74 **Somervell confidently** Somervell memo to Donald Nelson, 2 Aug. 1941, I, CEHO; "The Pentagon Project-EHD," 17, CEHO; Stimson diary, 14 Aug. 1941; U.S. Senate Subcommittee of the Committee on Appropriations, 77th Congress, 1st sess., Hearings on the First Supplemental National Defense Appropriations Bill for 1942, 8 Aug. 1941, 60–64; Ickes diary, 27 Aug. 1941, 5841.

75 **Clarke, the fine arts** Clarke letter to Senate, 2 Aug. 1941, NARA DC RG 66; Somervell, letter to Clarke, 5 Aug. 1941, I, CEHO.

75 **The newspapers had indeed** *Star*, 5, 6, and 7 Aug. 1941; *NYT*, 8 Aug. 1941; Leo Sheridan letter to Clarke, 7 Aug. 1941, NARA DC RG 66; Senate hearing, 31 July 1941.

76 **Barely noticed** Caemmerer letter to Clarke, 6 Aug. 1941, NARA DC RG 66; Senate hearing, 8 Aug. 1941, 150–1; Delano, telegram to A. E. Demaray, 7 Aug. 1941, NARA DC RG 66; *NYT*, 8 Aug. 1941; Ohl, *Supplying the Troops*, draft, 74, box 1310, OSD HO.

CHAPTER 5: A FIRST-CLASS BATTLE

A hell of a mess with Congress

79 **Brigadier General Brehon** Senate hearing, 8 Aug. 1941, 135–203; *Star*, 8 Aug. 1941; Ickes diary, 27 Aug. 1941, 5842; Clarke, oral history, 147, CU; *WP*, 9 and 12 Aug. 1941.

81 **But the only opinion** *WP*, 13 Aug. 1942 and 29 May 1946; Ickes diary, 27 Aug. 1941, 5842; *Star*, 13 and 14 Aug. 1941.

82 **On top of that** *WP*, 13 Aug. 1941; Ickes, letter to Stimson, 12 Aug. 1941, I, CEHO; Stimson, letter to Ickes, 19 Aug. 1941, I, CEHO; Frank C. Waldrop, *WTH*, 23 Aug. 1941.

Most shockingly extravagant proposal

83 **The Reverend Barney T. Phillips** *Cong. Rec.*, 14 Aug. 1941, 7111–13, 7132–45; *Star*, 15 Aug. 1941.

85 **Harold Ickes held** Ickes diary, 27 Aug. 1941, 5841; *WP*, 16 Aug. 1941; *Star*, 15 Aug. 1941.

85 **Clarke ceded battle** Clarke letter to Caemmerer, 15 Aug. 1941, NARA DC RG 66.

You've got to build it in a hurry

85 **"You've got to"** Paul Caraway, oral history, 1971, 10, MHI.

86 **Somervell had not waited** Minutes of staff conference, 15 Aug. 1941, box 700, NARA RG 92.

86 **Paul Hauck** "The Pentagon Project—EHD," 25, CEHO; Groves diary, 25 July 1941, entry 7530G, NARA RG 200.

86 **Bergstrom and his team** Colglazier, oral history, 37, MHI; architects' historical memo, NARA RG 200; Witmer biographical sketch, Witmer membership file, AIA; *Los Angeles Times*, Witmer obituary, 8 May 1973; Robert Farquhar membership file, AIA.

87 **Groves would oversee** Groves memo to Army Headquarters Commandant, 28 June 1946, Leslie R. Groves Collection, GCM Lib.

88 **Renshaw, from** Alan Renshaw, author interview, 6 Feb. 2004; *Assembly*, March 1981; Clarence Renshaw, F&R interview, VII, box 33, CEHO; F&R, *The Corps of Engineers*, 51; author visit, Wright Brothers National Memorial, 16 Aug. 2004.

88 **Assigned to the Washington** F&R, *The Corps of Engineers*, 280; Karen Byrne Kinsey, "Battling For Arlington House: To Lee or Not to Lee?" *Arlington Historical Magazine*, Oct. 2003.

88 **Renshaw had developed** Pagan, F&R interview, CEHO; Richard Groves, author interview; Furman, author interview.

89 **"I wasn't so sure"** Clarence Renshaw, F&R interview, CEHO.

This rape of Washington

89 **Bronzed and refreshed** Wilson, *The First Summit*, 201, 204–205; Roosevelt, *The Public Papers of Franklin D. Roosevelt*, 1941 vol., 319; Jon Meacham, *Franklin and Winston*, 122.

89 **His secretary of the interior** Ickes diary, 27 Aug. 1941, 5842; Delano telegram to Harold Smith, 16 Aug. 1941, OF 25, FDR Lib., Delano letter to FDR, 17 Aug. 1941, OF 25, FDR Lib.

90 **The newspapers** Washington *Sunday Star*, 17 Aug. 1941.

90 **Roosevelt already felt** Rhoads, "Franklin Roosevelt and Washington Architecture."

91 **On Monday, August 18** FDR, memo to Harold Smith, 18 Aug. 1941, OF 25, FDR Lib.

91 **Smith was only** Smith memorandum to the President, 19 Aug. 1941, Conferences with the President: 1941, Harold Smith papers, FDR Lib.

A mere formality

91 **The mood was euphoric** F&R, *The Corps of Engineers*, 435, Ohl, *Supplying the Troops*, 50; construction authorization, 19 Aug. 1941, I, CEHO; "The Pentagon Project—EHD," 17, CEHO.

91 **Groves and Renshaw were there** "Conference on New War Department Building," 19 Aug. 1941, I, CEHO.

I should be kept out of Heaven

92 **Across town at the White House** *WP,* 20 Aug. 1941; Roosevelt, *The Public Papers of Franklin D. Roosevelt,* 1941 vol., 325–33.

94 **News bulletins hit** Watson, memorandum for the president, 19 Aug. 1941, OF 25, FDR Lib.

94 **Gilmore Clarke read the news** Clarke letter to FDR, 20 Aug. 1941, NARA DC RG 66; *WP,* 21 Aug. 1941; *NYT,* 22 Aug. 1941; *New York Herald-Tribune,* 21 Aug. 1941.

94 **Indeed, Roosevelt** *NYT,* 20 Aug. 1941; *WP,* 20 Aug. 1941; Memorandums to the President, 20 and 25 Aug. 1941, OF 25, FDR Lib.

94 **Somervell scrambled** McCloy, interview with Eric Sevareid, 1975, John J. McCloy Papers, Archives and Special Collections, Amherst College Library; Stimson, *On Active Service,* 343.

95 **Somervell and McCloy reported** Somervell, memorandum to the Secretary of War, 20 Aug. 1941, NARA RG 107.

95 **"Put three shifts"** *Star,* 20 Aug. 1941.

95 **Emerging from the conference** *Star,* 21 Aug. 1941; summary of minutes of Quartermaster staff conference, 22 Aug. 1941, I, CEHO; *WP,* 22 Aug. 1941.

96 **"We are proceeding"** Somervell, memorandum to the Secretary of War, 20 Aug. 1941, NARA RG 107.

96 **That was news to McCloy** McCloy, memorandum for General Somervell, 26 Aug. 1941, NARA RG 107, McCloy papers, entry 182.

96 **Returning to Washington** Smith, memorandum to the president, 25 Aug. 1941, OF 25, FDR Lib.; *Star,* 25 Aug. 1941, *WP,* 26 Aug. 1941.

96 **The following afternoon** Franklin D. Roosevelt, *Complete Presidential Press Conferences of Franklin D. Roosevelt,* vol. 17–18, 113–116.

The whole thing is all up in the air

97 **No one could imagine** *Star,* 27 Aug. 1941, *WP,* 28 Aug. 1941; Caemmerer, letter to Francis P. Sullivan, Chairman, Committee on the National Capital, 26 Aug. 1941, NARA DC RG 66.

98 **That was not the lesson** Watson, memorandum to the President, 26 Aug. 1941, OF 25, FDR Lib.; *WP,* 28 Aug. 1941. *Star,* 27 Aug. 1941.

99 **Delano drafted an agreement** NCPPC minutes, 18 Sept. 1941, 65; NCPPC minutes, 17 Oct. 1941, 114; Delano, letter to Somervell, 11 Oct. 1941, I, CEHO.

99 **Consulting with McCloy** McCloy diary, 28 Aug. 1941, John J. McCloy Papers, Archives and Special Collections, Amherst College Library (hereafter McCloy

diary); "Memorandum for the President: Subject: War Department Building," 28 Aug. 1941, OF 25, FDR Lib.

100 "It is a compromise" *Star,* 29 Aug. 1941.

100 "I am going out" Roosevelt, *Presidential Press Conferences,* vol. 18, 127.

I'm still commander-in-chief

100 The president's limousine was waiting Vogel, "The Battle of Arlington," *WP,* 26 Apr. 1999.

100 Gilmore Clarke had received Clarke, oral history, 149–52, CU.

100 Shortly after finishing "The President's Day," International News Service; 30 Aug. 1941; *Star,* 30 Aug. 1941; Clarke, memorandum for the Commission of Fine Arts, 30 Aug. 1941, NARA DC RG 66.

101 "Gilmore . . ., don't you like it?" Clarke, oral history, 150, CU. All subsequent FDR quotes during the trip are drawn from Clarke's account unless otherwise noted.

102 Inspecting the site Jay Downer, letter to Delano, 2 Sept. 1941, NARA DC RG 66.

102 Roosevelt wanted to know *Ibid.*

102 The entourage rode Clarke, oral history, 152, CU.

103 Somervell had no intention Clarke, memorandum for the Commission of Fine Arts, 30 Aug. 1941, NARA DC RG 66; Clarke, oral history, 152, CU; Downer, letter to Delano, 2 Sept. 1941, NARA DC RG 66.

103 With that, the president "The President's Day," International News Service, 30 Aug. 1941.

CHAPTER 6: HELL'S BOTTOM

A hot time in the old town

105 As the southbound train Dorothy Ellis Lee, *A History of Arlington County, Virginia,* 33; Jack Hamilton Foster, "Crandal Mackey, Crusading Commonwealth's Attorney." *Arlington Historical Magazine,* 1984. Rose, *Arlington County, Virginia,* 150–156.

106 Jackson City, at least Jackson City history, vertical files, ACL; Rose, *Arlington County, Virginia,* 92–3; *Northern Virginia Sun,* 28 Aug. 1957; *Star,* 20 Jan. 1892; J. Elwood Clements, oral history, 1977, ACOHP.

106 Just inland, occupying Frank L. Ball, "The Arlington I Have Known," *Arlington Historical Magazine,* 1964; *WP,* 4 Dec. 1926.

107 By the turn Foster, "Crandal Mackey"; Ball, "The Arlington I Have Known." *WP,* 9 May 1904.

107 Jackson City was the prime Lee, *A History of Arlington,* 37–39, Foster, "Crandal Mackey."

The place where fish are caught

108 **The land where** Rose, *Arlington County, Virginia,* 9–15; Junior League of Washington, *The City of Washington: An Illustrated History,* 9–11; Arlington Historical Society, "Historic Arlington," on Arlington Historical Society Web site, www.arlingtonhistoricalsociety.org/learn/; Daniel Koski-Karell, "Historical and Archaeological Background Research of the GSA Pentagon Complex Project Area," 12–31, box 1312, OSD HO; "Final Environmental Assessment of the Pentagon Reservation Master Plan," 68–90, box 1312, OSD HO.

109 **The Civil War** Koski-Karell, "Historical and Archaeological Background Research"; Ruth Ward, "Life in Alexandria County During the Civil War," *The Arlington Historical Magazine,* 1984.

109 **A community of escaped slaves** Sherlock, "Arlington National Cemetery, Historic Background Southern Portion"; Roberta Schildt, "Freedman's Village: Arlington, Virginia, 1863–1900," *Arlington Historical Magazine,* 1984; Freedman's Village vertical file, ACL.

109 **Some residents** Susan Gilpin, unpublished paper on Queen City, 1984, Queen City vertical file, ACL; Schildt, "Freedman's Village." *Star,* 26 Jan., 1908.

110 **That was not the case with Hell's** *WP,* 25 June, 1910, 12 May 1923, 15 May 1925, 1 Dec. 1925, 28 Apr. 1926, 7 May 1926, 30 Apr. 1970.

110 **Nearby, on the old site** Arven H. Saunders, "Airports in Northern Virginia, Past and Present," *Arlington Historical Magazine,* 1967; Author visit, Arlington County Visitors Center.

110 **Constant burning** *WP,* 7 Oct. 1934, 13 Jan. 1957, 9 Aug. 1936.

110 **Legislation for a new airport** Saunders, "Airports in Northern Virginia."

110 **FDR, as usual** Rhoads, "Franklin D. Roosevelt and Washington Architecture"; Cowdrey, *A City for the Nation,* 55; *Star,* 20 Nov. 1940.

111 **There was only one problem** Reynolds, "John McShain—Builder." The plaque remains on the wall in the old terminal.

111 **Much change was afoot** *WP,* 17 Sept. 1941; "The Pentagon Project—ASF," NARA RG 160.

111 **The latter site** *Federal Architect,* Jan.–Apr. 1943; Sheilah Kast, "Not Everyone Thought It Was So Dreamy," *Star,* 1 Sept. 1975; Rayfield Barber, oral history, 1991, ACOHP; Perry West, oral history, 1975, ACOHP; Final Environmental Assessment of the Pentagon Reservation Master Plan," 82, box 1312, OSD HO.

111 **The whole county** NCPPC minutes, 29 July 1941, 23, 27; Rose, *Arlington County, Virginia,* 175–6, 197–203; *Star,* 25 July and 8 Nov. 1941; Arlington County Board minutes, 13 Nov. 1943.

112 **Faced now with the prospect** *WP,* 26 July 1941; Kast, "Not Everyone Thought It Was So Dreamy"; Senate hearing, 8 Aug. 1941, 195; *Star,* 25 July 1941.

112 **Somervell's building would require** John J. O'Brien, memorandum for Col. Clarence Renshaw, 31 July 1943, entry 5, box 1, NARA RG 200; "The Pentagon

Project-EHD," 36, CEHO; War Department press release, "General Plans Announced for New War Department Building in Arlington County, Va.", 7 Oct.
1941, I, CEHO.

A new pentagon

113 **The original rationale** "Basic Data on the Pentagon," IV, file 4, box 15, SDF,
NARA RG 160; Frierson, *The Pentagon*, 8–10 (see also draft manuscript, 11); *Architectural Record*, Jan. 1943; Witmer planning memorandum, OSD HO.

114 **Somervell liked it** Somervell, letter to William A. Delano, 11 Sept. 1941, I,
CEHO.

114 **Something else about a pentagon** "The Pentagon," Sept. 1942, 15, Witmer papers, OSD HO (hereafter "The Pentagon," Witmer papers); Leisenring, F&R interview, CEHO; Shelby Foote, *The Civil War: Fort Sumter to Perryville*, 49.

I should absolutely refuse to live in a building of that type

114 **Roosevelt made the first** Stimson diary, 29 Aug. 1941; Brinkley, *Washington Goes to War*, 72.

114 **Roosevelt had picked up** Downer letter to Delano, 2 Sept. 1941, NARA DC RG 66.

115 **Roosevelt's vision** Roosevelt, *Complete Presidential Press Conferences*, vol. 18, 127–29, 29 Aug. 1941.

115 **"Well, Mr. President"** Clarke, oral history, 153–154, CU.

115 **By the end** Downer, letter to Delano, 2 Sept. 1941, NARA DC RG 66.

I like that pentagon-shaped building

115 **Bergstrom arrived** *Washington Daily News*, 3 Sept. 1941; Minutes of meeting of the Commission of Fine Arts, 2 Sept. 1941, microfilm, NARA DC RG 66 (hereafter CFA minutes).

116 **"A pentagonal has never worked"** *Ibid.*

116 **Paul Philippe Cret** Rhoads, "Franklin D. Roosevelt and Washington Architecture"; "History of the National Naval Medical Center," NNMC; Philadelphia Architects and Buildings Project Web site, www.philadelphiabuildings.org/pab.

116 **"If one gets into"** CFA minutes, 2 Sept. 1941, NARA DC.

116 **Cret drew pencil sketches** Clarke, oral history, 152–53, CU.

116 **Somervell beat the commissioners** *Star*, 2 and 3 Sept. 1941; *Washington Daily News*, 3 Sept. 1941; "The President's Day," International News Service, 3 Sept. 1941; Pare Lorentz chronology, 2 Sept. 1941, FDR Lib.

117 **At 2:15 P.M.** Clarke, oral history, 153, CU; Clarke letter and accompanying report to FDR, 2 Sept. 1941, NARA DC RG 66; Pare Lorentz chronology, 2 Sept. 1941, FDR Lib.

117 **"You know, gentlemen"** Clarke, oral history, 153, CU.

A veil of secrecy falls

117 **Late that afternoon** Roosevelt, *Complete Presidential Press Conferences*, vol. 18, 2 Sept. 1941, 133–35.

118 **"It doesn't seem reasonable"** *WP*, 5 Sept. 1941.

118 **Somervell was cheery** *Star*, 4 Sept. 1941.

118 **The press did not fully** *Star*, 2 Sept. 1941.

118 **By Somervell's reckoning** Somervell memorandum for the assistant secretary of war, 3 Sept. 1941, SDF, NARA RG 160.

118 **Somervell told the press** *Washington Daily News*, 3 Sept. 1941; *Star*, 3 Sept. 1941; *WT-H*, 3 Sept. 1941; "The President's Day," International News Service, 4 Sept. 1941; Pare Lorentz chronology, 3 Sept. 1941, for Lib.

119 **The afternoon of September 4** "Minutes of conference on New War Department Building," 4 Sept. 1941, I, CEHO, FDR Lib.

119 **There was one more** Somervell memo to Chief, Bureau of Public Relations, 4 Sept. 1941, I, CEHO; Somervell memo to Surles, 5 Sept. 1941, I, CEHO.

119 **A veil of secrecy** "The Pentagon Project—EHD," 35, CEHO; F&R, *The Corps of Engineers*, 437.

CHAPTER 7: UNDER WAY

An army is marshaled

121 **Word was getting around fast** Stanley Nance Allan, author interviews, 2003–06; Stanley Nance Allan, "Building the Pentagon," lecture delivered to the Chicago Literary Club, 25 Nov. 2002. Allan went by the name "Joe" until after he left in Pentagon project in 1942.

122 **McShain had developed** Brauer, *The Man Who Built Washington*, 50.

122 **Hauck was a Pennsylvania-born** *WP*, Hauck obituary, 25 Jan. 1970; J. Lacey Reynolds, undated notes for "John McShain, Builder," VII, subseries 1, McShain papers, HML (hereafter Reynolds notes).

123 **Hauck was different** Polly McShain, author interview.

123 **McShain's treatment of Hauck** Reynolds notes, McShain papers, HML; Brauer, *The Man Who Built Washington*, 134.

The biggest white elephant in creation

123 **Roosevelt, after** Goodwin, *No Ordinary Time*, 271–2; Jan Pottker, *Sara and Eleanor*, 332; *NYT*, 9 Sept. 1941.

124 **In ordinary times** Frierson, *The Pentagon*, 8; Goldberg, *The Pentagon*, 44; Clarence Renshaw, memo to the Quartermaster General, 3 Sept. 1941, I, CEHO; George Malcolm White, "The Pentagon Drawings," 1993, 6.

124 **The key to building** *WP*, 23 Jan. 1951.

124 **as the contract required** Construction authorization, 6 Sept. 1941, I, CEHO; Witmer planning memorandum, OSD HO.

125 **The assembly-line** Ides van der Gracht, interview with George Malcolm White, 25–26 Jan. 1993, series 45.1, George M. White, RG 45, AOC (hereafter van der Gracht, White interview); McShain, address to The Society of American Military Engineers Philadelphia Post, 16 Mar. 1944, personal papers, McShain Papers, (hereafter McShain address to engineers).

125 **Hauck would have overall** *Ibid.;* Brauer, *The Man Who Built Washington*, 82. Leisenring, F&R interview, CEHO.

125 **At the site** *WT-H*, 3 Sept. 1941.

125 **With groundbreaking** Reynolds notes, 42, McShain papers, HML.

126 **On the eve** *Architectural Forum*, Sept. 1941.

September 11, 1941

126 **The heat finally broke** *WP*, 11 Sept. 1941.

126 **The new construction** Pentagon project audit, 22 Aug. 1942, I, CEHO; Groves diary, 11 Sept. 1941, entry 7530G, NARA RG 200.

126 **best part of the site** Groves letter to *The Journal of the Armed Forces*, 23 May 1968, entry 5, box 1, NARA RG 200; Stacie Condrell, author interview, Sept. 2003.

126 **Somervell had eight pile drivers** NCPPC minutes, 18 Sept. 1941, 71; "World's Largest Office Building," draft of article for *Engineering News-Record*, 16 Sept. 1942, I, CEHO; McShain address to engineers, McShain papers, HML.

127 **Regardless, the general** Somervell letter to William A. Delano, 11 Sept. 1941, I, CEHO.

127 **Alexander Surles, the Army chief** Somervell, memorandum to Surles, 10 Sept. 1941, I, CEHO; War Department press release, 11 Sept. 1941, SDF, NARA RG 160.

127 **In fact, the construction** Office of the Quartermaster General, memo to Office of the Under Secretary, 9 Sept. 1941, I, CEHO.

127 **Somervell was correct** Groves, "Notes on the Pentagon," NARA RG 200; W. D. Styer, memo to Somervell, 12 Sept. 1941, SDF, NARA RG 160; "Population of War Department Building," 7 Sept. 1941, Witmer notebook, Witmer papers, OSD HO.

128 **Stimson received "disturbing news"** Stimson diary, 11 Sept. 1941.

128 **At the White House** Burns, *The Soldier of Freedom*, 139.

128 **"The Nazi danger"** Roosevelt, *The Public Papers and Addresses of Franklin D. Roosevelt*, 1941 vol., 389.

128 **Roosevelt announced** Stimson diary, 11 Sept. 1941; Burns, *The Soldier of Freedom*, 141.

129 **"[W]hen you see a rattlesnake"** Roosevelt, *The Public Papers and Addresses of Franklin D. Roosevelt*, 1941 vol., 390.

Those damn pile drivers

129 **The pounding was incessant** Allan, "Building the Pentagon."

129 **Major Gar Davidson** Davidson, oral history, CEHO.

129 **The engineers had briefly considered** "The Pentagon," Witmer papers, 22, OSD HO; Lt. Col. Hugh Hester letter to Julius Amberg, 12 Dec. 1941, I, CEHO; Frierson, *The Pentagon*, draft, 30; Allan, "Building the Pentagon"; Allan, author interview; Condrell, author interview.

130 **After a week they had sunk** Furman, author interview; NCPPC minutes, 19 Sept. 1941, 69–71.

This infernal hole

130 **Somervell was indeed** *WT-H*, 8 Oct. 1941; *WP*, 31 Oct. 1941.

130 **The cool weather** *WP*, 1 Oct. 1941; Stimson diary, 16 Sept. 1941.

131 **"We'll have government clerks"** *WT-H*, 8 Oct. 1941.

131 **On September 19, Groves ordered** Groves memo to Renshaw, 19 Sept. 1941, I, CEHO; Hauck, letter to Renshaw, 23 Sept. 1941, I, box 17, CEHO; *Star*, 13 Sept. 1942.

131 **After two weeks** Edmund H. Leavey letter to Walter Wheeler, 3 Oct. 1941, I, CEHO; *Star*, 10 Oct. 1941.

131 **What was left of Hell's** Furman, author interview.

131 **Wrecking balls** *Ibid.;* Renshaw letter to Civil Aeronautics Administration, 22 Sept. 1941, I, CEHO; Furman, Notice to Flyers, I, CEHO.

132 **By early October** Allan, author interview; *WT-H*, 8 Oct. 1941; *WP*, 31 Oct. 1941.

132 **When construction started** "New War Department Building," undated report circa 1942, 3, Witmer papers, OSD HO; Frierson, *The Pentagon*, 16; architects' historical memo, NARA RG 200; "The Army's Giant 'Five-by-Five," *Popular Mechanics*, Mar. 1943. By comparison, 1.2 million cubic yards of earth and rock were excavated to build the World Trade Center.

132 **The excavation and grading** Furman, author interview; "Equipment Maintenance on Huge Earth Job," *ENR*, 2 July 1942; *Star*, 12 Oct. 1942; *WP*, 6 and 13 May, 1942.

133 **The Army had considered** Somervell memo the Chief of Engineers, 10 Sept. 1941, I, CEHO; Frierson, *The Pentagon*, 17.

133 **In the first weeks** "Concreting a 100-Acre Office Building," *ENR*, 4 June 1942.

133 **More than one million** Renshaw, memo to the Chief of Engineers, 5 July 1944, I, 16, CEHO; *WP*, 8 Nov. 1941.

We'd better leave town

134 **The original plan** House hearing, 22 July 1941, 507.

134 **The light-colored, fine-grained** Christina Pino-Marina, "Indiana Plant Makes its Mark on History," www.washingtonpost.com, 11 June 2002.

134 "I am sure" McShain letter to Groves, 30 July 1941, I, CEHO.

134 McShain had an ally J. B. Reinhalter letter to Somervell, 28 Aug. 1941, I, CEHO; Voorhees, F&R interview, CEHO; Groves comments, second draft, Chap. 13, 4–5, CEHO; Somervell letter to Rep. J. Harry McGregor, 18 Oct. 1941, I, CEHO.

135 The limestone debate F. E. Ross, "Architectural Concrete Work on the Pentagon Building," *Architectural Concrete*, 1943.

135 McShain and Groves thought it easiest F&R, *The Corps of Engineers*, 438; Ross, "Architectural Concrete Work on the Pentagon Building"; Groves comments, second draft, Chap. 13, 4–5, CEHO; Leisenring, F&R interview, CEHO.

135 McShain was beside himself Telephone transcript, McShain calling Groves, 21 Nov. 1941, I, CEHO; McShain letter to Renshaw, 2 Oct. 1941, I, CEHO; Groves, oral history with Pogue, second interview, GCM Lib.

135 Late on the morning "The President's Day," International News Service, 11 Oct. 1941; *Star*, 10 Oct. 1941; Edwin Watson, Memorandum for the President, 7 Oct. 1941, OF 25, FDR Lib.; F&R, *The Corps of Engineers*, 437.

135 Next Bergstrom made the case Telephone transcript, Groves calling McShain, 10 Oct. 1941.

136 The fight was not over *Ibid.;* Groves, oral history with Pogue, second interview, GCM Lib.; Groves comments, second draft, Chap. 13, 4–5, CEHO; Allan, author interview.

136 Inspecting the concrete Telephone transcript, McShain calling Groves, 14 Oct. 1941, I, CEHO.

136 Groves pressed Somervell Groves, oral history with Pogue, second interview, GCM Lib.

136 The president was "emphatic" Somervell, memorandum for General Watson, 5 Dec. 1941, OF 25, FDR Lib.

136 "Well, it's settled" Groves, oral history with Pogue, second interview, GCM Lib.

136 McShain, who prided Telephone transcript, McShain calling Groves, 21 Nov. 1941, I, CEHO.

It's going to be a whopper

136 Newspaper and magazine reporters George Holmes memo to Bureau of Public Relations, 7 Oct. 1941, I, CEHO.

137 Each face of the five-side War Department press release, "General Plans Announced for New War Department Building in Arlington County, Va.," 7 Oct. 1941, I, CEHO.

137 Reporters were further *WP*, 8 Oct. 1941.

137 The "so-called basement" Goldberg, *The Pentagon*, 44; "The Pentagon Telephone Conversations With General Groves Office Feb. '42 '43," Renshaw and Groves, 30 Apr. 1942, I, CEHO (hereafter The Pentagon Telephone Conversations—Groves).

137 Indeed, no information *Star*, 10 Oct. 1941.

138 Finally, leaving the White House *WT-H*, 11 Oct. 1941.

138 Conferring with local architects *Star*, 10 Oct. 1941.

138 The working papers of Witmer "Population of War Department Building," 7 Sept. 1941, Witmer notebook, Witmer papers, OSD HO.

138 Speaking to reporters *Star*, 10 Oct. 1941.

138 Somervell told Roosevelt Downer, letter to Delano, 2 Sept. 1941, NARA DC RG 66.

138 As for reporters' doubts *Star*, 10 Oct. 1941.

138 Skeptical reporters consulted *Washington Daily News*, 13 Oct. 1941; *Star*, 11 Oct. 1941. Though he had made no public announcement, Delano would soon tell Roosevelt he intended to retire from the commission he had fathered. The planning commission, Delano explained to his nephew, "no longer performed any planning functions" (Goldberg, "The Pentagon", 28).

139 "It was finally decided" *WT-H*, 11 Oct. 1941.

CHAPTER 8: THE VIEW FROM HIGH AND LOW

Lieutenant Furman's blimp ride

141 Lieutenant Bob Furman waited Furman, author interview.

141 The blimp was the only aircraft Renshaw, statement on use of Washington-Hoover Airport, 13 Oct. 1941, I, CEHO.

141 *Enterprise,* a 148-foot *WP*, 2 Feb. 1936, 8 Nov. 1941, and 12 Feb. 1942.

142 Furman knew time Furman, author interview.

143 Groves and Renshaw were impressed Richard Groves, author interview; Alan Renshaw, author interview; Norris, *Racing for the Bomb*, 287–88; Furman, author interview.

143 Now, as *Enterprise Ibid*.

143 Workers swarmed *Ibid.;* War Department aerial photograph, 22 Oct. 1941, Witmer papers, OSD HO; War Department press release, "New War Department Building," 1 Nov. 1941, I, CEHO.

McShain and Bergstrom go to war

144 Back on the ground Polly McShain, author interview; Telephone transcript, McShain calling Groves, 14 Oct. 1941, I, CEHO.

145 By October 28 Farrell, memo to Groves, 29 Oct. 1941, I, CEHO.

145 Every day Hauck McShain address to engineers, McShain papers, HML; Polly McShain, author interview.

145 Further complicating *Engineer Memoirs—Casey*, 41, 141. It was a fateful decision that took Casey to the Bataan Peninsula, where his engineering skills bought time

for ill-equipped and outnumbered American and Filipino troops; he later escaped
from Corregidor with MacArthur aboard a submarine to Australia.

145 **Worried about the growing** Farrell, memo to Groves, 29 Oct. 1941, I, CEHO.
AP, Farrell obituary, 11 Apr. 1967; Groves, "My Associations with Major General
Thomas F. Farrell," 12 Aug. 1968, NARA RG 200.

146 **Groves telephoned private** Groves, transcripts of telephone calls to Philadelphia
and Detroit, 3–5 Nov. 1941, I, CEHO.

146 **"It must be recognized"** Farrell, memo to Groves, 29 Oct. 1941, I, CEHO.

In the hangar

146 **All-out** van der Gracht, White interview, AOC; Somervell letter to Delano, 11
Sept. 1941, I, CEHO; White, "The Pentagon Drawings."

147 **"Mr. Delano said"** van der Gracht, White interview.

147 **He stood a shade** Ides van der Gracht membership file, AIA; White, author interview, 2004; White, "The Pentagon Drawings," 3; Delano letter to New York
State Education Department, 27 Oct. 1931, RG 45, series 45.1, AOC.

148 **"Okay, go to work"** van der Gracht, White interview.

148 **Larry Lemmon** Lawrence Clifton Lemmon, *Twentieth Century Sojourn*, 147–151.

148 **The drafting team** van der Gracht, White interview.

148 **More problematic, the warehouse** "The Pentagon," 9, Witmer papers, OSD
HO; Pentagon photographs, Witmer papers, OSD HO; White, "The Pentagon
Drawings," 6; Lemmon, *Twentieth Century Sojourn*, 152.

149 **The design force was approaching** "The Pentagon," 7–8, Witmer papers, OSD
HO; Lemmon, *Twentieth Century Sojourn*, 152.

149 **The drafting force was broken down** van der Gracht, White interview; Lemmon, *Twentieth Century Sojourn*, 152.

149 **Van der Gracht was a natural** van der Gracht, White interview.

149 **Van der Gracht issued a daily** *Ibid.*, White, author interview; Furman, author
interview.

150 **Behind van der Gracht's desk** van der Gracht, White interview.

150 **The draftsmen were using tools** White, "The Pentagon Drawings," 12; van der
Gracht, letter to George Malcolm White, 4 July 1993, RG 45, series 45.1, AOC.

150 **Drawings were issued nightly** "The Pentagon," 9–10, Witmer papers, OSD
HO; White, "The Pentagon Drawings," 6–8.

151 **The builders and Army** Furman, author interview; Polly McShain, author interview.

151 **"We were designing"** van der Gracht, White interview; "Basic Data on the Pentagon," III, 4, SDF, NARA RG 160. Leisenring, F&R interview; F&R, *The Corps
of Engineers*, 438.

151 **"How big should I"** Brinkley, *Washington Goes to War*, 73 (AIA membership
files and other documents spell Dickey's first name as Allen instead of Alan).

151 To curb the design chaos "Planning the Pentagon Building," 21 Oct. 1942, 4, Witmer papers, OSD HO; White, "The Pentagon Drawings," 10.

152 *Oh the General* undated, Witmer papers, OSD HO.

152 **Van der Gracht would make** van der Gracht, White interview.

A price to pay

153 **At the construction site** 1ˢᵗ Lt. Charles Smith, "Fatality report on Vernon S. Janney," 22 Oct. 1941, I, CEHO; *WP*, 16 Oct. 1941.

153 **Janney's death was the first** Lloyd Blanchard memo to Groves, 7 Nov. 1941, I, CEHO; *WP*, 6 Nov. 1941.

154 **Groves ordered Renshaw** Groves memo to Renshaw, 14 Nov. 1941, I, CEHO.

When push came to shove

154 **Somervell had picked** F&R, *The Corps of Engineers*, 522; *Star*, 6 Nov. 1941; Quartermaster General memo on conservation of critical materials, 24 Oct. 1941, I, CEHO.

154 **Industries and citizens** Somervell, letter to Capt. H. C. Whitehurst, 15 Sept. 1941, I, CEHO; Furman, author interview.

155 **Steel was most critical** F&R, *The Corps of Engineers*, 438; Maj. George H. Christensen, "Miscellaneous Data, Pentagon Building", 7 Oct. 1944, I, CEHO; Witmer planning memorandum, OSD HO; Colglazier, oral history, MHI; Alan Renshaw, author interview; "War Department Architects Saving Critical Materials," 30 Oct. 1941, I, CEHO.

155 **Furman was often sent** Furman, author interview.

156 **Officials with the Office** *Star*, 6, Nov. 1941.

156 **The OPM leak** W. B. Styer, memo, 6 Nov. 1941, I, CEHO; Col. Edmund Leavey, memo to Renshaw, 10 Nov. 1941, I, CEHO.

The gold rush

156 **The building's construction** Goldberg, *The Pentagon*, 56; Telephone transcript, Renshaw calling H. Waples, OPM, 10 Nov. 1941, I, CEHO.

156 **But OPM chief** F&R, *The Corps of Engineers*, 437; "The Pentagon Project— EHD," 24, CEHO; Numerous letters and telegrams from wood industry representatives sent in November 1941 on file in I, CEHO; Stimson, letter to Sen. Lister Hill, 3 Dec. 1941, I, CEHO.

157 **Other members of Congress** Smith letter to Somervell, 11 Oct. 1941, I, CEHO; Ramspeck letter to Styer, 2 Dec. 1941, I, CEHO; Bailey letter to Gen. Gregory, 6 Nov. 1941; Walter letter to Somervell, 28 Oct. 1941, I, CEHO; Somervell letter to Walter, 4 Nov. 1941; Bergstrom memo to Somervell, 10 Nov. 1941, I, CEHO; F&R, *The Corps of Engineers*, 437.

157 *The President, after his conversation* Watson memo to Somervell, 4 Dec. 1941, OF 25, FDR Lib.

157 **An exasperated Somervell refused** Somervell memo to Watson, 5 Dec. 1941, OF 25, FDR Lib.

158 **"Will you tell"** Roosevelt note to Watson, 5 Dec. 1941, OF 25, FDR Lib.

You can kind of out-slicker yourself

158 **On December 1, 1941** War Department press release, 2 Dec. 1941, Somervell papers, MHI; F&R, *The Corps of Engineers,* 472.

158 **The Corps of Engineers played a unique** Cowdrey, *A City for the Nation,* 34; *WP,* 17 Aug. 1941.

158 **The transfer was** F&R, *The Corps of Engineers,* 4–5, 239–241; Richard Groves, author interview.

159 **In mid-1941** F&R, *The Corps of Engineers,* 159, 462–3.

159 **Madigan quietly approached** *Ibid.;* Madigan, F&R interview, CEHO.

160 **Somervell's bid** F&R, *The Corps of Engineers,* 462–3; Eugene Reybold, F&R interview, 1959, VII, CEHO; *WP,* 21 May 1943; Groves, F&R interview, 1956, CEHO; Gregory, F&R interview, CEHO.

160 **Somervell was "mad"** Madigan, F&R interview; Ohl, *Supplying the Troops,* 53–54.

160 **Reybold, though, had no interest** Reybold interview, CEHO; F&R, *The Corps of Engineers,* 472–3.

160 **General Marshall considered** Marshall, oral history with Pogue, 14 Feb. 1957, GCM Lib.; Ohl, *Supplying the Troops,* 54.

161 **"We are right back"** Pagan interview, CEHO; F&R, *The Corps of Engineers,* 475.

Speed is paramount

161 **By the beginning** "The Pentagon Project EHD," 60, CEHO; F&R, *The Corps of Engineers,* 439; Furman, author interview.

162 **By late November** Farrell memo to Somervell, I, CEHO; Somervell order to Renshaw, 25 Nov. 1941, I, CEHO.

162 **The Commission of Fine Arts** CFA minutes, 14 Nov. 1941, NARA DC.

163 **Renshaw was also dealing** Davidson memo to Renshaw, 6 Dec. 1941, I, CEHO.

CHAPTER 9—THEY WOULDN'T DARE ATTACK PEARL HARBOR

Some devilry

165 **The tails set** Furman, author interview.

165 **In Washington** John J. McCloy, oral history, 1983, 2–3, oral history collection,

OSD HO; Marshall, *The Papers of George C. Marshall*, vol. 4, 4; Stimson diary, 7 Dec. 1941.

166 **The news caught Washington** *WP*, 8 Dec. 1941; *Star*, 8 Dec. 1941; Hart, *Washington at War*, 1–24.

167 **Helen McShane Bailey** Helen McShane Bailey, "The Office of the Chief of Staff, U.S. Army, in World War II: A Memoir," 7, Memories Project, GCM Lib.; Bailey, author interview, 10 July 2004; *WP*, 8 Dec. 1941.

167 **Inside the Munitions Building** McCloy, oral history, 5, OSD HO; Walter Isaacson and Evan Thomas, *The Wise Men*, 189; Handbook of Texas Online, s.v. Miles, Nelson Appelton, www.tsha.utexas.edu/handbook/online.

167 **At the White House** Brinkley, *Washington Goes to War*, 95; minutes of conference in Marshall's office, 8 Dec. 1941, entry 31, NARA RG 165; *WP*, 8 Dec. 1941; F&R, *The Corps of Engineers*, 477.

168 **Furman arrived** Furman, author interview.

Absolute necessity

168 **Walker had been on the job** Donald Walker, author interview, 15 Jan. 2004.

168 **After a stirring welcome** *The Public Papers of Franklin D. Roosevelt*, 1941 vol., 515; "The President's Busy Day," International News Service, 9 Dec. 1941.

169 **"Glad of it"** Walker, author interview.

169 **The decision was made** McShain autobiographical notes, 13, McShain papers, HML; Somervell letter to Rep. Clarence Cannon, 7 May 1942, SDF, NARA RG 160.

169 **The agreement that Frederic** Groves, "The Construction of the New War Department Office Building," 15 June 1942, prepared congressional testimony, Groves Collection, GCM Lib.

169 **Congressman who in November** F&R, *The Corps of Engineers*, 478; CFA minutes, 18 Dec. 1941, NARA DC RG 66.

169 **Within days** Renshaw, memo to Chief of Engineers, 17 Dec. 1941, I,CEHO; "Basic Data on the Pentagon," III, 7, SDF, NARA RG 160.

It's not fair to us to expect the impossible

170 **The pressure** Groves, "The Construction of the New War Department Office Building," GCM Lib.

170 **At Somervell's insistence** Renshaw, memorandum for Somervell, 22 Dec. 1941, SDF, NARA RG 160; Leisenring, F&R interview, CEHO.

170 **"Instructions were issued"** U.S. House Committee on Appropriations, Subcommittee on War Department, 77th Congress, 2nd sess., Hearings on the Military Establishment Appropriation Bill for 1943, 11 June 1941, 218 (hereafter House hearing, 15 June 1942).

170 **Bergstrom had to be brought** Renshaw, memorandum for Somervell, 22 Dec. 1941, SDF, NARA RG 160.

170 **"April first? It's going up"** Telephone transcript, McShain calling Groves, 23 Dec. 1941, I, CEHO.

Putting the screws to the delegees

171 **The strategy was simple** Richard Groves, author interview.

171 **Groves learned it from Somervell** *Engineer Memoirs—Hardin*, 106–7.

171 **"philosophy was to delegate"** William Lawren, *The General and the Bomb*, 61.

171 **Groves was not a screamer** Ken Nichols, *The Road to Trinity*, 102; Furman, author interview; Norris, *Racing for the Bomb*, 16; Teller, introduction to Groves, *Now It Can be Told*, vii.

171 **"Don't you ever praise"** Nichols, *The Road to Trinity*, 102.

171 **Groves had stenographers** Groves comments, 41–42, CEHO; Davidson letter Maj. Gen. A. C. Smith, VII, CEHO; Davidson, oral history, 160–1, CEHO; Davidson personnel file, CEHO; *NYT*, Davidson obituary, 27 Dec. 1992.

172 **Like one of his few heroes** Groves, *Now It Can be Told*, 28; Lawren, *The General and the Bomb*, 64. Davidson, oral history, 136, CEHO.

173 **John McShain bore** Polly McShain, author interview; Brauer, *The Man Who Built Washington*, 154–57.

173 **For Clarence Renshaw** Eileen Renshaw, author interview, 26 Feb. 2004; Furman, author interview.

173 **Groves was often** Groves, oral history with Pogue, second interview, GCM Lib.; Davidson, oral history, CEHO.

173 **Edwin Bergstrom** "Committee of Five" report, appendix A, minutes of the meeting of the AIA board of directors, 29 Oct.–1 Nov. 1941, AIA; Charles T. Ingham, letters to Bergstrom, 17 Dec. 1941, Bergstrom membership file, AIA; minutes of special meeting of AIA executive committee, 5 Feb. 1942, AIA.

174 **Somervell's three girls** Mary Anne Somervell Brenza, author interview, Feb. 31, 2004; Matter, author interview. *WT H*, 4 July 1941.

174 **McShain went to see Somervell** Telephone transcript, McShain calling Groves, 23 Dec. 1941, I, CEHO.

Remedy this situation

175 **With fears of a Japanese** van der Gracht, White interview, AOC; Furman, author interview.

175 **A team of engineers** memo to Robins, 17 Dec. 1941, I, CEHO; Robins memo to Somervell's office, 20 Dec. 1941, I, CEHO; telephone transcript, Major Donald Antes calling Renshaw, 22 Dec. 1941, I, CEHO.

176 **The pace inside** telephone transcript, McShain calling Groves, 23 Dec. 1941, I, CEHO; Leisenring, F&R interview, CEHO.

176 **Shortly before Christmas** McShain note to Groves, 21 Dec. 1941, I, CEHO; Hauck, letter to Renshaw, 31 Dec. 1941, I, CEHO.

176 On December 31 *Ibid.*

177 Groves received Groves memo to Renshaw, 31 Dec. 1942, I, CEHO.

Oh to hell with it

177 On the morning of Thursday Renshaw, note to Somervell, 1 Jan. 1942 and Somervell, note to Renshaw, 1 Jan. 1942, SDF, NARA RG 160; aerial photographs of site, 24 Dec. 1941, SDF, NARA RG 160.

177 Progress was soon evident audit report No. 2, 21 Jan., 1942, I, CEHO.

177 More than a half-century Condrell, author interview.

178 "The orders came through" van der Gracht, White interview, AOC.

178 Renshaw had received word telephone transcript, Major Donald Antes calling Renshaw, 22 Dec. 1941, I, CEHO; Renshaw memo to Chief of Engineers, 9 Jan. 1942, I, CEHO; Robins memo to Somervell's office, 9 Jan. 1942, I, CEHO.

178 Then Stimson Stimson memorandum for the president, 2 Jan. 1942, OF 25, FDR Lib.; FDR note to Stimson, 5 Jan. 1942, OF 25, FDR Lib.; telephone transcript, Groves calling Renshaw, 9 Jan. 1942, I, CEHO.

178 Each time the order Renshaw memo to Chief of Engineers, 9 Jan. 1942, I, CEHO; Robins memo to Somervell's office, 9 Jan. 1942, I, CEHO.

179 The proposal for the bomb shelter Stimson memorandum for the president, 14 Jan. 1942, OF 25, FDR Lib.; Harold Smith memorandum for the secretary of war, 17 Feb. 1942, OF 25, FDR Lib.

179 The resolution was a boost Col. F. S. Strong memo for Somervell, 21 Jan. 1942, SDF, NARA RG 160.

179 Perhaps the biggest Renshaw memo for Maj. Franklin Matthias, 11 Aug. 1942, I, CEHO; McShain address to engineers, McShain papers, HML.

A growing army of workers

179 More than six thousand audit report No. 2, 21 Jan., 1942, I, CEHO.

179 Any skilled laborer *WP*, 7 Mar. and 27 Apr. 1942; Hauck, letter to Rodmens' Local Union, 20 Feb. 1942, I, CEHO; Hank Neighbors, author interview, October 2003.

180 At the bottom Department of Labor memo, 2 Feb. 1942, I, CEHO; *Cong. Rec.*, 1 Oct. 1942, 7692; Neighbors, author interview; audit report No. 2, 21 Jan., 1942, I, CEHO; Allan, author interview.

180 As a payroll witness Neighbors, author interview.

180 Thousands of men Renshaw testimony, Office of the Inspector General, investigation report, 25 May 1942, box 1188, records of the Office of the Inspector General; NARA RG 159 (hereafter known as cafeteria IG report); Ralph Smith testimony, cafeteria IG report, NARA RG 159.

181 They had their hands Furman, author interview.

181 McShain figured audit report No. 2, 21 Jan., 1942, I, CEHO; Joseph A. Fox, "World's Largest Cafeteria to Feed 40,000 Nearing Completion," *Star*, 13 Sept. 1942.

181 Even finding the canteens Walker, author interview; Brian Kelly, "Pentagon Veterans Recall Construction Days," *Star,* 30 Apr. 1967.

All signifying chaos

181 "Washington in wartime" Dwight D. Eisenhower, *Crusade in Europe,* 16.

182 By 1941, the population "Engineers' Statement on Pentagon Roads System," 5 Jan. 1944, I, CEHO; Alden Stevens, "Washington: Blight on Democracy," *Harper's Magazine,* December 1941; Brinkley, *Washington Goes to War,* 105.

182 "A languid Southern town" *Ibid.,* xii.

182 A war mindset *WP,* 21 and 17 Dec. 1941.

182 The most immediate problem Stevens, "Washington: Blight on Democracy"; *WP,* 20 Jan. 1942.

182 Writer John Dos Passos John Dos Passos, *The State of the Nation,* 1943, excerpt in D.C. History Curriculum Project, *City of Magnificent Intentions,* 420.

182 Workers turning up *WP,* 27 Apr. 1942.

183 The government's need Roosevelt, *Complete Presidential Press Conferences,* vol. 18, 108.

183 A long gray line Marquis Childs, "Washington Is a State of Mind," 1942, in *Katharine Graham's Washington,* 288.

183 "It was said around town" Brinkley, *Washington Goes to War,* 117.

183 For all the dead Davidson, oral history, 155, CEHO; Colglazier, oral history, 51, MHI.

183 Somervell, on *Detroit News,* 7 May 1944; Somervell White House identification card, Somervell papers, MHI.

184 Anytime he put on Kerr, oral history, Smithsonian.

184 "Not many were fooled" Norris, *Racing for the Bomb,* 347.

All centered here

184 More than Marshall, memo for McIntyre, 3 Apr. 1942, Marshall papers, box 80, folder 32, GCM Lib; NCPPC minutes, 4 Feb. 1942, 4.

184 In late January, Roosevelt Renshaw, memo to Davidson, 31 Jan. 1942, I, CEHO; Howard Peterson memo to Coy, 6 Feb. 1942, and Coy memo for the president, 20 Feb. 1942, OF 25, FDR Lib.

CHAPTER 10: THE BIG PUSH

An overwhelming task

187 The concrete edifice Matter, author interview; Brenza, author interview; *WP,* 27 Jan. 1942.

188 General Marshall was informed Marshall note to Somervell, 26 Jan. 1942, GCM

Papers, box 85, Somervell folder, GCM Lib.; Stimson diary, 7 Feb. 1942; Somervell service records, Somervell papers, MHI.

188 **The loss** Matter, author interview.

188 **Four days after Pearl Harbor** Stimson diary, 11 Dec. 1941. The others Stimson mentioned were Jacob Devers, who would command the 6th Army Group in Europe, and Mark Clark, who would be deputy commander for the Allied landings in North Africa and would command the U.S. Fifth Army in Italy.

188 **Marshall, fed up** Pogue, *Ordeal and Hope,* 289–301; *The Papers of George Catlett Marshall,* 127–129; War Department press release, "Reorganization of the War Department," 2 Mar. 1942, Somervell papers, MHI.

189 **Learning in January** Ohl, *Supplying the Troops,* 60–2.

189 **On February 28** Pogue, *Ordeal and Hope,* 296–97, United States News, 27 Mar. 1942; *NYT,* Somervell obituary, 14 Feb. 1955.

189 **"I will say this"** Millett, *The Army Service Forces,* 7.

189 **At the suggestion of Marshall** Brenza, author interview; *Newsweek,* 7 Dec. 1942; Murphy, "Somervell of the S.O.S."

190 **Somervell soared** *Life,* 13 Apr. 1942; *Time,* 15 June 1942; *New York Daily News,* 17 Apr. 1942.

190 **In little over a year** Alfred Goldberg, author interview, 22 Jan. 2004; Somervell, letter to Marshall, 13 May 1952, Somervell papers, MHI.

190 **Somervell was again** Somervell, "Construction Goes to War," *The Constructor,* July 1942; Somervell remarks to Metropolitan Section of American Society of Civil Engineers, 20 Dec. 1944, Somervell addresses, vol. 4, MHI. Richard Groves, author interview.

190 **"The undertaking"** F&R, *The Corps of Engineers,* 499; Somervell, "The War Construction Job," *The Constructor,* July 1944, in Somervell addresses, vol. 4, MHI.

191 **Among many other** telephone transcript, Antes calling Renshaw, 20 Jan. 1942, I, CEHO.

191 **On March 25** Somervell, memo to Reybold, 25 Mar. 1942, I, CEHO.

191 **The next day** Strong, memo to Groves, 26 Mar. 1942, I, CEHO.

191 **Just when it looked** *WP,* 30 Mar. 1942; *Time,* 15 June 1942.

From the bottom of the Potomac River

191 **Slipping past Alexandria** C. E. Planck, "Potomac Blockade," *WP,* 22 Feb. 1942. The description and all quotations from the river scene comes from Planck's account.

192 **Builders were desperate** *WP,* 24 Jan. 1942; Furman, author interview.

193 **The War Department could indeed** Christensen, "Miscellaneous Data Pentagon Building" 7 Oct. 1944, I, CEHO; Frierson, *The Pentagon,* 17; The Skyscraper Museum Web site, www.skyscraper.org. The amount of concrete poured is surpassed by some enormous public-works projects, among them the Hoover Dam, which required three and a quarter million cubic yards of concrete. The Grand

Coulee Dam, the largest concrete structure in the United States, required twelve million cubic yards.

193 **The location chosen** "The Pentagon Building," *Airlanes*, Dec. 1942.

193 **The Pentagon was being built** Christensen, "Miscellaneous Data Pentagon Building" memo, 7 Oct. 1944, I, CEHO; Renshaw, letter to Christensen, 23 Sept. 1944, I, CEHO.

193 **Though the supply** *WP*, 24 Jan. 1942.

193 **Floating dredges** "Concreting a 100-Acre Office Building," *ENR*, 4 June 1942; "The Pentagon Building," *Airlanes*, Dec. 1942. F. E. Ross, "Architectural Concrete Work on the Pentagon Building," *Architectural Concrete*, 1943.

194 **Renshaw tried using** Furman, author interview.

195 **The constant pouring** Allan, author interview.

195 **The carpenters set up** Allan, "Building the Pentagon"; Allan, author interview.

195 **The mass-production techniques** Allan, "Building the Pentagon"; Allan, author interview.

196 **A sudden and unexpected** F&R, *The Corps of Engineers*, 546; *Cong. Rec.*, 29 Feb. 1944, 2105.

196 **After a spectacular fire** Douglas McKay memo to Groves, 13 Feb. 1942, I, CEHO; Groves memo to Renshaw, 24 Feb. 1942, I, CEHO; Furman, author interview. The five-alarm fire on Feb. 8, 1942, at the Hotel Statler at the corner of 16th and K streets required 350 firefighters to extinguish.

196 **Their emergency preparedness** *Star*, 14 June 1942; Furman, author interview.

Are there really guys buried down there?

196 **Given the vast size** Walker, author interview. Alan Renshaw, author interview.

197 **Such stories spread** Brockwell, letter to author, 8 Mar. 2004; Bill Immen, "The Pentagon . . . Fact and Fancy," 7 Oct. 1961; *Pentagram*, 14 June 1984; Alan Fogg, *Fairfax Journal*, 15 Aug. 1988; Marian Bailey, author interview, 1999.

197 **The stories** Furman, author interview; Alan Renshaw, author interview.

Don't slip on it

198 **Workers were dying** *WP*, 29 Mar. 1942.

198 **Inspecting the site** Blanchard, memo to Antes, 5 Dec. 1941, I, CEHO.

198 **Renshaw was unapologetic** *WP*, 29 Mar. 1942.

198 **Labor leaders** *Ibid.;* Stimson, letter to Hall, 20 June 1942, NARA RG 107.

199 **Further aggrieved** *WP*, 4 Mar. 1942.

199 **There were racial** Renshaw testimony, cafeteria IG report, NARA RG 159; McShain, letter to Renshaw, 18 May 1942, file 291.2, NARA RG 407; Furman, author interview.

199 **Discrimination created** telephone transcript, Antes calling Renshaw, 7 Mar. 1942, I, CEHO.

200 **The matter was not** 1936 Code of Virginia, Separation of Races, exhibit A, cafeteria IG report NARA RG 159; Goldberg, *The Pentagon*, 62; *WP*, 12 Mar. 1942.

The road network

200 **An enormous road network** Goldberg, *The Pentagon*, 66.

200 **When he had sold** NCPPC minutes, 29 July 1941, 2; *WP*, 4 Dec. 1941.

200 **Planners for the War** "Access to the World's Largest Building," *ENR*, 25 Mar. 1943; *WP*, 23 Sept. 1942; "The Pentagon," Witmer papers, OSD HO.

200 **The design included** National Register of Historic Places Inventory, Nomination Form for Federal Properties, Pentagon Office Building Complex, 1989, box 1312, OSD HO. Cloverleaf interchanges on the Pennsylvania Turnpike date to the 1930s.

201 **The basic plan** Thomas MacDonald letter to Rep. Albert Engel, 31 Dec. 1943, I, CEHO; NCPPC minutes, 29 July 1941, 41; "The Pentagon Project—ASF," 24, NARA RG 160.

201 **Roosevelt took care** Downer letter to Delano, 2 Sept. 1941, NARA DC RG 66; *Cong. Rec.* 29 Feb. 1944, 2105; "The Pentagon Telephone Conversations—Groves," Matthias and Renshaw, 10 Aug. 1942.

201 **To speed the work** Somervell letter to MacDonald, 28 Oct. 1941, I, CEHO; Clarke, oral history, 154–5, CU; architects' historical memo, NARA RG 200.

201 **Colonel Edmond Leavey** Colglazier, oral history, MHI.

202 **Groves had steamrolled** Drew Pearson, "Merry-Go-Round," *WP*, 22 May 1944.

202 **But the roads** Renshaw message to Somervell, 25 Feb. 1942, SDF, NARA RG 160; Renshaw letter to Baird Snyder, 20 Feb. 1942, SDF, NARA RG 160.

This was a nice little neighborhood

202 **To make it click** *WT-H*, 14 Feb. 1942.

202 **It was a small collection** Everett Norton, oral history, ACOHP; Kast, "Not Everyone Thought It Was So Dreamy"; Gilpin, unpublished paper on Queen City, 1984, Queen City vertical file, ACL.

203 **This was not seen** NCPPC minutes, 17 Oct. 1941, 120.

203 **Construction had been** *Star*, 12 Feb. 1942; Kast, "Not Everyone Thought It Was So Dreamy."

203 **"It was a predicament"** Gertrude Jeffress, author interview, April 2004.

203 **The desperate residents** *Star*, 12 Feb. 1942.

203 **Thomas MacDonald** *WT-H*, 14 Feb. 1942, *WP*, 14 Feb. 1942.

204 **There was little** Arlington County Board minutes, 7 Mar. 1942; *Star*, 7 and 8 Mar. 1942; *WP*, 14 Feb. 1942.

204 **"I remember his going crazy"** *WP*, 4 Nov. 1999.

204 **Renshaw was not concerned** "The Pentagon Telephone Conversations—Miscellaneous," Renshaw and O'Brien, 21 Mar. 1942, I, CEHO.

204 **At the end of the month** Jeffress, author interview; Celestine Dole, author interview, April 2004; *Star,* 24 Mar. 1942; *WT-H,* 14 Feb. 1942; *WP,* 4 Nov. 1999.

204 **With the families out** *Star,* Apr. 18, 1942.

205 **Fact sheets** "The Pentagon," visitors' pamphlet circa 2000.

205 **"Whoever said it was nothing"** Jeffress, author interview.

Some change, eh?

205 **With the arrival of spring** "Description of Sections A and B," 25 Apr. 1942, Witmer papers, OSD HO.

205 **So much limestone was needed** Pino-Marina, "Indiana Plant Makes Its Mark on History"; Gavin Hadden, memo to Groves, 16 Apr. 1945, I, CEHO; "Description of Sections A and B," Witmer papers, OSD HO.

205 **Each of the façades** *Ibid.;* Frierson, *The Pentagon,* 16.

206 **"This is how"** *Washington Daily News,* 23 Mar. 1942.

206 **The building was 40 percent** Renshaw, memo to Somervell, 9 Mar. 1942, SDF, NARA RG 160.

206 **peak at fifteen thousand** Office of the Chief of Engineers, "Comments on Statements of Congressman Albert J. Engel on the Pentagon," 7 Apr. 1944, 19, I, CEHO; *NYT,* 23 Apr. 2006; Goldberg, *The Pentagon,* 70; *Star,* 5 Apr. 1942.

206 **Renshaw—now** Renshaw memo to Somervell with accompanying photographs, 9 Mar. 1942, SDF, NARA RG 160.

206 **The architect** Groves to Renshaw, 26 Feb. 1942, I, CEHO; memo to Somervell, 8 Apr. 1942, SDF, NARA RG 160; Hauck letter to Renshaw, 10 Apr. 1942.

207 **The appropriations race** Bureau of the Budget, "Report Covering Pentagon Building," 31 Aug. 1942, K, I, CEHO; Bergstrom memo to Groves, "Chief Architect's Estimate of Cost," 7 Feb. 1942, I, CEHO; McShain memo to Col. Graham, 3 Apr. 1942; Hauck, letter to Renshaw, 16 Apr. 1942, I, CEHO.

207 **Somervell blew up** McShain letter to Somervell, 10 Apr. 1942 and Somervell reply 12 Apr. 1942, SDF, NARA RG 160.

207 **They would not** Renshaw memo to Chief of Engineers, 16 Apr. 1942, I, CEHO; "The Pentagon Telephone Conversations—Miscellaneous," Holmes and Renshaw, 4 Apr. 1942, I, CEHO.

207 **Renshaw had reported on March 28** Renshaw memo to Davidson, 28 Mar. 1942, I, CEHO.

208 **At War Department headquarters** Millett, *The Army Service Forces,* 369; Groves recollections of Styer, Groves collection, USMA; Renshaw memo to Styer, 20 Apr. 1942, I, CEHO; Groves memo to Styer, 21 Apr. 1942, I, CEHO; Styer memo to Adjutant General's office, 22 Apr. 1942, SDF, RG 160.

Gathered in haste from the four winds

209 **"Fellow Workers"** Bergstrom letter, 11 Apr. 1942, Witmer papers, OSD HO.

209 **At 10 A.M. on March 20** minutes of the special meeting of the Board of Directors, AIA, 19–22 Mar. 1942, 10, 12, 14–15, 45, AIA. The account of the hearing and all quotations come from the minutes.

210 **On March 28, the institute** AIA, confidential notice of disciplinary action, 28 Mar. 1942, I, CEHO.

210 **David Witmer** "Personnel principally responsible for design and construction," Oct. 1943, Hadden Notebook, I, CEHO.

211 *Gathered in haste* Bergstrom letter, 11 Apr. 1942, Witmer papers, OSD HO.

CHAPTER 11: THE PLANK WALKERS

Justifiable pride

213 **Joe Allan knew** Allan, author interview.

213 **Crews had worked** "The Pentagon," 11, Witmer papers, OSD HO; Renshaw letter to Joseph McNulty, 27 Apr. 1944, I, CEHO; *Federal Architect,* Jan.–Apr. 43; Holmes memo, 14 Sept. 1942, I, CEHO; Kast, "Not Everyone Thought It Was So Dreamy"; *Star,* 3 May 1942.

214 **All through the last** Allan, "Building the Pentagon"; Allan, author interview.

214 **More were arriving** Furman, author interview.

214 **Several hundred employees** War Department press release, 29 Apr. 1942, SDF, NARA RG 160; Downey, author interview.

215 **The employees "rattle"** *WP,* 3 May 1942.

215 **The newspapers** *Ibid.; WT-H,* 3 May 1942.

215 **A War Department press release** War Department press release, 29 Apr. 1942, SDF, NARA RG 160.

215 **From the day** House hearing, 22 July 1941, 508; Committee on Appropriations report 988, First Supplemental National Defense Appropriation Bill, 1942, 24 July 1941, 13; conference on New War Department Building, 19 Aug. 1941, I, CEHO; construction authorization, 6 Sept. 1941, I, CEHO; "The Pentagon," Witmer papers, 5, OSD HO

216 **"It is almost inconceivable"** *WP,* 4 May 1942.

216 **Somervell was exhilarated** Somervell memo for the Chief of Engineers, 30 Apr. 1942, I, CEHO.

216 **Somervell also sent** Somervell, "Memorandum for Mr. Hopkins," 30 Apr. 1942, SDF, NARA 160.

216 **Roosevelt and Hopkins** Renshaw memo to the Chief of Engineers, 4 May 1942.

216 **Touring the interior** Green, *Washington: A History of the Capital, 1800–1950,* vol. II, 477; Goldberg, *The Pentagon,* 62.

217 **A War Department employee** Renshaw, report of cafeteria incident to Groves, 19 May 1942, Army AG decimal files, file 291.2, NARA RG 407.

217 **Another confusing** War Department press release, 29 Apr. 1942, SDF, NARA RG 160; *Federal Architect,* Jan. 1943.

217 **Nine days after** Ulio memo, 9 May 1942, I, CEHO.

The plank walkers

217 **Even as the Pentagon's** Frierson, *The Pentagon,* 6; "The Pentagon," Witmer papers, 12, OSD HO. War Department press release, 29 Apr. 1942, SDF, NARA RG 160.

218 **Marjorie Hanshaw and her co-workers** Downey, author interview.

218 **Groves ordered** "The Pentagon Telephone Conversations—Groves," Groves calling Renshaw, 24 Apr. 1942

218 **The overriding taste** "Notes on the Pentagon," draft of article prepared by Lt. Col. Karl Detzer for Somervell, circa 1944, I, CEHO; Brinkley, *Washington Goes to War,* 73.

218 **Where there wasn't dust** Neighbors, author interview; Lucille Ramale, author interview, 6 Feb. 2004; Downey, author interview; *WT-H,* 9 June 1944.

219 **The ranks of War Department** *Star,* 7 June 1942; F&R, *The Corps of Engineers,* 512.

219 **Moving crews** Schintelin letter to administrations branch, 5 May 1942, 600.91, NARA RG 407.

219 **The employees were packed** Renshaw memo to Groves, 24 July 1942, I, CEHO; *Washington Daily News,* 30 Oct. 1942.

219 **Senior officers** Brinkley, *Washington Goes to War,* 113.

219 **"They're spoiling the outer"** "The Pentagon Telephone Conversations—Groves," Renshaw and Groves, 14 May 1942.

Overshooting the mark

220 **Somervell finally notified** Somervell, letter to Rep. Clarence Cannon, 7 May 1942, SDF, NARA RG 160; Groves, oral history with Pogue, second interview, GCM Lib.

220 **"I'm in favor"** F&R, *The Corps of Engineers,* 411.

220 **"You have overshot"** House hearing, 15 June 1942.

221 **"They listened to a $15 million"** "The Pentagon Telephone Conversations—Miscellaneous," Renshaw and Holmes, 16 June 1942.

Nothing is usual

221 **Like everyone else** Downey, author interview; Amy Iselin, ed., "Reminisces of Early Days," box 1303, OSD HO.

221 **Renshaw had come up** Alan Renshaw, author interview; Goldberg, *The Pentagon,* 60.

222 **Groves was skeptical** "The Pentagon Telephone Conversations—Groves," Groves calling Renshaw, 30 Apr. 1942.

My people are Americans

222 **Henry E. Bennett followed** Henry Bennett, statement to Judge William Hastie, 19 May 1942, Hastie papers, RG 107.

222 **A modest and serious-minded** Henry E. Bennett, Jr., author interview, August 2005; resume of Henry E. Bennett, courtesy Henry E. Bennett, Jr.

222 **Bennett sat at the table** Bennett statement to Hastie, 19 May 1942, Hastie papers, RG 107.

223 **a slight young man** Renshaw memo to Lt. Col. Benjamin Weisbrod, 8 Aug. 1942, Hastie papers, RG 107.

223 **Roosevelt's executive order** Renshaw memo to Chief of Engineers, 17 Mar. 1942, I, CEHO; W. P. McFarland, Industrial Foods, Inc., to Renshaw, 30 Mar. 1942, I, CEHO; McShain memo to Renshaw, 18 May 1942, file 291.2, NARA RG 407; Fox, "World's Largest Cafeteria to Feed 40,000 Nearing Completion."

223 **Whatever the legal** Bennett statement to Hastie, 19 May 1942, Hastie papers, RG 107; Bennett testimony, cafeteria IG report, NARA RG 159.

224 **The rebellion** McFarland and Horace Crump testimony cafeteria IG report, NARA RG 159.

224 **The chief of the Pentagon** Sumner Dodge and Alfred Lee testimony, cafeteria IG report, NARA RG 159; McShain memo to Renshaw, 18 May 1942, 5:30 P.M., file 291.2, NARA RG 407; Bennett statement to Hastie, 19 May 1942, Hastie papers, RG 107.

224 **On Monday** McShain memo to Renshaw, 18 May 1942, 10 A.M., file 291.2, NARA RG 407.

224 **Gladys Lancaster** Gladys Lancaster, Ruth Bush, and Laurel Carson testimony, cafeteria IG report, NARA RG 159.

225 **At 11:35** Bennett, Harold, Crump, and McFarland testimony, cafeteria IG report, NARA RG 159; Ristine report, 25 May 1942, cafeteria IG report, NARA RG 159; statement of Crump, 18 May 1942, file 291.2, NARA RG 407.

225 **Four officers rushed** Theodore Lee, Harold, Bennett, Carson, Charles Meisel, and Bush, testimony, cafeteria IG report, NARA RG 159; Bennett statement to Hastie, 19 May 1942, Hastie papers, NARA RG 107; statements of Crump, Lee, and J. A. McDaniel, 18 May 1942, file 291.2, NARA RG 407.

226 **Harold was staggering** Mildred Neal, Charles Bush, Carson, Bush testimony, cafeteria IG report, NARA RG 159; Bennett statement to Hastie, 19 May 1942, Hastie papers, RG 107.

226 **Back at the cafeteria** Theodore Lee testimony, cafeteria IG report, NARA RG 159; undated memo circa 18 May 1942, about visit of five Ordnance employees to Hastie's office, Hastie papers, NARA RG 107.

Integrating the Pentagon

226 **Judge William H. Hastie** *Ibid.*

226 **At thirty-seven, Hastie** *NYT,* Hastie obituary, 15 Apr. 1976; William Hastie, oral history, 1972, HST Lib.

227 **In his office** Bennett statement to Hastie, 19 May 1942, Hastie papers, NARA RG 107.

227 **The resulting investigation** Ristine report, 25 May 1942, cafeteria IG report, NARA RG 159; Bush, Harold, Evelyn Caines testimony, cafeteria IG report, NARA RG 159.

228 **In their testimony** Theodore Lee, McDaniel, Smith, and Crump testimony, cafeteria IG report, NARA RG 159; statements of Crump, Lee, and McDaniel, 18 May 1942, file 291.2, NARA RG 407.

228 **Moreover, Charles Meisel** Meisel testimony, cafeteria IG report, NARA RG 159.

228 **Hastie had to fight** Howard Peterson memo to Hastie, 29 June 1942, file 291.2, NARA RG 407; Hastie memo to the Under Secretary of War, 3 July 1942, cafeteria IG report, NARA RG 159.

228 **An aide to Patterson** memo about Howard Peterson, 30 July 1942, cafeteria IG report, NARA RG 159; Maj. Gen. Virgil Peterson memo on investigation to Howard Peterson, 14 Aug. 1942, cafeteria IG report, NARA RG 159; National Negro Congress, letter to Stimson, 22 May 1942, cafeteria IG report, NARA RG 159.

228 **Yet the rebellion** Renshaw report to Groves, 19 May 1942 and Reybold memo to Somervell, 19 May 1942, file 291.2, NARA RG 407. McFarland and Renshaw testimony, cafeteria IG report, NARA RG 159. After the war, Bennett continued his work on behalf of civil rights, serving as president of the NAACP in Gary, Indiana.

CHAPTER 12: HELL-AN-GONE

Miss Ten Thousand

231 **Opal Sheets did her best** Opal Sheets Belen, author interview, September 2003; *Washington Daily News,* 18 July 1942.

232 **McShain's workers** Field progress report, 15 June 1942, Records of the Office of Chief of Military History, entry 145, NARA RG 319.

232 **By the time** Adjutant General memo to Styer, 21 July 1942, I, CEHO.

232 **Critical days** Rick Atkinson, *An Army at Dawn,* 16; Murphy, "Somervell of the S.O.S."; McCloy, interview with Sevareid, Amherst College.

232 **McCloy had an idea** McCloy memo to Somervell, 13 July 1942, SDF, NARA RG 160.

233 **Reviewing McCloy's suggestion** Styer memo to Somervell, 14 July 1942, SDF, NARA RG 160.

233 **Without a doubt** *Cong. Rec.*, 29 Feb. 1944, 2106; conference about fifth floor, 16 July 1942, Witmer notebook, OSD HO.

233 **Groves notified Renshaw** "Pentagon Telephone Conversations—Groves," Renshaw and Groves, 14 and 15 July 1942, I, CEHO; Renshaw memo to Davidson, 17 July 1941, I, CEHO; "Pentagon Telephone Conversations—Miscellaneous," Renshaw and Davidson, 17 and 21 July 1942.

234 **Somervell soon issued** Somervell memo for the Chief of Engineers, 20 July 1942, I, CEHO; Col. W. A. Wood memo for the Chief of Engineers, 24 July 1942, SDF, NARA RG 160; Sidney Shalett, "Mammoth Cave, Washington, D.C." *NYT*, 27 June 1942.

234 **Army documents submitted** Gavin Hadden, memo to Renshaw, 15 Jan. 1944, I, CEHO; *Cong. Rec.*, 1 Oct. 1942, 7692.

234 **Nor was it the only** "Pentagon Telephone Conversations—Miscellaneous," Renshaw and Antes, 25 and 27 July, 1942.

234 **"Here's the story"** *Ibid.*

234 **Groves wanted Renshaw** "Pentagon Telephone Conversations—Groves," Renshaw and Matthias, 3 Aug. 1942; "Pentagon Telephone Conversations—Miscellaneous," Renshaw and Antes, 24 July 1942; Davidson memo to Renshaw about additional construction, 29 July 1942, I, CEHO; Col. Foster calling Groves, 22 July 1942, Groves papers, entry 5, box 1, NARA RG 200.

235 **"To get the whole"** "Pentagon Telephone Conversations—Miscellaneous," Renshaw and Mr. Sherman, 22 Aug. 1942.

McCloy, you blackmailer

235 **One problem** McCloy, Sevareid interview, Amherst College.

235 **Help came** *Ibid.;* Isaacson and Thomas, *The Wise Men*, 201; Steven Casey, "Franklin D. Roosevelt, Ernst 'Putzi' Hanfstaengl and the 'S-Project', June 1942–June 1944," *Journal of Contemporary History*, 1 July 2000.

235 **"So I sent back word"** McCloy, Sevareid interview, Amherst College.

236 **McCloy recalled** Isaacson and Thomas, *The Wise Men*, 201; McCloy, Sevareid interview, Amherst College.

Great strain

236 **Even as War Department** *Star*, 21 June 1942; *WP*, 21 June 1942. *Star*, 22 July, 1942.

236 **A heat wave** *WT-H*, 18 July 1942; Stimson diary, 29 July 1942; Stimson and Bundy, *On Active Service in Peace and War*, 411.

236 **Even Paul Hauck** McShain autobiographical notes, 14, VII, I, McShain papers, HML; Reynolds notes, 42, McShain papers HML; Brauer, *The Man Who Built Washington*, 84; Lew Edwards in 1984 McShain video, courtesy Polly McShain.

One day I'll be famous

237 **The job and the weather** McShain, letter to Groves, 20 Aug. 1942, entry 5, box 1, NARA RG 200; Polly McShain, author interview.

237 **Yet there was little** "Pentagon Telephone Conversations—Groves," Renshaw and Davidson, 19 Aug. 1942, and Renshaw and Groves, 19 Aug. 1942.

238 **Meanwhile, open warfare** "Pentagon Telephone Conversations—Groves," Groves and Renshaw, 29 July 1942; Wise Contracting Co. letter to Renshaw, 27 July 1942, I, CEHO; "Pentagon Telephone Conversations—Groves," Groves and Renshaw, 31 Aug. 1942; McShain letter to Renshaw, 30 July 1942, I, CEHO.

238 **Renshaw and Groves backed** "Pentagon Telephone Conversations—Groves," Groves and Renshaw, 31 Aug. and 1 Sept. 1942; Renshaw, memo to Chief of Engineers, 26 Aug. 1942, I, CEHO; H. E. Doyle, letter to Robins, 28 Aug. 1942, I, CEHO.

239 **However, the Virginia** Somervell and Woodrum, telephone transcript, 31 Aug. 1942, SDF, NARA RG 160.

239 **The limestone plaque** Hauck recollections on cornerstone, Oct. 1962, Pentagon vertical file, Pentagon Library; E. A. Rogner, *The Pentagon: A National Institution*, 27; "Pentagon Telephone Conversations—Groves," Renshaw and Matthias, 28 and 29 Aug. 1942; "Personnel principally responsible for design and construction," Oct. 1943, Hadden notebook, I, CEHO; Furman, author interview.

Hell-an-gone

239 **Why anyone** Richard E. Lauterbach, "The Pentagon Puzzle," *Life*, 24 May 1943; Immen, "The Pentagon . . . Fact and Fancy."

240 **the food operation** McShain address to engineers, McShain papers HML; Fox, "World's Largest Cafeteria to Feed 40,000 Nearing Completion"; J. H. Beswick, letter to the editor, *WP*, 12 Aug. 1942.

240 **Those eating** "Pentagon Telephone Conversations—Groves," Renshaw and Groves, 11 June 1942; *WP*, 13 June 1942; *Washington Daily News*, 13 June 1942; *WT-H*, 16 June 1942.

241 **Groves worried obsessively** "Pentagon Telephone Conversations—Groves," Groves and Renshaw, 3 June 1942; Pentagon Telephone Conversations—Groves," Groves and Renshaw, 30 July 1942.

241 **Still dissatisfied** Groves, memo to Renshaw, 6 Aug. 1942; "Pentagon Telephone Conversations—Miscellaneous," Antes and Renshaw, 7 Aug. 1942.

242 **The plank walkers reserved** Ramale, author interview.

242 **Air-conditioning** Frierson, *The Pentagon*, 18–19; "The Pentagon Building," *Airlanes;* "World's Largest Building Cooled by Sun Control," *Popular Science*, September 1943; Somervell memo to Donald Nelson, 20 Aug. 1941, I, CEHO; "Refrigeration Plant for the Pentagon," undated report, circa 1943, NARA RG 319; "Heating and Refrigeration Plant," sent to Renshaw 20 May 1944, I, CEHO.

242 **It was impossible** "Pentagon Telephone Conversations—Groves," Groves and Renshaw, 17 July 1941; Ulio memo, 10 Aug. 1942; SDF, NARA RG 160.

The situation here is tragic

243 **The final insult** *Washington Daily News*, 27 May 1942; *WP*, 2 Aug. 1942; McShain address at Rosemont College, 2 Apr. 1946, VII, McShain papers, HML; "Pentagon Telephone Conversations—Groves," Renshaw and Matthias, 7 Aug. 1942.

243 **Drivers who** Renshaw memo to Groves, 24 July 1942, I, CEHO; Iselin, ed., "Reminisces of Early Days."

243 **Nelson Clayton** Nelson H. Clayton, author interview, 23 Feb. 2004.

243 **In the evening** Kelly, "Pentagon Veterans Recall Construction Days"; *Star*, 2 Aug. 1942.

244 **The Capital Transit Company** Stimson letter to Nelson, 8 Mar. 1942, NARA RG 107; "New War Building Creates Huge Transportation Problem," *Star*, c. June 1942, I, CEHO; Downey, author interview.

244 **Getting to and from** *WP*, 7 Oct. 1942; *WT-H*, 24 July 1942; Henry F. Pringle, "My Thirty Days in the Pentagon," *The Saturday Evening Post*, 16 Oct. 1943; *WT-H*, 5 Sept. 1942.

The most fantastic operation

244 **General George Marshall** Furman, author interview; *Time*, 19 Oct. 1942; "Pentagon Telephone Conversations—Miscellaneous," Antes and Renshaw, 7 Aug. 1942; Pogue, *Organizer of Victory*, 30

245 **Hauck took Marshall** Reynolds notes, 42–3, McShain papers, HML.; field progress report, 31 Aug. 1942, NARA RG 319; *WP*, 2 Aug. 1942; "The Pentagon Building," *Airlanes;* McShain autobiographical notes, "The Pentagon," VII, McShain papers, HML.

245 **Even before its completion** *WP*, 17 Aug. 1941; Shalett, "Mammoth Cave"; "Inside the Five-sided Brain," *Time*, 2 July 1951.

246 **Among all the visitors** Bureau of the Budget, "Report Covering Pentagon Building," 31 Aug. 1942, I, CEHO; War Department press release, 13 July 1942, I, CEHO; House hearing, 15 June 1942, 219.

247 **"This project"** Bureau of the Budget, "Report Covering Pentagon Building," 31 Aug. 1942, I, CEHO.

CHAPTER 13: ONE OF THE WORST BLUNDERS OF THE WAR

Washington's demon investigator

249 **Engel was "Washington's demon"** Robert Humphreys, "The Man Who Astonished Washington," *Saturday Evening Post*, 9 Oct. 1943; *Time*, 12 July 1943; Engel

address to Washington Society of Engineers, 1 Oct. 1941, Somervell papers, MHI; F&R, *The Corps of Engineers*, 378–80.

250 **Armed with his findings** Humphreys, "The Man Who Astonished Washington"; Engel, address to Washington Society of Engineers, 1 Oct. 1941, Somervell papers, MHI.

250 **Engel was nothing** Humphreys, "The Man Who Astonished Washington."

250 **In early 1941** F&R, *The Corps of Engineers*, 379–80; *NYT*, 9 Mar. 1941.

250 **Engel did make it** F&R, *The Corps of Engineers*, 381.

251 **Somervell was irritated** *Ibid.;* Groves, oral history with Pogue, second interview.

The man on horseback

251 **Somervell by then** War Department Bureau of Public Relations, press digest, 18 Sept. 1942, Somervell papers, MHI; *Time*, 19 Oct. 1942.

251 **Somervell's rise** transcript of radio broadcast on WOL in Washington, 2 Mar. 1942, Somervell papers, MHI.

251 **Roosevelt's own** Ickes diary, 21 June 1942, 6720; Ohl, *Supplying the Troops*, 161–4; Ickes diary, 14 June 1942, 6715.

252 **Lunching with Roosevelt** Ickes diary, 10 Oct. 1942, 7064.

252 **Many in Washington** Rexford G. Tugwell, *The Democratic Roosevelt—A Biography of Franklin D. Roosevelt*, 568; Stimson and Bundy, *On Active Service in Peace and War*, 440; Charles R. Shrader, "World War II Logistics," *Parameters*, Spring 1995.

252 **Somervell was "one"** Murphy, "Somervell of the S.O.S."; Somervell address to Michigan industry group, 3 July 1942, Somervell addresses, vol. 1, Somervell papers, MHI; AP article in *WP*, 29 Sept. 1942.

253 **Somervell was driven by** Millett, *The Army Service Forces*, 366; *Newsweek*, 7 Dec. 1942, Somervell address to conference of commanding generals, S.O.S., 30 July 1942, Somervell addresses, vol. 1, Somervell papers, MHI; Murphy, "Somervell of the S.O.S."; Tugwell, *The Democratic Roosevelt*, 568.

253 **A request for munitions** Janney, "The Man Behind the Invasion."

253 **With the Army in need** Somervell, "Problems of Production in World War II," lecture to Industrial College of the Armed Forces, Washington, D.C., 18 Nov. 1946, 5, Somervell papers, MHI; Charles E. Funk, *Thereby Hangs A Tale: Stories of Curious Word Origins*, 30–31.

253 **"Prominent members"** Renshaw, F&R interview, I, CEHO.

The obstacle course

254 **Groves would later say** Groves, F&R interview, I, CEHO.

254 **"And there's no way"** "Pentagon Telephone Conversations—Groves," Groves and Renshaw, 14 July 1942.

254 **"He wanted the report"** "Pentagon Telephone Conversations—Groves," Davidson and Renshaw, 10 July 1942.

254 **Never mind that Somervell** House hearing, 22 July 1941, 505.

254 **The only problem** Groves, oral history with Pogue, second interview; Groves comments, 46, CEHO.

254 **"Groves had the idea"** "The Pentagon Telephone Conversations, Re: Congressman Engel Inquiry," Renshaw and Matthias, 22 Sept. 1942, I, CEHO (hereafter "Pentagon Telephone Conversations—Engel").

255 **The congressman fancied** Humphreys, "The Man Who Astonished Washington"; Groves, oral history with Pogue, second interview.

255 **Groves's strategy** Groves letter to McShain, 11 Dec. 1947, Groves papers, entry 7530B, box 6, NARA RG 200; Groves, oral history with Pogue, second interview; Groves diary, 24 June 1942, entry 7530G, NARA RG 200.

255 **Groves had certainly succeeded** "Pentagon Telephone Conversations—Engel," Renshaw and Matthias, 22 Sept. 1942; Renshaw, memo for Major Carl Sciple, 11 July 1941, I, CEHO.

A building unique in Washington

256 **Groves grew paranoid** "Pentagon Telephone Conversations—Engel," Renshaw and Antes, 24 Aug. 1942; House hearing, 15 June 1942, 220; Franklin Matthias, oral history, 1984, 14, CEHO; "Pentagon Telephone Conversations—Groves," Renshaw and Matthias, 25 Aug. 1942

256 **"Oh, that's ridiculous"** "Pentagon Telephone Conversations—Engel," Renshaw and Antes, 24 Aug. 1942.

256 **Marble had been used** *Ibid.;* "Basic Data on the Pentagon," III, 6, SDF, NARA RG 160; "Pentagon Telephone Conversations—Groves," Renshaw and Henry Thompson, 25 Aug. 1942.

256 **Somervell looked** "Pentagon Telephone Conversations—Groves," Renshaw and Matthias, 28 Aug. 1942; Groves, memo to Renshaw, 1 Sept. 1942.

257 **Witmer had also** "The Pentagon," Witmer papers, 14; Witmer planning memorandum, OSD HO.

257 **Groves cared not** House hearing, 15 June 1942, 219; Matthias, oral history, 10, CEHO; "Pentagon Telephone Conversations—Groves," Renshaw and Matthias, 3 Aug. 1942; Witmer planning memorandum, OSD HO.

257 **On September 11** "Pentagon Telephone Conversations—Groves," Renshaw and Groves, 11 Sept. 1942.

257 **His girth notwithstanding** Norris, *Racing for the Bomb,* 530; Groves, "For My Grandchildren," appendix V, by Gwen Groves Robinson, 295, Groves collection, USMA; Furman, author interview.

258 **"Maybe the next time"** telephone transcript, Col. Rehm calling Groves, 30 Jan. 1942, I, CEHO.

258 **Somervell had quashed** Somervell, memo for assistant chief of staff, 6 Aug. 1941, I, CEHO; Somervell, memo to Marshall, 27 July 1942, I, CEHO.

258 **Early in the construction** Groves memo to Army headquarters commandant, June 1946, Groves collection, GCM Lib.; telephone transcript, Rehm calling Groves, 30 Jan. 1942, I, CEHO; Capt. Biggs, memo to Renshaw about recreational facilities, 13 July 1942, I, CEHO; Richard Groves, author interview. The gym, known as the Pentagon Officers' Athletic Club, opened in January 1947 at the order of Eisenhower, then Army chief of staff, and operated until a new facility opened in 2004.

Groves seeks peace

258 **The job** Groves, "The Atom General Answers His Critics," *Saturday Evening Post,* 19 June 1948; "Recollections of Grace Williams Groves," Groves papers, MIII.

258 **He had been particularly** "Pentagon Telephone Conversations—Groves," Renshaw and Matthias, 3 Sept. 1942; *WT-H,* 11 Sept. 1942.

259 **"If we had competent"** "Pentagon Telephone Conversations—Groves," Renshaw, Hauck, Barker and Groves, 9 Sept. 1942.

259 **Most mornings** Norris, *Racing for the Bomb,* 2; "For My Grandchildren," appendix V, by Gwen Groves Robinson, 289, Groves collection, USMA.

259 **The job of constructing** Norris, *Racing for the Bomb,* 173; Groves, "The Atom General Answers His Critics."

259 **Groves was not alone** Norris, *Racing for the Bomb,* 162–4; Groves, recollections of Lucius Clay, Groves collection, USMA.

If you do the job right, it will win the war

260 **Groves was feeling** Groves, "The Atom General Answers His Critics"; Lawren, *The General and the Bomb,* 7.

260 **The day before** Groves, *Now It Can Be Told,* 3, "For My Grandchildren," appendix V, by Gwen Groves Robinson, 289, Groves Collection, USMA.

260 **"About that duty overseas"** Groves, "The Atom General Answers His Critics"; Groves, *Now It Can Be Told,* 3–4; Stephane Groueff, *Manhattan Project: The Untold Story of the Making of the Atomic Bomb,* 5; Nichols, *The Road to Trinity,* 49–50.

261 **The answer, ultimately** Groves, oral history with Pogue, first interview, GCM Lib.; Groves, F&R interview, 1964, CEHO; Groves impression of Manhattan Project associates, 1958, Groves collection, USMA.

261 **In the summer of 1942** Groves comments on Styer, Groves collection, West Point; Norris, *Racing for the Bomb,* 172; Nichols, *The Road to Trinity,* 49–50; Groves memo about 5 June 1961 conversation with Styer at West Point, Groves collection, USMA.

262 **Styer had a suggestion** *Ibid.;* Styer letter to Remington, 12 February 1968, VII, CEHO; Jones, *Manhattan: The Army and the Atomic Bomb,* 73–5.

262 **Yet Groves** Groves, impression of Manhattan Project associates, 1958, Groves collection, USMA.

Political dynamite

262 **Groves left Styer's** Groves, *Now It Can Be Told*, 19, 23–5; Nichols, *The Road to Trinity*, 51; Groueff, *Manhattan Project*, 15.

263 **Groves was moving fast** Groves, *Now It Can Be Told*, 4–5; Groves letter to Maj. Gen. A. C. Smith, 22 July 1955, with Groves's comments, VII, CEHO.

263 **The second reason** Groves, F&R interview, 1956, CEHO; Groves, *Now It Can Be Told*, 5.

263 **Somervell "very heartily"** Groves, F&R interview, 1964, CEHO; Groves, oral history with Pogue, second interview.

One of the worst blunders of the war

263 **The whole Pentagon project** Capt. Buysee memo to Antes about conference with Engel, 24 Sept. 1942, I, CEHO; "Pentagon Telephone Conversations—Engel," Engel and Renshaw, 21 Sept. 1942; field progress report, Pentagon building, 31 Aug. 1942, NARA RG 319.

264 **Renshaw could barely** "Pentagon Telephone Conversations—Engel," Renshaw and Rep. Lane Powers, 22 Sept. 1942.

264 **For some reason, Groves** "Pentagon Telephone Conversations—Engel," Renshaw and Matthias, 21 and 22 Sept. 1942.

264 **Renshaw replied** *Ibid;* field progress report, Pentagon building, 31 Mar. 1943, NARA RG 319.

265 **"Why don't you give Bill"** "Pentagon Telephone Conversations—Engel," Renshaw and Powers, 22 Sept. 1942.

265 **"I think he's going"** *Ibid*.

265 **On Thursday, October 1** *Cong. Rec.* 1 Oct. 1942, 7690–96; *WT-H*, 2 Oct. 1942.

265 **At Somervell's order** Groves memo to Somervell, 3 Oct. 1942, SDF, NARA RG 160; Groves diary, 1 and 2 Oct. 1942, entry 7530G NARA RG 200; Groves oral history with Pogue, second interview.

266 **Groves monitored** Groves memo to Somervell, 3 Oct. 1942, SDF, NARA RG 160; *Star*, 1 Oct. 1942; *WP*, 2 Oct. 1942, *WT-H*, 2 Oct. 1942; *Washington Daily News*, 1 Oct. 1942.

266 **The day after Engel's speech** Somervell letter to Woodrum, 2 Oct. 1942, I, CEHO; *Star*, 2 Oct. 1942; *WP*, 3 Oct. 1942, *WT-H*, 3 Oct. 1942.

266 **Engel declared himself** *WP*, 3 Oct. 1942; *Star*, 6 Oct. 1942.

266 **Yet there was no** Groves comments, 46, CEHO.

267 **"It is to be doubted"** *Star*, 5 Oct. 1942.

267 **It was not just** *WP*, 4 Oct. 1942; *Star*, 12 Oct. 1942; *WP*, 13 Oct. 1942.

267 **"Washington has many reasons"** *WP*, 4 Oct. 1942.

CHAPTER 14: THE RACE TO MOVE IN THE HIGH COMMAND

By command of General Somervell

269 **The race was on** Groves memo to Renshaw, 22 Oct. 1941, I, CEHO; field progress report, Pentagon building, 31 Mar. 1943, NARA RG 319.

269 **"If unfavorable weather"** Groves, memo to Renshaw, 22 Oct. 1941, I, CEHO.

269 **Just a few days** Memo to chief of staff about 1942 flood, 20 Oct. 1942, box 3, NARA RG 551; *Star,* 17 Oct. 1942; Stimson diary, 16 Oct. 1942; Price Day, "No Red Tape Fetters Army's Good Provider," *Baltimore Sun Sunday Magazine,* 5 Mar. 1944; *Newsweek,* 7 Dec. 1942; *NYT,* 17 Oct. 1942.

270 **Somervell was at the scene** *Star,* 17 Oct. 1942; *Newsweek,* 7 Dec. 1942; Day, "No Red Tape."

270 **The flood proved** *WP,* 18 Oct. 1942; *Star,* 17 Oct. 1942; National Weather Service Baltimore/Washington records for Potomac River at Washington, D.C. (Wisconsin Avenue/Georgetown). Unofficial records show the flood of 1889 cresting at 19.5 feet.

270 **"By command"** *Newsweek,* 7 Dec. 1942.

270 **The water spared the Pentagon** Journal of Military District of Washington, 17 Oct. 1941, NARA RG 551; Frierson, *The Pentagon,* 16; photographs of flooding, box 1317, OSD HO; *WP,* 23 Oct. 1942.

Our lives depend on that

271 **From outside, the Pentagon** "Pentagon Telephone Conversations—Groves," Groves and Renshaw, 30 Oct. 1942; Groves memo to Renshaw, 22 Oct. 1941, I, CEHO.

271 **Much exacting work** *Ibid.; Life,* 21 Dec. 1942; Groves memo to Styer, 9 July 1942, I, CEHO, Matthias, memo to Renshaw, 20 Oct. 1942, I, CEHO, *Star,* 14 Nov. 1942.

272 **Groves had been unsure** Voorhees, F&R interview, CEHO.

272 **Inspecting the building, Somervell** "Pentagon Telephone Conversations—Groves," Groves and Renshaw, 26 Aug. 1942.

272 **The same was true** "Pentagon Telephone Conversations—Groves," Groves and Renshaw, 31 Aug. 1942; "Pentagon Telephone Conversations—Groves," Renshaw and Matthias, 1 Sept. 1942.

273 **Most irritating of all** French memo to Chief of Engineers, 4 Nov. 1942, I, CEHO; Matthias memo to Renshaw, 6 Oct. 1942, I, CEHO; French memo to Renshaw, 31 Oct. 1942, I, CEHO; French memo to chief of engineers, 4 Nov. 1942; Major C. H. Humelinc memo to chief of engineers, 29 Oct. 1942.

274 **Renshaw appealed for help** Renshaw memo to Robins, 4 Nov. 1942, I, CEHO; Robins memo to chief signal officer, 11 Nov. 1942, I, CEHO.

274 **The first Signal Corps workers** George W. Good, Jr., e-mail to author, 9 Jan. 2004; Kelly, "Pentagon Veterans Recall Construction Days."

274 **Renshaw roared** "Pentagon Telephone Conversations—Groves," Renshaw and Matthias, 2 Oct. 1942.

This is the War Department

275 **The Pentagon had to be** *WP*, 12 Sept. 1941; Frierson, *The Pentagon*, 15.

276 **Frank E. Watts** Frank E. Watts, "Working in the Pentagon," 30 July 1994, box 1303, OSD HO; "Largest P.B.X. in the World," Nov. 1942, I, CEHO.

276 **Just before midnight** *WP*, 12 Sept. 1941; Clayton, author interview; Jim Fearson, "The Telephone in Northern Virginia from the Beginning to World War II," monograph; *WP*, 30 Apr. 1951.

276 **"It really was the eighth"** Marian Bailey, author interview; *WP*, 26 Mar. 1992; *Des Moines Register*, 20 Dec. 1992.

276 **Indeed, the switchboard** Military District of Washington memo, 4 Aug. 1942, NARA RG 551.

The whip

277 **"Certainly, even the greatest"** Groves comments, 115, CEHO.

277 **Groves had been consumed** Norris, *Racing for the Bomb*, 233–4.

277 **After writing the letter** Groves diary, 29–31 Oct. 1942, entry 7530 G, NARA RG 200; "Pentagon Telephone Conversations—Groves," Groves and Renshaw, 30 Oct. 1942.

277 **There were not enough trucks** *Ibid.;* War Department letter to Capital Excavating Co., 14 Nov. 1942, I, CEHO; Capt. F. T. Johnson, memo to Office of Judge Advocate General, 22 Oct. 1941, I, CEHO.

278 **On October 24** Atkinson, *An Army at Dawn*, 40.

278 **The timing of the move** War Department press release, 13 July 1942, I, CEHO; *WP*, 17 Sept. 1942.

278 **But in Stimson's own office** Helen McShane Bailey, author interview; John Connell, oral history, 1991, box 1311, OSD HO.

278 **Reporters were appalled** Fred Morrison, Radio Correspondents' Galleries, letter to Stimson, 24 Sept. 1942, I, CEHO; Stimson letter to Clifford A. Provost, National Press Club, 21 Sept. 1942, I, CEHO.

Carry me back to Old Virginny

279 **Yet Admiral Ernest King** Stimson diary, 31 Oct. 1942.

279 **The cantankerous** Eric Larrabee, *Commander in Chief: Franklin Delano Roosevelt, His Lieutenants, and Their War*, 155, 193–4; Stimson diary, 31 Oct. 1942.

280 **Stimson was often dismayed** Stimson and Bundy, *On Active Service in Peace and War*, 194.

280 **The secretary of war was pleased** Stimson diary, 31 Oct. 1942; Larrabee, *Commander in Chief*, 171.

280 **Marshall, even more** Stimson diary, 31 Oct. 1942; Pogue, *Organizer of Victory*, 42.

281 **Open-faced** Goodwin, *No Ordinary Time*, 71; *WP*, 29 and 30 Apr. 1944.

281 **Knox responded warmly** Stimson diary, 2 Nov. 1942; King letter to Marshall, 26 May 1944, Otto L. Nelson Papers, GCM Lib.

281 **After their meeting** Stimson diary, 2 Nov. 1942; *Star*, 3 Nov. 1942; Furman, author interview.

281 **At a press conference** *Star*, 3 and 4 Nov. 1942; *WP*, 4 Nov. 1942.

282 **The admirals were less pleased** *Washington Daily News*, 4 Nov, 1942; *WP*, 6 Nov. 1942.

282 **Some Navy employees** "Pentagon Building, 1941–1944," vertical files, MLK Lib.

282 *Carry me back WP*, 6 Nov. 1942.

The real opening of the Pentagon

283 **The convoys started rolling** memo, 31 Oct. 1942, NARA RG 107; memo for commanding general, Military District of Washington, 7 Nov. 1942, NARA RG 107; "Early Occupants' Introductions," about Robert Sanders, fiftieth-anniversary preparations, box 1303, OSD HO; Brinkley, *Washington Goes to War*, 73.

283 **The invasion of North Africa** Stimson diary, 7, 9, 15 Nov. 1942.

283 **At 4 P.M. Saturday** War Department memo, 19 Nov. 1942, NARA RG 407; Pogue, *Organizer of Victory*, 38.

284 **Inspecting his new** Merrill Pasco, oral history with Pogue, GCM Lib.; author visit, George C. Marshall Museum, Lexington, Va., 6 May 2004; *NYT*, 3 Oct. 1943; *The Papers of George Catlett Marshall*, vol. 3, xxix, 439–40.

284 **Stimson arrived the next day** Stimson diary, 16 Nov. 1942; *Life*, 21 Dec. 1942; *Star*, 14 Nov. 1942; Isaacson and Thomas, *The Wise Men*, 192.

285 **The high command** William T. Sexton, undated interview, Forrest C. Pogue Collection, GCM Lib.; Helen McShane Bailey, author interview.

Those damned admirals

285 **Stimson was hoping** Stimson diary, 19, 20, 24 Nov. 1942; McCloy diary, 12 Nov. 1942; *WP*, 1 Dec. 1942.

286 **The press was starting** *Star*, 21 Nov. 1942; Stimson diary, 20 Nov. 1942.

207 **The beleaguered Renshaw** Renshaw memo to Chief of Engineers, 3 Nov. 1942, box 702, NARA RG 77; Renshaw memo to Groves, 20 Nov. 1942, entry 5, box 1,

NARA RG 200; Alan Renshaw, author interview; Stimson letter to Roosevelt, 28 Nov. 1942, OF 380, FDR Lib.

287 **Marshall told Stimson** Stimson diary, 24 and 26 Nov. 1942.

288 **Stimson set to writing** Stimson diary, 28 Nov. 1942; Stimson, letter to Roosevelt, 28 Nov. 1942, OF 380, FDR Lib.

288 **Roosevelt sent his regrets** Roosevelt letter to Stimson, 29 Nov. 1942, President's Secretary's File: Stimson, FDR Lib.; "Federal Diary," *WP*, 2 Dec. 1942.

288 **Knox announced** *Star*, 1 Dec. 1942; *WP*, 1 Dec. 1942. Pogue observed that "the Army had revenge of a sort, for the public assumed that all the services were operating from the Pentagon. The building became so identified with the direction of the war that many later writers had difficulty realizing that it was not there from the beginning. As a result occasional subsequent accounts of the attack at Pearl Harbor had officers rushing up and down in confusion in the fabled—and then uncompleted—Pentagon maze." Pogue, *Organizer of Victory*, 42.

288 **The Navy had legitimate** telephone transcript, Styer and Adm. Robinson, 14 Dec. 1942, entry 2, Styer, SDF, NARA RG 160; Pogue, *Organizer of Victory*, 42; Goldberg, *The Pentagon*, 157.

Lost perpendicularly and horizontally

289 **dozens of Army officers** *WP*, 2 and 3 Dec. 1942; *Star*, 2 Dec. 1942; McCloy diary, 2 Dec. 1942.

289 *We are in the Pentagon* Dorothy Potter Benedict, letter to the editor, *WP*, 21 Nov. 1942.

289 **Newspapers reported** AP, 17 Oct. 1942; Lauterbach, "The Pentagon Puzzle"; "Race Between Claustrophobia and Agoraphobia for Those Pent Up in Washington's Pentagon," *Newsweek*, 15 Feb. 1943.

290 **"The generals are right"** G. Dorrance, letter to the editor, *WP*, 3 Nov. 1942.

290 **"Looming across"** *Life*, 21 Dec. 1942.

290 **Somervell was impervious** Brenza, author interview; Somervell letter to van der Gracht, 12 Sept. 1942, series 45.1, White, RG 45, AOC; *WP*, 3 Nov. 1942.

290 **Those least impressed** Hastie memo to Under Secretary of War, 31 Oct. 1942 Hastie papers, NARA RG 107.

291 **It was not an isolated** Laura Freeman and Constance J. Riley, letter to Hastie, 9 July 1942; investigation of reports of segregation on buses at Pentagon, 12 Nov. 1942; memo to secretary of war, 16 Dec. 1942, all in Hastie papers, NARA RG 107.

291 **In January, he would resign** *NYT*, Hastie obituary, 15 Apr. 1976; Hastie, oral history, HST Lib.

291 **"It is ironic"** Dorothy J. Williams, letter to chief of ordnance, August 1943, NARA RG 107.

The glorious chords of free men singing

291 **By Christmas Eve** War Department press release, 22 Dec. 1942, SDF, NARA RG 160; Stimson diary, 24 Dec. 1942; Gene Gurney, *The Pentagon: A Pictorial Story,* 11.

292 **A vast crowd** *Star,* 25 Dec. 1942; *Washington Daily News,* 25 Dec. 1942; Frierson, *The Pentagon,* 12; program for Christmas celebration, 24 Dec. 1942, SDF, NARA RG 160; Stimson diary, 24 Dec. 1942.

292 **Somervell spoke first** Somervell remarks, 24 Dec. 1942, entry 18, box 88, SDF, NARA RG 160.

293 **Stimson was relieved** Stimson remarks, 24 Dec. 1942, Henry L. Stimson Papers, Manuscript Division, LOC; Stimson diary, 24 Dec. 1942.

293 **As darkness approached** Program for Christmas celebration, 24 Dec. 1942, SDF, NARA RG 160; *Washington Daily News,* 25 Dec. 1942.

CHAPTER 15: HEADQUARTERS FOR THE WAR

Able and fearless constructors

295 **The Pentagon was still not** "The Pentagon Telephone Conversations—Miscellaneous," Renshaw and McShain, 4 Feb. 1943; memo to adjutant general, 17 Dec. 1942, SDF, NARA RG 160; Furman, author interview.

295 **The goal** Groves memo to Styer, 1 Jan. 1943, entry 5, box 1, NARA RG 200; field progress report, 31 Mar. 1943, NARA RG 319.

296 **thousands of employees** "Occupancy During Construction of the Pentagon," undated graph, I, CEHO. The population as of Jan. 15 was 26,086.

296 **The main holdup** checklist of work to be completed, 7 Jan. 1943, I, CEHO; McShain, Doyle, and Paschall, letter to Groves, 14 Jan. 1943, I, CEHO.

296 **The auditor** Bureau of the Budget, "Report Covering Pentagon Building," 31 Aug. 1942, I, CEHO. It is perhaps more appropriate to consider the building's opening to be Apr. 30, 1942, when the first employees moved in, or Nov. 14, 1942, when the secretary of war moved in.

The Pentagon

296 **In the Pentagon** Frierson, *The Pentagon,* draft, 25, Records of the Office of Chief of Military History, entry 145, NARA RG 319.

296 **Originally proposed** memo to the chief of engineers, 17 Jan. 1944, I, CEHO; Hadden report to Renshaw, 14 Jan. 1944, I, CEHO.

297 **At a price** Goldberg, *The Pentagon,* 112; "Estimate—Pentagon Building," 8 Jan. 1943, Records of the Office of Chief of Military History, entry 145, NARA RG 319; Commissioner of Public Buildings, letter to Woodrum, 15 Mar. 1944,

entry 145, NARA RG 319; Defense Project Agency audit, 22 Aug. 1942, I, CEHO.

297 **the Pentagon's first cost** Jacob Weisberg, "Edifice Wrecked," *The New Republic*, 1 Apr. 1991.

297 **Upon its creation** Charles E. Brownell, Calder Loth, William M.S. Rasmussen, and Richard Guy Wilson, *The Making of Virginia Architecture*, 400.

297 **As time goes on** Surles memo about designation of War Department headquarters, 12 Feb. 1943, box 3905, NARA RG 407.

297 **not everyone** *Complete Presidential Press Conferences of Franklin D. Roosevelt*, vol. 19–20, 11 Dec. 1942, 292; *WP*, 7 Mar. 1943; Hadden, memo with suggested revisions to "Basic Data on the Pentagon," 28 Sept. 1943, I, CEHO.

The miraculous takes a little longer

298 **At the Casablanca conference** Burns, *The Soldier of Freedom*, 323; Pogue, *Organizer of Victory*, 23, 31, 182, 209.

298 **Marshall's routine** *Life*, 3 Jan. 1944; Russell Lynes letter to Pogue, 8 Mar. 1961, GCM Lib.; Cora Thomas, oral history with Pogue, 1961, GCM Lib.; author visit, Gen. Lib., 6 May 2004; Pogue, *Organizer of Victory*, 55–61.

299 **Early on the agenda** Handy oral history, GCM Lib.; Pogue, *Organizer of Victory*, 65–66; *NYT*, 3 Oct. 43; *Life*, 3 Jan. 1944.

299 **Somervell was a frequent** Millett, *The Army Service Forces*, 174; Styer memo to Somervell, 8 May 1942, SDF, NARA 160; Styer memo about move to Pentagon, 30 Sept. 1942, I, CEHO; Murphy, "Somervell of the S.O.S."; Frierson, *The Pentagon*, 14.

300 **There was no downtime** *Newsweek*, 7 Dec. 1942; "The S.O.S." *Fortune*, Sept. 1942; Murphy, "Somervell of the S.O.S."; *Saturday Evening Post*, 16 Oct. 1943.

301 **Attending the Casablanca** Eisenhower, *Crusade in Europe*, 149; Eisenhower address at Pentagon, 10 June 1946, Somervell papers, MHI; Janney, "The Man Behind the Invasion"; *NYT*, 7 Aug. 1943.

A foretaste of the future

301 **Just arriving** "Pentagon Building," *Architectural Forum*, Jan. 1943.

302 **Most people** "A Visit to the Pentagon Building," *Baltimore Evening Sun*, 8 March 1943; Frierson, *The Pentagon*, draft, 13.

302 **"Here is the picture"** "Pentagon Building," *Architectural Forum*.

302 **The terminal** "The Army's Giant 'Five-by-Five,' " *Popular Mechanics; Star*, 8 and 9 Nov. 1942; *WT-H*, 10 Nov. 1942; Frierson, *The Pentagon*, draft, 13.

302 **At the top** *The Pentagon: A Description of the World's Largest Office Building*. 1954, 5, OSD HO; "Pentagon Building," *Architectural Forum;* Frierson, *The Penta-*

gon, draft, 13; Carl Rose, "My Life in Pentagonia," *New York Times Magazine,* 7 May 1944; "The Pentagon," Witmer papers, 16.

303 **A reception desk** *Star,* 23 Jan. 1943; Frierson, *The Pentagon,* 11.

303 **Once past security** Alden P. Armagnac, "Nerve Center of the Fighting Forces," *Popular Science,* Feb. 1943; Frierson, *The Pentagon,* 12–15; Gurney, *The Pentagon,* 90–92; "Pentagon Building," *Architectural Forum;* "The Army's Giant 'Five-by-Five," *Popular Mechanics.*

304 **The fifth floor** Conference on fifth floor, 16 July 1942, Witmer notebook, OSD HO; National Register of Historic Places Inventory, 4, OSD HO; Goldberg, *The Pentagon,* 97.

304 **The first floor** Rogner, *The Pentagon,* 20; "Pentagon Building," *Architectural Forum;* Gurney, *The Pentagon,* 13.

304 **Most unnatural were the basement** Rogner, *The Pentagon,* 19; Condrell, author interview; Frierson, *The Pentagon,* 16; Christensen, "Miscellaneous Data Pentagon Building" memo, 7 Oct. 1944, I, CEHO.

305 **The building's low setting** Benjamin Forgey, "The Pentagon at 40," *WP,* 15 Jan. 1983.

305 **Likewise, from** National Register of Historic Places Inventory, 3–6, 20–22, OSD HO; Forgey, "The Pentagon at 40"; *Federal Architect,* Jan.–Apr. 1943.

306 **None of this** "Pentagon Building," *Architectural Forum;* "Race Between Claustrophobia and Agoraphobia," *Newsweek;* Shalett, "Mammoth Cave, Washington, D.C."

306 **David Witmer** Witmer planning memorandum, OSD HO.

306 **"The world's largest"** Frierson, *The Pentagon,* 5.

A little chiseling

307 **The building was completed** Maj. Charles Smith memo to Groves about landscaping work, 14 Feb. 1943, I, CEHO; field progress report, 31 Mar. 1943, RG 319; "The Pentagon," Witmer papers, 7; F&R, *The Corps of Engineers,* 266; "Basic Data on the Pentagon," III, 6 NARA RG 160; Groves, "A Few Facts on the Pentagon," circa 1968, Groves papers, entry 5, box 1, NARA RG 200.

307 **"The General figures"** "Pentagon Telephone Conversations—Groves," Renshaw and Matthias, 17 Feb. 1943.

308 **That accounting trick** *Cong. Rec.,* 29 Feb. 1944, 2104–05; *Time,* 22 Feb. 1943.

308 **Groves responded** Groves memo to Renshaw, 9 Apr. 1943, entry 5, box 1, NARA RG 200.

308 **"almost entirely"** Shalett, "Mammoth Cave, Washington, D.C."

I prefer not mentioning our fee

308 **Constructing a building** Groves memo, 16 Mar. 1943, entry 5, box 1, NARA RG 200.

308   **Groves mercilessly** *Ibid.;* "Basic Data on the Pentagon," IV, 4, NARA RG 160; McShain address to engineers, McShain papers, HML.

309   **Perhaps to soften** *WP,* 17 Apr. 1943; *Star,* 18 Apr. 1943.

309   **"I prefer not mentioning"** McShain letter to Billy Sams, 28 June 1978, VII, McShain papers, HML. McShain's biographer, Carl Brauer, suggests that McShain's fee after further negotiations may have been closer to $500,000, though the figure does not appear in War Department documents. Brauer also reports that McShain's profits were increased because he apparently owned a sizable interest in Potts & Callahan, which did most of the excavating and grading work. Brauer, *The Man Who Built Washington,* 87–88.

309   **Pierre L'Enfant may have designed** Brauer, *The Man Who Built Washington,* xi; excerpt from broadcast on radio station WRC, 9 Dec. 1949, VII, McShain papers, HML. In addition to the Pentagon, Jefferson Memorial, National Airport, and various federal buildings, McShain built the John F. Kennedy Center for the Performing Arts. He renovated the White House during the Truman administration and completed the National Shrine of the Immaculate Conception, one of the largest cathedrals in the world. But the glory that McShain accrued in Washington proved ephemeral. When he died in 1989, "the man who built Washington" rated a four-inch obituary buried deep in the *Washington Post,* more than ten days after the fact. McShain had dissolved his business in the late 1970s and left most of his considerable fortune to Catholic charities. *Exegi Monumentum Aere Perennius* was the title of the homily given at his memorial mass at Rosemont College outside Philadelphia. It was a Latin verse from the poet Horace that McShain had read seventy years earlier as a student at Georgetown University: "I have built a monument more lasting than bronze."

A Herculean enterprise

309   **By late spring** Groves memo to Renshaw, 18 Feb. 1943, entry 5, box 1, RG 200; Col. H. W. Isbell memo to Col. O. L. Nelson, 27 Apr. 1943, I, CEHO; Nelson memo to Styer, 28 Apr. 1943, I, CEHO; "Building Engineer for the Pentagon," 17 May 1943, entry 5, box 1, RG 200; Renshaw memo to Farrell, 24 May 1943, I, CEHO.

310   **As the project wound down** "The Society of the Pentagon, Roster of the Membership," Sept. 1942, Somervell papers, MHI; *Star,* 30 May 1943; van der Gracht, White interview.

310   **Van der Gracht had been commissioned** Renshaw letter to van der Gracht, 12 Aug. 1942, series 45.1, White, RG 45, AOC; van der Gracht service records, series 45.1, White, RG 45, AOC; van der Gracht, White interview.

311   **McShain's performance** McShain autobiographical notes, 20–21, VII, I, McShain papers HML; Polly McShain, author interview; Brauer, *The Man Who Built Washington,* 89. Groves recalled discussing such a proposition with McShain and

Somervell but placed the discussion shortly after Pearl Harbor. Groves "Seabees" memo, 29 Mar. 1967, Groves collection, USMA.

311 **Renshaw, to his disappointment** Furman, author interview; Alan Renshaw, author interview; Renshaw biographical file, CEHO; *Star,* Jan. 1945.

311 **Groves had his eye** Furman, author interview; Norris, *Racing for the Bomb,* 287–91, 299–307.

312 **For a while, Major Furman** Furman, author interview.

We take 'em back

312 **The end of April** *WP,* 28 Apr. 1943; *Star,* 28 Apr. 1943.

313 **"Pentagon's Lucky 30,814"** *WP,* 9 July 1943.

313 **Even the Pentagon's six** War Department press release, 29 Apr. 1943, SDF, NARA RG 160; *WP,* 8 Apr. 1944.

313 **The layers of dust** War Department press release, 22 Dec. 1942, SDF, NARA RG 160; Jeffress, author interview; Dole, author interview.

314 **Despite the Pentagon's size** *The Pentagon: A Description of the World's Largest Office Building,* 4.

314 **The road network** War Department press release, 29 Apr. 1943, SDF, NARA RG 160; *WP,* 22 Mar. 1942; *WP,* 26 Apr. 1944.

314 **Even the once-ugly courtyard** *Star,* 30 May 1943; *Washington Daily News,* 23 July 1943.

314 **Movie stars** *NYT,* 28 Oct. 1943; *WP,* 28 Oct. 1943; *Star,* 23 Jan. 1943; *WT-H,* 16 June 1943; Drew Pearson, "Washington Merry-Go-Round," 3 July 1943.

314 **On the concourse** War Department press release, 29 Apr. 1943, SDF, NARA RG 160; *Publishers Weekly,* 18 Sept. 1943; Isbell, memo about concessions, 19 Feb. 1944, SDF, NARA RG 160; *Star,* 2 June and 23 Aug. 1943; *WP,* 28 Apr. and 2 June 1943.

315 **Tall and erect, General Henri** *Time,* 2 July 1951.

Somervell's Folly

315 **In the spring of 1943** Engel letter to Somervell, 20 Apr. 1943, I, CEHO; Somervell letter to Engel, 28 Apr. 1943, I, CEHO; Hadden, memo to Renshaw, 30 Apr. 1943, entry 5, box 1, NARA RG 200.

316 **Equally alarming** Hugh Fulton letters to Julius H. Amberg, 16 June, 21 June, and 3 Aug. 1943, I, CEHO; Fulton letter to Amberg, 7 July 1943, NARA RG 107.

316 **"I was watching you"** Hauck memo to McShain, 13 Jan. 1950, VII, McShain papers, HML; Manning memo to McShain, 10 Jan. 1950, VII; McShain papers; McShain notes about 31 Dec. 1949 meeting with Truman, VII, McShain papers, HML.

316 **On Capitol Hill** telephone transcript, Renshaw and Col. Chapin, 8 Jan. 1944, I, CEHO; Renshaw memo to Hadden, 17 Jan. 1944, I, CEHO; *Cong. Rec.,* 29 Feb. 1944, 2102–10; *Star,* 29 Feb. 1944.

316 **Somervell telephoned Renshaw** telephone transcript, Somervell and Renshaw, 29 Feb. 1944, I, CEHO; Somervell 1944 appointment book, 29 Feb. 1944, Somervell papers, MHI.

317 **Engel nonetheless** *Cong Rec.*, 6 Mar. 1944, 2288–92; "Comments on Statements of Congressman Albert J. Engel on the Pentagon, 6 March 1944," Office of the Chief of Engineers, 7 Apr. 1944, I, CEHO.

317 **Once again, Engel's attacks** United Press, 29 Feb. 1944; *Newsweek*, 20 Mar. 1944.

317 **Even the German press** *"Das Somervell-Narrenhaus in Washington,"* 24 Feb. 1944, copy with translation in entry 18, Karl Detzer file, SDF, NARA RG 160.

317 **Other congressmen** United Press article in *NYT*, 7 Feb. 1944.

CHAPTER 16: WHAT TO DO WITH THE PENTAGON

I no longer consider the Pentagon a safe shelter

319 **As the clock counted** Groves, *Now It Can Be Told*, 295–6; Lawren, *The General and the Bomb*, 215–17; Groves memo to the secretary of war, 18 July 1945, appendix VIII, 436, *Now It Can Be Told*.

319 **"If our gadget"** F&R, *The Corps of Engineers*, 661.

319 **Somervell was no more** Groves, *Now It Can Be Told*, 70.

320 **No one could be sure** Groves, *Now It Can Be Told*, 291; Richard Rhodes, *The Making of the Atomic Bomb*, 652.

320 **"What the hell"** Rhodes, *The Making of the Atomic Bomb*, 666.

320 **"During most of these hours"** Groves memo to the secretary of war, 18 July 1945, appendix VIII, 438–9, *Now It Can Be Told*.

320 **Accompanied by Vannevar Bush** *Ibid.;* Groves, 438, 294–8.

321 **"The war is over"** *Ibid.*, 298.

321 **Groves boarded a plane** *Ibid.*, 302–4; Norris, *Racing for the Bomb*, 407.

321 **In graphic and, for Groves** Groves, memo to the secretary of war, 18 July 1945, appendix VIII, 433–4, *Now It Can Be Told*.

I just plum forgot

321 **On the morning of August 6** Groves, *Now It Can Be Told*, 321–4.

322 **Marshall wanted Groves** *Ibid.*, 324–30.

323 **At 11 A.M., the announcement** McCullough, *Truman*, 455.

323 **Groves soon ran into Somervell** Groves, oral history with Pogue, first interview.

How did you know Truman was going to be president?

323 **Somervell waited** Millett, *The Army Service Forces*, 419; *Newsweek*, 7 Dec. 1942.

323 **In 1943, a little** AP article in *WP*, 16 Mar. 1943; Matter, author interview. At Bel-

court, Louise had been one of the girls eyeing the young West Point cadet when he was home on holidays. Louise Wartmann and her husband, Henry, a Florida citrus packing company owner, had befriended the Somervells in Ocala in 1935, when the Army engineer was building the soon-aborted Florida ship canal. Both widowed and each with three daughters, they were married in Ocala on March 15, 1943, with Fat Styer serving as the general's best man. Roosevelt telegrammed Somervell with congratulations for the "good news from the South."

323 **Though only fifty-three** Ohl, *Supplying the Troops*, 250; Handy, memo to Marshall, 5 Jan. 1944, box 65, folder 43, Marshall papers, GCM Lib.

324 **At 7 P.M., the announcement** Millett, *The Army Service Forces*, 419. The Services of Supply name was changed to Army Service Forces on Mar. 12, 1943.

324 **The vast supply empire** Janney, "The Man Behind the Invasion"; *NYT*, 14 Feb. 1955; Eisenhower address at Pentagon, 10 June 1946, Somervell papers, MHI.

324 **Somervell signed a second** Millett, *The Army Service Forces*, 419; Somervell memo to Marshall, 18 Aug. 1945, Somervell papers, MHI.

324 **Somervell "looked very sorrowful"** Groves, oral history with Pogue, second interview.

325 **In the Somervell family** Brehon Somervell Griswold, author interview, 8 Mar. 2004.

325 **Despite all the criticism** *WT-H*, 25 Sept. 1943; Ohl, *Supplying the Troops*, 250; Robert E. Sherwood, *Roosevelt and Hopkins: An Intimate History*, 758–62.

325 **Two weeks after** Pearson, "The Washington Merry-Go-Round," *WP*, 27 Apr. 1945.

325 **It was obvious by then** Ohl, *Supplying the Troops*, 250; *WP*, 19 June 1945; Hart, *Washington at War*, 260–1; Stimson diary, 18 June 1945; McCloy diary, 18 June 1945.

326 **"So strategist"** Somervell speech, Army-Navy Staff College, 24 Feb. 1944, Somervell addresses, vol. V, MHI.

We can only leave with the greatest feeling of pride

326 **On September 20** *WP*, 21 Sept. 1945; War Department press release, 21 Nov. 1945.

326 **Henry Stimson was leaving** Godfrey Hodgson, *The Colonel: The Life and Wars of Henry Stimson*, 350; McCloy, remarks at time of dedication of the Marshall Corridor in the Pentagon, 20 Apr. 1976, McCloy papers, Amherst College.

326 **On his final morning** Stimson diary, 21 Sept. 1945; Hodgson, *The Colonel*, 367.

327 **The Pentagon bade farewell** *WP*, 27 Nov. 1945; McCullough, *Truman*, 472; *Time*, 3 Jan. 1944; Stimson and Bundy, *On Active Service*, 441; Pogue, *Organizer of Victory*, 321, xi.

327 **Somervell's departure** War Department press release, 21 Nov. 1945.

327 **Marshall was disappointed** Millett, *The Army Service Forces*, 419; Marshall, oral histories with Pogue, 13 Nov. 1956 and 14 Feb. 1957.

327 **From Highhold** Stimson, letter to Somervell, 13 Nov. 1945, Somervell papers, MHI; Millett, *The Army Service Forces*, 420.

328 **There were rumors** *Newsweek*, 1 Oct. 1945; Karl Detzer, undated anecdote, circa 1946, Somervell papers, MHI.

328 **"[N]ow that the play"** Katherine King, letter to Somervell, 7 June 1946, Somervell papers, MHI.

Hell in a handbasket

328 **It was well into October** Furman, author interview.

329 **The Pentagon was put** *Star*, 7 Sept. 1945 and 22 Mar. 1946.

329 **Before long** *Star*, 17 Feb. 1946.

329 **The population of the building** Goldberg, *The Pentagon*, 158, 185; War Department press release, 29 Apr. 1943, SDF, NARA RG 160; "Pentagon Telephone Conversations—Groves," Renshaw and Matthias, 7 Aug. 1942; Inspector General's Office report on space in Pentagon, 26 Aug. 1943, box 963, NARA RG 159.

330 **Even Eisenhower** Eisenhower, *At Ease: Stories I Tell to Friends*, 315–16.

What to do with the Pentagon

330 **The question now** Immen, "The Pentagon . . . Fact and Fancy"; Joe McCarthy, "Our Miraculous Pentagon," *Holiday*, Mar. 1952; Lauterbach, "The Pentagon Puzzle."

330 **Other suggestions** *WP*, 20 Aug. 1944; *Washington Daily News*, 24 Oct. 1945; *Star*, 13 Mar. 1945.

331 **Whatever the price** Engel press release, 29 Feb. 1944, I, CEHO; Goldberg, *The Pentagon*, 112; "Estimate—Pentagon Building," 8 Jan. 1943, entry 145, NARA RG 319; Defense Project Agency audit, 22 Aug. 1942, I, CEHO; "Comments on Statements of Congressman Albert J. Engel on the Pentagon, 29 February 1944," Office of the Chief of Engineers, 7 Apr. 1944, I, CEHO.

331 **"It is probable"** *Ibid*.

331 **Failure to tell Congress** "Problems Related to Pentagon Project," SDF, NARA RG 160.

331 **The War Department produced several** "The Pentagon Project-ASF"; NARA RG 160; "Basic Data on the Pentagon," SDF, NARA RG 160; memo to Somervell about "The Pentagon Project," 28 July 1944, I, CEHO.

332 **"Imagine what"** "The Pentagon Saves Lives," Lt. Col. Karl Detzer, draft, Jan. 1944, I, CEHO.

332 **Still, the Pentagon had failed** Goldberg, *The Pentagon*, 165; "The Pentagon," Office of the Chief of Engineers, draft, 1 May 1944, I, CEHO.

The eighth wonder of the world

332 **Little more than** *War Times*, 31 Aug. 1945; *Star*, 2 Sept. 1945, *WP*, 2 Sept. 1945.

332 **It was George Marshall** King letter to Marshall, 26 May 1944; Nelson memo to

McNarney, 7 June 1944; Marshall note, Nov. 1945; Patterson letter to secretary of state, 19 Nov. 1945; Forrestal letter to Patterson, 29 Nov. 1945, all in Otto L. Nelson Papers, GCM Lib.

If we get a decent peace

334 **Franklin D. Roosevelt had also** Roosevelt, memo to Smith, 8 Jan. 1945, OF 380, FDR Lib.

PART II
CHAPTER 17: NO DECENT PEACE

I want to take the oath

339 **At 9:45 A.M.** Steven L. Rearden, *History of the Office of the Secretary of Defense: The Formative Years, 1947–1950*, 1; *Time*, 29 Sept. 1947; *WP*, 18 Sept. 1947; *NYT*, 18 Sept. 1947.

339 **President Harry Truman had hoped** Rearden, *The Formative Years*, 1; Clark Clifford with Richard Holbrooke, *Counsel to the President: A Memoir*, 159; Allan R. Millett and Peter Maslowski, *For the Common Defense: A Military History of the United States of America*, 495.

340 **Truman, alarmed** James Forrestal, *The Forrestal Diaries*, 313.

340 **Minutes before noon** *Time*, 29 Sept. 1947; *NYT*, 18 Sept. 1947.

340 **A broken nose** C. W. Borklund, *Men of the Pentagon: From Forrestal to McNamara*, 12; Eisenhower, *At Ease*, 330; Jonathan Daniels, quoted in *Time*, 31 Jan. 1964.

340 **Amid "an atmosphere"** Clifford, *Counsel to the President*, 159; Rearden, *The Formative Years*, 1–2.

340 **Forrestal crossed** J. S. Davitt, memo to Wilfred J. McNeil, 22 July 1947, box 510 D, OSD HO; *WP*, 29 July 1947; Forrestal, *The Forrestal Diaries*, 295; Borklund, *Men of the Pentagon*, 45; Marx Leva, minutes of meeting, 1 Aug. 1947, 2 Aug. 1947, boxes 513/4, OSD HO.

341 **A Navy band** *NYT*, 24 Sept. 1947; *WP*, 24 Sept. 1947.

341 **Forrestal's advisers wanted** Leva, minutes of meeting, 1 Aug. 1947, 2 Aug. 1947, boxes 513/4, OSD HO; minutes of meeting, 15 Aug. 1947, boxes 513/4, OSD HO.

341 **"This is National Defense"** *WP*, 22 Sept. 1947; *Star*, 23 and 28 Oct., 1947.

341 **Most noteworthy** Marx Leva, oral history, 1970, HST Lib.

The biggest cemetery for dead cats in the world

342 **The New War Department Building** Goldberg, *The Pentagon*, 4; *Star*, 20 June 1947.

342 **The tenuous wartime alliance** Rearden, *The Formative Years*, 3–4, 9; Millett and Maslowski, *For the Common Defense*, 496–7.

342 **It was a sweeping** Rearden, *The Formative Years,* 12; Forrestal, *The Forrestal Diaries,* 314.

343 **The atmosphere lent urgency** Townsend Hoopes and Douglas Brinkley, *Driven Patriot: The Life and Times of James Forrestal,* 321, 327; Clifford, *Counsel to the President,* 153, 146; Rearden, *The Formative Years,* 20.

343 **"They have a propaganda"** Clifford, *Counsel to the President,* 156.

343 **The son of an immigrant** Borklund, *Men of the Pentagon,* 12.

344 **After seven years** Clifford, *Counsel to the President,* 149–51; Clark M. Clifford, oral history, 19 Apr. 1971, HST Lib.; Hoopes and Brinkley, *Driven Patriot,* 334–5; Arnold A. Rogow, *James Forrestal: A Study of Personality, Politics, and Policy,* 223.

344 **Truman may have been tempted** Clifford, *Counsel to the President,* 153–55; Rearden, *The Formative Years,* 22; Clifford, oral history, 19 Apr. 1971, HST Lib.

344 **Forrestal was not Truman's first** Forrestal, *Forrestal Diaries,* 295; Hoopes and Brinkley, *Driven Patriot,* 351; Rearden, *The Formative Years,* 4; Clifford, *Counsel to the President,* 158; Clifford, oral history, 23 Mar. 1971, HST Lib.

345 **Forrestal, for his part** Hoopes and Brinkley, *Driven Patriot,* 350; Cecilia Stiles Cornell, "James V. Forrestal and American National Security Policy, 1940–49," 312; Hanson W. Baldwin, "Big Boss of the Pentagon," *NYT,* 29 Aug. 1948; Borklund, *Men of the Pentagon,* 38.

345 **Forrestal had his own** Forrestal, *Forrestal Diaries,* 299.

When the soul's life is gone

345 **Forrestal brought forty-five** Rearden, *The Formative Years,* 6; House hearings on H.R. 2319, 79th Cong. 2nd Sess., 1946, p. 109–110, excerpt in box 510, OSD HO.

345 **It was immediately clear** Borklund, *Men of the Pentagon,* 157; Rearden, *The Formative Years,* 32, 61; Hoopes and Brinkley, *Driven Patriot,* 356; Roger R. Trask and Alfred Goldberg, *The Department of Defense, 1947–1997,* 10.

346 **"Well, have a nice"** Borklund, *Men of the Pentagon,* 15.

346 **Forrestal lacked authority** Hoopes and Brinkley, *Driven Patriot,* 360–4.

346 **Even getting the Navy** Leva, minutes of meeting of Forrestal staff on 1 Aug. 1947, 2 Aug. 1947, boxes 513/4, OSD HO; Cramer, *Washington Daily News,* 4 Aug. 1947.

346 **Forrestal saw the Navy's absence** Forrestal, "Report to the President from the Secretary of Defense," 28 Feb. 1948, OSD HO; OSD press release, "Navy Top Level Officials Begin Move to Pentagon," 11 Aug. 1948, OSD HO; National Military Establishment Office of Public Information press release, 24 Aug. 1948, OSD HO; *NYT,* 12 Aug. 1948; Goldberg, *The Pentagon,* 163.

347 **Of all the military** Ronald Schiller, "That Amazing Monster, The Pentagon," *Pageant,* Dec. 1951; Gidget Fuentes, "Making Way for the Corps (at the Pentagon)," *Marine Corps Times,* 1 Jan. 1996; Otto Kreisher, "Marine Boss No Longer in Annex," *San Diego Union-Tribune,* 12 Jan. 1996; John Hamre, author interview, 27 Feb. 2006.

347 Getting the Navy Rearden, *The Formative Years*, 38–9.

347 As Forrestal's frustration Clifford, *Counsel to the President*, 160; Hoopes and Brinkley, *Driven Patriot*, 422–4; Clifford, oral history, 19 Apr. 1971, HST Lib.

348 Forrestal's anxiety McCullough, *Truman*, 736–8; Clifford, *Counsel to the President*, 173; Hoopes and Brinkley, *Driven Patriot*, 428–31, 437; Clifford, oral history, 19 Apr. 1971, HST Lib.

348 Shortly before his inauguration Hoopes and Brinkley, *Driven Patriot*, 438–9, 423, 443; Rearden, *The Formative Years*, 46.

348 "Ike, I simply can't" Eisenhower, *At Ease*, 333.

349 Johnson was sworn in Keith D. McFarland and David L. Roll, *Louis Johnson and the Arming of America: The Roosevelt and Truman Years*, 151; *NYT*, 29 Mar. 1949; *WP*, 29 Mar. 1949; Clifford, *Counsel to the President*, 173; Leva, oral history, HST Lib.; Rogow, *James Forrestal*, 3–4.

349 Alarmed friends arranged Rogow, *James Forrestal*, 5–8; Hoopes and Brinkley, *Driven Patriot*, 450–54, 460.

350 On the night of May 21 Hoopes and Brinkley, *Driven Patriot*, 463–5; Rogow, *James Forrestal*, 17–18.

I want that office

350 Big, bluff, backslapping Borklund, *Men of the Pentagon*, 65–66; "Master of the Pentagon," *Time*, 6 June 1949; McCullough, *Truman*, 742.

351 Moving into Forrestal's office Louis H. Renfrow, oral history, 1971, 114–116, HST Lib.; McFarland and Roll, *Louis Johnson*, 149–150; Rearden, *The Formative Years*, 48; Leva, oral history, HST Lib.

351 The biggest desk Jack Raymond, *Power at the Pentagon*, 8; Goldberg memo with attached desk inventory, 13 Jan. 2005, OSD HO.

351 Renfrow informed Army Secretary Renfrow, oral history, 1971, 114–116, HST Lib., *WP*, 10 Apr. 1949, Leva, oral history, HST Lib. Johnson's suite in 3E 880 encompassed the suite that had been used by Stimson, which had been originally known as 3E-884 based on the number on one of several doors that led to that suite. For many years, the numbering style included a hyphen. In recent years, the hyphen has been dropped.

351 Johnson did not stop *WP*, 16 Apr. 1949; *Star*, 28 Sept. 1951; AP, 29 Mar. 1959; *WP*, 28 July 1957; OSD press release, 29 Mar. 1949, OSD HO; Renfrow, oral history, 119, HST Lib.; *Time*, 6 June 1949.

352 Disruptive as it all *Time*, 2 July 1951; *NYT*, 15 July 1951; Goldberg, "The Pentagon," 164; OSD fact sheet about "The Tank," June 1984, box 1303, OSD HO. The name "Tank" was carried over from its original location during World War II, when the combined chiefs met in the Public Health Building at Constitution Avenue and 19th Street. The entrance to the conference room was down a flight of stairs and through an arched portal, which gave the impression of entering a tank.

352 **The most important command** *Time*, 2 July 1951; *WP*, 23 July 1951.

353 **The threat of a nuclear attack** Millett and Maslowski, *For the Common Defense*, 499; Lawren, *The General and the Bomb*, 267; Norris, *Racing for the Bomb*, 674.

353 **The news immediately rekindled** *WP*, 28 Sept. 1949; *WP*, 25 Mar. 1951; "Army discloses data on sub-Pentagon," *ENR*, 13 Nov. 1952. "Site R" is short for Raven Rock Mountain.

353 **George Marshall** Schiller, "That Amazing Monster, The Pentagon."

354 **Pentagonians—as employees** C. B. Overman, "I Run the World's Biggest Building," *American Magazine*, June 1951; Harry Gabbett, "Gen. Somervell's 'Folly' Proves Itself Despite Jeers of Critics," *WP*, 18 Aug. 1954; *WP*, 8 June 1994; DoD press release, 9 Sept. 1997.

We weren't ready to fight

354 **Louis Johnson** Borklund, *Men of the Pentagon*, 65–88; McCullough, *Truman*, 741.

354 **In Omar Bradley's view** Omar N. Bradley and Clay Blair, *A General's Life: An Autobiography by General of the Army Omar N. Bradley*, 503.

354 **Taking the opposite approach** *Time*, 6 June 1949; Millett and Maslowski, *For the Common Defense*, 504–505; Rearden, *The Formative Years*, 47–65.

354 **Poorly trained** Brad Smith, author interview, June 2000; Steve Vogel, "Unprepared to Fight," *WP*, 19 June 2000.

355 **The pathetic state** Trask and Goldberg, *The Department of Defense*, 63; McCullough, *Truman*, 742.

355 **George C. Marshall had been vacationing** Forrest C. Pogue, *George C. Marshall: Statesman*, 420; Borklund, *Men of the Pentagon*, 89.

355 **On September 21** *Ibid.* 101; Mark A. Stoler, *George C. Marshall: Soldier-Statesman of the American Century*, 183.

355 **Marshall went to work** Borklund, *Men of the Pentagon*, 6, 89, 112; *WP*, 1 Oct. 1950; Trask and Goldberg, *The Department of Defense*, 63.

356 **Inside the Pentagon** Goldberg, *The Pentagon*, 165; *NYT*, 17 Sept. 1950; *NYT*, 14 Feb. 1954.

He served America magnificently

356 **Truman, through an intermediary** Truman letter to Somervell, 23 Apr. 1951; Somervell letter to Marshall, undated copy, circa 1951, Somervell letter to Truman, 25 Apr. 1951, all in Somervell papers, MHI; Ohl, *Supplying the Troops*, 250.

357 **After his retirement** Ohl, *Supplying the Troops*, 252, 257–9.

357 **Somervell, belying** Somervell letter to Maj. Gen. W. A. Wood, Jr., 2 June 1952, Somervell papers, MHI.

357 **Somervell did take** Matter, author interview; Gabbett, "Gen. Somervell's 'Folly' Proves Itself"; *Star*, 9 Sept. 1951; Maj. Robert B. McBane, "The Pentagon

Makes Sense," Army Information Digest, Jan. 1947, copy in McShain papers, HML; Somervell letter to Marshall McNeil, 16 Jan. 1947, Somervell papers, MHI.

358 **To an artist** Somervell letter to Orland Campbell, 27 Aug. 1954, Somervell papers, MHI.

358 **Several weeks later** Matter, author interview; Ohl, *Supplying the Troops*, 260; Styer, Somervell obituary, *Assembly*, October 1955; Delano letter to the editor, *New York Herald-Tribune*, 16 Feb. 1955; *NYT, WP*, and *Star*, 14 Feb. 1955.

358 **Newspapers were filled** *WP*, 15 Feb. 1955; *Memphis Commercial Appeal*, Feb. 1955; *Sun*, 15 Feb. 1955.

358 **front rank of Allied** Shrader, "World War II Logistics."

358 **"I would start out"** Marshall, oral history with Pogue, 14 Feb. 1957.

359 **On February 17, 1955** *WP*, 18 Feb. 1955; *WP*, 14 Feb. 1955.

Water flowed like money

359 **Somervell's folly had** *WP*, 13 Jan. 1957; *The Pentagon: A Description of the World's Largest Office Building*, 1–9.

359 **"Anyone, from a four-star"** Pawel Monat, with John Dille, *Spy in the U.S.*, 91–92.

360 **It was not just spies** Overman, "I Run the World's Biggest Building"; Gabbett, "Gen. Somervell's 'Folly' Proves Itself."

360 **Building supervisors** Overman, "I Run the World's Biggest Building"; *WP*, 29 June 1958; *WP*, 14 Apr. 1959.

361 **Three months later** *WP*, 3 July, 1959; *Star*, 3 July, 1959; *WP*, 4 Aug. 1959. Among the reporters who covered the fire for the *Post* was Tom Wolfe, then beginning his career as a writer.

I don't give a damn what John Paul Jones would have done

362 **By October 24, 1962** Henry L. Trewhitt, *McNamara*, 107; Dino A. Brugioni, *Eyeball to Eyeball: The Inside Story of the Cuban Missile Crisis*, 415, 398; Raymond, *Power at the Pentagon*, 10–12.

362 **A private elevator** Ibid.; Goldberg, *The Pentagon*, 144; National Military Command Center System history draft, NMCC, 18 Aug. 1986, OSD HO.

362 **The reality was strange enough** George C. Wilson, "From Strangelovian to Prosaic," *WP*, 10 July 1976; Raymond, *Power at the Pentagon*, 10–12.

363 **Yet the National Military** Brugioni, *Eyeball to Eyeball*, 399–400.

363 **"It was a means"** Transcript, forum on Fortieth Anniversary of the Cuban Missile Crisis, 18 Oct. 2002, Harvard University, John F. Kennedy School of Government, www.iop.harvard.edu/pdfs/transcripts/cuban_missile_crisis_10.18.02.pdf, (hereafter fortieth anniversary transcript, Harvard).

363 **At 9:15 that evening** Elie Abel, *The Missile Crisis*, 154; Brugioni, *Eyeball to Eyeball*, 384, 416.

363 **Anderson—at fifty-five** Brugioni, *Eyeball to Eyeball*, 271.

363 **"Mr. Secretary, the Navy"** Roswell L. Gilpatric, oral history interview, 27 May 1970, 60–61, John F. Kennedy Presidential Library; Abel, *The Missile Crisis,* 154–6; fortieth anniversary transcript, Harvard; Lawrence S. Kaplan, Ronald O. Landa, Edward J. Drea, *The McNamara Ascendancy, 1961–1965,* 212–13. Anderson later described the incident as less of a confrontation.

364 **McNamara angrily returned** Brugioni, 416.

364 **Navy destroyers continued** *Ibid.; Virginian-Pilot,* 10 Nov. 2002.

364 **"Maybe the war"** *NYT,* 14 Oct. 2002.

CHAPTER 18: THE BATTLE OF THE PENTAGON

You had to be scared

367 **Under the cover of darkness** "The Anti-Vietnam War Demonstration at Washington, D.C. 21–22 October 1967, After Action Report," draft, 7 Nov. 1967, 52, Office of the Deputy Chief of Staff for Military Operations, box 3, Anti-War Demonstrations, March on the Pentagon, CMH (hereafter Army AAR draft); Phil Entrekin, author interview, Apr. 2006; *NYT,* 22 Nov. 1967; "After Action Report, Operation Cabinet Maker," 13 Nov. 1967, 14, Headquarters Military District of Washington, box 4, Anti-War Demonstrations, March on the Pentagon, CMH (hereafter MDW AAR); Nick Adde, "Solving the Puzzle Palace," *Army Times,* 13 Oct. 1986; Allen Woode, "How the Pentagon Stopped Worrying and Learned to Love Peace Marchers," *Ramparts,* Feb. 1968.

367 **Inside the green-carpeted** Army AAR draft, 37, 79, 62–4; Woode, "How the Pentagon Stopped Worrying." Woode noted that maps of Vietnam remained up elsewhere in the operations center.

368 **All day, minute-by-minute** Army Operations Center log, 20–21 Oct. 1967, Anti-War Demonstrations, March on the Pentagon, CMH (hereafter Army ops log); Paul J. Scheips, *The Role of Federal Military Forces in Domestic Disorders, 1945–1992,* 248, 255.

368 **As the first demonstrators** Army AAR draft, 52; Office of the Under Secretary of the Army Journal, 21 Oct. 1967, Anti-War Demonstrations, March on the Pentagon, CMH, 5 (hereafter OUSA journal).

368 **Colonel Ernie Graves felt uneasy** Graves, author interviews, 12 Feb. 2004 and 7 Dec. 2005; Scheips, *The Role of Federal Military Forces,* 249.

369 **McNamara and Under Secretary** Robert McNamara, author interview, 11 Jan. 2006.

369 **A line of MPs** Army AAR draft, 34, 50; MDW AAR, 14.

369 **A northeast wind** George C. Wilson, "Chronology of Pentagon's Biggest, Strangest Siege," *WP,* 23 Oct. 1967.

369 **McNamara went to** McNamara, author's interview; Reis Kash, e-mail to author, 6 Apr. 2006; Reis Kash, author interview 14 Apr. 2006.

369 **"Christ, yes,"** Paul Hendrickson, "McNamara: Specters of Vietnam," *WP*, 10 May 1984; Robert S. McNamara with Brian VanDeMark, *In Retrospect: The Tragedy and Lessons of Vietnam*, 305.

The true and high church

370 **By October, more than 13,000** Paul Hendrickson, *The Living and the Dead: Robert McNamara and Five Lives of a Lost War*, 334–5; George C. Herring, *LBJ and Vietnam: A Different Kind of War*, 141; Selected Manpower Statistics, FY 1986, DoD.

370 **"were going to face"** Norman Mailer, *The Armies of the Night*, 113–4.

370 **There had been previous** Paul Hendrickson, "Daughter of the Flames," *WP*, 2 Dec. 1985; Hendrickson, *The Living and the Dead*, 187–91; McNamara, *In Retrospect*, 216–217.

370 **By 1967, protests** *WP*, 16 Feb. 1997; Tom Wells, *The War Within: America's Battle over Vietnam*, 122–3.

371 **The march on the Pentagon** Scheips, *The Role of Federal Military Forces*.

371 **A healthy dose** AP article in *Fayetteville Observer*, 15 Oct. 1967; Abbie Hoffman, *Soon to be a Major Motion Picture*, 131–2.

371 **Not everyone** Scheips, *The Role of Federal Military Forces*, 235; Army AAR draft, 1–2; *NYT*, 28 July 1967. The speech was delivered at St. Stephen and the Incarnation Episcopal Church.

372 **"This confrontation"** *Ibid.*, foreword.

372 **This "extraordinary"** Herring, *LBJ and Vietnam*, 142; Scheips, *The Role of Federal Military Forces*, 248; Seymour M. Hersh, "Files Disclose More Army Snooping Under Johnson," *NYT*, 1 Sept. 1972.

372 **In the days before** Army AAR draft, 45–47; Hollis memo, 18 Oct. 1967, box 2, Anti-War Demonstrations, March on the Pentagon, CMH; Scheips, *The Role of Federal Military Forces*, 251, 255, 258; MDW AAR, 14; *WP*, 20 Oct. 1967; *NYT*, 22 Nov. 1967; Army ops log, 20–21 Oct. 1967.

373 **For all the extraordinary** McGiffert memo to McNamara, 21 Oct. 1967, box 3, Anti-War Demonstrations, March on the Pentagon, CMH.

373 **The zeal to show** MDW AAR, 29; McNamara, *In Retrospect*, 303; Army AAR draft, 36–38; Col. George M. Bush memo to McGiffert, "Lessons Learned October 20–22 Demonstration," 26 Oct. 1967, Anti-War Demonstrations, March on the Pentagon, CMH; McGiffert after action evaluation, 26 Oct. 1967, Anti-War Demonstrations, March on the Pentagon, CMH.

374 **The day before the march** "Orientation of Military Commanders by the Chief of Staff Army," 20 Oct. 1967, box 3, Anti-War Demonstrations, March on the Pentagon, CMH; *WP*, Johnson obituary, 28 Sept. 1983.

The situation became extremely fluid

374   **A vast cross-section** Scheips, *The Role of Federal Military Forces*, 255–8; *WP*, 29 Oct. 1967; Bruce Jackson, "The Battle of the Pentagon"; MDW AAR, annex B-1.

375   **Marching at the front** Scheips, *The Role of Federal Military Forces*, 257; Jackson, "The Battle of the Pentagon"; Louis Cassels, "Analysis 10/22," UPI, 22 Oct. 1967.

375   **High on spirit** Mailer, *The Armies of the Night*, 106–110, 117.

375   **The route marked by police** Permit issued to demonstrators, MDW AAR, annex E-1; Wells, *The War Within*, 189; Woode, "How the Pentagon Stopped Worrying"; McGiffert, after-action evaluation, 26 Oct. 1967, Anti-War Demonstrations, March on the Pentagon, CMH.

375   **"No enemy was visible"** Mailer, *The Armies of the Night*, 119.

375   **Walter Teague** Teague, author interview, 19 Jan. 2006; Jim Hoagland, "Protest Leaders Faded at Pentagon," *WP*, 23 Oct. 1967; Wells, *The War Within*, 196; MDW AAR, 14–15.

376   **It was quickly apparent** *Ibid.*, 24; Teague, author interview.

376   **O'Malley, the operational** Army AAR draft, 55.

377   **From his office** OUSA journal, 21 Oct. 1967.

377   **The crowd at the Mall** Army AAR draft, 55–57; OUSA journal, 21 Oct. 1967; letter of instruction to O'Malley, 19 Oct. 1967, Anti-War Demonstrations, March on the Pentagon, CMH.

377   **The violence was kept** MDW AAR, 15; McGiffert, after-action evaluation, CMH.

377   **At the rope barriers** James Reston, "Everyone is a Loser," *NYT*, 23 Oct. 1967; Cassels, "Analysis 10/22"; MDW AAR, 29, CMH.

378   **Captain Phil Entrekin** Entrekin, author interview.

378   **Ernie Graves** Graves, author interview.

Out, demons, out!

378   **Elsewhere, the crowd** Marty Jezer, *Abbie Hoffman, American Rebel*, 118; Hoffman, *Soon to be a Major Motion Picture*, 134.

378   **Nearby in the North** "Exorcising the Pentagon," on the Fugs' official Web site, www.thefugs.com/history_fugs.html; Mailer, *The Armies of the Night*, 119.

378   **Hippies danced** Jackson, "The Battle of the Pentagon."

379   **Some women** Frank Naughton, author interview, April 2006; Woode, "How the Pentagon Stopped Worrying"; McNamara, *In Retrospect*, 304; Entrekin, author interview.

The holy of holies

379   **The first round of trouble** Army AAR draft, 57.

379   **Frank Naughton** Naughton, author interview.

379 A platoon of MPs MDW AAR, 15, 23; Army ops journal, 21 Oct. 1967, CMH; WP, 22 Oct. 1967; Jackson, "The Battle of the Pentagon."

380 The protesters who had reached Bill Ayers, author interview, 23 Jan. 2006; Bill Ayers, Fugitive Days, 11.

380 Inside, McGiffert Army AAR draft, 57; Wilson, "Chronology of Pentagon's Biggest, Strangest Siege"; MDW AAR, 15, CMH.

380 It was not enough Army AAR draft, 59, CMH; Wilson, "Chronology of Pentagon's Biggest, Strangest Siege"; Hoagland, "Protest Leaders Faded at Pentagon"; Mailer, The Armies of the Night, 252.

381 The "Seventh-Corridor Rush" Army AAR draft, 59; MDW AAR, 16, CMH; Wilson, "Chronology of Pentagon's Biggest, Strangest Siege"; NYT, 22 Oct. 1967; Kash, author interview.

381 The Mall plaza remained Ayers, author interview; Wilson, "Chronology of Pentagon's Biggest, Strangest Siege"; OUSA Journal, 21 Oct. 1967, CMH.

381 In the operations OUSA journal, 21 Oct. 1967, CMH; Army AAR draft, 59–61, CMH.

382 Most protesters Carl Bernstein and Robert G. Kaiser, "2000 Protesters Spend Night at Pentagon—Cold, Hopeful," WP, 23 Oct. 1967; Mailer, The Armies of the Night, 268; Army ops log, 21 Oct. 1967, CMH.

382 Boredom and hunger Mailer, The Armies of the Night, 268.

382 Ayers celebrated Ayers, Fugitive Days, 11; Ayers, author interview; MDW investigation, 30 Oct, 1967, Anti-War Demonstrations, March on the Pentagon, CMH; NYT, 22 Oct. 1967.

382 "Isn't it beautiful?" Graves, author interview.

Swept away

383 As the night wore on Army AAR draft, 61–62, CMH.

383 Trouble flared Ibid., 61–5; Jackson, "The Battle of the Pentagon"; Mailer, The Armies of the Night, 272–8; Kash, author interview; Wilson, "Chronology of Pentagon's Biggest, Strangest Siege"; NYT, McShane obituary, 24 Dec. 1968; OUSA journal, 21–22 Oct. 1967, CMH.

383 By dawn Wilson, "Chronology of Pentagon's Biggest, Strangest Siege"; Army AAR draft, 69–70, CMH.

384 Within minutes, crews Ibid., 71; WP, 24 Oct. 1967; Wells, The War Within, 203. The 82nd Airborne brigade, which never left Andrews, flew back to Fort Bragg Sunday afternoon. Ironically, given the Pentagon's priority on image, some reports incorrectly stated—and many demonstrators believed—that 82nd Airborne paratroopers defended the building. Some accounts have the first marchers arriving at the Pentagon to find it ringed by the bayonet-wielding troops of the 82nd

384 O'Malley was seething OUSA journal, 22 Oct. 1967, CMH; Bush, memo to

McGiffert, "Lessons Learned October 20–22 Demonstration," 26 Oct. 1967, Anti-War Demonstrations, March on the Pentagon, CMH; McGiffert, after-action evaluation, 26 Oct. 1967, Anti-War Demonstrations, March on the Pentagon, CMH.

384 **The antiwar movement** Wells, *The War Within*, 203.

A full load

385 **Robert McNamara was waiting** Will Sparks, "Memorandum for the Record Concerning Secretary McNamara's Departure Ceremony," 29 Feb. 1968, Lyndon Baines Johnson Library, copy courtesy of Paul Hendrickson (hereafter Sparks elevator memo); Hendrickson, *The Living and the Dead*, 345–6; McNamara, *In Retrospect*, 380; David Halberstam, *The Best and the Brightest*, 645; OSD memo about elevator malfunction, 1 Mar. 1968, copy courtesy Ed Drea.

385 **Out on the River terrace** *Star*, 29 Feb. 1969; *NYT*, 1 Mar. 1968.

385 **Johnson and McNamara, accompanied** Sparks elevator memo; Deborah Shapley, *Promise and Power: The Life and Times of Robert McNamara*, vii.

385 **McNamara, as always** Sparks elevator memo.

386 **Waiting outside** *Star*, 29 Feb. 1969; *NYT*, 29 Feb. 1968.

386 **Watching McNamara's** Trewhitt, *McNamara*, 271; Joseph A. Califano, Jr., *The Triumph & Tragedy of Lyndon Johnson: The White House Years*, 249; McNamara, *In Retrospect*, 313; Shapley, *Promise and Power*, 415; Clifford, *Counsel to the President*, 487.

386 **Inside the Pentagon elevator** Sparks elevator memo.

387 **"At least this didn't happen"** Clifford, *Counsel to the President*, 487.

387 **The ordeal was not** *Time*, 8 Mar. 1968; Sparks elevator memo; *NYT*, 1 Mar. 1968; Hendrickson, "McNamara: Specters of Vietnam"; McNamara, *In Retrospect*, 316.

387 **McNamara had served** Clifford, *Counsel to the President*, 459–60; Trask and Goldberg, *The Department of Defense*, 78, 83; Hendrickson, "McNamara: Specters of Vietnam."

388 **"God, it was symbolic"** *Ibid*.

The bastards were going to get it

388 **Much had happened** Ayers, *Fugitive Days*, 262–3; Dinitia Smith, "No Regrets for a Love of Explosives," *NYT*, 11 Sept. 2001.

388 **The Weatherman** *WP*, 20 May 1972; Smith, "No Regrets for a Love of Explosives."

388 **"The Pentagon was ground zero"** Ayers, *Fugitive Days*, 256.

389 **A team of three Weathermen** *Ibid.*, 259–60; Michael Getler, "The Pentagon: Huge Building Is No Fortress," *WP*, 20 May 1972.

389 **Ayers awaited** Ayers, *Fugitive Days*, 256.

390 **Rita Campbell and her cleaning ladies** Rita Campbell, author interview, 8 Dec. 2005.

390 **At 12:42 A.M.** *WP,* 19 May 1972; *Star,* 19 May 1972; Ayers, *Fugitive Days,* 260–1.

390 **In her office** Campbell, author interview; Adde, "Solving the Puzzle Palace."

391 **The explosion had blown** *WP,* 20 May 1972; *Star,* 19 May 1972.

391 **Campbell was frantic** Campbell, author interview.

391 **Later that day** AP, 19 May 1972; *WP,* 20 May 1972; Campbell, author interview.

391 **At his safe house** Ayers, *Fugitive Days,* 257, 262; Ayers, author interview.

391 **Terrorism had struck** Ayers, *Fugitive Days,* 263; Campbell, author interview.

Does anyone know what really exists down here?

392 **Air Force Lieutenant Colonel Alan Renshaw** Alan Renshaw, author interview; *WP,* 20 May 1972; *WP,* 27 Mar. 1981.

392 **Clarence Renshaw had gone on** *Assembly,* Mar. 1981; Alan Renshaw, author interview. Clarence Renshaw died in 1980 at the age of seventy-three.

393 **The Pentagon was aging** OSD, "A Status Report to Congress on the Renovation of the Pentagon," 1 Mar. 1994 OSD HO (hereafter 1994 Pentagon renovation report); Goldberg, *The Pentagon,* 137.

393 **The great office bays** Gurney, *The Pentagon,* 117; Walt Freeman, interview with Charles W. Hall, 1992. Dick Groves, living in retirement in an apartment on Connecticut Avenue in Washington, considered it "very stupid to chop it all up, because it screwed up the heating and air-conditioning and all that," according to his son, Richard Groves. Until his death on July 13, 1970, Groves retained an intense proprietary interest in the Pentagon.

393 **Soon after taking office** Donald Rumsfeld, author interview, 19 Apr. 2006; *WP,* 10 Jan. 1981; *Star,* 1 Apr. 1964; Goldberg, *The Pentagon,* 125; *WP,* 5 Sept. 1977; David O. Cooke, oral history with Goldberg, 20 Nov. 1989, oral history collection, OSD HO.

394 **The corridors** General Accounting Office, report to Congress, "Actions Needed to Prevent Further Deterioration and Obsolescence," May 1991 (hereafter GAO buildings report, 1991); Freeman, Hall interview.

394 **In 1984, Steve Carter** Steve Carter, author interview, 18 Nov. 2005.

394 **The basement was worse** "The History of the Pentagon Building Condition," Pentagon Renovation Program Web site, http://renovation.pentagon.mil/history-condition.htm (hereafter PENREN Web site); Carter, author interview; *WP,* 26 June 1992. Stanley "Joe" Nance Allan, who had worked as a carpenter on the original Pentagon construction, returned to the site in 1967 to oversee architectural design at the Pentagon Metro Station as project manager for Harry Weese Associates. "At the beginning, strangely enough, we discovered that the original pile foundation drawings for the Pentagon were nowhere to be found," he said (Allan, "Building the Pentagon").

CHAPTER 19: THE REMAKING OF THE PENTAGON

If we're lucky the floods will be shallow

397 **It was C-Day** Michael R. Gordon and Bernard E. Trainor, *The Generals' War: The Inside Story of the Conflict in the Gulf,* 54–55; H. Norman Schwarzkopf with Peter Petre, *It Doesn't Take a Hero,* 310. Colin Powell with Joseph E. Persico, *My American Journey,* 467.

397 **The Army and Air Force** Carter, author interview; Weisberg, "Edifice Wrecked."

398 **"speed bumps"** Colin Powell, author interview, 3 Feb. 2006.

398 **The coffee** Carter, author interview; Freeman, Hall interview; *WP,* 8 Aug. 1990; GAO buildings report, 1991, 23.

399 **Electricians Bobby McCloud** Bobby McCloud, author interview, 29 Nov. 2005; Reimund Schuster, author interview, 16 Feb. 2006.

399 **The smoky fire** *WP,* 8 Aug. 1990; "The History of the Pentagon Building Condition," PENREN Web site; GAO buildings report, 1991, 23.

399 **Mechanical engineers** Freeman, Hall interview; Weisberg, "Edifice Wrecked."

The horror board

400 **Doc Cooke would later say** *WP,* 27 June 2002; *Army Times,* 20 Mar. 1990; Carter, author interview.

400 **David O. Cooke had many** Cooke, Goldberg oral history, 11 Jan. 1990.

400 **Colin Powell had learned early** Powell, *My American Journey,* 299–300; Powell, author interview.

401 **Defense secretaries and their staffs** Paul Haselbush, author interview, 16 June 2003; Bob Woodward, *The Commanders,* 71; Secretary of Defense William S. Cohen, Cooke award presentation, 21 Jan. 1999, on Pentagon Web site, www .defenselink.mil/speeches; Carter, author interview.

401 **The Pentagon did not meet any** OSD, "A Report to Congress on the Pentagon Renovation Program," 1 March 1993, 10–13, box 1304, OSD HO (hereafter 1993 Pentagon renovation report); Lee Evey, DoD news briefing on Pentagon renovation, 15 Sept. 2001 (hereafter Evey briefing 15 Sept. 2001; this and all DoD news briefings dating after October 1994 are available at www.defenselink.mil/transcripts); "Fixer Upper," *Government Executive,* Aug. 2000; *USA Today,* 28 Jan. 2000. The few passenger elevators that had been added to the building over the years were restricted to the executive suites.

401 **The asbestos used** *WP,* 29 Jan. 1985; 1993 Pentagon renovation report, 9.

401 **Throughout the building** Ken Ringle, "Five-Sided Home of Megathink Blithely Ignores 40th Birthday," *WP,* 15 Jan. 1983; *WP,* 18 Jan. 1985; Charles W. Hall, "The

Rat Patrol; Ever-Growing Rodent Population Gains Ground at the Pentagon," 15 Dec. 1991.

402 **The General Services Administration** Freeman, Hall interview; GAO buildings report, 1991, 34; Judith Havemann, "Pentagon's Maintenance Woes: A Boiling Issue for GSA," *WP*, 27 Mar. 1990; Weisberg, "Edifice Wrecked."

402 **With GSA showing little** Haselbush, author interview; A. L. Singleton, "Mayor of the Pentagon," *Government Executive*, Sept. 1995; GAO buildings report, 1991, 2, 4, 15. The other one was the Department of Agriculture South Building.

402 **Cooke requested that Congress** J. B. Hudson, author interview, 2003; "Miserable Offices," Government Executive, May 1990; "Pentagon Transfer and Renovation Chronology," David O. Cooke papers, OSD HO; 1994 Pentagon renovation report, 33, OSD HO.

403 **The timing turned out** Freeman, Hall interview; David Hackworth, "The Pentagon's $2 Billion Face Lift," *San Francisco Examiner*, 15 July 1994.

403 **Several months before** Cooke, statement before the U.S. Senate Committee on Armed Services Subcommittee on Military Readiness and Defense Infrastructure, 20 May 1993, box 1304, OSD HO; Singleton, "Mayor of the Pentagon."

A certain respectability

403 **"one of the most complex"** Myron P. Curzan, "Report on Pentagon Renovation Project," 14 May 1996, Cooke papers, OSD HO.

403 **The plan began with** Sherrie Winston, "Pentagon Contractors Divide and Conquer," *ENR*, 4 Sept. 2000; 1994 Pentagon renovation report, 22, OSD HO; Cooke letter to Rep. Patricia Schroeder, 17 Apr. 1990, box 1304, OSD HO; *Pentagram*, 18 Oct. 1990.

404 **Later, when it** Pentagon Renovation briefing, "Getting Back to Basics," 22 Oct. 1999, Cooke papers, OSD HO; Evey briefing, 15 Sept. 2001, DoD.

405 **The fiftieth anniversary** Charles W. Hall, "Pentagon Fetes Five Decades in Five Sides," *WP*, 13 May 1993; minutes of the Pentagon fiftieth-anniversary steering group, 26 Oct. 1992 and 23 Apr. 1993, box 1303, OSD HO; Glenn Flood, author interview, Feb. 2006.

405 **The Eiffel tower** AP, "Pentagon Celebrates 50th Birthday, 12 May 1993.

405 **The building so reviled** National Register of Historic Places Inventory, 19, 23, 27, OSD HO.

They wanted the noise to stop

406 **It was shades of 1942** *The Renovator*, Jan. and Feb. 1995, box 1304, OSD HO.

406 **Construction of a new** *The Renovator*, Dec. 1994; Carter, author interview; Lee Evey, author interview, 28 Nov. 2005. The original contractor, the George Hyman Construction Company of Bethesda, Md., merged with Clark in October 2005.

406 **The first work** *The Renovator,* Dec. 1994; "The History of the Pentagon Building Condition," PENREN Web site; Frank Probst, author interview, 22 Nov. 2005.

407 **It was not long before other** Ken Catlow, author interview, 10 Nov. 2005.

407 **The real trouble began** Carter, author interview.

407 **The message was not** DoD news briefing, 16 Mar. 1995; Hamre, author interview.

408 **The work already under contract** John Deutch, Pentagon renovation memo, 9 Mar. 1995, box 1304, OSD HO; Gilbert A. Lewthwaite, "Pentagon face lift at age 52," Baltimore *Sun,* 26 Nov. 1995; Catlow, author interview; *Pentagram,* 22 Mar. 1996.

408 **Doc Cooke had a new generation** Carter, author interview; Deutch, e-mail to author, 11 Feb. 2006.

408 **The review continued** Hamre, author interview; *The Renovator,* Feb. 1997.

409 **At the rate the program** "Problems with Pentagon Renovation Projects," Federal Facilities Division, 23 Jan. 1997, Cooke papers, OSD HO.

409 **But that was not the worst** *Ibid.;* "Sewer Line Corrections," Pentagon renovation program, 14 Aug. 1997, OSD HO; Probst, author interview.

409 **"The program wasn't looked"** *Ibid.*

409 **Hamre, who had succeeded** Hamre, author interview.

The psychology major

409 **Walker Lee Evey knew nothing** Evey, author interviews, 9 July 2002 and 28 Nov. 2005; Steve Vogel, "From Ruins, Pentagon Rises Renewed," 8 Sept. 2002; Evey resume, 2002, author's papers; Hamre, author interview.

410 **On November 17, 1997** Evey, author interview, 2005; *WP,* 7 June 2005.

410 **Hamre and Cooke** Hamre, author interview; "Notes on organizational structure," undated memo, Cooke papers, OSD HO; Evey, author interview, 2005.

411 **Hamre "asked Air Force"** *Ibid.*

411 **Back in his office** *Ibid.; WP,* 17 Nov. 1997.

411 **Hamre warmly ushered** Evey, author interview, 2005; Hamre, author interview.

Whistling in the dark

412 **On his first morning** Evey, author interviews, 2002 and 2005.

412 **In subsequent days** Catlow, author interview; Evey, author interview, 2005.

412 **At one of his first** *Ibid.*

413 **"This guy's lost it"** Probst, author interview.

413 **The first sign** Evey, author interview, 2005.

The Big Bash

413 **The Big Bash** *The Renovator,* Feb/Mar. 1998; Hamre, author interview.

414 **Wedge 1** Evey, author interview, 2002; Catlow, author interview.

414 **It was easier said** Winston, "Pentagon Contractors Divide and Conquer"; "Wedge 1," PENREN Web site, http://renovation.pentagon.mil/projects-W1.htm

414 **As the work continued** Evey, author interviews, 2002 and 2005; Vogel, "From Ruins, Pentagon Rises Renewed"; Les Hunkele, author interview, 9 Dec. 2005.

415 **Evey soon hit a brick wall** *Ibid.;* Catlow, author interview; Brian Dziekonski, author interview, 10 Nov. 2005; Evey, author interview, 2005; Probst, author interview; Allyn Kilsheimer, author interview, Aug. 2002; Winston, "Pentagon Contractors Divide and Conquer."

Terrorists don't arrive on buses

415 **At about 10:30 A.M.** *WP,* 13 Aug. 1998; Steve Coll, *Ghost Wars: The Secret History of the CIA, Afghanistan, and Bin Laden, From the Soviet Invasion to September 10, 2001,* 403–4, 406–412; Peter L. Bergen, *Holy War, Inc., Inside the Secret World of Osama bin Laden,* 108; *Time,* 24 Aug. 1998.

416 **In his office, Doc Cooke** John Jester, author interview, 30 Nov. 2005; 1993 Pentagon renovation report, 17, OSD HO; 1994 Pentagon renovation report, 12, OSD HO.

416 **Cooke had been pushing** Cooke, statement before the U.S. Senate Committee on Armed Services Subcommittee on Military Readiness and Defense Infrastructure," 20 May 1993, box 1304, OSD HO, 1994 Pentagon renovation report, 29; Jester, author interview.

416 **The embassy bombings** Evey, author interview, 2005; Jester, author interview; *The Renovator,* Winter 2001.

417 **The loading docks were hardly** Evey, author interview, 2005; Catlow, author interview; American Society of Civil Engineers. *The Pentagon Building Performance Report,* 6, (hereafter ASCE *Building Performance Report*); Evey briefing, 15 Sept. 2001, DoD.

417 **Putting blast-resistant** Evey, author interview, 2003 and 2005; Rudy DeLeon, Pentagon security memo draft, June 2000, box 1304, OSD HO; Georgine Glatz, author interview, 22 Mar. 2006; *ENR,* 14 Sept. 2001.

417 **The tougher problem** Evey, author interview, 2005; Catlow, author interview; Jester, author interview; Glatz, author interview; *ENR,* 24 Sept. 2001; *60 Minutes II,* 28 Nov. 2001.

417 **The Pentagon's bus-and-subway** Haselbush, author interview; Freeman, Hall interview; *NYT,* 17 Dec. 1983; *NYT,* 11 Mar. 1987; *Pentagram,* Apr. 1987; Evey briefing, 15 Sept. 2001, DoD; *WP,* 5 Sept. 1977; *The Renovator,* Jan./Feb. 2002; *Pentagram,* 28 Feb. 1997; Lyndsey Layton and Steven Ginsberg, "Pentagon to Move Bus Station," *WP,* 14 Apr. 2000.

From an old VW Bug to a big Cadillac

418 **The Arleigh Burke Bell** *Pentagram,* 6 Sept. 2002.

418 **Everything else in the Navy Command** Kevin Shaeffer, e-mail to author, 14

Dec. 2005; Shaeffer, "My Ring Story," *Shipmate,* Sept. 2002; Jo Becker, Steve Vogel, and Michael E. Ruane, "Aboard Room 1D457," *WP,* 16 Sept. 2001; William Wertz, author interview, 15 Sept. 2001.

419 **Wedge 1 was on cost** *The Renovator,* winter 2001; Winston, "Pentagon Contractors Divide and Conquer."

419 **The Remote Delivery Facility** *The Renovator,* winter 2001; Evey, author interview, 2005; Jester, author interview; Dziekonski, author interview. In the interim since the march, the lawn had been paved over for a parking lot.

420 **Evey, for his part** Evey, author interview, 2002.

420 **By September 10** *The Renovator,* Jan./Feb. 2002; *Government Executive,* May 2002; Evey, author interview, 2005. Probst, author interview.

CHAPTER 20: SEPTEMBER 11, 2001

I'm never going to see my boys again

423 **Frank Probst checked the new** Probst, author interview: ASCE *Building Performance Report,* 13; Vince Crawley, "Fortress Reborn," *Army Times,* 16 Sept. 2002.

It's headed toward the Pentagon

424 **American Airlines Flight 77** *The 9/11 Commission Report: Final Report of the National Commission on Terrorist Attacks Upon the United States,* 8; Debra Burlingame, author interview, Sept. 2003.

424 **The Boeing 757** ASCE *Building Performance Report,* 12; Marc Fisher and Don Phillips, "On Flight 77: Our Plane is Being Hijacked," *WP,* 12 Sept. 2001; Annie Gowen and Avis Thomas-Lester, "Family Was Starting Exciting Adventure," *WP,* 20 Sept. 2001; Rudi Williams, "Scholarship honors young attack victim," American Forces Press Service, 6 Sept. 2002; Hamil Harris, "1,000 Recall Studious, Fun-Loving 11-Year-Old," *WP,* 21 Sept. 2001; Ted Olson, *CNN Larry King Weekend,* 6 Jan. 2002.

425 **Hani Hanjour** *The 9/11 Commission Report,* 226.

425 **The idea had been proposed** *Ibid.,* 153–5.

425 **Hanjour was joined** *Ibid.,* 3–4.

426 **The hijackers made their move** *Ibid.,* 8–9.

426 **In the back of the plane** *Ibid.,* 9; Olson, *CNN Larry King Weekend,* 6 Jan. 2002.

426 **At 9:32, air traffic** *The 9/11 Commission Report,* 25, 9, 39; Lieutenant Colonel Robert Rossow, *Uncommon Strength: The Story of the Office of the Army Deputy Chief of Staff for Personnel During the Attack on the Pentagon, 11 September 2001,* 13.

426 **But the aircraft was heading** *The 9/11 Commission Report,* 9; Richard Cox, interview with Margaret Roth, 22 May 2002.

427 **In the last seconds** ASCE *Building Performance Report*, 12; *The* (Allentown, Pa.) *Morning Call*, 11 Sept. 2003.

Something can happen in this world

427 **"My God!"** Becker, et al., "Aboard Room 1D457."

427 **It was the first inkling** *Ibid.;* Shaeffer, e-mail to author; Shaeffer, "My Ring Story."

427 **The lead item** Rowan Scarborough, "Pentagon Staff to Be Trimmed by 15 Percent," *Washington Times,* in DoD "Current News Early Bird," 11 Sept. 2001; Smith, "No Regrets for a Love of Explosives," 11 Sept. 2001.

428 **Shaeffer and his branch** Shaeffer, e-mail to author; Shaeffer, "My Ring Story."

428 **On the opposite** Rumsfeld, author interview, 19 Apr. 2006; Paul Wolfowitz, OSD interview, 19 Apr. 2002, OSD HO; Rumsfeld statement, *The 9/11 Commission: Proceedings and Analysis, Book 3,* 191.

428 **Below Rumsfeld's office** *The 9/11 Commission Report*, 37; Leidig testimony and statement, *The 9/11 Commission: Proceedings and Analysis, Book 4,* 594, 651.

429 **In the Building Operations Center** Carter, author interview; Jester, author interview; Bradley Graham, "Pentagon Unprepared for 'Something We Had Never Even Thought Of,' " *WP,* 16 Sept. 2001; *The 9/11 Commission Report,* 37. The information received by the command center was not about American 77 but instead American 11, which had already crashed into the World Trade Center.

429 **Despite the flurry** Col. Phil McNair, author interview, 25 July 2002; Paul Gonzales, author interview, 6 Mar. 2002; Steve Vogel, "Survivors Healed, but Not Whole," *WP,* 11 Mar. 2002.

I don't want to get burnt again

429 **Frank Probst—on the ground** Probst, author interview.

430 **Alan Wallace** Alan Wallace, interview with Margaret Roth, 2002; *Newsweek,* 27 Sept. 2001.

A rapidly moving avalanche

431 **Army Specialist Chin** Martha Carden, author interview, July 2002; McNair, author interview; Office of the Deputy Chief of Staff for Personnel, "The U.S. Army DCSPER Newsletter, 9-11 Memorial Special Edition," Feb. 2002; Esther Schrader, "At the Pentagon, 'Not Just an Assignment,' " *Los Angeles Times,* 26 Aug. 2002; *The Tulsa World,* 8 Sept. 2002.

431 **The Boeing 757** ASCE *Building Performance Report*, 40–41; Rossow, *Uncommon Strength,* 17.

431 **The avalanche burst** *Ibid.;* Glatz, author interview; ASCE *Building Performance Report*, 39, 50, 12; *The Renovator*, Jan./Feb. 02.

432 **The fuselage in essence** ASCE *Building Performance Report,* 40–1; FBI evidence report, "First Floor—West," author's possession; Steve Vogel, "Lost and, Sometimes, Never Found," *WP,* 13 Sept. 2002.

Hail Mary full of grace. Help me out of this place

432 **In the Navy Command Center** Shaeffer, "My Ring Story"; Shaeffer, e-mail to author; Earl Swift, "Inside the Pentagon on 9/11," *The Virginian-Pilot,* 7–10 Sept. 2002.

433 **In the adjacent DIA** Gonzales, Aaron Cooper, Dave Lanagan, Patty Pague, Dan Hooton, interview with author, 6 Mar. 2002; Vogel, "Survivors Healed, but Not Whole."

There are people behind me

434 **In the Building Operations** Carter, author interview.

434 **Nearby, confusion reigned** Ted Anderson, author interview, 23 July 2002; Karen Baker, e-mail to author, 19 Aug. 2002; Michael E. Ruane, Steve Vogel, Manny Fernandez, Patricia Davis, and Avis Thomas-Lester, "Inch by Inch," *WP,* 8 Sept. 2002.

435 **Two women had jumped** Anderson, author interview; Swift, "Inside the Pentagon on 9/11."

435 **Reentering the door** Anderson, author interview.

436 **Anderson and Braman carried** *Ibid.;* Swift, "Inside the Pentagon on 9/11"; James Schwartz, author interview, 15 Mar. 2006; Ruane et al, "Inch by Inch."

I'm alive

436 **Colonel Phil McNair felt** McNair, author interview; Rossow, *Uncommon Strength,* 39–45; Glatz, author interview; Swift, "Inside the Pentagon on 9/11."

437 **Unlike Ted Anderson** McNair, author interview; Nancy McNair, author interview, August 2002.

437 **McNair heard a voice** McNair, author interview; Swift, "Inside the Pentagon on 9/11"; Rossow, *Uncommon Strength,* 45.

438 **On the first floor, the DIA** Gonzales, author interview; Vogel, "Survivors Healed, but Not Whole."

438 **In the adjacent Navy** Shaeffer, "My Ring Story"; Swift, "Inside the Pentagon on 9/11."

It was just a smoking, burning mess

439 **Rumsfeld had been in the midst** Rumsfeld, author interview.

439 **Hundreds of employees** Payam Zeraat, interview with Margaret Roth, 22 May 2002; Wallace, Roth interview; *WP,* 12 Sept. 2001; Rumsfeld, author interview; Charles Fowler, author interview, 11 Sept. 2001.

440 **Rumsfeld was stunned** Rumsfeld, author interview.

440 **Rumsfeld's instinctive rush** David Von Drehle, "Wrestling With History," *WP*, 13 Nov. 2005; *The 9/11 Commission: Proceedings and Analysis, Book 4*, 564; *The 9/11 Commission Report*, 43–4.

440 **At 10:15 A.M., Rumsfeld walked** Torie Clarke, *Lipstick on a Pig: Winning in the No-Spin Era by Someone Who Knows the Game*, 221.

440 **Fifteen minutes later** *The 9/11 Commission Report*, 43–4, 37–38; DoD news briefing, 12 Sept. 2001; Rumsfeld, author interview.

441 **As Rumsfeld conferred** *The 9/11 Commission Report*, 44, William J. Haynes, OSD interview, 8 Apr. 2003, OSD HO; Wolfowitz, OSD interview; Rumsfeld, OSD interview, 23 Dec. 2002, OSD HO; Rumsfeld, author interview.

That's when I saw real fear

441 **The first Arlington County** Arlington County, "After-Action Report on the Response to the September 11 Terrorist Attack on the Pentagon," 2002, A-8-10 (hereafter Arlington AAR); Mike Smith, interview with Margaret Roth, 2002.

442 **Outside, Arlington County Fire Captain** Arlington AAR, A-66; Schwartz, author interview; Alfred Goldberg, Sarandis Papadopoulos, Diane Putney, Nancy Berlage and Rebecca Welch, *Pentagon 9/11*, Washington D.C.: Office of the Secretary of Defense, Historical Office, 2007, 19; Smith, Roth interview; Capt. Jim McKay, interview with Margaret Roth, 2002, ASCE *Building Performance Report*, 13; Anderson, author interview.

443 **Fifteen minutes after rescue** Arlington AAR, C-46, I-10, *WP*, 12 Sept. 2001; Jester, author interview.

The plane is five minutes out

443 **Inside the Pentagon** Carter, author interview; John Irby, DoD news briefing, 14 Sept. 2001.

Let me know in case I picked the wrong side

444 **Colonel Phil McNair made it** McNair, author interview; Rossow, *Uncommon Strength*, 60–1; Swift, "Inside the Pentagon on 9/11."

445 **Some three hundred employees and rescue** Arlington AAR, B-4; Gonzales, author interview.

445 **McNair saw doctors** McNair, author interview; Swift, "Inside the Pentagon on 9/11."

445 **Steve Carter, reaching** Carter, author interview.

I guess that will be us doing the shooting

445 **At Andrews Air Force Base** David F. Wherley, Jr., author interview, 2 Apr. 2002; Steve Vogel, "Flights of Vigilance Over the Capital," *WP*, 8 Apr. 2002.

446 **Wherley called the Secret Service** *Ibid.; The 9/11 Commission Report,* 44. Wherley, author interview.

446 **Three of the squadron's** Marc Sasseville, author interview, 29 Mar. 2002; Vogel, "Flights of Vigilance Over the Capital"; Heather Penney, author interview, 29 Mar. 2002; Wherley, author interview.

Well, a little too late

447 **In the Pentagon courtyard** Carter, author interview; Bruce Hackert, interview with Margaret Roth, 22 May 2002.

447 **United Airlines Flight 93** *The 9/11 Commission Report,* 33, 41; Arlington AAR, C-46.

448 **At 10:38 A.M.** Arlington AAR, appendix 1, A-31; Schwartz, author interview.

448 **The evacuation** *The 9/11 Commission Report,* 31, 41.

448 **"We are sure"** *Ibid.,* 45

Tell me exactly where it hit

449 **Lee Evey pulled** Evey, author interview, 2002; Vogel, "From Ruins, Pentagon Rises Renewed."

449 **From a purely analytical** Evey, author interview, 21 Sept. 2001; Steve Vogel, "New Pentagon Pays Off," *WP,* 23 Sept. 2001; Evey, DoD news briefing, 15 Sept. 2001; *The Renovator,* Jan/Feb. 2002; McKay, Roth interview.

449 **The plane struck** ASCE *Building Performance Report,* 24–26; *ENR,* 24 Sept. 2001; Probst, author interview; Leo J. Titus, Jr., "A Review of the Temporary Shoring Used to Stabilize the Pentagon After the Terrorist Attacks of September 11th, 2001," 9–10.

449 **All the command centers** PENREN, "Incident Impact, Program Challenges, Required Decisions," Dec. 2001, Evey papers.

450 **"It really hurt"** Downey, author interview.

450 **Most remarkably, the plane** Evey, author interview, 2001; Vogel, "New Pentagon Pays Off"; Evey briefing, 15 Sept. 2001, DoD; Glatz, author interview.

I'm not running anymore

450 **The plane's path** McNair, author interview; Gonzales, author interview; Shaeffer, "My Ring Story."

451 **They had made it out** Smith, Roth interview; Schwartz, author interview.

451 **It was unlike any fire** *Ibid.;* Smith, Roth interview; ASCE *Building Performance Report,* 42–3; James Glanz and Eric Lipton, *City in the Sky: The Rise and Fall of the World Trade Center,* 253; DoD news briefing, 12 Sept. 2002; Arlington AAR, A-16.

451 **Those watching the scene** *Ibid.,* A-8; Smith, Roth interview.

452 **The five-story collapse zone** Larry Collins, "Collapse Rescue Operations at

The Pentagon 9-11 Attack: A Case Study on Urban Search and Rescue Disaster Response," 6; Smith, Roth interview.

452 **At 2 P.M. the evacuation** Arlington AAR, A-30, appendix 1; Smith, Roth interview; Schwartz, author interview; Mike Baker, interview with Margaret Roth, 22 May 2002.

452 **After the all-clear** Smith, Roth interview.

452 **rescuers were not finding anybody** Schwartz, author interview; Titus, "A Review of the Temporary Shoring," 7–8; Collins, "Collapse Rescue Operations," 10–11; *Newsweek,* 27 Sept. 2001.

452 **Out front, Lieutenant Colonel Ted Anderson** Anderson, author interview; Ruane et al, "Inch by Inch"; FBI evidence report, "Pentagon—First Floor West."

They would have won

453 **Inside the National Military** Rumsfeld, author interview; Rumsfeld, OSD interview; Schwartz, author interview; Wolfowitz, OSD interview; Bob Woodward, *Bush at War,* 25.

453 **Rumsfeld decided** Rumsfeld, author interview.

453 **Fire commanders decided** Schwartz, author interview; Anderson, author interview; Carter, author interview; Clarke, *Lipstick on a Pig,* 222–3.

454 **Despite the problems, Rumsfeld** Rumsfeld, author interview; author's notes, DoD news briefing, 11 Sept. 2001; Clarke, *Lipstick on a Pig,* 229–31.

454 **Schwartz was astonished** Schwartz, author interview; Arlington AAR, A-65; Carter, author interview.

Nobody left

455 **Lee Evey had driven** Evey, author interview, 2002; Vogel, "From Ruins, Pentagon Rises Renewed."

455 **In Evey's absence** Michael Sullivan, daily log of activities, 11 Sept. 2001, Evey papers; Sullivan, OSD interview, 18 Oct. 2001, OSD HO; *Government Executive,* May 2002; Evey, "Failure No Option at Pentagon," 1 Sept. 2002, *Building Design and Construction;* Evey briefing, 15 Sept. 2001, DoD; Hunkele, author interview.

455 **When the call came** Kilsheimer, author interview; Vogel, "From Ruins, Pentagon Rises Renewed"; Hunkele, author interview.

456 **Evey had never heard** Evey, author interview, 2002; Kilsheimer, author interview; Titus, "A Review of the Temporary Shoring," 27.

456 **Kilsheimer met** Kilsheimer, author interview; Lt. Gen. Carl Strock, remarks at Phoenix Project reunion, 11 Sept. 2006, Vogel, "From Ruins, Pentagon Rises Renewed"; Strock, CEHO interviews, Sept.–Oct. 2002, CEHO.

456 That night, Evey addressed *Building Design and Construction,* 1 July 2002; Evey, author interview, 2005.

CHAPTER 21: THE PHOENIX PROJECT

The Pentagon had held

459 The orange glow Anderson, author interview; author's notes from scene, 11 and 12 Sept. 2001.

459 Some ten thousand workers Steve Vogel, "Defiant Workers Return to Posts at the Pentagon," *WP,* 13 Sept. 2001; Glenn Flood, e-mail to author, 16 Mar. 2006; Anderson, author interview.

460 Donald Rumsfeld, back in Rumsfeld, address to troops and DoD personnel, 12 Sept. 2001, OSD; Rumsfeld, DoD news briefing, 12 Sept. 2001.

460 The ones most impressed Carter, author interview; Irby, DoD news briefing, 14 Sept. 2001.

460 It was hardly business Vogel, "Defiant Workers Return to Posts at the Pentagon"; Schwartz, author interview; Arlington Fire Chief Ed Plaugher, DoD news briefing, 12 Sept. 2001.

460 An American flag James T. Jackson, author interview, 16 Mar. 2006; Schwartz, author interview.

Hell's Kitchen

461 By the afternoon of September 12 Schwartz, author interview; *WP,* 13 Sept. 2001; *NYT,* 14 Sept. 2001.

461 The chaos of the first Author's notes, visit to site, 13 Sept. 2001; Arthur Santana, "Helping and Hoping, a Man Resolves to Rescue His Wife," *WP,* 13 Sept. 2001.

461 Arlington police detective Don Fortunato, interview with Margaret Roth, 24 May 2002.

462 Rescuers had not officially Kilsheimer, author interview; Vogel, "From Ruins, Pentagon Rises Renewed." Collins, "Collapse Rescue Operations," 6.

462 Shoring had begun Titus, "A Review of the Temporary Shoring," 17–19.

462 Rescuers methodically Collins, "Collapse Rescue Operations," 6–7.

462 Shoring had begun Titus, "A Review of the Temporary Shoring," 17–19.

462 Rescuers methodically Collins, "Collapse Rescue Operations," 6–7.

463 Whenever a body was found *Ibid.,* 8; Command Sergeant Major Aubrey Butts, author interview, 13 Sept. 2001.

463 A large area Collins, "Collapse Rescue Operations," 9–11, Kilsheimer, author interview.

You make it happen

464 Unlike in New York Evey, author interview, 2002; *WP,* 25 June 2002.

464 **Even as search** Hunkele, author interview; Kilsheimer, author interview; Evey notes, 13 Sept. 2001, Evey papers.

464 **Cooke refused** *Ibid.;* Evey notes, 17 Sept. 2001, Evey papers.

464 **The Corps was asked** *The Renovator,* Mar. 2002; Evey, DoD news briefing, 7 Mar. 2002 (hereafter Evey briefing, 7 Mar. 2002).

464 **Evey quickly selected AMEC** OSD press release, 15 Sept. 2001 (this and all OSD press releases from October 1994 on are available at www.defenselink.mil/ releases); Evey, memo to deputy secretary of defense, 14 Sept. 2001, Evey papers.

465 **The main question was who** Evey, author interview, 2002; Kilsheimer, author interview; Schwartz, author interview; Vogel, "From Ruins, Pentagon Rises Renewed"; Kilsheimer, remarks to Fairfax County Department Works and Environmental Services conference, 2 Apr. 2004 (hereafter Kilsheimer Fairfax remarks); FBI Special Agent Garrett MacKenzie, remarks at Phoenix Project reunion, 11 Sept. 2006.

465 **Kilsheimer was exactly** Evey, author interview, 2002; Catlow, author interview; *ENR,* 4 Feb. 2002.

465 **On Friday, September 14** Evey, author interview, 2002; Kilsheimer, author interview.

Only by the grace of God

466 **That Sunday night** Evey, author interview, 2002; Vogel, "From Ruins, Pentagon Rises Renewed."

466 **After five days at the site** *Ibid.;* Kilsheimer, author interview.

466 **The first step** *Ibid.;* Evey briefing, 7 Mar. 2002, DoD; ASCE *Building Performance Report,* 9, 58.

466 **Core samples** Evey briefing, 7 Mar. 2002, DoD; Kerry Hall, "Concrete Autopsy Helps Strengthen the Pentagon," *National Geographic Today,* 9 July 2002.

467 **It meant many** Kilsheimer, author interview; Kilsheimer, OSD interview, 29 Oct. 2001.

467 **It was surprising** ASCE *Building Performance Report,* 1, 4; Baltimore *Sun,* 22 Sept. 2001; Paul Mlakar, author interview, 11 May 2006. A similar team was sent to the World Trade Center.

Remains

467 **At 8:45 in the morning** *WP,* 22 Sept. 2001; "Inside the Wire," Military District of Washington public affairs, 26 Sept. 2001.

468 **The Army had lost the most** *Ibid.;* DoD casualty updates, Sept.–Oct. 2001, www.defenselink.mil/news; Steve Vogel, "Tear-Stained Spreadsheets," *WP,* 10 Oct. 2001.

468 **The search for remains** Arlington AAR, C-55-56; Steve Vogel, "On the Job

Amid the Surreal," *WP,* 30 Sept. 2001; Zeraat, Roth interview; Major Ed Monarez, interview with Margaret Roth, 2002.

I would certainly be dead now

469 **The same day the FBI** Vogel, "New Pentagon Pays Off"; author's notes from tour with Evey, 21 Sept. 2001; AP, 6 Oct. 2001; *The Renovator,* summer 2002.

469 **Three days earlier** Peter Murphy, e-mail to Evey, 19 Sept. 2001, PENREN; Steve Vogel, "Retaking a Lost Position," *WP,* 16 Aug. 2002. The flag was rescued on September 13, marched out of the Pentagon by Marines and soldiers, and in December 2001 orbited Earth aboard the space shuttle *Endeavour.*

470 **Many had similar stories** Susan Morrisey Livingstone letter to Cooke and Evey, 18 Sept. 2001, Evey papers; Stephen Pietropaoli e-mail to Evey, 14 Sept. 2001, Evey papers; ASCE *Building Performance Report,* 16–7, 44; Titus, "A Review of the Temporary Shoring," 14–15; Vogel, "Retaking a Lost Position"; *Today's Facility Manager,* September 2002; Goldberg, author interview, Mar. 2006; Glatz, author interview.

470 **But there were other stories** *Ibid.;* Evey, author interview, 2002, 2005; Glatz, e-mail to Evey, 24 Sept. 2001, Evey papers; McNair, author interview; *The Renovator,* Mar. 2002.

470 **The blast-resistant windows** Glatz, author interview; *The Renovator,* Jan./Feb 2002.

470 **The big open-bay** Glatz, author interview.

471 **Most disturbing** *Ibid.;* Schwartz, author interview; Evey, author interviews, 2002, 2005; *The Renovator,* Mar. 2002.

471 **The main problem** Glatz, author interview; Rossow, *Uncommon Strength,* xi–xii, 22, 55; McNair, author interview.

Somebody could fly into the doughnut hole

472 **Evey's initial reaction** Evey, author interview, 2002; Schwartz, author interview.

472 **Some of the fixes** Evey, author interview, 2002; Evey briefings, 7 Mar. and 11 June 2002, DoD; *The Renovator,* Mar. 2002; Glatz, author interview; Michael Sullivan, author interview, Sept. 2003; Steve Vogel, "Workers Push to Fortify Military Headquarters," *WP,* 7 Sept. 2003.

472 **the safety upgrades were similar** Robins memo to Somervell's office, 20 Dec. 1941, I, CEHO.

472 **Representative John Murtha** Michael Sullivan, e-mail to Wendy Thompson and Stacie Condrell, 26 Oct. 2001, Evey papers; Evey e-mail to Cooke, 2 Nov. 2001, Evey papers; Evey briefing, 7 Mar. 2002, DoD.

473 **Security officials decided** Jester, author interview; Haselbush, author interview; Sullivan, author interview; Vogel, "Workers Push to Fortify Military Headquarters."

473 **The original renovation plan** "Incident Impact, Program Challenges, Required Decisions," PENREN, Dec. 2001, Evey papers; Catlow, author interview; Evey, author interview, 2005.

473 **In October, Wolfowitz** Wolfowitz, "Chemical, Biological and Radiological (CBR) Protection and Response for Pentagon Personnel," 26 Oct. 2001, Evey papers.

473 **To Evey's astonishment** Evey, e-mails to John Batiste, 1, 2, and 3 Oct. 2001, Evey papers; Batiste, e-mails to Evey, 1 and 2 Oct. 2001, Evey papers.

474 **Batiste scheduled** Evey, author interview, 2005; Wolfowitz, OSD interview.

474 **"You don't think"** Rumsfeld, author interview.

Are you nuts?

474 **The crash scene** *WP*, 3 Oct. 2001; Evey, author interview, 2002; Vogel, "From Ruins, Pentagon Rises Renewed." The section is based on this account.

474 **crews kept working** *Ibid.;* Lynne Perri, "Pentagon Waging a Massive Effort," *USA Today*, 23 Nov. 2001; Kilsheimer Fairfax remarks; *The Renovator*, Mar. 2002.

474 **Kilsheimer was worried** Kilsheimer, author interview; Pat Riley, author interview, 20 Mar. 2006; Pino-Marina, "Indiana Plant Makes its Mark on History"; Kilsheimer Fairfax remarks.

475 **All around the site** Will Colston, author interview, August 2002; Evey, author interview, 2002.

475 **Evey considered the idea** *Ibid.;* Vogel, "From Ruins, Pentagon Rises Renewed." Evey briefing, 15 Sept. 2001, DoD; Sullivan, daily log of activities, 12 Sept. 2001, Evey papers; Kilsheimer, OSD interview.

475 **On October 5** Evey, CNN.com, 5 Oct. 2001; Evey, author interview, 2002; Vogel, "From Ruins, Pentagon Rises Renewed."

475 **"Are you nuts?"** *Ibid.*

The view from Arlington

475 **Demolition began** Ruane et al, "Inch by Inch."

476 **Employees inside** Perri, "Pentagon waging a massive effort"; Steve Vogel, "Pentagon Halfway Back in Countdown from Inferno," 10 Mar. 2002; Kilsheimer, OSD interview.

476 **Most estimates of how long** Evey briefings, 7 Mar. and 11 June 2002, DoD; Kilsheimer, author interview; PENREN incident status briefing, 31 Oct. 2001, Evey papers.

476 **From the gravesites** McNair, author interview; Ruane et al, "Inch by Inch."

I'm not leaving until this damn place is rebuilt

476 **Kilsheimer felt it too** Kilsheimer, Washington Building Congress Bulletin, Sept.

2002; Kilsheimer, OSD interview; Evey briefing, 7 Mar. 2002, DoD; Vogel, "From Ruins, Pentagon Rises Renewed."

477 **It was time** *Ibid.;* Hunkele, author interview; Evey, author interview, 2002.

477 **Thousands of Phoenix Project** Kilsheimer, author interview.

477 **As was the case** Perri, "Pentagon Waging a Massive Effort"; "CBS Morning News," 21 Dec. 2001; Mary Beth Sheridan, "U.S. Symbol, Latino Muscle," *WP,* 4 Apr. 2002; Fredrick Kunkle, "At Pentagon, Healing and Rebuilding," *WP,* 22 Jan. 2002; Carter, author interview; Catlow, author interview; Evey, author interview, 2002; Stephen Ludden, author interview, 3 Apr. 2006.

478 **Everyone worked with purpose** Fredrick Kunkle, "On the Job With Pride and Pain," *WP,* 18 Feb. 2002; Travis Fox, "Rebuilding a Fortress, Rebuilding a Life," 16 Aug. 2002, washingtonpost.com; "The Early Show," CBS, 11 Mar. 2002; Wilmington *News-Journal,* 11 Apr. 2002.

The odd couple

479 **Evey and Kilsheimer** Kilsheimer, author interview; Vogel, "From Ruins, Pentagon Rises Renewed."

479 **Working seven days a week** *Ibid.;* Evey e-mail about Kilsheimer, 28 Nov. 2001, Evey papers; Ori Nir, "A Son of Survivors Raises the Pentagon from the Ashes," *Forward,* 20 Sept. 2002; Kilsheimer, OSD interview; Kilsheimer Fairfax remarks.

480 **Whenever questions were raised** *Ibid.;* Evey, author interview, 2005.

480 **Evey considered himself** *Ibid.*

481 **Steve Carter** Carter, author interview.

481 **Of course, it was easy** *Ibid.;* Evey, author interview, 2005.

Out of the ground

481 **In the new year** Vogel, "From Ruins, Pentagon Rises Renewed"; Anderson, author interview.

481 **By mid-January** *ENR,* 4 Feb. 2002; Kilsheimer, author interview; Ludden, author interview; Evey briefing, 7 Mar. 2002, DoD.

482 **Modern construction techniques** *Ibid.;* Kilsheimer, Washington Building Congress Bulletin, Sept. 2002; Carter, author interview.

483 **By late February** Evey briefing, 7 Mar. 2002, DoD; Pino-Marina, "Indiana Plant Makes its Mark on History"; Riley, author interview; "Limestone on Way to Pentagon," *The* (Bloomington, Indiana) *Herald Times,* 20 Dec. 2001.

483 **On February 25** Ruane et al, "Inch by Inch"; Evey briefing, 11 June 2002, DoD; Evey, author interview, 2002.

The countdown clock

484 **Evey changed the schedule** Evey briefing, 7 Mar. 2002, DoD; Vogel, "Pentagon Halfway Back in Countdown From Inferno"; *WP,* 12 Mar. 2002.

484 **On April 5, the last** Armed Forces Information Service, 5 Apr. 2002.

484 **On June 11** Evey briefing, 11 June 2002, DoD; Steve Vogel, "Final Stone Placed in Pentagon's Exterior," *WP,* 12 June 2002; *The Renovator,* summer 2002.

People needed to remember

485 **Peter Murphy's knees** Peter Murphy, author interview, 15 Aug. 2002; Vogel, "Retaking a Lost Position."

486 **Earlier, Evey overheard** Evey, author interview, 2002.

486 **Murphy had been astonished** Murphy, author interview, 15 Aug. 2002; Vogel, "Retaking a Lost Position."

486 **"They felt they had"** Evey, remarks on fifth anniversary of 9/11, posted on www.nightofthephoenix.com, Sept. 2006.

EPILOGUE

September 11, 2001

489 **Except for the wind** Steve Vogel and Fredrick Kunkle, "Day of Remembrance and Celebration," *WP,* 12 Sept. 2002.

489 **When Secretary of Defense Donald Rumsfeld** John Tierney, "Honoring Those Lost and Celebrating a New Symbol of Resistance," *NYT,* 12 Sept. 2002; Andrea Stone, "Mourners Shaky but Present Strong Face," *USA Today,* 12 Sept. 2002; Rumsfeld remarks at Pentagon memorial ceremony, 11 Sept. 2002, www.defenselink.mil/speeches.

490 **"As long as terrorists"** Bush remarks at the Pentagon, White House Web site, www.whitehouse.gov/news/releases/2002/09/20020911.html; Stone, "Mourners Shaky but Present Strong Face."

490 **Doe Cooke was conspicuous** *WP,* 27 June 2002; *WP,* 18 July 2002; AP, 12 July 2002; Powell, author interview.

491 **Lee Evey would retire** Evey, author interview, 2002; Evey, remarks to PENREN program, 9 Oct. 2003, author's notes; *WP,* 16 Oct. 2003.

491 **Allyn Kilsheimer** Kilsheimer, author interview.

491 **The Pentagon ceremony** Vogel and Kunkle, "Day of Remembrance and Celebration"; Armed Forces Information Service, 11 Sept. 2002; *The Renovator,* Fall/Winter 2002; Wolfowitz remarks at ceremony honoring Pentagon builders, 11 Sept. 2002, www.defenselink.mil/speeches.

A $5 billion affair

492 **The work** Catlow, author interview.

492 **Upon the official completion** *Ibid.;* Vogel, "Workers Push to Fortify Military Headquarters"; OSD, "A Status Report to Congress on the Renovation of the Pen-

tagon," 1 Mar. 2005, PENREN; Douglas Johnson, Defense Facilities Directorate program manager, tour of roof, 10 Nov. 2005.

492 **Further adding to the tally** Catlow, author interview; PENREN "Command Communications Survivability Program" briefing, July 2002, Evey papers.

492 **the Pentagon command centers** Sullivan, e-mail to Charles T. Horner about accelerated renovation, 30 Oct. 2001, Evey papers; Evey, author interview 30 Mar. 2006; Catlow, author interview; Vogel, "Workers Push to Fortify Military Headquarters"; author's tour of basement work, September 2003.

493 **Rumsfeld had seized** Rumsfeld, author interview; Vogel, "Workers Push to Fortify Military Headquarters"; Sullivan, author interview; Catlow, author interview; *Defense Daily,* 23 Oct. 2003; *Defense Daily,* 3 Dec. 2003; Lt. Col. T. V. Johnson, Office of the Joint Chiefs of Staff, e-mail to author, 7 July 2006; Navy News Service, 11 Sept. 2002.

493 **Various extras were thrown** author's tours of athletic center and conference center site, Nov. 2005; *The Renovator,* Mar. 2004, Oct. 2005, Oct. 2006.

493 **By 2007** Catlow, author interview; Bill Hopper, PENREN, e-mail to author 30 June 2006; *The Renovator,* November 2005. Catlow retired in September 2006 and was replaced as director by Sajeel Ahmed.

494 **In November 2005** Rumsfeld, author interview; Michael B. Donley memo to Rumsfeld, 10 Nov. 2005, OSD; Evey, author interview.

494 **Ironically, despite the billions** Catlow, author interview; "Population of the Pentagon, 1942–1990," OSD HO.

494 **Despite the safety** author interviews with Pentagon employees; Hamre, author interview.

We claim this ground

495 **The project moved swiftly** U.S. Army Corps of Engineers Baltimore District, press release, 20 May 2002; Steve Vogel, "For Pentagon, A Memorial 'Like No Other,' " *WP,* 4 Mar. 2003.

495 **When the design** *Ibid.;* Timothy Dwyer, "Something Personal in Stainless Steel," *WP,* 8 Mar. 2005; Donley memo to Rumsfeld, 10 Nov. 2005; Jim Laychak, author interview, 15 June 2006; Julie Beckman, author interview, 15 June 2006; Pentagon Memorial Web site, www.pentagonmemorial.net. Information about donations for the memorial is available at the Web site.

496 **On June 15, 2006** Pentagon Memorial groundbreaking, author's notes, 15 June 2006; Lisa Dolan, author interview, 15 June 2006; Tom Heidenberger, author interview, 15 June 2006; Laychak, author interview; Rumsfeld, author interview.

497 **Yet when Rumsfeld spoke** Kris Fisher, author interview, 15 June 2006; Rumsfeld remarks, Pentagon groundbreaking ceremony, 15 June 2006, www.defenselink.mil/speeches; *WP,* 16 June 2006.

497 **Nearby, Abraham Scott** Abraham Scott, author interview, 15 June 2006.

For the ages

497 On January 23, 2003 Mlakar, author interview; James Glanz, "Lessons Drawn from Attack on Pentagon May Stay Secret," *NYT,* 5 Nov. 2002; Jester, author interview.

498 The report affirmed ASCE *Building Performance Report,* 1–2, 23, 44; Mlakar, author interview; *NYT,* 23 Jan. 2003; Glatz, author interview.

498 The building's structural redundancy ASCE *Building Performance Report,* 58–9; Mlakar, author interview.

499 Moreover, the Pentagon had *Ibid.;* ASCE *Building Performance Report,* 9–10, 41, 49, 58–9.

499 "It makes a strong column" Walker, author interview, 5 Dec. 2005; ASCE *Building Performance Report,* 58.

499 Two columns in particular *Ibid.,* 49.

SELECTED
BIBLIOGRAPHY

BOOKS

Abel, Elie. *The Missile Crisis*. Philadelphia: J. B. Lippincott Co., 1966.

Atkinson, Rick. *An Army at Dawn: The War in North Africa, 1942–1943*. New York: Henry Holt, 2002.

Ayers, Bill. *Fugitive Days*. Boston: Beacon Press, 2001.

Bergen, Peter L. *Holy War, Inc.: Inside the Secret World of Osama bin Laden,* New York: The Free Press, 2001.

Bigler, Philip. *In Honored Glory: Arlington National Cemetery: The Final Post*. Clearwater, Fla.: Vandamere Press, 1987.

Borklund, C. W. *Men of the Pentagon: From Forrestal to McNamara*. New York: Frederick A. Praeger, 1966.

Bradley, Omar N. and Clay Blair. *A General's Life: An Autobiography by General of the Army Omar N. Bradley*. New York: Simon and Schuster, 1983.

Brauer, Carl M. *The Man Who Built Washington: A Life of John McShain*. Wilmington, De.: Hagley Museum and Library, 1996.

Brinkley, David. *Washington Goes to War*. New York: Ballantine Books, 1989.

Brownell, Charles E., Calder Loth, William M.S. Rasmussen, and Richard Guy Wilson. *The Making of Virginia Architecture*. Richmond: Virginia Museum of Fine Arts, 1992.

Brugioni, Dino A. *Eyeball to Eyeball: The Inside Story of the Cuban Missile Crisis*. New York: Random House, 1991.

Burns, James MacGregor. *Roosevelt: The Lion and the Fox*. New York: Harcourt, Brace and Co., 1956.

———. *Roosevelt: The Soldier of Freedom, 1940–1945*. New York: Harcourt Brace Jovanovich, Inc., 1970.

Califano, Joseph A., Jr. *The Triumph and Tragedy of Lyndon Johnson: The White House Years*. New York: Simon & Schuster, 1991.

Childs, Marquis. "Washington Is a State of Mind," 1942, in *Katharine Graham's Washington*. New York: Alfred A. Knopf, 2002.

Chronology of World War II: The Day by Day Illustrated Record, 1939–45. Compiled by Christopher Argyle. New York: Exeter Books, 1980.

Clarke, Torie. *Lipstick on a Pig: Winning in the No-Spin Era by Someone Who Knows the Game*. New York: Free Press, 2006.

Clifford, Clark with Richard Holbrooke. *Counsel to the President: A Memoir*. New York: Random House, 1991.

Coll, Steve. *Ghost Wars: The Secret History of the CIA, Afghanistan, and Bin Laden, From the Soviet Invasion to September 10, 2001*. New York: The Penguin Press, 2004.

Cowdrey, Albert E. *A City for the Nation: The Army Engineers and the Building of Washington, D.C., 1790–1967*. Washington, D.C.: Office of the Chief of Engineers, U.S. Army Corps of Engineers, 1979.

Eisenhower, Dwight D. *Crusade in Europe*. Garden City, N.Y.: Doubleday, 1948.

———. *At Ease: Stories I Tell to Friends*. Garden City, N.Y.: Doubleday, 1967.

Fine, Lenore and Jesse A. Remington. *The Corps of Engineers: Construction in the United States*. Washington, D.C.: Office of the Chief of Military History, U.S. Army, 1972.

Foote, Shelby. *The Civil War: Fort Sumter to Perryville*. New York: Vintage Books, 1958.

Forrestal, James. *The Forrestal Diaries*. Edited by Walter Millis. New York: The Viking Press, 1951.

Fowle, Barry W., ed. *Builders and Fighters: U.S. Army Engineers in World War II*. Fort Belvoir, Va.: Office of History, United States Army Corps of Engineers, 1992.

Glanz, James and Eric Lipton. *City in the Sky: The Rise and Fall of the World Trade Center*. New York: Henry Holt and Co., 2003.

Goldberg, Alfred. *The Pentagon: The First Fifty Years*. Washington, D.C.: Historical Office, Office of the Secretary of Defense, 1992.

Goodwin, Doris Kearns. *No Ordinary Time: Franklin and Eleanor Roosevelt: The Home Front in World War II*. New York: Simon & Schuster, 1994.

Gordon, Michael R. and Bernard E. Trainor. *The Generals' War: The Inside Story of the Conflict in the Gulf*. Boston: Little, Brown and Co., 1995.

Graham, Katharine. *Katharine Graham's Washington*. New York: Alfred A. Knopf, 1992.

Green, Constance McLaughlin. *Washington: A History of the Capital, 1800–1950*. Princeton, N.J.: Princeton University Press, 1962.

Groueff, Stephane. *Manhattan Project: The Untold Story of the Making of the Atomic Bomb.* Boston: Little, Brown, 1967.

Groves, Leslie R. *Now It Can Be Told: The Story of the Manhattan Project.* 1962. Introd. Edward Teller. New York: Da Capo Press, 1983.

Gurney, Gene. *The Pentagon: The Nerve Center of United States Defenses Throughout the World: A Pictorial Story.* New York: Crown Publishers, 1964.

Gutheim, Frederick. *Worthy of the Nation: The History of Planning for the National Capital.* Washington, D.C.: National Capital Planning Commission and Smithsonian Institution Press, 1977.

Halberstam, David. *The Best and the Brightest,* twentieth-anniversary ed. New York: Ballantine Books, 1993.

Hart, Scott. *Washington at War: 1941–1945.* Englewood Cliffs, N.J.: Prentice-Hall, 1970.

Hendrickson, Paul. *The Living and the Dead: Robert McNamara and Five Lives of a Lost War.* New York: Alfred A. Knopf, 1996.

Herring, George C. *LBJ and Vietnam: A Different Kind of War.* Austin, Tx.: University of Texas Press, 1994.

Hodgson, Godfrey. *The Colonel: The Life and Wars of Henry Stimson, 1867–1950.* 1990. Boston: Northeastern University Press, 1992.

Hoffman, Abbie. *Soon to Be a Major Motion Picture.* New York: Perigee Books, 1980.

Hoopes, Townsend and Douglas Brinkley. *Driven Patriot: The Life and Times of James Forrestal.* New York: Alfred A. Knopf, 1992.

Isaacson, Walter and Evan Thomas. *The Wise Men: Six Friends and the World They Made.* New York: Simon & Schuster, 1986.

Jackson, Bruce, "The Battle of the Pentagon." In *Who We Are: An Atlantic Chronicle of the United States and Vietnam.* Robert Manning and Michael Janeway, eds. Boston: Little, Brown, 1969.

Jones, Vincent C. *Manhattan: The Army and the Atomic Bomb.* Washington, D.C.: Center of Military History, U.S. Army, 1985.

Junior League of Washington. *The City of Washington: An Illustrated History.* Thomas Froncek, ed. New York: Alfred A. Knopf, 1977.

Kaplan, Lawrence S., Ronald D. Landa, and Edward J. Drea. *The McNamara Ascendancy, 1961–1965.* Washington, D.C.: Historical Office, Office of the Secretary of Defense, 2006.

Kohler, Sue A. *The Commission of Fine Arts: A Brief History, 1910–1995.* Washington, D.C.: U.S. Government Printing Office, 1996.

Larrabee, Eric. *Commander in Chief: Franklin Delano Roosevelt, His Lieutenants, and Their War.* New York: Simon & Schuster, 1987.

Lawren, William. *The General and the Bomb: A Biography of General Leslie R. Groves, Director of the Manhattan Project.* New York: Dodd, Mead & Co., 1988.

Lee, Dorothy Ellis. *A History of Arlington County Virginia.* Richmond, Va.: The Dietz Press, 1946.

Mailer, Norman. *The Armies of the Night*. 1968. New York: Plume, 1994.

Marshall, George Catlett. *The Papers of George Catlett Marshall*, vols. 2–3. Larry I. Bland, ed. Baltimore: The Johns Hopkins University Press, 1986, 1991.

McCullough, David. *Truman*. New York: Simon & Schuster, 1992.

McFarland, Keith D. and David L. Roll. *Louis Johnson and the Arming of America: The Roosevelt and Truman Years*. Bloomington, Ind.: Indiana University Press, 2005.

McNamara, Robert S. with Brian VanDeMark. *In Retrospect: The Tragedy and Lessons of Vietnam*. New York: Times Books-Random House, 1995.

Melder, Keith, ed. *City of Magnificent Intentions: A History of the District of Columbia*. Second ed. Washington, D.C.: Intac, Inc. for Associates in Renewal of Education, 1997.

Millett, Allan R. and Peter Maslowski. *For the Common Defense: A Military History of the United States of America*. Rev. ed. New York: The Free Press, 1994.

Millet, John D. *The Organization and Role of the Army Service Forces*. Washington, D.C.: Office of the Chief of Military History, Department of the Army, 1954.

Monat, Pawel with John Dille. *Spy in the U.S.* London: Frederick Muller, 1964.

Nichols, Kenneth D. *The Road to Trinity*. New York: William Morrow, 1987.

Norris, Robert S. *Racing for the Bomb: General Leslie R. Groves, The Manhattan Project's Indispensable Man*. South Royalton, Vt.: Steerforth Press, 2002.

Ohl, John Kennedy. *Supplying the Troops: General Somervell and American Logistics in WWII*. DeKalb, Ill.: Northern Illinois University Press, 1994.

Passonneau, Joseph R. *Washington Through Two Centuries: A History in Maps and Images*. New York: The Monacelli Press, 2004.

Pogue, Forrest C. *George C. Marshall: Ordeal and Hope, 1939–1942*. 1966. New York: Penguin Books, 1993.

———. *George C. Marshall: Organizer of Victory, 1943–1945*. 1973. New York: Penguin Books, 1993.

———. *George C. Marshall: Statesman, 1945–1949*. New York: Viking, 1980.

Pottker, Jan. *Sara and Eleanor: The Story of Sara Delano Roosevelt and Her Daughter-in-Law, Eleanor Roosevelt*. New York: St. Martin's Press, 2004.

Powell, Colin with Joseph E. Persico. *My American Journey*. New York: Random House, 1995.

Raymond, Jack. *Power at the Pentagon*. New York: Harper & Row, 1964.

Rearden, Steven L. *History of the Office of the Secretary of Defense: The Formative Years, 1947–1950*. Washington, D.C.: Office of the Secretary of Defense, Historical Office, 1984.

Rhoads, William B. "Franklin Roosevelt and Washington Architecture." In *Records of the Columbia Historical Society of Washington, D.C., Volume 52*. J. Kirkpatrick Flack, ed. Charlottesville: The University Press of Virginia, 1989.

Rhodes, Richard. *The Making of the Atomic Bomb*. New York: Simon & Schuster, 1986.

Roberts, Chalmers M. *Washington, Past and Present: A Pictorial History of the Nation's Capital*. Washington, D.C.: Public Affairs Press, 1949–1950.

Rogner, E. A. *The Pentagon: "A National Institution."* Alexandria, Va.: D'OR Press, 1984.

Rogow, Arnold A. *James Forrestal: A Study of Personality, Politics, and Policy.* New York: The Macmillan Co., 1963.

Roosevelt, Franklin D. *Complete Presidential Press Conferences of Franklin D. Roosevelt,* volumes 17–18, 1941. New York: Da Capo Press, 1972.

Roosevelt, Franklin D. *The Public Papers and Addresses of Franklin D. Roosevelt, 1941.* Samuel I. Rosenman, ed. New York: Harper & Bros., 1950.

Rose, C. B., Jr. *Arlington County, Virginia: A History.* Arlington, Va.: Arlington Historical Society, 1976.

Rossow, Robert. *Uncommon Strength: The Story of the Office of the Army Deputy Chief of Staff for Personnel During the Attack on the Pentagon, 11 September 2001.* Washington, D.C.: Office of the Deputy Chief of Staff, G-1, Department of the Army, 2004.

Scheips, Paul J. *The Role of Federal Military Forces in Domestic Disorders, 1945–1992.* Washington, D.C.: Center of Military History, United States Army, 2005.

Schwarzkopf, H. Norman with Peter Petre. *It Doesn't Take a Hero.* New York: Linda Grey/Bantam Books, 1992.

Scott, Pamela. *Capital Engineers: The U.S. Army Corps of Engineers in the Development of Washington, D.C., 1790–2004.* Alexandria, Va.: Office of History, U.S. Army Corps of Engineers, 2005.

Shapley, Deborah. *Promise and Power: The Life and Times of Robert McNamara.* Boston: Little, Brown, 1993.

Sherwood, Robert E. *Roosevelt and Hopkins: An Intimate History.* New York: Harper & Bros., 1948.

Smith, Jean Edward. *Lucius D. Clay: An American Life.* New York: Henry Holt, 1990.

Stimson, Henry L., and McGeorge Bundy. *On Active Service in Peace and War.* New York: Harper & Bros., 1948.

Stoler, Mark A. *George C. Marshall: Soldier Statesman of the American Century.* New York: Twayne, 1989.

Trask, Roger R. and Alfred Goldberg. *The Department of Defense, 1947–1997: Organization and Leaders.* Washington, D.C.: Historical Office, Office of the Secretary of Defense, 1997.

Trewhitt, Henry L. *McNamara.* New York: Harper & Row, 1971.

Tugwell, Rexford G. *The Democratic Roosevelt: A Biography of Franklin D. Roosevelt.* Garden City, N.Y.: Doubleday, 1957.

Twichell, Heath. *Northwest Epic: The Building of the Alaska Highway.* New York: St. Martin's Press, 1992.

Wells, Tom. *The War Within: America's Battle over Vietnam.* Berkeley, Calif: University of California Press, 1994.

Wilson, Theodore A. *The First Summit: Roosevelt and Churchill at Placentia Bay, 1941.* Revised ed. Lawrence, Kan.: University Press of Kansas, 1941 and 1991.

Woodward, Bob. *The Commanders.* New York: Simon & Schuster, 1991.

———. *Bush at War.* New York: Simon & Schuster, 2002.

PERIODICALS

"Access to the World's Largest Building." *ENR.* 25 Mar. 1943.

Armagnac, Alden P. "Nerve Center of the Fighting Forces." *Popular Science,* Feb. 1943.

"The Army's Giant 'Five-by-Five.' " *Popular Mechanics,* Mar. 1943.

"The Army Raises a Ghost." *Time,* 18 Aug. 1941.

"The Army's Pentagon Building." *Architectural Record,* Jan. 1943.

Ball, Frank L. "The Arlington I Have Known." *Arlington Historical Magazine,* 1964.

Casey, Steven. "Franklin D. Roosevelt, Ernst 'Putzi' Hanfstaengl and the 'S-Project', June 1942–June 1944." *Journal of Contemporary History,* 2000.

"Concreting a 100-Acre Office Building." *ENR,* 4 June 1942.

Dunbar, L. D. "Army Man at Work," parts I and II. *The New Yorker,* 10 and 17 Feb. 1940.

"Equipment Maintenance on Huge Earth Job." *ENR,* 2 July 1942.

Foster, Jack Hamilton. "Crandal Mackey, Crusading Commonwealth's Attorney." *Arlington Historical Magazine,* 1984.

Gerrity, John. "He Changed the Face of Washington." *Nation's Business,* Jan. 1952.

Groves, Leslie R. "The Atom General Answers His Critics." *Saturday Evening Post,* 19 June 1948.

Humphreys, Robert. "The Man Who Astonished Washington." *Saturday Evening Post,* 9 Oct. 1943.

Immen, Bill. "The Pentagon . . . Fact and Fancy." *Army-Navy-Air Force Register,* 7 Oct. 1961.

Janney, John. "The Man Behind the Invasion." *American Magazine,* June 1944.

Kinsey, Karen Byrne. "Battling for Arlington House: To Lee or Not to Lee?" *Arlington Historical Magazine,* October 2003.

Lauterbach, Richard E. "The Pentagon Puzzle." *Life,* 24 May 1943.

McBane, Robert B. "The Pentagon Makes Sense." *Army Information Digest,* Jan. 1947.

McCarthy, Joe. "Our Miraculous Pentagon." *Holiday,* Mar. 1952.

Murphy, Charles J. V. "Somervell of the S.O.S." *Life,* 8 May 1943.

"Pentagon Building." *Architectural Forum,* Jan. 1943.

"The Pentagon Building." *Airlanes,* Dec. 1942.

"The Pentagon Building." *The Federal Architect,* Jan.–Apr. 1943.

Overman, C. B. "I Run the World's Biggest Building." *American Magazine,* June 1951.

"Planning the World's Largest Building." *ENR,* 22 Oct. 1942.

"Race Between Claustrophobia and Agoraphobia for Those Pent Up in Washington's Pentagon." *Newsweek,* 15 Feb. 1943.

Rasmussen, Wayne D. and Vivian Wiser. "Arlington—An Agricultural Experiment Farm in a Changing Era." *Arlington Historical Magazine*, 1966.

Ross, F. E. "Architectural Concrete Work on the Pentagon Building." *Architectural Concrete*, 1943.

Sargent, James E., "Clifton A. Woodrum of Virginia." *The Virginia Magazine of History and Biography*, July 1981.

Saunders, Arven H. "Airports in Northern Virginia, Past and Present." *Arlington Historical Magazine*, 1967.

Schiller, Ronald. "That Amazing Monster, the Pentagon." *Pageant*, Dec. 1951.

Schildt, Roberta. "Freedman's Village: Arlington, Virginia, 1863–1900." *Arlington Historical Magazine*, 1984.

Shaeffer, Kevin. "My Ring Story." *Shipmate*, Sept. 2002.

Shrader, Charles R. "World War II Logistics." *Parameters*, Spring 1995.

Singleton, A. L. "Mayor of the Pentagon." *Government Executive*, Sept. 1995.

"The S.O.S." *Fortune*, Sept. 1942.

Somervell, Brehon. "The Engineer and Defense Construction." *Engineer Society Magazine*, 2 Feb. 1942.

———. "Construction Goes to War." *The Constructor*, July 1942.

Stevens, Alden. "Washington: Blight on Democracy." *Harper's Magazine*, Dec. 1941.

"Stimson's New Offices." *Life*, 21 Dec. 1942.

Ward, Ruth. "Life in Alexandria County During the Civil War." *Arlington Historical Magazine*, 1984.

Webb, Willard J. "Building the Pentagon in Arlington." *Arlington Historical Magazine*, Oct. 1984.

Weisberg, Jacob. "Edifice Wrecked." *The New Republic*, 1 Apr. 1991.

Winston, Sherrie. "Pentagon Contractors Divide and Conquer." *ENR*, 4 Sept. 2000.

Woode, Allen. "How the Pentagon Stopped Worrying and Learned to Love Peace Marchers." *Ramparts*, Feb. 1968.

NEWSPAPERS

Adde, Nick. "Solving the Puzzle Palace." *Army Times*, 13 Oct. 1986.

Becker, Jo, Steve Vogel, and Michael E. Ruane. "Aboard Room 1D457." *WP*, 16 Sept. 2001.

Day, Price. "No Red Tape Fetters Army's Good Provider." *Baltimore Sun Sunday Magazine*, 5 Mar. 1944.

Ditzen, L. Stuart. "Billion Dollar Builder—Philadelphia's John McShain." *Philadelphia Bulletin*, 8 Aug. 1976.

Forgey, Benjamin. "The Pentagon at 40." *WP*, 15 Jan. 1983.

Fox, Joseph A. "World's Largest Cafeteria to Feed 40,000 Nearing Completion." *Star*, 13 Sept. 1942.

Gabbett, Harry. "Gen. Somervell's 'Folly' Proves Itself Despite Jeers of Critics." *WP,* 18 Aug. 1954.

Hall, Charles W. "Pentagon Fetes Five Decades in Five Sides." *WP,* 13 May 1993.

Hendrickson, Paul. "McNamara: Specters of Vietnam." *WP,* 10 May 1984.

Huxtable, Ada Louise. "Pentagon: A Cosy Fortress." *NYT,* 16 Apr. 1968.

Infield, Tom. "The 5 Sides at 50." *The Philadelphia Inquirer,* 15 Jan. 1993.

Kast, Sheilah. "Not Everyone Thought It Was So Dreamy." *Star,* 1 Sept. 1975.

Kelly, Brian. "Pentagon Veterans Recall Construction Days." *Star,* 30 Apr. 1967.

Lewthwaite, Gilbert A. "Pentagon face lift at age 52." Baltimore *Sun,* 26 Nov. 1995.

Perri, Lynne. "Pentagon Waging a Massive Effort." *USA Today,* 23 Nov. 2001.

Pino-Marina, Christina. "Indiana Plant Makes its Mark on History." Washingtonpost .com, 11 June 2002.

Planck, C. E. "Potomac Blockade." *WP,* 22 Feb. 1942.

Ringle, Ken. "Five-Sided Home of Megathink Blithely Ignores 40th Birthday." *WP,* 15 Jan. 1983.

Rose, Carl. "My Life in Pentagonia." *NYT Magazine,* 7 May 1944.

Ruane, Michael E., Steve Vogel, Manny Fernandez, Patricia Davis, and Avis Thomas-Lester, "Inch by Inch." *WP,* 8 Sept. 2002.

Shalett, Sidney. "Mammoth Cave, Washington, D.C." *NYT,* 27 June 1942.

Smith, Dinitia. "No Regrets for a Love of Explosives." *NYT,* 11 Sept. 2001.

Swift, Earl, "Inside the Pentagon on 9/11." *The Virginian-Pilot,* 7–10 Sept. 2002.

Vogel, Steve. "The Battle of Arlington: How the Pentagon Got Built." *WP,* 26 Apr. 1999.

———. "Defiant Workers Return to Posts at the Pentagon." *WP,* 13 Sept. 2001.

———. "New Pentagon Pays Off." *WP,* 23 Sept. 2001.

———. "Pentagon Halfway Back in Countdown From Inferno." *WP,* 10 Mar. 2002.

———. "Survivors Healed, but Not Whole." *WP,* 11 Mar. 2002.

———. "Flights of Vigilance Over the Capital." *WP,* 8 Apr. 2002.

———. "Retaking a Lost Position." *WP,* 16 Aug. 2002.

———. "From Ruins, Pentagon Rises Renewed." *WP,* 8 Sept. 2002.

———. "Workers Push to Fortify Military Headquarters." *WP,* 7 Sept. 2003.

Vogel, Steve and Fredrick Kunkle, "Day of Remembrance and Celebration." *WP,* 12 Sept. 2002.

"War Building 'Blitz' Leaves Capital Stunned and Confused." *Star,* 13 Aug. 1941.

Wilson, George C. "Chronology of Pentagon's Biggest, Strangest Siege." *WP,* 23 Oct. 1967.

COLLECTIONS

(Note: Many of the periodical and newspaper articles listed in the bibliography and notes are included in collections housed in the archives listed below, in particular the Corps of

Engineers Office of History, the Martin Luther King Library, the Hagley Museum and Library, the OSD Historical Office, and the Pentagon Library. Many issues of *The Renovator* and articles from *The Pentagram* can be found in the latter two collections.)

American Institute of Architects Library and Archives, Washington, D.C.: AIA board minutes; Baldwin Memorial Files; Membership files for George Edwin Bergstrom, Ides van der Gracht, and David Witmer.

Amherst College Library, Archives and Special Collections, Amherst, Mass.: Papers of John J. McCloy.

Architect of the Capitol, Washington, D.C.: George M. White papers.

Arlington Central Library, Virginia Room, Arlington, Va.: Arlington County Oral History Project; vertical file.

Franklin D. Roosevelt Library, Hyde Park, N.Y.: Papers of Franklin D. Roosevelt; Harry L. Hopkins; Harold Smith; Samuel I. Rosenman; Franklin D. Roosevelt Library, Inc.; vertical file.

George C. Marshall Library, Lexington, Va.: George C. Marshall Collection; George C. Marshall Papers; Leslie R. Groves Collection; Otto Nelson Papers; T. T. Handy Papers; William T. Sexton Papers; Memories Project.

Hagley Museum and Library, Wilmington, De.: Papers of John McShain.

Library of Congress, Manuscript Division, Washington D.C.: Harold L. Ickes diary; Henry L. Stimson diary and papers (original at Sterling Library, Manuscript and Archives, Yale University).

Martin Luther King Jr. Memorial Library, Washingtoniana Division, Washington, D.C.: The Washington *Star* Collection; vertical files on "Pentagon Building."

National Archives, Modern Military Records, College Park, Md.: Records of the Office of the Commanding General, Army Services Forces (RG 160); Papers of Leslie R. Groves (RG 200); Records of the Office of the Chief of Staff (RG 165); Records of the Office of the Secretary of War (RG 107); Records of the Office of the Chief of Engineers (RG 77); Records of the Adjutant General's Office (RG 407); Records of the Office of the Quartermaster General (RG 92); Records of the United States Army Center of Military History (RG 319); Records of the Military District of Washington (RG 551); Records of the Office of the Inspector General, Army (RG 159).

National Archives, Washington, D.C.: Records of the Commission of Fine Arts (RG 66); Records of the National Capital Park and Planning Commission (RG 328).

Office of the Secretary of Defense Historical Office, Rosslyn, Va.: Subject files, boxes 1303–1317, 510–514; David O. Cooke Papers; Oral History Collection.

Pentagon Library, Arlington, Va.: Vertical files on the Pentagon.

U.S. Army Corps of Engineers, Office of History, Fort Belvoir, Va.: General Military Files (I, boxes 16–20); Military Construction in Continental United States (VII, boxes 32–34).

U.S. Army Military History Institute, Carlisle, Pa.: Papers of Brehon Burke Somervell; Leslie R. Groves—diaries and papers; Senior Officer Oral History Program.

Walker Lee Evey: personal papers, courtesy of Lee Evey.

Washington Post, Washington, D.C.: Clip files and photograph files.

U.S. Military Academy, West Point, N.Y.: Leslie R. Groves Collection.

PERSONAL PAPERS AND REMINISCENCES

Allan, Stanley Nance. "Building the Pentagon." Lecture delivered to the Chicago Literary Club, 25 Nov. 2002.

Bailey, Helen McShane. "The Office of the Chief of Staff, U.S. Army, in World War II: A Memoir." 2001. Memories Project, GCM Lib.

Casey, Hugh J. *Engineer Memoirs.* Washington, D.C.: Office of History, U.S. Army Corps of Engineers, 1993.

Davidson, Garrison. "Grandpa Gar—The Saga of One Soldier as Told to His Grandchildren." 1974, CEHO.

Graves, Ernest Jr., "Recollections of General Brehon Somervell." Memorandum to author, 12 Feb. 2004.

Groves, Leslie R. "Comments of Lt. Gen. Leslie R. Groves on MS, Construction in the United States." 1955, 1963, 1965. CEHO.

Hardin, John R. *Engineer Memoirs.* Washington, D.C.: Office of History, U.S. Army Corps of Engineers, 1981.

Hoge, William M. *Engineer Memoirs.* Washington, D.C.: Office of History, U.S. Army Corps of Engineers, 1993.

Iselin, Amy L., ed. "Reminisces of the Early Days of the Pentagon." Washington Headquarters Services, 1993, OSD HO.

Lee, John C. H. "Service Reminiscences of Lt. Gen. John C. H. Lee." n.d. MHI.

Lemmon, Lawrence Clifton. "Twentieth Century Sojourn—The Story of My Life." Published privately, 1989 (courtesy Ruth Lemmon Ferrill).

McShain, John. "Hyde Park: A Memoir—1939–40." McShain papers, HML.

———. Autobiographical notes, post-1971 HML.

Somervell, Brehon B. "General Brehon B. Somervell Public Addresses," vols. 1–4. 1941–1945, MHI.

REPORTS AND DOCUMENTS

American Society of Civil Engineers. *The Pentagon Building Performance Report: January 2003.* Reston, Va.: American Society of Civil Engineers, 2003.

Arlington County. "After-Action Report on the Response to the September 11 Terrorist Attack on the Pentagon," 2002.

Army Service Forces, Control Division. "The Pentagon Project," 25 June 1944. Copies in box 15, file 4, SDF, NARA RG 160 and box 1310, OSD HO.

Bureau of the Budget, "Report Covering Pentagon Building," 31 Aug. 1942, I, CEHO.

Department of the Army, Office of the Deputy Chief of Staff for Military Operations. "The Anti-Vietnam War Demonstration at Washington, D.C. 21–22 October 1967, After Action Report," draft, 7 Nov. 1967. Box 3, Anti-War Demonstrations, March on the Pentagon, CMH.

Department of Defense, Washington Headquarters Service. "Final Environmental Assessment of the Pentagon Reservation Master Plan." Prepared by DMJM-3DI, 28 May 1991.

Headquarters Military District of Washington. "After Action Report, Operation Cabinet Maker," 13 Nov. 1967, box 4, Anti War Demonstrations, March on the Pentagon, CMH.

Koski-Karell, Daniel. Technical Report. Historical and Archaeological Background Research of the GSA Pentagon Complex Project Area. Submitted to David Volkert and Associates, Inc., Bethesda, Md., 3 Jan. 1986. Box 1312, OSD HO.

National Register of Historic Places Inventory—Nomination Form for Federal Properties. Pentagon Office Building Complex. Prepared by Daniel Koski-Karell, Karell Archaeological Services, 15 June 1989. Box 1312, OSD HO.

Office of the Chief of Engineers. "Basic Data on the Pentagon." Washington, D.C., 21 Dec. 1943. SDF, NARA RG 160.

Office of the Chief of Engineers, "Comments on Statements of Congressman Albert J. Engel on the Pentagon, 29 February 1944" and "Comments on Statements of Congressman Albert J. Engel on the Pentagon, 6 March 1944," 7 Apr. 1944, I, CEHO.

Office of the Inspector General, investigation report, 25 May 1942. Box 1188, NARA RG 159.

Office of the Secretary of Defense. "A Status Report to Congress on the Renovation of the Pentagon," 2005, PENREN.

Office of the Secretary of Defense. "A Report to Congress on the Pentagon Renovation Program," 1993, 1994. Washington, D.C.: Office of the Secretary of Defense, 1993, 1994, OSD HO.

The Pentagon Telephone Conversations. "With General Groves Office—Feb. '42–'43"; "Miscellaneous 3/42–6/43"; "Re: Congressman Engel Inquiry," I, CEHO.

Report of the Secretary of War to the President, 1939, 1941. Washington, D.C.: United States Government Printing Office, 1939, 1941.

United States General Accounting Office. "Report to the Chairman, Subcommittee on Public Buildings and Grounds, Committee on Public Works and Transportation, House of Representatives Federal Buildings, Actions Needed to Prevent Further Deterioration and Obsolescence." Washington, D.C.: United States General Accounting Office, 1991.

U.S. Army Corps of Engineers, Engineer Historical Division. "The Pentagon Project,"
I, box 16, CEHO (three draft versions).

*The 9/11 Commission Report: Final Report of the National Commission on Terrorist Attacks
Upon the United States.* New York: W.W. Norton & Co., 2004.

The 9/11 Commission: Proceedings and Analysis. Books 3–4, Seventeenth Volume, Second Series, Terrorism: Documents of International & Local Control. James R. Holbein, ed. Dobbs Ferry, N.Y.: Oceana Publications, 2005.

MISCELLANY

Collins, Larry. "Collapse Rescue Operations at The Pentagon 9-11 Attack: A Case Study on Urban Search and Rescue Disaster Response." www.ukfssart.org.uk/files/pentagon.

Cornell, Cecilia Stiles. "James V. Forrestal and American National Security Policy, 1940–1949." Dissertation. Nashville, Tenn.: Vanderbilt University, 1987. Pentagon Library.

Department of Defense, Office of Public Information. "The Pentagon: A Description of the World's Largest Office Building," 1954, OSD HO.

Fearson, Jim. "The Telephone in Northern Virginia from the Beginning to World War II." Monograph, May 1993. Courtesy Jim Fearson.

Frierson, William. *The Pentagon.* The Pentagon Post Restaurant Council, Washington DC., 1944. Copies in box 1311, OSD HO and CMH. See also manuscript draft, Records of the Office of Chief of Military History, entry 145, NARA RG 319.

Gilpin, Susan. Paper on Queen City, 1984, Queen City vertical file, ACL.

Hammond, Christina J. "Chapter III, The Architect, George Edwin Bergstrom," from "The Italian-style Garden at Kimberly Crest" manuscript, Baldwin Memorial Files, AIA.

"The Pentagon." Two-volume booklet prepared by Pentagon architects, Sept. 1942. SDF, NARA RG 160; OSD HO; AOC.

Reynolds, J. Lacey. "John McShain, Builder," draft of article c. 1949. McShain papers, HML.

Titus, Leo J., Jr. "A Review of the Temporary Shoring Used to Stabilize the Pentagon After the Terrorist Attacks of September 11th, 2001." University of Maryland, Department of Civil Engineering, 2002.

White, George Malcolm. "The Pentagon Drawings." 1993. Box 1303, OSD HO.

AUTHOR INTERVIEWS

Part I—Stanley Nance Allan; Helen McShane Bailey; Marian Bailey; Henry E. Bennett, Jr.; Cecil Belcher; Opal Sheets Belen; Mary Anne Somervell Brenza; Nelson Clayton; Vera Pounds Dickerson; Celestine Dole; Marjorie Hanshaw Downey; Robert Furman; Alfred Goldberg; Ernest Graves, Jr.; Richard Groves; Brehon Somervell Griswold; Byron Henderson; Gertrude Jeffress; Connie Somervell Matter; Polly McShain; Thomas Munyan; Hank Neighbors; Lucille Ramale; Alan Renshaw; Elaine Renshaw; Socrates Thomas Stathes; Donald Walker; Rubye Olson Youngblood.

Part II—Ted Anderson; Bill Ayers; Julie Beckman; Ken Blackshaw; Debra Burlingame; Aubrey Butts; Rita Campbell; Martha Carden; Steve Carter; Ken Catlow; Will Colston; Stacie Condrell; Aaron Cooper; John Deutch (e-mail); Lisa Dolan; Brian Dziekonski; Phil Entrekin; Lee Evey; Kris Fisher; Georgine Glatz; Paul Gonzales; John Hamre; Paul Haselbush; Tom Heidenberger; Dan Hooton; J. B. Hudson; Les Hunkele; James T. Jackson; John Jester; Douglas Johnson; Reis Kash; Allyn Kilsheimer; Dave Lanagan; Jim Laychak; Stephen Ludden; Brian Maguire; Carl Mahnken; Paul Mlakar; Bobby McCloud; Phil McNair; Nancy McNair; Robert McNamara; Peter Murphy; Frank Naughton; David Osterhout; Patty Pague; Heather Penney; Colin Powell; Frank Probst; Pat Riley; Donald Rumsfeld; Marc Sasseville; Reimund Schuster; Jim Schwartz; Abraham Scott; Kevin Shaeffer (e-mail); Brad Smith; Michael Sullivan; Walter Teague; William Wertz; David F. Wherley, Jr.; Richard Guy Wilson. (*Note: Some interviews for Part II were conducted on behalf of* The Washington Post.)

Margaret Roth interviews: Mike Baker; Fred Calvert; Richard Cox; Don Fortunato; Bruce Hackert; Louise and Mike Kurtz; Jim McKay; Ed Monarez; Mike Smith; Alan Wallace; Payam Zeraat.

Charles W. Hall interview for The Washington Post: Walt Freeman.

INTERVIEW SUMMARIES AND ORAL HISTORY TRANSCRIPTS

Amherst College Library, Archives and Special Collections: John J. McCloy, interview by Eric Sevareid.

Architect of the Capitol: Ides van der Gracht, interview by George M. White.

Arlington Central Library, Arlington County Oral History Project: Rayfield Barber; J. Elwood Clements; Louise Gray; Ruth Jones; Everett Norton; Ellen Puterbaugh; Katherine Ross; George Vollin; Perry West.

Columbia University Oral History Research Office: Horace M. Albright; Gilmore Clarke.

George C. Marshall Library: Interviews by Forrest Pogue: Leslie Groves; T. T. Handy; Merrill Pasco; William T. Sexton; George C. Marshall; Joseph McNarney; Maxwell Taylor, Cora Thomas. *Other:* Mona Nason.

Hagley Museum and Library: John McShain, interview by Harold Wiegand.

John F. Kennedy Presidential Library and Museum: Roswell L. Gilpatric.

U.S. Army Military History Institute: Paul Caraway; Lucius Clay; Robert Colglazier.

Office of the Secretary of Defense Historical Office: John J. McCloy; John Connell; David O. Cooke; William Haynes; Allyn Kilsheimer; Donald Rumsfeld; Mike Sullivan; Paul Wolfowitz.

Smithsonian Archives of American Art: Florence Kerr.

Harry S. Truman Presidential Museum and Library: Clark Clifford; Matthew Connelly; William Hastie; Donald Dawson; Marx Leva; Louis H. Renfrow; Stuart Symington.

U.S. Army Corps of Engineers, Office of History: Interviews by Lenore Fine and Jesse Remington: Donald Antes; James Burns; Winnie Cox; W. A. Danielson; F.J.C. Dresser; Christian Dreyer; Edmund Gregory; Leslie Groves; John Hardin; Charles Hartman (letter); John Hogan; Luther Leisenring; Michael Madigan; John J. McCloy (memo); Mary Pagan; Clarence Renshaw; Eugene Reybold; Julian Schley; August Sperl; Wilhelm Styer (letter); E. G. Thomas; Harry S. Truman; Rigby Valliant; Stephen Voorhees. *Other:* Hugh Casey (letter); Garrison Davidson; Gavin Hadden (letter); Franklin Matthias; Richard C. Moore (letter); Kenneth Nichols; Carl Strock; Frederick Strong.

INDEX

Page numbers in *italics* refer to illustrations.

PHOTO © TIFFANY AYERS

STEVE VOGEL is a veteran military reporter for *The Washington Post* who covered the U.S. war in Iraq as an embedded journalist with an Army airborne brigade. His coverage of the U.S. war in Afghanistan was part of a package of *Washington Post* stories selected as a finalist for the 2002 Pulitzer Prize. Vogel covered the September 11 terrorist attack on the Pentagon and subsequently reported in depth on the victims of the attack and the building's reconstruction.

Based overseas from 1989 through 1994 and reporting for the *Post* and *Army Times*, he covered the fall of the Berlin Wall and the first Gulf War, as well as military operations in Somalia, Rwanda, and the Balkans. His reporting has won journalism awards and resulted in many memorable stories, including *Washington Post Magazine* cover stories on military test pilots, police 911 operators, and emergency workers in a Washington, D.C., hospital. A 1982 graduate of the College of William and Mary, he received a master's degree in international public policy from Johns Hopkins University's School of Advanced International Studies in 1998. Vogel lives in Washington, D.C., with his wife and two young children.